Cost and management accounting level 2

O. O. Joshua

Cost and management accounting level 2

N Coulthurst and L McAulay

The Chartered Association of Certified Accountants

Longman

PUBLISHED BY LONGMAN GROUP UK LTD IN CO-OPERATION
WITH THE CHARTERED ASSOCIATION OF CERTIFIED ACCOUNTANTS

ISBN 0 85121 5076

Published by

Longman Law, Tax and Finance Division
Longman Group UK Limited
21–27 Lamb's Conduit Street, London WC1N 3NJ

Associated Offices

Australia Longman Professional Publishing (Pty) Limited
130 Phillip Street, Sydney, NSW 2000

Hong Kong Longman Group (Far East) Limited
Cornwall House, 18th Floor, Taikoo Trading Estate,
Tong Chong Street, Quarry Bay

Malaysia Longman Malaysia Sdn Bhd
No 3 Jalan Kilang A, Off Jalan Penchala,
Petaling Jaya, Selangor, Malaysia

Singapore Longman Singapore Publishers (Pte) Ltd
25 First Lok Yang Road, Singapore 2262

USA Longman Group (USA) Inc
500 North Dearborn Street, Chicago, Illinois 60610

A CIP catalogue record for this book is available from the British Library.

Printed in Great Britain at The Bath Press, Avon

For further information and enquiries please contact your local Longman office.

Europe, Latin America, Iran
Please contact our International
Sales Department
Longman House
Burnt Mill
Harlow
Essex CM20 2JE

Arab World
Longman Arab World Centre
Butros Bustani Street
Zokak el Blat
PO Box 11–945
Beirut
Lebanon

New Sphinx Publishing Co. Ltd.
3 Shawarby Street
Kasr el Nil
Cairo
Egypt

Librairie Sayegh
Salhie Street
PO Box 704
Damascus
Syria

Longman Arab World Centre
Al-Hajairi Building
Amir Mohammed Street
PO Box 6587
Amman
Jordan

Longman Arab World Centre
15th Street
PO Box 1391
Khartoum
Sudan

Cameroon
M A W Ngoumbah
BP 537
Limbe
Cameroon

Australia
Longman Cheshire Pty Ltd.
Longman Cheshire House
Kings Gardens
91–97 Coventry Street
South Melbourne
Victoria 3205

Botswana
Longman Botswana (Pty) Ltd.
PO Box 1083
Gaborone

Canada
James D Lang
Marketing Manager
Carswell Legal Publications
2330 Midland Avenue
Agincourt
Ontario
MIS 1P7

Ghana
Sedco Publishing Co. Ltd.
Sedco House
PO Box 2051
Tabon Street
North Ridge
Accra

Hong Kong
Longman Group (Far East) Ltd.
18th Floor Cornwall House
Taikoo Trading Estate
Tong Chong Street
Quarry Bay

India
Orient Longman Limited
5–9–41/1 Bashir Bagh
Hyderabad 500 029

UBS Publishers Distributors
5 Ansari Road
PO Box 7051
New Delhi 110 002

Japan
Longman Penguin Japan Co. Ltd.
Yamaguchi Building
2–12–9 Kanda Jimbocho
Chiyoda-ku
Tokyo 101

Kenya
Longman Kenya Ltd.
PO Box 18033
Funzi Road, Industrial Area
Nairobi

Lesotho
Longman Lesotho (Pty) Ltd.
PO Box 1174
Maseru, 100

Malawi
Dzuka Publishing Co. Ltd.
Blantyre Printing & Publishing
Co. Ltd. PMB 39
Blantyre

Malaysia
Longman Malaysia Sdn, Berhad
No. 3 Jalan Kilang A
Off Jalan Penchala
Petaling Jaya
Selangor

New Zealand
Longman Paul Ltd.
Private Bag
Takapuna
Auckland 9

Nigeria
Longman Nigeria Ltd.
52 Oba Akran Avenue
Private Mail Bag 21036
Ikeja
Lagos

Pakistan
Tahir M Lodhi
Regional Manager
Butterworths
7 Jahangir Street
Islamia Park
Poonch Road
Lahore

Singapore
Longman Singapore
Publishers Pte Ltd.
25 First Lok Yang Road
Off International Road
Jurong Town
Singapore 22

South Africa
Maskew Miller Longman (Pty) Ltd.
PO Box 396
Howard Drive
Pinelands 7405
Cape Town 8000

Swaziland
Longman Swaziland Ltd.
PO Box 2207
Manzni

Tanzania
Ben & Co. Ltd.
PO Box 3164
Dar-es-Salaam

USA
Longman Trade USA.
Caroline House Inc.
520 North Dearborn Street
Chicago
Illinois 60610

Transnational Publishers, Inc.
PO Box 7282
Ardsley-on-Hudson
NY 10503

West Indies
Longman Caribbean (Trinidad) Ltd.
Boundary Road
San Juan
Trinidad

Longman Jamaica Ltd.
PO Box 489
95 Newport Boulevard
Newport West
Kingston 10
Jamaica

Mr Louis A Forde
'Suncrest'
Sunrise Drive
Pine Gardens
St Michael
Barbados

Zimbabwe
Longman Zimbabwe (PVT) Ltd.
PO Box ST 125
Southerton
Harare

Acknowledgements

The following are acknowledged for material and quotations used within the text of the book:

The Accountant's Magazine the official journal of the Institute of Chartered Accountants of Scotland.

ACCA Students' Newsletter (December 1984) courtesy of the Certified Accountants Educational Trust.

Oxford English Dictionary.

Best of Business International, Vol 1 No 1, Winter 1988/9, 'Renaissance Man', by Roger Elgin, published by Whittle Communications International (UK) Limited, Conway Street, London.

John Sizer, An Insight into Management Accounting, Penguin.

Charles Handy, Understanding Organisations, Penguin.

Clive Emmanuel and David Otley, Accounting for Management Control, Van Nostrand Reinhold.

Colin Drury, Management and Cost Accounting, Van Nostrand Reinhold.

R Likert, New Patterns of Management, McGraw Hill.

D McGregor, The Human Side of Enterprise, McGraw Hill.

ACCA Examiner for December 1986 paper, suggested answer.

L Cheek, Zero Based Budgeting Comes of Age.

Management Accounting—Official Terminology, The Chartered Institute of Management Accountants.

C T Horngren and G Foster, Cost Accounting: a Managerial Emphasis, Prentice Hall International.

The following are acknowledged for ideas used in the text which have been referenced by name:

R N Anthony.

H A Simon.

Astley and Van de Ven, 1983, Central Perspectives and Debates in Organisational Theory, Administrative Science Quarterly.

Macintosh, N B, 1985, The Social Software of Accounting and Information Systems, Wiley.

Lapin, L L, 1973, Statistics for Modern Business Decisions, Harcourt Brace Jovanovich.

Argyris, C, 1953, Human Problems with Budgets, Harvard Business Review, January–February 1953, 97–110.

Hopwood, A G, 1976, Accountancy and Human Behaviour, Prentice Hall.

Hopwood, A G, 1978, Towards an Organisational Perspective for the Study of Accounting and Information Systems, Accounting, Organisations and Society, 3(1), 3–14.

Dopuch, N, Birnberg, J G and Demski, J, 1974, Cost Accounting: Data for Management's Decisions.

Trist, E L and Bamforth, K W, 1951, Some Social and psychological Consequences of the Longwall Method of Coal-getting, Human Relations, vol 4, no 1, pp 6–24 and 37–8.

Otley, D, 1987, Budgeting for Management Control, Management Accounting, (May), Vol 65, No 5.

Phyrrh, P A, 1970, Zero Base Budgeting, Harvard Business Review, November–December, 111–121.

McHugh, A K and Sparks, J R, 1983, The Forecasting Dilemma, Management Accounting, (March), Vol 61, No 3.

Sizer, J, Perspectives in Management Accounting, The Institute of Cost and Management Accountants.

Sizer, J and Coulthurst, N, (editors), A Casebook of British Management Accounting, Institute of Chartered Accountants in England and Wales.

The following are acknowledged for their general influence, although no specific reference is provided in the text:

Arnold, J and Hope, A, Accounting for Managerial Decisions, Prentice Hall International.

Kaplan, R, Advanced Management Accounting, Prentice Hall International.

Mepham, M, Accounting Models, Polytech.

Preface

This book has been written with those students of Accountancy who are preparing for Paper 2.4, Cost and Management Accounting II, of the Chartered Association of Certified Accountants particularly in mind. However, as the syllabus for this examination paper is largely common, in both content and depth, with those on Management Accounting for the final examination stages of the other professional accounting bodies, the book is appropriate also for students of these bodies. Indeed, it can also be used as the basis for accounting degree (and equivalent) studies. It is appropriate as a specialist Management Accounting course for those who have already done an introductory course, or for those who are doing a specialist course without much of the detailed mechanics of cost accounting.

Thorough study of the book should enable a student to meet the broad objectives of the Paper 2.4 syllabus, which are stated by the ACCA to be to:

'ensure a student has the ability to prepare and analyse accounting data and is able to:
— apply it in a range of planning, control and decision-making situations;
— assess its relevance, strengths and weaknesses;
— consider how its use may be amended to accommodate change.'

Overall, the purpose of the book is not simply to give a detailed exposition and illustration of management accounting techniques, but to attempt to show whether, why and when the various techniques should be used to form a co-ordinated whole in terms of total company financial planning and control. In doing this it will be demonstrated that management accounting is indeed multi-disciplined, requiring the student to draw upon knowledge previously acquired in not only financial and cost accounting, but also economics, quantitative techniques, social sciences, industrial relations, organisation theory, marketing, auditing, taxation and law.

It is important that this text provides an adequate coverage of the subject within the broad boundaries indicated by the ACCA Paper 2.4 syllabus and by past examination questions. This the authors have sought to do and also to incorporate developments which are taking place which may well affect the content of future examination papers and the syllabus when next rewritten. The syllabus at this level is especially open to interpretation regarding both content and depth, and to the emphasis of the examiner at a particular time. The Paper 2.4 syllabus also underwent some significant change in December 1988, especially with the introduction of capital investment decision-making, including the use of DCF techniques. The syllabus has, in addition, been completely rewritten and the nature and emphasis of the examination paper changed in December 1987 with the appointment of a new examiner. Students must be careful, therefore, when analysing and interpreting past examination papers.

Besides the need to be conversant with the various management accounting techniques, there is a need to understand their theoretical basis, the concepts which underpin them, and their limitations as well as their applications. It should be noted that questions may incorporate 'appraisal of the environment in which the Management Accountant functions and in which specific management accounting techniques are utilised.' An appreciation of the working environment in which management accounting operates is in any case a necessary aspect of the subject. Students should also view Management Accounting as part of an overall information system and not in isolation. It is not restricted to monetary measurements alone, but also includes relevant physical measurements, for example, scrap expressed in litres or as a percentage of input quantity.

Section 1 provides an introduction to the study of Cost and Management Accounting. Chapters 1 and 2 seek to provide a framework and an environmental setting in which the subject can be most successfully studied. They contrast management accounting with financial accounting and goes on to outline the scope and application of cost and management accounting, the place of the management accountant, and the environment within which he/she works. Finally the question of whether management accounting itself may be economical, efficient and effective in the provision of its service to management is raised. Chapters 3 and 4 consider cost behaviour and cost-volume-profit analysis. These provide a firm foundation for the studies which follow.

The remainder of the book seeks to build upon the foundations laid in the introduction and in the student's earlier studies of cost and management accounting, either for Paper 1.2, Cost and Management Accounting I, or for qualifications providing exemption from this paper. The syllabus requirements of Cost and Management Accounting II provide some revision of cost accounting, as well as extending previous coverage and building upon the introduction to decision-making and to planning and control provided by the Level 1 course and examination.

Section 2, 'Cost Accumulation and Performance Measurement' provides coverage of the framework of routine information provision, broadly meeting the requirements of Sections 1 and 5 (part) of the syllabus. The section considers the detailed recording and processing of information within the cost accounting system, including the issues involved in determining how costs are allocated and apportioned (for example, material cost allocation, overhead apportionment and absorption) and the influence on the collection of information imposed by the nature of the business (for example, specific order or job costing, operation or process costing). Performance measures are considered, including cost, profit, and investment performance, and in relation to customers/outlets as well as products/divisions. Also the issues determining the way in which the overall information is presented to management (ie, marginal or absorption costing) are addressed. The examination of the points at issue between marginal and absorption costing prepares the way for the ground to be covered in Sections 3 and 4.

Section 3 of the book, 'Decision Making', covers the subject matter contained in Section 4 of the Paper 2.4 syllabus. The section considers initially the general approach to decision-making. The importance of specifying objectives and developing strategies and long-term plans for the achievement of objectives is stressed, and consideration is given to the important concepts involved in identifying relevant information for decision-making, leading to the development of a general framework for analysis. The section then provides examples of particular types of short-term decision and identifies the factors influencing their analysis. This is followed by coverage of certain aspects of capital investment decision-making–the appraisal techniques available and the identification and presentation of relevant information, both in general and in particular choice situations. The special problems posed in decision-making by the existence of inflation and uncertainty, and possible solutions to these problems, are also considered.

Section 4 of the book 'Planning and Control' covers the subject matter contained in Sections 2 and 3 of the syllabus and also builds on the introduction to Section 5 provided earlier in the book. The section covers planning and control systems and the assistance they provide in achieving one of the important objectives of management accounting, viz: effective, efficient and economic management of the organisation's activities on a routine basis. This includes planning at the strategic as well as tactical level. The section will look at different types of budgets and standards and their preparation, variance analysis and the organisational implications of such systems.

Where appropriate, chapters contain worked examples and self-assessment questions at stages of the text with fully worked answers. These enable the student to test his/her understanding of parts of a chapter before moving on, and help to promote active learning. The self-assessment questions should be seen as further worked examples which can be attempted initially without any reference to the answer provided. At the end of each chapter there is a selection of further exercises, and, in some cases, objective tests. These together cover as much of the text as possible and provide a test of understanding of the whole chapter. In the case of the further exercises, material from earlier chapters, or even an introduction to material covered later, may be included. The intention is to promote a questioning, intelligent response to the subject matter, rather than a passive recall of statements made in the text.

Supplementary recommended reading material is not provided, as comprehensive study of the book should prepare the student adequately for the examination. The literature has grown enormously such that it is difficult to be selective whilst keeping reading lists within the constraints of time available to the average student. The interested student should explore different views and approaches in the literature.

Contents

		Page
Preface		ix
Section 1		
1	**An introduction to cost and management accounting**	3
1.1	Business accounting	3
1.2	Cost and management accounting v financial accounting	7
1.2.1	Objective	7
1.2.2	Method	8
1.2.3	Type of information	8
1.2.4	Amount of information	8
1.2.5	Responsibility/controllability	9
1.2.6	Information provision	9
1.2.7	Work environment/communication	9
1.3	Cost and management accounting in perspective	10
1.4	The scope of cost and management accounting	10
1.5	The application of cost and management accounting	11
1.6	The place of the management accountant	12
	Summary	12
2	**The environment and utility of cost and management accounting**	15
2.1	Manufacturing environment	15
2.1.1	A new manufacturing philosophy	15
2.1.2	Technologies and concepts available	16
2.2	Organisational environment	17
2.3	Information technology	18
2.3.1	Impact on management accounting	18
2.3.2	Technology and data/information processing	18
2.3.3	Information strategy	19
2.3.4	Impact on management accountants	20
2.4	Economy, efficiency and effectiveness	20
2.5	A review of theory and practice	20
	Summary	21
3	**Cost behaviour**	23
3.1	Cost behaviour patterns	23
3.2	Factors affecting cost behaviour patterns	24
3.2.1	Nature of the expense	24
3.2.2	Time period	26
3.2.3	Level of, and change in, activity	26
3.2.4	Attributability of costs	27
3.2.5	Efficiency and input prices	27
3.2.6	Other factors	27
3.2.7	Summary	28
3.3	Cost behaviour over time	30
3.4	The learning effect	30

3.4.1 The learning curve 30
3.4.2 Calculating labour productivity 32
3.4.3 Learning applications 34
3.5 Estimating cost behaviour 34
3.5.1 Accounts classification method 34
3.5.2 Scattergraph 35
3.5.3 High-low method 36
3.5.4 Visual line of best fit 36
3.5.5 Least-squares regression 36
3.5.6 Goodness of fit 39
Summary 40
Exercises 41

4 Cost-volume-profit analysis 47
4.1 Assumptions of CVP analysis 47
4.2 CVP relationships 47
4.3 Cost volume profit charts 51
4.4 Operating and financial leverage 52
4.4.1 Operating leverage 52
4.4.2 Financial leverage 53
4.4.3 Combined leverage 54
4.5 Accountant's v economist's CVP model 55
4.5.1 Content 55
4.5.2 Purpose 56
4.6 Utility of accountant's model 57
Summary 58
Exercises 58

Section 2
5 General framework of cost accounting routine information provision 63
5.1 Useful information 63
5.2 Routine information requirements and provision 65
5.3 Information requirements 66
5.3.1 Content 66
5.3.2 Form 67
5.4 Information provision 69
5.4.1 Processing requirements 70
5.4.2 Relationship with the financial accounts 72
5.4.3 Cost coding and cost classification 74
Summary 75
Exercises 76

6 The processing of input costs 79
6.1 Input costs 79
6.2 Direct versus indirect product costs 79
6.2.1 Traceability 79
6.2.2 Fairness 80
6.2.3 Practicality 80
6.2.4 Cost behaviour 80
6.3 Direct product/service costs 80
6.3.1 Direct materials 81
6.3.2 Direct labour 81
6.3.3 The flow of direct materials and direct labour costs 82
6.4 Overheads in outline 82
6.4.1 The process of production overhead pricing 83

6.4.2 The process of non-production overhead pricing 85
6.5 Allocation, apportionment and absorption issues 85
6.5.1 Responsibility centres 86
6.5.2 Whether overhead is apportioned from one centre to another 87
6.5.3 How overhead is apportioned from one centre to another 88
6.5.4 Inter-servicing apportionment 89
6.5.5 Absorption method 90
6.5.6 Predetermined or actual absorption rates 91
6.5.7 Resource base 92
6.5.8 Absorption or marginal costing 94
6.6 Costing in the new technology environment 94
6.6.1 The new environment 94
6.6.2 Existing accounting deficiencies 95
6.6.3 Towards accounting solutions 96
6.7 Non-monetary measures 98
Summary 98
Exercises 99

7 Relating values to outputs 105
7.1 Valuation bases 105
7.2 Costing methods 105
7.3 Cost units 106
7.4 Valuation principles 107
7.5 Short illustrative examples 107
7.6 Customer costs and profitability 112
7.6.1 General information requirements 112
7.6.2 Identifying customer's costs 113
Summary 113
Exercises 114

8 Absorption costing versus marginal costing 119
8.1 Information provided 119
8.2 Issues 120
8.2.1 Overhead apportionment and absorption 120
8.2.2 Stock valuation 120
8.2.3 Income determination 120
8.2.4 Presentation of management information 124
8.2.5 The ability to split total cost into fixed and variable categories 130
8.2.6 Whether contribution analysis on its own is sufficient 130
8.3 Beyond absorption and marginal 130
8.3.1 Decision objects 131
8.3.2 Decision events 131
8.3.3 Time horizons 131
8.3.4 Decision information 132
Summary 134
Exercises 134

9 Application in service organisations 143
9.1 Service costing generally 143
9.2 Transport costing 144
9.2.1 Cost centres 144
9.2.2 Cost units 144
9.3 Higher education 145
9.3.1 Description of accounting practice 145
9.3.2 Recommendations for the future 146

9.3.3 The common cost problem 146
9.4 The Health Service 146
9.4.1 Hospital management and accounting (early 1980s) 147
9.4.2 Hospital management and accounting (late 1980s) 147
9.5 Accounting in retail organisations 148
9.5.1 Unique features and difficulties 148
9.5.2 Accounting and technological developments 148
9.5.3 Direct product profitability 149
9.5.4 Store performance 151
Summary 151
Exercises 151

10 Measurement of divisional performance 157
10.1 Divisionalisation 157
10.1.1 Types of organisational division 157
10.1.2 Interactions 158
10.1.3 Independence: centralisation and decentralisation 158
10.2 Cost, profit and investment centres 159
10.2.1 Cost centres 159
10.2.2 Profit centres 161
10.2.3 Investment centres 162
10.3 Sub-optimisation 162
10.4 Monetary and non-monetary measures 164
10.4.1 Physical quantities 164
10.4.2 Percentages and ratios 164
10.4.3 Indices 165
10.5 Quantitative and qualitative measures 166
10.6 Inter-divisional comparisons 166
Summary 167
Exercises 168

Section 3
11 Decision-making in context 173
11.1 Elements of decisions 173
11.2 Necessary conditions for optimal decision-making 173
11.3 The economic model 174
11.4 Ends rationality 175
11.5 Means rationality 177
11.5.1 Objectives 177
11.5.2 All possible courses of action must be known 178
11.5.3 Information concerning the effect of alternative courses of action must be available, identified, and expressed in a manner consistent with the means of expressing objectives 178
11.5.4 Information must be evaluated in such a way that a decision can be taken on the best alternative 179
11.5.5 Decisions, once taken must be successfully executed; potential must be realised 179
11.6 The nature of decisions 179
11.6.1 Structure 180
11.6.2 Choice 180
11.6.3 Quantification 180
11.6.4 Time period 181
11.7 Quantitative decisions and the economic model 181
11.8 Conclusions 183
Summary 183

12 The differential costing process 185
12.1 Differential costing 185
12.2 Avoidable costs and benefits 185
12.3 Concepts in analysis 186
12.4 Summary of terms 187
12.5 A framework for analysis 188
12.6 The framework illustrated 188
12.6.1 Problem 188
12.6.2 Alternatives 188
12.6.3 Base 188
12.6.4 Avoidable costs and benefits 189
12.6.5 Analysis 189
12.7 Alternative analysis 190
12.8 Opportunity costs and benefits 191
12.9 Choice of base 192
12.10 Difficulties and limitation of analysis 194
12.10.1 Availability of, and ability to identify and analyse, information 194
12.10.2 Presentation and communication of information 195
12.10.3 Conflict between decision data and control data 196
12.10.4 Longer-term consequences 197
12.11 The difficulties illustrated 197
12.11.1 Problem 197
12.11.2 Solution 197
12.11.3 Conclusions 198
Summary 199

13 Short-term decision-making—problem situations 201
13.1 Problem situations 201
13.2 What to produce and sell 202
13.3 How much to produce and sell 204
13.4 Where/how to sell 207
13.5 Where/how to produce 208
13.6 Whether to produce and sell 210
Summary 211

14 Short-term decision-making allocation of scarce resources 217
14.1 Limiting factor situations 217
14.2 Limiting factor illustration (single constraint) 217
14.2.1 Problem 218
14.2.2 Solution 218
14.2.3 Changed assumptions 223
14.3 Limiting factor illustration (two or more constraints) 226
14.3.1 Problem 226
14.3.2 Solution 227
14.3.3 Changed assumptions 235
Summary 236
Exercises 236

15 Pricing decisions 241
15.1 The economic approach to pricing 241
15.1.1 Market structures 241
15.1.2 Profit elasticity of demand 242
15.1.3 Profit elasticity 244
15.1.4 Establishing optimal price and output 247

15.1.5 Limitations of economic theory 251
15.1.6 Sensitivity analysis 253
15.2 Cost based approaches to pricing 253
15.2.1 Long-run cost plus 254
15.2.2 Short-run cost plus 254
15.3 Pricing in practice 255
Summary 256
Exercises 256

16 Capital investment decision-making—appraisal techniques 263
16.1 Methods of analysis 263
16.1.1 Accounting rate of return 264
16.1.2 Discounted cash flow 265
16.1.3 Payback 269
16.2 Appraisal techniques and differing projects 269
16.3 Techniques compared 270
16.3.1 Accounting rate of return 270
16.3.2 Discounted cash flow 271
16.3.3 Payback 271
16.4 Appraisal techniques in practice 272
16.5 DCF in perspective 272
16.5.1 Ease of use and extent of understanding of different appraisal techniques 272
16.5.2 Closeness of substitutes 273
16.5.3 Difficulties or misapplication in appraisal 275
16.5.4 Part played by computation in decision-making 275
16.5.5 Objectives other than long-term profit 276
16.5.6 Conclusions 276
16.6 Calculation of the IRR—interpolation and extrapolation 276
16.7 Calculation of the internal rate of return—short cuts 279
16.7.1 Average discount factor 279
16.7.2 Cumulative discount factor 280
16.8 Relative ranking of projects: IRR v NPV 281
Summary 284
Exercises 284

17 Capital investment decision-making: identification, analysis and presentation of information 287
17.1 Types of decisions 287
17.2 Expansion 287
17.2.1 Sensitivity analysis 289
17.2.2 Working capital 289
17.3 Modernisation 290
17.3.1 Benefits from new technology 291
17.3.2 Operating cost savings 291
17.3.3 Reduced stockholding 291
17.3.4 Flexibility 292
17.3.5 Quality 292
17.3.6 Delivery 292
17.3.7 Investment and alternatives 292
17.4 Replacement 293
17.5 Inflation 295
17.6 Difficulties and limitation of analysis 298
17.6.1 Conflict between decision data and control data 298
17.6.2 Longer-term consequences 299
Summary 300
Exercises 300

18 Uncertainty and decision-making 305
18.1 Risk and uncertainty 305
18.2 Stating the problem 306
18.3 Resolving decision-making problems 308
18.3.1 The maximin criterion 308
18.3.2 Simulation 309
18.3.3 Expected value and decision trees 311
18.3.4 Minimax opportunity loss 312
18.4 The value of perfect information 313
18.5 Discrete and continuous distributions 313
18.6 Joint probabilities 317
18.7 Reducing uncertainty 318
Summary 319
Exercises 319

Section 4 323
19 Planning, control and evaluation; an outline 325
19.1 Definitions 325
19.1.1 Planning 325
19.1.2 Control 326
19.1.3 Evaluation 327
19.2 Formal accounting control mechanisms 329
19.2.1 Internal control 329
19.2.2 Cybernetic control 330
Summary 334
Exercises 335

20 Information for long- and short-term planning and control 337
20.1 A framework for long- and short-term information needs 337
20.1.1 Strategic planning 337
20.1.2 Operational control 339
20.1.3 Management control 340
20.2 Information 342
20.2.1 Data and information 343
20.2.2 Communications theory 343
Summary 345
Exercises 346

21 Organisational implications of management accounting systems 347
21.1 The debate on organisational theory 347
21.2 The negative impacts of controls 348
21.2.1 The contribution of Argyris 348
21.2.2 Other contributions 349
21.3 Organisational structure and management style 350
21.3.1 Organisational structure, the environment and accounting systems design 350
21.3.2 Management style 352
21.4 Groups, participation and bargaining 354
21.4.1 Becker and Green 354
21.4.2 Hofstede 355
21.4.3 Schiff and Lewin 355
21.5 Motivation and the individual 356
21.5.1 Expectancy theory 356
21.5.2 Aspiration levels 357
21.6 Design of accounting information systems 359
Summary 360
Exercises 361

22 Variance data for planning and control 363
22.1 Variance analysis 363
22.1.1 Variance analysis definition 363
22.1.2 Implications for management information 364
22.2 One factor analysis 366
22.2.1 Calculation 366
22.2.2 Examples 366
22.3 Two factor analysis 368
22.3.1 Calculation 368
22.3.2 Conventional two factor analysis 370
22.3.3 A procedure for two factor variance analysis 370
22.3.4 Two factor variance formulae 371
22.4 Three factor analysis 372
22.4.1 A statement of the basic problem 372
22.4.2 A three factor analysis 372
Summary 374
Exercises 375

23 Budgets: preparation, procedures and purposes 379
23.1 Objectives 379
23.1.1 Statement of objectives 379
23.1.2 Discussion: the conflicting nature of objectives 381
23.2 Preparation 381
23.2.1 The iterative nature of budget preparation 381
23.2.2 Subsidiary and master budget formulation 382
23.3 Procedures 386
23.3.1 Cash budgeting 386
23.3.2 Standard costing and budget formulation 388
23.3.3 Fixed and flexible budgets and standard costs 388
23.3.4 Zero-based budgeting 389
23.3.5 Management by objectives 391
23.3.6 Management audits 391
23.3.7 Forecasting 392
23.3.8 Financial models 394
Summary 395
Exercises 395

24 Standards: preparation, procedures and purposes 405
24.1 Preparing standard costs 405
24.1.1 The meaning of standard cost 405
24.1.2 Approaches to establishing standards; engineered costs 407
24.1.3 Overheads 409
24.1.4 Wastage, scrap and by-products 409
24.1.5 Types of standard 411
24.1.6 Inflation 412
24.1.7 Product and service costs 412
24.2 Operating standard costing systems 413
24.2.1 Cost recording systems 413
24.2.2 Feedback and efficiency for responsibility centres 414
24.2.3 Investigations 415
24.3 Purposes of standard costing 416
24.3.1 Decision-making 416
24.3.2 Planning 416
24.3.3 Control 416
24.3.4 Performance evaluation 417

24.3.5 Financial accounting 417
Summary 417
Exercises 417

25 Standard costing variance analysis 421
25.1 Absorption costing 424
25.1.1 Raw materials 424
25.1.2 Direct labour 427
25.1.3 Variable overheads 428
25.1.4 Fixed overheads 429
25.1.5 Sales variances 430
25.1.6 Quality cost variance 432
25.1.7 Profit or operating statement 432
25.2 Marginal costing 433
Summary 435
Exercises 435

26 Interpreting and investigating variances 441
26.1 Interpreting variances 441
26.2 Investigating variances 442
26.2.1 Heuristics 443
26.2.2 Trends 443
26.2.3 Control charts 444
26.2.4 Decision tree approach 445
26.2.5 Decision theory approach (game theory) 447
26.3 Discussion 447
Summary 448
Exercises 448

27 Uncertainty: impact and responses in budgets and standards 451
27.1 Probability, simulation and sensitivity analysis 451
27.1.1 Three-tier budgeting 451
27.1.2 Decision trees and joint probabilities 452
27.1.3 Simulation 452
27.1.4 Sensitivity analysis 453
27.2 Ex ante revision of budgets and standards 455
27.2.1 Continuous budgeting and rolling forecasts 455
27.2.2 Revision of standards 456
27.3 Ex post revision of budgets and standards 457
27.3.1 Planning and operating variances 458
Summary 459
Exercises 459

28 Transfer pricing and performance evaluation 463
28.1 Transfer pricing: purposes 463
28.2 Transfer pricing methods 464
28.2.1 Absorption cost based transfer prices 465
28.2.2 Variable cost based transfer prices 466
28.2.3 Market value based transfer prices 466
28.2.4 Negotiated prices 466
28.2.5 Linear programming based transfers 467
28.3 Critique of performance measurement 467
Summary 472
Exercises 473

Solutions to questions 477

June 1989 ACCA Cost and Management Accounting II Paper 645

Authors' model answers to June 1989 Examination 651

Index 667

(Coupon for latest ACCA examination paper questions and answers supplied at back of book.)

Section 1

INTRODUCTION

This first section provides an introduction to the study of cost and management accounting. In Chapter 1 cost and management accounting is contrasted with financial accounting, and the scope of the subject matter, together with the place of the management accountant within an organisation, are outlined. Chapter 2 considers the wider organisation setting and environment of cost and management accounting. It is important that the subject is viewed in the widest possible context, and certainly a broad organisational context, because of the many influences on cost and management accounting information provision. This is followed, in Chapter 3, by the study of cost behaviour patterns and cost estimation. An understanding of cost behaviour patterns, and an ability to project likely cost behaviour in a particular situation, are important in cost and management accounting and are relevant to much of the study in the book. Chapter 4 provides an introduction to cost — volume — profit analysis, which is expanded upon later in the book and which is based upon simplified cost behaviour assumptions.

An Introduction to Cost and Management Accounting

INTRODUCTION

The overall purpose of this opening chapter is to provide an introduction to cost and management accounting. A brief summary of business accounting is provided with an illustration of financial accounting statements and their interpretation. Cost and management accounting is then contrasted with financial accounting with significant differences noted. The chapter goes on to consider briefly the scope, in terms of subject matter, of cost and management accounting, and its application in different types of business. Finally, attention is given to the place of the management accountant within an organisation's structure.

1.1 BUSINESS ACCOUNTING

Business accounting has a very important influence on the conduct of economic affairs, serving the needs of both external and internal users of financial information (ie, both the providers of funds to business and the managers of those funds). It is possible that they (ie, funds providers and managers) are one and the same, although increasingly ownership has become divorced from management as businesses have grown in size.

The basic accounting process which is designed to satisfy the requirements of external users, the stewardship function, is called financial accounting. It is concerned with recording the transactions that take place between a business enterprise and the outside world, resulting in the acquisition and use of resources.

Periodically, through preparation of accounting statements, the overall outcome of these past efforts is reported to the owners of the business. The accounting statements comprise the Profit and Loss Account, which establishes the net outcome in terms of profit or loss of carrying on business for a period, the Balance Sheet, which shows the financial position of the business in terms of assets and liabilities at a particular date, and statements of cash and funds flow. The use of accounting to measure the economic progress of firms is a significant factor influencing the share transaction behaviour of the financial community.

Financial accounting applies to every type of business which can be depicted on a co-ordinate system with two axes, representing two basic aspects of business and its accounting. One aspect is how a business is financed and managed; the other aspect is where the funds are invested within the business (see Figure 1.1).

FIGURE 1.1 **Types of Business**

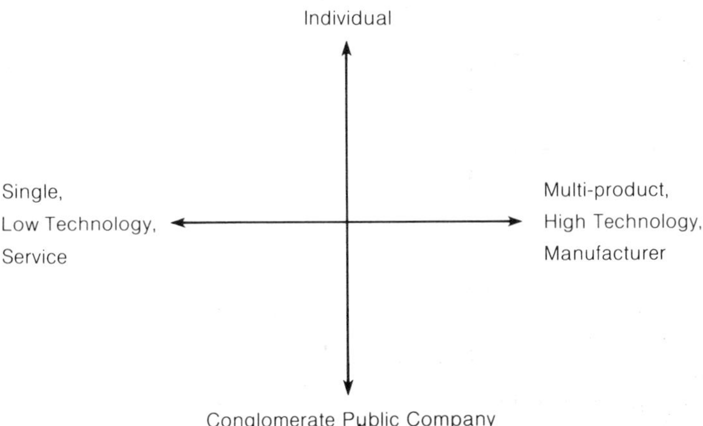

The financing and management of a business can be shown as ranging from at one extreme, individual ownership, to at the other extreme, a conglomerate public company. The axis encompasses different ownership structures, including partnership and private company, which also reflect differences in management. As far as investment of funds is concerned a variety of businesses are to be found. They can be differentiated in various ways. Three significant factors are identified here as having an influence on the investment of funds. The three factors are whether the business is in a service or manufacturing industry, the number of services/products provided and the level of technology applied. The axis shows at one extreme a single, low-technology service, and at the other,

FIGURE 1.2 **Financial Accounting System (Manufacturing Business)**

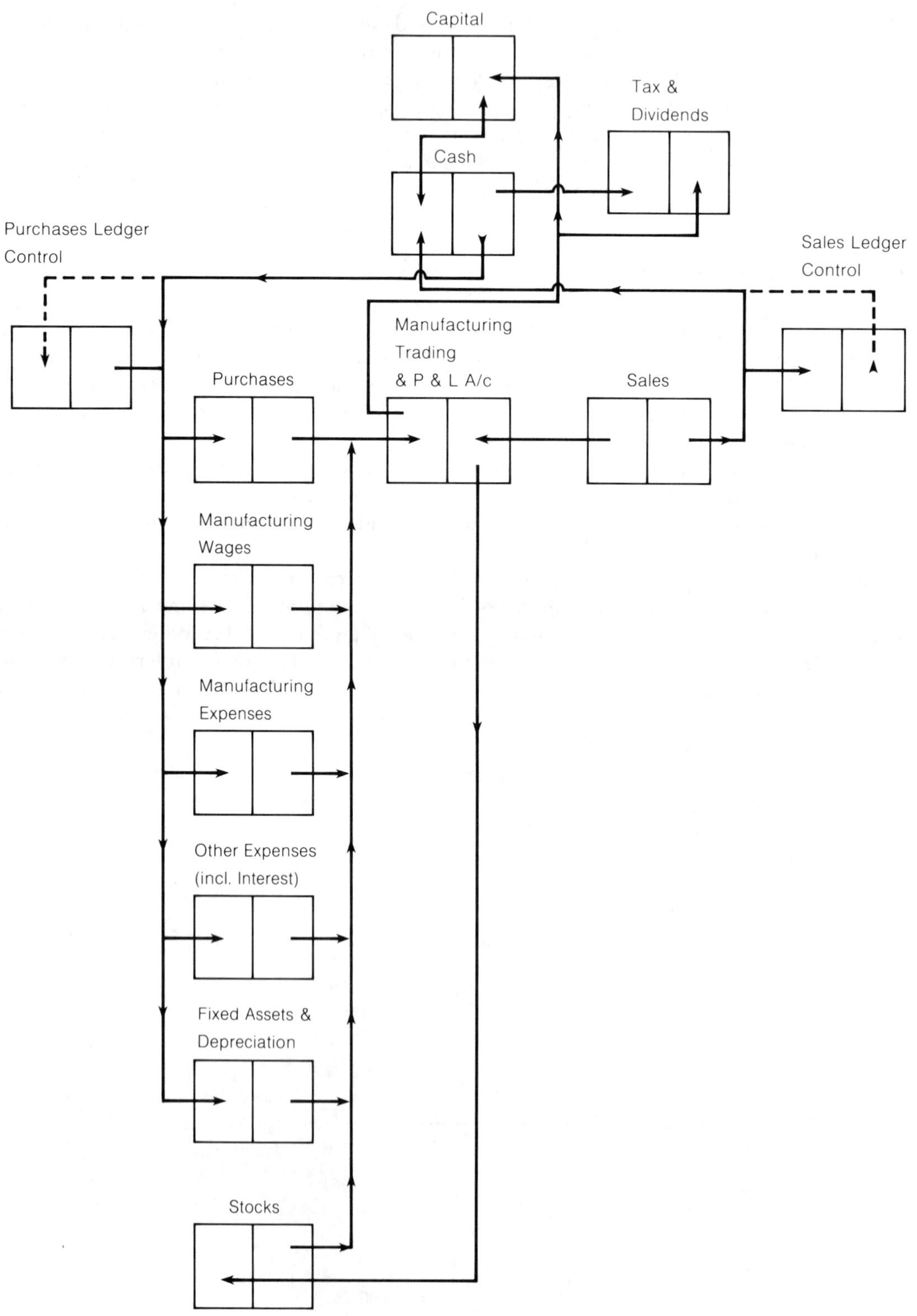

a multi-product, high-technology manufacturer. For example, service industries take on more of the characteristics of the manufacturer ie, large premises, machinery, significant materials as well as labour costs, as they move along the axis towards the manufacturing end.

The accounting information flow for a manufacturing business is demonstrated in Figure 1.2.

The variety of sources of funds affects the complexity of recording, and also influences the contents of the Profit and Loss Account and Balance Sheet. As far as the investment of funds is concerned, a variety of resources are acquired and consumed. In accounting for these resources, the major issue in financial accounting is that of product versus period costs. Product costs are those that are assigned to a product and are charged in the Profit and Loss Account in the period in which the product is sold. Period costs are charged against profit in the period in which they are incurred.

An issue arises where stock exists at the end of an accounting period, ie, where resources acquired have not all been converted into sales. Stock valuation is sometimes achieved by adoption of a simplified approach. For example, a trader may value stock of goods at their basic cost and not include a share of other costs incurred in acquiring and storing them. With a manufacturer this is not as straightforward, as many different costs are incurred in manufacturing an item of stock. Internal transfers of cost are required in order to identify the various costs incurred in the manufacturing process with the output of completed goods, and thus adequately fulfil accounting's stewardship function. This provides one of the objectives of cost accounting.

Self-assessment question 1.1

The following illustration is provided as revision of the financial accounting process and statements.

A company operates a small transport fleet which provides distribution services to local industry. The Trial Balance of the Company drawn up at the end of the financial year just ended was as follows:

	£	£
Share Capital		40,000
Reserves		30,800
Bank Loan		20,000
Sales		119,500
Purchases of fuel and oil	19,160	
Drivers' wages	32,730	
Repairs and maintenance	4,040	
Office salaries and expenses	34,790	
Road tax	820	
Insurance	3,960	
Office buildings	62,500	
Vehicles	45,000	
Office equipment	3,600	
Accumulated depreciation:		
Office buildings		8,750
Vehicles		21,270
Office equipment		850
Stock of fuel and oil	1,840	
Debtors	34,240	
Creditors for fuel and oil		3,240
Balance at Bank	1,730	
	£244,410	£244,410

The following additional information was available relevant to the preparation of accounts for the year:

1 No adjustment had been made in the accounts for interest charged on the bank loan during the year. Bank statements for the period revealed that total interest of £2,400 had been charged direct to the company's current account.

2 Fixed assets are depreciated as follows:
Office buildings— 2% of cost per annum
Office equipment—5% of cost per annum
Vehicles—charge for the year £8,880
3 Stock of fuel and oil at the end of the year was £1,960.
4 Road tax prepaid was £200.
5 Insurance prepaid was £360. Of the adjusted amount for the year 1/10th related to the insurance of office buildings and equipment.
6 Office expenses accrued were estimated at £630.
7 The rate of corporate tax on profits is 50%.
8 It was proposed to pay a dividend of £2,000 to shareholders.

The Profit and Loss Account for the year and Balance Sheet at the end of the year, produced from the above information (with comparative figures for the previous year) are as follows:

Profit and Loss Account

	For the year just ended		For the previous year	
	£	£	£	£
Sales		119,500		93,420
Less: Cost of Sales				
Fuel & oil	19,040		13,300	
Drivers' wages	32,730		22,710	
Repairs & maintenance	4,040		3,860	
Road tax	620		540	
Vehicle insurance	3,240		2,520	
Depreciation of vehicles	8,880	68,550	7,230	50,160
Gross Profit		50,950		43,260
Less: Office salaries & expenses	35,420		29,060	
Building & equipment insurance	360		300	
Depreciation of office buildings	1,250		1,250	
Depreciation of office equipment	180	37,210	150	30,760
Net Profit before Interest & Tax		13,740		12,500
Less: Interest on bank loan		2,400		1,500
Net Profit Before Tax		11,340		11,000
Less: Taxation		5,670		5,500
Net Profit After Tax		5,670		5,500
Less: Dividend		2,000		2,000
Retained Profit for the Year		£3,670		£3,500

Balance Sheet

	End of year		End of previous year	
	£	£	£	£
Fixed Assets				
Office buildings	62,500		62,500	
Less: Accumulated depreciation	10,000	52,500	8,750	53,750
Vehicles	45,000		39,000	
Less: Accumulated depreciation	30,150	14,850	28,270	10,730
Office equipment	3,600		3,000	
Less: Accumulated depreciation	1,030	2,570	850	2,150
		69,920		66,630
Net Current Assets				
Current Assets				
Stock of fuel and oil	1,960		1,840	
Debtors	34,240		22,140	
Prepaid expenses	560		400	
	36,760		24,380	

	£	£	£	£
Less: **Current Liabilities**				
Bank overdraft	670		1,760	
Tax	5,670		5,500	
Dividend	2,000		2,000	
Creditors	3,240		3,130	
Accrued expenses	630		820	
	12,210		13,210	
		24,550		11,170
		94,470		77,800
Financed by:				
Share capital	40,000		32,000	
Reserves	34,470	74,470	30,800	62,800
Bank loan		20,000		15,000
		94,470		77,800

On seeing the above results, the Managing Director and major shareholder of the company (known to be fond of testing the financial awareness of you, his General Manager) makes the following comments:

'We have done well. Profit has increased compared with last year. That's progress.'
'There's no reason why the dividend should not be increased. If we make a profit we may as well give it to the shareholders.'
'Depreciation is accumulating nicely in the balance sheet. We can use this to replace assets when they wear out.'

Required:
(a) Respond fully to each of the above comments made by your managing director (where appropriate, figures should be provided to justify your response).
(b) Indicate (by putting a figure in the appropriate box(es) in the table below) what effect the following changes in the information already provided, would have on the company's bank balance at the year-end and/or profit before tax for the year just ended:

	Increases Bank Balance/ Reduces Overdraft	Increases Profit Before Tax	Decreases Bank Balance/ Increases Overdraft	Decreases Profit Before Tax
(i) Debtors £36,000				
(ii) Interest on bank loan £2,500				
(iii) Further share issue £5,000				
(iv) Office expenses accrued £930				
(v) Stock of fuel & oil at the end of the year £2,000				
(vi) Purchase of additional office equipment £1,000				

Answers on page 479

1.2 COST AND MANAGEMENT ACCOUNTING V FINANCIAL ACCOUNTING

1.2.1 Objective

Arguments exist as to whether the requirement to place a value on manufactured stock was a primary motivation for the birth of cost accounting. Whether or not it was, in addition to the stock valuation requirement, demands have increasingly come from within business for more financial information to be provided. Along with the divorce in management from ownership has come growth in both size and diversity of business organisations, increasing value and complexity of fixed assets, widening markets for products, greater variety of customers, and increasing competition. All these have brought demands for more information to be provided to management on a frequent basis. This is the province of cost and management accounting. Management accounting is wholly concerned with meeting the needs of internal users of financial information, who make decisions about resources and seek to plan and control their use. Cost accounting provides the database not just for inventory valuation, but also for the management accounting information provision. Indeed, the provision of cost accounting information should be influenced primarily by usefulness of information to management. Stock valuation should be regarded as a by-product of cost accounting rather than the reason for it.

There is thus a fundamental difference of objective between financial accounting and cost and management accounting. Whereas financial accounting is concerned with reporting periodically to the owners of the business the overall outcome, in terms of profit or loss, resulting from the use of resources, cost and management accounting is concerned with the provision of regular and detailed information to management, structured and analysed in such a way that resources may be acquired and used as economically, efficiently and effectively as possible in the pursuit of an organisation's objectives.

Other differences between cost and management accounting and financial accounting follow from this fundamental difference of objective.

1.2.2 Method

Financial accounting has one purpose and one set of rules or generally accepted principles. This is a necessary condition of external reporting; if there are no rules then little sense can be made universally of the information. Objectivity and verifiability are essential to understanding.

Cost and management accounting on the other hand is not constrained in the same way by such generally accepted principles. Information is arranged according to the needs of particular managers at particular times in particular organisations. Instead of being confined to following highly structured practices, the management accountant is expected to recognise information that is useful for specific managerial purposes. This may be referred to as a 'conditional' truth approach, the principle of different costs for different purposes. This can be contrasted with the 'absolute' truth of financial accounting, which follows clearly laid down rules in establishing costs. The absolute truth also typified the early approaches to cost accounting.

1.2.3 Type of information

A key distinction is between the past and the future. Whilst financial accounting is concerned with recording what has happened, cost and management accounting on the other hand has a forward-looking aspect. Plans can only be made, and decisions taken, concerning the future; control can only be arranged for something that is going to happen. The view is taken that where something has already happened it is too late for management to take decisive action to do anything about it.

Thus in trying to ensure the long-run survival of a business, whilst past and current information may be of relevance, the organisation will be especially concerned with what will happen tomorrow. External parties are of course also interested in the future. However, it is management who have the task of shaping it. The emphasis must always be on providing information so that managers can take positive actions which influence what is going to happen rather than reacting to the events that have happened in order to cope with the situation that these events have brought about.

1.2.4 Amount of information

Financial accounting analyses expenditure according to the nature of the outlays and not to the activity for whose use the expense has been incurred, other than a broad functional classification eg manufacturing, distribution, selling, administration. It merely records values at the interface between the organisation and the outside world.

Cost and management accounting is concerned with internal movements of value, amplifying the analysis in the financial accounts by giving an operational analysis relating outlays to departments and to products. It is generally, therefore, of a more detailed nature than financial accounting.

Much of the coverage of this book will be at a detailed level. Such detail will be a necessary database within organisations, and will be particularly appropriate for lower-level management for planning and control and for tactical decisions. More senior managers, however, would generally require some aggregation of such information. At the highest level, the information would be used for strategic planning and control.

1.2.5 Responsibility/controllability

Cost and management accounting is concerned with identifying costs and revenues not just with physical locations but also with people. This is responsibility accounting and is a further important contrast with financial accounting. The aim is to assist and monitor decisions that individuals/groups make.

There must as far as possible be clear responsibility for actions within a business organisation. Cost identification and attribution should then be consistent with this responsibility. However, it must be realised that in practice divisions of responsibility are rarely absolutely clear. In most organisations there are many interdependencies and shared responsibilities which arise inevitably in their operation.

As a result the consequences of actions in one area affect other areas. For example, a purchasing manager may lose quantity discount on the purchase of a material following a reduction in demand. On another material the manager may buy inferior quality in order to achieve the standard price set; product rejects increase. Whilst he/she is responsible for purchasing, aspects of the purchasing job are influenced by others ie, outside his/her control. Equally actions that are taken by the manager affect the results of others. Care has to be taken in assigning responsibility for costs incurred. Responsibility should be consistent with controllability.

1.2.6 Information provision

The financial accountant is the provider of financial accounting information which demonstrates past performance and financial situation. As noted earlier, this he/she can do, and only he/she can do, as custodian of the information which is put together on clearly established principles.

The management accountant, however, should not be looked upon necessarily as the provider of management accounting information, as he/she is very often not the most qualified to provide it. Rather, the management accountant frequently needs to act more as a prober, investigator, and consolidator, skilled in asking the right questions of personnel involved in production, marketing, engineering, purchasing etc. He/she also needs to be skilled in the analysis of data.

1.2.7 Work environment/communication

It follows from the above that a feature of the cost and management accountant's work is that he/she must work in close contact with managers throughout the organisation in all other functional areas, assisting them in planning and controlling the future. It is necessary to take a multi-discipline approach, and to ensure that information, the assumptions on which it is based, and the situations where it may be used are effectively communicated. Communication is a vital element in the cost and management accountant's work.

The financial accountant on the other hand can work to a greater extent in isolation from the rest of the management team, and has less need therefore to be concerned with, or understand, the other functional areas of a business in order to carry out the job effectively.

1.3 COST AND MANAGEMENT ACCOUNTING IN PERSPECTIVE

In summary, cost and management accounting has gradually taken accounting from its concern with keeping an overall record of past events to a means of helping businesses determine their detailed future and in a variety of situations. The emphasis is on economic reality, relevance and timeliness more than objectivity and verifiability which are of particular importance in financial accounting.

In the course of development, cost and management accounting has incorporated other base disciplines, drawing upon the concepts of economics, the techniques of operational research, organisation principles and the behavioural views of human resources management, in order to provide assistance to other functional managers in determining the production, marketing, selling and distribution of their products and services.

It must, however, be recognised that:

1 The degree of accuracy in much accounting data, especially cost and management accounting data, is more apparent than real. Accountancy is frequently much more a matter of judgement than of absolute truth. The only certainty about the future is that it is uncertain.
2 Management accounting is not *the* management control system, but only part of it.
3 Systems and figures themselves do not do anything; ultimately it is the management in the organisation who take (or fail to take) the necessary action. Management accounting can help good managers to function more effectively but cannot replace them.
4 The routine cost and management accounting system cannot satisfy the information requirements of all situations. A degree of rigidity and inflexibility is inevitable. Ad hoc information will also be required and the need for it should be recognised.

1.4 THE SCOPE OF COST AND MANAGEMENT ACCOUNTING

Cost and management accounting was described earlier as the provision of regular and detailed information to management so that resources may be acquired and used as economically, efficiently and effectively as possible.

Simon et al, in a well-known study in the early 1950s, identified three basic types of information needed by management:

1 Score-keeping
2 Attention-directing
3 Problem-solving

Score-keeping information is provided by the cost accounting system and answers the question 'How well have we done?' Attention-directing covers the use of accounting information to provide a stimulus for management decision-making and action. Problem-solving covers the use of accounting information to provide a basis for actually making decisions. It should be seen as not just solving problems but also taking advantage of opportunities. Attention-directing is also enabled by the comparison of actual results against a previously agreed target.

As was explained in the preface, the subject matter in this book, reflecting the scope of cost and management accounting, is divided into three further main sections, following this introductory section.

Section 2, 'Cost Accumulation and Performance Measurement' provides coverage of the framework of routine information provision essentially satisfying the requirement for score-keeping information. The aim should be to organise the information in such a way that will be most useful to management. It is made useful by:

1 indicating areas for attention and providing a basis for information estimation for particular decisions and for their post-audit, and
2 providing a framework for the planning of resources, the co-ordination of decisions, the setting of targets of performance, and the necessary feedback in order to measure progress against overall plans.

Section 3, 'Decision-Making' covers the subject matter outlined in 1. above, considering the decision-making process, especially the identification of relevant information and its analysis. This covers both attention-directing and problem-solving aspects.

The types of decisions taken, and their information requirements, should shape as far as possible the cost accounting system, so that attention is directed in the right way and so that a basis is provided for identifying relevant information. It is important that decisions taken are in the best interests of the business as a whole. Sectional profit should not be increased by any action that reduces the total business profit. It should be considered whether the system provides relevant information for a decision, as this not only affects the ability to make the decision but the incentive also, given the feedback that will be provided by the accounting system after the event. However, it is important to appreciate that as decisions are varied and not infrequently ad hoc, the cost accounting system can only provide a general framework.

Section 4, 'Planning and Control' covers the subject matter outlined in 2. above, considering budgeting systems which provide a better basis for attention-directing and a framework within which decisions can be co-ordinated. It is important that managers:

1 know what they are expected to achieve;
2 know what they are achieving;
3 are provided with a measure which is consistent with their responsibilities, and ability to control ie, profit/costs should be as independent as possible of performance efficiency and managerial decisions elsewhere in the business.

Thus managers should not only know what they are expected to achieve, and what they are achieving, but have the power to regulate what is happening.

It should be clear from the outline provided above that cost and management accounting is concerned with influencing human behaviour through the figures it provides. The behavioural consequences of information provision are thus paramount and behavioural considerations are an essential ongoing aspect of the study of the subject.

1.5 THE APPLICATION OF COST AND MANAGEMENT ACCOUNTING

Cost and management accounting is appropriate for all businesses, whether large or small, manufacturing or service, and regardless of their ownership structure. However, greater scope for more extensive cost analysis, and thus also for subsequent use of information, is provided by a manufacturing environment. As a result such an environment often occupies centre stage in textbooks and examination questions, especially in the area of cost accumulation.

In this text, the manufacturing environment will be given prominence for the reasons already stated and also due to the fact that, in many industries, it is undergoing particularly rapid change as a result of advances in computer technology applied to manufacturing and due to changes in philosophy. This has implications for both accounting and organisation systems. It is important to appreciate the variety of situations that exist and the influence that the particular situation has on costing method.

Service industry environments, however, will also be considered. Whilst generally offering less scope for extensive cost analysis they provide considerable potential for effective management accounting. They have been rather neglected in the literature. What distinguishes a manufacturing organisation from a service organisation is the existence of a manufactured physical product. Service organisations towards the manufacturing half of the continuum discussed earlier will have many of the characteristics of a manufacturer. For example a shoe repairer will have premises and machinery, and will incur significant materials as well as labour costs.

The importance of service industries has grown with increasing average wealth. The world market for services is nearly one-third of manufactured goods. The leisure industry for example has been a major growth industry in both the public and private sectors of the economy. Other significant growth areas include the computer industry, where computer services have been prominent, financial services, and retailing.

Many of the accounting methods employed in commercial organisations can be adapted to welfare or non-profit organisations. The important thing is to be clear what the objectives of the organisation are. Once established, the role of cost and management accounting will be to assist in their successful achievement. Where profit, as traditionally measured by a commercial organisation, is not the objective, other measures of benefits are required. Concepts such as value for money may be used to measure performance. Cost efficiency will be equally important.

1.6 THE PLACE OF THE MANAGEMENT ACCOUNTANT

A major determinant of how the management accountant performs the role can be his/her position within the organisation structure, especially to whom he/she reports. For example, a management accountant in a purely accounting department which is ultimately responsible as a function to the financial director may conceive the role differently from one who is a member of a multi-functional team reporting to a business unit manager.

A second aspect of structure may be the physical location of management accountants. Should they be located in a specialist accounting department or alongside the managers who they serve? The question is likely to be relevant only in situations where management accountants are in a specialist department as far as the organisation structure is concerned. Where the management accountant is structured as part of a multi-functional team then location within the business unit is likely to follow.

There are thus three possible types of structural and locational arrangement:

1 Fully decentralised, where the management accountant reports to a non-accounting manager and is also located within the multi-functional unit.
2 Partly decentralised, where the management accountant is structured within a specialist accounting department but is located within a multi-functional unit.
3 Fully centralised, where the management accountant is both structured and located within a specialist accounting department.

Interaction between accountants and managers is likely to be greatest in fully decentralised units. Also, there are likely to be fewer conflicts and greater attention to accounting information, which may be more favourably received. Certainly the management accountant in such situations is in a better position to provide assistance to management and fulfil the attention-directing and problem-solving roles. This may, however, result in the pursuit of narrow goals, sometimes in conflict with other units. Decentralisation can mean more conflicting demands on the management accountant between central accounting and the management accountant's non-accounting superiors.

Centralisation on the other hand is likely to result in less interaction between accountants and managers. It will be more difficult to establish the necessary relationship if centralised, especially if this is locationally. Centralisation is likely to lead to greater emphasis on score-keeping. This may be desirable, however, if this aspect of the management accountant's role is to be emphasised. It enables the management accountant to be more of a watchdog for top managers, a means by which hierarchical control may be imposed. Centralised accounting also permits specialisation and greater guidance and control, preventing the pursuit of narrow goals.

Other factors which affect the arrangement are the size of units and the size of the business as a whole, the relative cost of alternative arrangements, the question of career structure, and the personalities involved at a particular time. Sometimes a half-way solution is reached, physically locating the management accountants within the business units served, whilst maintaining line reporting through the accounting function. A further factor, however, is the degree of centralisation/decentralisation of the organisation structure as a whole. If it is centralised along functional lines the management accountants will also operate in a centralised functional unit. Overall, organisation structure and location can affect management accounting and its effectiveness.

SUMMARY

Cost and management accounting is that branch of business accounting which seeks to provide useful information within a business in order to facilitate its effective management. Cost and management accounting has a fundamental difference of objective compared with financial accounting. Other significant differences arise as a result. In contrast to financial accounting there are fewer rules, greater concern with the future, more detailed information, assignment of responsibility for different aspects of performance, greater involvement with others in generating information, and as a result, a requirement to be more familiar with other functional aspects of the business, and to communicate effectively with other functional managers.

Cost and management accounting seeks to provide three basic types of information viz score-keeping, attention-directing, and problem-solving. The subject matter covered in this book under the section headings 'Cost Accumulation and Performance Measurement', 'Decision-Making', and 'Planning and Control' seeks to satisfy the information requirement. The requirement exists, and can be satisfied, in a wide range of businesses. Degree of success may be influenced by the place of the management accountant within the organisation. A number of factors which may be influential should be recognised.

This chapter has been essentially introductory. It provides a background for the studies in the remainder of the book. For this reason end-of-chapter exercises are not provided.

The Environment and Utility of Cost and Management Accounting

INTRODUCTION

The nature of management accounting changes as a result of changes in the environment in which it operates. Advances in manufacturing technology for example can have an important impact. In addition, in order to appreciate fully the influences on management accounting, it is necessary to put it into a wider organisational setting. Another significant factor is the development of information technology; it is desirable to have some appreciation of the available technology and of the impact that the technology has had, and will continue to have, on management accounting information provision.

A brief description of changes in the manufacturing environment, and a consideration of the effect of organisational setting and information technology on management accounting are provided in this chapter. This is followed by a brief review of both the theory and practice of management accounting, asking whether it serves the needs of management adequately at minimum cost.

2.1 MANUFACTURING ENVIRONMENT

2.1.1 A new manufacturing philosophy

In order to compete effectively, many companies engaged in manufacturing must be capable of producing increasingly sophisticated products of the highest quality and with first-class service, but at low cost. They must also have the flexibility to cope with shorter product and equipment life cycles, and with demands for greater product variety, the combined effects of greater competition and more discriminating customers. To achieve this the production process in many industries has had to change in order to improve quality, reduce set-up times, increase manufacturing flexibility, overcome restrictive work-force rules and reduce randomness caused by uncertain supply, poor quality and erratic machine performance.

Indeed, in many industries manufacturing philosophy is undergoing quite dramatic change. In many respects the wheel is turning full circle with a return to small–batch production of complete products on flexible equipment, instead of the large–batch mass production of parts of products in specialised processes which has been relatively commonplace. The economics of volume versus variety have radically shifted.

A major factor, but by no means the only factor, which has brought about this change in economic logic, has been the advances in computer technology applied to manufacturing. Whilst throughout the history of manufacturing there has been a steady trend of substituting machinery for labour, the pace of change has altered dramatically over the last few years.

Automated manufacturing and the use of computers in design and production management is not new, but inflexibility hitherto restricted their application to volume production of a few products. The great advance has been in flexibility as well as in developments in technology generally. Concepts of Just In Time (JIT) and Total Quality Control (TQC) have also become established which, to a certain extent regardless of computer technology, have pointed the way to a new manufacturing philosophy and organisation.

The ACARD report expressed the view that 'those firms which do not make use of these technologies risk being overtaken by competitors achieving superior quality at lower cost'. It is important to add, however, that it is obviously wrong to invest for the sake of it. Automation is not a panacea. It should also be recognised that significant benefits may be achievable as a result of change in thinking, for example JIT concepts, as much as from capital investment. The level of capital investment required is not necessarily large. It is important though to consider advanced manufacturing technology (AMT) investment possibilities and to reject them only for the right reasons.

2.1.2 Technologies and concepts available

It is important to stress at the outset that AMT relates to the technology of the manufacturing process and not to the technology of the product. It is certainly not confined to high technology products. Neither is the potential confined to only the largest firms. The main areas of AMT are in Computer–Aided Design (CAD), Computer–Aided Manufacture (CAM), Flexible Manufacturing Systems (FMS) and Computer–Integrated Manufacture (CIM).

CAD systems enable drawings to be constructed on a VDU screen and subsequently stored, manipulated and updated electronically. CAM systems support production engineering by defining operating sequences and part routing, creating control tapes for Computer Numerically Controlled (CNC) machines, establishing requirements for fixtures, tooling, etc and simulating operations prior to 'first-off' machining. FMS consist of sets or 'cells' of computerised numerical controlled machining stations with automated and integrated systems for tool changing, workpiece transfer and loading, and inspection. Computer based systems are also available for inventory control, production planning and control, stores and parts issue and testing. The ultimate goal is to link all facets of an enterprise ie design, purchasing, production planning and control, machining, assembly, inspection, marketing and accounting, through a common database to provide CIM.

The new technology is operating in practice although there are only a few instances of all elements of the factory of the future. On a general level investment in computerised manufacturing technology has been the key factor in the recovery of the UK textile industry. Aero engine and automobile manufacture are other examples of industries where extensive use of AMT has been made.

Concepts of JIT and TQC have also had an impact on production systems. JIT Manufacture is a production system which utilises modern technology but is not dependent upon it. It is based on the principle of organising manufacturing plants along product lines rather than by specialisation of function, with production being demand driven, such that in the absence of demand no production takes place. It is a pull through rather than a push through system. This has the effect of reducing work-in progress and finished goods stocks, and requirements for space. A lot of emphasis is placed on preventive machine maintenance and manufacturing flexibility. In contrast, push through systems have been commonplace with emphasis on large batch production making the fullest possible use of production capacity.

The same JIT principles applied to raw materials and bought-in components has a similar effect on stock and space requirements. This depends upon being able economically to reduce order quantities and upon frequent and reliable delivery schedules, reduced and highly reliable lead times, and consistent quality of material. It requires a very close relationship with suppliers with local sourcing wherever possible, and pushes quality and reliability back to the supplier.

The ideal state of JIT purchasing and production would be a stockless system, where material/product is purchased/produced just as it is needed for the next stage. Whilst the concept of JIT is not practical or feasible for all companies, very real opportunities do exist to reduce stocks and thus the cash cycle. Success is dependent upon the effective co-ordination of the different stages of manufacture and the availability of materials.

The objective of TQC is to eliminate waste and improve quality in all areas of an organisation in order to reduce cost and improve the quality of products and services. Higher quality should be a driving force in the new manufacturing environment. The time has gone when low price served as the primary basis for competition, with quality defined as a standard level of acceptability. There is also an increasing realisation that poor quality is a significant cost driver. Quality is not expensive, non-quality is.

Like JIT, the potential for TQC is improved by AMT which to summarise can be thought of as consisting of three levels: the stand-alone piece of equipment, the cell, and the fully integrated factory.

2.2 ORGANISATIONAL ENVIRONMENT

The study of management accounting should consider the broader context of the organisational environment within which the management accounting system operates. Organisation refers to the way that activities of people are co-ordinated to achieve a goal. Organisation structure indicates the division of responsibility and authority. This has a major influence on information needs and also on how information is used in conjunction with objectives and targets. Information needs determine the structure of data collection and processing.

Traditional approaches to organisation design developed 'rational' models of the organisation, using a closed systems approach. The organisation was considered apart from its external environment. The scientific management theories formulated by Taylor, the administrative theories of Fayol, and to some extent the bureaucratic theories of Weber are examples of closed system approaches to organisational design. In the same way approaches to management accounting systems design have also traditionally used a closed system approach.

Alternative approaches to organisational analysis have been provided by general systems research, and, more recently, by contingency theories of organisational processes. Contingency theory research on organisations suggests that the collection, provision and determination of requisite decision information will be affected by a wide variety of situational and behavioural factors. There are complex interactions between parts of the organisation and between the organisation and its external environment. Systems must be viewed as 'open' rather than 'closed'. Contingency theory provides a framework for understanding the design of management accounting systems by examining such systems in the context of the environment, organisation structure and technology within which they operate.

Hierarchical organisation structures on functional lines and/or business (divisional) lines are common. The size and type of organisation will be an influence. In a functional structure one problem is ensuring that functional goals are consistent with organisational goals. The implications of particular actions on the business as a whole may not be appreciated, or an individual manager may not be sufficiently concerned. For example, a goal of sales maximisation for the selling function may mean too many products which is a cost to production. Functional goals should be a subset of organisational goals for effective management. Clear specification of organisational goals is paramount. If they are unstated or unclear, adequate performance measurement is impossible.

In a divisional structure, although goals should be entirely consistent with those of the organisation as a whole, the question is whether divisional behaviour, although to the benefit of the division, is to the net benefit of the company eg a decision by a division to buy-in from outside rather than from another division. Ultimately the managing director can take an overall organisation view, but only the largest decisions will be taken at that level. In any case such involvement could have adverse motivational consequences.

The more dynamic, uncertain and competitive the environment facing a business, the more flexible the organisation structure needs to be in order to permit and encourage adaptive, pro-active and inventive management. In the new manufacturing environment described earlier, manufacturing must reflect its central role. It is no longer responsible for delivering what marketing demands or the engineer designs; manufacturing and its capabilities have become increasingly central to the strategic positioning of the firm. The manufacturing manager will have a far more complex, sophisticated and demanding job, and thus needs to be better represented at senior levels. Engineers likewise; it is necessary to get away from the 'oily rag' syndrome.

The task of management accounting is to establish appropriate measures of performance in each area of the business. This requires awareness of the types of decisions taken and of information relevant to their choice, as well as awareness of goals and organisation structure.

A further environmental factor is communication. Good communication between departments is of great importance, with close working relationships needed, for example between manufacturing and marketing, research and development and design. Changes in organisation structure, or personnel, should be made where necessary to create stronger links. Communication is a major influence on the success of information systems, including management accounting. The important questions that should be asked are—does the information get passed on, in unimpeded form, and more important in management accounting, is it understood?

Finally, it is important to recognise that organisations have a culture. Organisational culture goes further than structure, goals, and communication. There may in addition, and independently, be differences between organisations in atmosphere, attitudes and general behaviour. This can influence the effectiveness of management accounting.

2.3 INFORMATION TECHNOLOGY

2.3.1 Impact on management accounting

An ongoing revolution in information technology (IT) has continued to exert a profound influence on accounting information systems, (as well as all other types of information systems), especially management accounting. The driving force has been the computer. Computing now dominates many aspects of accounting life. In virtually all organisations, whatever their size, the computer is responsible for processing accounting transactions and preparing accounting reports. There has been a huge growth in the ability to collect and manipulate large volumes of data. This is not just for routine purposes, but increasingly on an ad hoc basis, as computers become smaller, faster, more reliable, more user friendly, more flexible, and less expensive. If properly used, advances in information technology now enable:

1. Greater flexibility of information provision, with increasing opportunities for tailoring reports to user and use, and thus more focused information.
2. More frequent availability of information. Weekly reports rather than, or as well as, monthly reports, may be provided and be the particular focus of attention.
3. More detailed information with more comprehensive and comprehensible reports.
4. Faster feedback of information. Actual results can be identified much more quickly and rapid comparisons can be made against budget.
5. Reduced emphasis on routine reporting, with greater exception reporting, and substitution of highly selective management reports.
6. Information to be produced relatively cheaply. The computing revolution of the past two decades has removed significant barriers to the design and implementation of effective management accounting systems through the reduction of costs of information collection and processing.
7. More widespread access to databases. Many managers now have a terminal on their desk linked to mainframe systems which are more user friendly. The development of personal computers and spreadsheet packages has also provided widespread and easier access.
8. New information to be provided. For example, in the retail industry, the introduction of electronic point of sale technology now enables sales of individual items to be identified accurately, losses to be known, the effect of pricing/promotion decisions to be gauged, and space to be more effectively utilised.
9. Sensitivity analysis to be carried out. The computer model and availability of terminal access may enable 'what if' questions to be asked and answered.

Overall, IT offers significant opportunities for management accountants to perform their existing functions better. It is not, however, without its dangers. At its worst it has resulted in mountains of paper and information overload. Also, too frequently, the information generated from computer systems is no more than a summary of transaction data. The technology is useful and valuable but only so long as the information being collected and disseminated is appropriate, and reaches the manager at the right time, in the right place, in the right form, and for the right reasons. Another problem for many organisations is that computer systems have grown over time and often comprise a collection of separate systems with different hardware and software. They do not easily provide the flexibility required and offered by brand new computer systems. Difficult decisions are whether to carry on adapting the existing systems or whether to make major investment in new systems.

2.3.2 Technology and data/information processing

A particular feature of the development of technology has been the increasing use of desk-top terminals linked to mainframe computer systems. They are now widespread, enabling decision-support systems to be made available to senior managers through accessibility of both accounting and non-accounting information from an organisation's database. The terminal has given immediate input and output access, potentially to anybody in the organisation. Output can be easily organised in different forms eg tables, graphs. This has had a profound effect not just on the availability of information but also on the way it is acquired and used. Microcomputers, which have enabled the development of small, inexpensive and user-oriented computer systems, have also become very prominent.

Software packages range from complete management accounting routine reporting packages for mainframe application to discrete packages for use on microcomputers. Choosing the right software is more difficult, but at the same time more important, because there are many accounting packages to choose from which, once chosen, will have a fundamental influence on management accounting information provision for years to come. Spreadsheet packages, which are software packages for microcomputers, have figured prominently in computer development. They enable the user to create small financial models without the need for any programming knowledge and without any necessary link with mainframe applications. They are versatile, powerful, and user–friendly.

It is important to differentiate between 'data' and 'information'. 'Data' are facts and figures about events. They are input to an information system and then stored and/or processed. 'Information' is the combination of data into a form that has a particular relevance in the planning and control process. Computers frequently perform the necessary data processing steps and have tremendous storage capacity. What is in store can be readily called upon for further processing or updating, to produce management information. The task of cost and management accounting is to collect data and ensure that it is put together to provide useful information. Data are the raw material from which information is produced.

Many data processing applications in business and accounting consist of the updating of master files on the occurrence of transactions or other file activity, which is called file maintenance. Due to the high volume of input which is typical of many business data processing applications, it is common in business systems for transactions to be accumulated in batches that are processed at given time intervals or after the batch reaches a certain size. This method of data processing is referred to as batch processing.

Alternatively, individual transactions can be processed through a computer system as they occur. This is called on-line processing. The advantage of on-line processing is that files are kept up-to-date at all times. With batch processing this may only be once a day, once a week, etc. On-line processing also avoids the need for batching operations. However, the software for on-line processing is generally considerably more expensive, and more machine time is required for a given set of transactions.

2.3.3 Information strategy

The introduction and utilisation of new technology should follow from a coherent information strategy based on the individual needs of the people running the business. Defining this calls for a detailed analysis of the decisions people make, the information requirements of such decisions, and the source of such information within the business. Managers need to be fully aware of their decision-making role, and hence the information that they need, and of the role which they play in satisfying the information needs of others.

Organisations should regard information systems and their associated technology as investments. This brings the need to assess viability in terms of contribution to the business. Expected benefits should be identified (a list of potential benefits was provided earlier) and compared with purchase, implementation, and running costs associated with computerisation.

Considerable amounts of money are being spent on technology more as an act of faith than as a strategic necessity. If technology is not harnessed to satisfy the information needs of the business then the problem of sheer volume may result. This arises because:

1 The computer facility is available and will tend to be used to provide more and more information.
2 A report, once set up, will continue unless, and until, action is taken to stop it.

2.3.4 Impact on management accountants

The skills requirements of the modern accountant are changing. The ability to use computers is becoming a necessity rather than a luxury. This does not mean that accountants and accountancy students have to rethink the basic concepts. The knowledge base remains largely unaltered.

2.4 ECONOMY, EFFICIENCY AND EFFECTIVENESS

The objective of any organisation, and of separate tasks within each organisation, will be to achieve effectiveness, efficiency and economy. In general there is no direct link between them, although they are clearly related. Separate measures of each are therefore required, and will form important aspects of the study of cost and management accounting through this book.

Economy is the level of input resources applied to a particular task.

Efficiency is the relationship between the resources applied to a task and the output of work generated.

Effectiveness is the relationship between the output generated and the output desired (the objective).

The same tests can be applied to management accounting itself. Is it economical, efficient and effective? ie, Does it serve the needs of management adequately at minimum cost? A view on the state of management accounting theory and practice is required.

2.5 A REVIEW OF THEORY AND PRACTICE

Many researchers have identified a considerable gap between theory and practice. Kaplan, for example, believes that efforts to introduce new competitive manufacturing technologies and modern management methods are hampered in many cases by obsolete accounting and control systems—systems that distort product costs, fail to provide key non-financial data, and are dominated by external reporting requirements. His views have been echoed by many other distinguished academics who have presented a somewhat gloomy picture of the state of the art.

It is certainly true that some things which are conventionally practised are difficult to defend in theory. The practice of fixed overhead apportionment, especially based on fairly arbitrary apportionment bases, is not uncommon yet is traditionally criticised in the literature. It could be argued, however, that it provides a very approximate indication of long-run costs and is thus useful. It depends very much on how and when the information is used. Also, in Scapens' view, 'until the role of management accounting practice is better understood, it is extremely difficult to make prescriptive statements regarding the usefulness of new or revised accounting methods. We cannot even say that contribution approaches are to be preferred in practice to methods which include allocated overheads—as is claimed in most management accounting textbooks'. There has been no dramatic change since he expressed this view.

Coulthurst, in his study with Sizer of management accounting practices, concluded that managements made a conscious selection of elements of theory which are practical and useful in their own particular circumstances. It is all too easy to assume that theory is correct and level criticism at practice. To be practical and thus applicable, a model must possess both prescriptive (normative) validity and descriptive (empirical) validity. In other words the model must be based not only upon how people in theory should behave, but also upon how in practice they are reasonably capable of behaving. Theory may be too advanced for practical application. This is certainly a criticism levelled by many practitioners.

It is important to recognise also that information is not costless. Recognition of this fact leads to the realisation that practitioners cannot necessarily be criticised simply because they choose to ignore the conventional wisdom of management accounting. The use of simple techniques or rules-of-thumb can represent optimal responses to the cost and benefits of information provision. However, if information cost is a primary reason for any gap between theory and practice, then technology should enable the gap to close. The response to information cost is a further reason why it is necessary to study actual practice, rather than prescribe what it should be. It is no use presenting complex models, even if they are capable of application, which assume that information generation has no cost.

Also, even if there is no apparent gap between theory and practice, this in itself is not justification of the theory. Both may be slow to respond to changes in the environment or may be a victim of their historical development. For example, as far as the environment is concerned, the prescriptive accounting literature has been slow to face up to the challenges posed by changes in the organisation and technology of manufacturing. Kaplan especially has highlighted this failing, stating that '. . . the cost accounting implications of these more advanced production control systems have barely been investigated, and, as a result, our cost accounting textbooks continue to describe production processes using extremely simplified models . . . It is unlikely that our current accounting graduates will have any understanding of the complex production environment in which cost accounting must be applied today'.

The pattern of historical development has also inevitably had an important influence on both theory and practice. Management accounting's score-keeping role has developed over a long period of time but very much as a by-product of transaction based systems, heavily influenced by the requirements of external reporting. In the authors' view, there is, as a result, a lack of any clear integration between decision-making concepts and routine information provision, and a failure to consider sufficiently factors which should influence that provision. The result is that routine information provision may not provide a useful basis for decision-making. The flexibility to provide for different decision situations is lacking and thus the conditional truth philosophy has been inadequately fulfilled.

Another result of the historical development of cost accounting has been the emphasis on financial measures of performance. Insufficient attention has been given to the development of non-financial measures.

There are two further areas where the management accounting literature could be criticised. There is in general a failure to reflect the changes in information technology which are not only making more information available faster, but reducing the emphasis on routine reporting as such and substituting for it highly selective management reports backed up by facilities for more flexible reporting on demand. There are thus increasing opportunities for tailoring reports to user and use.

Finally, the terminology of management accounting has developed in a rather confusing way for students. There are conceptual difficulties because terms, especially the term 'cost', have many different usages and meanings according to the situation in which the terms are used. Sometimes the terms are synonymous; at others almost but not quite synonymous. What is particularly confusing for students, however, is the inconsistent use, and sometimes misuse, of cost terminology. Many terms used in accountancy are capable of misinterpretation and even accountants disagree as to the precise meaning to be given to a particular term. Also, as Horngren notes, 'you may encounter terms such as allocate, re-allocate, trace, assign, distribute, redistribute, load, apportion, and re-apportion being used interchangeably to describe the same accounting practice'. CIMA have produced an official terminology booklet. However, this does not solve the problem of the plethora of confused and inconsistent terminology in the literature, as many serious deficiencies of detail exist.

SUMMARY

It is important that the subject of management accounting is viewed in the widest possible context, and certainly in a broad organisational context, because of the many influences on management accounting information provision. The introduction to the coverage of management accounting will be expanded upon throughout the book.

It is hoped that the foregoing review of theory and practice does not make the subject more difficult for students. It is important to recognise, however, that management accounting is not fully developed and does not consist simply of separate neat compartments. Whilst presentation of the subject as a set of weakly related topics may be convenient for writing the material and for teaching, this may not be most useful for learning and for effective practice.

Theory and practice may diverge for a variety of reasons. Some criticisms of both may be well founded. It is hoped that this book will provide some reconciliation of theory and practice, and provide a bridge for students who not infrequently complain that what they do at work is nothing like what they are taught.

It is important continually to advance the prescriptive literature. This cannot be without regard to what is reasonably practical. It is necessary also for the prescriptive literature to keep abreast of, and learn from, developments that take place in practice. Management accountants are breaking out of a strait-jacket which left them as providers principally of conventional costing information. The result is quicker, more relevant, and more intelligently presented and discussed information. This is itself the result of pressures to meet changing management needs, of a gradual realisation on the part of management accountants themselves, and of advances in, and availability of, technology.

The challenge is collectively to devise systems and performance measures that support strategic objectives and are consistent with factors peculiar, and critical, to the success of particular businesses.

This chapter has provided further introduction to the study of cost and management accounting. As with Chapter 1 end-of-chapter exercises are not provided.

Cost Behaviour

INTRODUCTION

Costs, like human beings, have varying behaviour patterns. The term 'cost behaviour' refers to the extent to which an organisation's costs respond to a change in the level of activity.

An understanding of cost behaviour patterns, and an ability to project likely cost behaviour in a particular situation, are essential for planning, decision-making and control, and require an understanding of different input/output relationships ie, the relationship between resources utilised and amount of work done. It is important, therefore, as part of the introduction to the studies in this book, to consider these relationships and their effect on cost behaviour, and also to describe and illustrate the various methods of identifying behaviour patterns.

3.1 COST BEHAVIOUR PATTERNS

It can be stated that an increase in activity for an organisation as a whole will result in an increase in total cost. The more work there is to be done, the more resources will be required to do it. The converse is equally true; lower costs will be incurred at lower levels of activity. However, although costs do move in sympathy with activity changes, the cost movements tend to be less sensitive than the activity changes. Total costs contain different cost elements with different behaviour patterns which result in an overall pattern of behaviour somewhere between the following two extremes: proportionality variable costs and absolutely fixed costs.

Figure 3.1 provides a graphical demonstration of a variable cost; total costs change in proportion to the change in activity. Another feature of such a situation is that the unit cost remains unchanged (ie, it is a constant cost per unit of activity). This is because, for each unit of work carried out, the same unit quantity of a particular resource is required, and can be obtained, at the same unit price. Input/output relationships, (ie, between resources required and work to be carried out), can be clearly established and are unchanging, and resources are divisible (ie, can be utilised in small quantities). This may be referred to as an 'engineered' variable cost, so termed because the input/output relationship can be clearly established.

FIGURE 3.1 **Variable cost**

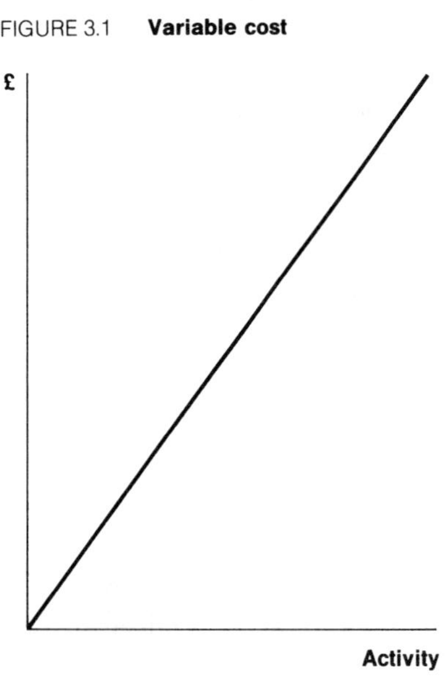

Figure 3.2 provides a graphical demonstration of a fixed cost; total costs remain unaffected by a change in activity. Another feature of such a situation is that the unit cost changes as activity changes, because the same total quantity of a resource is required at the same cost whatever the activity. This may be because resources are not divisible; the cost may be termed a 'capacity' fixed cost (or alternatively 'committed' fixed cost) reflecting the capability to sustain activity. It may on the other hand be because input/output relationships are difficult to establish and a decision is taken to use resources at a particular level. Such a cost may be termed a 'discretionary' fixed cost (also known as 'managed' or 'programmed' fixed cost).

FIGURE 3.2 **Fixed cost**

Some individual cost elements may display characteristics in common with one or other of the two extremes described and illustrated graphically above; other cost elements will display patterns of behaviour between the two extremes. Together all cost elements produce a total cost which will also lie somewhere between.

3.2 FACTORS AFFECTING COST BEHAVIOUR PATTERNS

Activity will not alone influence costs. There are several other factors which may influence input/output relationships, and thus cost behaviour patterns in general, and/or cost behaviour in a particular situation. These factors can be listed as:

1 Nature of the expense.
2 Time period under consideration.
3 Level of activity in relation to normal capacity.
4 Relative size of the change in activity.
5 Attributability of costs.
6 Efficiency.
7 Price paid for inputs.
8 Nature of the organisation's activities.
9 Management policy, judgement, and control.
10 Random factors.

The influence of these factors on cost behaviour is considered below.

3.2.1 Nature of the expense

Consideration of the nature of the expense could be expected to shed some light on likely input/output relationships. As noted earlier, whilst total costs are unlikely to increase/decrease in direct proportion to the increase/decrease in activity, some individual cost elements may display such behavioural characteristics. Simple raw material costs are an example, because they have a clear unit input/output relationship; there is a clear relationship and resources are divisible. This would be a variable cost with a pattern of behaviour as demonstrated in Figure 3.1 if unit prices are also unaffected by activity. The availability of quantity discounts produces more complex cost/volume relationships (see 3.2.5 below).

With other costs the input/output relationship may be reasonably clear but resources may not be divisible, for example rent and rates paid for factory or office space. As a result changes in the resource take place intermittently in a step function (see Figure 3.3). This is referred to as a step-fixed cost; for long periods the cost is fixed, whilst changes may take place, if capacity allows, in activity. In the time period under consideration, for example, one year, it may well be a fixed cost with a pattern of behaviour as demonstrated in Figure 3.2.

FIGURE 3.3 **Step—Fixed cost**

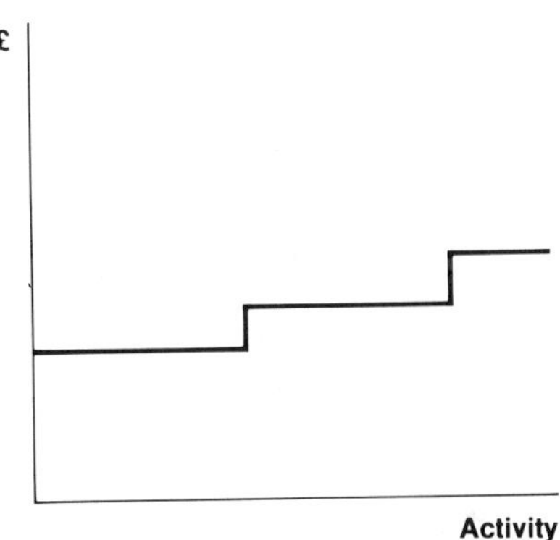

Other resources may be fairly divisible but not infinitely so. Labour paid on a day rate is an example, especially if the total number of employees is relatively large and operations are labour intensive. An increase/decrease of one employee is likely to have a step effect on costs, although payment systems and working hour systems will also have an influence. This is more in the nature of a step-variable cost (see Figure 3.4).

FIGURE 3.4 **Step—Variable cost**

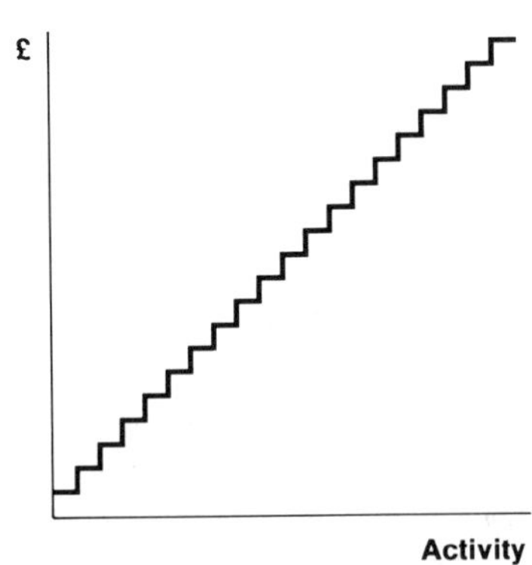

Some costs by their nature may have both fixed and variable elements, and are referred to as mixed costs (see Figure 3.5). The fixed element represents the minimum cost of supplying a service. The variable element is that portion of the mixed cost that is influenced by changes in activity, for example vehicle rental at a fixed cost plus a rate per mile. Electricity and telephone expenses, with a basic fixed standing charge/rental are other examples of mixed costs.

Thus costs by their nature may tend towards one or other of the two extremes of cost behaviour pattern in a particular time period. However, awareness of the nature of the expense is insufficient on its own to identify cost behaviour pattern. A particular cost does not have a particular pattern per se; the factors discussed below may also have an influence.

FIGURE 3.5 **Mixed cost**

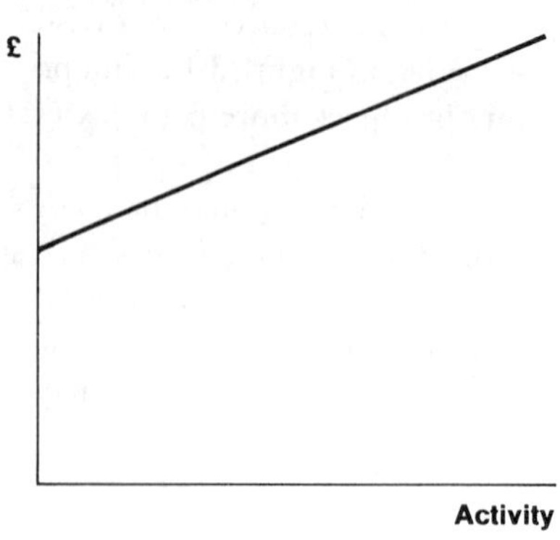

3.2.2 Time period

The time period will influence cost behaviour. The shorter the time period under consideration the more that costs will display the characteristics of a capacity fixed cost. Resources such as machinery, buildings and even labour, may be impossible to change in such a short period; at the same time there may be changes in activity, especially if this is a reduction. The longer the time period the more that input resources, and thus costs, are likely to change in response to a change in activity. In the long-run all costs are subject to variation as levels of activity change.

3.2.3 Level of, and change in, activity

The level of activity in relation to normal capacity and the relative change in activity are factors which will have an influence on cost behaviour in a particular situation. If spare capacity exists then changes in the level of activity will not affect those costs associated with resources which are already committed. If, on the other hand, activity is already at or close to normal capacity, then additional resources will be required for increased activity, for example premiums paid for overtime or additional space rented. If the change in activity is relatively small this may be more easily accommodated with existing resources than if a larger change was being considered. For example, a 1% change in activity may have a rather different effect on costs than a 10% change, apart from the obvious differences in scale. The span of control of a supervisor may accommodate small changes; larger changes, especially if permanent, may result in a change in the number of supervisors.

The above are factors which influence the degree of fixity of costs ie, they provide variations on Figure 3.2 (eg Figure 3.3). Other factors influence the extent of their variability ie, provide variations on Figure 3.1 (eg Figure 3.4).

3.2.4 Attributability of costs

Costs which are attributable to particular activities as opposed to being jointly incurred for several activities will be more directly affected by the introduction/elimination of an activity. For example, if a product which has been manufactured in its own facility (including separate site) is discontinued and not replaced, certain previously fixed costs would be avoided. They would be less easily avoided if incurred jointly. Discontinuation of a major product may be a significant change in activity level, but, if contemplated, cost behaviour would be influenced by the extent to which costs are attributable to the particular activity.

3.2.5 Efficiency and input prices

Efficiency will influence cost variability, as will the price of input resources. For example, whilst raw material costs directly associated with production will display variable characteristics, especially for small changes in activity, if output changes are large, the variable cost may not be linear. This could arise from increasing or decreasing marginal physical productivity, or from a change in input factor prices related to different quantities. Input prices may be influenced for example by the size of the purchase order; at higher levels of activity quantity discounts may be obtained due to increased purchase quantities. Inflation is also a factor which affects input prices over time. Physical productivity will be influenced by the experience of employees, the degree of pressure exerted, and the pressure imposed by production requirements. Overall, on an individual cost, there may be economies, or even diseconomies, of scale.

Labour directly concerned with production may also tend to vary with output, although as noted earlier this could be in a step-variable way. Input/output relationships may be clear. However, as with raw materials, productivity may change over time or at different levels of activity, and input prices may not be constant. With labour, input prices will depend upon the particular payment scheme (for example, a bonus scheme may be in operation) and upon whether shift premiums or overtime apply. Labour productivity will be influenced by similar factors as those affecting raw materials. The learning curve is a particular phenomenon which will be considered later in the chapter. Motivation will also be a factor.

3.2.6 Other factors

There are, finally, some additional factors which may influence cost behaviour patterns. The nature of an organisation's activities is one; for example, the degree of capital intensity in production. When an organisation utilizes fully automatic machinery the worker becomes a machine minder and may take on more of the characteristics of a fixed cost.

The nature of an organisation's activities sets the broad framework. Management policy influences the framework; for example policy decisions regarding part-time workers, overtime, payment systems, redundancy, use of machinery rather than labour. Thus, there is an element of management discretion determining how costs behave. Once the discretion has been exercised in some cases it is difficult to reverse. For example, once machinery has been purchased and installed it will generally have an influence for years to come. Certain costs become committed fixed costs as a result. Some are committed by the organisation as a whole; others by particular activities. This affects the level at which they can be avoided as was noted in 3.2.4 above.

Other costs are not only discretionary as to whether they are incurred in preference to some alternative resource, but are also discretionary as to whether they are incurred at all, and at what level. Once a decision is taken they will generally be incurred regardless of activity but only until such time as the decision is changed. There is no long-term commitment. Advertising costs are an example of a cost which is largely discretionary. There is generally a lack of any clear relationship between input and output ie, advertising expenditure and sales. It is far more a question of judgement. General administration costs have elements of discretion, certainly as to the optimum level of cost to be incurred. It is possible that discretion is exercised in such a way that costs vary with output. A business may make a decision to spend a certain percentage of sales on for example research and development, or training. It may incur expenditure on sales promotion for example in such a way that it is directly linked to sales eg, money off, gift with purchase. How discretion is exercised, and how frequently, will be a factor in cost behaviour.

The degree of control exercised over costs will also have an influence on their behaviour. It may be a factor in achieving productivity improvements, or at least ensuring that productivity is maintained; for example if unit costs are monitored closely over time and feature prominently in progress meetings with staff. The use of budgets may have a restraining effect on administration costs as activity expands, compared with a situation where no such controls are applied. The ability to anticipate work requirements, and thus obtain the level of resources required, is also a control element. Lastly, random factors such as strikes or weather conditions may have an influence on cost behaviour.

3.2.7 Summary

Cost behaviour patterns and likely cost behaviour in a particular situation are not easy to identify and anticipate. However, they are important aspects of management accounting. If a business is going to be in the best possible position to anticipate the likely outcome, in terms of cost incurrence, of taking different courses of action, an awareness of cost behaviour influences and patterns is essential. As a result, decisions can be taken on a sound basis, resource requirements can be better anticipated, and more effective control can be exercised through a comparison of actual results against a clearly–reasoned target. The key questions in order to determine general behaviour patterns are twofold:

1 Are resources fairly divisible?
2 Are there clear input/output relationships?

If the answer to both questions is yes, the cost will have a behaviour pattern at, or towards, the variable extreme. If the answer to question one is 'no', the cost will have a behaviour pattern towards the fixed extreme. If the answer to question two is 'no', the costs become more discretionary, and once decided will frequently be relatively fixed (see Figure 3.6). Various other situational factors (eg, efficiency, spare capacity, time period) will more precisely determine cost behaviour for a particular cost at a particular time.

Figure 3.6 attempts to display the different types of cost behaviour alongside the major influences on cost incurrence.

'Engineered variable costs' (top left–hand corner) are variable with activity. Input/output relationships are clear and resources are divisible. If resources are divisible, but without a clear input/output relationship, they may still be largely variable with activity but cost incurrence becomes due more to discretion being exercised. There are unlikely to be any costs close to the top right–hand corner.

As resources become less divisible, even if input/output relationships are clear (eg machinery), costs become more fixed, eventually (at the bottom left–hand corner of Figure 3.6) becoming 'capacity fixed costs'. As the input/output relationship becomes less clear, and if resources are not easily divisible, costs become 'discretionary fixed' eg an advertising campaign (bottom right–hand corner). A number of costs are likely to fall into the middle ground largely dependent upon divisibility and input/output relationship.

FIGURE 3.6 **Cost behaviour grid**

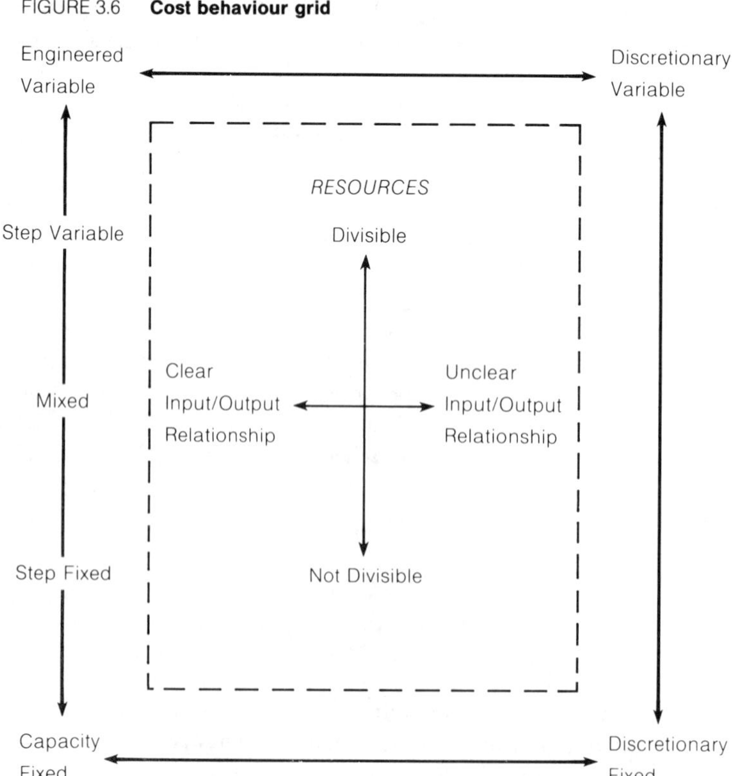

Self-assessment question 3.1

(a) Sketch on a single graph the general pattern of the cost per unit of production over a range of output for each of:

(i) variable cost

(ii) fixed cost

(iii) total cost

(b) Comment on the following: 'fixed costs are really variable: the more you produce the less they become'.

(c) For each of the cost items listed below:

(i) Sketch a graph to indicate the behaviour of the expense (ie total cost in relation to activity) in the short-term.

(ii) Place each item in the appropriate box on the following cost behaviour grid (assume that the grid is similar to that shown in Figure 3.6).

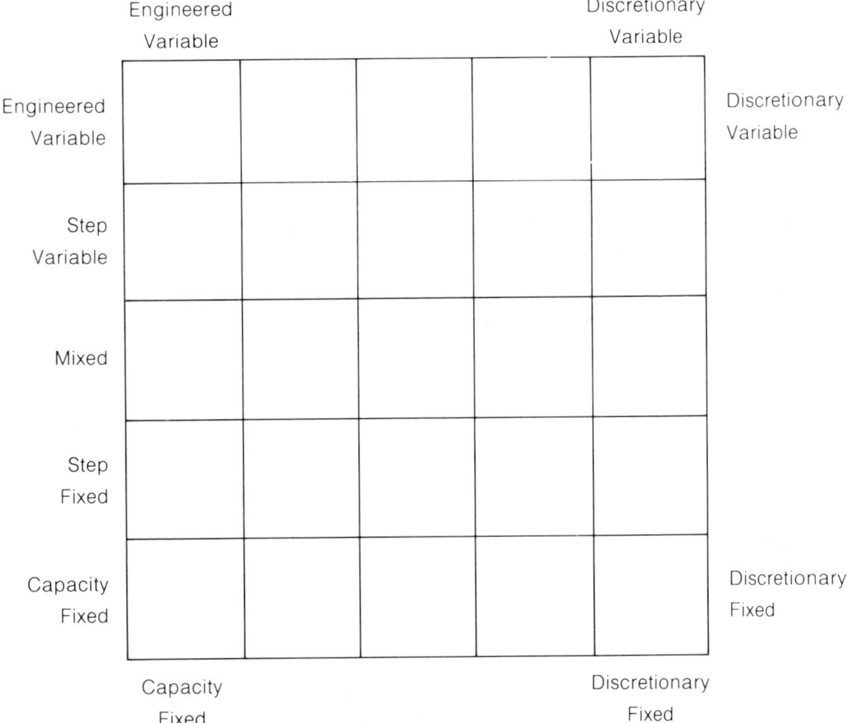

Cost items:

- Supervisory labour in a small capital–intensive plant, with three departments each requiring a supervisor.
- Supervisory labour in a large, labour intensive plant where management judgement and past experience determines that a supervisor will be required for every ten employees.
- Routine preventive maintenance that involves replacement of parts on a planned maintenance schedule in relation to the age of equipment, on the basis of statistical evidence of cost effective maintenance provided by the supplier.
- Plant repair where the age, rather than utilisation, of plant is a significant factor.
- Direct materials, with a quantity discount available on additional purchases beyond the mid-point of the activity range.
- Routine after sales check and rectification if required.
- Sales force costs, where the number of salesmen are adjusted over time in line with sales.
- Expenditure on public relations.

Answers on page 481

3.3 COST BEHAVIOUR OVER TIME

Consideration has been given to the effect on costs of operating at differing levels of activity in a particular time period. Also of interest is cost behaviour over time in relation to cumulative activity.

Fixed costs will tend to be repeated in real terms (ie, common purchasing power) each time period at the same level regardless of the level of activity, although over time they inevitably become susceptible to change, especially if activity levels change to a significant extent. If, for example, activity increases consistently, additional resources will be required from time to time shifting fixed costs on to a new higher level. Inflation will increase costs further, (both fixed and variable), in money terms. Cost–cutting exercises will have the effect of reducing costs.

Total variable costs will tend to increase in real terms over time in proportion to cumulative activity; unit variable costs in real terms would remain unchanged. However, changes in efficiency may occur over time in response to changes in the level of activity. For example, economies of scale may result from increases in activity. Also, improvements in efficiency may result from repetition of an operation, due to the learning effect ie, the more an activity is carried out the more proficient an individual becomes at that activity, through the experience/skills gained. This is likely to have an effect on labour costs particularly.

3.4 THE LEARNING EFFECT

In the earliest stages of the learning process, progress is substantial. Whilst improvement continues thereafter, with an individual becoming more and more proficient at an operation the more it is repeated, the rate of learning progressively slows as there is an ever-diminishing amount of experience/skills still to be acquired. This holds true irrespective of the task performed.

Work study engineers have long recognised the learning phenomenon, but it was not appreciated until the late 1930s that the rate of improvement is regular enough to be predictable. Observations on aircraft assembly led to the conclusion that every time output doubled, the manpower requirement fell by about 20% per unit. Unit costs were thus modelled as an exponential function of cumulative activity producing a learning curve when plotted graphically. The situation where unit costs reduce by 20% every time cumulative output doubles is known as an 80% learning curve. The learning effect is usually expressed in such a way, ie a stated % learning curve denoting the effect on average hours per unit for a doubling of output.

3.4.1 The learning curve

The table below shows the application of an 80% learning curve. A sequence of production quantities, with each quantity doubling the previous cumulative production quantity, is shown. The average labour hours per batch of 10 units for the cumulative production is reduced by 20% at each doubling of output. A further feature is that the hours required for the incremental output, in order to double cumulative production, are 60% of the hours required for the previous cumulative production. The marginal improvement (40%) is always twice the improvement in the cumulative average (20%).

Thus:

Order Number	Number of Units		Cumulative Hours		Incremental Hours for Order
	On Order	Cumulative	Per Batch of 10 units	Total	
1	10	10	10.00	10.00	10.00
2	10	20	x 80% = 8.00	16.00	x 60% = 6.00
3	20	40	x 80% = 6.40	25.60	x 60% = 9.60
4	40	80	x 80% = 5.12	40.96	x 60% = 15.36
5	80	160	x 80% = 4.10	65.60	x 60% = 24.65
6	160	320	x 80% = 3.28	104.96	x 60% = 39.36

Figure 3.7 demonstrates the characteristic shape of the learning curve, with cumulative average hours plotted against cumulative production quantity.

FIGURE 3.7 **80% Learning curve**

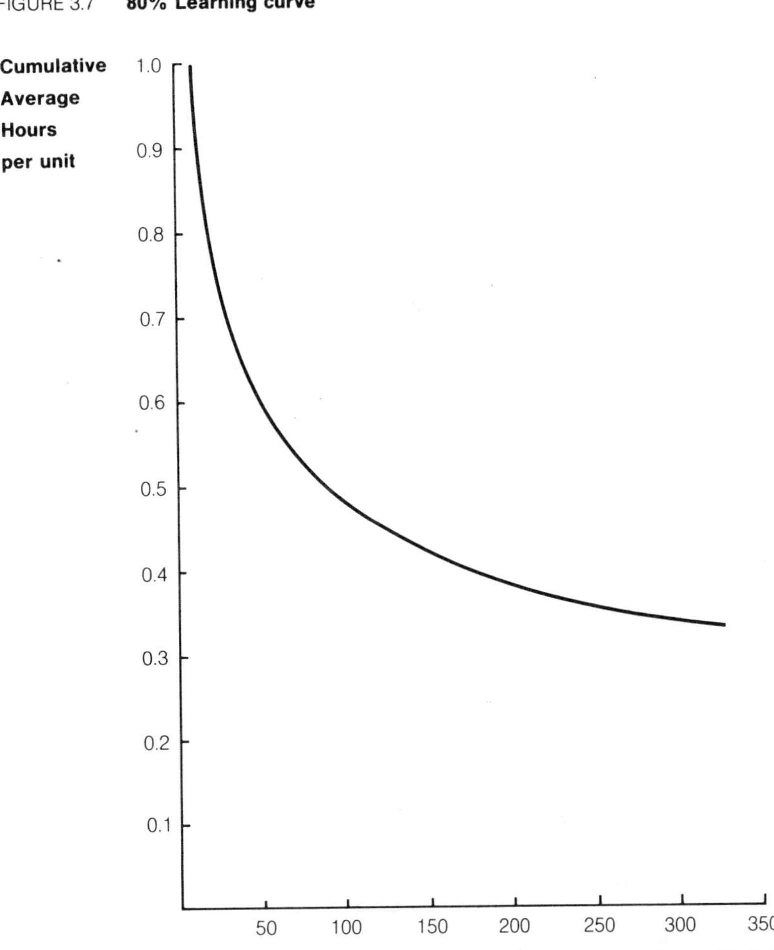

As can be seen the curve dips at a sharp angle at first and then slopes gently as the constant improvement has a smaller and smaller effect on the absolute level of cost, whilst at the same time being extended over larger and larger doubled output quantities.

Cumulative cost may be very sensitive to different learning effects, especially if the learning continues for some time. If, in the above example, 85% or 90% learning effects are applied instead, cumulative hours for the six orders would be:

Order No	**Cumulative Units**	**Cumulative Hours**	
		85%	**90%**
1	10	10	10
2	20	17	18
3	40	28.9	32.4
4	80	49.1	58.3
5	160	83.5	105.0
6	320	142.0	189.0

Cumulative hours, and therefore cumulative labour cost, at 85% and 90% learning effects are 35% and 80% respectively above those at 80% learning effect, if learning continues for six orders.

The minimum possible learning curve in theory is just above 50%. A 50% learning curve would suggest that the incremental hours to double output are zero.

Order Number	Number of Units		Cumulative Hours		Incremental Hours for Order
	On Order	Cumulative	Per Batch of 10 units	Total	
1	10	10	10.00	10.00	10.00
2	10	20	× 50% = 5.00	10.00	× 0% = 0
3	20	40	× 50% = 2.50	10.00	× 0% = 0

It is unrealistic to expect the learning curve in any situation to be near 50%. The more an activity is machine paced the more the learning curve approaches 100%.

It is difficult to see the consistency in the rate of learning when data is plotted on ordinary arithmetical graph paper. However, the curve is reduced to a straight line on double log graph paper, because as the sequence (unit quantities) increases in geometric progression (ie, 10, 20, 40, 80, 160, etc), the variable (time) decreases in the same manner (1.0, 0.8, 0.64, 0.512, etc).

3.4.2 Calculating labour productivity

The learning effect may be expressed by an exponential function as:

$Y_1 = ax^b$

where

Y_1 = labour productivity measured in terms of average number of hours per batch for output of x batches.
a = number of hours for the first batch.
x = cumulative batches.
b = index of the rate of increase in productivity due to learning.

The model thus describes the manner in which productivity increases with increasing output, throughout the learning period.

The index b has a value between the limits of zero and one. When b = 0 productivity remains constant, ie there is no learning effect. The rate of learning becomes larger as b approaches one. The index b is measured in terms of the log of the learning rate (for a doubling of output), divided by the log of 2 (the output multiple). For an 80% learning effect this is:

$$\frac{\log 0.8}{\log 2}$$

$$= \frac{-0.0969}{0.3010}$$

$$= -0.322$$

Hence for an 80% learning curve:

$Y_1 = ax^{-0.322}$

An alternative expression of the learning effect, in terms of total cumulative hours rather than cumulative average hours per batch, is:

$Y_2 = Y_1\, x = ax^{1-b}$

where:

Y_2 = labour productivity measured in terms of total cumulative number of hours for output of x batches.

Thus with an 80% learning effect cumulative hours for output of x batches would be:

$ax^{0.678}$.

The learning effect expressed in terms of Y_1 or Y_2 is useful for estimating the number of hours, and therefore cost, associated with differing levels of output, given an assumption about the rate of productivity due to learning.

Refer to the earlier example demonstrating an 80% learning effect. The average time per batch (and also per unit), and the cumulative hours, required for output of say 32 batches (320 units) could be calculated using the above formulae:

Average time per batch $(Y_1) = 10.0 \times 32^{-0.322}$

$\log Y_1 = \log 10.0 - 0.322 \log 32$

$= 0.515$

$Y_1 = 3.28$ hrs per batch (or 0.328 hrs per unit)

Cumulative time for 32 batches $(Y_2) = 10.0 \times 32^{0.678}$

$\log Y_2 = \log 10.0 + 0.678 \log 32$

$= 2.021$

$Y_2 = 104.96$ hours.

Alternatively, having already established Y_1,Y_2 can be calculated as $0.328 \times 320 = 104.96$ (or 3.28×32).

Self-assessment question 3.2

A company has commenced a new operation which, from past experience of similar operations, would be expected to have a 90% learning curve, which should continue over the cumulative output currently under consideration. The first batch of output took 120 hours to complete. Successive batches will be of the same size as the first batch.

Required:

(a) Graph the learning curve for values of x = 1, 2, 4, 8 and 16 (where x equals the cumulative batches produced).

(b) Calculate the cumulative average hours per batch when 10 and 20 batches have been completed respectively.

(c) Without reference to your answer to **(b)**, calculate the total cumulative hours for the production of 10 batches.

(d) Calculate the additional hours expected to be required in order to increase cumulative output from 10 to 20 batches.

Answers on page 482

3.4.3 Learning applications

Learning curve theory is more applicable when labour is a significant element in an operation, where there is the opportunity for repetition, and/or where operations are subject to frequent change. The rate of learning achieved will depend upon a number of variables, the two most significant being the ability of the individual concerned and the complexity of the task.

One of the difficulties of using the learning curve model is knowing when the learning phase will cease. After the learning period a steady state of output will tend to occur where no further reductions are possible without the introduction of new methods or new technology. Another serious problem of applying the learning curve model, when used as a planning tool, is the estimation of the model parameters 'a' and 'b'. Past experience may help but the same elements may not exist in the future.

3.5 ESTIMATING COST BEHAVIOUR

3.5.1 Accounts classification method

Cost behaviour patterns may be estimated by applying judgement based upon the nature of the particular expense, and awareness of, and judgement on, the other factors influencing cost behaviour which have been considered in this chapter. Historical data of expense (measured in common purchasing power terms) in relation to activity, will also assist that overall judgement.

If no simple pattern of behaviour can be discerned from past data, and/or if judgement based upon the nature of the expense and general behavioural influences is difficult, a number of other methods are available which attempt to identify cost behaviour patterns from empirical data.

Methods considered will be limited to those which establish a linear relationship and thus a cost equation of the form $y = ax + b$ where:

y = total period cost.

a = variable cost per unit of activity.

b = the level of fixed cost.

x = the level of activity.

Each method assumes, therefore, that a straightforward causal relationship exists between activity and cost (measured in common purchasing power terms). It should be stressed at the outset that such a simple relationship is unlikely to apply in practice. Such an analysis may, however, provide a sound basis for further examination.

3.5.2 Scattergraph

A useful preliminary step would be to prepare a scattergraph showing the relationship between the dependent variable (total cost) and the independent variable (activity). The scattergraph will provide a basis for judging whether it is reasonable to estimate a simple linear relationship between the two variables, or whether a more complex relationship may prevail.

As an example, let us assume that the following information has been obtained for a cost item over a 12-month period. Costs are measured in common purchasing power terms, which means that actual costs incurred must be adjusted to a base value by the application of an inflation factor.

Month	Cost (£)	Activity (units)
1	55,000	2,260
2	46,600	1,540
3	53,800	1,820
4	49,600	1,900
5	52,200	2,340
6	58,200	2,320
7	54,600	2,060
8	55,200	2,400
9	42,200	1,540
10	43,400	1,560
11	60,400	2,580
12	54,600	2,120

Figure 3.8 plots the values on a scattergraph.

FIGURE 3.8 **Scattergraph**

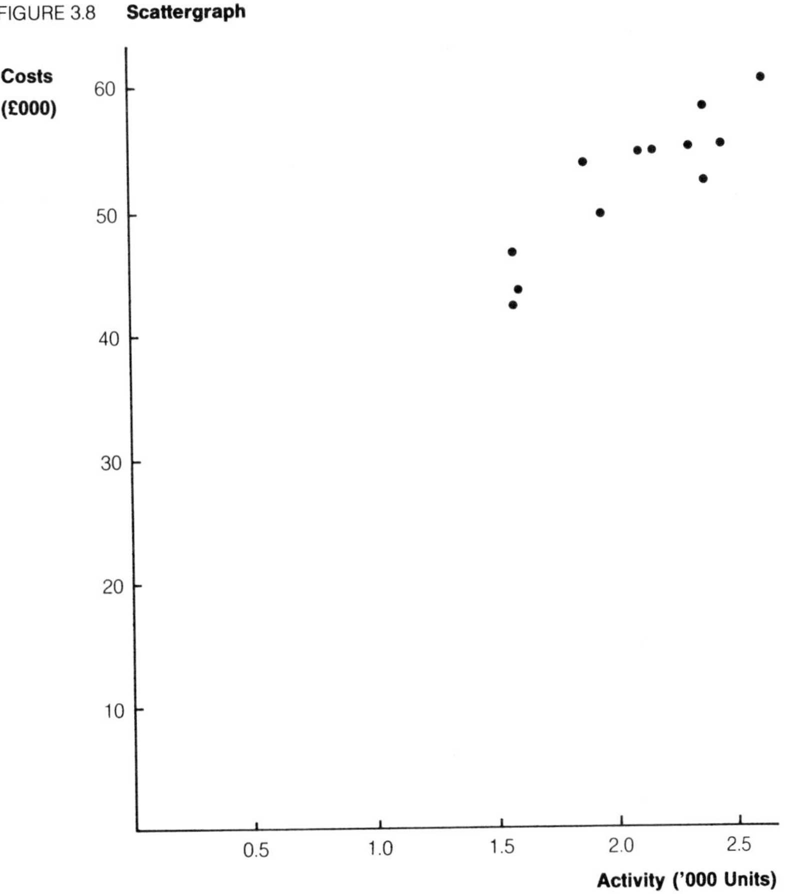

3.5.3 High-low method

The high-low method provides a quick, but as a result approximate, estimate of the linear relationship between cost and activity. The method takes the highest and lowest values, ignoring all others, and uses these to establish the cost equation, $y = ax + b$.

When the line depicting the relationship between cost and activity is drawn on the scattergraph, a is the slope of the line and b is the y intercept (where $x = 0$). 'a' and 'b' are calculated from the highest values (y_2 and x_2) and the lowest values (y_1 and x_1) as follows:

$$a = \frac{y_2 - y_1}{x_2 - x_1}$$

and

$$b = y - ax$$

Using the information from the scattergraph (Figure 3.8),

$$a = \frac{60{,}400 - 42{,}200}{2{,}580 - 1{,}540}$$

$$= \frac{18{,}200}{1{,}040}$$

$$= £17.5 \text{ per unit.}$$

b = 60,400 – (2,580 × 17.5)

= £15,250

or £42,200 – (1,540 × 17.5)

= £15,250.

The line can be drawn on the scattergraph to join the highest and lowest points (see Figure 3.9). The line cuts the y axis at £15,250, the level of fixed cost calculated above.

The advantage of the high-low method is its simplicity. Its disadvantage is that it uses only the two extreme observations to fit the data, which may not represent typical operating conditions.

FIGURE 3.9 **High-low method**

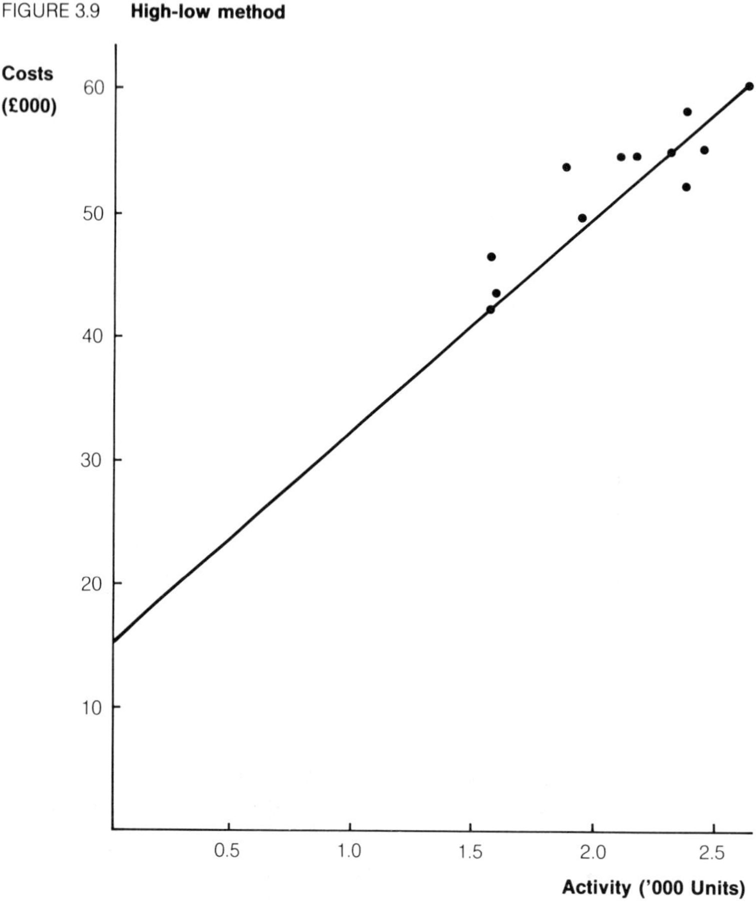

3.5.4 Visual line of best fit

An alternative method of fitting an approximate linear relationship to the data plotted on the scattergraph is to visually draw a line between the points plotted, which seems best to fit the data. Whilst clearly subjective, compared with the high-low method, it does enable all the data to be taken into account in making judgement about the 'line of best fit'. It is difficult, however, to judge correctly the slope of the line.

The line can be continued back to the y intercept enabling the level of fixed cost to be determined. An additional step is then required in order to calculate unit variable cost. This can be determined by measuring the gradient of the line or by taking any other point on the line read from the graph and used in much the same way as the high-low method calculations.

3.5.5 Least-squares regression

Regression analysis provides a statistical line of best fit by minimising the sum of the squares of the vertical distances from each point plotted to the estimated line.

The ordinary least-squares regression minimises

$$\sum_t (y_t - ax_t - b)^2$$

'a' and 'b' can be calculated by solving the following two equations (known as the Normal Equations)

$$\Sigma y = a\Sigma x + bn$$

$$\Sigma xy = a\Sigma x^2 + b\Sigma x$$

where:

n = the number of observations

Σx = the sum of the observations of the independent variable (activity)

and Σy = the sum of the observations of the dependent variable (total cost).

Alternatively the coefficients a and b can be calculated directly as:

$$a = \frac{n\,\Sigma\,xy - \Sigma\,x\,\Sigma\,y}{n\,\Sigma\,x^2 - (\Sigma\,x)^2}$$

$$b = \frac{\Sigma\,y\,\Sigma\,x^2 - \Sigma\,x\,\Sigma\,xy}{n\,\Sigma\,x^2 - (\Sigma\,x)^2}$$

If preferred the coefficients can be calculated as follows:

$$a = \frac{\Sigma\,(x_t - \bar{x})(y_t - \bar{y})}{\Sigma\,(x_t - \bar{x})^2}$$

$$b = \bar{y} - a\bar{x}$$

where:

$$\bar{x} = \frac{\Sigma\,x}{n}$$

$$\bar{y} = \frac{\Sigma\,y}{n}$$

Calculations:

Activity (x)	**Cost (y)**	**xy 000's**	**x^2 000's**
2260	55000	124300	5107.6
1540	46600	71764	2371.6
1820	53800	97916	3312.4
1900	49600	94240	3610.0
2340	52200	122148	5475.6
2320	58200	135024	5382.4
2060	54600	112476	4243.6
2400	55200	132480	5760.0
1540	42200	64988	2371.6
1560	43400	67704	2433.6
2580	60400	155832	6656.4
2120	54600	115752	4494.4
$\Sigma x = 24{,}440$	$\Sigma y = 625{,}800$	$\Sigma xy = 1{,}294{,}624$	$\Sigma x^2 = 51219.2$

number of observations = 12

(i) Using the normal equations:

625,800 = 24,440a + 12b ①

1,294,624,000 = 51,219,200a + 24440b ②

Multiplying equation ① by 2036.6:

∴ 1,274,546,000 = 49,776,133a + 24440b ③

Deducting equation ③ from equation ②:

20,078,000 = 1,443,067a

a = 13.9134

Substituting for a in equation ①

625,800 = 340,043 + 12b

285,757 = 12b

b = 23,813

(ii) Using the second set of equations for calculating the coefficients:

$$a = \frac{(12 \times 1{,}294{,}624{,}000) - (24{,}440 \times 625{,}800)}{(12 \times 51{,}219{,}200) - 24440^2}$$

$$= 13.9134$$

$$b = \frac{(625{,}800 \times 51{,}219{,}200) - (24440 \times 1{,}294{,}624{,}000)}{(12 \times 51219.2) - 24440^2}$$

$$= 23{,}813$$

Thus variable costs are £13.9134 per unit and fixed cost £23,813 per month. In order to plot the regression line a further reference point is required. If activity is say 2,500 units, total cost is £58,597 ((2500 × £13.9134) + £23,813). The regression line is plotted in Figure 3.10.

FIGURE 3.10 **Least–squares regression**

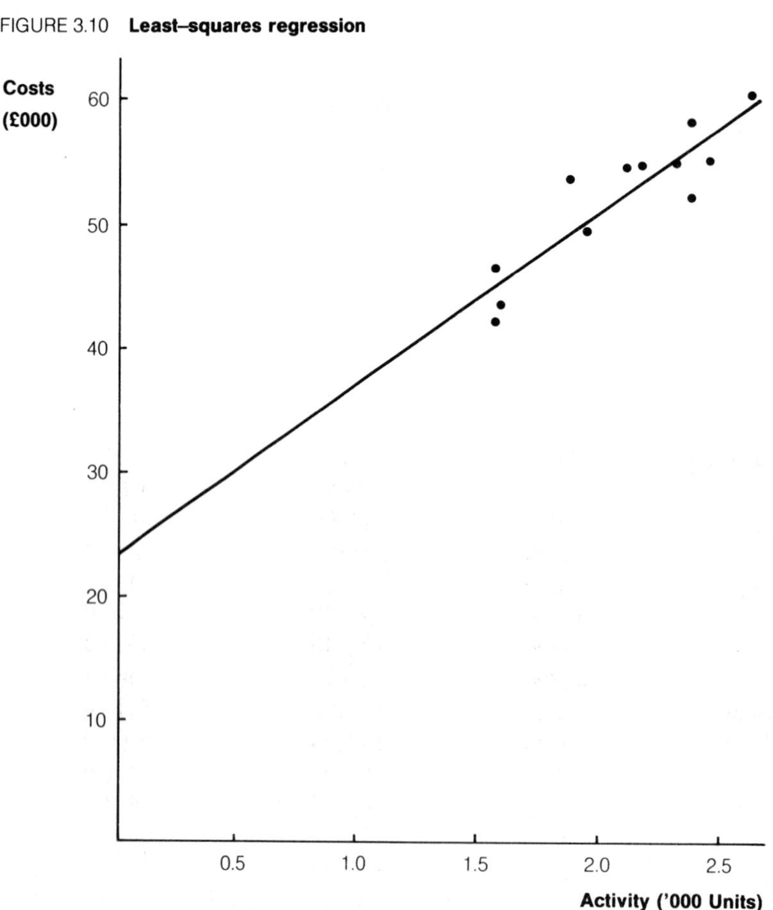

It should be noted that the coefficients provided by the least-squares analysis are substantially different from those calculated using the high-low method.

3.5.6 Goodness of fit

A cost line, and thus cost behaviour pattern, can be established using the various methods above, from any set of data. Whether the values obtained for unit variable cost and total fixed cost are of practical use depends upon whether there is a clear causal relationship and sufficient evidence of correlation. Whilst it is reasonable to assume that there is a causal relationship between activity and cost, the question is whether it is as straightforward as that suggested by the linear relationship, and by the particular cost function calculated. Even if there is a linear relationship the values produced by the methods illustrated in this section, including the least-squares regression, may be wrong due to any unrepresentative data used. In regression analysis the squaring process gives considerable prominence to large fluctuations.

The cost function determined by regression analysis can be tested to establish how well the estimated relationship explains the variation in the observations. The coefficient of correlation, r, measures the extent to which the output variable explains the changes in total costs, and may be measured by the following formula:

$$r = \frac{n\Sigma xy - \Sigma x \Sigma y}{\sqrt{n\Sigma x^2 - (\Sigma x)^2}\sqrt{n\Sigma y^2 - (\Sigma y)^2}}$$

Using the figures as before, and with a calculation of Σy^2 as 32,985,160,000:

$$r = \frac{(12 \times 1{,}294{,}624{,}000) - (24440 \times 625800)}{\sqrt{(12 \times 51{,}219{,}200) - 24440^2} \times \sqrt{(12 \times 32{,}985{,}160{,}000 - 625800^2}}$$

$$= 0.894$$

This suggests a relatively strong linear relationship between the x and y values, but the real significance of a particular r value can only be judged by considering the number of observations. The t-test, the calculation of which is outside the scope of this book, provides a means of judging the significance of an r value calculated from a given number of observations.

The coefficient of determination, r^2, calculates what proportion of the variation in the actual values of y (total cost) may be predicted by changes in the value of x (activity), using the regression coefficients. If all the scatter of the dependent variable is explained by the regression line, the explained variation is equal to the total variation and the coefficient of determination is equal to 1 (or 100%). The line would have perfect predictability. Otherwise r^2 will be between 0 and 1 (or between 0% and 100%).

In the illustration provided:

$$r^2 = 0.894^2$$
$$= 0.799$$

79.9% of the variations in costs may be predicted by changes in the activity level. Factors other than activity could, therefore, be said to influence costs to the extent of 20.1%.

Self-assessment question 3.3

A company has spare manufacturing capacity on one of its machines and the management accountant has been asked to advise sales and marketing management of the hourly rate that should be applied in establishing the viability and required pricing of any additional work that can be obtained. A preliminary analysis undertaken, based on costs and activity over the previous eight weeks, has determined that the average cost per hour is £45.54. The cost and activity data are as follows:

Week	Cost(£)	Activity(hrs)
1	990	20
2	1050	24
3	950	18
4	1005	22
5	1110	30
6	1080	25
7	855	15
8	1020	23

Required:
As management accountant, analyse the figures given above and advise sales and marketing management.

Answers on page 483

In situations where a low r^2 is obtained, consideration should be given to whether a cost function with a single independent variable provides a sufficiently reliable estimate of total costs. A cost function with two or more independent variables requires multiple regression. This is outside the scope of the book. Also outside the scope of the book is the establishment of non-linear cost functions. A particular non-linear model that was recognised earlier in the chapter was the learning curve phenomenon. Output data could be used to estimate the learning rate. It should be stressed that any such calculations, and estimates of costs and resource requirements based upon them, should be viewed with particular caution because of the potential effect of error.

SUMMARY

This chapter has provided an introduction to cost behaviour. It is important to recognise that cost incurrence is not simply dependent upon the level of activity but upon a number of other factors which result in a variety of different behaviour patterns when costs are plotted against activity. The behaviour patterns may be non-linear as well as linear and dependent upon such factors as the nature of the expense, where the divisibility of the resource and the ability to identify clear input/output relationships will be influential; the time period; the level of activity in relation to capacity; the relative size of the change in activity, the attributability of costs; efficiency; the price paid for resources; the nature of an organisation's activities; management policy, judgement and control; as well as certain random factors. An appreciation of the factors affecting cost behaviour and of the different behaviour patterns, provides an essential basis for planning, decision-making and control.

Efficiency over time will be an important factor in influencing successive behaviour patterns. A particular aspect, which may be influential, is the learning process. The rate of improvement in efficiency as a result of learning may be regular enough to be predictable.

A variety of methods are available for estimating particular cost behaviour patterns, especially for establishing a cost equation of the form $y = ax + b$, which assumes a linear, and thus straightforward causal, relationship between activity and cost. It should be recognised that such cost equations should only be used for cost estimation and cost control where they are felt to provide a reasonable approximation.

EXERCISES

Exercise 3.1

It is commonly agreed that cost behaviour is much more complex than is allowed for in the conventional cost accounting model and that costs cannot always be divided into fixed or variable categories.

Describe some alternative forms of cost behaviour that may be relevant for the management accountant. Consider the extent to which cost accounting systems are based on the linear cost function assumption and discuss the proposition that such an assumption can be a serious defect.

(*ACCA Management Accounting, June 1985*)

Answer on page 486

Exercise 3.2

A company is tendering for a contract for the production of 310 units of a particular product. The product, although in certain operational respects similar to other products currently manufactured by the company, is nevertheless expected to be subject to a learning effect. Past experience indicates that an 80% learning curve may reasonably be expected on relevant aspects of the work. Learning is expected to continue over the cumulative activity required to complete the contract.

The contract will be completed in stages with an initial order of 100 units, and then further orders of 80, 70, and 60 units respectively.

The company estimates the following unit costs for the initial order of 100 units:

Direct materials: £62.30 per unit
Direct labour:
  Department A: 2.5 hours at £4.00 per hour
  Department B: 9.5 hours at £4.50 per hour
Variable overhead:
  Department A: £2.00 per machine hour
  Department B: £1.10 per direct labour hour
Fixed overhead:
  Department A: £14.60 per machine hour
  Department B: £2.40 per direct labour hour

The work in Department A requires the use of advanced manufacturing technology. The volume of output is machine controlled and 1.5 machine hours are required per unit of output. Department B is labour intensive and operator efficiency is a major determinant of the volume of output.

An 80% learning effect results in the following relationship between cumulative volume (x), expressed as a multiple of the initial order quantity, and average unit cost (y), expressed as a percentage of the average unit cost of the initial order.

x	y
1.0	100
1.1	96.9
1.2	93.3
1.3	91.7
1.4	89.5
1.5	87.6
1.6	86.1
1.7	84.4
1.8	83.0
1.9	81.5
2.0	80.0
2.1	78.9
2.2	77.8
2.3	76.8
2.4	76.0
2.5	74.9
2.6	74.0
2.7	73.2
2.8	72.3
2.9	71.5
3.0	70.7
3.1	70.0

Required:
Calculate the expected cost per unit for:
(i) the initial order of 100 units and for each of the second, third, and fourth orders.
(ii) the whole contract

Answers on page 488

Exercise 3.3

Gray Ltd will commence operations at the beginning of the year and the budgets for activity and costs for the first 3 quarters of operation are shown below.

Budgets—Quarters I-III			
	QI	*QII*	*QIII*
Period covered—months	1–3	4–6	7–9
Activity	(000's)	(000's)	(000's)
Sales—units	9	17	15
Production—units	10	20	15
Costs	(£000's)	(£000's)	(£000's)
Direct materials—A	50	100	75
—B	40	80	60
Production labour	180	285	230
Factory overheads—excluding depreciation	80	110	95
Depreciation of production machinery	14	14	14
Administration expenses	30	30	30
Selling and distribution expenses	29	37	35
TOTAL COSTS	423	656	539

The figures in the budgets for quarters I to III reflect Gray's cost structures which have the following major features:
(i) the fixed element of any cost is completely independent of activity levels;
(ii) any variable element of each cost displays a simple linear relationship to volume except that the variable labour costs become 50% higher for activity in excess of 19,000 units per quarter due to the necessity for overtime working;
(iii) the variable element of selling and distribution expenses is a function of sales, *ALL* other costs with a variable element are a function of production volume.

In quarter IV the sales volume could range from an extreme low volume of 15,000 units to an extreme high volume of 21,000 units but with a most likely volume of 18,000 units. In month 9 it will be possible to estimate accurately sales for quarter IV and the production level for that quarter will be set equal to the sales volume. Activity for each quarter is spread evenly throughout that quarter.

Cost structures will remain the same in quarters I to III but are expected to differ in quarter IV *only* in the following respects:
(i) Material A will rise in price by 20%.
(ii) All production labour wage rates will rise by $12\frac{1}{2}$%.
(iii) Variable labour input per unit of output will decrease, due to the learning curve effect, such that only 80% of the previous labour input per unit of output is required in quarter IV. The threshold for overtime working remains at 19,000 units per quarter.
(iv) Fixed factory overheads and the fixed element of selling and distribution costs will each rise by 20%. (The variable element of selling and distribution costs will be unaltered.)

The effect of these changes is considered too small to require a change in the standard cost per unit of £30 which is used for stock valuation.

Sales price in quarter IV, £40, will be identical to the price charged in the previous three quarters. All sales are made on terms which are strictly net and allow two months' credit. However, the actual payment pattern expected will lead to:

70% of all sales being paid in accordance with the credit terms.
100% of all sales being paid for within 3 months.

All cash expenses relating to production are paid for in the month production takes place and similarly expenses relating to selling and distribution are paid for in the month of sale.

Required:

(a) Produce a statement which analyses, under each cost classification given in the budgets, the variable cost per unit and the fixed costs which will be effective in quarter IV.

(b) Prepare a flexible budget of estimated production costs for quarter IV. The budget should be drawn up with step points which will facilitate simple interpolation of costs for production levels between those presented in the budget and will also show expected costs for the most likely production level.

(c) **(i)** Prepare statements showing the profit and the cash flow to be derived during quarter IV at the expected, extreme high and extreme low levels of activity.

(ii) Briefly comment on the reasons for any differences between the behaviour of cash flow and profit at the three levels of activity.

(*ACCA Management Accounting, June 1980*)

Answers on page 489

Exercise 3.4

Stobo plc must decide whether to produce and sell either Product X or Product Y in the coming period.

The estimated demand probabilities for the period and the selling prices which have been set are as follows:

	Product X		**Product Y**	
Selling price per unit	£75		£150	
Sales (units)	5,600	1,400	3,200	1,600
Probability	0·6	0·4	0·3	0·7

The average direct material cost per product unit is expected to vary according to quantity purchased as follows:

Product X		**Product Y**	
Units Purchased up to—	*Average Material Cost per unit* £	*Units Purchased up to—*	*Average Material Cost per unit* £
1,000	6·50	1,000	33
2,000	6·00	2,000	30
3,000	5·50	3,000	28
4,000	5·00	4,000	26
5,000	4·75		
6,000	4·50		

Each product would pass through two departments—making and finishing—where the maximum available labour hours are sufficient for all possible quantities. It may be assumed that labour hours which are paid for are balanced by natural wastage, so that labour hours which are surplus to actual production requirements do not need to be paid for.

The labour operations are subject to a learning curve effect of 80% for Product X and 90% for Product Y which would apply in both the making and finishing departments.

Initial batch sizes will be 700 units for Product X and 800 units for Product Y. For these sizes, the hours required per product unit are as follows:

	Product X	**Product Y**
	Hours per unit	*Hours per unit*
Making department	4	5
Finishing department	3	4

Wages are paid at £4 per hour in the making department and £3.75 per hour in the finishing department.

Variable overheads would be incurred at 200% on productive wage costs for the making department and 250% on productive wage costs for the finishing department.

Company fixed overheads are normally apportioned to products as a percentage of sales revenue. During the coming period, when total sales revenue of Stobo plc is estimated at £12,000,000, the overheads have been budgeted at 17.5% of sales revenue. The fixed overheads which would be avoidable if Products X or Y were not produced are as follows:

Product X	£36,000
Product Y	£5,000

Production would be adjusted to equate with sales in the period and the purchase of raw material would be matched with production requirements.

Required:

(a) Showing all relevant calculations, explain which product Stobo plc should produce and sell.

(b) Showing all relevant calculations, explain how the choice of product might be affected if the maximum available labour hours must be retained and paid for in the making and finishing departments but all other conditions are as above.

(*ACCA Management Accounting, December 1987*)

(*Answers provided in lecturer's manual*)

Exercise 3.5

The diagrams below represent nine cost-volume relationships. They have been drawn on the following bases and assumptions:

1 the independent variable is productive activity;
2 the dependent variable is total cost;
3 the graphs are not necessarily drawn to scale;
4 the zero point is at the intersection of the axes;
5 the period being considered is a year;
6 each relationship which is represented should be interpreted as being independent of those shown on other diagrams.

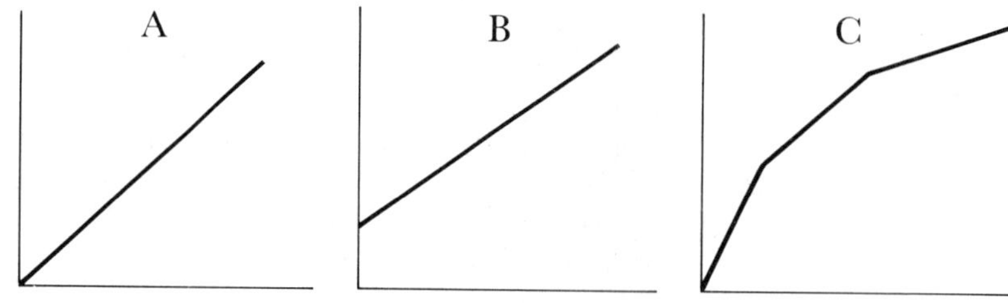

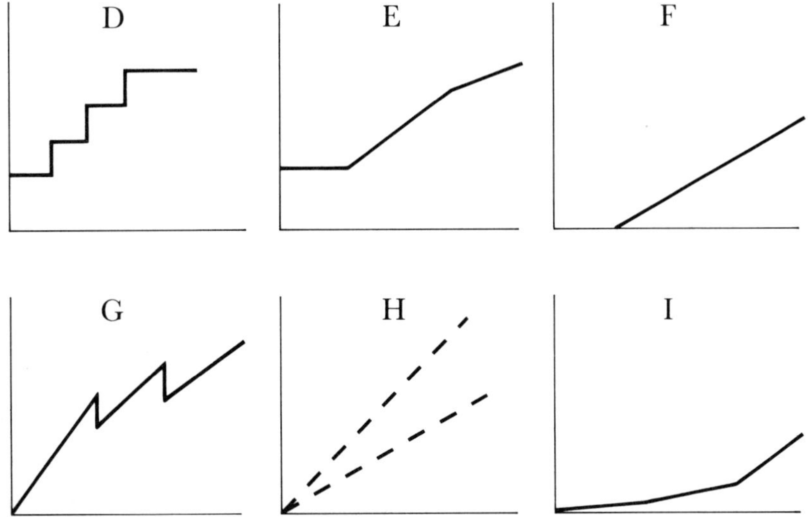

Required:

(a) A brief statement of which relationship each diagram could represent, together with an example, taken either from your reading or own experiences, of a cost that could follow the pattern illustrated. In your answer, clearly indicate which diagram you are discussing.

(c 12 marks)

(b) A brief discussion of how a knowledge of the major cost-volume relationships can be helpful to the management accountant.

(c 8 marks)
(Total 20 marks)

(*ACCA Management Accounting, June 1977*)

(*Answers provided in lecturer's manual*)

Cost—Volume—Profit Analysis

INTRODUCTION

The many factors affecting cost behaviour were considered in the previous chapter. In particular situations, costs will tend either to be fixed regardless of activity, or will tend to vary largely in line with activity. Whilst this may not be exactly so for either classification, it may be reasonable and useful, as a start point to providing management with more information (and as a further introduction to the study of management accounting), to make some simplifying assumptions about cost behaviour which divides them into fixed and variable compartments. This simple dichotomy, and a widening of the analysis to include revenue and profit in the linear model, can be used to carry out analysis of profit/volume relationships for an organisation (later in the book this is extended to more detailed analysis). Such analysis is called 'Cost-Volume-Profit' (CVP) Analysis, sometimes rather restrictedly referred to as 'Break-Even Analysis'.

This final introductory chapter considers the use of the CVP model (the 'accountant's' model), and in contrast to the 'economist's' cost behaviour model.

4.1 ASSUMPTIONS OF CVP ANALYSIS

An important and necessary assumption for CVP analysis concerns the time period. This will have an important influence on the location of costs as fixed or variable and whether they are in practice at the extremes. Generally any analysis carried out will be a short-term analysis, the short-term usually being defined as the annual accounting cycle, during which time an overall framework of facilities will be largely determined. Analysis over a shorter time horizon is of course possible. It is necessary also, in dividing costs between fixed and variable, to take account of the nature of the firm's activities and management policy/judgement, which will influence fixed/variable in the specific case, as well as considering the nature of the cost per se. An implicit assumption in the basic CVP model is that there will be a constant level of efficiency and constant prices.

4.2 CVP RELATIONSHIPS

From the basic expression of profit,

Revenue – Costs = Profit,

the split of costs into fixed and variable compartments in CVP analysis enables the formula to be extended. A new term 'contribution' is used to describe the amount of profit generated from the relationship between revenue and variable costs. Each additional pound (£) of sales will require additional variable costs; the difference between them provides a contribution towards the fixed costs and profit.

Thus:

Revenue – Variable Costs = Contribution

Contribution – Fixed Costs = Profit.

For CVP analysis it is also necessary to express contribution in relation to sales, for example how much contribution is generated per £ of sales. (The alternative expression of contribution per unit of sales will be considered later). Profit can then be expressed as:

(Revenue × Contribution per £ of sales) – Fixed Costs = Profit

There are thus four variables. In CVP analysis, assumptions are made about three of them in order to determine the fourth. If assumptions are being made about revenue, contribution rate, and fixed costs in order to determine profit, then the above formula will be used. However, for more general analysis the formula can be usefully restated as:

Revenue × Contribution per £ of sales = Fixed Costs + Profit.

The above formula can be more easily manipulated to suit the purpose.

In a narrow sense, CVP analysis is concerned with determining the break-even point, which is the point of zero profit, ie where contribution from sales just covers fixed costs. Assumptions are made not only about profit (ie zero), but also about the level of fixed costs and the rate of contribution, in order to calculate the break-even point sales. As profit is zero, break-even sales can be calculated as:

$$\frac{\text{Fixed Costs}}{\text{Contribution per £ of sales.}} = \text{Break-even sales revenue}$$

More generally, if the analysis is of sales required in order to achieve various levels of profit, given assumptions again about the contribution/sales ratio and the level of fixed costs, then the formula is:

$$\frac{\text{Fixed Costs + Desired Profit}}{\text{Contribution per £ of sales}} = \text{Sales revenue required}$$

In order to illustrate the use of the above formulae, assume that the summary profit and loss account of a business for a year is as follows:

	£
Sales revenue	1,000,000
Total costs	900,000
Net profit	100,000

Assume also that an analysis of costs has revealed that £300,000 is fixed for the period regardless of activity. The contribution generated by sales during the period is therefore £400,000 (ie £1,000,000 sales revenue − £600,000 variable costs), at a rate of £0.40 per £ of sales (ie £400,000 contribution ÷ £1,000,000 sales revenue).

Thus the break-even sales revenue of A Ltd is:

$$\frac{300,000}{0.4} = £750,000$$

This can be confirmed by the following calculation:

	£	**% of sales**
Sales revenue	750,000	100
less Variable costs	450,000	60
Contribution	300,000	40
Less Fixed costs	300,000	40
Net profit	—	—

If it is desired to know the sales required in order to generate say a 20% increase in profit (from the level of £100,000), or the level of sales that would result in a 20% reduction in profits, the following calculations are required:

For a 20% increase in net profit to £120,000, the required contribution is £420,000 (ie £300,000 fixed costs + £120,000 net profit). Required sales revenue is:

$$\frac{420{,}000}{0.4} = £1{,}050{,}000$$

A 20% reduction in net profit to £80,000, would require contribution of £380,000 (ie £300,000 fixed costs + £80,000 net profit) and sales of:

$$\frac{380{,}000}{0.4} = £950{,}000$$

It can be seen that a change in sales of £50,000 (ie ± 5%) changes profit by £20,000 (ie ± 20%). The percentage change in profit depends upon the base profit used (see Section 4.4.1). The important thing to recognize is that profit is changed in absolute terms according to the contribution rate, ie extra profit of £20,000 requires extra sales of £50,000 because the contribution rate is £0.40 per £ of sales.

The analysis may also be used to calculate the profit derived from different levels of sales, or to calculate the effect of different levels of fixed and variable costs.

CVP analysis can be carried out using contribution per unit (instead of contribution per £ of sales), where a single product is produced and sold or where units provide a meaningful measure in a product mix situation. The break-even point, for example, is calculated as:

$$\frac{\text{Fixed Costs}}{\text{Contribution per unit}} = \text{Break-even sales units}$$

(see Exercises 4.2 and 4.3 for further illustrations).

A further concept that arises in CVP analysis is that of the 'Margin of Safety'. The margin of safety is any excess of expected/actual sales over and above the sales required to break even. The excess may be expressed as a percentage of expected/actual sales. The margin of safety provides an indication of the reduction in sales that would be necessary for the business to only just break even.

In the above illustration the margin of safety for the year is:

£1,000,000 − £750,000 = £250,000
which is

$$\frac{250{,}000}{1{,}000{,}000} \times 100\% \text{ (ie 25\%) of actual sales.}$$

The contribution/sales ratio, the margin of safety, and the net profit/sales ratio can be linked as follows:

Contribution/sales ratio × Margin of Safety = Profit/sales ratio.

In the illustration provided, when sales are £1,000,000, the profit/sales ratio is 10% $\left(\frac{100{,}000}{1{,}000{,}000} \times 100\%\right)$. Thus:

40% × 25% = 10%

If sales are reduced to say £900,000 net profit becomes:

Contribution	£360,000	(£900,000 × 40%)
Fixed costs	£300,000	
Net profit	£ 60,000	($6.\dot{6}\%$)

The margin of safety becomes £150,000 (£900,000 − £750,000) which is $16.\dot{6}\%$ of sales. Thus:

$40\% \times 16.\dot{6}\% = 6.\dot{6}\%$

Self-assessment question 4.1

Two businesses A Ltd and B Ltd have made the following estimates for the year ahead:

	A Ltd	B Ltd
Sales (£'000)	6,000	6,000
Variable costs (% of sales)	60%	40%
Fixed costs (£'000)	1,800	3,000

Required:

(a) Calculate the expected net profit, break-even point and margin of safety of each business for the year ahead.

(b) Calculate the level of sales at which each business would earn £250,000 net profit.

(c) Calculate the level of sales required by each business in order to achieve budgeted profit, if selling prices were increased by 10% with no change in cost behaviour.

(d) At budgeted selling prices, state which business is likely to earn greater profits, and give reasons why, if:

- **(i)** sales are higher than expected
- **(ii)** sales are lower than expected

(e) Calculate at what common level of sales the profits of A Ltd and B Ltd would be equal if A Ltd's costs comprised:
Variable Costs 55% of sales
Fixed Costs £2,000,000

Answers on page 492

In carrying out different cost volume profit analyses, the basic assumptions must be recognised. The key general assumptions about costs are that they are either variable (in direct proportion to volume) or else fixed, and can be accurately separated into one or other category in the short-term. Further assumptions, that are implicit in such a dichotomy, are that efficiency and input prices are constant over the range of activity.

FIGURE 4.1 **Cost-volume-profit chart**

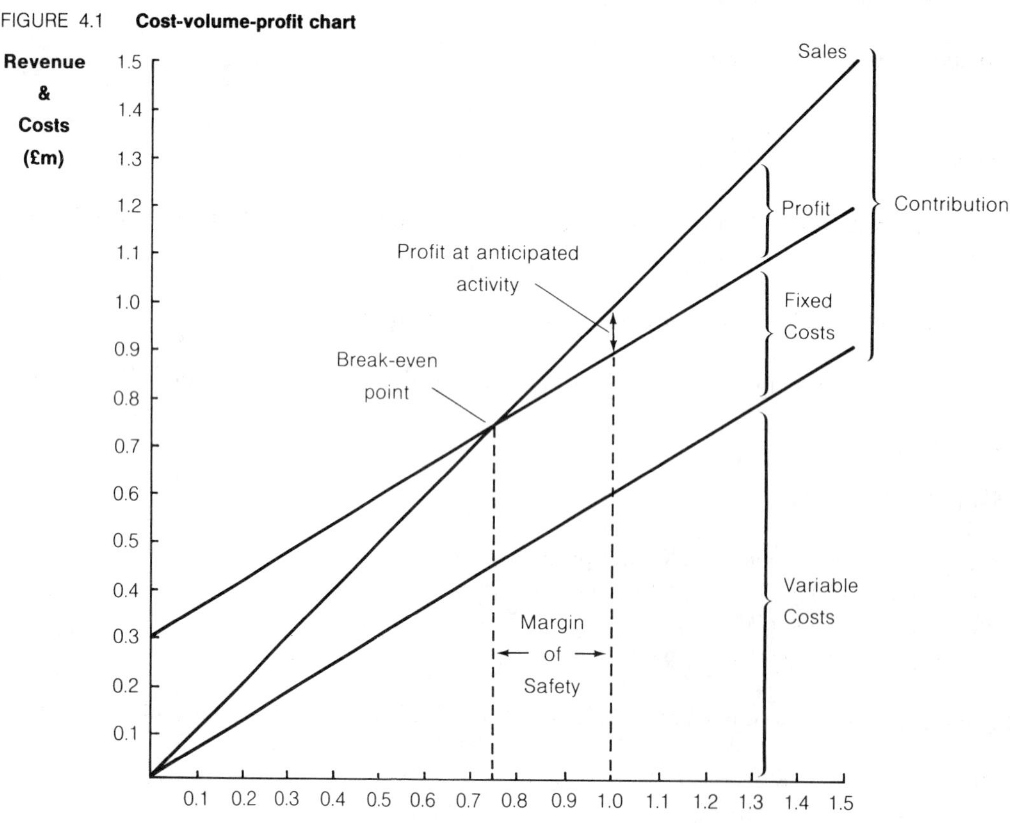

In any particular analysis, assumptions are also made about all but one of the following: the level of profit, the level of fixed costs, sales revenue, and contribution in relation to sales, which itself requires assumptions about selling prices, the sales mix, and the level of variable costs. Selling prices and sales mix are assumed constant over the range of activity.

A further necessary assumption, for a business to report profits for a period (using absorption costing) consistent with the results of CVP analysis, is that the level of production and sales are equal. If production and sales are not equal, through the build-up or reduction of finished goods stocks, profit will be affected by changes in the fixed production overhead absorbed in stock. (This is examined further in Chapter 8.) Even if production and sales are equal, changes in overhead absorption rates over time will also affect profit.

4.3 COST VOLUME PROFIT CHARTS

A useful way of presenting the general CVP relationships to management is through the use of charts. The relationships in the above illustration can be presented on a cost-volume-profit chart (Figure 4.1).

The above is a complete CVP chart showing the relationship between sales revenue, variable and fixed costs, contribution, and net profit as different activity levels. However, contribution and net profit values cannot be easily read from the chart as the difference between sales revenue and costs needs to be considered in each case.

In order to demonstrate contribution more clearly, a contribution line can be plotted directly, replacing the sales revenue and variable cost lines. This is shown below (Figure 4.2) and is often referred to as a 'contribution volume chart'.

Net profit still cannot be read directly from such a chart. In order to highlight the effect on profit of different levels of activity, a net profit line can be plotted directly, replacing the contribution and fixed cost lines. This is shown below (Figure 4.3) and is often referred to as a 'profit volume chart'.

FIGURE 4.2 **Contribution volume chart**

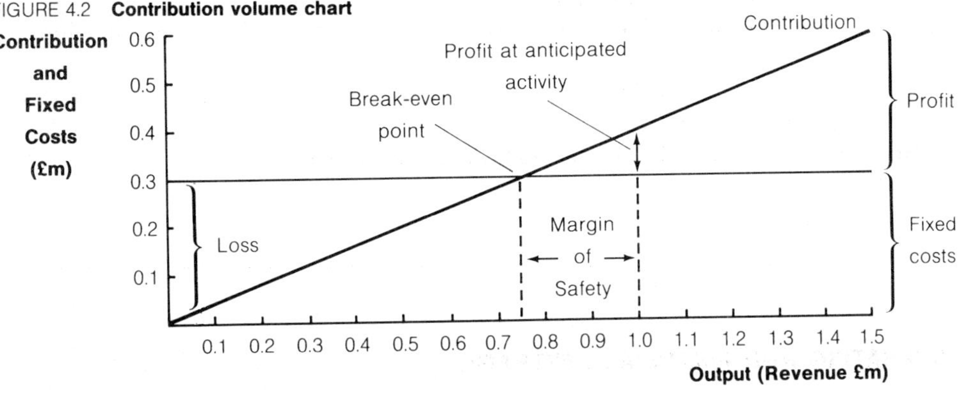

FIGURE 4.3 **Profit volume chart**

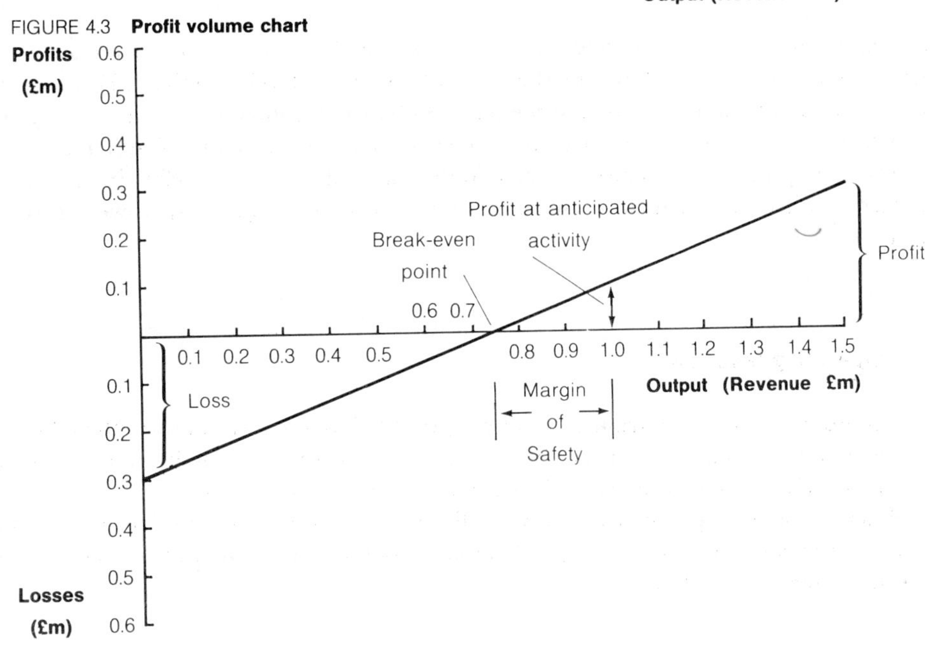

Self-assessment question 4.2

A company has prepared a budget for the year ahead which comprises the following revenue and cost expectations:

	£000
Sales	4,200
Raw materials	1,810
Production labour	800
Other production expenses	1,000
Distribution expenses	400
Administration expenses	500

Cost behaviour is estimated as follows:

	Variable	**Fixed**
Raw materials	100%	—
Production labour	80%	20%
Other production expenses	20%	80%
Distribution expenses	75%	25%
Administration expenses	10%	90%

Required:

a Prepare a graph to show expected profit-volume relationships for the year ahead, clearly indicating the break-even point and the margin of safety.

b Draw separate profit-volume charts to demonstrate, in general terms, the effect on the break-even point and the margin of safety of:

(i) an increase in fixed costs, which is less than compensated by a reduction in variable costs.

(ii) an increase in selling price with a resultant decrease in sales volume, and a reduction in fixed cost.

(iii) an increase in sales volume and an increase in variable cost.

Answers on page 493

4.4 OPERATING AND FINANCIAL LEVERAGE

Measured in absolute terms, a given increase in sales will lead to particular monetary increases in contribution and profit, which will be the same whatever the level of activity. However, the relative change in net profit will be different to the relative change in contribution and will depend upon the particular level of activity before the change. This is because of the fixity of certain costs in the short-term. The change in profit can be considered at the stages of both profit before interest and also profit after interest, where the fixed costs associated with interest bearing capital, as well as fixed operating costs, are considered.

4.4.1 Operating leverage

The relationship between contribution and net profit before interest indicates the relative change in profit before interest that would result from a particular relative change in contribution, affected by the existence of fixed operating costs. This is termed 'operating leverage'.

Refer to the example of A Ltd used earlier in the chapter. In addition to the profit and loss accounts as presented, the effect of $\pm$ 10% in sales volume, with selling prices and costs unchanged, has been calculated as follows:

	−10% £000	Normal £000	+10% £000
Sales	900	1,000	1,100
Variable costs	540	600	660
Contribution	360	400	440
Fixed costs	300	300	300
Net profit	60	100	140

At the normal level, the operating leverage is 4, which can be calculated as:

$$\frac{\text{\% change in profit}}{\text{\% change in contribution}}$$

$$= \frac{40\%}{10\%}$$

For a given percentage change in contribution, net profit will change by a factor of 4.

A simpler calculation of operating leverage is:

$$\frac{\text{Contribution}}{\text{Profit}} = \frac{£400{,}000}{£100{,}000}$$

At the −10% level, the operating leverage is increased. A change in sales of £100,000 and contribution of £40,000 now represents 11.1% of existing business and would change profit by 66.7% $\left(\frac{40000}{60000} \times 100\%\right)$. Operating leverage is 6, ie $\frac{(66.7\%)}{(11.1\%)}$. Alternatively this can be calculated as $\frac{£360{,}000}{£60{,}000}$.

At the +10% level, the operating leverage is reduced. A change in sales of £100,000 and contribution of £40,000 now represents 9.1% of existing business and would change profit by 28.6% $\left(\frac{40000}{140000} \times 100\%\right)$. Operating leverage is 3.14 $\frac{(28.6\%)}{(9.1\%)}$. Alternatively this can be calculated as $\frac{£440{,}000}{£140{,}000}$.

Operating leverage is dependent not only upon the existing level of activity, as demonstrated in the above calculations, but also upon the relationship between variable and fixed costs. In the above example, if at the normal level £100,000 is switched from variable to fixed costs, contribution becomes £500,000. A 10% increase in sales and contribution now results in a profit increase of 50% $\left(\frac{50{,}000}{100{,}000} \times 100\%\right)$. Operating leverage is $5\left(\frac{50\%}{10\%}\right)$.

4.4.2 Financial leverage

Net profit can be measured both before and after fixed interest payments. The relationship between profit before interest and profit after interest indicates the relative change in profit after interest that would result from a particular relative change in profit before interest affected by the existence of fixed interest payments. This is termed 'financial leverage'.

Using the example of A Ltd, it will be assumed that costs of interest bearing, as opposed to share, capital total £30,000 for the period.

Thus:

	−10% £000	Normal £000	+10% £000
Profit before interest	60	100	140
Interest	30	30	30
Profit after interest	30	70	110

At the normal level the financial leverage is 1.43 which can be calculated as:

$$\frac{\%\text{ change in profit after interest}}{\%\text{ change in profit before interest}}$$

$$= \frac{57\%}{40\%}$$

For a given percentage change in profit before interest, profit after interest will change by a factor of 1.43.

A simpler calculation of financial leverage is:

$$\frac{\text{Profit before interest}}{\text{Profit after interest}} \quad \text{ie} \quad \frac{\pounds 100{,}000}{\pounds 70{,}000}$$

At the −10% level, financial leverage is increased. Financial leverage is 2 (£60,000 ÷ £30,000). At the +10% level, financial leverage is reduced to 1.27 (£140,000 ÷ £110,000).

As with operating leverage, financial leverage is dependent upon the existing level of activity, as demonstrated in the above calculations. It is also dependent upon the relationship between fixed interest capital and share capital.

It has been assumed that interest bearing capital and interest payments are fixed in the short-term. The level of activity, influencing working capital requirements, may enable and/or necessitate some flexibility in interest bearing capital. This, however, is unlikely to have a significant effect on the calculations made above.

4.4.3 Combined leverage

The relationship between contribution and profit after interest indicates the relative change in profit after interest that would result from a particular relative change in contribution. This is the combined operating and financial leverage.

At the normal level of activity, the combined leverage is 5.7, which can be calculated as:

$$\frac{\%\text{ change in profit after interest}}{\%\text{ change in contribution}}$$

$$= \frac{57\%}{10\%}$$

For a given percentage change in contribution, profit after interest will change by a factor of 5.7.

Alternatively the combined leverage can be calculated as:

$$\frac{\text{Contribution}}{\text{Profit after interest}} = \frac{\pounds 400{,}000}{\pounds 70{,}000}$$

Combined leverage of 5.7 is the product of the operating leverage and the financial leverage (ie, 4 × 1.43). At the −10% and +10% levels of activity, the combined leverage is 12 (6 × 2) and 4(3.14 × 1.27) respectively. This demonstrates that in relative terms a change in activity can have a dramatic effect on profit available for shareholders.

Generally, the usefulness of the calculations depends upon the appropriateness of a linear model to represent the price-output-cost relationships of the firm, and the extent to which the requirement for capital, and the proportion funded by fixed interest capital, remains unchanged over a range of activity. In practice, a change in activity may be brought about by a change in selling price which alters the volume-profit relationships. The model may, nevertheless, provide a very useful indication of the magnification effect of both types of leverage, in particular at lower activity levels.

Self-assessment question 4.3

A company has prepared a budget for the year ahead with the following sales, costs and profit projections:

	£000
Sales	9,600
Variable Operating Costs	3,840
Fixed Operating Costs	4,320
Interest Payable	400
Profit	1,040

Required:
Calculate, and comment upon, the company's operating and financial leverage.

Answer provided on page 495

4.5 ACCOUNTANT'S V ECONOMIST'S CVP MODEL

The accountant's model for CVP analysis can be compared with the economist's model of cost and revenue behaviour, representing typical short-run economic relationships under conditions of imperfect competition. Differences of both content and also purpose exist between them.

4.5.1 Content

There are obvious differences of content which can be seen from the depiction of the respective models below (Figures 4.4 and 4.5).

FIGURE 4.4 **The accountant's CVP model**

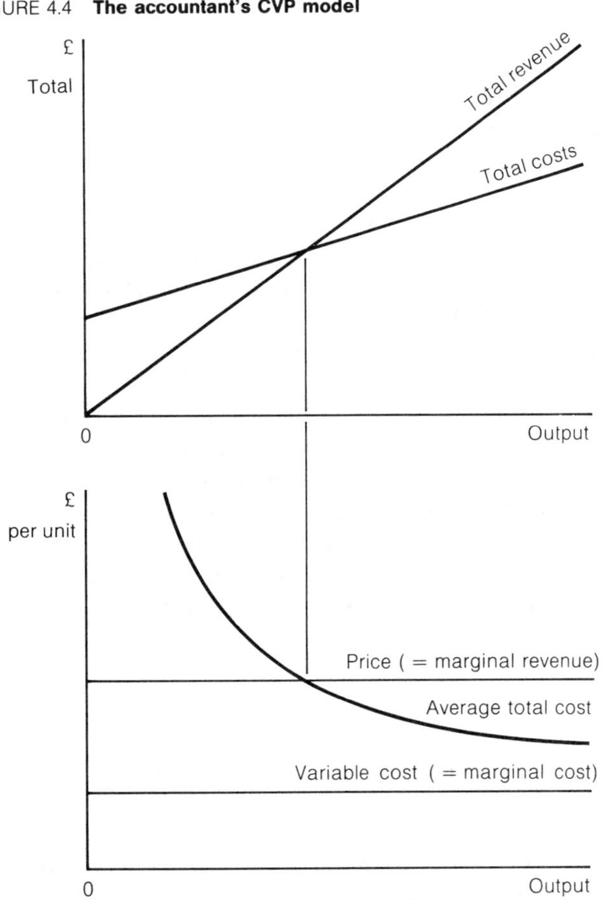

FIGURE 4.5 **The economist's CVP model**

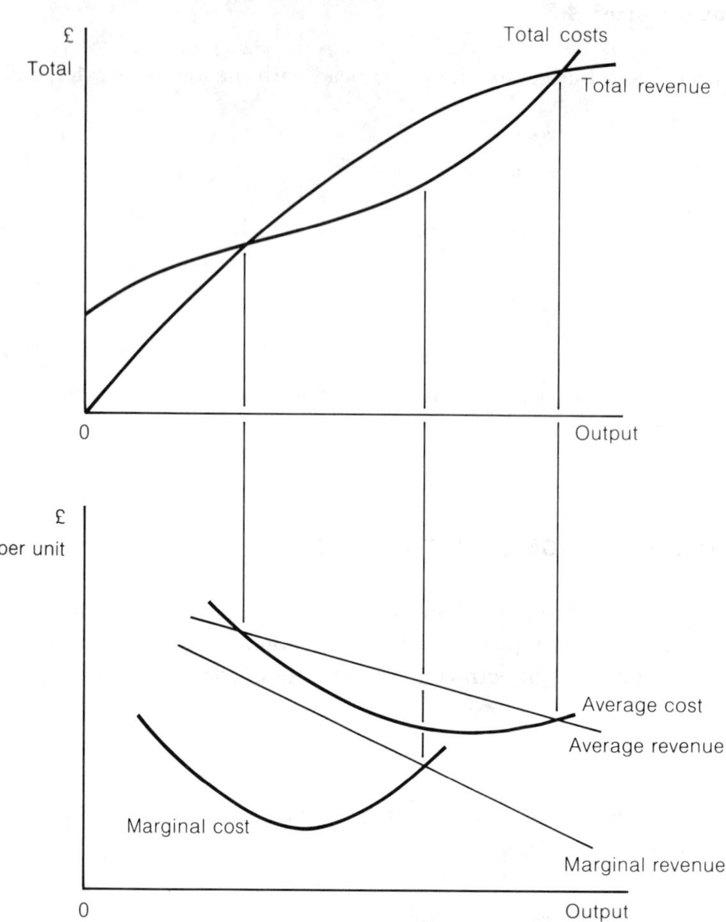

The accountant's CVP model assumes that either costs are fixed in total regardless of the level of activity or else vary in proportion to activity. It also assumes that revenue will increase in proportion to activity ie unit selling price is assumed constant.

By contrast, the economist's model assumes curvi-linear functions. Unit variable cost changes with the level of activity; fixed costs are also likely to change over the activity range. In total, average unit cost declines due to economies of scale in a more complex relationship with activity than that assumed in the accountant's model. Unlike the accountant's model, the economist's model reaches a point where unit costs start to increase due to diseconomies. As far as the revenue function is concerned, the economist's model assumes that additional sales can only be generated at reduced prices, and thus marginal and average revenue decline.

Another difference between the accountant's and economist's models, which is less obvious, is the absence in the accountant's model, and inclusion in the economist's model, of the cost of capital employed. In the accountant's model, the break-even point for example, is the point at which sales revenue equals total costs. Whilst this means that operating costs would be covered, financing costs are not considered. A firm would find that it had not in fact broken-even because of the cost of borrowing, and because no return at all would be provided for the owners. The economist's model, on the other hand, makes provision in cost for a normal profit to be earned.

4.5.2 Purpose

Before criticising the accountant's model as being too over simplified it should be recognised that the respective models have a fundamental difference of purpose. The accountant's model enables general cost-volume-profit analysis to be carried out in practical situations. This can be allied to sensitivity analysis, enabling the effect of changed assumptions about different variables to be estimated. The economist's model on the other hand is a single purpose prescriptive model. It provides a summary explanation of profit maximising behaviour, showing how cost and revenue behaviour determine the optimum price/output decision. Profit is maximised at the combination of selling price and output at which marginal revenue is equal to marginal cost.

4.6 UTILITY OF ACCOUNTANT'S MODEL

Given the difference in purpose outlined above, are the differences in content justified? First, it must be recognised that whilst the economist's model provides a useful conceptual framework for understanding the considerations which affect profit maximisation, it is not a technique for supplying management with the right answer. In practice, it may be impossible to derive the revenue function even for a single product firm. The accountant may have volume forecasts provided by marketing management at a limited range of discrete prices for different products. Whilst this could be used to try to derive a revenue function over the relevant range of activity, as the estimates would all be uncertain a broader analysis would only realistically be possible and would be preferred anyway for decision-making purposes.

This is achieved by carrying out a series of different cost-volume-profit analyses, one at each different selling price for each product. The contribution to be derived at different volume levels for each selling price is calculated. Judgement can then be exercised on the 'best' price, by considering the sensitivity of contribution to changed assumptions about selling price and volume. The revenue function depicted in the accountant's model is therefore reasonable as long as it is recognised that each function is based upon a particular selling price, and is not an attempt to derive *the* revenue function. The approach in practice is an iterative one.

As far as costs are concerned there is no reason why different functions could not be portrayed if it is felt to be possible and necessary for the analysis being carried out. In some cases, however, the simplicity of the traditional cost-volume-profit chart is its greatest asset.

The imperfections of cost-volume-profit analysis are not simply the question of whether the functions assumed are oversimplified but the problem of uncertainty in cost (and revenue) estimation if the analysis is used for planning purposes. One possibility is to introduce cost and revenue bands, ie upper and lower limits, based on optimistic and pessimistic views of the future.

The charts are only likely to be reasonable indicators of cost-volume-profit relationships for activity within a reasonable range of average production, say 80% to 120%. This could be more clearly demonstrated on the chart by limiting the analysis to such a range of activity. Within the relevant range the cost behaviour assumptions may be reasonable, and in any case could be refined if better information is available. The economic model covers a range of activity sufficient to cause significant changes in efficiency.

The question remains as to whether the ignorance in the accountant's model of the cost of capital can be justified. However, this is a weakness of the traditional cost-volume-profit model which can be rectified. An additional dimension can be introduced onto the chart to reflect the cost of capital (see Figure 4.6).

FIGURE 4.6 **Profit volume chart (including return on capital)**

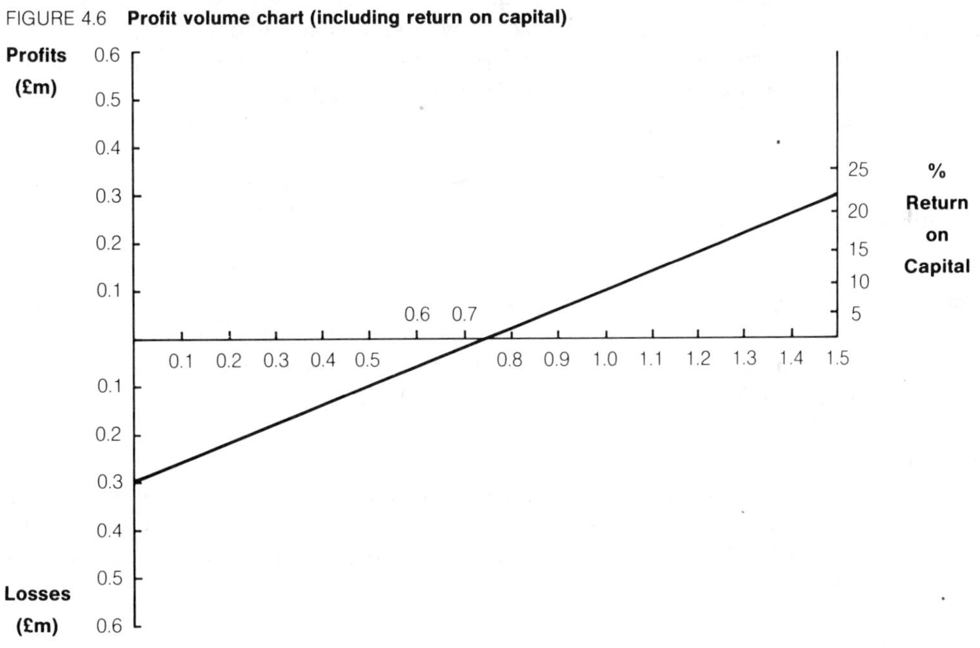

Consideration can then be given to not only whether total revenue covers total cost, but whether the excess of revenue over cost provides an adequate return on capital. The above chart reflects the fact that capital employed will vary with activity due to differing requirements for working capital at different activity levels. The return will not increase in direct proportion to increases in activity above the break-even level.

Self-assessment question 4.4

The accountant's break-even chart offends against many of the economist's basic assumptions as to the shape of costs and revenue curves. Some economists have attacked the use of such a break-even chart, stating that its underlying assumptions are so unsound that no practical analysis should be based upon it.

Required:
Describe the principal differences between the accountant and the economist in relation to break-even charts and discuss the extent to which the accountant is justified in using these charts.

(*ACCA*, *Management Accounting*, *June 1975*).

Answer on page 495

SUMMARY

The accountant's CVP model can be said to stand up fairly well to any criticisms arising from a direct comparison with the economist's model particularly within the range of activity that is likely to be relevant in practice. The economist's model provides a prescriptive model of profit maximising behaviour; the accountant's model is a practical model for analysing general cost-volume-profit relationships. When it is derived from an extensive analysis of costs, and as long as its limitations are sufficiently recognised, the accountant's model becomes a useful technique for management use, providing a flexible set of projections of cost and revenues under different scenarios. It must be remembered that it is only possible to display the information available; analysis based on imperfect information is likely to be better than no analysis at all. Ultimately it is important to consider whether adequate returns on capital are achieved. Recognition of this fact has been lacking in the accountant's cost-volume-profit model.

The simple dichotomy of cost behaviour into fixed and variable classifications, and the resulting cost-volume-profit relationships which have been established in this chapter, provide a flexible basis for examining and explaining general factors influential in organisation performance.

Further consideration of cost-volume-profit analysis will be provided in later chapters, particularly Chapters 8, 15 and 18.

EXERCISES

Exercise 4.1

'A break-even chart must be interpreted in the light of the limitations of its under-lying assumptions . . .'. (From *Cost Accounting*: *a managerial emphasis* by C. T. Horngren.)

Required:
(a) Discuss the extent to which the above statement is valid and both describe and briefly appraise the reasons for SIX of the most important underlying assumptions of break-even analysis.
(b) For any THREE of the underlying assumptions provided in answer to (a) above, give an example of circumstances in which that assumption is violated. Indicate the nature of the

violation and the extent to which the break-even chart can be adapted to allow for this violation.

(*ACCA, Management Accounting, December 1979*)

Answers on page 495

Exercise 4.2

Part Works Ltd. is a publishing company which specialises in the production of part work publications. The company recently introduced special single publications to enable it to extend the life of some of its more successful ventures. One such publication is to follow on from the extremely successful 'Silver Fingers' part work.

The costing for this single publication, which as yet is unnamed and referred to as Silver Fingers A, is as follows:

1 Preparation costs, commissioning authors, photographers, composition, blocks, etc, for whatever quantity of the publication is produced, will be £3,000.

2 Printing costs £8 per hundred up to 25,000 and then £4 per hundred for any further copies. The reduction in costs coming about because of less spoilt work and scrapping of paper during longer print runs.

3 Binding and other finishing costs £100 per 5,000 whatever quantity is produced.

The publication is to be sold direct to newsagents and similar retailers at a fixed price of 20p each, to retail at a price of 25p.

Required:

(a) A table showing the production costs for 15,000, 20,000, 25,000, 30,000 and 35,000 of Silver Fingers A, together with the average costs per 5,000 copies of each quantity. Show the marginal costs for each increment.

(b) Draw a break-even chart for the publication and from this derive the break-even point. Check the accuracy of your graph by calculating the break-even point.

(c) Part Works Ltd. has already printed 35,000 copies of a publication with similar costs to Silver Fingers A. This has not sold as well as expected and the firm has 10,000 copies left which seem likely to remain unsold. A dealer, who specialises in market trading, offers to buy these for £600. What factors should be considered before deciding whether or not to accept the offer? What difference would it have made if the offer had been for £100?

(*ACCA, Management Accounting, June 1975*)

Answers on page 497

Exercise 4.3

Nettab Ltd. manufactures a single product which sells at £1.20 per unit. The variable cost of this product is 60p per unit. At present the fixed expenses of the organisation are £30,000 per annum.

Nettab is currently selling its full productive capacity of 100,000 units per annum at what the company's directors believe is the optimum price-volume relationship for the product.

However, they are considering selling the product under an additional brand name. While being virtually identical from the manufacturing point of view brands will be differentiated by the packaging and the marketing approaches adopted.

Sales of the existing and the new brand when both are priced at 90p per unit are expected to total 300,000 units.

The introduction of the additional brand will require the firm to increase its productive capacity. To do this will increase Nettab's fixed costs to £60,000 per annum. However as this will involve some re-equipment there will be economies of operation arising which will reduce variable costs to 50p per unit.

Required:

(a) Present the above information graphically.

(b) For both the existing situation and the proposed scheme calculate (i) the break-even point, (ii) the profit, (iii) the margin of safety and (iv) the sales required under the proposed scheme to maintain the present profit position. In relation to these situations discuss whether the proposed scheme will improve the companies position.

(c) Briefly discuss the criticisms that the economist would make of the accountant's break-even graph. Do these criticisms invalidate its use in practical situations?

Answers on page 498

SECTION 2

COST ACCUMULATION AND PERFORMANCE MEASUREMENT

This section seeks to lay a foundation of routine cost accounting upon which management accounting's role, in providing management with accounting information for the purposes of planning, decision-making and control, can be built. Chapter 5 considers the general issues influencing cost accounting information provision. Chapters 6 and 7 then deal in more detail with aspects of the processing of input costs (Chapter 6) and their relationship to output (Chapter 7). Chapter 8 returns to consider in more detail the issues influencing the choice between absorption and marginal costing methods, which are first introduced in Chapter 5. In Chapter 9 particular attention is given to service organisations to balance the emphasis placed in earlier chapters on a manufacturing environment. Examples of particular service industries are used to illustrate the applicability of the concepts introduced in this second section of the book, and to provide illustrations of differences between service and manufacturing environments. Finally, Chapter 10 deals with performance measurement on a broader-scale where the issues influencing divisional performance measurement are introduced.

General Framework of Cost Accounting Routine Information Provision

INTRODUCTION

The recording of data in the cost accounting system (as an extension of the financial accounts) provides the basis for the provision of accounting information for management for the purposes of planning, decision-making and control. For information to be available for presentation to management for these purposes, data must first be recorded and accumulated in an appropriate way. This chapter seeks to provide a general framework for such information provision which is built upon in the rest of the section.

Information provision is considered both from the point of view of what general information is required, where both content, (for example product profitability), and form, (for example absorption versus marginal costing), are considered, and also from the point of view of how the information may be provided, where the processing requirements in the cost accounts, the relationship between the cost and financial accounts, and the requirements of cost coding and cost classification are considered. First the characteristics of useful information are outlined.

5.1 USEFUL INFORMATION

The criteria that should influence the provision of cost and management accounting information, and which can be used to judge its usefulness, have become broadly accepted as:

1 **Economic reality**:
Economic reality is the prime requirement of management accounting information. It may mean adjusting conventionally prepared accounting information, for example to reflect future rather than past values.

2 **Relevance**:
Information must be relevant for particular purposes and to particular persons. For example information relevant to a particular division will depend entirely on the circumstances and should reflect the true economic value of those factors that will be affected according to the course of action selected. The management accountant should try to ensure that irrelevant information is filtered. Another aspect of relevance is the degree of detail; different levels of management will have different requirements for degree of detail.

3 **Timeliness**:
Information must be produced in time for it to be used effectively. This is another feature which is especially important for management accounting information. Reports should be sent out as soon as possible following the end of the period to which they relate, and in sufficient time for effective use to be made of them.

4 **Cost Effectiveness**:
In management accounting, decisions have to be made about information requirements. One influential factor should be the cost of obtaining information; value for money should always be considered.

5 **Understandability**:
For a person to effectively receive information, it must be processed at a cognitive level. Financial accounting reports are made more readily understandable through the use of commonly accepted rules and conventions. This is not the case in management accounting where good communication, especially from financial to non-financial personnel, will be a significant influence on

understandability. Information should be well presented, where the use of charts, diagrams and tables may be appropriate, and should avoid jargon and unnecessary technical terms.

6 **Comparability**:
An important criterion for the evaluation of performance is the comparability of information for a period with other information. This may be comparison with other periods, with comparable activities, or with targets set. Comparability of information with that of previous time periods may be improved by using price indices in order to allow for the impact of inflation. Relative values, for example through the use of percentages, may at times provide better comparability than absolute values.

7 **Objectivity**:
Subjectivity should be minimised, although it cannot be avoided entirely. Information which is objective is acceptable to the majority of people; information which is subjective reflects the views and judgements of one person. Subjective information is particularly at risk from the effects of distortion; the message received by one person may not be the message intended by the person sending the message, because each holds personal views which may differ. A feature of management accounting information, because of its future orientation, is that it will be more subjective than financial accounting information.

8 **Verifiability**:
Verifiability is particularly important in financial accounting, justifying for example the importance of the audit trail or the need to verify balance sheet data through third parties, such as the debtors circularisation procedure, stock check, or fixed asset audit. If information is to be used for planning, decision-making and control it must also be verifiable, in a different sense, from source documentation. This does not mean that its value will be known with certainty, but ensures that it at least has a sound basis. This also has an influence on objectivity.

9 **Reliability**:
Information to be reliable must be as accurate as possible, which may be improved by the way in which it is collected, or by the checking procedures which are used. For example, the automatic recording of machine operating time and idle time will be more reliable than the completion of machine log sheets by the supervisor. Clear instructions as to how information is to be classified and coded will improve its reliability. The use of standard documentation will mean that information reporting takes place in a consistent manner which should improve its reliability.

There may be some conflict between the criteria, especially between those that are of primary importance in management accounting and those that have greater weighting in financial accounting. For example, timeliness of information provision is an important factor in management accounting but may be in conflict with other criteria. Information may be issued in incomplete form in the interests of timeliness; greater understanding could be achieved by delaying the issue of information until it could be presented in report form with explanatory notes. Information may also be issued before sufficient time has been allowed in which to verify its accuracy or to enable its comparability with other information to be properly analysed.

Economic reality may conflict with objectivity and reliability; the essence of economic reality is its future orientation which inevitably increases subjectivity and reduces accuracy. Relevance may conflict with understandability; the conditional truth of information of relevance in management accounting places greater reliance on effective communication. Cost effectiveness may conflict with reliability; in order for information to be cost effective some accuracy may be foregone.

Self-assessment question 5.1

Management accounting information should comply with a number of criteria including verifiability, objectivity, timeliness, comparability, reliability, understandability and relevance if it is to be useful in planning, control and decision making.

Required:

(a) Explain the meaning of each of the criteria named above.

(b) Give a brief explanation of how the criteria detailed in (1) might be in conflict with each other giving examples to illustrate where such conflict might arise.

(ACCA, Management Accounting, June 1988, adapted)

Answers on page 502

5.2 ROUTINE INFORMATION REQUIREMENTS AND PROVISION

In general terms, cost accounting is concerned with placing values on internal transactions, which represent transfers of value throughout an organisation. Internal transactions reflect the conversion of input resources to outputs of goods or services. Outputs include goods and services provided from one area of an organisation to another as well as those provided to the organisation's external customers. Figure 5.1 illustrates the general cost movements within an organisation.

FIGURE 5.1 **Illustration of cost movements**

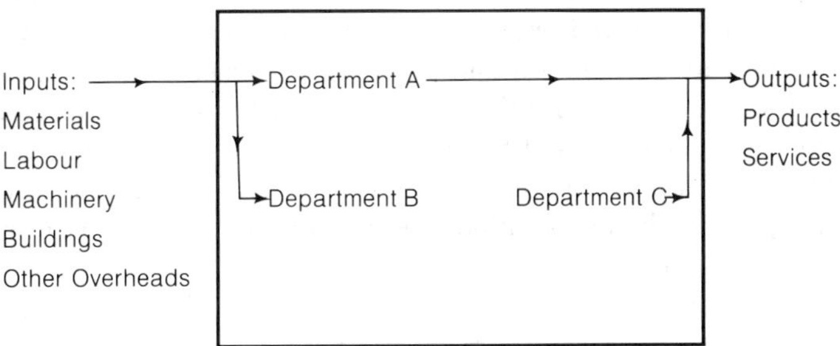

Ideally general information requirements of cost and management accounting should be specified in such a way as to suit all organisations and purposes. However, it seems impossible to generalise about cost accounting system requirements. The problem is that information is used in different types of organisation and for a variety of purposes. Also a particular purpose may not be known in advance; information itself may prompt the question. For example poor performance in a particular area of the business may prompt the question as to whether the activity should be discontinued. Quite specific information relevant to the discontinuation of that activity, taking into account its particular situation and links with other activities in the organisation, will be required.

Information requirements of different organisations vary not only because they have differing characteristics and identified needs for information, but also because the needs of a particular organisation are likely to be so varied that they cannot all be satisfied by a routine recording system. It may be impossible, therefore, to specify the required system, not only in general for all organisations, but also for particular types of organisation, and even for a particular organisation. In certain respects one can only discuss the issues that should influence. This is also partly true of financial accounting, for example what depreciation method to use, but to a much lesser extent.

In cost and management accounting an organisation has far more autonomy to determine its own systems specifications. The question is not simply 'how is information *provided* in the *general* case ie, for all organisations?' as is the case with financial accounting, but 'how is information *best* provided in the *specific* case ie, for a particular organisation?' Each organisation must consider:

1 What information is required for effective planning, decision-making and control?
2 How that information is to be provided?

The answers to the first will determine the information output from the cost accounts. The answers to the second will determine the information processing requirements in order to achieve the information output specified by the first.

5.3 INFORMATION REQUIREMENTS

In considering general information requirements there are two issues:

1 What information *content* is required? eg, product profitability, customer profitability, departmental performance.
2 What *form* should it take? eg, absorption versus marginal costing.

5.3.1 Content

It is difficult to specify the required content of the cost accounting system (or any information system) without first of all being clear what objectives the organisation is seeking to achieve (or parts of the organisation). An objective of achieving at least a satisfactory profit will figure prominently in many organisation's objectives, (or in the case of non-profit organisations, value for money). Indeed without such objectives a cost accounting system, and indeed any form of money accounting system, would have no rationale.

Thus, ultimately, measures of profit are required in relation to different aspects of the business. The question is what aspects, in what detail, and how often? Traditionally, the aspect of business has been the individual products or services that the organisation sells, or convenient groupings of the same, as this has conveniently followed (especially in the case of manufactured products) from the use of cost accounting for inventory valuation and profit measurement. Increasingly, interest has been shown in, and the management accounting system has sought to provide, information on the profitability of different customers or of different sales areas. Detail required, and provided, will be influenced by the number of different products, services or customers, and/or useful groupings of the same. Frequency of reporting should be influenced by the utility of the information for planning, decision-making and control purposes.

Measuring profit in relation to products, or customers, or sales areas, is a measurement of the organisation's performance in respect of its final output. Many activities in an organisation provide product or service at an intermediate stage of that process and the question arises as to how their performance will be measured. Each could be a separate responsibility area and it is necessary to consider carefully what those responsibility areas should be, what they are responsible for, and how best to measure their performance. Effectiveness (getting tasks completed in order to meet objectives), and cost efficiency (the relationship between input resources and completed tasks) may well act as proxies for profit for areas of the business where profit cannot easily be measured or where it is inappropriate. Non-financial measures should be considered also. However, it may be difficult to establish a clear objective for these activities, and it may be difficult both to measure output, and to relate input resources to output, in a meaningful and useful way. Further, the cost of gathering information must be considered in relation to benefits.

The term 'cost objective' is used to describe any activity for which a separate measurement of costs is desired. The measurement of the profit generated by each of the different final outputs of an organisation requires the establishment of cost units, and the identification of costs (and revenues) in relation to cost units. A 'cost unit' may be defined as a quantitative unit of product or service in relation to which costs are ascertained.

Areas of a business which provide product or service to other areas of that business, and which are often measured on cost performance alone as they do not directly generate sales and thus profit, are termed 'cost centres'. A 'cost centre' may be defined as a location, person, or item of equipment in relation to which costs are ascertained. Costs are identified, and analysed, at the level of the cost centre as a whole. It may, however, be possible and useful to establish a cost unit for the centre which can provide the basis for charging for the service and a means of cost control.

It may be possible also, and may be judged useful, to establish a value for the output of intermediate areas of the business which is other than cost, attempting to reflect the true value of the output. Cost centres become profit centres, or even investment centres. An investment centre is one whose performance is measured not simply as revenue minus costs, but where the ensuring profit is related to the capital employed required to generate it. Thus, for example, product may pass from one department in a factory to another at a transfer price which seeks to reflect market value at that point.

Service departments, for example computer operations, may establish a value for their service, and thus a charge for users which again is based upon market values, rather than simply cost. Influential factors should be whether market values can be reasonably established, and if so, whether the use of such measures leads to desired behaviour of all concerned.

There is a great deal of flexibility, therefore, in designing a cost accounting system because it is difficult to clearly specify ideal information needs. Each organisation must establish its own information needs in the context of its own particular circumstances. The purpose of this section has been to emphasise this fact and to raise the important general questions that need to be asked when considering the required information content of cost accounting systems. The availability of information at reasonable cost is also an important consideration.

Self-assessment question 5.2

The management of a transport company is considering introducing a cost accounting system. The company owns a fleet of forty lorries operating from five depots located across the country and is engaged in transporting the finished goods from a number of industrial customers.

Required:
Outline how a costing system could assist the management of such an organisation and what information could usefully be provided.

Answer on page 502

5.3.2 Form

The identification of the profitability, and/or cost, of different areas of a business is a prime purpose of any internal accounting system. Without this information, management will have little knowledge of the areas from which the business derives its profit and, therefore, will not be in a position to allocate properly the resources of the firm in terms of selling effort and production capacity. But this begs the questions to what is the correct measure of cost, and thus profit, to use in measuring performance. Traditionally the measure of cost which has been adopted is that of total cost (or fully absorbed cost), because an organisation will only make a profit once all costs have been recovered. Under full absorption costing, part of every cost incurred is identified in some way with output units. This is undeniably the long-term situation, in the sense that products must generate revenue to cover all costs in order to justify their continued and permanent existence.

The attempt to depart from a traditional functional classification of costs in absorption costing, to provide a behavioural classification of costs is called marginal (or variable) costing. This is an extension of the assumptions made in the cost volume profit analysis that was covered in Section 1 on the assumption that while some costs will be heavily influenced by activity in the short term and thus properly identified with output units, other costs will tend to remain relatively fixed, unaffected by the level of activity over such a time period. In a marginal costing system the contribution of individual products is highlighted. Together they make a contribution towards the total fixed costs of the organisation.

The contrasting formats of these two approaches, ie, absorption and marginal costing, are illustrated in the outline of the identification of product performance (for a manufacturing organisation) shown in Figure 5.2. In a service organisation the cost of sales would include those costs closely related to the service provided. The behavioural classification and the emphasis on contribution in the marginal costing statement can be contrasted with the functional classification and total cost apportionment of the absorption format.

FIGURE 5.2 **Product Performance Measurement: Contrasting Absorption and Marginal Costing.**

ABSORPTION COSTING

Trading and Profit and Loss Account

	Product 1	Product 2	Total
	£	£	£
Sales	X	X	X
Less: Manufacturing Cost of Sales	X	X	X
Gross Profit	X	X	X
Less: Selling and Administrative Overhead	X	X	X
Net Profit	X	X	X

MARGINAL COSTING

Income Statement

	Product 1	Product 2	Total
	£	£	£
Sales	X	X	X
Less: Variable Cost of Sales	X	X	X
Contribution	X	X	X
Less: Fixed Overheads			X
Net Profit			X

A second question regarding the form that the required information should take is whether absolute or relative measures (or both) should be provided. Both have a part to play in performance measurement. Absolute measures provide information on total costs and revenues, which may provide an indication of the scale of operations and thus effectiveness, for example total sales. Relative measures show the relationship between one aspect of the business and another, for example the cost of resources consumed divided by the output achieved with those resources. Whereas absolute measures provide, for example, a measure of the cost of cost centres, relative measures provide a measure of costs in relation to cost units. Both cost centres and cost units are cost objectives, which as noted earlier, comprise any activity for which a separate measurement of costs is desired.

Self-assessment question 5.3

In Chapter 1 an illustration was provided of a small transport company providing distribution services to local industry. The company provides two main types of distribution service—container distribution of consumer products on a contract basis, and a parcel delivery service by transit van. You have the following additional information at your disposal.

1 Sales:
Container lorries £96,780
Parcel vans £22,720

2 Fuel & Oil:
Container lorries £16,450
Parcel vans £ 2,590

3 Drivers' wages: All drivers are paid at the same standard rate per hour for normal time. Hours worked by drivers on the two main services were:
Container lorries 5500 hrs
Parcel vans 3600 hrs
Overtime premiums paid to drivers on the container service amounted to £2,700.

4 Repairs and Maintenance:
Container lorries £3,120
Parcel vans £ 920

5 Road tax:
Container lorries £ 310
Parcel vans £ 310

6 Vehicle insurance:
Container lorries £2,010
Parcel vans £1,230

7 Depreciation: Depreciation of vehicles is considered to be a function of both usage and time. The charge for usage is based on an hourly rate applied to drivers' hours. The hourly rate for each service is:
Container lorries £0.6/hr
Parcel vans £0.3/hr
The balance of depreciation is considered to be a function of time and is based on a percentage of the cost of vehicles.
The same percentage rate is applied to all vehicles.
Capital costs are split:
Container lorries £30,000
Parcel vans £15,000

8 Office salaries and expenses: Office salaries and expenses include rates of £2,800 and heating and lighting of £4,600. Office floor space is divided equally between the two services. The remainder of the office salaries and expenses (ie, excluding rates and heating and lighting) have displayed a tendency over recent years to increase to a certain extent with sales revenue. Available information reveals:

	Year 1	**Year 2**	**Year 3**	**Year 4** (*current yr*)
Remainder of office salaries & expenses	£26,470	£26,365	£26,695	£ 28,020
Sales revenue	£88,500	£86,400	£93,000	£119,500

The fixed element of these remaining costs is considered to be fairly split between the two services in the ratio 8:2.

Required:
From the profit and loss account provided in the illustration in Chapter 1, and from the above additional information:

(a) Provide a breakdown of the profit and loss account for the year in order to identify separately the net profit before interest and tax generated by each of the two main services.
(b) Prepare what you consider to be a reasonable approximation of a marginal cost statement, identifying the contribution generated by each of the services.
(c) Comment upon the profitability of the two services and also the relative merits of these different statements.

Answers on page 503

5.4 INFORMATION PROVISION

Having established information requirements, following a consideration of both content and form, it is necessary to set up the required recording system. There are two broad considerations:

1 The processing requirements within the cost accounts.
2 The relationship of the cost accounting system with the financial accounts.

5.4.1 Processing requirements

Figure 5.3 repeats the outline provided in Chapter 1 of a financial accounting system for a manufacturing organisation. In a service organisation there would not be a finished stock account; the costs of services are charged to the Trading and Profit and Loss Account when complete.

FIGURE 5.3 **Financial accounting system—(manufacturing business)**

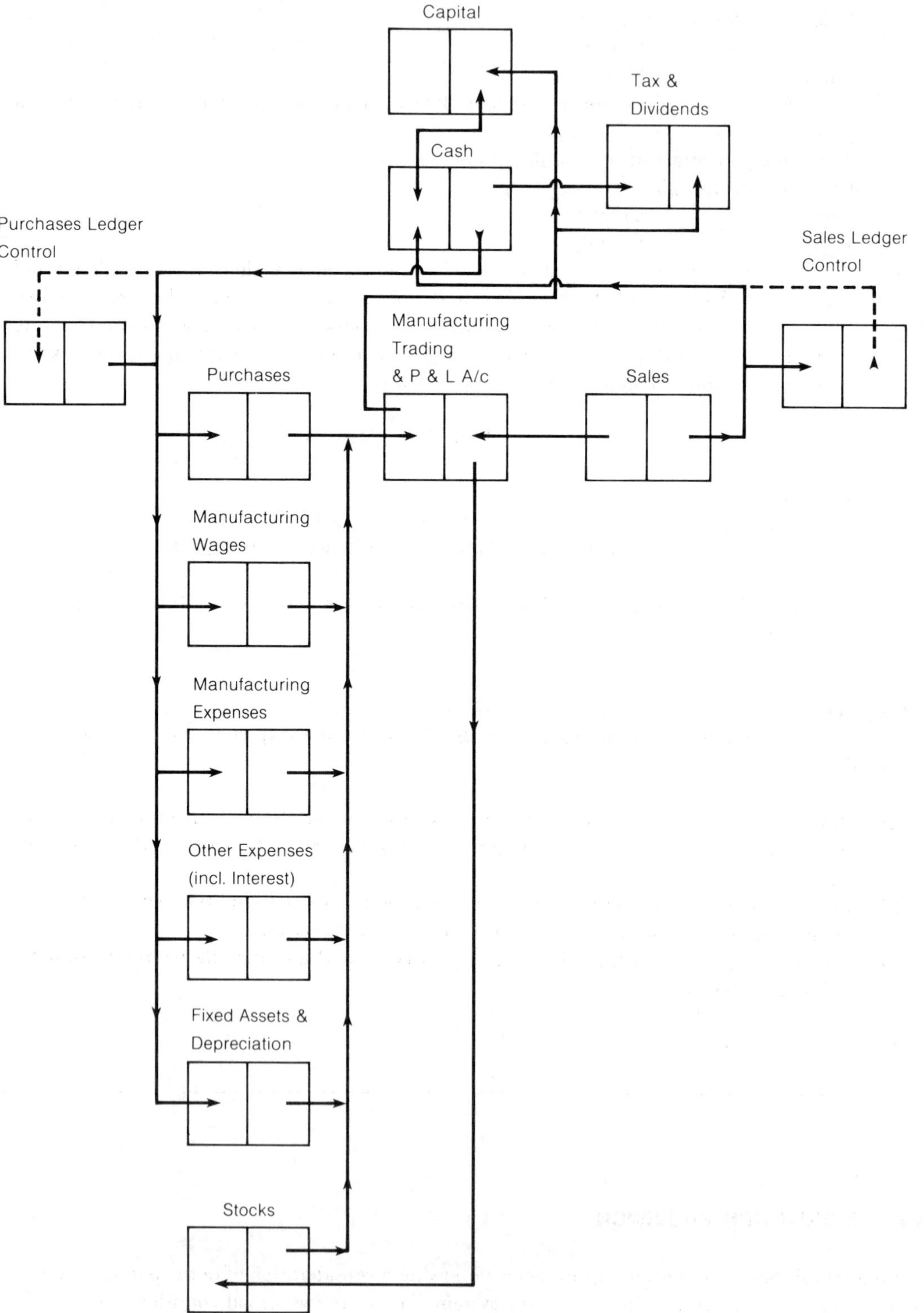

Figure 5.4 shows an outline of a cost accounting system for a manufacturer, using absorption costing.

FIGURE 5.4 **Cost accounting system—absorption costing (manufacturing business)**

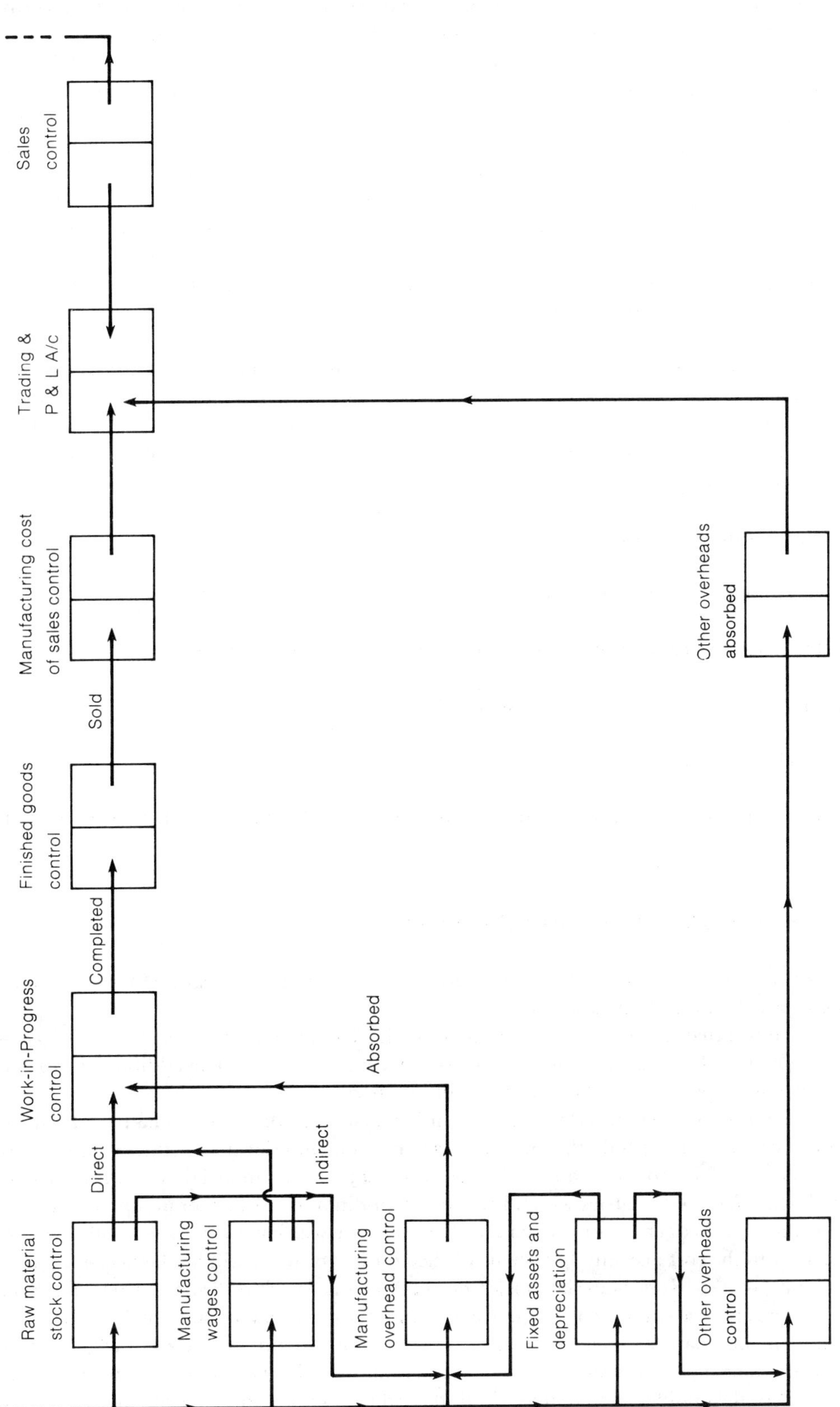

The distinguishing features in comparison with the diagram showing the financial accounting system are:

1. The continuous recording of both inputs and outputs. A cost accounting system records internal transfers of value, for example the use of labour to produce a part-finished product in a particular area of the factory. Values are placed continuously on the outcome of the use of input resources, so that costs are passed on from one stage of an organisation to another.
2. The association of costs with different activities in an organisation. As noted earlier in this chapter, a cost objective is any activity for which a separate measurement of costs is desired. This is less clear from the diagram because it is at a summary level.
3. The distinction between direct and indirect costs. Direct costs are those that can be allocated to a particular cost centre or cost unit. Indirect costs are those that cannot be so allocated, but instead need to be apportioned, ie, shared over more than one cost centre or cost unit.
4. The widespread use of control accounts. These are used to provide a summary of information contained in separate sections of the cost accounts.

An important influence on the processing requirement in the cost accounts is the content and form required. For example, a marginal costing system will dictate a different processing of information as demonstrated by Figure 5.5. More detailed processing considerations will be partly influenced by more detailed characteristics of the particular organisation and partly by what more detailed information it requires.

Further questions are:

What cost units are to be established?

Which costs are direct and which indirect in relation to final cost units?

How are direct costs recorded and passed on?

How are indirect costs recorded and passed on?

Consideration will be given to each of these questions in subsequent chapters in this section.

5.4.2 Relationship with the financial accounts

The cost and financial accounting systems may operate as either an integrated system, as interlocking systems, or as completely separate systems.

An integrated accounting system is a single, comprehensive accounting system with the integration of the financial accounts and the cost accounts together. The addition of cost accounting requirements simply adds to the level of detail required.

In contrast to this, interlocking accounting systems, which have many variants, establish separate cost accounts outside the financial accounts. The interlocking of the two systems is carried out by the use of control accounts in each set of accounts. The financial accounting system has the normal debit and credit entries within itself and in addition has a memorandum account frequently termed the Cost Ledger Control Account. This account will have posted to it all items which are transferred to the cost accounting system. In the cost ledger there will be the necessary accounts for costing purposes eg, Raw Material Stock Control Account, Work-in-Progress Control Account, and, in addition, an account which is equal and opposite to the memorandum Cost Ledger Control Account in the financial (general) ledger. This control account in the cost ledger is termed the Financial (General) Ledger Control Account. It is an essential element of the cost ledger because it forms part of the double entry system within the ledger, enables the financial and cost ledgers to be interlocked, and avoids duplication of accounts which are not required for costing purposes. For example, in the cost accounts the purchase of raw materials on credit would be debited to the raw material stock account: a credit to the financial ledger control account avoids duplication of the creditor's accounts.

FIGURE 5.5 **Cost accounting system—marginal costing (manufacturing business)**

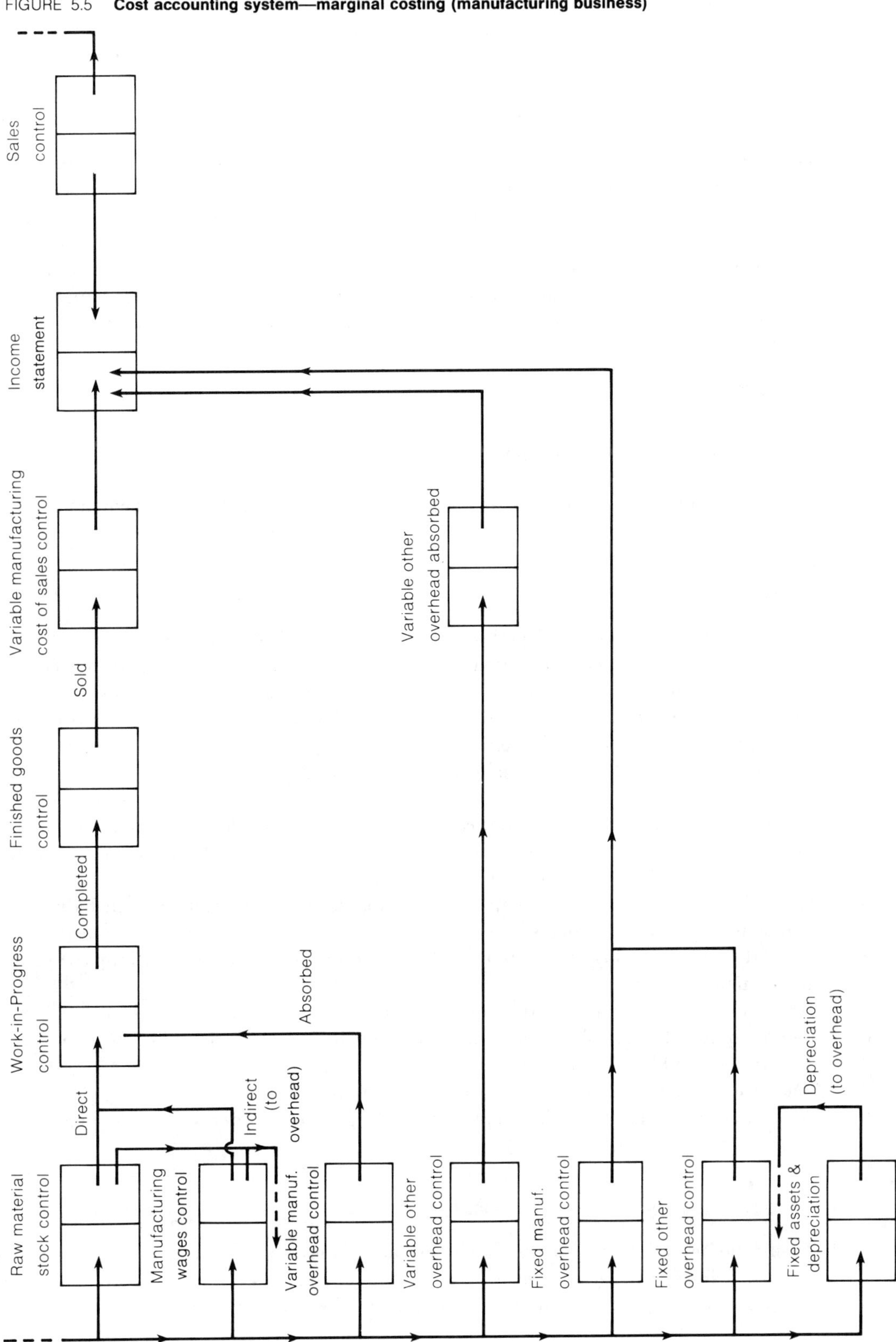

At one time, integration was commonly viewed as a desirable aim. A single system would be expected to reduce costs and obviate the need for any reconciliation. However, the conventions of financial accounting will tend to take precedence in such a system which may restrict the usefulness of information, in any case restricted by its historic transaction basis, for management purposes. The move to an interlocking system, although somewhat removed from the financial accounts, cannot however free the cost accounts, and thus the basis for management accounting information, from the shackles of financial accounting conventions.

The differing requirements of cost and management accounting have become increasingly recognised with a realisation that they may be best accommodated by a completely separate information system. The financial accounting system would have sufficient cost accounting to satisfy the minimum requirements of scorekeeping for both external and internal users. The separate cost and management accounting system would then have no necessary processing requirements for financial accounting purposes, thus enabling a move away from financial accounting conventions, especially historic cost and the transaction basis. Stock valuation becomes irrelevant and unnecessary: it is not even a by-product of the system. As a result particular attention can be placed upon economic reality, relevance, timeliness, and understandability, with selective use of information which will be increasingly available as an on-line data base for management.

5.4.3 Cost coding and cost classification

Important features of information processing in any cost accounting system are adequate cost coding and cost classification.

COST CODING

A code can be defined as a system of symbols designed to be applied to a classified set of items. Cost coding is symbols applied to sets of cost items, giving a brief accurate reference and thus facilitating entry, collation and analysis of items in the accounts. In particular, items or sets of items can be separated from each other, with descriptions reduced to a few symbols. This reduces processing time and data storage in computer based systems.

The following will be features of good cost coding systems:

1 All items should have only one code; each code should be used for only one item.
2 The notation used in the coding system should avoid ambiguity; for example, numbers and letters should not be capable of confusion (1 and 0 are examples).
3 The coding structure for a set of items must be capable of including all items, including making provision for possible new items.
4 The code should be as brief as possible, while having sufficient symbols to encompass and clearly differentiate all items.
5 Symbols for a set of items should be of equal length and structure.
6 Where possible the code should have a symbol which is an abbreviation of the item.
7 A clear and complete index should be kept.
8 There should be centralised control over the establishment of codes.
9 Where possible, codes should be preprinted on documents in order to help minimise error.

COST CLASSIFICATION

Cost classification is the process of arranging cost items into groups according to their degree of similarity. Cost items can be similar in several different respects, the particular classification depending upon the purposes of grouping costs together. The different purposes of the cost accounts are:

1 stock valuation and income determination
2 decision making
3 planning and control.

A particularly important distinction in stock valuation is between product costs and period costs. Product costs are those costs which are deemed to have been incurred in getting stock to its present location and condition and thus used to place a value on the stock carried forward to a future accounting period. In a manufacturing organisation all manufacturing costs are regarded as product costs. Period costs are those costs which are not included in the stock valuation and as a result are treated as expenses in the period in which they are incurred.

Other classifications, which are used to sort and separate costs for profit reporting and stock valuation purposes, are according to type (eg, material, labour) or function (eg, manufacturing, administration, selling). These classifications are also useful for the purposes of decision-making and planning and control.

An important classification for decision-making is according to behavioural characteristics. As has been explained before, some costs tend to vary with the output level of a particular activity; other costs are incurred because of having an activity, but are largely unaffected by its output level. Raw materials used in a manufactured product are an example of the first; rent and rates paid on a factory an example of the second. A necessary and important assumption concerns the time period. In the long run all costs become to some extent variable. The classification of costs as fixed or variable is on the assumption of its use for short-term decision making for which it provides relevant information. Such a classification is also very important for planning and control purposes.

A general concept which is more broadly relevant for decision-making is the classification of costs as being either avoidable or unavoidable. Avoidable costs are those that are not necessarily going to be incurred, and whose incurrence depends, therefore, on the course of action chosen. These are the costs that are relevant to determining choice in that particular situation. Another similar classification method is to distinguish between relevant and irrelevant costs. These classifications, ie, avoidable/unavoidable and relevant/irrelevant, can only be general in nature; particular costs are classified into one or other grouping according to the circumstances of each particular case. For example, the cost of renting a factory is relevant and thus avoidable in a decision as to whether expansion of factory space should be made; it is irrelevant and unavoidable if the decision is how to use existing space. For this reason such classifications would not be expected to be found in routine cost accounting systems.

An aspect of planning and control is the identification of responsibility for cost incurrence. The classification of costs into controllable and uncontrollable groupings is important. All costs are controllable at some management level. At lower levels fewer costs are controllable but more detailed analysis is required. Thus, what costs are controllable by a particular manager can only be determined in each particular organisational situation.

A classification of costs which is relevant to income determination, decision-making and planning and control, is according to directness. The distinction between direct and indirect costs was made earlier in the chapter. This helps to identify those costs that are solely attributable to a particular activity. Ultimately all costs are directly attributable to the organisation as a whole. Certain costs become indirect, and have to be shared between activities, as the organisation is divided into smaller units. The classification of costs as direct or indirect has some similarity to the controllable/uncontrollable groupings. However, the emphasis of direct/indirect is on activities rather than people and is particularly used in the context of product costing, where the term 'direct cost' is conventionally applied to those costs which can be solely attributed to particular cost units (produced).

SUMMARY

Before establishing a cost accounting system for an organisation it is important to clearly identify information requirements which will form the basis for planning, decision making and control. Information requirements of different organisations vary. Each organisation must consider their general information requirements and also how the required information will be provided by the system. Information requirements involve consideration of content, (eg, product profitability, customer profitability), and form (eg, absorption costing versus marginal costing). Processing requirements will be considered in some detail in subsequent chapters in this section. Whatever the cost accounting system cost coding and cost classification will be essential features.

This chapter has provided an introduction to the issues affecting the operation of a cost accounting system. The exercises that follow provide an illustration of some of these issues, preparing the way for the more detailed considerations that follow in the remaining chapters in this section.

EXERCISES

Exercise 5.1

A multiple retailer owns a hundred large department stores selling a wide range of household products. The company also operates four regional depots at which the goods, purchased from outside manufacturers, are stored, repacked and finally distributed by the company's own fleet of lorries to the particular stores in that region. In addition there is one head office at which the necessary central management and administrative activities are performed.

Required:
A discussion of the type of information the cost and management accountant could produce to assist the management of the company with particular reference to the provision of information in respect of:

(i) planning and decision-making activities
(ii) controlling and evaluating activities.

Answer on page 504

Exercise 5.2

The management of a large manufacturing company are considering introducing a system of job costing into their Plant Maintenance and Repair Department. At present all the expenses incurred by this department, which is regarded as a service function to the production departments, are collected and apportioned to the production department under the expense heading 'General Works Expenses'.

Required:

(a) Describe the benefits to the company which may result from introducing a job costing system into the Plant Maintenance and Repair Department.
(b) Outline the information and procedures required in order to establish the total cost of individual repair or maintenance jobs.

Answer on page 505

Exercise 5.3

The XY Engineering Company operates a job order absorption costing system. Although a wide variety of work is undertaken it has been found useful to distinguish two categories of work, these are referred to as X jobs and Y jobs.

The company's manufacturing activities are carried out in two production departments, X department and Y department. These departments are dealt with as cost centres in the company's costing system. Most of the manufacturing for X jobs is carried out in department X and most of the work on Y jobs is carried out in department Y. There is, however, a certain amount of inter-departmental work and this is charged for at cost, as estimated by the costing system. Department X is more capital intensive than department Y.

Service department expenses, direct labour overtime premiums and administrative overheads are charged to jobs by means of a plant wide overhead absorption rate. For the past year the absorption rate has been £15 per direct labour hour.

At present department X is working at 90% of full capacity whereas department Y is regularly working overtime.

During the past year some concern has been expressed over the profitability of the average Y job. It seems that, whereas X jobs average 22% profit on sales value, the corresponding percentage for Y jobs is 12. The manager of department Y disputes the use of the profit percentage of sales value to assess the relative profitability of the two departments. He points out that his department's annual profit is 10% higher than that of department X.

Required:

(a) To comment on the suitability of the costing system for providing information on the relative profitability of the two types of product and the use of the profit on sales value percentage as a measure of relative profitability;

(b) To advise the management on improvements to their costing system. Do not suggest a standard costing system, but specifically include in your report your views on the merits of a profit centre system.

(*ACCA, Management Accounting, December 1984*)

(*Answers provided in lecturer's manual*)

The Processing of Input Costs

INTRODUCTION

The previous chapter established a general framework for providing cost information for business management purposes. This chapter and the next explore in more detail the processing requirements in order to satisfy the management information need. The recording and valuing of all input resources acquired by a business will be considered in this chapter. The methods, and issues, affecting the valuation of a business's output is the subject of the next chapter.

First of all the distinction is made between direct and indirect costs, classifications of cost which were introduced in the previous chapter. The recording and processing of direct and indirect costs are then considered in turn. Recording and processing of costs is a particularly lengthy task in the case of indirect costs because by their very nature they are more difficult than direct costs to value. The text provides some revision of, and seeks to build upon, material covered in previous studies. The changing requirements for the processing of input costs, especially indirect costs, arising from developments in manufacturing and information technology are considered at the end of the chapter. Such changes are likely to increase the utility of non-monetary measures which should in any case be seen as an important part of cost and management accounting.

6.1 INPUT COSTS

Costs are incurred in acquiring a range of resources. These will be used within a business either directly or indirectly in providing output of goods or services. In a manufacturing organisation, the major general categories of resource are materials, labour, machinery and buildings. In service organisations, machinery is likely to be far less significant and labour more so. Many costs are incurred in either providing these resources or in obtaining additional resources required as a result of their use eg having acquired a building it requires lighting and heating. These may collectively be termed input costs.

It was stated in the previous chapter that direct costs are those that can be traced directly to any cost objective. As the cost objective under analysis narrows the direct costs become fewer and thus the indirect costs greater, in number. For example, while the factory manager's salary is a direct cost of the factory as a whole it is indirect in relation to any particular department in the factory. Direct product costs are those that can be, and are felt justifiably, charged to the cost unit. Collectively they are termed prime costs and generally comprise part of material and labour cost only. All other costs are normally indirect in relation to the cost unit and are termed overheads. They may be classified by function, and/or by behaviour, as well as by type.

There are two aspects to the processing of input costs which apply regardless of whether the costs are for materials, labour or some other resources, whether they are direct or indirect, or whether they are fixed or variable. First, control needs to be exercised over the expense itself. Second, the resources have to be passed on to form part of total product costs, where further control is later exercised in relation to output.

6.2 DIRECT VERSUS INDIRECT PRODUCT COSTS

6.2.1 Traceability

An obvious influence on the direct/indirect dichotomy is the ability to trace a cost specifically to a particular cost unit. Certain costs by their nature will tend to be classified as direct (for example, raw materials that go into the products of a manufacturing organisation) and others as indirect (for example, the managing director's salary). However, it should be appreciated that the nature of the business, and the cost unit chosen, will be determinants of the ability to charge a cost as direct. For example, the hire of a crane for use on a building contract at a particular site could be traced as a direct cost of the work being carried out on the site, but if the crane is used as part of the general services of a factory, the hire would be regarded as an indirect expense, because it would probably benefit more than one cost unit. Although the nature of an expense will always be an important determinant of traceability, the nature of the business and the particular cost unit may also have an influence.

6.2.2 Fairness

Traceability is not the only factor influencing the direct/indirect dichotomy. The question of fairness also arises. An example here would be overtime. If adequate records are kept it should be possible to trace both the overtime hours worked by operatives directly involved in production, and also the cost of those hours (including overtime premium), to a particular cost unit. If the overtime is being worked as a special requirement of a particular job then it would seem right to charge the cost of overtime working in this way. If, on the other hand, overtime is being worked as a general consequence of the overall level of activity, then it would seem fairer to treat the overtime premium as an indirect cost to be shared over all production, whether undertaken in normal or overtime hours. The work carried out in overtime hours is merely a consequence of general production scheduling. The important factor in judging fairness is the underlying cause of cost incurrence.

6.2.3 Practicality

Some expenses could be traced to a particular cost unit if sufficient time and trouble were devoted to the task of analysis, but frequently the advantages to be gained by recording the required information would be outweighed by the cost of obtaining the information. For example, small and inexpensive materials used as part of a manufactured product, eg, the glue used to attach labels to a batch of canned food products, would normally be treated as an indirect cost. Some costs are not traced directly to a cost unit because it is impractical to do so.

6.2.4 Cost behaviour

Another influence on the charging of product costs as direct/indirect may be cost behaviour. Even if a cost is traceable to a product it may nevertheless have to be treated as an indirect cost in relation to a particular amount of production of that product if the cost has a relatively fixed element, or at least is only incurred intermittently. For example, even if a particular machine is used exclusively for one product, the depreciation and maintenance costs of the machine would be shared out amongst the units produced over a fairly long period, or alternatively treated as a total period cost of the product. Thus the behaviour of the cost, although not preventing a cost being traced directly to a product, may prevent direct traceability to the cost unit. Nevertheless, direct should not be confused with variable costs; the terms have different meanings. Direct costs are determined largely by traceability; variable costs are determined by cost behaviour alone. Some direct costs will not be variable, especially the shorter the time period being considered. Some variable costs are not generally traceable, for example, power.

6.3 DIRECT PRODUCT/SERVICE COSTS

Only brief attention will be given to direct costs. Certain aspects of their control are not the concern of accounting. Where cost accounting has a contribution to make it is assumed that this has been comprehensively covered in earlier studies or is covered later in the book. The purpose here is simply to summarise the important aspects. Several end of chapter exercises provide a guide to examination questions asked and a basis for revision.

6.3.1 Direct materials

Direct materials control is the system that tries to ensure the provision of the required quantity of materials, of the required quality, at the required time and at minimum cost. Bad control causes excess stock or shortages; too much variety; wrong quality, quantity and/or price; theft, breakage and/or deterioration; misuse of floor space; idle time; and bad costing. It may also have implications for labour control.

The important aspects of direct materials control are:

1 Scheduling of requirements
2 When and how much to purchase
3 Ordering
4 Receiving and inspecting
5 Storing
6 Issuing

It is assumed that students are familiar with the operation of the different pricing methods, (ie FIFO, LIFO, average, standard, and replacement), and with the variety of records/documents that are used in accounting for materials (e.g. purchase requisition, purchase order, delivery/receiving note, invoice, bin card, store requisition).

Some of the aspects listed above are more the concern of accounting than others. Management accounting is concerned with the scheduling of requirements as part of the planning of resources and with assisting in the determination of optimum stock and purchase quantities. These aspects are considered later in the book. Financial accounting will have some involvement in the processes of ordering, receiving and inspecting in order to ensure that the acquisition and payment of resources are properly conducted and authorised. Cost accounting is principally concerned with the aspects of storing and issuing. As a by-product of the cost accounting system the valuation of issues will also influence profit determination and stock valuation in the financial accounts. Aspects of storing with which the cost accountant will be concerned will be the use of space, and levels of stock discrepancy, breakage and deterioration.

On the question of valuation, cost accounting (and management accounting) may well be in conflict with financial accounting. For example, in the financial accounts the use of FIFO for pricing of issues is likely to be favoured as it leads, in an inflationary environment, to increased profits, (compared with alternative methods), and balance sheet stock valuation at latest prices. In the cost accounts profit would be overstated in real terms if the FIFO method is used for pricing issues, which is misleading if used as the basis for planning and decision-making. The issue price for management accounting purposes should be based upon opportunity cost, which in the majority of situations may be coincident with replacement cost (ie a current rather than a historic cost).

Further aspects of material control, once direct materials are merged with other resources in the production process (if a manufacturing organisation), which are of concern in cost and management accounting, are when to use the resources in production and how much to produce, and also concern about the efficiency of use in production. These aspects will be considered later.

6.3.2 Direct labour

Direct labour is that labour which is directly concerned with a particular product or service. In a manufacturing organisation this is normally restricted to certain production labour costs as other functional labour, such as administration or selling, will usually be used for the benefit of more than one product jointly. In a service organisation direct labour is that labour which can be directly traced to a cost unit, however that is determined for the service in question. This section considers, in outline, what is involved in direct labour control, (some of which is relevant to indirect labour also), and the contribution of accounting to such control.

The general objective of direct labour control is similar to that for materials, namely to ensure the provision of the required quantity of labour, of the required quality, at the required time and at minimum cost. However it is rather more qualitative in measurement, ie subjective, especially the desired balance between quality and cost, and also the judgement of quality itself. Quality is influenced by investment in training, which is an additional cost. A further factor affecting cost is the organisation's objectives regarding their employee's reward in relation to the organisation's performance.

The important aspects of direct labour control are:

1 Scheduling of requirements
2 Selection
3 Payment schemes
4 Training
5 Organisation
6 Labour records

Accounting has less of a role to play in direct labour control, and in the control of labour generally, because many aspects are outside the scope of accounting and because control is more susceptible to inter-personal relationships and skills. Cost accounting will be involved in the keeping of labour records which enable direct labour costs to be monitored and charged to cost units. In contrast to the issuing of materials, the major consideration is whether the resource is direct or indirect, rather than how to price it. Management accounting has a broader role to play. It is especially important to appreciate, and to contribute to the positive enhancement of, the behavioural implications of different aspects of labour control, and the behavioural implications of management accounting systems, methods and procedures.

As with materials, it is assumed that the student is familiar with different payment systems and with the process of direct labour recording and charging. Accounting records/documents include employee record cards, clock cards, time sheets, and job cards.

A further important aspect of labour control, which is of concern in cost and management accounting once direct labour is merged with other resources in the production process, is its efficiency. This will be considered later.

6.3.3 The flow of direct materials and direct labour costs

Figures 6.1 and 6.2 demonstrate in outline the flow of direct materials and direct labour costs, and the initial recording and charging of indirect materials and labour costs. Resources are recorded into the organisation and are then identified upon use either directly with the output to which they contribute, the cost unit, or in the case of indirect costs, with the appropriate cost centre.

6.4 OVERHEADS IN OUTLINE

Indirect costs are incurred across all functions of an organisation whether production, warehousing, distribution, selling or administration. The function which attracts by far the most attention in the cost and management accounting literature is production. The reason for this is probably because sharing of production overheads is required in order to establish product costs for stock valuation and thus profit reporting. However, non-production overheads collectively comprise a very significant part of total costs and require attention, as do production overheads, in order to ensure effectiveness, efficiency, and value for money.

All overheads are incurred in the provision of services either from one section of the organisation to another, or for the organisation's final customers. As such they may be looked upon as separate businesses each of which should be concerned to provide its own particular service to the optimum. The cost and management accounting requirement for each internal service may thus be regarded in principle as being identical to those of a similar service organisation, apart from the reduced significance of each individual internal service in the context of the organisation as a whole.

Consideration is given firstly to the treatment of overheads collectively, a process which seeks to assist in the establishment of product costs and also to assist control over the separate activities involved. This latter aspect, ie control, is especially important in the case of overheads as unlike direct materials and direct labour, control over overhead costs can only really be exercised at the cost centre level rather than within product costs.

FIGURE 6.1 **Flow of material costs**

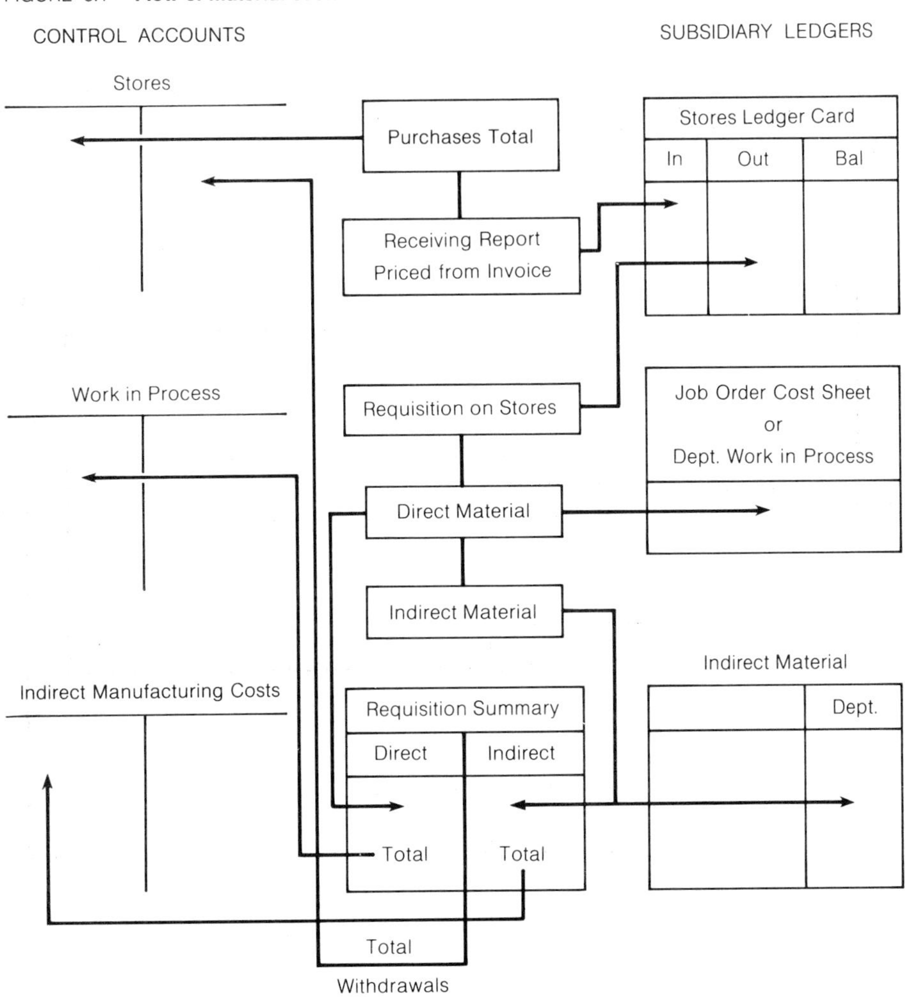

6.4.1 The process of production overhead pricing

As was explained earlier, overheads represent those costs which cannot be traced, or which it would be unfair or impractical to trace, directly to cost units. The task of sharing is considerably reduced if a marginal costing rather than an absorption costing system is in operation, as only variable production overheads have to be shared out.

The process of recording indirect manufacturing costs is shown in Figure 6.3 on page 86.

The process of sharing out production overheads can be summarised as follows (and see Figure 6.4 on page 87):

Overheads consisting of: Indirect materials
Indirect labour
and
Indirect expenses

are ALLOCATED to responsibility centres
APPORTIONED from service centres to users of the service
ABSORBED into cost units, using a method chosen from the following bases:

1 Cost per unit
2 Percentage of a direct cost/revenue
3 Hourly rate

Absorption rates may be established in advance of the accounting period based on anticipated overhead expenditure and activity.

FIGURE 6.2 **Flow of labour costs**

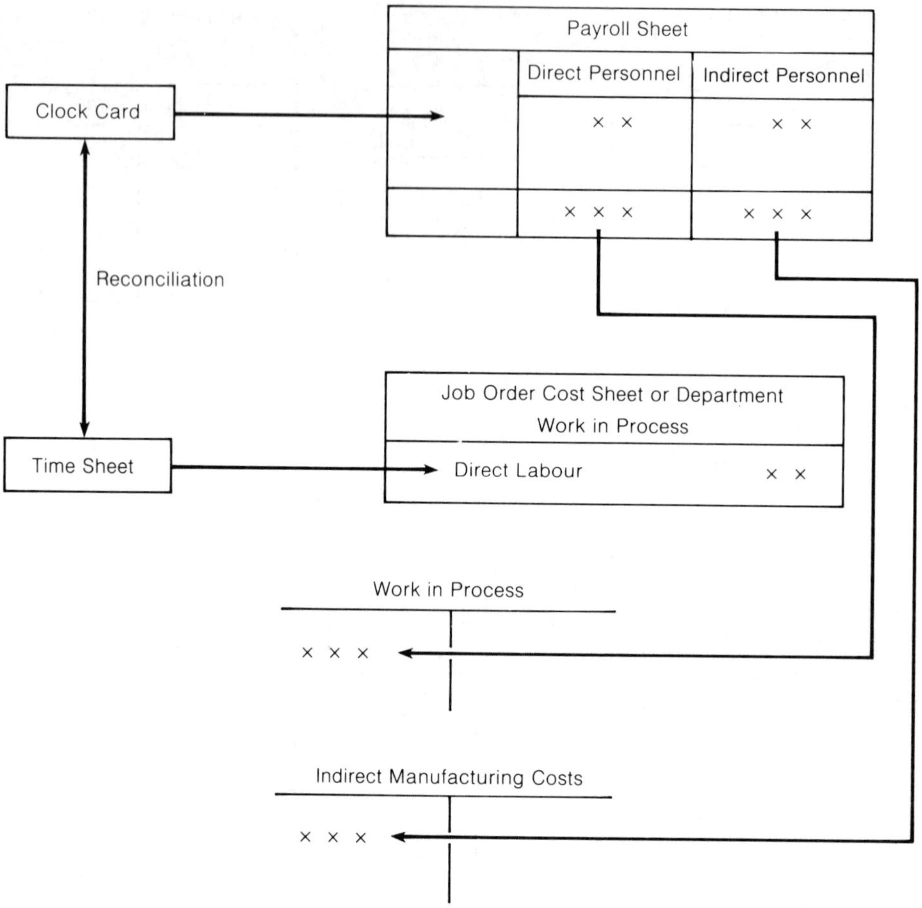

Self-assessment question 6.1

The following overhead costs were budgeted in a manufacturing company for a period:

	Indirect materials £000	Indirect labour £000	Other expenses £000	Total £000
Production department A	12	60	—	72
Production department B	24	40	—	64
Production department C	16	80	—	96
Service department X	8	20	—	28
Service department Y	12	40	—	52
General factory	12	88	220	320
	84	328	220	632

Overheads incurred are not expected to be affected by changes in activity in the short-term. General factory and service department costs are apportioned as follows:

	Production department			Service department		Total
	A	B	C	X	Y	
	%	%	%	%	%	%
General factory	35	20	30	5	10	100
Service dept X	25	20	40	—	15	100
Service dept Y	15	45	40	—	—	100

The company uses predetermined departmental direct labour hour rates for absorption of overhead into product costs.
Direct labour hours for the period were:

	Production department		
	A	B	C
Budgeted	20,000	40,000	30,000
Actual	21,200	38,600	28,100

Overheads incurred during the period were as follows:

	£
Indirect materials	85,000
Indirect labour	332,000
Other expenses	217,000
	634,000

Required:
(a) Calculate the overhead absorption rate for each production department for the period.
(b) Prepare the overhead control account for the period.
(c) Provide an explanation for any under/over absorption.

Answers on page 507

6.4.2 The process of non-production overhead pricing

Non-production overheads are those incurred in storing the finished product, marketing and selling it, distributing it, and in the general administration of the business as a whole. As such the overheads become, to differing degrees, remote from the final cost unit (the product). For service organisations, which have no finished stock, such overheads comprise total indirect costs.

It is important to recognise that each separate area of activity should be considered, whatever its function, with a view to establishing cost analysis systems which facilitate both control over the particular functional activity and also costing of those aspects of the business which utilise the function and thus resources. This may be the costing of different products; it may also be the costing of different customers/outlets for the products. Such analysis should have regard also to the cost of establishing, maintaining and operating such systems. It may be both too difficult and impractical to adopt sophisticated cost analysis methods.

6.5 ALLOCATION, APPORTIONMENT AND ABSORPTION ISSUES

The factors affecting the process of production overhead allocation, apportionment and absorption, and the sharing of non-production overheads also, are:

1. The responsibility centres established
2. Whether overhead is apportioned from one centre to another
3. How overhead is apportioned from one centre to another
4. Inter-servicing apportionment
5. The absorption method chosen
6. Whether predetermined or actual absorption rates are applied
7. The resource base chosen
8. Whether absorption costing or marginal costing is employed.

These eight factors will now be considered in turn. In many cases reference will be to a manufacturing environment, but the issues and principles frequently have universal application.

FIGURE 6.3 **Recording indirect manufacturing costs**

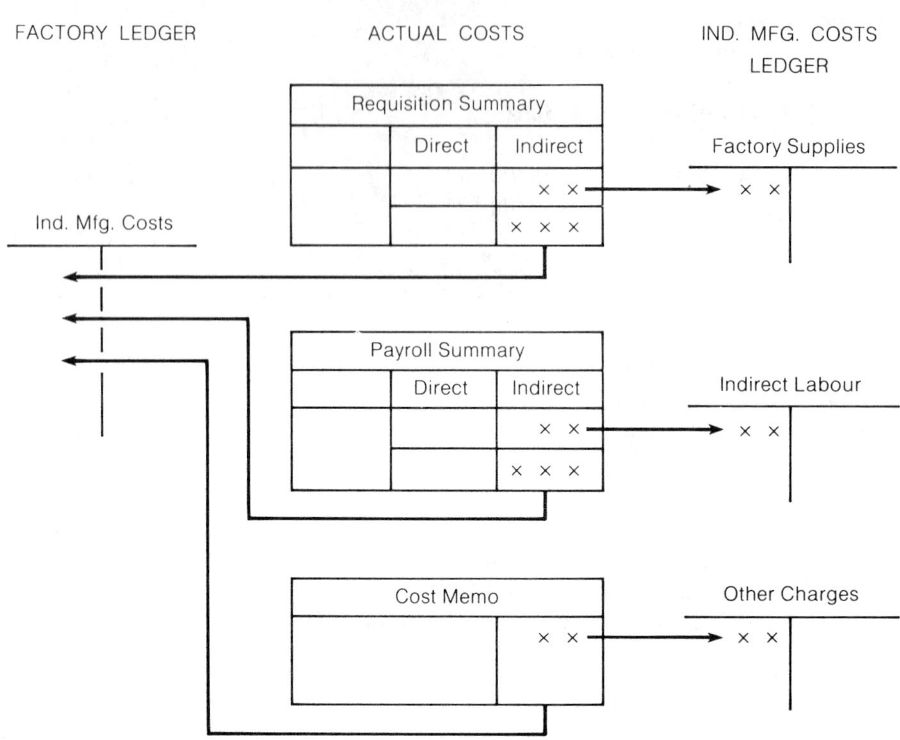

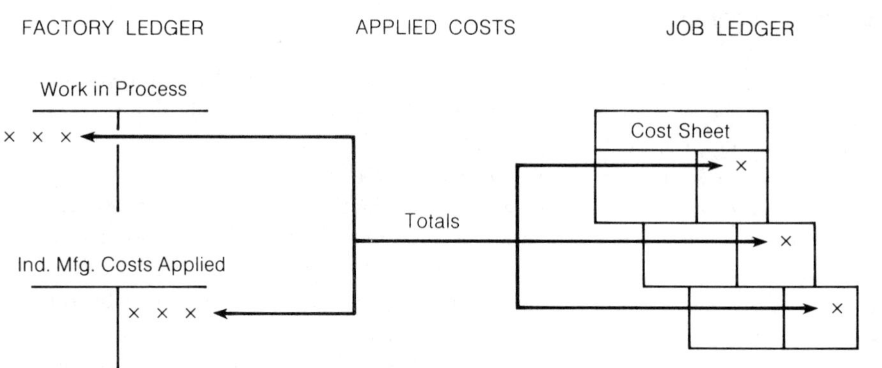

6.5.1 Responsibility centres

If a business manufactures only one product, or all jobs spend an equal amount of time in each department and use the same amount of resources, then a blanket overhead absorption rate, ie a single rate for the whole factory, would yield the same production overhead costs per unit as separate overhead absorption rates for each separate production centre within the overall production operation. It may be argued, in such a hypothetical situation, that a blanket rate would be sufficient and that separate cost centres are not required. However, this neglects the necessity to exercise control over overhead expenditure in each separate area of the business. It is the case also that the more the total production operation can be divided into separately identifiable parts for the analysis of overhead expenditure, not only is control over each part facilitated, but the sharing of those costs to different cost units should be more reasonable.

Responsibility centres within production may include for example, the canteen, maintenance, quality control, material handling and several production departments each involved in a different stage of production or producing different products. The service cost centres that should ideally be

FIGURE 6.4 **Sharing of production overheads**

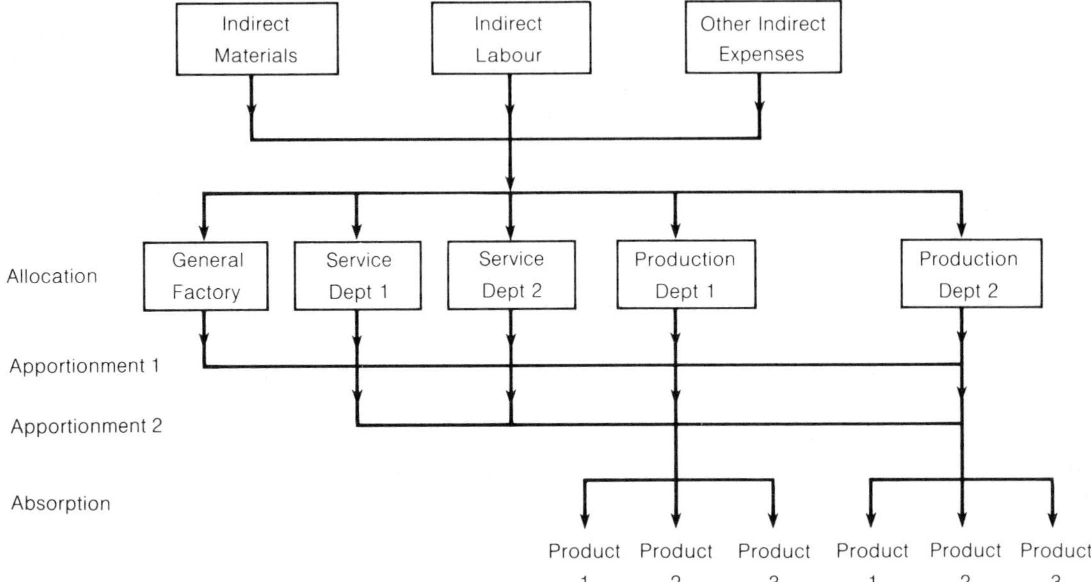

established may be fairly obvious although they may not necessarily be synonymous with departments. At the same time the cost of providing the information breakdown must be considered. The information analysed at this level must be of some use, which means that somebody must be capable of being held responsible for the expenditure, which must therefore as far as possible be within his/her control. The production cost centres required will also be influenced by the nature of the production operations and products.

6.5.2 Whether overhead is apportioned from one centre to another

Each responsibility centre can be looked upon as a separate business. Thus, in a way, the same questions can be asked regarding required information as with a business as a whole ie, what information is required? How should it be provided?

In considering what information is required for the effective control of one small area of activity, the cost of providing sophisticated analysis may outweigh the benefits, and thus influence whether any apportionment of overhead is made from one centre to another. Other factors affecting whether such apportionment of overhead is made are:

1. Whether input/output relationships are sufficiently clear. If relationships are unclear the cost may not be passed on, as apportionment is unlikely to increase product cost reliability or enable improved cost centre controls.
2. The extent of the choice as to whether, and as to how much, a centre uses another centre's services. If choice is not available, the buying centre cannot be held responsible for price and thus are not in a position to control their own costs.
3. Where the responsibility centre is in the production/ administration process. For example, the cost of the factory personnel department may be shared out over production departments because product cost reliability is improved; the cost of the general personnel department may not be shared out over other administration departments, because this could not be expected to influence product cost reliability.
4. It may be wished to stimulate demand for a service where potential user departments have some discretion over its use: for example, to stimulate demand for ad hoc computer analysis of data from the computer centre. This could be achieved by not charging for a service.
5. Whether indiscriminate use of a service is encouraged if no charge is made.
6. Whether there may be adverse consequences in terms of employee motivation as a result of apportionment. For example, assume that a manager is made responsible for a cost budget which includes a share of computer centre costs, whose apportionment is based on numbers of employees. Adverse motivational consequences may result if an increase in computer charges

occurs because the costs of the computer centre increase, or because employee numbers in other departments decline. The manager may be less motivated to achieve budget, may be forced to reduce expenditure elsewhere with unfavourable consequences in order to achieve budget, or may seek to obtain the computer service elsewhere at additional cost to the company as a whole. Key factors affecting employee motivation will be whether the extent of responsibility for different costs can be, and is, clearly established, and whether charges reflect economic reality.

Thus apportionment should not be automatic. The question should be 'is it useful for the cost?'

6.5.3 How overhead is apportioned from one centre to another

As far as the 'how?' is concerned, the apportionment method depends upon the particular relationship between input and output. In production, certain overheads can only be allocated to the factory as a whole, and thus require a factory wide apportionment which will depend upon the nature of the expense. Value of materials, numbers of employees, value of plant and machinery, or floor area could be used, reflecting the influence of materials, labour, machinery and buildings on overhead cost.

Bases for apportioning individual responsibility centre costs will depend upon the input/output relationship determined. This may result in costs being charged in relation to particular uses of the service. A maintenance department, for example, will carry out a variety of work which can be classified under four main categories:

1 Routine maintenance carried out in accordance with a planned schedule.
2 Capital work such as involvement in the installation of plant and machinery or the construction of buildings.
3 Small repair jobs, found during routine maintenance or at the request of other departments.
4 Major repairs and alterations at the request of other departments and sometimes on a planned schedule.

Particular maintenance and repair work carried out may be charged with actual materials used and the maintenance labour hours taken. Such charging is based on specific order (job) costing principles. This may be worthwhile in the case of 2. and 4. above (ie, capital work and major repairs) but less justified in the case of routine maintenance and minor repairs. The indirect costs of the maintenance department, and of other departments treated in this way, would be charged on the basis of some unit of the department's activity, for example maintenance labour hours.

Alternatively, a responsibility centre's costs may be charged out to the different departments using the service, based upon an agreed split of total costs. The cost of routine maintenance work, for example, could be charged in this way. This has the advantage of simplicity but is likely to be more arbitrary. Having agreed a budget figure this may be charged without reference to actual costs. This has the advantage that users know exactly what they will be charged, actual costs do not have to be shared, and the providing department is left to explain any variation in costs from budget. Against this it could be argued that, in the short-term, users will have no regard to economy in their use of the service as their costs are unaffected. However, if actual costs are charged, there is less incentive for the service department manager to control the cost of the service and inefficiencies in the provision of the service are passed on to users. Product costs may also be inflated which may affect the ability to obtain business.

A responsibility centre's costs could instead be charged out at an average rate per unit. For example, factory canteen costs may be charged to production departments at an average rate per person. Such charging is based on operation (process) costing principles. Having established an average rate per unit in the budget (a form of standard) this may be applied throughout a period, with the advantage that actual costs do not have to be shared. With a standard rate the charge made reflects increased or reduced use of the service, and inefficiencies are not passed on thus providing some measure of the providing department's efficiency.

It may also be considered whether a department's activities could, and should, be charged out at other than actual/budgeted cost. Charging could be based on market value for work done, rather than on cost, if such a value can be established. Market value may reflect opportunity cost where the service has limited capacity and the possibility of selling the service outside the company exists. The possibility of charging a market value will be explored further in Chapter 10. Frequently, however, costs incurred in providing the service, rather than any market value, will be the opportunity cost. This begs the question as to whether total or marginal costs should be used. If surplus capacity exists in the providing department there may be an argument in the short-term for charging marginal cost.

With reference to the earlier discussion of maintenance costs, as a by-product of the cost accounts the maintenance department should keep a set of plant records, giving details of breakdowns, repairs and maintenance of individual items of plant and machinery. This will be useful in managing an asset over its useful life, including planned maintenance and replacement. Such asset management is termed terotechnology.

Because of the difficulty of establishing input/output relationships, responsibility centre cost apportionment may be fairly arbitrary. This can result in:

1 Inadequate control over service costs.
2 Operating inefficiencies being passed on to users.
3 Relative changes of departmental use of services not being reflected.
4 Unreliable product costs.

This can lead to sub-optimal behaviour. If greater attention to cost apportionment is not felt to be justified then it is important to clearly recognise that it is being done for the purpose of product costing only, and then only as a guide to long-term costs.

Self-assessment question 6.2

(a) When considering the way in which service department costs should be controlled, the management accountant must consider a range of aims.
Identify and comment briefly on THREE such aims.

(b) A charge may be made to user departments for the provision of a service by a service department, using any of the following charge bases:
(i) Total actual cost;
(ii) Standard absorption cost;
(iii) Variable cost;
(iv) Opportunity cost;
(v) No charge.
For any FOUR of the above bases, comment on the circumstances in which their use might be appropriate and describe problems associated with their use.

(*ACCA, Management Accounting, December 1988*)

Answers on page 508

6.5.4 Inter-servicing apportionment

A further question that arises in determining the 'how'? of overhead apportionment is how to apportion service department costs where these departments provide services for each other. There are three main methods of dealing with the inter-servicing problem, which it is assumed have been covered in earlier studies:

1 The elimination method.
2 The repeated distribution method.
3 The algebraic method.

The elimination method apportions the cost of service cost centres between users in turn, but once they have been apportioned the cost centres are eliminated from any subsequent apportionment.

It is usual to begin with the service cost centre serving the greatest number of other service cost centres, with the amount of costs also being a factor in establishing priority.

The repeated distribution method, unlike the elimination method, does not eliminate a cost centre from the apportionment process. Having apportioned a particular service centre's costs, it can subsequently pick up a share of other service centre costs, thus necessitating a repeat of the process. This continues until the amounts involved are insignificant, and can be as a result slow and cumbersome, especially for students in examination.

The algebraic method provides a mathematical solution to the repeated distribution problem, but the solution becomes increasingly complex as more service cost centres are involved. Students should be capable of providing a mathematical solution, in a two reciprocal service cost centre situation, using simultaneous equations.

The choice of method will depend upon:

1 The number of other departments serviced.
2 The size of the overhead expenditure.
3 The percentage of the total service provided to other service departments.
4 Whether cost apportionment assists overhead control or whether it is simply used to establish product costs.
5 The amount of work involved.
6 The extent to which product cost reliability is affected.

The use of the repeated distribution method provides an apportionment of overhead which seems very logical and precise. However, much depends upon the bases of apportionment which can be quite arbitrary. The differences in apportionment caused by using the elimination method, rather than the repeated distribution method, may be quite trivial when compared to the differences which could be caused by using alternative apportionment bases.

Self-assessment question 6.3

Refer back to self-assessment question 6.1. The apportionment of Service Department Y costs has been revised to include an apportionment to Service Department X as follows:

Production Department			**Service Department**	**Total**
A	B	C	X	
%	%	%	%	%
15	35	30	20	100

Required:
Calculate the budgeted overhead attributable to each of the three production departments for the period using:
(i) the elimination method
(ii) the repeated distribution method
(iii) the algebraic method.

Answers on page 509

6.5.5 Absorption method

Overheads are absorbed into cost units using a method chosen from the following bases:

1 Cost per unit.
2 Percentage of a direct cost/revenue.
3 Hourly rate.

The particular method(s) chosen depend(s) upon the dominant element of cost and upon how it is best used to absorb overheads. It is assumed that the use of the different methods has been adequately covered in previous studies. The following self-assessment question will test recall of the subject.

Self-assessment question 6.4

(a) Specify and explain the factors to be considered in determining whether to utilise a single, factory wide recovery rate for all production overheads or a separate rate for each cost centre, production or service department.

(b) Describe three methods of determining fixed overhead recovery rates and specify the circumstances under which each method is superior to the other methods mentioned.

(*ACCA, Management Accounting, June 1981*)

Answers on page 510

6.5.6 Predetermined or actual absorption rates

It is usual to establish overhead absorption rates in advance because:

1. Overhead incurrence and production activity may be independent and may take place unevenly during a period. It is confusing and not at all useful to have constantly fluctuating rates and thus changing product costs.
2. It enables product costs to be established as production takes place and not some time after the event.
3. It is less time consuming as the establishment of absorption rates is required less frequently.
4. It provides a better basis for control.

The establishment of predetermined overhead rates is not directly associated with budgeting. Even if an organisation has no formal budgeting system the question of overhead absorption arises.

The establishment of predetermined rates means that estimated, rather than actual, costs are used to transfer overheads from their incurrence in different areas of production into the costs associated with final output when production takes place. Ultimately, however, actual costs, not estimated costs, have to be charged. A comparison has to be made between actual overhead costs incurred and those charged to production. Differences will inevitably occur either because costs incurred, or because actual activity, differ from that expected. The two may be related. Increased activity is likely to result in increased costs but it is unlikely to be in the same proportions. Resource requirements are likely in any case to vary from expectation. Overheads will, therefore, be either underabsorbed (where actual costs exceed those absorbed) or over-absorbed (where costs absorbed exceed those incurred).

There are three possible treatments of under- or over-absorbed production overheads. The remaining balance of overheads may be:

1. retained as a balance on the overhead control account for the following period.
2. transferred to profit and loss account in the period.
3. shared between period profit and closing stock.

Under or over-absorbed overhead may be retained as a balance in the short-term, ie from one month to another in the accounting period, if it is due to fluctuations in activity and/or costs incurred which are expected to even out by the end of the period. If on the other hand, a balance remains at the end of the period, or the under- or over-absorption in the short term is not expected to reverse, then the balance should be transferred to the profit and loss account. Transfer of a share in order to adjust the value of stock may be justified in principle (see next section re resource base) but is unlikely to be felt worthwhile in practice.

These are primarily concerns of financial accounting. For management purposes, it is important that product costs bear the appropriate share of overheads, and that the basis for their determination is understood. The important thing with over- or under-absorption is to determine the underlying cause. The cause is important for control.

Predetermined rates may be similarly applied to non-production overheads with under-/over-absorbed balances either retained in the short term or immediately transferred to profit/loss. Alternatively, whilst non-production overheads may be periodically apportioned to products, they may not form part of the routine cost accounting system.

6.5.7 Resource base

The resource base is the denominator in the absorption rate calculation ie it is the number of units, or hours, or the amount of direct costs that are divided into the overhead cost to establish the absorption rate.
It may be based on:

1 Resource availability
or
2 Resource utilisation

Resource availability requires a measure of what activity could be with the facilities that exist/are likely to exist. The measure could be of:

1(a) Maximum capacity
or
2(b) Practical capacity

Maximum capacity assumes continuous operation at peak efficiency. Practical capacity establishes a measure of activity which assumes continuous operation at expected efficiency.

Resource utilisation requires a measure of what activity is likely to be or of what it actually was. The measure could be of:

2(a) Normal activity
or
2(b) Annual activity

Normal activity is a measure of the long-run annual average activity expected. It is intended to smooth any fluctuations in activity from one year to another. The annual activity (or shorter period if desired) is based on actual activity/expected activity for the period in question. The use of annual activity smoothes any fluctuations from period to period within a year.

The rationale for using a measure of resource availability, rather than resource utilisation, is that is provides an indication of what unit costs could be if full use was made of resources available, and it highlights, through under-absorption, the cost of spare capacity. An idle capacity cost would be budgeted. Against this, it could be argued, however, that unit costs are understated, especially if maximum capacity is used as the resource base. Measures of resources, other than actual utilisation, may also be difficult to determine. For example, measures of capacity are affected by working hours available, which can be altered by overtime and/or shift patterns.

The choice of resource base may affect the treatment of under- or over-absorbed overhead balances. Where the resource base reflects resource availability, rather than utilisation, overheads are likely to be under-absorbed. That part of the balance due to difference between actual activity and theoretical capacity should not be carried forward, except to the extent that it may be attributable to closing stock. Where normal activity is used, there may be a stronger argument for delaying the transfer of under- or over- absorbed balances beyond the accounting period. There is likely to be much less argument for apportioning part of the balance to closing stock, because it already reflects normal cost.

Self-assessment question 6.5

A divisionalised company sets profit goals for its divisions but otherwise allows the divisional managers to establish their own budgets making their own decisions as to selling prices and production plans. The profit target for the Alemouth Division has been set at £500,000 for the forthcoming year. The profit for the year which is just ending is estimated at £1,000,000 but the central planning department has accepted the report of an independent market survey that predicts a 50% drop in customer demand for the division's products from the 'normal' level that has existed for some years past. The division makes a range of products. The summarised profit and loss account for the year just ending is as follows:

Estimated Profit and Loss Account

	£	£
Sales		2,500,000
Opening Stock	100,000	
Production Costs	1,000,000	
	1,100,000	
Less		
Closing Stock	100,000	
		1,000,000
		1,500,000
Administrative Costs		500,000
Estimated Profit		1,000,000

The target profit is regarded with some consternation and the divisional manager believes that it is not achievable. He proposes to budget for the predicted sales reduction of 50% but for a planned level of production of only 20% below the current year's figure. Lower levels of production appear to move the division even further from the target profit so he proposes to abandon the division's 'optimal' stock control system and to build up finished goods stocks in the hope that demand will improve. The budgeted figure for Administrative Costs is to be drastically cut from £500,000 to £300,000. He has prepared the following Budgeted Profit and Loss Account for his plan:

Budgeted Profit and Loss Account

(*manager's proposal*)

	£	£
Sales		1,250,000
Opening Stock	100,000	
Production Costs	900,000	
	1,000,000	
Less		
Closing Stock	450,000	
		550,000
		700,000
Administrative Costs		300,000
Estimated Profit		400,000

The manager has valued the closing finished goods stock at average actual production cost; this basis is allowed by the group's accounting procedures manual but its adoption is opposed by the divisional accountant. The accountant claims that a fairer basis is 'normal' average production cost.

The divisional accountant also argues against the rationale of the proposed budget. He suggests that the division should try to stimulate demand by a general 10% price cut. The market survey suggested that such a cut would allow the division to sell 75% of its current level in physical terms. He argues that if demand is 25% down then budgeted closing stocks should also be 25% down, as compared to present levels.

Required:

(a) to compare the alternative methods of valuing stock given in the question:

(b) to explain why the manager's calculations show that reductions in the budgeted level of production move the division further away from its target profit; and

(c) to draft the budgeted profit and loss account for the accountant's proposals (with closing stock valued at 'normal' average production cost).

(*ACCA*, *Management Accounting*, *December 1984*)

Answers on page 511

6.5.8 Absorption or marginal costing

The issues considered above affecting the allocation, apportionment and absorption of overheads, will all have an effect on the cost accounting process. One final influence is whether an absorption costing or a marginal costing system is employed. This obviously has an important effect on the recording process.

If a marginal costing system is used then all fixed overheads are allocated in the normal way to responsibility centres. They are not then charged to user areas. If they are fixed in the short-term, exponents of marginal costing argue that cost control is best exercised in the area where the cost can be allocated. They also argue that product costs should only include the cost of those resources that are variable with short-term changes in activity.

The implication for cost recording is that the majority of production overheads are not apportioned from one responsibility centre to another and are not absorbed into product cost. The process is thus considerably simplified. Fixed costs would simply be charged against profit for the organisation as a whole in the period in which they are incurred.

6.6 COSTING IN THE NEW TECHNOLOGY ENVIRONMENT

The changes that are taking place in the manufacturing environment were outlined in Chapter 2. These changes are affecting cost accounting requirements due to new priorities in the factory, to a changed relationship between direct and indirect costs, to increasing fixed costs and to the need to reconsider traditional overhead apportionment and absorption methods. This final section of the chapter considers the implications for cost accounting of these changes.

6.6.1 The new environment

The application of the concepts of Just in Time and Total Quality, and investment in computer technology applied to manufacturing, are changing the workplace. Manufacturing businesses have to be capable of manufacturing increasingly sophisticated products of the highest quality and with first class service, but at low cost. They must also have the flexibility to cope with shorter product and equipment life cycles, and with demands for greater product variety, the combined effects of greater competition and more discriminating customers.

This requirement has necessitated changes in the production process to improve quality, reduce set up times, increase manufacturing flexibility, overcome restrictive work-force rules and reduce randomness caused by uncertain supply, poor quality and erratic machine performance.

The result has been a new philosophy and, where relevant and justified, capital investment, which has enabled and encouraged a return to small batch production of complete products on flexible equipment, instead of the large batch, mass production of parts of products in specialised processes. Investment in advanced manufacturing technology is not necessarily essential in order to remain competitive. The principles of JIT and TQC may be capable of application and may yield sufficient benefit, without investment. Also, management style and labour relations appear to be at least as important in raising efficiency as is technology.

Within the manufacturing function, because the factory's capabilities and constraints are changed, how it is organised must also change. Fewer people will be needed for operations with a change in the balance between manual and non manual, but they must be better trained and more highly skilled. Industrial relations will also need to change. The greater integration and cooperation of design and production, and of maintenance and production, also means less separation of skills, and thus a flexible and adaptable workforce, as well as flexible and adaptable plant, is required. Work will be more of a team approach, with shop floor personnel becoming machine minders rather than machine users, and thus many conventional payment systems will become redundant.

There must be the necessary management and organisation to make it work. The emphasis on quality, low inventory, flexibility and delivery performance, and the changes in manufacturing organisation and technology themselves, call for new performance measures and changes in organisation structure. At the same time the advances in information technology provide tremendous opportunities for gathering, analysing, and presenting cost and management accounting information and at much reduced cost.

6.6.2 Existing accounting deficiencies

In Kaplan's view (expressed in his book (with Johnson) 'Relevance Lost, The Rise and Fall of Management Accounting') typical 1980's cost accounting systems are helpful neither for product costing nor for operational cost control. Whilst all the systems are installed and running on computers, few show any difference in design philosophy to reflect the increased computational power of digital computers. They claim that many cost accounting systems incorporate simplifying assumptions, (for example overhead costs are combined into large, frequently plant-wide overhead pools with direct labour used as the absorption method), which were heavily influenced by previously limited processing power.

Most companies, Kaplan asserts, still use the same cost accounting and management control systems that were developed decades ago for a competitive environment drastically different to that of today. He also believes that these inadequacies in existing performance measurement systems are hindering many firms transition to the organisation and technology required for the new industrial competition.

The accounting literature has also failed, generally, to face up to the challenges to accounting information provision posed by these changes in the organisation and technology of manufacture and the new competitive demands. To quote Kaplan, 'the cost accounting implications of . . . more advanced production control systems have barely been investigated and, as a result, our cost accounting textbooks continue to describe production processes using extremely simplified models . . . It is unlikely that our current accounting graduates will have any understanding of the complex production environment in which cost accounting must be applied today.'

It is not simply that the computational power of modern computers has not been recognised. Overhead treatment results from the fact that scorekeeping is frequently undertaken and described within a framework of accounting logic rather than economic logic. In traditional cost accounting systems, manufacturing overhead is often treated as an oncost receiving too little attention because it may be less significant than direct costs. Non-production overheads have frequently been even more neglected.

The traditional approach to overhead absorption is to calculate a rate per direct labour hour within a department/factory and then apply it to the number of direct labour hours expended on a particular piece of work. This works fairly well in a labour paced manufacturing environment where machines function as tools to assist production workers. It will, however, provide unsatisfactory results in an automated environment, where the work is machine paced. There is no possible cause and effect relationship.

Not only does the relationship between overhead and direct labour hours become especially tenuous in such a scenario, but small savings in time can have a large influence on product cost, as overhead rates become very large. As a result although direct labour cost may be low, saving here is the best way to reduce apparent product cost because of the effect on overhead absorption. Thus too much attention may be devoted to a relatively unimportant cost. Reduction in overhead absorption is likely to result without any real reduction in overhead expenditure.

There is, as a result, in general a lack of any clear integration between decision making concepts and routine information provision, and a failure to consider sufficiently factors which should influence that provision. Routine information provision may not, therefore, provide a useful basis for decision making. This is serious because information provided to management will be a vital prompt and a source of information for decision making.

6.6.3 Towards accounting solutions

OVERHEAD ABSORPTION

As technology changes, and as service becomes more important, so indirect costs represent a higher proportion of total costs. Not only are the number of what were direct personnel reduced, but the nature of the work changes such that direct labour is very often no longer direct in relation to the product. Thus the profile of indirect costs, which will now comprise all conversion (value added) costs in manufacturing, will be raised. The grouping of all conversion costs means that there will be consistent treatment of, and no argument about, such things as overtime premiums, holiday pay, waiting time etc as all labour costs are included in the indirect category.

Along with this change in the relationship between direct and indirect costs it should also be recognised that direct labour hours are no longer the critical resource constraint in the new factory, nor even an adequate surrogate for capacity. Machine centres provide the capacity and the major source of indirect costs. Thus, new measures will have to be found, and based on machine utilisation and other non-labour measures of activity. Machine time has not traditionally been used, even in many cases where factory automation may be relatively high, because of the added clerical cost and the difficulty of computing machine time on individual jobs.

Sizer and Coulthurst (Case Studies in Management Accounting) provide an example, in their case study of Rolls Royce Manufacturing, of a company coming to terms with the problem. The company has progressively moved from standard direct labour time to machine cycle time for absorbing overheads. This is resulting in significant benefits, such as more reliable product costs and project costing, and improved sourcing decisions, inventory control and management control information.

It is questionable, however, whether overhead absorption as traditionally practiced is useful, and therefore necessary, especially in the environment of the new factory. The only reason for overhead absorption is in order to determine product cost which can be used for stock valuation and as a guide to long run cost. A very detailed and continuous system of full absorption costing is unnecessary in order to satisfy both of these requirements. Stock can be valued by approximate means every 6 months or so. A more detailed exercise say annually, could be carried out to share overheads over products in order to determine an approximate long run cost. In between times any changes in total overhead expenditure or total output could be used to make approximate adjustments if required.

PRODUCT COSTS

Several factors point to a reduced requirement for total product cost information in the new factory environment. First, stocks of work-in-progress and finished goods may be substantially reduced and thus the stock valuation exercise will reduce in significance and complexity. Second, depreciation becomes an even bigger share of total indirect cost. Its inclusion in product cost based on an arbitrary write-off method, and historic cost, provides no indication of the true economic cost. Third, with direct costs (and variable costs) comprising little more than raw materials, the reliability of total product cost information will be even more questionable. Fourth, with production along product lines, the system of sharing out overheads and absorbing them at different stages of manufacture does not apply.

If production of similar products is organised in machining centres, more overheads will become directly allocatable to a particular product group. Non directly allocatable overheads could be shared out to product groups on an annual basis. This would provide a measure of performance in relation to the investment in the machining centre. Is any further analysis of costs useful? It would also incidentally make stock valuation easier. It is time that a lot of the age old routines are seriously questioned. Do they really help in the cycle of planning, decision making and control? A lot of wasted time, effort, and expense may be devoted to them, and the arbitrary allocation of expenses may not only be pointless but also damaging.

Another change will be in costing method. As batch sizes are reduced and the number of batches increased, it takes on more of the characteristics of the job costing environment. However, job costing is unnecessary even if overhead absorption is carried out. The volume of paperwork and the time taken in recording would be prohibitive, and to no useful end whatsoever. Costing will take on the characteristics of process costing with costs collected and averaged over time where unit product costs are required. (Job and process costing are considered in the next chapter).

It is likely, however, that in most cases factories do not become totally automated in one stroke. Thus a firm's cost accounting systems should accommodate both man and machine paced environments and provide useful comparative data.

COST/BENEFIT RELATIONSHIPS

It was stated earlier that the profile of indirect costs will be raised, as they represent an increased proportion of costs. It was also suggested that hitherto the absorption of overhead may have deflected attention from the source of such costs. Attention needs to be directed to the monitoring of the costs of different departments and areas of manufacturing overhead expenditure, and further to the establishment of cost/benefit relationships.

All indirect costs (in relation to products) are in fact allocatable somewhere. It is at this level that attention needs to be focused as this is the level at which the majority of indirect costs may be altered by action. By investigating in detail the demands placed upon different factory departments, it will frequently be found that cost drivers are more than just physical volume of production, and that there may be several cost drivers within a given cost centre. Similar insights are likely to be gained from an examination of non-production departments.

A further benefit that could be derived from adopting a different approach, which seeks to concentrate attention on identifying cost drivers, is that the true cost of providing product variety may be found. The benefits of variety are often over-estimated and their cost under-estimated because routine accounting systems inevitably fail to adjust for three main factors: complexity sensitive variable costs; creeping fixed costs; and the effect of substitution. These factors are considered further in the paragraphs that follow.

Product variety inevitably results in greater machine downtime due to changeover and breakdown, plus higher waste levels. Warehouse and distribution costs result from higher stock levels for slow moving products together with increased handling and shipping costs for split pallets.

Higher costs, generally regarded as fixed, will be incurred for product variety due to extra space requirements (for example in the warehouse) and the need for more production and ancilliary staff to cope with the extra products. More salesmen and marketing staff are also likely to be required and many central administration costs increase as there are more products to be invoiced, more codes to put on computer systems, more complicated planning etc.

The substitution effect is difficult to measure. However, for any product service where similar alternatives are also provided by the same business, an element of substitution would occur if the product/service offering was reduced. This should be recognised.

It is certainly the case that marketing management have been encouraged to extend product variety because the true benefits and costs have not hitherto been measured. Whilst in the new manufacturing environment the cost of variety will decline, all business should still be concerned to establish an optimum product mix, which should be influenced by the cost of variety. Direct product profitability, a new concept of profit measurement being applied in retailing (see chapter 9), is improving cost identification and, where applied, is generally leading to some product rationalisation. Manufacturers as well as retailers should look to use the concept constructively.

From the foregoing it will be clear that non-production overheads (ie warehouse, distribution, marketing, sales and administration cost) also require adequate data collection and analysis. Both theory and practice have concentrated on production/bought-in product costs, again driven by the external requirement for stock valuation. It is important to look for cost/benefit relationships in all of these non-production areas in order to monitor costs and establish optimum levels of expenditure. The important question is whether costs add sufficient value.

6.7 NON–MONETARY MEASURES

Cost and management accounting should be concerned with non-monetary as well as monetary measures, as certain aspects of business are not easy to measure or interpret in financial terms. The requirement for non-monetary measures is likely to grow, as factors such as quality, reliability and delivery performance are increasingly seen as a crucial aspect of competition and thus relevant to strategy. Information, for example, on deliveries not made on time, the number of sub-standard products, quantities of material wasted, amount of rework, the frequency and length of machine breakdowns, non-productive labour time, the launch time for new products, and the number and gravity of customer complaints and returns, should be part of the accounting routine. The measures may express performance in absolute quantity terms, for example the number of sub-standard products, or in relative terms, for example sub-standard products as a proportion of total output.

It should be recognised that quality is an important aspect of all work carried out by all functions within an organisation. All have levels of service/quality as well as levels of cost. The question is what is the optimum level of quality in relation to cost? Concentration on quality could in fact reveal that in many areas high quality may be less costly because of the implications of poor quality. Zero defects can minimise total cost. Peters and Waterman, in their book 'In Search of Excellence' state that the excellent companies are permeated by an almost neurotic philosophy that requires every level of management to seek higher quality.

Thus higher quality should be a driving force. Within the factory the absence of good materials, highly trained and motivated labour, and well-maintained equipment, will increase the costs of non-quality such as scrap, rework, excess inventory, equipment breakdown, customer complaints, product replacements/refunds. Thus appropriate measures must be found. It is also important that other measures of performance do not encourage non-quality eg the material purchase price variance may encourage the purchase of cheaper, but poorer quality, materials with the result that the rest of the company may incur costs of non-quality as a result.

Non-monetary measures can also be used for other factors. For example, the level of stock and stock turnover will provide an indication of the ability to achieve JIT targets. Set-up times can be compared with those expected. Reduction in non value-added activities will provide an indication of whether certain planned cost reductions have been achieved. Labour turnover can be used as a measure of aspects of labour welfare.

One reason for the use of non-monetary measures for some of the factors mentioned above is that very often monetary measurement will be more difficult or even impossible. In any case, non-monetary measures often have more direct relevance to employees, and thus have greater impact. They may also be easier to interpret by management, available more quickly, and enable better comparisons to be made of relative operational efficiency, for example the level of losses between processes. Another reason for encouraging non-monetary measures, although the monetary consequences may need to be evaluated also, is because they are unaffected over time by variations in the relative prices of input factors caused especially by inflation. Thus it is useful to measure factory productivity in terms of output per direct labour hour, or direct labour hours per unit. The change in manufacturing operations resulting from investment in advanced manufacturing technology is, however, likely to make such measures less useful. But other measures need to be found, one of which may be a measure of total factor productivity.

The use of non-monetary measures, as well as monetary measures, in the measurement of divisional performance is considered in Chapter 10.

SUMMARY

This chapter has considered the factors affecting the processing of input costs, incurred in acquiring resources used within a business, in the cost accounts in order to provide the necessary basis for planning and controlling such costs, and for establishing the cost, and where relevant profitability, of the business' output. The establishment of output costs, and profit, is the subject of the next chapter.

Accounting for indirect product costs has been given particular attention because, by their nature, such costs cannot be easily related to the cost unit. The various steps in the process, and the factors affecting each step, have been explained. Finally, the chapter has considered the implications for cost accounting, as yet not fully developed, of changes in the factory environment resulting from the application of the concepts of Just in Time and Total Quality, and from investment in computerised manufacturing technology.

EXERCISES

Exercise 6.1

The Spot-On Company manufacture 'dotties'. The bin card for this product states that the maximum stock holding for it is 15,000 and the minimum 5,000.

Four materials are used in the manufacture of dotties and information currently available about these materials is as follows:

Material	Number of kilos required to produce one dottie	Information on bin card (in kilos)		
		on hand	maximum	minimum
Doh	2	3,000	7,000	2,000
Ray	3	3,000	12,000	3,000
Mee	1	5,000	7,000	2,000
Fah	5	20,000	20,000	5,000

Information from various departments within the Spot-On Company about dotties is:

Raw Material Store

2,000 kilos of Doh and 1,000 kilos of Fah in the store have been reserved for work already in progress.

Finished Goods Store

The stock of dotties is 5,000 but 1,000 are on order and still have to be withdrawn from the store and sent to the warehouse for despatch.

Production Control

2,000 dotties are in the process of manufacture and all the materials necessary to produce these have been either reserved or issued.

Sales Department

Orders have just been received for 10,000 dotties which are to be delivered as quickly as possible, but so far the orders concerned have been processed no further than the sales department.

Required:

(a) Prepare statements for management which clearly show workings for:

- **(i)** the size of the production order to be placed, to bring stocks to a maximum,
- **(ii)** details of the quantities of materials which need to be issued with the production order,
- **(iii)** information of the purchase order which will have to be placed to bring the stock of raw materials up to the maximum holdings required for each of them.

(b) In the table showing information on raw materials it can be seen that although twice as much Doh is required in the production of dotties than Mee, the maximum and minimum stock holdings shown on the bin card for these materials is the same. Briefly state the factors that the firm would have taken into consideration when arriving at the maximum and minimum levels of stock holdings shown, and with reference to Doh and Mee explain how these factors may have caused the maximum and minimum stock levels to be the same.

(*ACCA, Management Accounting, December* 1975)

Answers on page 512

Exercise 6.2

On receiving his departmental performance report for a month, the supervisor of production department A in an engineering company noted that, although most of his actual expenditures were fairly close to budget, there were three items on which his variances were very adverse:

1 machinery maintenance;
2 power;
3 materials handling.

He discussed with the cost accountant how these variances had arisen and was told as stated below:

1 The maintenance department kept records of the time worked on all maintenance jobs. The total monthly cost of the maintenance department was then apportioned to each department on the basis of the time spent on work done by them in the month.
2 The company generates its own electrical power and the total costs of doing so are calculated and apportioned to each department on the basis of total direct wages. During the month the direct wages of department A were higher than the average for the year, whilst those for the other departments were lower than average. As a result a large proportion of total power costs was charged to department A.
3 An analysis of the time sheets of the materials handling department revealed that a large proportion of the high costs for the month charged to department A arose from one particular job. Due to an error on the part of the design department, the whole of the job had had to be re-worked by department A during the month and sent back to the assembly department one piece at a time, thus incurring additional materials handling.

Required:
(a) Discuss the validity of the arguments which support the view that the costs of service departments in a firm should be charged eventually to the production departments which use the services.
(b) Discuss in respect of each of the three expenses in the situation described above:
  (i) to what extent you consider the treatment in the departmental performance report was ineffective from a budgeting control point of view.
  (ii) what other treatment might have been given to improve the effectiveness of the report.

Answers on page 514

Exercise 6.3

The Isis Engineering Company operates a job order costing system which includes the use of predetermined overhead absorption rates. The company has two service cost centres and two production cost centres. The production cost centre overheads are charged to jobs via direct labour hour rates which are currently £3.10 per hour in production cost centre A and £11.00 per hour in production cost centre B. The calculations involved in determining these rates have excluded any consideration of the services that are provided by each service cost centre to the other.

The bases used to charge general factory overhead and service cost centre expenses to the production cost centres are as follows:

1 general factory overhead is apportioned on the basis of the floor area used by each of the production and service cost centres,
2 the expenses of service cost centre 1 are charged out on the basis of the number of personnel in each production cost centre,

3 the expenses of service cost centre 2 are charged out on the basis of the usage of its services by each production cost centre.

The company's overhead absorption rates are revised annually prior to the beginning of each year, using an analysis of the outcome of the current year and the draft plans and forecasts for the forthcoming year. The revised rates for next year are to be based on the following data:

	General Factory Overhead	*Service Cost Centres* 1	2	*Production Cost Centres* *A*	*B*
Budgeted Overhead for next year (before any reallocation)	£210,000	£93,800	£38,600	£182,800	£124,800
% of factory floor area	—	5	10	15	70
% of factory personnel	—	10	18	63	9
Estimated usage of services of service cost centre 2 in forthcoming year	—	1,000 hrs	—	4,000 hrs	25,000 hrs
Budgeted direct labour hours for next year (to be used to calculate next year's absorption rates)	—	—	—	120,000 hrs	20,000 hrs
Budgeted direct labour hours for current year (these figures were used in the calculation of this year's absorption rates)	—	—	—	100,000 hrs	30,000 hrs

Required:

(a) Ignoring the question of reciprocal charges between the service cost centres, you are required to calculate the revised overhead absorption rates for the two production cost centres. Use the company's established procedures.

(b) Comment on the extent of the differences between the current overhead absorption rates and those you have calculated in your answer to (a). Set out the likely reasons for these differences.

(c) Each service cost centre provides services to the other. Recalculate next year's overhead absorption rates recognising the existence of such reciprocal services and assuming that they can be measured on the same bases as those used to allocate costs to the production cost centres.

(d) Assume that:

(i) General factory overhead is a fixed cost.

(ii) Service cost centre 1 is concerned with inspection and quality control with its budgeted expenses (before any reallocations) being 10% fixed and 90% variable.

(iii) Service cost centre 2 is the company's plant maintenance section with its budgeted expenses (before any reallocations) being 90% fixed and 10% variable.

(iv) Production cost centre A is labour intensive with its budgeted overhead (before any reallocation) being 90% fixed and 10% variable.

(v) Production cost centre B is highly mechanised with its budgeted overhead (before any reallocations) being 20% fixed and 80% variable.

In the light of these assumptions, comment on the cost apportionment and absorption calculations made in parts (a) and (c) and suggest any improvements that you would consider appropriate.

(*ACCA*, *Management Accounting*, *June 1983*)

Answers on page 515

Exercise 6.4

A factory has three production departments and three service departments. The budgeted overhead costs for the year are:

	Consumable supplies £	Indirect labour £	Depreciation of machiney £
Production departments			
Machine shop: A	31,500	24,200	60,000
B	45,500	22,750	41,000
Assembly	10,500	49,550	16,000
Service departments			
Stores	7,000	20,500	8,000
Engineering service	21,000	26,700	20,000
General service	8,000	37,600	8,000

In addition to the above, general factory overheads comprise:

	£
Insurance of machinery	20,000
Insurance of building	9,000
Power	18,000
Heat & light	15,000
Rent & rates	35,250

The following data are also available:

	Book value of machinery £	Area sq ft	Effective horse-power hours %	Production capacity Direct labour hours	Production capacity Machine hours
Machine shop: A	300,000	5,000	50	200,000	40,000
B	225,000	6,000	30	150,000	50,000
Assembly	60,000	8,000	5	300,000	5,000
Stores	30,000	2,000	—		
Engineering service	90,000	2,500	15		
General service	30,000	1,500	—		

The value of issues of direct materials from stores to production departments are in the same proportion as shown above for consumable supplies. Service department costs are apportioned to prodution departments using the elimination method.

Required:

(a) Prepare an overhead analysis sheet showing the bases of any apportionments of overhead.
(b) Calculate suitable overhead absorption rates for the production departments.
(c) Calculate the overhead to be absorbed by a product which has the following times spent in different departments per hundred units produced:

	Direct labour hours	Machine hours
Machine shop: A	9	2
B	8	3
Assembly	12	0.5

(d) Explain how a budgeted idle capacity cost could arise and comment on its relevance to management.

(e) The factory manager has suggested that 'as the actual overheads incurred and units produced are usually different from budget and, as a consequence, profits at each month-end are distorted by over/under absorbed overheads, it would be more accurate to calculate the actual overhead cost per unit each month-end by dividing the total number of all units actually produced during the month into the actual overheads incurred'.

Critically examine the factory manager's suggestion.

(*Answers in lecturer's manual*)

Exercise 6.5

(a) Itemise FOUR reasons why it might be appropriate to express some management accounting information in non-monetary terms and give a specific example to illustrate each.

(b) Explain how inaccuracy may exist in each of the following management accounting information situations and how such inaccuracy may be minimised:

(i) Analysis of costs into fixed and variable components.

(ii) Calculation of fixed overhead absorption rate.

(iii) Calculation of material cost per product unit for inclusion in a product price quotation.

(*ACCA Management Accounting, December 1988*)

(*Answers in lecturer's manual*)

Relating Values to Outputs

INTRODUCTION

The processing of input costs was considered in the previous chapter. Cost accumulation was brought to the point where costs could be related to final products or services provided to the organisation's customers. This chapter considers the final stage of cost accumulation. This stage is concerned with the valuation of departmental output and the implications of including a profit element in order to encourage departmental managers to pursue profit motives. The main content of the chapter reviews output valuation bases and methods, considers the principles involved in the technical aspects of output valuation and provides some short illustrations. Students are expected to consider costing methods and principles in relation to the impacts they can have on managers and the organisation as a whole. The material presented builds on knowledge which students have thoroughly explored at earlier levels of study and therefore contains a high degree of revision.

7.1 VALUATION BASES

Cost based approaches include historic cost, replacement cost and standard cost, all of which can relate to either marginal or absorption principles. In addition, opportunity costs may be included in the evaluation of output through the consideration of costs and benefits of other alternatives. Cost valuation of output in this chapter will assume that historic costs are applied. Later in the book, section 4 will consider standard costs. Consideration of the concept and use of opportunity costs and replacement costs will also be delayed, until section 3.

Historic cost is inherently an input based valuation. The terms materials, labour and overheads all refer to resources consumed. These inputs are processed in order to produce outputs such as finished goods or services. The total of inputs is related to outputs with the aim of "balancing" total inputs, perhaps as detailed in financial accounts, with total output values. A manufacturing company buys raw materials, labour and machinery to produce finished items for sale to customers. In this case, costs of materials, labour and overheads are divided between finished products so that the cost of each different product can be ascertained. In the case of a hospital, costs of doctors, nurses, buildings, equipment and consumables can be divided between patients according to the nature of illnesses. Costing methods take the accumulation of costs from the point reached in the previous chapter through to the determination of product, service or departmental output cost.

Market–based valuations of output may be applied to create a profit or loss situation. Input values do not balance in relation to output values. Where the total of output values exceeds input values, a profit is said to have arisen. Market values may be applied to the goods and services sold to customers or to individual departments within the organisation. In the case of sales to customers, the market value is given by the sales price. In the case of transfers between departments, a transfer price is established. A rationale for introducing transfer prices is to motivate managers to create profits through their managerial activities. In some cases, valuation is carried out on a net residual value basis, representing the difference between the final sales value and the cost of processing to the point of sale. Residual value is important to the accounting treatment of by-products.

7.2 COSTING METHODS

Costing methods relate to the type of business in which a particular organisation engages.

Organisations such as manufacturers of biscuits, textiles or automobiles may have production lines devoted to a product range which is reasonably static, at least in the short term. An individual product item will not differ significantly from other items. A wheatmeal biscuit produced by a particular manufacturer does not significantly differ from other wheatmeal biscuits. Continuous operation or process costing systems are appropriate to such organisations.

Organisations such as manufacturers of roads, ships or furniture may produce finished goods to order. There would be little evidence to assume that one road is the same as another road, in cost terms. Specific order or job costing would be appropriate to such organisations. At a departmental level, the specific order method of costing can be applied in circumstances such as research and development, where project codes can be used to accumulate costs. Where specific orders relate to more than one financial year and an element of profit is involved, problems regarding the amount of profit to take into each year arise. It is customary to use the term contract costing to describe the particular problems which occur.

Essentially, for continuous operation costing, departmental or process costs for a period are divided between output units. This gives rise to a cost per unit for the period which can be compared with budgeted cost per unit or with previous periods results, for instance, to monitor the extent to which costs are under control. For specific order costing, costs are classified according to a specific order reference over the period during which the order is being processed. Once the order has been completed, costs are added up to give the total product cost. This general approach is applicable to both job and contract costing. The general principle underpinning costing methods is that:

1 where products are homogeneous, or similar to each other, costs can be divided by product units to provide a product cost;

2 where products are heterogeneous, or different to each other, costs must be coded to individual products and summed to provide a product cost.

Not all organisations neatly fit the continuous operation or specific order models. The nature of production programming may necessitate that a single production line or process should accommodate a large number of different products. A single production run processes a production batch. Batches of homogeneous products are produced. Each batch differs from the next batch processed but the production of a single product will be made up of a number of batches produced during a particular period. It is possible to treat each batch as a separate, specific order. The batch is costed according to specific order methods and the total cost of a batch is divided by the number of units produced to give a cost per unit. Batch costing combines both specific order and continuous operation methods, therefore. However, in practice, standard process costing appears to offer a suitable alternative in some batch costing situations. Standard process costing is illustrated in section 4 of the book.

Services may be costed according either to specific order or continuous operation methods, depending on the situation. Professional services may be costed by the hour in businesses where an hourly charge is made to clients. Firms of accountants may charge different rates for work done, depending on the level of expertise and experience required. An incomplete records exercise for a particular client may be treated as a specific order. Each accountant working on the exercise would code their time to a client or job reference. Once the exercise is complete, hours can be multiplied by hourly values and summed to give total costs and charges. Alternatively, in the leisure industry, a charge is commonly made on entry to a leisure park in the United Kingdom. Assessing the reasonableness of the charge can be checked either through a profit and loss statement or by taking the total cost for the park for each period and dividing by the number of customers. Where charges are made for different areas of the leisure park, the cost of each area could be divided by the number of customers.

Fundamentally, historic costs can only either be divided by the number of production units for a period or classified according to product through a coding process. Costing method is concerned with whether costs should be divided equally between output units or added up to give different costs for individual products. The nature of the costing method applicable to particular circumstances is intimately connected with the nature of the cost unit.

7.3 COST UNITS

In specific order costing, the concept of cost unit is of little importance. Each separate order represents a single cost unit described in terms of the nature of the order. A cost unit for the shipbuilding unit would be an individual ship. Direct costs are accumulated in relation to each cost unit.

In simple continuous operation costing situations, the cost unit is a single unit of the product being processed. Units may be measured in physical unit terms: kilograms, litres, or metres, for instance. For a milk bottling plant, the total cost of the plant can be divided by the number of litres bottled to give a cost per litre. In some service situations, the association of cost with cost unit can be similarly straightforward. The cost of a student in higher education can be determined by designating a student as a cost unit and dividing the total number of students in higher education into the total cost of higher education. If the cost of individual departments in individual institutions is required, costs would first be accumulated by department and then divided by the number of students within the department.

Some service industries find it difficult to specify a simple cost unit because of cost behaviour factors. In road haulage, for instance, costs may depend upon both the distance travelled and the weight of the load. A heavier load may require a larger and more expensive vehicle to transport it to its destination. The tonne-mile, a composite cost unit, is used in this situation. Weight is multiplied by distance to provide a total quantity of units of work for a particular period and this is divided into the total cost. Similarly, passenger-mile is used in passenger transport industries.

7.4 VALUATION PRINCIPLES

The two main principles which are followed at the technical level of associating values with outputs are that losses should become associated with good units of production and that normal levels of cost should be ascertained. This chapter will not debate or justify these principles, but one aim of this book is to illustrate by example how the principles need to be modified to respond to current management assumptions such as zero defects in quality management. For now, perhaps the easiest way of understanding these principles is given by the need to determine cost based selling prices. Theory and practice suggest the need to pass on unavoidable costs to customers in order to maintain profitability but to avoid passing on costs caused by abnormal circumstances, such as seasonal variations in overhead absorption rates, since this can adversely affect customer relationships. A customer may accept a selling price which reflects an acceptable level of materials wastage or machine down-time, but is likely to be confused where selling prices in June are higher than selling prices in February. Additionally, it may be considered unfair to charge customers with costs arising from an unacceptable level of wastage or machine down-time and, in competitive situations, passing costs of inefficiency can lead to lost custom. From a financial accounting perspective, SSAP 9 expects stocks to be valued in accordance with the normality principle. Abnormal costs, included in closing stock valuations, have the effect of increasing profits and should not therefore be reflected in product costs for reasons of prudency.

7.5 SHORT ILLUSTRATIVE EXAMPLES

Example 7.1 Specific order costing

Aye PLC is in the road construction industry. It allocates a contract number upon receipt of an order and codes all materials and labour records by contract number. Summarised records for materials for the most recent week are as follows:

Material content of work-in-progress, brought forward:

Contract 1106	£29,007
1107	£289,790
1108	£115,089
1110	£11,909

Material requisitions for the period:

Requisition number	Contract number	Amount £
197076	1108	13,476
197077	1111	4,819
197078	1107	29,110
197079	1108	30,121

During the week, contract number 1107 was completed and an invoice for £400,000 was raised for the material content of the order.

In order to calculate output values, costs are allocated to contracts through materials and labour recording systems, and an allowance for overhead absorption is made. Allocation is achieved through coding. Overhead absorption progresses according to the principles described in the previous chapter. Once coding and absorption mechanisms have been established, the process of output valuation is one of summation.

For example, the material content of work in progress valuation of contract number 1108 is derived by adding £115,089, £13,476 and £30,121. Completed output for the week has a sales value of £400,000 and a cost of £318,900 (289,790 + 29,110).

Example 7.2 Specific order costing and financial accounts

Geeco PLC carries out machine repairs for a variety of customers. A summary of work carried out in June 19 × 9, as reported in the cost accounts, is provided below, together with financial accounting figures for the same period.

	Cost brought forward	*Materials costs*	*Conversion costs*
	£	£	£
Job number 38	3,000	3,480	5,770
52	—	7,350	1,290
90	—	170	8,940

Conversion costs include labour and overhead, which is recovered at the rate of 100% of direct labour cost. Jobs 38 and 90 were completed during the period.

Manufacturing, trading and profit and loss account

		£
Opening stock of materials		1,000
Purchases		13,000
		14,000
less closing stock of materials		2,000
		12,000
Direct labour		8,000
Production overheads		10,000
		30,000
add opening stock of w.i.p	3,000	
less closing stock of w.i.p	8,640	(5,640)
Cost of goods manufactured		24,360

Self-assessment question 7.1

Attempt to check the differences between the cost accounting record of jobs and the financial accounting profit statement before reading the answer which follows.

The cost accounts value the output of the period as the accumulation of costs on jobs which have been completed. Incomplete jobs represent work in progress, as shown in the financial accounts. The cost accounting valuation of output is thus the total costs of jobs 38 and 90, £21,360. Financial accounts show a cost of goods manufactured figure of £24,360 which can be reconciled to the cost valuation of output, for control purposes, as follows:

Output per financial accounts:		£24,360
less: raw material stock discrepancy	£1,000	
under absorption of overhead	£2,000	£ 3,000
Cost valuation of output		£21,360

Raw material discrepancy:
The financial accounts show a material cost of £12,000 where only £11,000 has been charged to jobs

through the cost accounting system.
Under absorption of overhead:

Overheads incurred		£10,000
Overheads absorbed	(total conversion costs are £16,000 of which labour cost must be £8,000)	£ 8,000
		£ 2,000

Investigation and interpretation of these reconciliation differences provides a means by which control of the organisation can be exercised. Labour costs are not investigated since all costs have been charged to jobs and therefore passed to customers. If labour were to be inefficient, this would reflect in lost business following from customers finding that competitors charged lower prices for repairs. Some consideration of output levels, output market values and output cost values would be necessary for a complete picture of efficiency and effectiveness in this situation, therefore.

Example 7.3 Profit in continuous operation costing

Aitch PLC produces a finished item by passing raw materials through two processes. The output from process A can be sold for £5 per kilogram but Aitch prefers process A to pass all of its production through to process B. Process B sells its production for £8 per kilogram. At the beginning of last month there were no stocks in work in progress. Losses do not occur in either process A or B. A batch of 5,000 kg. was found to be at the beginning of process B at the end of the financial period. No finished goods were in stock at either the beginning or the end of the period. Costs and activity figures for last month are as follows:

Raw materials consumed	30,000 kg.
Production from process A	30,000 kg.
Production from process B	25,000 kg.
Process A costs	£120,000
Process B costs	£ 50,000
Process A accounts would show:	
(Debits)	
Costs	£120,000
Profit	£ 30,000
(Credits)	
Value of output (30,000 kg @ £5)	£150,000
Process B accounts would show:	
(Debits)	
Input from process A	£150,000
Costs	£ 50,000
Profit	£ 25,000
(Credits)	
Value of output (25,000 kg @ £8)	£200,000
Value of stock (5,000 kg @ £5)	£ 25,000

The profit per unit in process A is £5 less the cost per unit of £4 (£120,000/30,000). The £1 per unit profit is earned on each unit produced by A, giving a total profit of £30,000 and motivating the process A to produce as much as possible to minimise fixed cost per unit and to maximise profit from selling a higher volume to process B.

Process B incurs costs from A of £5 and incurs costs of £2(£50,000/25,000). When this total cost of £7 is deducted from the selling price of £8, a profit of £1 per unit is shown, which when multiplied by the output of 25,000 gives a total profit of £25,000.

Stocks are valued at £5 because this was the cost to process B. This contains a profit element of £1 per kilogram, so that the profit for the company as a whole can be calculated:

Profit in process A	£30,000
Profit in process B	£25,000
	£55,000
less: profit in stock	£ 5,000
Company profit	£50,000

Self-assessment question 7.2

Check the calculation of profit in stock, given above, and produce a manufacturing and trading account to show that the profit for the company as a whole is £50,000.

Answer in lecturer's manual

Example 7.4 Continuous operation costing and inventories

Jay PLC produces two products by passing a single raw material through three processes. Information for June 19 × 9 is provided below:

Process A:	Materials and conversion costs:	£ 85,000
	Output, units	500,000
Process B:	Conversion costs:	£ 15,000
	Output, units	450,000
	Closing stock, units	50,000
Process C:	Opening stock, 30,000 units, 60% complete	£ 6,907
	Conversion costs:	£22,750
	Output, Product X, units	230,000
	Product Y, units	230,000
	Closing stock, 20,000 units, 65% complete	

The opening stock in process C comprises costs transferred from previous processes of £6,480 and process C conversion costs of £427. Product X is sold at £0.40 per unit and product Y is sold at £0.20 per unit.

This example illustrates three problems of divisibility which can arise for processing situations:

1 In process A, the total value of output is £85,000 since all input leaves the process during the period. The cost per unit is given by dividing the output units into the output value, giving £0.17. This is an average; individual products may have cost more or less than £0.17. It is important that Jay's individual product is homogeneous, or similar, in every respect; if a customer requests an expensive, special variation on the basic product and that variation is incorporated into the averaging, information will not entirely reflect processing realities.

2 Where stocks arise, costs will need to be taken into stock valuations as well as output values. In process B, costs amount to £100,000 (£85,000 transferred from process 1 and £15,000 incurred in the process). This should be divided between output and closing stock. Assuming that the closing stock is complete and awaiting transfer to process 3, the £100,000 should be split between 50,000 units, giving £0.20 per unit and valuations of £90,000 for output and £10,000 for closing stocks.

Process C illustrates the situation where both opening and closing stocks are incomplete for conversion costs. Two assumptions are possible and each assumption leads to a different calculation for output value.

Under the first in first out assumption, all opening stock values are included in the value of output. Costs incurred during the period are spread between output values and closing stock. This necessitates a calculation of cost per unit for the period, taking the costs for the period (£90,000 transferred from process B and £22,750 conversion costs) and the amount of work carried out during the period, calculated as an equivalent number of completed units. For conversion costs, process 3 processes 455,000 equivalent units:

	Equivalent units
Production	460,000
less: work carried out on opening stock in previous period (60% of 30,000 units)	18,000
	442,000

add: work carried out on	
closing stock (65% of 20,000)	13,000
	455,000

The resulting cost per unit is £0.25 in total. This is used to value closing stocks, units started and completed during the period and the cost of completing work on opening stocks.

The second assumption, usually termed the weighted average approach, spreads costs of both opening stock and the period over output and closing stocks, taking into account the stage of completion of closing stocks. Section 4 provides further consideration of the treatment of equivalent units.

3 On occasions, products are interdependent in that they arise from a common use of resources. The production of one product depends upon production of the other product; neither can be made in isolation from each other. An example is given in transport, where several different trains or types of train make use of the same line of track. To arrive at an absorption cost for a particular train or service, a basis for dividing the cost of the track must be devised. Jay produces two products from the same process and thus has this problem of common costs, arising from the output of joint products from process C. Output values of £0.25 per unit for the 460,000 units of output must be split between products X and Y in order to place a value on those products held in finished goods stock. Such a split is generally acknowledged to be arbitrary and so dangers arise from using cost per unit of X or Y in planning, control or decision situations.

Self-assessment question 7.3

Process costing and the joint product problem are covered in detail at previous examination stages. Using revision of this basic material and the principle outlined above, produce accounts for Jay, illustrating the FIFO and Weighted average approaches to process costing. Allocate joint costs to products on the basis of number of units (physical measure basis) and the sales value of output.

Answer in lecturer's manual

Example 7.5 Normality and associating costs of losses

The calculations illustrated in this section are normally associated with continuous operation costing. It could be argued, however, that the underlying principle is also applicable to specific order costing. Some refinement of the usual approach would be necessary to incorporate a normal rather than an actual level of losses into specific order costs.

Kay PLC expects to lose 10% of its production due to inevitable scrap, saleable at values between nil and £0.20 per kilogram, depending on market conditions. During March, 19X9, it processed 100,000 kilograms at a cost of £100,000 and produced 88,000 kilograms of first quality output. Scrap was placed into stock pending later sale at the expected normal selling price of £0.15.

At one extreme, 88,000 kilograms could be considered to have cost £100,000, a cost per unit of £1.136 which could be recovered in selling prices. This extreme makes no allowance for a possible saleable value and makes no allowance for the fact that Kay was inefficient during May, wasting 2,000 kilograms more than normal (12,000 kilograms were wasted but an input of 100,000 kilograms would normally see waste of only 10,000 kilograms, 10% of input).

Applying prudence, the view could be taken that the scrap may be sold at £nil and the cost of abnormal scrap should be excluded from the valuation of output. This would give a cost per unit of £100,000 / 90,000, £1.1111, for use in selling price decisions and stock valuations. This would provide a value of £2,222.22 (2,000 units at cost) which would be reported to management as the cost of abnormal scrap, a measurement of efficiency in the processing of materials.

Applying the full principle of normality, the value of normal scrap would be deducted from the cost of the process before the calculation of output value. This would give a process cost of £98,500 for a normal production of 90,000 units, a cost of £1.094. Abnormal scrap would be shown as costing £2,188.89. A separate account, or accounts, would be maintained to show the values collected from the sale of scrap in comparison with the amounts taken into the process account.

Dopuch, Birnberg and Demski show a variation on the processing of normal costs which permits the reporting of the cost of normal losses. Following the normality principle, the following calculations would be made:

Cost per unit, based on input units, is determined:

Costs	£100,000
Units	100,000
Cost per unit	£1.00

The cost per unit is used to measure the cost of normal losses, output, abnormal losses and stocks:

Cost of normal losses:	£10,000 (10,000 units @ £1)
Output	£88,000
Abnormal losses	£2,000

The cost of normal losses is then spread between output, abnormal losses and any stocks, which are also valued initially at £1.
Additional cost per unit arising from normal loss:

£10,000/90,000 units
£0.111

Cost of output, abnormal waste and stocks:

£1.000 + £0.111 per unit

This provides the same outcome as in the previous approach, but it is claimed that this approach brings the cost of normal AND abnormal losses to management's attention. This should be seen as providing information to motivate improvements in quality.

A more extreme approach is to adopt the zero defects assumption, where no allowance is made for losses, even where some normal loss is anticipated. It has been claimed that such an approach motivates managers to reduce wastage, with effective results; wastage reduces significantly. The cost per unit would be £1, the output value would be £88,000, no value for wastage would be passed to customers and the cost of abnormal wastage would be reported as £12,000, with a possible reduction for the sales value of scrap. The production manager would be held responsible for £12,000 under this approach, as opposed to approximately £2,200 under the previous approaches. Stock values and hence profits would be reduced, providing a "bottom line" motivation to improve quality performance and hence profit.

It should be noted that a variety of approaches is possible in real world situations, each having different impacts on levels of motivation to improve performance within the organisation. Examination questions at this level of study demand flexibility on the part of the student in applying general principles. The emphasis is on the ability to respond to situations presented in examination questions rather than memorising procedures for set past examination question patterns. Examination questions specify exactly the requirements of the case studies presented. It is essential that the underlying principle be followed.

A proportion of the loss in value associated with wastage, scrap, or by products is added to the cost of main products in a manner which reflects the objectives of the costing system, be it to provide a value for output, a stock value or to motivate managers.

This will be further illustrated in relation to standard costing.

7.6 CUSTOMER COSTS AND PROFITABILITY

The emphasis of this book has so far been on the identification and analysis of products and departments. Such information should provide a basis for answering such questions as 'which products should be offered for sale', 'how should they be manufactured and accounted for' and 'what should the selling price of a particular product be?'. These are not the only questions which should be raised and answered by reference to cost and profit information. Other questions include: 'who should the business be selling to, and on what terms?', 'how should the business be selling to particular outlets?' and 'to which market segments should the business be selling?'. Here, the orientation is towards the customer rather than towards the product. Such an orientation has been relatively neglected in academic books on management accounting and requires an alternative approach to outputs than that provided by valuing products alone.

7.6.1 General information requirements

Information could be re-orientated towards outlets as opposed to products. Through the use of information technology developments, such as the use of computers by accountants, it is possible not only to relate costs to products, but also to customers, although there is little evidence of companies taking advantages of such opportunities. Management may be informally aware that some customers are relatively economic to service, whilst others provide practical difficulties such as small and fragmented ordering. Measuring costs on an outlet basis provides a means by which difficult customers can bear a fair share of the costs of the distribution, marketing and administrative costs, for example, in order to inform decisions of the kind listed above.

There may be advantages to be gained from integrating existing management accounting data, with its emphasis on products and production, into marketing information systems. These can incorporate output related information in addition to product specific information. Outlet analysis may include profitability by geographical area, by individual customer or by customer's location.

7.6.2 Identifying customers costs

Customer profitability analysis requires the ability to allocate specific customer costs to specific customers. A fundamental question which should be answered is 'what aspect of the relationship with the customer does this cost support and how does it vary with activity levels and customer characteristics?'. Small deliveries, cost of breaking bulk and serving the administrative and stock needs of small customers may all represent significant costs which are traceable to individual customers. Different areas of business may have different levels of customer cost. Specific aspects of these differences include the following:

1 the standards of customer service which it is desired to achieve;
2 the extent to which an order is routine and can be planned. One-off or urgent orders incur greater costs and may be associated with a small number of customers;
3 distribution cost savings may be achievable by arranging for supply outlets to be in close proximity to customers. Regional distribution centres may ensure that customers are served more efficiently and effectively;
4 channels of distribution: decisions on the operation of own transport fleets, or on the use of external distribution transport may be influenced by customer location and requirement patterns;
5 the method of obtaining orders, for instance, by means of direct selling or indirect selling. What role is to be played by the company's sales force in relation to specific types of customer?;
6 the size of order;
7 the number of orders;
8 storage and handling requirements;
9 whether special purchasing arrangements are required; do some customers insist upon particular product or packaging changes?;
10 settlement terms; do certain customers delay payment of invoices and thereby increase cash flow and interest cost problems? A debtors analysis may be produced with sufficient information to analyse financing costs direct to individual customers. An opportunity cost may be appropriate, where the output value shows the saving in interest charges related to the customer paying according to normal settlement terms, 30 days perhaps.
11 inventory; is certain stock held for specific customers? If so, what are the costs of holding those items in relation to customer profitability?

The implementation of customer profitability poses a range of challenges to the management accountant. Each element of customer cost must be considered in relation to appropriate cost driver(s), such as the number or size of orders. A complex apportionment arrangement may arise, necessitating the use of computing facilities to provide reliable and valid results. Where sufficient knowledge is gained about specific cost drivers, it may be appropriate to pass specific cost items to specific customers through appropriate pricing structures, subject to normal business practice of ensuring that advantageous custom is not lost to competitors. Judgements could be made on the viability of individual customers. Customers could be encouraged to enter into distribution arrangements of mutual advantage to the customer and to the business.

SUMMARY

Values may be placed upon outputs in terms of products, departments or customers. There are alternative ways of valuing outputs, each of which have an impact on motivation within the organisation or on relationships with customers through profitability or selling price decisions. These alternatives are based on a relatively small number of principles, but these principles interact to produce a surprising number of considerations, even in small illustrations. Costs may be accumulated within recording systems or divided between cost units, depending on the type of situation. Outputs may be valued on a cost basis or a market value basis, depending on whether it is desirable to show a profit result. Inputs are checked against outputs to ensure that a given situation has been fully accounted for. Technical accounting considerations give rise to values which are reported to management and which are used to manage enterprises.

EXERCISES

Exercise 7.1

Stover Chemicals operates four manufacturing processes. Process 1 yields three joint products (X, Y and Z) in fixed proportions. Although each of these products could be sold at the split-off point (and there exists a ready market for each in this state) they are normally processed further; X in process 2, Y in process 3 and Z in process 4. This additional processing enhances their saleable values as follows:

Selling prices per litre

	X	Y	Z
Product sold at split-off point	£0.80	£0.30	£1.30
Product sold after further processing	£1.20	£0.70	£1.75

The process accounts for the last operating period, when the plant was operating at full capacity, can be summarised as follows:

Process 1

	Litres	£		Litres	£
Opening stock	4000	1,200	Production:		
Material	99000	9,900	X to process 2	50000	25,000
Conversion		39,500	Y to process 3	30000	15,000
			Z to process 4	20000	10,000
			Closing stock	3000	600
	103000	£50,600		103000	£50,600

Process 2

	Litres	£		Litres	£
Opening stock	2000	1,267	Sales	50000	60,000
Process 1	50000	25,000	Closing stock	2000	1,267
Conversion		13,333			
Profit/loss		21,667			
	52000	£61,267		52000	£61,267

Process 3

	Litres	£		Litres	£
Opening stock	1000	650	Sales	30000	21,000
Process 1	30000	15,000	Closing stock	1000	650
Conversion		9,000			
			Profit/loss		3,000
	31000	£24,650		31000	£24,650

Process 4

	Litres	£		Litres	£
Opening stock	2000	1,700	Sales	20000	35,000
Process 1	20000	10,000	Closing stock	2000	1,700
Conversion		14,000			
Profit/loss		11,000			
	22000	£36,700		22000	£36,700

The costs incurred and the processing efficiency for the period to which the above accounts relate, can be assumed to be representative of current conditions. The joint costs in process 1 have been apportioned on the basis of the output (in litres) of X, Y and Z. All work in progress is complete as far as material content is concerned and (except for the closing work in progress in process 1) it is half processed. The closing work in progress in process 1 is one quarter processed.

You are required:

(a) To restate the process accounts using sales values at the split-off point as the basis for the joint cost allocation.

(b) To restate the process accounts using the sales values at the split-off point as transfer prices in transferring production from process 1 to the other processes.

(c) To discuss the utility of each of the three versions of the process accounts in terms of the relative profitability of products and the effect of the accounting treatment on the actions of managers.

(*ACCA, Management Accounting, June 1982, adapted*)

Answers in lecturer's manual

Exercise 7.2

A chemical manufacturer operates a process that yields two joint products, A and B, and a toxic waste product C. The standard formula used is as follows:

Inputs
8 kilos of chemical Y
10 kilos of chemical Z
Outputs
10 kilos of A (joint product)
5 kilos of B (joint product)
3 kilos of C (joint product)

The joint products are separated at the end of the process but the waste product is extracted from a batch of the mixture at an even rate throughout the processing. Products A and B require further processing before they are saleable. At present C is segregated in waste bins and collected periodically by an outside contractor who charges £2 per kilo for his services.

The following details relate to the last accounting period:

Main process	
Opening work in progress	1,650 kilos half-processed £2,950 (materials £2,100 conversion cost £250 waste disposal £600)
Opening stock of C	500 kilos
Closing work in progress	1,650 kilos half-processed
Input of Y	9,600 kilos costing £19,200
Input of Z	12,000 kilos costing £ 6,000
Processing labour	£ 1,440
Processing expense	£ 4,560
Payments for waste disposal	£ 6,500
Transfers to finished processes:	
A	12,000 kilos
B	6,000 kilos
Finishing process for A	
Opening work in progress	500 kilos half-processed £1,219 (materials £1,200 conversion £19)
Processing labour	£ 300
Processing expense	£ 600
Closing work in progress	500 kilos half-processed

Finished production	12,000 kilos
Finishing process for B	
Opening work in process	1,800 kilos half-processed £3,825 (materials £2,880 conversion £405)
Processing labour	£1,170
Processing expense	£1,755
Closing work in progress	800 kilos half-processed
Finished production	7,000 kilos

In the foregoing the work in progress stocks are fully complete as far as the material content is concerned. The established selling prices are £3 per kilo for product A and £2.40 per kilo for product B.

Required:

(a) You are required to write up the three Process Accounts for the accounting period, using the relative sales value method for the apportionment of the joint costs. The waste disposal expense is to be accrued and charged to the main process account whenever a fresh batch of raw material is fed into the process.

(*ACCA, Management Accounting, December 1983*)

Answer in lecturer's manual

Exercise 7.3

In process costing, spoilage can be normal or abnormal. Explain the alternative methods for accounting for such occurrences.

(*ACCA, Management Accounting June 1987*)

Answer in lecturer's manual

Exercise 7.4

A company manufactures two joint products in a single process. One is sold as a garden fertiliser, the other is a synthetic fuel which is sold to external customers but which can also be used to heat greenhouses in which the company grows fruit and vegetables all year round as a subsidiary market venture. Information relating to the previous 12–month period is as follows:

(i) 1,600,000 kilos of garden fertiliser were produced and then sold at £3·00 per kilo. Joint costs are apportioned between the garden fertiliser and the synthetic fuel on a physical units (weight) basis. The fertiliser has a contribution to sales ratio of 40 % after such apportionment. There are no direct costs of fertiliser sales or production.

(ii) The synthetic fuel represents 20 % of the total weight of output from the manufacturing process. A wholesaler bought 160,000 kilos at £1·40 per kilo under a long-term contract which stipulates that its availability to him will not be reduced below 100,000 kilos per annum. There is no other external market for the fuel. Fixed administrative, selling and distribution costs incurred specifically as a result of the fuel sales to the wholesaler totalled £40,000. That part of the fuel production which was sold to the wholesaler incurred additional variable costs for packaging of £1·20 per kilo.

(iii) The remaining synthetic fuel was used to heat the company greenhouses. The greenhouses produced 5 kilos of fruit and vegetables per kilo of fuel. The fruit and vegetables were sold at an average of £0·50 per kilo. Total direct costs of fruit and vegetable production were £520,000. Direct costs included a fixed labour cost of £100,000 which is avoidable if fruit and vegetable production ceases, the remainder being variable with the quantity produced.

A notional fuel charge of £1·40 per kilo of fuel is made to fruit and vegetable production. This notional charge is in addition to the direct costs detailed above.

(iv) Further company fixed costs were apportioned to the products as follows:

	£
Garden fertiliser	720,000
Synthetic fuel	18,000
Fruit and vegetables	90,000

The above data was used to produce a profit and loss analysis for the 12–month period for each of three areas of operation viz.

1 Garden fertiliser
2 Synthetic fuel (including external sales and transfers to the greenhouses at £1·40 per kilo).
3 Fruit and vegetables (incorporating the deduction of any notional charges).

Required:

(a) Prepare a summary statement showing the profit or loss reported in each of the three areas of operation detailed above.

(b) Calculate the percentage reduction in the fixed costs of £40,000 which would have been required before the synthetic fuel sales for the previous 12–month period would have resulted in a net benefit to the company.

(c) Calculate the net benefit or loss which sales of fruit and vegetables caused the company in the previous 12–month period.

(*ACCA, Management Accounting, June 1988, adapted*)

Answers in lecturer's manual

Absorption Costing Versus Marginal Costing

INTRODUCTION

Previous chapters in the book have attempted to provide a view of the cost accounting process, not as an objective, purely mechanical, process, but one where issues affecting the sort of information required and how it is provided need to be considered, in an effort to provide information that will be useful as a basis for management accounting and in a changing environment.

This chapter returns to consider the arguments influencing the choice of the overall form that cost accounting information should take ie the contrast between absorption costing and marginal costing. These two forms of cost accounting information were contrasted in Chapter 5, but discussion in subsequent chapters of other aspects of cost accounting, and illustrations provided, have in the main assumed the existence of an absorption costing system. This should not have been taken as an indication that absorption costing is to be preferred.

After reviewing the issues between absorption and marginal costing the chapter explores whether it may be possible to provide more flexible information in order to better meet the varied requirements for information for decision-making purposes.

8.1 INFORMATION PROVIDED

Marginal costing as a system appears to emphasise the behavioural aspects of costs, albeit rather simplistically, the recognition and understanding of which are important to the effective, efficient and economic operation of a business. Because absorption costing identifies all costs with units of output, and maintains a functional analysis of costs rather the behavioural analysis provided in marginal costing, it is commonly assumed that absorption costing ignores the behavioural characteristics of costs.

However, this is not really true. In their own way both marginal and absorption costing are interested in cost behaviour. This can be seen by considering their objectives as far as management information is concerned.

Objectives:

Absorption costing seeks to identify total cost per unit (ie the long-term variable cost per unit).

Marginal costing seeks to identify the short-term variable cost per unit.

Thus, there is no such thing as a fixed cost or a variable cost per se. Costs are only fixed or variable given assumptions about the conditions under which the analysis is being made. Both absorption and marginal costing make certain assumptions about those conditions.

In the case of absorption costing, in addition to assuming a long-term situation, it must be recognised that it is based on a specific situation ie, a particular level of activity. Unit costs established in a routine cost accounting system depend upon the level of activity assumed due to the inclusion of short-term fixed costs. Unit costs thus change as activity changes. The accuracy of unit costs established under absorption costing is also particularly dependent upon the accuracy of overhead apportionment.

In addition to assuming a short-term situation, marginal costing assumes that capacity is fixed over the time period concerned, and thus certain costs are fixed as a result, that changes in activity will be within a reasonable range, that efficiency will remain constant, and that there will be no economies of scale. It depends on the correct identification of cost behaviour patterns and, to a much lesser extent than absorption costing, on the accuracy of overhead apportionment.

8.2 ISSUES

The points at issue between absorption and marginal costing are sixfold:

1. Overhead apportionment and absorption.
2. Stock valuation.
3. Income determination.
4. Presentation of management information.
5. The ability to split total cost into fixed and variable categories.
6. Whether contribution analysis on its own is sufficient.

Each of these points is considered below.

8.2.1 Overhead apportionment and absorption

An advantage that can be claimed for marginal costing is that it eliminates the need to apportion and absorb fixed overheads which is a considerable task. Also, when predetermined overhead rates are used, there is the added complication of under- or over-recovery of overhead costs.

8.2.2 Stock valuation

The contrasting treatment of fixed production overhead costs is reflected in the valuation of inventory. The conventional criterion for establishing which costs of a manufacturing firm are to be attached to inventory is whether or not the cost is connected with the manufacturing process. Under absorption costing therefore a share of the fixed production costs incurred in a period will be carried forward in the value of work-in-progress or finished goods on hand at the end of the period. This is clearly recommended by SSAP9 which states that 'the costs of stocks and work-in-progress should comprise the expenditure which has been incurred in the normal course of business in bringing the product or service to its present location and condition. Such costs will include all related production overheads, even though they may accrue on a time basis'

In contrast, in marginal costing the fixed production overheads are treated as period costs ie they are charged against the profit of the period during which they are incurred. Exponents of absorption costing, and of the principle established in SSAP9, would claim that stock is undervalued in marginal costing.

The above, however, should be seen as a financial accounting issue, which has nothing to do with the utility of information for management. The requirements of financial accounting should not be allowed to dictate the form of the information provided in the cost and management accounts. The requirements of financial accounting can be met by adjustment to the cost accounts if a marginal costing system is employed.

8.2.3 Income determination

This is directly connected to the previous issue concerning stock valuation. Any change in stock valuation will affect profit. The issue here is the relationship between sales volume and profit. There is a closer relationship in marginal costing than absorption costing. This is because, in absorption costing, the level of production, as well as the level of sales, can influence profit. The profits of a period are affected by changes in the absorption of fixed overhead resulting from the building-up or reducing of stocks.

In periods where production exceeds sales, the profit reported by absorption costing is greater than that reported by marginal costing. This is because of the stock build-up and thus the increased fixed overhead in stock. The reverse is true where sales exceed production. In periods where sales and production are equal, the two methods would produce the same profit. Finally, in periods where sales volume is constant but production fluctuates, marginal costing gives identical profits because it is unaffected by stock changes.

Example 8.1

A company has drawn up plans for the total number of units to be produced and sold, covering the next three periods, as follows:

	Period 1	Period 2	Period 3
Sales ('000 units)	100	60	140
Production ('000 units)	100	160	40

Unit selling price and variable production costs are expected to be:

	£/unit
Selling price	6.00
Variable production costs	5.00

Fixed production overheads and total selling and administrative costs (assumed to be fixed) are expected to be £80,000 and £20,000 respectively per period. The fixed production overhead absorption rate per unit is based on practical production capacity of 200,000 units per period. The rate is thus £0.40 per unit (ie, £80,000 ÷ 200,000 units).

A profit and loss account prepared on an absorption costing basis for each of the three periods would be as follows:

	Period 1	Period 2	Period 3
	£000	*£000*	*£000*
Sales	600	360	840
less:			
Variable production cost of sales	(500)	(300)	(700)
Fixed production overhead absorbed on sales	(40)	(24)	(56)
	(540)	(324)	(756)
Gross profit	60	36	84
less:			
Selling and administration overhead	(20)	(20)	(20)
Net profit before adjustment	40	16	64
Under–absorbed production overhead	(40)	(16)	(64)
Net profit	—	—	—

The profit and loss accounts have been prepared on the basis that no under-absorbed production overhead balances will be carried forward from one period to another. Under-absorption results from planned production being less than practical capacity, ie

Period 1 100,000 units × £0.40/unit = £40,000
Period 2 40,000 units × £0.40/unit = £16,000
Period 3 160,000 units × £0.40/unit = £64,000

It would seem, from the profit and loss accounts, that the firm will just break-even in each accounting period, despite the widely differing sales and the fact that costs and prices remain unchanged. This does not make sense but nevertheless is a financial accounting fact (based on the assumptions reasonably made in this situation) which results from the important influence that production, as well as sales, has on profit under absorption costing.

The sales break-even point, determined using marginal costing, is 100,000 units calculated as:

$$\frac{£100,000 \text{ (fixed costs)}}{£1.00 \text{ (contribution per unit)}}$$

This occurs in Period 1, where marginal costing results are consistent with those shown by absorption costing. This is because production and sales are planned to be equal in Period 1.

Over the three periods marginal costing would produce the following results:

	Period 1	**Period 2**	**Period 3**
	£000	*£000*	*£000*
Sales	600	360	840
less:			
Variable production cost of sales	(500)	(300)	(700)
Contribution	100	60	140
Less:			
Fixed production overhead	(80)	(80)	(80)
Fixed selling and administration overhead	(20)	(20)	(20)
	(100)	(100)	(100)
Net profit/loss	—	(40)	40

In Period 2 a loss occurs because sales are below break-even. In Period 3 a profit occurs because sales are above break-even. Sales are either 40,000 units above or below break-even resulting in contribution gain or loss of £40,000 (ie, 40,000 units × £1.00 per unit).

The results of the absorption and marginal costing approaches can be reconciled as follows:

	Period 1	**Period 2**	**Period 3**
	£000	*£000*	*£000*
Profit/(Loss) under absorption costing	–	–	–
± Change in fixed production overhead absorbed in stock	–	(40)	40
Profit/(Loss) under marginal costing	–	(40)	40

In Period 2 production exceeds sales by 100,000 units and thus £40,000 absorbed overheads are included in the increased stock. In Period 3 sales exceeds production and thus 100,000 units are taken from stock.

The above illustrates the effect on profit, using absorption costing, of including a share of fixed production overheads in stock when stock levels are changing. The particular production overhead absorption method used will have an important influence on profit/(loss). An alternative approach to fixed production overhead absorption could have been to base it on normal activity over the three periods. Normal activity (average over the three periods) is 100,000 units per annum which results in an absorption rate of £0.80 per unit, instead of £0.40 per unit when based on practical capacity. If this rate is used, and over/under absorbed overhead balances are written-off each period, the profit and loss account becomes:

	Period 1	**Period 2**	**Period 3**
	£000	*£000*	*£000*
Sales	600	360	840
less:			
Variable production cost of sales	(500)	(300)	(700)
Fixed production overhead absorbed on sales	(80)	(48)	(112)
	(580)	(348)	(812)
Gross profit	20	12	28

less:			
Selling and administration overhead	(20)	(20)	(20)
Net profit before adjustment	–	(8)	8
Over/(under) absorbed production overhead	–	48	(48)
Net profit/(loss)	–	40	(40)

Over/under absorption results from planned production being different to normal activity ie

Period 2 + 60,000 units × £0.80/unit = £48,000
Period 3 – 60,000 units × 0.80/unit = (£48,000)

This produces an even more ridiculous situation where a profit of £40,000 is made when sales are £360,000, and a £40,000 loss occurs when sales are £840,000.

The results may once again be reconciled via fixed overhead absorbed in stock:

	Period 1	**Period 2**	**Period 3**
	£000	*£000*	*£000*
Profit/(Loss) under absorption costing	–	40	(40)
± Change in fixed production overhead absorbed in stock	–	(80)	80
Profit/(Loss) under marginal costing	–	(40)	40

The above change in fixed production overhead included in stock is twice the amount calculated previously as the absorption rate is now £0.80 per unit (rather than £0.40).

Returning to the arguments between absorption and marginal costing in relation to income determination. The issue is one of timing. When are costs brought to account? It could be argued that when a proportion of fixed overhead is carried forward in stock valuation, as in absorption costing, the real effect of selling below or above the level of production capacity tends to be obscured as fixed overhead incurred in one period is reflected in cost of sales in a subsequent period. However, whatever the arguments, the financial accounts require the inclusion of a share of fixed production overheads. It is possible, therefore, to affect profits through the building-up or reduction of stocks.

It is thus a motivational issue. Absorption costing may encourage over production, and thus inefficiency, in order to increase profits in the short-term. Any comparisons of overall performance made from period to period in the management accounts are better made if the accounts are based on marginal costing principles. It is important to be clear, if interpreting the financial accounts, what effect any change in the level of stocks has had. It should be noted, however, that other changes from period to period, (eg selling prices, sales mix, levels of costs, margins), are going to render comparisons difficult anyway.

Self-assessment question 8.1

Mahler Products has two manufacturing departments each producing a single standardised product. The data for unit cost and selling price of these products are as follows:

		Department **A**		Department **B**
		£		£
Direct material cost		4		6
Direct labour cost		2		4
Variable manufacturing overheads		2		4
Fixed manufacturing overheads		12		16
Factory cost		20		30
Profit mark-up	50%	10	25%	7.50
Selling price		30		37.50

The factory cost figures are used in the departmental accounts for the valuation of finished goods stock.

The department profit and loss accounts have been prepared for the year to 30 June 1985. These are given below separately for the two halves of the year.

Mahler Products

Departmental profit and loss accounts Year to 30 June 1985

	1 July–31 December 1984 Department **A** £'000	1984 Department **B** £'000	1 January–30 June 1985 Department **A** £'000	1985 Department **B** £'000
Sales revenue	300	750	375	675
Manufacturing costs				
Direct material	52	114	30	132
Direct labour	26	76	15	88
Variable overheads	26	76	15	88
Fixed overheads	132	304	132	304
Factory cost of production	236	570	192	612
Add				
Opening stock of finished goods	60	210	120	180
	296	780	312	792
Less				
Closing stock of finished goods	120	180	20	300
Factory cost of goods sold	176	600	292	492
Administrative and selling costs	30	100	30	100
	206	700	322	592
Net Profit	94	50	53	83

The total sales revenue was the same in each six monthly period but in the second half of the year the company increased the sales of Department **A** (which has the higher profit mark-up) and reduced the sales of Department **B** (which has the lower profit mark-up). An increase in company profits for the second six months was anticipated but the profit achieved was £8,000 lower for the second half of the year than for the first half. The profit for Deparment **A** fell by £41,000 while the profit for Department **B** rose by £33,000. There has been no change in prices of inputs or outputs.

Required:

(a) to explain the situation described in the last paragraph—illustrate your answer with appropriate supporting calculations, and

(b) to redraft the departmental profit and loss accounts using marginal cost to value unsold stock.

(*ACCA, Management Accounting, December 1985*)

Answers on page 518

8.2.4 Presentation of management information

By far the most significant issue concerns the presentation of management information. It is unarguable that identification of product/service costs and profit are essential information in any management accounting system both for routine planning and control of organisation costs and profit, and for decision-making. Certainly, amongst other things, without this information management will have little knowledge of the areas from which the business derives its profit and, therefore, will not be in a position to allocate properly the resources of the firm in terms of selling effort and production capacity.

Most managers asked to define the profit on one of their products/services would say that it is the difference between selling price and cost. But this begs the question as to what is the right level of cost to use. Traditionally the measure has been total cost, as profit will only be earned when all costs have been recovered in sales.

The concept of there being a particular total unit cost, however, is valid only in a static situation, whereas management is interested in dynamic situations. As soon as activity changes, total unit cost changes because, although it is an approximate long-term variable cost, resources are not easily divisible. Certainly total costs obtained by absorption costing can be quite confusing to management. In any case, even if the information provides a reasonable approximation of long-term unit costs, long-term decisions should be appraised properly over their life taking into account the time value of money.

In addition to the problem of dependence of total unit costs on volume, and the need to correctly appraise long-term decisions, an additional problem with absorption costing is that it does not identify relevant variables in the short-term. As fixed assets and fixed costs cannot be changed in the short-term, they cannot assist short-term decisions. At best they will have a neutral effect. At worst they may:

1 Cause frustration, and actually be a disincentive, either because management feel that fixed assets and fixed costs, although measured, are beyond their control in the short-term, or because such information is part of the feedback provided by the accounting system which is inconsistent with the basis on which decisions have been correctly taken.

2 Encourage decisions to be taken which are not in the best interests of the organisation as a whole, because:
  - **(i)** information is not available in the right form to prompt and assist decisions.
  - **(ii)** incorrect information is used in decision-making through ignorance.
  - **(iii)** management play by the rules and take decisions according to how the outcome will be measured.

In view of the above, the presentation of information in marginal costing would seem to offer more than the alternative absorption costing. Its concentration on short-term variables would seem to highlight those factors which are relevant on an on-going basis. It could be argued that marginal costing:

1 provides a better measure of short-term profitability, as fixed costs are commitments already made.

2 facilitates the control of costs, by considering more the behaviour of costs at cost centre level.

3 provides the necessary control over, and motivation to, management.

4 facilitates an assessment of the effect on profit of operating at different activity levels, and with varying product mix, and thus provides a rational basis upon which management can formulate its plans for the utilization of resources and the allocation of priorities.

Example 8.2

The Multi-Unit Furniture Company manufactures a range of 5 units which may be bought separately by customers and put together to form different sizes and shapes of cupboards, dressing tables, etc. Sales of the units are at the following prices:

A–£20, B–£24, C–£30, D–£35, E–£40

The variable manufacturing costs are:
A–£12, B–£14, C–£18, D–£24, E–£24

Selling and distribution costs per unit are as follows:
A–£1.50, B–£1.25, C–£1.00, D–£1.50, E–£1.25

and in addition salesmen receive 5 per cent commission on all sales.

Fixed charges for the year are estimated to be £87,000, shared amongst the five products as follows:

A–£24,000
B–£27,000
C–£20,000
D–£10,000
E–£ 6,000

Total sales are forecast to be 13,500 units for the year. The pattern of units sold accords with the following ratio:

A–4, B–5, C–3, D–2, E–1

The profitability of the five products can be measured and displayed in various ways. Taking an approximate long-term view from the figures provided, through a full absorption analysis, but at the same time using a marginal costing format in order to demonstrate the contribution generated by individual products, the profitability of the five products in absolute money terms is as follows:

Product	**A**	**B**	**C**	**D**	**E**	**Total**
	£000	**£000**	**£000**	**£000**	**£000**	**£000**
Sales	72	108	81	63	36	360
Variable costs	52.2	74	55.4	49	24.5	255.1
Contribution	19.8	34	25.6	14	11.5	104.9
Fixed costs	24	27	20	10	6	87
Net profit/(loss)	(4.2)	7	5.6	4	5.5	17.9
Sales units	3,600	4,500	2,700	1,800	900	13,500

In the long term, on current levels of activity and based on the cost apportionment assumptions made, Product A makes a loss. The remaining four products are profitable, with Product B the most profitable and Product D the least profitable. In terms of contribution, Product A appears to be satisfactory. Product B is especially attractive, followed by Product C, with Products D and E least attractive. Sales volume is a significant factor influencing relative profitability in absolute terms. It is useful to consider the total monies generated by different products as a guide to their relative profitability and importance.

Also useful and influential are measures of relative profitability, where profit (net profit or contribution) is measured either per unit of sales, or per £ of sales. This is demonstrated in the following table:

Product	**A**		**B**		**C**		**D**		**E**	
	£/unit	**% of sales**	**£/unit**	**% of sales**	**£/unit**	**% of sales**	**£/unit**	**% of sales**	**£/unit**	**% of sales**
Selling price	20	100	24	100	30	100	35	100	40	100
Less variable costs:										
Manufacturing	12		14		18		24		24	
Selling and distribution	2.50		2.45		2.50		3.25		3.25	
	14.50	72.5	16.45	68.5	20.50	68.3	27.25	77.9	27.25	68.1
Contribution	5.50	27.5	7.55	31.5	9.50	31.7	7.75	22.1	12.75	31.9
Fixed costs	6.67	33.3	6	25	7.41	24.7	5.55	15.8	6.67	16.7
Net profit/(loss)	(1.17)	(5.8)	1.55	6.5	2.09	7	2.20	6.3	6.08	15.2

Without the weighting provided by the volume of sales, Product B is considerably less profitable in comparison with the other products. In the long run, however measured, effort should be directed behind Product E. It is not only very profitable per £ of sales where the selling price of £40 is an influential factor, but also, in comparison with the other products, per unit of sales. This is in some contrast to its position using the absolute profit measures.

In the short term, the contribution analysis reveals a somewhat different picture, certainly when profitability is measured in terms of contribution % of sales. Products B, C and E are almost equally profitable with Product D in particular lagging behind. With contribution measured per unit of sales Product E is again prominent, with Product C well ahead of the other products. Product A lags some way behind.

There would thus appear to be conflicting advice as to which is the most profitable product, and as to their order of ranking. Is profit to be based on an absolute or relative measure, and if a relative measure, on profit measured per unit or per £ of sales? Is an approximate long-term view to be taken, or are short-term measures based on contribution required?

There is no simple single answer. It depends upon the objective of the exercise. However, it should be stressed again that measures of long-run profitability are very dependent, in relative as well as absolute terms, upon arbitrary cost apportionment and upon the volume of business. The contribution analysis provided by marginal costing is more reliable as an indicator of profitability, (although it must be recognised that it is a short-term measure), and is not dependent in relative terms on the volume of business. Whilst absolute contribution provides a guide to the overall significance of a product, measures of relative contribution will be especially useful when planning the allocation of resources in the short term. Contribution per unit and contribution per £ of sales provide alternative ways of looking at relative profitability and the implications of a reallocation of resources.

The contribution of the different products in both relative and absolute terms can be demonstrated on a Contribution Volume chart. Relative contribution can be demonstrated per unit or per £ of sales. Cumulative contribution plotted on the CVP chart is established by taking each product in turn according to their ranking based on relative contribution, starting with the most profitable. Figure 8.1 demonstrates a Contribution Volume chart based on contribution per unit.

FIGURE 8.1 **Contribution and fixed costs (£000)**

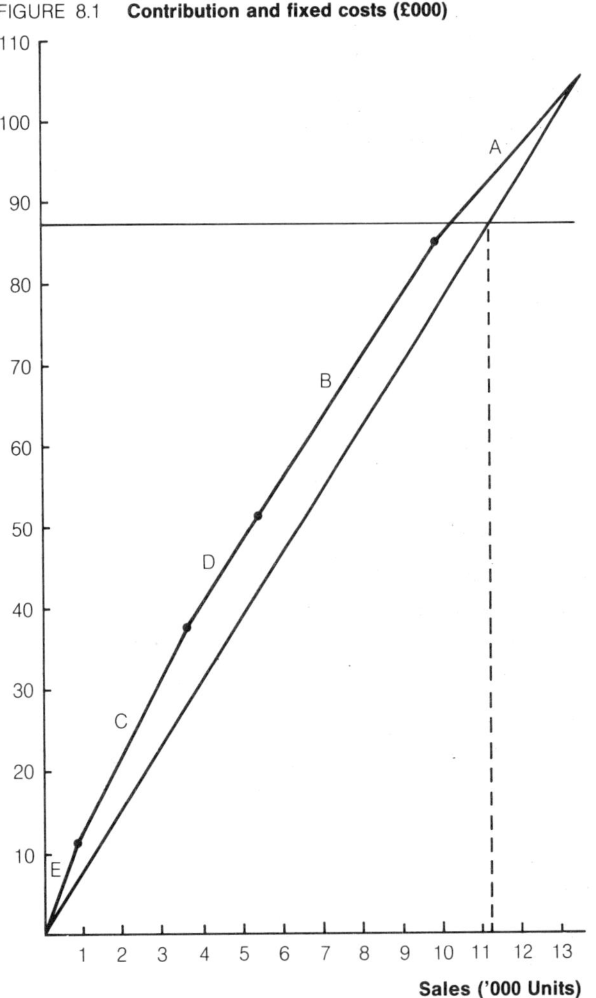

The slope of the average line reflects the average contribution per unit based on the forecast mix. The slope of the cumulative contribution line at any point reflects the contribution per unit of the product plotted at that point in comparison with other products. The length of the line for each product provides a guide to its absolute contribution in comparison with other products.

The contribution analysis, provided in this example, can be used to calculate a break-even point of the business and the effect on profit of changes in volume, mix and/or prices. For example, a break-even point can be calculated, based on the forecast mix of sales, as follows:

1 Average contribution per unit $= \frac{£104{,}900}{13{,}500} = £7.77/\text{unit}.$

This can be derived from the individual products as follows:

A	£5.50 × 4/15 =	1.47
B	£7.55 × 5/15 =	2.52
C	£9.50 × 3/15 =	1.90
D	£7.75 × 2/15 =	1.03
E	£12.75 × 1/15 =	0.85
		£7.77

Break-even point $= \frac{£87{,}000}{£7.77}$

= 11,197 (Sales units)

2 Average contribution per £ of sales $= \frac{£104{,}900}{£360{,}000}$

= £0.2914

This can be derived from the individual products as follows:

A	£0.275 × 4/15 =	0.0733
B	£0.315 × 5/15 =	0.1050
C	£0.317 × 3/15 =	0.0634
D	£0.221 × 2/15 =	0.0295
E	£0.319 × 1/15 =	0.0212
		£0.2914

Break-even point $= \frac{£87{,}000}{£0.2914}$

= £298,559 (Sales revenue)

The company will break even if it sells 11,197 units (see Figure 8.1) and at a total sales value of £298,969. This is 83% of forecast sales. The company will only break-even at this point, however, if the sales mix remains unchanged ie, the sales of each product would have to be 83% of forecast sales. Changed assumptions can be made about the variables in the forecast. For example, if instead the pattern of sales is forecast in the following revised ratio:
A – 4, B – 3, C – 5, D – 2, E – 1
(ie, a shift in sales between Products B and C).
The change in total sales and contribution is:

	Sales	**Contribution**
Product B	– 1800 units	– 1800 units
	× £24/unit	× £7.55/unit
	= – £43,200	= – £13,590
Product C	+ 1800 units	+ 1800 units
	× £30/unit	× £9.50/unit
	= + £54,000	= + £17,100
Net effect	+ £10,800	+ £3,510

Total profit and loss account becomes, if sales are still forecast at 13,500 units:

	£000
Sales	370.8
Variable Costs	262.4
Contribution	108.4
Fixed Costs	87.0
Net Profit	21.4

A revised break-even point can be calculated:

Average contribution per unit $= \frac{£108,400}{13,500}$

$= £8.03/\text{unit}$

Average contribution per £ of sales $= \frac{£108,400}{£370,800}$

$= £0.2924$

Break-even point $= \frac{£87,000}{£8.03} = 10,834$ units

or $\frac{£87,000}{£0.2924} = £297,538$

If total sales were still forecast at 13,500 units, the break-even point represents 80% of forecast sales.

The above provides just one illustration of the use of cost-volume-profit analysis in multi-product situations. The data can be manipulated in a variety of ways in order to indicate the effect of changed assumptions.

Self-assessment question 8.2

A company manufactures and sells three products X, Y, and Z. From the accounts of the year just ended the following information is available:

Product	Selling price (£ per unit)	Contribution/ sales ratio (%)	Proportion of total Sales Revenue (%)
X	10.00	35%	50%
Y	6.00	60%	35%
Z	8.00	45%	15%

Total fixed costs and total sales revenue are £330,000 and £900,000 respectively. Forecasts for the following period include the following changes:

(1) a reduction in selling price of Product Y to £5.50 per unit with no change in unit variable costs.

(2) total sales revenue of £938,450 in the following mix:

Product X	50%
Product Y	40%
Product Z	10%

No other changes are expected.

Required:
You are required to analyse the profit performance for the year just ended and also that expected for the year ahead. Prepare a profit volume chart, comparing the two-year performance, in order to assist your analysis.

Answer on page 519

8.2.5 The ability to split total cost into fixed and variable categories

The methods that were considered in Chapter 3 can be used to divide costs into fixed and variable elements. It must be recognised that the methods themselves will produce an estimate only of the fixed/variable dichotomy which will anyway, in many cases, be an oversimplification of the cost behaviour pattern in practice.

Care must be taken to recognise situations where the information provided by marginal costing may reasonably be used. The analysis may remain valid over a range of situations but this will depend upon the size of the change in activity and the particular level of activity in relation to capacity. Greater sophistication is always possible if reliable information can be found. The fact remains that an imperfect expression of a correct principle is likely to be of more value to management in planning, decision making, and control than information based on an inappropriate principle.

8.2.6 Whether contribution analysis on its own is sufficient

It must be recognised that contribution analysis on its own does ignore longer-term implications. Although fixed costs are ultimately considered, this is only at cost centre, and at an aggregate, level, for example in CVP analysis. It could be argued that this is insufficient, even though investment in fixed assets will have to pass a long-term investment hurdle elsewhere. Although absorption costing on its own has serious deficiencies, it may be useful from time to time to provide an indication of long-run costs (as was illustrated in Example 8.2).

It is important also to consider at what stage fixed costs become avoidable. Some may, for example, be attributable to particular products and thus become avoidable if the product is discontinued. Absorption costing should be seen as an extension of, rather than a substitute for, marginal costing. This does not need to be part of the routine cost accounting system, but could be carried out say once a year, in order to provide an indication of the full cost of different products/services/outlets, etc. This exercise would utilise the detailed analysis of expenditure at cost centre level which was discussed in Chapter 5.

A feature of factories applying advanced manufacturing technology will be an even higher level of fixed, sunk and joint costs which will bring both the short-term (marginal) analysis and the long-term (full absorption) analysis into sharper focus. There will be tremendous scope and flexibility with marginal business. At the same time it will be impossible to rely entirely on contribution as a measure. It will be essential to have a view, at least from time to time, of the longer term situation.

8.3 BEYOND ABSORPTION AND MARGINAL

A question remains, however, as to whether the analysis still remains rather inflexible. Changes in information technology are not only making more information available faster, but are enabling much more sophisticated gathering, analysis and presentation of information. Also, another feature of the more advanced information technology is its reduced emphasis on routine reporting as such, substituting for it highly selective management reports backed up by facilities for more flexible reporting on demand, at much reduced cost. The opportunity now exists to establish more sophisticated and flexible information databases that can be used for management accounting less routinely and quite apart from the financial accounting process.

It will always be difficult to provide routine cost and management accounting information which is directly appropriate for decision making because of the wide range of decisions taken. The challenge is to devise systems and performance indicators that support strategic objectives and are consistent with factors critical to the success of the particular business, and also to provide practical information that addresses as wide a range of decision situations as possible. The contingency philosophy of 'different costs for different purposes' should be practised.

A framework for more flexible information provision could be based upon the recognition that different types of decisions (decision events) may be taken in relation to decision objects and over different time horizons. A decision relevant information system would thus have three dimensions.

1 Decision objects
2 Decision events
3 Time horizons

8.3.1 Decision objects

It is important to recognise that costs (and benefits) have ownership, ie they arise in relation to an object about which decisions are made. The object may be the business as a whole or it may, for example, be a factory, a department within a factory, a machine in a department, a product or a customer. They are all objects in relation to which decisions will be taken and thus in relation to which information will be required. The concept of decision objects replaces that of cost objectives in conventional cost accounting.

8.3.2 Decision events

The second factor that is important in influencing the provision of information is the nature of the decisions that are taken in relation to decision objects. These are here termed 'decision events'. The major events in relation to decision objects are:

1 A change in the level of activity of a decision object, eg increasing the production of an existing product;
2 a change in how decision objects are performed, eg the introduction of new technology into an existing operation;
3 the addition or deletion of decision objects, eg the adding of a new product.

If the above three categories cover the major decision events then they can provide the basis for routine information provision.

8.3.3 Time horizons

The third element influencing decision-relevant routine information provision is time. Economic theory specifies two time assumptions: the short-term and the long-term. The distinction is that in the long-term the time value of money becomes significant and more costs and benefits become subject to variation according to course of action selected, and are thus relevant. However, the economic distinction between the short-term and long-term is, in practical terms, rather stark. Three time dimensions may be useful:

1 **Short-term**: This is where decisions to be taken only have implications for a short period ahead, eg up to a few months. The decision must be considered within the framework of existing facilities provided. Whether costs will be affected will be influenced in a particular situation by the type of business involved and the nature of its costs and facilities. It is likely that some costs, in addition to those related to fixed asset commitments, will be largely unavoidable. The short-term time horizon would only relate to decision events in (a) above, ie a change in the level of activity of a decision object.
2 **Medium-term**: This is where decisions to be taken have somewhat longer-term implications, eg several months or even a few years. Decisions would still be taken within a framework of existing facilities but all costs other than those which result from fixed asset commitments would most likely be affected. The medium-term horizon could relate to any of the three decision events described above. This would be the case if capital investment/divestment decisions were not involved.
3 **Long-term**: This is where decisions to be taken have implications over many years. The framework of existing facilities would be subject to alteration, eg a permanent change in the level of activity of a decision object would have implications in the long-term for the size of factory, plant, sales force, etc. Thus capital investment decisions would exclusively fall into this category and may relate to any of the three decision events described above.

Within each of the above time periods and for each of the decision events there may be problems of creeping incrementalism. The decision event being considered may not, on its own over the particular time horizon, have implications for certain resources. Several similar events together over the same time horizon may, however, begin to have an effect on such resources. Thus information for decision events over each time horizon may have to be presented in two different ways, ie first on the assumption of the event in isolation and second on the assumption of several such events together.

8.3.4 Decision information

Information relevant to any decision object depends upon whether costs and benefits are avoidable according to event and time. The concept of avoidability will be considered in section 3 of the book; Decision-Making. Whilst the concepts of direct/indirect and fixed/variable remain useful, a less rigid use of such concepts will be required in the establishment of avoidable costs. If avoidable costs associated with a range of decisions can be identified within a routine data base, management will have a much improved basis for decision-making. The objective in providing routine information to management should be to try to achieve as much flexibility as possible. The events and time periods described above are suggested as a general framework for the identification of routine information in relation to decision objects.

Example 8.3

The following example provides an illustration of more flexible information provision and use. The information provided below relates to a company making and selling four different products.

Product	Selling Price **(£/unit)**	Contribution/ Sales ratio **(%)**	Attributable Fixed Costs per period **(£000)**
A	6.00	60%	270
B	8.00	50%	180
C	10.00	30%	290
D	12.00	40%	300

General fixed costs total £1,500,000 per period and are shared amongst the four products in proportion to units sold. Total sales per period are expected to be 900,000 units, in the following proportions:

Product A 15%
Product B 15%
Product C 50%
Product D 20%

The following advertising costs per period are included in the attributable fixed costs:

Product A £100,000
Product B £ 60,000
Product C £180,000
Product D £180,000

Depreciation of plant and machinery which has ten years remaining useful life, but which would have negligible disposal value is included in fixed costs as follows:

	Attributable Fixed Costs	**General Fixed Costs**
Product A	£60,000	
Product B	£60,000	
Product C	£70,000	
Product D	£70,000	
	£260,000	£600,000

The following table analyses the profitability of the four products in as much detail as possible from the information provided. In considering the long-term profitability of the four products, as has been stressed before, it must be recognised that the information as presented is influenced by the assumptions made concerning overhead apportionment and by the particular activity level. A change in the level of activity may have a significant effect on long-term profitability in both absolute and relative terms.

	PRODUCT A			PRODUCT B			PRODUCT C			PRODUCT D			TOTAL	
Sales Units	135,000			135,000			450,000			180,000			900,000	
	£000	£/ Unit	% of Sales	£000	£/ Unit	% of Sales	£000	£/ Unit	% of Sales	£000	£/ Unit	% of Sales	£000	% of Sales
Sales Revenue	810	6.00	100	1,080	8.00	100	4,500	10.00	100	2,160	12.00	100	8,550	100
Variable Costs	(324)			(540)			(3,150)			(1,296)			(5,310)	
Contribution	486	3.60	60	540	4.00	50	1,350	3.00	30	864	4.80	40	3,240	38
Attributable Fixed Costs:														
Discretionary (Advertising)	(100)			(60)			(180)			(180)			(520)	
	386	2.86	48	480	3.56	44	1,170	2.60	26	684	3.80	32	2,720	32
Capacity (Misc)	(110)			(60)			(40)			(50)			(260)	
	276	2.12	34	420	3.11	39	1,130	2.51	25	634	3.52	29	2,460	29
Capacity (Depr'n)	(60)			(60)			(70)			(70)			(260)	
Attributable Profit	216	1.60	27	360	2.67	33	1,060	2.36	24	564	3.13	26	2,200	26
Add Back Depr'n	60			60			70			70			260	
Less:														
General Fixed Costs: Miscellaneous	(135)			(135)			(450)			(180)			(900)	
	141	1.04	17	285	2.64	26	680	1.51	15	454	2.52	21	1,560	18
Depr'n	(90)			(90)			(300)			(120)			(600)	
Attributable Depr'n	(60)			(60)			(70)			(70)			(260)	
NET PROFIT	(9)	(0.07)	(1)	135	1.00	13	310	0.69	7	264	1.47	12	700	8

In the long term, at the activity levels assumed, Products C and D are most profitable in absolute terms. In relative terms, Product B is significantly more profitable than Product C, with Product D again prominent. There should be some concern about the profitability of Product A. However, as fixed assets are already committed, have a significant remaining useful life, and negligible disposal value, depreciation is not relevant to decisions made, assuming also that spare capacity exists and will continue to do so. Thus adjusted long-term profit figures are provided before depreciation. Product B is now the most profitable in relative terms and Product A is now acceptable.

The analysis discussed above provides a view of the long-term situation. In the short and medium term, decisions made on individual products will have little impact upon the level of general resources provided (the general fixed costs). However, certain fixed costs are attributable to particular products and thus would be avoided in the event of the products being discontinued. It is useful to identify attributable profits and to differentiate between fixed costs which are discretionary (and thus which can easily be changed), and those which are incurred as a result of the capacity provided. Further, depreciation is considered separately as the cost is already committed.

At this level the lower–volume/lower–selling–price products become more attractive when measured in relative profit terms, as they increasingly lose the burden of fixed costs. Profit net of miscellaneous capacity fixed costs is relevant to decisions concerning the future of individual products. Profit net of discretionary fixed costs should be used for decisions concerning the level of advertising.

Having made a commitment to advertising, contribution should be the focus of attention in the short term. The higher volume products (Products C and D) are dominant in absolute terms despite their lower contribution/sales ratios. Products A and B have significantly higher contribution/sales ratios, but are not dominant in contribution per unit terms because of their lower unit selling prices.

Information should be presented to management according to the purpose for which it is required. It is important to have a flexible attitude and approach which recognises the different decision events and time periods that may be appropriate.

SUMMARY

Absorption and marginal costing systems have been contrasted in this chapter. In summary, marginal costing has been useful in taking management accounting from the provision of detailed information on past performance to the provision of information that will be useful in helping to plan and control the future through its emphasis on the contribution to fixed costs generated in the short term by different activities.

Two questions should however be asked, and satisfactorily answered, before the conclusion can be reached that marginal costing is to be preferred for management purposes:

Is contribution analysis too oversimplified?

Is contribution analysis sufficient?

It is always important to recognise the assumptions which underlie marginal costing analysis. With these in mind it is possible to recognise those situations where the information can be reasonably used. Absorption costing may be useful from time to time to provide an indication of the long-term situation. Absorption costing should be seen as an extension of, rather than a substitute for, marginal costing, especially as in the new factory environment the amount of variable costs are diminishing.

It should be considered whether greater flexibility can be built into routine information provision in order to recognise the varied requirements for information for decision-making purposes. The chapter has explored how more flexible information may be provided by recognising the different types of decisions that may be required in relation to decision objects and over different time horizons, and the information that may be relevant in these varied situations.

EXERCISES

Exercise 8.1

In product costing the costs attributed to each unit of production may be calculated by using either

(i) absorption costing, or

(ii) marginal (or direct or variable) costing.

Similarly, in departmental cost or profit reports the fixed costs of overhead or service departments may be allocated to production departments as an integral part of the production departments' costs or else segregated in some form.

Required:

(a) Describe absorption and marginal (or direct or variable) costing and outline the strengths and weaknesses of each method.

(b) For any three of the following, explain why and to what extent each of the costing techniques is useful in providing relevant cost information for

(i) Control purposes
(ii) Decision–making
(iii) Planning
(iv) Pricing
(v) Stock valuation

(*ACCA, Management Accounting, June 1979*)

Answer in lecturer's manual

Exercise 8.2

Synchrodot Ltd manufactures two standard products, product 1 selling at £15 and product 2 selling at £18. A standard absorption costing system is in operation and summarised details of the unit cost standards are as follows:

Standard Cost Data—Summary

	Product 1	**Product 2**
	£	£
Direct Material Cost	2	3
Direct Labour Cost	1	2
Overhead (Fixed and Variable)	7	9
	£10	£14

The budgeted fixed factory overhead for Synchrodot Ltd is £180,000 (per quarter) for product 1 and £480,000 (per quarter) for product 2. This apportionment to product lines is achieved by using a variety of 'appropriate' bases for individual expense categories, eg floor space for rates, number of workstaff for supervisory salaries etc. The fixed overhead is absorbed into production using practical capacity as the basis and any volume variance is written off (or credited) to the Profit and Loss Account in the quarter in which it occurs. Any planned volume variance in the quarterly budgets is dealt with similarly. The practical capacity per quarter is 30,000 units for product 1 and 60,000 units for product 2.

At the March board meeting the draft budgeted income statement for the April/May/June quarter is presented for consideration. This shows the following:

Budgeted Income Statement
for April, May and June 1981

		Product 1		**Product 2**
Budgeted Sales Quantity		30,000 *units*		57,000 *units*
Budgeted Production Quantity		24,000 *units*		60,000 *units*
Budgeted Sales Revenue		£450,000		£1,026,000
Budgeted Production Costs				
Direct Material		£48,000		£180,000
Direct Labour		24,000		120,000
Factory Overhead		204,000		540,000
		£276,000		£840,000
Add:				
Budgeted Finished Goods Stock at 1 April 1981	(8,000 units)	80,000	(3,000 units)	42,000
		£356,000		£882,000

Less:				
Budgeted Finished Goods Stock at 30 June 1981	(2,000 units)	20,000	(6,000 units)	84,000
Budgeted Manufacturing Cost of Budgeted Sales		£336,000		£798,000
Budgeted Manufacturing Profit		£114,000		£228,000
Budgeted Administrative and Selling Costs (fixed)		30,000		48,000
Budgeted Profit		£84,000		£180,000

The statement causes consternation at the board meeting because it seems to show that product 2 contributes much more profit than product 1 and yet this has not previously been apparent.

The Sales Director is perplexed and he points out that the budgeted sales programme for the forthcoming quarter is identical with that accepted for the current quarter (January/February/March) and yet the budget for the current quarter shows a budgeted profit of £120,000 for each product line and the actual results seem to be in line with the budget.

The Production Director emphasises that identical assumptions, as to unit variable costs, selling prices and manufacturing efficiency, underly both budgets but there has been a change in the budgeted production pattern. He produces the following table:

Budgeted Production	**Product 1**	**Product 2**
January/February/March	30,000 units	52,500 units
April/May/June	24,000 units	60,000 units

He urges that the company's budgeting procedures be overhauled as he can see no reason why the quarter's profit should be £24,000 up on the previous quarter and why the net profit for product 1 should fall from £4.00 to £2.80 per unit sold, whereas, for product 2 it should rise from £2.11 to £3.16.

Required:

(a) Reconstruct the company's budget for the January/February/March quarter.

(b) Restate the budgets (for both quarters) using standard marginal cost as the stock valuation basis.

(c) Comment on the queries raised by the Sales Director and the Production Director and on the varying profit figures disclosed by the alternative budgets.

(*ACCA*, *Management Accounting*, *June 1982*)

Answers on page 521

Exercise 8.3

At the initial planning meeting of Walton Ltd it was tentatively agreed that the sales mix in the forthcoming year would result in each of the three products generating the following proportions of total sales revenues:

Product	*Percentage of sales revenue produced* %
A	20
B	20
C	60
	100

Utilising the above figures the management accountant produced a budgeted product profitability report on a full cost basis as follows:

Budgeted Product Profitability Report

	Product					
	A £		*B* £		*C* £	
Sales price—per unit		10		20		25
Costs—per unit						
direct materials		1.5		2.0		6.0
direct labour		1.0		2.0		2.5
variable overhead		3.0		4.0		4.0
fixed overhead		1.0		2.0		8.0
depreciation:						
general	–		1.0		3.0	
variable	1.5	1.5	4.0	5.0	–	3.0
Total costs—per unit		8.0		15.0		23.5
Profit—per unit		£2.0		£5.0		£1.5

The management accountant's explanation of the report included the following:

1 The report is based on total sales of £5 million—which is the best estimate of sales for the forthcoming year.

2 Sales and production are intended to be equal hence there will be no change in the stock levels.

3 Planned production and sales are in total less than normal capacity and so the figures utilised in the product profitability report will lead, at the level of sales on which the report is based, to an under-recovery of fixed production overheads as follows:

	£
Fixed overheads	70,000
General depreciation	20,000

4 Apart from the planned under-recovery mentioned above, all production overheads are included in the product profitability report.

5 'General' depreciation is the time based depreciation of production machinery and is independent of activity levels. 'Variable' depreciation is the depletion of rights purchased 3 years ago which entitle Walton to produce products *A* and *B* which are patented in the U.S.A. These rights entitle Walton to produce an agreed limited number of products *A* and *B* over a further seven years—however, at current and planned rates of production, the quantity limit will be exhausted within three or four years.

6 Non production overheads are excluded from the report. These amount to:

	£
Salaries	140,000
Accommodation expenses	40,000
Depreciation of office buildings (in accordance with S.S.A.P. 12)	70,000

7 Apart from depreciation all other expenses involve cash flow.

8 Following an agreement with trade union representatives concerning guaranteed payments to production workers, it is decided to treat the labour costs inherent in this original plan as a fixed cost.

The managing director is concerned that the plans rely heavily on product *C* which has the lowest profit per unit and asks whether it would be possible to reduce the dependence on product *C*. The marketing manager feels that total sales value will be unaltered if the sales mix were changed, with less emphasis on *C* and more on the profitable product *B*, and suggests that the following production and sales mix would be feasible:

Product	*Percentage of sales revenue produced*
	%
A	20
B	50
C	30

This alternative will not alter selling price or variable costs per unit and fixed costs will also be unaltered. The marketing manager is reluctant, for competitive and strategic reasons, to reduce the sales revenue of any product below 20% of total sales.

The managing director states, 'Walton needs profit and cash flow therefore I hope both the original and revised plans provide these'.

Required:

(a) Calculate the profit and cash flow implied by the original plan.

(b) (i) Calculate the sales required in order that the revised plan produces a profit and cash flow equal to that derived in (a) above.

(ii) Advise Walton of the best plan to pursue if the objective is to maximise

(1) profit

(2) cash flow.

(c) List and comment on the three major practical difficulties in the analysis you have pursued above. To what extent do these deficiencies reduce the usefulness of your results?

(*ACCA*, *Management Accounting*, *December 1981*)

Answers on page 523

Exercise 8.4

The budgeted product profitability report of Midland Ltd for each of its products for the forthcoming year is as shown in the table on the opposite page:

The management accountant provides the following additional information concerning the basis on which the above report was prepared:

1 Material costs are a combination of variable material cost and a 10% surcharge which is added to the basic variable material cost in order to recover the fixed costs of storage and stores administration.

2 Labour is to be considered a variable cost.

3 Fixed production overhead comprises some directly attributable fixed costs which are allocated to their appropriate product together with an apportionment of general fixed production overhead. The general fixed production overhead amounts to £3,000,000 and is apportioned in proportion to labour costs ie 50% of labour costs. Of the attributable fixed production overhead, depreciation of specific plant and equipment is as follows:

product	*V*	£50,000
	W	£150,000
	X	£300,000
	Y	—
	Z	£10,000

For product *Y*, specific plant and equipment is hired (on an annual contract) at a fixed charge of £200,000 per annum.

4 Transport charge comprises a fixed cost of £450,000 and a variable charge. The fixed cost is apportioned to products in proportion to their material costs.

5 Selling and advertising expenses comprise advertising expenses directly related, and therefore directly attributed, to each product and a sales commission which equals 5% of sales revenues.

Product	*V* (£000)	*W* (£000)	*X* (£000)	*Y* (£000)	*Z* (£000)	*Total* (£000)
Sales	£4,400	£4,900	£6,500	£5,100	£9,100	£30,000
Manufacturing costs						
Materials	220	660	1,320	1,100	1,650	4,950
Labour	500	800	1,500	1,400	1,800	6,000
Production overhead—variable	250	350	400	500	720	2,220
Production overhead—fixed	350	600	1,100	1,000	950	4,000
	1,320	2,410	4,320	4,000	5,120	17,170
Transport and delivery costs						
Transport	120	360	720	600	650	2,450
Packaging	200	100	200	100	300	900
	320	460	920	700	950	3,350
Selling and advertising expenses	720	545	525	555	755	3,100
Administration	660	735	975	765	1,365	4,500
Total cost	£3,020	£4,150	£6,740	£6,020	£8,190	£28,120
PROFIT	£1,380	£750	£(240)	£(920)	£910	£1,880

Advertising costs are avoidable fixed costs.

6 Administration is a fixed cost and is apportioned in proportion to sales revenue.

7 Packaging is a variable cost.

The managing director feels that products *X* and *Y* should not be produced as they both result in a loss.

The marketing manager makes two points:

(1) Sales of any product can be increased by up to 40% of the sales figures contained in the above report merely by pursuing an additional extensive advertising campaign. If any product were selected to have its sales increased the additional advertising campaign would cost three times the currently planned cost of advertising that product. The relationship between advertising costs and increased sales applies to each product and is a proportional relationship, eg sales could increase by 20% if advertising were increased by 150%.

(2) By reducing sales (and production) of product *X* the demand for *either V* or *W* will rise depending upon which product is offered as a substitute for *X*. If *V* is offered as the substitute then each £1 reduction in sales of *X* will cause an increase in sales of *V* of £0.45. If *W* is the substitute then each £1 reduction in sales of *X* will cause an increase in sales of *W* of £0.50.

Required:

(a) Advise the managing director of the desirability of ceasing production of products *X* and *Y* and prepare a statement which shows the effect that not producing *X* and *Y* will have on the profits of Midland Ltd.

(b) (i) Show the effect of pursuing the advertising campaign mentioned by the marketing manager in order to increase sales of each product by 40%. Indicate which products it would be worthwhile advertising. (ii) If only £1,200,000 is available for advertising indicate which products should then be advertised?

(c) Should sales (and production) of *X* be reduced in favour of either *V* or *W*? If so, which product should be offered as a substitute for *X*? Show the effect of reducing sales of *X* to zero.

(*ACCA, Management Accounting, December 1979, adapted*)

Answers on page 526

Exercise 8.5

The Miozip Company operates an absorption costing system which incorporates a factory-wide overhead absorption rate per direct labour hour. For 1980 and 1981 this rate was £2.10 per hour. The fixed factory overhead for 1981 was £600,000 and this would have been fully absorbed if the company had operated at full capacity, which is estimated at 400,000 direct labour hours. Unfortunately, only 200,000 hours were worked in that year so that the overhead was seriously under-absorbed. Fixed factory overheads are expected to be unchanged in 1982 and 1983.

The outcome for 1981 was a loss of £70,000 and the management believed that a major cause of this loss was the low overhead absorption rate which had led the company to quote selling prices which were uneconomic.

For 1982 the overhead absorption rate was increased to £3.60 per direct labour hour and selling prices were raised in line with the established pricing procedures which involve adding a profit mark-up of 50% onto the full factory cost of the company's products. The new selling prices were also charged on the stock of finished goods held at the beginning of 1982.

In December 1982 the company's accountant prepares an estimated Profit and Loss Account for 1982 and a budgeted Profit and Loss Account for 1983. Although sales were considered to be depressed in 1981, they were even lower in 1982 but, nevertheless, it seems that the company will make a profit for that year. A worrying feature of the estimated accounts is the high level of finished goods stock held and the 1983 budget provides for a reduction in the stock level at 31 December 1983 to the (physical) level which obtained at the 1 January 1981. Budgeted sales for 1983 are set at the 1982 sales level.

The summarised profit statements for the three years to 31 December 1983 are as follows:

Summarised Profit and Loss Accounts

	Actual 1981		*Estimated 1982*		*Budgeted 1983*	
	£	£	£	£	£	£
Sales Revenue		1,350,000		1,316,250		1,316,250
Opening Stock of Finished Goods	100,000		200,000		357,500	
Factory Cost of Production	1,000,000		975,000		650,000	
	1,100,000		1,175,000		1,007,500	
Less: Closing Stock of Finished Goods	200,000		357,500		130,000	
Factory Cost of Goods Sold		900,000		817,500		877,500
		450,000		498,750		438,750
Less: Factory Overhead Under-absorbed		300,000		150,000		300,000
		150,000		348,750		138,750
Administrative and Financial Costs		220,000		220,000		220,000
		Loss (£70,000)		£128,750		Loss (£81,250)

(a) You are required to write a short report to the board of Miozip explaining why the budgeted outcome for 1983 is so different from that of 1982 when the Sales Revenue is the same for both years.

(b) Restate the Profit and Loss Account for 1981, the estimated Profit and Loss Account for 1982 and the Budgeted Profit and Loss Account for 1983 using marginal factory cost for stock valuation purposes.

(c) Comment on the problems which *may* follow from a decision to increase the overhead absorption rate in conditions when cost plus pricing is used and overhead is currently under-absorbed.

(d) Explain why the majority of businesses use full costing systems whilst most management accounting theorists favour marginal costing.

N.B. Assume in your answers to this question that the value of the £ and the efficiency of the company have been constant over the period under review.

(*ACCA, Management Accounting, December 1982*)

(*Answers in lecturer's manual*)

Exercise 8.6

The product range of Cotten Ltd consists of 3 product lines. The estimates of some variable costs, sales prices and the tentative activity levels for the forthcoming year are:

	Product		
	K	L	M
Production and sales—units (000's)	50	40	40
Per unit details	£	£	£
Sales price	10	15	20
Costs—labour	2	2	6
materials	1	3	3
delivery costs	2	1	3

There will be no opening stocks of any product at the beginning of the year and it is intended that sales will equal production.

In addition to the above costs there is also expected to be variable production overhead, which will be 50% of the direct labour cost, and the following production and non-production overheads:

		(£000's)
(i)	Assembly area occupancy costs	60
(ii)	Operating and depreciation costs of production machinery	50
(iii)	Other production overheads	234
(iv)	Selling expenses	85
(v)	Administrative expenses	95
(vi)	Advertising costs	76

Apart from cost (iii), all costs (i)–(vi) are fixed and cannot be reduced or avoided unless all activity ceases. Costs (iv)–(vi) will not increase over the feasible range of activity levels and costs (i)–(iii) will only increase if additional factory capacity and machinery are installed. 'Other production overheads' comprise some costs specific to a particular product line and some general production overheads—none of these costs depend on the level of activity except that the specific production overheads for each product could be avoided if production of that product ceased entirely.

The managing director feels that as all Cotten's activities are caused by the 3 product types all costs should be allocated between those products and this would enable a useful product profitability report to be prepared.

In the discussions between the managing director and the management accountant concerning the problems of apportioning the fixed costs to individual products, the following points emerge:

(i) The tentative plans imply the following proportional usage of the factory space used in the assembly function and of the production machinery:

% of total usage

	K	L	M
Assembly capacity	50	40	10
Production machinery	10	30	60

The proposed activity levels leave little assembly and machinery capacity unused. Any increase or decrease in activity levels will cause a corresponding increase or decrease in assembly and machinery usage.

(ii) Selling expenses relate to salaries and other costs of sales staff. It is generally agreed among sales staff that although each *unit* of K and L is equally difficult to sell, it requires twice the time and effort to sell each *unit* of M.

(iii) The 'other production overheads' which are specific to each product are:

	(£000's)
K	30
L	15
M	5

(iv) Those 'other production overheads' which are not specific to any one product line are thought to be difficult to apportion. However it is suggested that apportionment in accordance with variable production costs is likely to be the most suitable method.

(v) Administrative expenses and advertising costs relate to all activities and are not specific to any product line. The suggested method of apportionment is in accordance with sales revenues.

The managing director points out that although the tentative plans are likely to be adhered to it is possible that these will be changed following a further planning meeting. At this further planning meeting it may be decided to increase the activity of some products, and perhaps reduce or cease production of others, in order to increase the expected profit. However any increase in activity may cause the constraint on assembly capacity or production machinery to become operative.

Required:

(a) Provide, preferably in a single statement in tabular form, the following:

- **(i)** the profit of each product line calculated in accordance with the wishes of the managing director, and
- **(ii)** information which will be useful at the forthcoming planning meeting in assisting any discussions concerning expansion, contraction or cessation of product lines.

(b) Use the information produced in (a) above to

- **(i)** show separately for each product line the effect on profit of
  - **(a)** a 10% increase in activity, and
  - **(b)** complete cessation of that product line, and
- **(ii)** rank the products in order of their desirability from the viewpoint of maximising profit under conditions where the constraints on
  - **(a)** assembly capacity, and
  - **(b)** production machinery

  are *separately* operative. Assume all three product lines are produced.

(c) Using the tentative plans show the cost per unit of each product for the purposes of stock valuation in accordance with the absorption costing approach of S.S.A.P. 9 to be used in the event of any stock remaining at the year end.

Explain, but do not attempt to calculate, the effect of any change in activity levels on the per unit stock valuation figures derived. Give an example of one major factor which could alter the per unit stock valuation figures in the context of Cotten's plans and cost structures.

(*ACCA, Management Accounting, December 1980*)

(*Answers in lecturer's manual*)

Application in Service Organisations

INTRODUCTION

In earlier chapters, the factors influencing the costing and performance measurement of those areas of a business which provide a service to direct product costs were considered. In order to measure performance, each service area may be considered as a separate business. The performance measure depends upon the ability to provide meaningful links between input of resources and output of service.

The same issues occur within organisations whose final output is in the form of a service, (rather than a physical product), when considering how best to measure and control the performance of the individual services provided to customers. The difference is that greater investment in providing information on the performance of the different services is required because of its greater importance in the management of the organisation. Service costing is of increasing importance because the proportion of the economy devoted to the service sector has been growing, and that devoted to manufacturing shrinking.

Earlier chapters have largely neglected the service industry environment, attention having been centred upon manufacturing situations. This chapter considers the application of the principles, established in earlier chapters, in service organisations. Following the identification of general features of service costing this is done by discussion of a variety of different service industries. Numerical illustrations are provided via the end of chapter exercises. In examinations students will not be expected to have a specialist knowledge of different industries, manufacturing or service. Details relevant to a particular business situation may, however, be provided and students asked to discuss and/or illustrate information requirements.

9.1 SERVICE COSTING GENERALLY

It has been seen, in manufacturing, that the costing system used will depend upon whether the business carries out a continuous series of individual operations or undertakes separate jobs. No new costing methods are involved with services, merely application of the methods already described. The main costing decisions, therefore, will be:

1 What cost units are made available to the customer?
2 What cost centres should be established?
3 What costs are directly identifiable with cost units?
4 How should the costs of the individual cost centres be associated with the cost units?

Some service organisations establish cost accounting systems along single order costing principles. Each service provided to the customer is separately costed. Businesses providing services such as plumbing or electrical services are examples. In a similar way, in principle, to a manufacturing organisation, direct costs may include materials and labour. Other businesses may use a single order costing system but with only labour as a direct cost eg management consultants, accountants, solicitors. A transport business may also be costed in this way.

However, although labour (driver's time) could be treated as a direct cost it may be considered inappropriate to cost different jobs according to time taken because of the many factors affecting time in each individual case. The question of fairness in determining direct/indirect cost relationships may thus be an influence in the costing of service organisations also. As a result, a system of averaging may be used based on some other factor (eg, miles travelled in the case of the transport business). This is a form of operation costing.

A feature of service organisations generally is that the ratio of indirect to direct costs, and of short-term fixed costs to variable costs, in relation to cost units will often be high. The question of indirect cost treatment is especially important in service organisations. Also, indirect costs will tend to be common to all services provided by the organisation rather than attributable to particular ones. A third distinguishing feature of service organisation costing in comparison with cost accounting in manufacturing organisations, is frequently the absence of an obvious cost unit. The cost unit in manufacturing is a unit of physical product. The cost unit in service organisations is less concrete and thus may be less easy to establish.

The combination of the above three features makes cost accounting in service organisations more difficult. Unfortunately, and perhaps partly because of this fact, service costing has been largely ignored in the cost and management accounting literature. The most likely reason for this, however, can be traced once again to the origins of cost accounting in response to the requirements for stock valuation in manufacturing organisations. Service organisations could be neglected because of the absence of manufactured stock.

Several different service industry environments are now considered in order to illustrate the features described above, and the general application of costing principles, in public as well as private sector situations, non-profit as well as profit seeking.

9.2 TRANSPORT COSTING

Transport operations cover a wide range of service businesses concerned with the transportation of goods or passengers in both the private and public sectors. A transport company situation was provided in Chapter 5 (self-assessment question 5.2) as an illustration of general cost accounting information requirements. A further transport example was used in the same chapter to introduce the contrasting formats of absorption and marginal costing.

9.2.1 Cost centres

Cost centres are established within three broad areas of activity. First, as with any business, the functions of administration, and of marketing and selling, will be required. A number of cost centres will be required, according to the size of the business and individuals' responsibility within it. Second, cost centres will be required to collect costs incurred in vehicle maintenance (if carried out within the business). The cost centres should be established so as to reflect individual responsibility and to enable relevant costs to be passed on to the different services provided to customers. Within cost centres maintenance costs may be collected by vehicle/vehicle type. Third, cost centres will be required for vehicle operations, to identify costs that will be used to establish the cost, and profitability, of the different services provided to customers. Different cost centres may be established for different vehicles/vehicle types, for different customers, for different routes, or for different types of work. In addition to the collection of costs, output information will be required, for example kilometres travelled, weight carried, type of load, number of passengers.

9.2.2 Cost units

The cost unit will depend upon the nature of the transport service provided to customers. Where uniform standard loads are carried, the cost unit is likely to be kilometres travelled, and operation costing methods will be used to establish the average cost per kilometre of a vehicle, or group of similar vehicles, over a period. If the transport operator carries different loads, the cost unit may be a composite one, (either tonne/kilometre or passenger/kilometre), in order to establish the average cost of carrying one tonne (or one passenger) for one kilometre.

Operation costing methods may thus be employed to establish the average cost per unit. Single order costing methods could then be used to establish the total cost for a particular job. If the cost unit is kilometre travelled, total cost would be obtained by multiplying the cost per unit by the number of kilometres for the journey. Thus, for example, the cost of hiring out a coach would be identified as being the same regardless of the number of passengers carried. If the cost unit is passenger/kilometre, the total cost would be obtained by multiplying the cost per unit by the product of kilometres travelled and passengers carried. The cost unit used may be influenced by the basis for charging customers.

The total costs of operating vehicles include fixed costs such as insurance, road tax and administration, variable costs such as fuel and oil, and various other costs somewhere between the two extremes. Significant 'other' costs are labour, maintenance and depreciation. Drivers' wages are essentially a time cost but overtime and overnight allowances depend on activity. Also, as activity expands or contracts, a change in the number of vehicles, and thus drivers, can be brought about. Vehicle maintenance and depreciation are also partly a function of activity and partly of time. The number, and proportion, of costs that are relatively fixed in the short-term are likely to be high and thus the utilisation of capacity has a major influence on unit costs.

9.3 HIGHER EDUCATION

Higher education provides an example of a service industry which is predominantly, in the UK, in the public sector and non-profit seeking.

Broadly speaking, there are two aims of higher education: to teach and to research. These aims are accepted throughout the world. The ways in which accountancy can further these aims may be diverse and presenting a world view acceptable to all may not be possible. For the purpose of this review, it is proposed to take a view of the United Kingdom universities in the mid 1980's because there is clear evidence of approaches and opinions in a documentary form. The Jarrett Report was released in March 1985 and contains a description of accounting practice and recommendations for the future. The salient features of the report are summarised below, together with a discussion of the common cost problem, as it affects higher education in general.

9.3.1 Description of accounting practice

The committee meeting under the chairmanship of Jarrett, conducted a survey of practice in United Kingdom universities with the following findings:

1 Strategy and long-term planning were not key elements in the management of universities. Objectives were defined in broad terms and took the form of a general statement of intent to 'maintain and improve the quality of teaching and research across all subjects'. There was little consideration of the alternative ways of meeting objectives.

2 Resources were allocated between departments and schools in a way which did not appear to relate closely to objectives. The division of resources between teaching and research was problematic.

3 Costs were analysed by type alone, under broad functional headings (staff costs, departmental running costs, equipment grants, minor works, for example).

4 Quantitative and qualitative performance measures, such as the quality of research, were used in the decision about how to allocate resources, but quantitative performance measures usually merely supplement the qualitative judgements made by colleagues on performance and views about short-term political pressures. A range of non-financial and qualitative performance measures are available to a single university. There remains a potential debate on the appropriateness and form of financial measures. Input measures include: results of school examinations for students attending the university, research grants and unit costs. Output indicators include: quality of research, publications, the number and quality of successful students and their employability.

5 Much information was available but it was 'used for administration and not for management'.

6 Financial information differed in quality in terms of timeliness and consistency of format.

7 Non-academic departments such as library or central computing facilities did not always have detailed budgets. Heads of academic departments were usually only able to control part of the expenditure for which they were held responsible.

8 One university was found to have a departmental profit and loss statement.

9 There was substantial reliance on informal feedback and a lack of formal accountability.

This list shows the concern of the Jarrett committee with a number of the issues raised in this book so far. Some issues, particularly the strategic element and the significance of feedback, will be considered in detail in later chapters. Based on this assessment, the Jarrett committee formed an opinion about the strengths and weaknesses of accounting within universities. They were concerned about the possibility that resources might be wasted. They were concerned about a lack of formal planning processes and an emphasis on maintaining past distributions of resource. If a department had been allocated big resources in the past, there would be every chance that high levels of resourcing would be available for the future, irrespective of future needs. The need for clear objectives was stressed by the committee. A means for improving university management was seen to be an appropriate level of de-centralisation supported by a suitable accounting system.

9.3.2 Recommendations for the future

The following recommendations were made:

1 The Government should provide broad policy guidelines and information on longer term funding to allow universities to plan strategically.
2 The senior management of universities should communicate its views clearly and encourage best management practices.
3 A range of input and output performance indicators should be developed to allow comparison between universities and between departments within universities.
4 Universities should make their own arrangements for strategic planning, resource allocation and accountability. Resources should be allocated in accordance with a sound planning approach.
5 Budget centres should be made responsible for results in comparison with budgets.
6 Reliable and consistent performance indicators should be used by universities.
7 Cost consciousness should be improved and absorption costing applied more often in charging situations.

One of the implications for the universities of the Jarrett report is the adoption of cost centre accounting, allied to budgeting at the cost centre level. It is anticipated that accounting procedures will contribute significantly to improvements in the future effectiveness, efficiency and economy of the universities in order to ensure value for money from the point of view of society as a whole.

9.3.3 The common cost problem

Up to about 80% of the cost of higher education represents a common cost in terms of output. The major example of this is the salaries of teachers. The cost of teachers' salaries must be associated with research and courses, for cost centre accounting to be implemented effectively. A single teacher may spend part of the time on research, part of the time on teaching a variety of courses within the department and part of the time on teaching courses for other departments. There are problems concerned with determining a time base. Time sheets are not completed as a matter of routine. Contracts of employment are flexible and some teachers may become so engrossed in their subject area as to unwittingly spend virtually every waking hour on a work related activity. Other teachers may discharge the minimum requirements of their jobs. There are problems concerned with the value base necessary to calculate a cost per hour to apply to the cost of a course, for instance. Teachers are paid according to a system whereby the maximum pay for a particular job is not achieved until 35–40 years of age or older. Younger teachers are therefore less expensive. Expensive teachers are those who have been promoted to higher scales. If cost centre accounting is to be adopted on an historical, absorption costing basis, then there will be a motivation to place younger teachers, who have not been promoted, onto those courses which a department wishes to continue or expand. There may be no natural link between academic objectives, in terms of the future of courses, and financial reporting.

A variety of means have been suggested for accounting for the common cost problem, but it remains a difficult area in both servicing and manufacturing situations.

9.4 THE HEALTH SERVICE

The story of accounting in the British Health Service over the past decade has been a story of changing managerial structure. The Health Service has developed a complex organisational structure and a complex terminology, the detail of which is not relevant to an understanding of the issues pertinent to this chapter. For the purposes of this chapter, in order to minimise complexity in describing some of the numerous contemporary initiatives it will be assumed that the accounting system operates for each individual hospital. A hospital comprises medical staff, in direct contact with patients, and service staff, providing a service to medical staff. Examples of medical staff include doctors and nurses. Examples of service staff include the meals and laundry services.

9.4.1 Hospital management and accounting (early 1980s)

The early years of the 1980s saw the hospital managed through 'consensus'. Committees comprising medical and services department representatives would meet and take decisions. Cost centres were established for individual medical and service functions, with cost centre heads being made responsible for maintaining cost levels within budget. Computerised systems were gradually developed to process much of the routine budgeting and historic cost analysis. Direct costs of functions were taken to cost centres so that at first sight departmental heads were accountable for controllable costs, which they had authorised by signing appropriate purchase orders and invoices.

From the accounting point of view, there are two problems with the consensus management arrangements. These arise from interdependence and independence. The primary objective underpinning consensus management concerned the level of patient care. Service departments would place the objective of patient care above that of cost control or cost reduction. Patients created complex conditions of interdependence as service departments served each other, and medical departments, with the quality of care in mind. A simple case to come out of one survey concerned the packaging of cotton wool for use by nurses in treating patients. Some patients required more cotton wool than others. The packing department agreed with medical departments that an excess of cotton wool would be preferable to a nurse having insufficient. In explaining an overspending in the packing cost centre, therefore, the managers would state that the medical department needed the cotton wool. The medical department would explain that wasted cotton wool is necessary to meet the needs of patients as a whole. Additionally, the cotton wool would be purchased by a centralised purchasing department and could be subjected to centralised instruction regarding hygiene quality. The independence of the packing department is therefore in question.

9.4.2 Hospital management and accounting (late 1980s)

Government initiatives, through committees and reports associated with Griffiths and Korner, has led to criticism of consensus management and the development of patient costing. It was felt that to operate effectively, hospitals should appoint individuals to take responsibility and manage the necessary patient care. Consensus management has been replaced by management by hospital managers.

Patient costing illustrates the application of costing methods to a service organisation. Medical costs are allocated or apportioned to wards. Patients within wards, or segmentations of wards, share a common type of health problem or specialty. By dividing ward costs by numbers of patients a cost per patient by specialty can be calculated. Service departments, and central costs, such as buildings, are similarly traced to patients through a process of apportionment. The problem of common costs arises in practice. A ward may minister to more than one specialty. Buildings' costs are common to all patients. Numerous alternative bases of cost apportionment are apparent at a detailed level. Patient costing, therefore, requires a high level of skill from the accountants who make judgements about apportionment bases, in order to provide value for money information.

On academic grounds, patient costing has certain fundamental problems to overcome:

1 the problem of common costs, especially in relation to decision–making, has not yet been satisfactorily overcome in manufacturing situations of comparable complexity in terms of interdependence and independence.
2 early studies suggested that the cost of patient costing would be low. To achieve benefits to exceed even modest costs requires the commitment of hospital staff. Media reports that some doctors are unhappy about the operation of budgets and cost controls. Dysfunctional consequences of changing accounting systems must be carefully managed.
3 the evidence on the ability of management to pursue the dual objectives of cost control and patient care for an ageing population is unclear.

The Health Service accounting systems are changing emphasis from the monitoring of direct costs of individual functions to monitoring absorption costs with patients as the cost unit. With this change is coming a change in the people within hospitals who assume responsibility and accountablity. Both accounting systems are problematic in terms of both technical aspects and the effects on people.

9.5 ACCOUNTING IN RETAIL ORGANISATIONS

Retailing provides a further example of a service industry with its own unique features and accounting aspects. Both accounting within a store and also accounting for each store as a whole are important. Accounting for different aspects within a store has provided the greatest problems, and developments in this area provide the focus for the coverage below.

9.5.1 Unique features and difficulties

Retailing has had two special accounting problems which are not to be found in other organisations.

First, there has been a problem of identifying sales, and thus profitability, of different products/product groups. Whilst supplies to retail outlets (stores) can be recorded accurately, no direct measure has generally been available of product sales. In the long-run, even if opening and closing stocks in stores, as well as supplies to stores, are known, units sold cannot be determined by product/product group because stock losses through breakage and pilfering may have occurred. Determining the value of sales is further complicated where price changes take place during the period. Stocks are, in any case, difficult to determine accurately at a particular point in time if there are many products and several outlets. In the short-term, eg from week to week or month to month, it has been even more difficult to establish a break-down of sales by product/product group, which is critical to the effective use of space, and for justification of promotional offers.

A second accounting problem for many retailers results from the very large number of different products which are frequently stocked and thus sold and the fact that the inventory may be constantly changing. It increases considerably the difficulties of both providing and interpreting product information. The greater the number of products the greater the difficulty also in establishing an analysis of sales. Complexity is increased for retailers with a large number of outlets, of differing size, in different locations.

A further accounting problem, which generally retailers have in common with other service organisations is the proportion of costs which are common to the organisation as a whole and which are, therefore, difficult to apportion to products/product groups. This problem is also exacerbated the greater the number of products.

9.5.2 Accounting and technological developments

Because of the above accounting problems, the measure of product/product group profitability traditionally established in retail organisations has been gross profit on supplies to stores. All this is changing as a result of two very significant developments resulting from advances in computer technology.

First, the advent of computer hardware and software capable of handling the detailed analysis of product moving through the distribution chain to point of sale has enabled a closer quantification of the different elements, and the establishment of product costs other than the cost of the goods themselves. This analysis is called Direct Product Profitability, and will be considered in more detail below.

The second significant development has been the introduction of electronic point of sale (EPOS) equipment at store check out points, capable of distinguishing, clearly and immediately, between the sale of different products, both units and value. It is especially useful not only in identifying sales of a product, but also the response of sales to changes in the marketing mix, eg, pricing trials, changes in space allocation, sales promotions.

Together DPP and EPOS are enabling the establishment of product sales as well as supplies, with profitability on sales determined after the inclusion of other than simply the cost of the goods. Further consideration is now given to DPP.

9.5.3 Direct product profitability

ESTABLISHMENT OF DIRECT PRODUCT PROFITS

The concept of Direct Product Profitability (DPP) is not new. It basically follows absorption costing principles in seeking to establish product profitability for retailers. Product profit is measured as sales minus direct product cost. However, product costs are not 'direct' as applied in a manufacturing organisation and thus the term can be confusing. In the retail operation the only 'direct' product cost, as earlier defined in relation to manufacturers, is the cost of the goods for resale, which is already deducted from sales in the traditional measure of gross profit. DPP adds a share of indirect costs to the cost of the goods. This normally includes store labour, store space, and other store operating costs, inventory carrying costs, promotion, and where the retailer also fulfils the wholesaling function, warehousing and distribution costs.

Such analysis has been until recently extremely difficult, time consuming and costly, and therefore not done. However, increasingly the availability of computer technology has enabled DPP to be carried out. Data regarding item characteristics and throughput during a period (say 12 months) are combined with the costs of activities that those products gave rise to during the same time period. A complex set of rules within the system calculates the amount of workload associated with an item's throughput from which the cost is then derived. This should reflect the complexity of warehousing and distribution operations, the variation in size of products/stores, breadth of inventory carried and so on.

This complexity means that the cost of an activity per single item handled will be different in different circumstances. Take order picking in the warehouse as an example. For a store large enough to take a full order of something, the time per order will clearly be different from an order where, for example, only two singles are required for a much smaller store.

Thus, the Product Profitability system uses a large amount of item information. At each stage of a product's passage through the network of warehousing, distribution and selling, item characteristics (eg, unit cubic volume; warehouse, semi-direct or direct supply; level of throughput; size of store order; normal or allocation supply; type of transit container and finished package) are taken into account to produce a fair and reasonable charge for the workload associated with the item.

The costs involved in getting an item to the store, and the costs of handling it in store, will not be directly related to the value of the item. The physical and logistical characteristics of the item—its size, weight, level of throughput and the way it is handled—determine the amount of workload associated with the item and thence the charge it attracts.

Although in principle similar to absorption costing, DPP has become a more refined and sophisticated method of establishing product costs because of its development in conjunction with advances in computer technology, and because of the rationale that has been adopted. Traditional absorption costing systems have much to learn from DPP.

The sheer volume of data, and the complexity of the task, generally restricts the frequency of analysis to once or twice a year. However, known changes can be allowed for manually if required, although the characteristics of products and their handling do not change frequently.

Ideally the DPP system will also have a modelling facility. Rules and relationships are established on a database. To produce an estimated profit contribution for an item, a small number of parameters would have to be estimated. It inevitably requires careful interpretation. It does not supplement the need for judgement in decision-making and cannot provide all the answers to all possible queries.

UTILITY OF DPP

Critics of absorption costing would also question the validity of the DPP approach. However, four factors should be recognised. First, it should be seen particularly as a guide to the long-run allocation of resources and thus an aid in strategic planning rather than for short-term tactical decisions. Secondly, space is a limiting factor and thus ultimately profit in relation to space will be the crucial measure. As a result the apportionment of space costs, which will be largely fixed, will have no effect on comparisons of profitability from one product to another. The third factor to recognise is that certain costs, which tend to remain fixed and are remote from the product, (for example, general administration, general store labour), would normally be excluded from DPP. Finally, marginal costing may also be usefully applied to product profit analysis. A shorter-term view can be taken of cost variability in order to assist tactical decision-making in the retailing environment.

If properly used, DPP provides an invaluable decision-support system. Its more specific uses include:

1 Helping to determine whether to add/drop product ranges. In the long-run, products must make a sufficient contribution to the space that they occupy in store (and in the warehouse also). Identifying the contribution using DPP provides a guide to the longer-term situation and enables a clearer view to be formed as to the relative contributions of different types of merchandise. A more clearly defined strategy and a more sharply focused product offering should result.

   One of the most revealing aspects of DPP for retailers, has been the highlighting of the high costs of stockholding and related storage and rehandling costs. Despite an initial high gross profit margin, products may well have a negative DPP contribution. It is important to appreciate the variability of the different costs included and over what time horizon.

2 Helping to determine mix within ranges of products. The cost of having variety is not reflected by gross profit. DPP measures draw greater attention to the question of product mix and its space allocation. EPOS provides the means to test the effect of making changes, particularly to reduce variety.

3 Providing a better understanding of the business and of the incidence of cost, especially to buyers. As a result buyers, in consultation with suppliers, may discuss the possibility of changing product characteristics in order to reduce cost. Outer packaging size may be increased for high volume lines or reduced for slow movers. Product configuration may even be changed in order to provide easier handling, distribution and display. Customer appeal has to be weighed against bad pallet fit, damage, delay and cost in the distribution chain, and ultimately poor presentation at the point of sale.

   This is relevant to manufacturers as well as to retailers and goes far beyond the more traditional value engineering which simply looked for cheaper materials whilst maintaining functional capability and aesthetic appeal. It is important for manufacturers to consider the implications for wholesalers and retailers of aspects of the product's shape and packaging, and thus to consider costs right through to the point of sale. Changes made can result in reduced packaging and packing costs for the manufacturer and savings in the retailer operation in the areas of labour, space and inventory as the product passes through the warehouse, transport and store environments.

   DPP also provides a good indication of the economics of bulky low value products, and of having different pack sizes of the same product. Again, manufacturers may find DPP useful in providing an indication of the true cost of variety, and may even point to improvements in their own absorption costing. It certainly helps to direct attention to other than simply the costing of the manufacturing operation.

4 Use in margin negotiations with suppliers. Clear demonstration of the DPP implications of different products, (according to gross profit margin, configuration and size), may enable retailer margins to be increased.

5 Determining the true profitability of promotions. DPP has helped to measure the true cost of 'added value' promotions, where the added value was an additional item stuck to the side of the original pack. The costs of handling, the frequently reduced percentage margin and on a reduced selling price, and the loss of sales of alternative packs with easier handling and higher margins, may well offset the increased volume that may be generated by the promotion. Rapid feedback from EPOS equipment has also helped in such decisions.

6 The detailed structure of the DPP process, (ie sophisticated absorption costing), provides management (eg buying teams), with an increased appreciation of the practical side of the way other functions perform their duties.

7 Helping to maximise return on space. Store space is one of the biggest costs and is the overriding limiting factor. DPP information can be used to reallocate display space between product groups, ranges or brands, and to manipulate the quality of space. The final measure of DPP performance will be profit in relation to space (limiting factor problems generally are explored in Chapter 14).

   However, it is difficult to determine the optimum use of space. For example, poor performance may be because insufficient space has been allocated to a product/product range for it to establish the necessary authority. An increase in space may result in an increase in DPP per unit of space. In other situations the reverse may be the case. It is also difficult to measure, and reflect in DPP analysis, the quality of space. For example, certain parts of the store have more passing traffic, generating greater customer awareness, and impulse purchase. Investment in EPOS equipment enables limited experimentation to be carried out which may provide useful information to assist in space allocation.

Thus DPP has provided considerable benefits for those retailers who have developed it. It is not, however, a panacea, as for example the above discussion about space allocation shows, and it is not without its difficulties. The quality of information is dependent upon the ability to identify input/output relationships. Ultimately cost apportionment assumptions have to be made. Because of its complexity and the cost of operating the DPP system it provides an infrequent, and only broad, indication of profit incidence on ranges of products and cannot be expected to provide rapid response to changed tactics on individual products. It also tends to provide a bias against variety, because of its emphasis on cost. An adequate range of products is necessary in order to provide authority and sufficient choice for the consumer.

DPP has, however, much to offer those who appreciate what it can be reasonably used for. The kinds of decisions are not new; DPP has provided much better quantification and has had a significant effect on management thinking.

9.5.4 Store performance

A further important aspect of retail accounting is the measurement of store performance. This is much more straightforward. Total sales and cost of sales can be relatively easily identified and many more costs are directly allocatable at store level. From this information contribution and attributable profit can be determined. In addition, it may be decided to approximate each store's net profit performance through the apportionment of central costs of administration, marketing, warehousing and distribution. This is more problematic and arbitrary, but some costs, for example warehousing and distribution, may be accumulated via the DPP system.

The performance of a store can be judged on its own merits in relation to budget/target. It may also be judged in relation to the performance of other stores.

SUMMARY

This chapter has considered the application of cost accounting principles, and the establishment of profitability/value for money, in service as opposed to manufacturing organisations. A variety of different service industries have been examined in order not only to redress the balance of earlier chapters' concentration on the manufacturing environment, but also to illustrate the wide variety of service organisations and their particular accounting problems.

The exercises that follow provide numerical illustrations of some of the service environments that have been examined and provide further examples of situations where the principles will be applied.

EXERCISES

Exercise 9.1

The costs of operating a wholesale warehouse include the following:

Wages and salaries
Rent and rates
Depreciation of fixtures, fittings and equipment
Depreciation of fork lift trucks
Property repairs
Light, heat and power
Packaging supplies
Telephone
General administration

You are required to discuss:

(a) the cost centres that may usefully be established in the wholesale warehouse

(b) the performance indicators which might be used for the control of costs.

Answers on page 528

Exercise 9.2

(a) Describe the characteristics of service costing.

(b) A transport business with a fleet of four similar vehicles is working at 80% of practical capacity for three-quarters of the time. For the remainder of the time operations are at 60% of practical capacity. Measured in operating hours, practical capacity of the business is 8,000 per annum; this is equivalent to 160,000 kilometres.

Operating costs of the business are as follows:
Vehicle depreciation, £4,000 per vehicle, per annum.
Basic maintenance, £110 per vehicle, per 6 monthly service.
Spares/replacement parts, £100 per '000 kilometres.
Vehicle licence, £140 per vehicle, per annum.
Vehicle insurance, £450 per vehicle, per annum.
Tyre replacements after 40,000 kilometres, six at £90 each.
Fuel, £0.40 per litre.
Average kilometres per litre, 4.0.
Drivers, £8,000 per annum each (four drivers are employed at all times, on a time rate basis).
General administration costs, £19,700 per annum (these are absorbed into the cost of jobs at 25% of total cost before general administration).

Required:

(a) Define the term 'cost unit' and discuss appropriate cost unit(s) for the transport business.

(b) Demonstrate on a graph the total cost per kilometre from 60% to 100% of practical capacity (plot costs at intervals of 8,000 kilometres).

(c) If jobs are costed based upon unit costs per kilometre (to 3 decimal places of a £) at 80% of practical capacity, calculate the extent of the fixed overhead under-absorption in a year.

(d) Calculate the variable and total costs that would be charged to a job if it requires one vehicle driving 64 kilometres.

Answers on page 528

Exercise 9.3

A polytechnic offers a range of degree courses. The polytechnic organisation structure consists of three faculties each with a number of teaching departments. In addition, there is a polytechnic administrative/management function and a central services function.

The following cost information is available for the year ended 30 June 1987:

(i) *Occupancy costs*: Total: £1,500,000. Such costs are apportioned on the basis of area used which is:

	Square feet
Faculties	7,500
Teaching departments	20,000
Administration/management	7,000
Central services	3,000

(ii) *Administration/management costs*: Direct costs: £1,775,000.
Indirect costs: an apportionment of occupancy costs.
Direct and indirect costs are charged to degree courses on a percentage basis.

(iii) *Faculty costs*: Direct costs: £700,000.
Indirect costs: an apportionment of occupancy costs and central service costs.

Direct and indirect costs are charged to teaching departments.

(iv) *Teaching departments*: Direct costs: £5,525,000.
Indirect costs: an apportionment of occupancy costs and central service costs plus all faculty costs.
Direct and indirect costs are charged to degree courses on a percentage basis.

(v) *Central services*: Direct costs: £1,000,000.
Indirect costs: an apportionment of occupancy costs.

Direct and indirect costs of central services have, in previous years been charged to users on a percentage basis. A study has now been completed which has estimated what user areas would have paid external suppliers for the same services on an individual basis. For the year ended 30 June 1987, the apportionment of the central services cost is to be recalculated in a manner which recognises the cost savings achieved by using the central services facilities instead of using external service companies. This is to be done by apportioning the overall savings to user areas in proportion to their share of the estimated external costs.

The estimated external costs of service provision are as follows:

	£000
Faculties	240
Teaching departments	800
Degree courses:	
Business studies	32
Mechanical engineering	48
Catering studies	32
All other degrees	448
	1,600

(vi) Additional data relating to the degree courses are as follows:

	Business Studies	*Degree course Mechanical Engineering*	*Catering Studies*
Number of graduates	80	50	120
Apportioned costs (as % of totals)			
Teaching departments	3%	2·5%	7%
Administration/management	2·5%	5%	4%

Central services are to be apportioned as detailed in (v) above.
The total number of graduates from the polytechnic in the year to 30 June 1987 was 2,500.

Required:

(a) Prepare a flow diagram which shows the apportionment of costs to user areas. No values need be shown.

(b) Calculate the average cost per graduate, for the year ended 30 June 1987, for the polytechnic and for each of the degrees in business studies, mechanical engineering, and catering studies, showing all relevant cost analysis.

(c) Suggest reasons for any differences in the average cost per graduate from one degree to another, and discuss briefly the relevance of such information to the polytechnic management.

(*ACCA, Management Accounting, June 1988*)

Answers on page 530

Exercise 9.4

Mr Lane, with his two sons, trades as Lanes Stores, a small family departmental store business with four major departments. Because of increased competition the business has not been doing very well during recent years.

In fact, the last year's trading results show a loss of £750, the first time that the firm has not made a profit in its history.

Mr Lane calls a family meeting to discuss the following summarised Trading and Profit and Loss Account and departmental accounts:

Summary Trading and Profit & Loss Account for the year ended 31 March 1976

(all figures in thousands)

	£	£
Sales		397
Less: Cost of Sales		308
Gross Profit		89
Less: Expenses		
Direct		
Departmental Wages	57	
Departmental Expenses	3	
Advertising	7·75	
	67·75	
Indirect		
Delivery Expenses	5	
Administrative Expenses	6	
Miscellaneous Expenses	2	
Finance Charges	1	
Management Fees	8	
	22.00	
		89·75
Net Loss		(0.75)

Departmental accounts for the year ended 31 March 1976

(all figures in thousands)

	Departments			
	Furniture	*Hardware*	*Drapery*	*Clothing*
	£	£	£	£
Sales	178	80	40	99
Purchases	160	60	30	60
Opening Stock	30	30	30	42
Closing Stock	34	30	34	36
Direct Expenses				
Wages	13	12	14	18
Expenses	1	0·5	0·5	1
Advertising	3	0·5	0·25	4
Selling Floor Space	35%	20%	15%	30%

At the meeting it was pointed out that the performance of some departments had been affected by the competition more adversely than others, so perhaps one such department could be closed to enable the others to be expanded.

It was also suggested that the firm had entered a situation where because margins were falling, these needed to be increased, yet the very effect of doing this would raise prices to make the firm even more uncompetitive with the various national group retailers who had recently opened up stores in the district.

Required:

(a) The preparation of an operating report which includes pertinent ratios, to provide management with more helpful information in their decision making than that shown above.

(b) Indicate matters which would justify further consideration and give your comments. Refer specifically to any limitations in the form of the information which is available.

(*ACCA, Management Accounting, December 1976*)

(*Answers in lecturer's manual*)

Exercise 9.5

As a recently appointed management accountant to a company operating a chain of food supermarkets you have noticed that the local retail managers appear to over-emphasize the importance of gross margin percentages, have a lack of attention to costs generated by particular sections, and tend to ignore any distinction between fixed and variable costs.

Required:

You are required to prepare an explanatory paper for the future guidance of retail managers clearly setting out how they should aim to maximise their profit contributions within the normal constraints of the trade.

(*Answers in lecturer's manual*)

Exercise 9.6

Adne Ltd is a small retail chain with five branches clustered together in a district of Ireland. The following figures have been extracted from its previous year's accounts:

Retail shop (all figures in £'000s)	*C*	*G*	*L*	*N*	*Y*
Sales	45	60	90	180	120
Staff costs	8	11	14	23	17
Occupancy*	2	5	6	12	7

*Including branch rents, rates, heat, insurance, etc.

Future results are expected to approximate to these if management's current policies are continued.

Head office costs of £15,000 per annum are divided equally between the five branches. In addition, annual advertising costs of £10,000 are apportioned to shops on a sales related basis as follows:

highest shop —£4,000;
two lowest shops —£1,000 each;
each remaining shop—£2,000 each

Adne Ltd's gross profit ratio is one-third on sales. All purchases are obtained from a voluntary group of which the company is a member. Once a member firm's purchases exceed £300,000 in any one year, an additional 10% discount is allowed on all the purchases that it makes from the voluntary group. All purchases are delivered to head office, which distribute these to branches. Annual distribution costs are fixed, at £5,000 per annum, and are apportioned equally between branches.

A recent analysis of the operations of branches, based on the above methods of accounting for items, shows that one branch makes a loss, while another branch is just in a break-even situation.

Required:

(a) A comparative branch profit and loss statement drawn up on the basis indicated above.

(b) Your analysis of the situation, providing a comparative branch statement in a form which will help the decision maker, together with brief comments on the possible actions that the management of the company could take in the future.

(*ACCA, Management Accounting, December 1978*)

Answers on page 532

Measurement of Divisional Performance

INTRODUCTION

Organisations may take the decision to manage their affairs by forming divisions and entrusting the running of those divisions to responsible managers. Performance at divisional level is measured to provide information from which activities can be controlled, plans can be made and decisions can be taken. This chapter provides an introductory coverage of the management accounting implications of organising on a divisional basis and developing performance measures. Examples are provided to illustrate the relationship between performance measurement, the management of divisions and the management of the company as a whole.

By the end of the chapter, the student should be able to:

1 list typical performance measures of both a monetary and non-monetary nature, including physical quantities, percentages, ratios and indices;

2 explain the nature of cost, profit and investment centres and appreciate the problem of sub-optimisation;

3 state the need for qualitative rather than quantitative measurements of performance in appropriate circumstances;

4 interpret performance of individual divisions based on inter divisional comparisons.

10.1 DIVISIONALISATION

10.1.1 Types of organisational division

The general aim of divisionalisation can be explained in terms of specialisation and the division of duties in order to form a logical grouping around common interests. Common interests may be concerned with functionality, geographical location, product grouping or market segmentation.

Organisations may form groupings based on functions; marketing, production, research and development and accounting groups may be formed, for instance. Such groupings can bring people together to share common interests, expertise and experience. Social interaction, between, say, accountants, can be promoted to the benefit of the company as a whole. Accounting problems can be shared. Innovative ideas can be developed. Expertise and experience can be pooled to promote synergy; two accountants working together can bring a combination of interests so that the company gains access to a greater level of resource than that provided by the accountants working in isolation from each other.

It is not uncommon to find organisations which have formed divisions based on a geographical, product group or market segment basis. A multinational company may need to divisionalise on a geographical basis. European, North American, Asian and African divisions may be established to allow the company to overcome the problems of geographical distance, for example. These problems may be ones of culture, logistics or communication. Local knowledge of social, political and economic trends may aid a multinational company in forming plans. Decision making may be improved through detailed, local knowledge of relevant costs and conditions. Control may be improved from a knowledge of the likely impacts of control measures on people, taking into account social factors. Divisionalisation by product grouping or market segment may help an organisation to manage its products or markets more effectively. The board games industry, for example, has increasingly turned its attention to the adult audience in recent years, through games such as Trivial Pursuit or Scruples. In this case, divisionalisation based on the age of the potential market may provide a natural organisational structure. Publishers may divisionalise into business, science, arts, fiction and biography, for instance, where each division may represent a different product group or meet the needs of a different market segment.

In general, organisations take decisions on the most appropriate form of divisionalisation and create groupings based on the form chosen. The separate groups within the organisation will then have a life of their own, subject to the fact that they are still a part of the whole organisation and may inter-relate with other parts. Ways in which divisions inter-relate lead to a consideration of two important aspects of divisionalisation; the way in which divisions interact and the extent to which divisions are independent of centralised control.

10.1.2 Interactions

Two extreme types of interaction are described by the terms vertical and horizontal integration. Within vertically integrated organisations, the output from one division becomes the input for another division, and both divisions contribute to the same product range. Boots PLC, for instance, operates some manufacturing units which provide finished items for the retailing division. Manufacturing and retailing divisions are vertically integrated. A textile company such as Courtaulds will have a number of divisions, some of which will sell finished products to other divisions within the group of companies. A yarn manufacturing company may sell to a garment manufacturing company. A garment manufacturing company may package finished goods under the name of another group company and sell to that company, which will function as a distribution outlet. The yarn manufacturer, the garment manufacturer and the distributor are vertically integrated. Alternatively, ICI have divisions involved in the textile industry and the paint industry, for instance. Textiles and paint divisions are horizontally integrated. Within horizontally integrated organisations, trading occurs primarily with external organisations. The textile division would sell textiles to one market; the paint division would sell paint to another market. The paint division may sell paint to the textile division (for building maintenance, perhaps) and the textile division may sell garments to the paint division (staff uniforms, perhaps) but the primary purpose of divisions is to create finished items for different markets. Complex companies may have a range of interactions between divisions; some divisions may be vertically integrated, some divisions may be horizontally integrated. A single division may in some circumstances be vertically integrated and in other circumstances may be horizontally integrated. Interactions between divisions can become complex.

The significance of interactions, from the point of view of the measurement of performance, arises from the extent to which each division can control its own destiny. In principle, the management accountant should ensure that divisions are in a position to control that for which they are held responsible. This may be more difficult where divisions interact.

10.1.3 Independence: centralisation and decentralisation

At one extreme, a decentralised organisation allows divisional managers to fully plan, control and take decisions for their divisions. At the other extreme, a centralised organisation plans, controls and takes decisions on a company basis, perhaps through the mechanism of a head office. Divisional managers would be accountable and responsible, but would not be able to control their own situations in terms of determining actions for themselves. In centralised organisations, divisional managers comply with plans, controls and decisions made for them: in decentralised organisations, divisional managers manage their own affairs fully, are autonomous and independent of central control.

Real organisations are likely to fall somewhere between these two extremes. This leads to decisions regarding the extent to which each division can be allowed to be autonomous; the degree to which management functions are delegated to divisional managers. This implies a level of control over divisional management which can be reflected in management accounting systems. Experience has shown that organisational problems can arise from accounting systems which show a manager to be performing poorly for an aspect of management over which no control is exercised at divisional level. Is it fair to criticise a divisional manager for paying more for raw materials than expected, if all raw materials are purchased through a centralised purchasing function? Can a divisional manager be blamed for poor profitability when a centralised marketing function has an important impact on divisional sales? Degrees of centralisation and decentralisation can be expected to influence the way in which performance measures should be developed and interpreted.

10.2 COST, PROFIT AND INVESTMENT CENTRES

10.2.1 Cost centres

The concept of a cost centre was explained in Chapter 5. In the context of divisional performance, a cost centre is a division of an organisation which is held responsible for costs alone. Investments and revenues, where these exist, are completely managed on a centralised basis; Head Office may operate a centralised marketing function and take decisions on investment on new fixed assets. Targets for spending may typically be set by budgets, which become authorisation for expenditure. Once the budget has been finalised, the divisional manager is permitted to spend up to the limit imposed by the budget and may be rewarded for underspending.

Cost centre approaches are suitable where costs alone are managed at divisional level. Vertically integrated organisations may take the view that there is no fair way of deciding on prices to transfer goods from one division to the next and may thus decide to operate on a cost centre basis. Other organisations may not have a measurable output. These include public service sector organisations. In the British Health Service, for instance, there have been substantial initiatives to increase the extent to which cost centre principles are applied. Specialty costing systems allocate costs to patient groupings. This provides information for possible use in comparing performance between hospitals and between divisions within hospitals.

Extreme examples show the drawback to the use of cost centres. Imagine a divisional manager, appraised on a cost centre basis, who faces the problem of overspending on an advertising budget. An opportunity arises to commit expenditure on a campaign which will generate £500,000 for a cost of £250,000. Spending £250,000 would lead to an adverse variance against budget of £120,000. The rational manager, knowing that performance is based on the ability to remain within budget, would decide not to undertake the advertising campaign, or would risk postponing the campaign until the following year. Cost centre accounting can therefore lead to a failure to pursue advantageous projects. Now imagine another division which is instructed that where underspending against budget occurs, the following year's budget will be set equal to the current year's expenditure. Towards the end of the year, the manager notices that some underspending is likely to arise because requirements for that particular year have been lower than normal. A rational response is to spend money in order to ensure that actual expenditure equals budgeted expenditure, even though the spending is not necessary. Both of these examples are taken from real situations but the organisations are not named to maintain confidentiality. The detailed consideration of the operation of budgeting systems is the subject of Section 4 of the book.

A final effect of cost centre performance measurement arises from the technical process of charging costs to cost centres. Similar issues arise as with the measurement of departmental cost centre performance which was considered in Chapter 6. Where centralised costs are apportioned to divisions, divisional managers may be affected by the basis of the apportionment chosen by the accountant. Consider the following example:

Example 10.1

Costcheck PLC appraises its two divisions on a cost centre basis. Data for last month is provided below:

	Division A	Division B
Direct divisional costs	£356,000	£873,000
Floor area, square metres	30,000	20,000
Number of employees	1,200	1,800
Total budgeted costs	£500,000	£950,000

In addition to direct divisional costs, managers are expected to be charged with their share of centralised computing costs. These were £150,000 for the period. In the absence of a suitable means for charging computer services to divisions, the accountant of division A has argued that the number of employees is the most accurate means of apportioning costs.

Were the advice of the division A accountant to be followed, the costs of the two divisions would be as follows:

	Division A	Division B
Direct divisional costs	£356,000	£873,000
Computer services	£ 60,000	£ 90,000
	£416,000	£963,000
Total budgeted costs	£500,000	£950,000

Division B appears to have over-spent its budget and its performance is poor in cost centre terms. A rational response to this state of affairs would be for division B to negotiate with division A and gain agreement to the proposal that computer service costs would be more accurately accounted for on a floor area basis. Agreement on this proposal would provide the following results:

	Division A	Division B
Direct divisional costs	£356,000	£873,000
Computer services	£ 90,000	£ 60,000
	£446,000	£933,000
Total budgeted costs	£500,000	£950,000

Division B's performance now appears to be satisfactory. The need for accounting judgement on matters such as apportionment implies that performance measures partly reflect divisional success or failure and partly reflect accounting assumptions.

An attempt to overcome the problem shown in the above example is to give divisional managers responsibility for only those costs over which they have control, in this case direct divisional costs only. This avoids the need to bargain or apply judgement to account for centralised costs. The performance of the computer services manager would be measured according to the ability to control costs in the same way that divisional performancce would be measured. However, divisions may influence centralised costs; the level of demand for computer services may be determined partly by Head Office and partly by divisional requirements. The effect of providing a free service to divisions may lead to divisions making uneconomic demands on centralised functions. This in turn may lead to the development of charging systems, perhaps based on computer processing time or reports produced, which in turn require judgement to establish.

These charging systems may themselves be costly to operate. The effect of operating cost centres may be to increase the costs of administering performance measurement systems beyond the level of savings achievable. The interaction between accounting judgement, controllability, methods of analysing costs and the cost motive illustrate some of the difficulties of designing systems and draw attention to the potential dysfunctional consequences of performance measurement. A system is dysfunctional if, by its operation, it defeats the objectives it was set up to meet. In this example, the objective of cost control may lead to increased spending.

Where central charges are allocated to divisions, it is important to ensure a consistent basis of charging for both budget and actual calculations. In example 10.1, if the budgeted figures had included a computer department charge based on number of employees, then the actual level of spending at divisional level should be apportioned on the basis of number of employees. However, interpretation of overspending would need to consider the extent to which the computer department itself had met budgeted cost targets. Knowledge of the budgeted and actual costs for individual categories of expenditure, together with knowledge of the basis for allocating costs to responsibility centres, is necessary for a full interpretation of the situation.

Although examples have shown a comparison of actual results with budget there are other means by which costs can be assessed for cost centre purposes. These include:

1 **Trends**. The movement of costs over time can be monitored. An upward trend may suggest that costs need to be brought under control.
2 **Cost per unit of output**. British hospitals are involved in accounting for costs per patient for different categories of illness, for example. The trend of cost per patient can show the need to take action in relation to particular kinds of cost. For a particular illness, a particular hospital may use a particular drug treatment which is cheaper and yet equally effective to that used by another hospital. Cost per patient for different hospitals may provide useful information from which costs may be controlled more effectively.

3 **Inter-divisional comparison.** One division can be compared with another. Expenditure on management accounting services at divisional level, for instance, could be compared, perhaps using a percentage of turnover to compensate for differences in activity levels between divisions.

4 **Inter-company comparisons.** Where information of a sufficiently detailed and uniform nature exists, one company may compare its divisions' results with the norm for the industry, by using data from comparable companies.

5 **Standard costing variance analysis.** Favourable variances may imply good performance, in cost centre terms. Adverse variances may imply poor performance. This subject is more fully covered in section 4, later in the book.

10.2.2 Profit centres

Under profit centre arrangements, divisional managers are responsible for both costs and revenues. Profit may be measured in absolute terms (a £ figure) or in relative terms (as a percentage of turnover). Divisional managers are held accountable for sales as well as costs. Decisions on investments are taken at Head Office level.

The profit centre approach seeks to promote the adoption of the profit motive throughout the organisation. It is suitable for organisations which include a measure of profit amongst their objectives. In vertically integrated organisations, this implies that selling prices must be established for transfers from one division to the next. In horizontally integrated divisions, a fair charge must be levied for services or products provided between divisions. These selling prices or charges are known as transfer prices and will be discussed in greater detail in section 4 of the book.

Profit centre approaches overcome some of the limitations of cost centre approaches but can create additional problems. To return to the examples described under the cost centre section, a profit centre manager would be motivated to bring an advertising campaign into operation where the resulting contribution from sales exceeded the costs of the campaign. Managers would be motivated to incur costs only where commensurate levels of profit result. By emphasising the profit motive, managers would be motivated to commit resources only where profit implications appear to be beneficial. However, where transfer prices are necessary, the determination of appropriate output prices can present a challenge to the designer of performance measurement systems. The performance of a division may reflect the power of the division to bargain for advantageous transfer prices rather than the ability of the manager to manage, or the ability of the division to guarantee the future success of the company as a whole. The principle of making divisional managers accountable for controllable costs alone should be extended to include controllable revenues, but it may be difficult to ensure that each manager retains control over transfer prices. The profit centre approach may also discourage investment. This is illustrated by the following example.

Example 10.2

Profitmore Group PLC operates a system of profit centre performance measurement. Its divisions differ in size considerably but are all expected to achieve a net profit margin of at least 10%. The Unsure division is considering an investment decision which will generate an extra turnover of £900,000 per annum for an investment of £250,000 in high technology machinery. Profits for the first year of operation are expected to be £50,250 but these could rise to £100,000 per annum within three years. The division currently shows an annual profit of £330,000 from a turnover of £3 million.

The division is currently showing a net profit margin of 11% (330,000/3,000,000). A decision to invest in high technology machinery would produce a net profit margin in the first year of 9.75% (380,250/3,900,000), less than the 10% necessary to meet performance appraisal requirements. Given that there would be uncertainty about the ability of the project to ensure compliance with profit targets in the longer term, a rational decision might be to reject the investment proposal. This may be dysfunctional because the return on investment may be attractive, at between 20% and 40% per annum throughout the life of the project.

Profit centre performance can be assessed in terms of budgeted targets, trends, norms for the company and norms for the industry, in much the same way that cost centres can be appraised. Additionally, divisions can be assessed in terms of margin of safety, the difference between current activity levels and break-even, potential to create profits for the future, given by long-term profit plans, or in relation to risk; the more risk involved in a particular venture, the higher the profits would be required to be.

10.2.3 Investment centres

Investment centres provide divisional managers with responsibilities for investments as well as costs and revenues. It is normal to measure divisional performance by relating profitability to investment. The following example contrasts Return on Capital Employed (ROCE) with performance as measured on cost centre or profit centre criteria.

Example 10.3

Budgeted and actual results for a division which is evaluated on an investment centre basis are provided below. ROCE is used to measure performance and is determined by expressing net profit as a percentage of capital employed.

	Budget	**Actual**
	£	**£**
Capital employed	900,000	1,000,000
Turnover	3,600,000	5,000,000
Total costs	3,420,000	4,775,000
Net Profit	180,000	225,000
Net Profit Margin	5.0%	4.5%
ROCE	20.0%	22.5%

On a cost centre basis, the division is considerably overspent and thus performing badly. On a profit margin basis, the division is performing badly, although in terms of absolute profit, the division has improved on its budgeted profit. However, the ROCE is 22.5%, compared with a budget of 20%; on an investment centre basis, the division is performing well.

Divisional managers are encouraged to plan, control and make decisions for the costs, revenues and investments with which they are entrusted. Where a company can break its total capital employed into separate divisional figures and where investments, revenues and costs can be controlled at divisional level, investment centre appraisal has the advantage of motivating managers to optimise both profit and investment decisions. An investment would be undertaken at divisional level where it leads to an improvement in divisional ROCE, for example. This promotes the taking of advantageous decisions at divisional level, where detailed local knowledge can be brought to bear. Central management may not have detailed knowledge of the processes operating at divisional level, especially where an organisation has diversified into a range of different technologies. However, section 3 of this book explains that ROCE based decisions are known to lead to incorrect investments in a number of circumstances.

The problems of controllability, cost analysis and determination of transfer prices apply equally to investment centres as to profit centres. For investments to be controllable at divisional level, investment decisions must be made at divisional level. This may not be possible where the company as a whole has access to limited investment resources and where final decisions on investments are made at Head Office. It appears to be normal for financing to be managed on a company wide basis and for divisions to compete for investment funds. Once funds are allocated to divisions, use of those funds can be made the responsibility of divisional management. Controllability is concerned with the ability to compete for the scarce resource of investment funds, in this case. A manager who feels that central management do not allocate funds in an appropriate manner may cease to be motivated to expend effort on investment decisions.

Investment centres can be appraised in similar ways to profit centres: through budgets, trends, future potential or in relation to risk, for instance. Risky projects are normally associated with a requirement for higher returns.

10.3 SUB-OPTIMISATION

Sub-optimisation arises where a division optimises its own performance to the detriment of the performance of the company as a whole. The example which follows relates to investment centres. This example also shows how systems design can seek to overcome problems such as sub-optimisation.

Example 10.4

Investment PLC expects its divisions to show a 20% return on investment (ROI). Its Bestresults division produced the following results for the most recent reporting period:

Profit	£ 30,000
Investment	£100,000

This performance of 30% ROI is the best in the company and the divisional director has high expectations of promotion in the near future to the company's main board. The nearest rival is achieving an ROI of 28%.

Bestresults division is considering an investment decision which will provide an additional £8,500 per annum from an investment of £40,000, an ROI of 21.25%.

The divisional director will be motivated to reject the investment opportunity because it reduces divisional profit to a lower level than its rival (an ROI of 27.5% results from acceptance (38,500/140,000)). This decision is sub-optimal as the company wishes to take on investments which will achieve returns in excess of 20%.

The residual income approach overcomes sub-optimisation in this particular situation. Residual income is an alternative investment centre measure to that provided by ROI. It is an absolute measure, rather than the relative measure provided by the profit as a percentage of investment. Residual income is the profit remaining after a charge is made for notional interest, determined on a company wide basis. For example 10.3, it is appropriate to charge divisions 20% of divisional investment. The following calculation shows that the divisional director would be motivated to accept the investment proposal.

	Residual income before new investment	**Residual income after new investment**
	£	**£**
Profit	30,000	38,500
Interest charge:		
20% of £100,000	20,000	
20% of £140,000		28,000
Residual income	10,000	10,500

Performance is seen to improve as a consequence of accepting the investment opportunity. Divisions are encouraged by this approach to increase the absolute value of their residual income and the divisional director will accept the proposal. This should ensure the improved performance of the company as a whole. The results of ROI and residual income can be contrasted with cash flow based techniques, as shown in section 3.

Self-assessment question 10.1

Merrycare Group PLC is considering introducing performance measures in order to assess its five divisions. Each division is a company in its own right, with its own share capital and board of directors. Each division is in a different type of business and has a significantly different turnover and capital employed. There is a well established line of promotion from divisional company directorship to Merrycare Group PLC directorship. The company is fully decentralised and each of its divisions is completely autonomous, even in terms of making financial arrangements, subject to maintaining Merrycare's status as Group Holding company. You have been requested to act as consultant to Merrycare and to recommend a suitable approach to performance measurement.

How would your answer have differed if you had received the additional information that the group was vertically integrated?

(*Answer in lecturer's manual*)

Self-assessment question 10.2

The Merrycare Group PLC decides to set up investment centres and calculates that it requires a return on investment of at least 25% to improve overall performance. The Helpcare Division has recently rejected an investment project which would have provided profits of £26,000 per annum for an outlay of £100,000. Explain the implications of this decision.

(*Answer in lecturer's manual*)

10.4 MONETARY AND NON-MONETARY MEASURES

Measures may be of a monetary or non-monetary nature. Measures based on cost, profit and investment are monetary measures. It has been argued for some years that money is a common measurement, which is well understood by most users of accounting information, and is thus a sound basis for the appraisal of performance. This point of view, however, is the subject of debate. Some authorities believe that monetary measures alone do not always provide fair results. Non-monetary measures have been suggested as a means to improve performance measurement at divisional level. These can be classified into four groupings: physical quantities, percentages, ratios, and indices, examples of which are listed in separate sections below.

10.4.1 Physical quantities

The following list of measures is not intended to be comprehensive but illustrates some of the possible approaches to be found in practice.

1 *Size of order book*; the quantity of outstanding orders may be an indication of the future prospects of a company, or of its ability to meet customers order requirements.
2 *Number of units sold*; these can be analysed by product or market segment so that trend in sales turnover can be traced over a long time span. The use of quantity sold rather than sales turnover can avoid problems associated with inflation, where a monetary measure may show increases despite a decline in the number of units sold.
3 *Number of units produced*; as a measure of productivity and the ability of the manufacturing function to meet sales requirements, the number of units produced may be reported on a daily or weekly basis.
4 *Quantities of production wasted*; this may be given as a weight or as a number of units, depending on the type of production operation. This can be used as a measure of quality. The zero defects principle should motivate managers to strive for a result showing no wastage.
5 *Quantities of units returned by customers*; a measure of quality, probably analysed by product category and cause of return.
6 *Non-productive labour or machine hours*; analysed by cause.
7 *Number of customers visited by salesmen*; a possible measure of the productivity of a salesforce.
8 *Number of key depressions*; computers can be programmed to count up the number of times keys are pressed on a keyboard. This measure can be used to assess the productivity of an individual keyboard operator.

10.4.2 Percentages and ratios

Examples include:

1 *Wastage*; measured as a percentage of input or output. A measure of quality. Industry or company norms are to be found in certain instances.
2 *Labour turnover*; possibly a measure of labour relations.
3 *Productivity*; the relationship between the quantity of production and the inputs required for that production, in terms of production per employee or production per direct hour, for example.
4 *Market share*; the quantity or value of the market held by the organisation is expressed as a percentage of the total market. This may be a measure of marketing performance.

5 *Debtors collection period*; the relationship between debtors and sales. This is a measure of the performance of the credit control department.

6 *For charities, the percentage of administrative costs to funding*; this percentage can have important implications for the ability of a charity to secure funds in Britain and is used, for instance, as a measure of performance in reporting to funding sources or regulatory bodies. There is an assumption that charity funds should be spent on the people or other purposes originally designated as the charity objectives. Ideally, it is perceived that the percentage should be zero, a point indirectly brought to the British public's attention in the recent, national "Comic Relief" fund raising activity.

10.4.3 Indices

A famous index of performance at national level is provided by the calculation of inflation. Inflation is calculated by taking the prices of certain household inputs such as food, heating and lighting or housing costs, and applying a weighting to each input so as to arrive at a composite index at discrete points in time. The increase in the index between one date and the corresponding date in the previous year is measured in percentage terms and the resulting figure is referred to as the inflation for the period.

Those variables which are considered to be important in measuring performance are weighted and aggregated to provide a calculated number. The change in this particular number is then monitored. Consider the following example:

Example 10.5

A company wishes to assess its efficiency by relating all inputs to outputs. Its inputs comprise raw materials, labour, power and fixed assets. It has two products as outputs. Details of results for three periods are give below:

	Period 1	Period 2	Period 3
Sales of product A	£30,000	£38,000	£35,000
-units	60,000	95,000	77,500
Sales of product B	£130,000	£75,000	£90,000
-units	130,000	70,000	95,000
Raw material weight	10,000	10,500	13,000
Labour hours	4,000	7,500	6,500
Power costs	£7,000	£10,000	£10,000
Book value of assets	£95,000	£96,000	£94,000

Judgements have been applied to the way in which input and output indices should be constructed and the weightings to be applied. It has been determined that the most appropriate calculation of output should be given by weighting the units sold in a ratio of 3:1 for products A and B respectively. Inputs should be weighted equally.

Calculations of an appropriate index for this example are as follows:

	Period 1				Period 2			Period 3		
Outputs:										
	A 60,000	3	180,000		95,000	3	285,000	77,500	3	232,500
	B 130,000	1	130,000		70,000	1	70,000	95,000	1	95,000
			310,000				355,000			327,500
Inputs, each weighted 1:										
Raw materials			10,000				10,500			13,000
Labour			4,000				7,500			6,500
Power			7,000				10,000			10,000
Assets			95,000				96,000			94,000
			116,000				124,000			123,500
Weighted output			310,000				355,000			327,500
Weighted input			116,000				124,000			123,500
Efficiency			2.67241				2.86290			2.65182
Index			100				107			99

Note the ability of the index to summarise a mass of potentially confusing detail into one apparently simple measure. Period 2 performance is clearly better than performance in the other two periods. Notice also the significance of the judgement regarding the way in which outputs were included (in units rather than £) and the weightings for both input and output factors. There appears to be room for disagreement in detail about the way in which the calculation should be made and difficulty in interpreting the exact meaning of a particular figure. Some experimental work, in applying similar ideas to those presented here, has been reported from the USA with apparently encouraging results. Managers claim to understand such measures more readily than monetary measures and appear to be motivated to improve performance.

10.5 QUANTITATIVE AND QUALITATIVE MEASURES

Financial and non-financial measures which have so far been considered are all of a quantitative nature; performance is reduced to figures which are interpreted to form an impression of level of relative success or failure. Some commentators on performance measurement have pointed out that real life cannot simply be reduced to numbers and that there is a need for qualitative measures. These are concerned with aspects of performance such as relationships with customers, quality of industrial relations or the contribution of individuals to a community.

Qualitative measures may lack the degree of objectivity attributed to quantitative measures. To be reliable, qualitative measures need a degree of consensus amongst those people who are given responsibility to consider performance. Imagine the assessment of a student at the end of a course. Quantitative measures would include marks gained in assignments or projects, marks gained in examinations and possibly attendance times as a proportion of possible attendance time. A student scoring 90% in coursework, 90% in the examination and attending 100% of lectures will clearly pass. At some level, a pass requirement can be stipulated as a decision rule to interpret the performance of borderline students. A student averaging 50% in coursework and examinations, and attending 75% of lectures may be considered worthy of a pass. Opponents of assessment schemes such as these point out that quantitative measurements do not necessarily reveal the abilities and potential of all students. It may be desirable to assess a student's ability to relate to other students; accountants need to work with other people in organisations, for instance. Students' performance could be measured in qualitative terms by collecting the opinions of all lecturers on the skills of particular students. If all lecturers feel that accounting student A has excellent interpersonal skills, the student may be allowed to pass. However, the situation where lecturers disagree about accounting student B, for instance can be difficult to resolve.

An example of a well established qualitative measurement is given by staff appraisal schemes. These may be established so that a head of department offers judgements on the qualities of departmental staff. To use the student analogy, this is equivalent to one lecturer passing or failing all students based on personal opinion. It can be expected that the quality of such an approach to performance measurement will depend upon the interaction between the head of department and the departmental staff. A poor head of department may provide a good appraisal for a member of staff who is a personal friend or one who possesses particular skills that the head of department relies upon, such as the ability to construct spreadsheet models, for instance. It is not uncommon to find grievance procedures built into staff appraisal schemes to allow for situations where the opinions of individual members of staff differ from the judgement of the head of department.

10.6 INTER-DIVISIONAL COMPARISONS

The following example illustrates how divisions can be compared with each other in order to measure performance. For the sake of illustration, it is assumed that only financial data is available.

Example 10.6

The following data has been extracted from the monthly accounts of Emm and Enn, two divisions of the Letters Group PLC.

	Emm	**Enn**
	£'000	**£'000**
Sales	4500	1240
Cost of sales	2250	744
Gross profit	2250	496

	Emm	Enn
	£'000	£'000
Administrative costs	450	40
Marketing costs	1575	20
Research and development	90	372
Net Profit	135	64
Fixed assets	1500	124
Stocks	40	62
Debtors	300	234
Creditors	490	100
Capital Employed	1350	320

The company as a whole expects to achieve a net profit margin of 10% and a return on investment of 20%. Both divisions have succeeded in spending within their budgets and costs for the period under investigation are comparable with previous periods.

It is useful to consider the performance of these two divisions in relation to each other, the company as a whole and in relation to cost centre, profit centre and investment centre approaches.

From a cost centre basis, both divisions appear to be performing satisfactorily. It is clear that division Emm spends considerably more than division Enn and the company might thus believe that it will be better rewarded by monitoring the performance of Emm more closely than by monitoring division Enn.

From a profit centre basis, both divisions earn profits. However, both divisions underperform in comparison with company profit margin and Emm performs less well than Enn.

From an investment centre perspective, Emm underperforms against both Enn and the company wide position, whilst Enn complies with company requirements.

Self-assessment question 10.3

Calculate a full range of measures of performance, including, for instance, individual costs compared with turnover and stock and debtors days, in order to provide an explanation of the performance of Emm, in comparison with Enn.

(*Answer in lecturer's manual*)

Inter-divisional comparisons can be converted into 'league tables' where the most successful divisions appear at the top of the table, as measured by company criteria such as cost savings or profit performance. Such summaries make success and failure ratings explicit. This has consequences for the organisation in terms of the effect on people. The aim would be to motivate low performing divisions to improve. One danger might be that low performing divisions lose morale and perform even less well until they are eventually closed. This situation may be dysfunctional where the potential future for some low performers is good. By rewarding short-term success of some divisions, the long-term potential for other divisions may be sacrificed in some circumstances.

SUMMARY

Organisations create divisional structures to bring about a logical grouping of activities in search of improved overall performance. Performance of each division can be measured in terms of a cost centre, profit centre or investment centre approach. The potential benefits to be gained from such measurement arise from improved planning, control and decision making. They may promote cost consciousness, the profit motive or the desire to invest in favourable projects. Unfortunately, the implementation of these approaches can lead to dysfunctional decision making and sub-optimisation. Financial measures alone may not provide a complete picture of divisional performance and some non-financial and qualitative measures may be introduced to aid the process of interpreting divisional success. Once measures have been established, comparison can be made with organisational criteria such as budgeted targets or the performance of other divisions. Divisional performance measurement, including transfer pricing, is considered further in Section 4.

EXERCISES

Exercise 10.1

Discuss the main techniques which have been suggested for the evaluation of the financial aspects of the performance of

1 cost centres
2 profit centres.

(*ACCA, Management Accounting, December 1985*)

(*Answers in lecturer's manual*)

Exercise 10.2

From an accounting point of perspective an organisational unit of an accounting entity may be a cost centre or a profit centre or an investment centre. Explain these categories, describe the strengths and weaknesses of each and the conditions in which each would be most appropriate if the aim is to develop efficient planning and control procedures.

(*ACCA, Management Accounting, June 1983*)

(*Answers in lecturer's manual*)

Exercise 10.3

Divisionalisation is a common form of organisational arrangement but there is some diversity of opinion as to the best measure of divisional performance.

Discuss this topic and describe and compare the main performance measures that have been suggested.

(*ACCA, Management Accounting, June 1982*)

(*Answer in lecturer's manual*)

Exercise 10.4

'The measurement of performance is a fundamental partof the management process.'

Discuss this statement and outline the major forms of performance measurement available to management

(*Answer in lecturer's manual*)

Exercise 10.5

The following table of results has been extracted from the monthly management accounts of Basil plc, a company comprising ten divisions.

	Division G	Division J
Sales	£3,000,000	£10,000,000
Gross Profit	£1,000,000	£ 5,000,000
Net Profit	£ 500,000	£ 900,000
Employees	100	100
Number of employees leaving and being replaced	3	5
Materials wastage	8%	2%
Fixed assets	£1,500,000	£ 3,000,000
Capital Employed	£2,500,000	£ 3,600,000

Required:

(a) Comment on the performance of these two divisions

(b) The management of Basil plc expect its managers to maximise sales and net profit and minimise labour turnover and materials wastage. Outline a method for constructing a single index which would show the relative performance of divisions G and J in these areas.

(c) Division J is considering an investment of £500,000 which would provide a profit of £120,000 per annum. Explain the suboptimisation implications of this situation.

(d) Explain the significance of qualitative measures of performance.

(*Answer in lecturer's manual*)

Section 3

DECISION-MAKING

The previous section of the book provided an examination of cost accumulation and performance measurement, with the primary objective that information be organised and structured so as to provide a basis for ad hoc decision-making, and for drawing up plans and exercising control over a business's activities in general.

This section considers how decisions should be made with particular emphasis on the identification, analysis and evaluation of quantitative information. This will be examined and illustrated in a variety of decision-making situations covering different types of decisions, of both a long-term and short-term nature.

In some cases particular mathematical models are employed and thus there are close links with paper 2.6 'Quantitative Analysis'. Students are advised in the study guide for Cost and Management Accounting II to study Quantitative Analysis before or at the same time as paper 2.4.

Decision-Making In Context

INTRODUCTION

This introductory chapter of the section provides, and examines, a model of the decision-making process which will become a framework for the rest of the section. The different stages in the process are identified and difficulties at each stage examined, both in general and in respect of different types of decisions. Consideration is also given to business objectives, which shape the process.

No self-assessment questions or end-of-chapter exercises are included as it is an introductory chapter. The chapters that follow in this section include questions and exercises which build upon the foundations laid.

11.1 ELEMENTS OF DECISIONS

Decisions are taken in response to identified opportunities or problems. Each decision requires the selection of one from two or more alternatives even if the only other alternative is to do nothing (ie alternatives must always, by definition, be mutually exclusive; at the same time if there are no alternatives, there is thus no choice and no decision to make).
Decisions have the following elements:

1 Objectives
2 Alternatives
3 Information
4 Evaluation
5 Execution

Decisions taken will depend upon the information available and identified, how it is evaluated, and on what the decision taker is hoping to achieve, (ie objective). The objective is a prerequisite for the consideration of alternatives, the processing of information and of evaluation, as it may shape the sort of opportunities or problems that are sought/identified, what information is relevant, and how it is evaluated. Whether or not the objective is achieved will depend not just upon how good the decision is but also upon how well it is executed.

11.2 NECESSARY CONDITIONS FOR OPTIMAL DECISION-MAKING

Having identified decision elements it is possible to specify necessary conditions under which a business ought to achieve optimal decision-making:

1 The business (and decision-takers within it) must have a clear and consistent objective and express it in such a way that the acceptability of alternative courses of action can be assessed.
2 All possible courses of action must be known. This includes the identification both of opportunities/problems and of ways of taking advantage of/solving them.
3 Information concerning the effect of such courses of action must be available, correctly identified and expressed in a manner consistent with the means of expressing objectives.
4 The information must be correctly evaluated and alternatives compared with each other, and with the criterion of acceptability, in order to reach a decision on the best alternative.
5 Decisions, once taken, must be successfully executed.

This would seem to be a rational process (ie reasonable and sensible). If these conditions were met, decisions could be taken objectively through computation, and ought to lead to optimality.

However, the above prescription is very general. Rationality depends upon both ends and means ie upon the objective as well as the process for achieving it. The precise nature of the process (means) will depend upon the business objective(s) (ends). The sort of information that is relevant and the nature of the evaluation will be especially affected.

It would seem reasonable to suggest that decision-making in business must have a profit motive. Certainly traditional economic theory argues that the only objective of a business organisation is the pursuit of maximum profit. A more detailed prescriptive model of rational decision-making can be established on the assumption of a profit maximising objective. This is termed the economic model.

Before describing and assessing the economic model it should be recognised that business decisions are extremely varied. Only certain decisions could be expected to be made with recourse to management accounting data and with reference to the economic model. The nature of decisions, with a consideration of different possible categorisations, will be described later in the chapter. One of these categorisations is according to the extent to which decision alternatives can be quantified. In the sections that follow it should be recognised that the economic model is prescribed for decision situations that enable quantification in profit terms.

11.3 THE ECONOMIC MODEL

From the necessary conditions for optimal decision-making specified above it is possible to prescribe more precisely how management ought to make decisions if their objective is to maximise the business's profits.

The first requirement is to establish the criterion for judging profit acceptability ie the minimum profit return that is required to satisfy the providers of capital. Then all decision situations must be identified, and all alternative courses of action for each situation, together with their anticipated benefits and costs. The decision process would then consist of choosing from among the alternative actions, through evaluation of their overall long-term profit consequences. The opportunity selected would be that offering the highest return over and above the criterion of acceptability. Having made the decision it must be implemented correctly.

This may be called a prescriptive economic model of the decision-making process; a model of economic rationality. Is this prescription reasonable? One questionable feature is the assumption of certainty of outcome. The only thing certain about the future is that it is uncertain. A recognition of uncertainty regarding the future leads to an adjustment to the above prescription of economic decision-making behaviour for a business.

Rather than single estimates of the factors affected by a particular course of action, the consequences of taking each course of action under each possible state of the world should be assessed, together with the likelihood of each state occurring. The opportunity selected should be that offering the highest expected monetary value. This is the product of different possible outcomes and their probability of occurrence. If situations are repetitive, if possible outcomes stay the same, and if successive decision probabilities do not change, the expected monetary value reflects the long-run result.

However, in practice many situations are one-off situations. Even if uncertainties are measured there is no guarantee of the long-term result. A single project may be large enough to have a significant influence on the business. Also, even if other projects of similar size are available (or the investor has a portfolio of investments), they are unlikely to balance uncertainties because if a particular state of the world occurs it may affect all projects similarly.

As the long-run average result cannot be guaranteed (ie uncertainty still exists even if possible outcomes and probabilities of occurrence are accurate) an adjustment to the expected monetary value model is required because money and satisfaction may not be linearly related. Many people seem to display diminishing marginal satisfaction for money. This will be reflected in their attitude to uncertainty in one-off situations. They may thus be more inclined to choose an alternative with a lower expected monetary value if it also reduces the possibility of particularly adverse outcomes when considered in conjunction with other investments. Such a refinement may be called the Expected Profit Utility Model. Preferences need to be expressed in terms of satisfaction (utility) rather than money.

This is a refinement to the criterion of acceptability, ie it is based upon profit utility, rather than pure profit maximisation, in an uncertain world. Decision-takers who are more concerned to avoid possible consequences worse than the expected value, rather than to accept possible consequences better than the expected value, are said to be risk averse (ie the term 'risk' is here associated only with events turning out worse than expected). It should be noted that the term 'risk' is also popularly used in texts to describe a situation where the probability of all different possible outcomes can be established, as opposed to 'uncertainty' where the likelihood of possible outcomes occurring is unknown.

If profit utility maximisation is the objective of a business, the necessary conditions for optimal decision-making (ie, the prescription of what management *ought* to do) become:

1 The profit utility maximisation objective must be expressed in behavioural terms. Required profit returns must be established and the attitude to risk quantified.
2 All possible courses of future action must be identified.
3 Information must be identified concerning the likely economic effect of such future actions, and expressed in terms of profit utility.
4 This information must be evaluated so that the anticipated outcome of alternatives can be compared with each other, and with the criterion of acceptability, in order for a decision to be taken.
5 A final vital ingredient in successful decision-making is to ensure that decisions turn out as planned. Even if estimates of the future are reasonable it is necessary to exercise effective control over the implementation and outcome of projects.

The above process still places emphasis on quantitative evaluation and decisions by computation. The question can be asked again as to whether this is a reasonable prescription. To be practical, and thus useful, a model must possess not only prescriptive (normative) validity, ie how people should make decisions based on sound theoretical reasoning, but also descriptive (empirical) validity ie how in practice they do make decisions, or at least are reasonably capable of doing so.

What is required is a theory which proves a reasonable standard to which decision-makers might aspire. There is nothing more practical than a good theory; it is a guide to action. The validity of the economic model established above can be questioned in two main respects:

1 Is the assumption of an objective of profit utility maximisation valid? ie is it 'ends' rational?
2 Are the general stages in the model, leading to emphasis on evaluation, and decision by computation, valid? ie is it 'means' rational?

11.4 ENDS RATIONALITY

Does the earlier prescription of profit utility maximisation reflect what an organisation's objectives are or should be?

In looking for an objective which is characteristic of all firms, profit is undoubtedly of widest applicability, as was noted earlier. Certainly, the economic theory of the firm emphasises profit maximisation as an objective, apparently to the exclusion of more psychologically oriented goals such as employee satisfaction and motivation, customer and community relationships, and personal attitudes.

However, even if profit maximisation is the prime objective of a business enterprise it is vital to recognise the importance of these more psychologically oriented goals as secondary goals important in the achievement of profit maximisation. Behavioural factors impinge considerably on the activities of all firms such that no decisions can be taken without full consideration of the possible economic consequences of these factors. As Briston and Liversidge state:

'The firm is a complex system strongly influenced by the attitudes and behaviour of its participants with the result that what appears to be an optimal decision in the abstract may prove to be sub-optimal when implemented, due to the unfavourable response which it generates from those whom it affects. Behavioural factors have a major influence upon all activities of a firm and must thus be taken into account whenever decisions are being analysed, made or implemented.'

This emphasises not so much the possible existence of other objectives for their own sake but the possible behavioural implications of action for future profit. It also highlights the difficulty of the means, (ie the process of deciding). In fact the idea of maximisation should not be taken too literally.

The reason why maximisation is retained in economic theory is that definite predictions are more readily available with it than without it. It is a basis for prediction rather than prescription. Nevertheless, it is surely a reasonable belief that the interests of firms will be better served by a bigger profit than a smaller one. Satisficing (ie earning a satisfactory level of profit) may be a more workable objective, however, and can incorporate the concept of risk attitude considered earlier.

Further considerations would tend to confirm this. Because of uncertainty in the future, a business enterprise will never in practice know if, and when, it is maximising its profit. This of course does not prevent the organisation adopting a decision criterion which would lead to the selection of the most profitable from a range of alternatives, but does suggest the need for greater realism in setting objectives. Setting a satisficing objective also enables other objectives to be pursued. Empirical evidence collected by many researchers indicates that additional objectives other than profit, which are pursued, are sales maximisation, growth and increase in market share. Indeed, many firms tend to state their primary objective in terms of sales or market share. However this is in fact often because it is a good substitute for profit. Research has found a positive correlation between a firm's market share and its profitability (return on investment). Also, if firms explicitly recognise the importance of more psychologically oriented goals, this is frequently because of the potential consequences for profitability, ie they may well not be separate and potentially conflicting objectives. However, it is unlikely that objectives (if a firm has more than one) can ever be perfectly positively correlated (eg profit, sales maximisation, employee satisfaction).

Potentially dysfunctional, however, is the pursuit of individual objectives which are inconsistent with those of the organisation as a whole. This would demonstrate a lack of goal conguence. For example, sales and marketing management may pursue increased sales with insufficient regard for the profit consequences; production management may seek to increase output in order to recover overheads, or to achieve greater productivity with insufficient regard for sales; top management may be interested more in prestige or technical excellence which may not be of concern directly to the shareholders; individual decision-takers may want a quick improvement in performance to improve their standing, which may be costly in the long-term and not sustainable; reward/performance evaluation systems, if not structured carefully, can encourage decisions to be taken which are not in the best interests of the business as a whole. However, none of the above would be prescribed. They describe, however, behaviour that can occur in practice. They are examples of misapplication.

A further problem for business organisations in setting objectives, and in attempting to achieve them, is the problem of balancing long-term potential against the requirements for short-term profit. Whilst long-term profitability is indisputably important, the effect of major investment decisions on annual profits from year to year must also be considered. Major projects may well take some time to realise their full potential, with a possible adverse effect on reported profits in early years. Also, if at a particular time projects are being financed by increased borrowing rather than, for example, from retained profits, the requirement to pay high interest charges to finance the capital investment in early years may have a particularly damaging effect on the profit remaining for shareholders and on measures of such profitability, especially earnings per share. This is important because the return to the shareholder is a combination of two factors: the return that will be earned on the investment in the form of dividends and the capital gain that will be made through the increasing value of the shares. Whilst it is true that the latter factor will be largely influenced by the long-term trend in earnings, it is not exclusively so. The way in which the earnings accrue to the shareholders will also have some influence on the share price. Also, total disregard for short-run considerations could create not only adverse effects on the price of the company's shares but also on its ability to raise funds (and thus exploit future investment opportunities), the cost of those funds, and its vulnerability to take-over. However, short-term profit pressures may lead to neglect of research, advertising and promotion, and training, and to postponed investment.

Finally, it should be recognised that there are differences between the approach to evaluation of projects by the firm and the approach that is adopted for public projects. Compared with the appraisal of private industry projects, the appraisal of public projects extends the scope of the analysis by considering the effect on the whole community, rather than the effects just on the individual firm, and in non-economic as well as economic terms. This is likely to impose constraints on the quest for profit, and also call for a wider definition of profit utility.

The well-being of various classes of people—shareholders, lenders, employees, customers and society at large—will be affected in different ways by the decisions of a firm. If the objective of the firm is profit maximisation for its shareholders, other groups may be adversely (or favourably) affected by such an objective. What about the effect on lenders, other companies, the community? Is it in the interests of lenders (and the community) that firms borrow money in periods of high inflation at the interest rate prevailing? Is it in the interests of other firms and ultimately the community, that a firm introduces a new product in direct competition to the products of other firms especially where spare capacity exists within the industry? Is it in the interests of the community that a firm makes employees redundant in an area of high unemployment?

It could be argued that firms should have more of a social conscience in setting objectives and taking decisions to achieve those objectives. In the absence of a social conscience, Government can take steps to encourage or even force firms to take decisions in the interests of outsiders, whose livelihood will not affect the existence of the firm. Grants may be used to encourage investment or subsidise employment, or legislation passed to restrict pollution or enforce product safety standards or safety at work, but there remain considerable areas of difference between apparent corporate well-being and community well-being.

A further point is that high profitability can be achieved by paying inadequate wages and avoiding costs by neglecting responsibilities to employees generally. This is likely to be less relevant where employees are unionised. Moreover paying higher wages and improving working conditions may increase worker productivity and ultimately profit.

Each business must define its own objectives, which ought to satisfy the needs of those groups whose co-operation makes the continued existence of the business possible (ie shareholders, management, employees, and customers), and must have regard to the needs of the community at large. Although long-term profit will be of primary importance other objectives may also have an influence and may call for some sacrifice of long-term profit. The need for stability for example recognises the importance of such things as risk and shorter-term patterns of earnings and thus is often somewhat in conflict with long-term profit. A balance is required.

Nevertheless, long-term profit, with allowance for attitude to risk, is likely to remain an important objective. If other objectives are broadly consistent with this, or do not have a significant influence in most cases, the ends outlined earlier remain rational. Decisions can be taken by computation if the means are also found to be rational. If, however, other objectives are conflicting and are also of significant importance, judgement and inspiration take over from decisions by computation and the detailed means will change.

11.5 MEANS RATIONALITY

On the assumption that long-term profit utility maximisation remains valid as an objective, are the means for achieving that objective, which were outlined earlier in this chapter, also rational and thus valid?

11.5.1 Objectives

Having determined an organisation's objectives, to be operational they must be stated in behavioural terms. There are three necessary elements of such a measure:

1 the particular attribute that is chosen as the measure (eg profit);
2 the yardstick, or scale, by which the attribute is measured (eg profit as a percentage of capital employed); and
3 the goal—the particular value on the scale which the firm seeks to attain (eg 20%).

The measure is not only necessary to enable judgement of progress towards objectives, but as a criterion for judging the acceptability of future alternative courses of action in the first place. No decisions can be taken regarding the future without some clear indication of what is to be regarded as acceptable, eg what is the minimum acceptable rate of return on capital investment? It may be that the criteria for judging the acceptability of alternative courses of action and the overall benchmark for judging progress may differ, ie it is possible to set as an overall objective a target which is difficult to attain but, at the same time for decision-making purposes, set a criterion of acceptability at a lower level.

Unfortunately a situation simply does not exist whereby there is a specified rate of interest at which desired transactions take place. A composite rate needs to be established, taking into account the cost of the separate sources of funds to the business and their part respectively in the capital mix. Taxation, inflation, risk and gearing will all be important considerations. A further consideration, once a weighted average cost of capital has been established, is the relationship that should exist between this cost of capital and the measure that should be used to judge the viability of an investment project. Are they one and the same? For example, a firm will invest in projects which do not make a direct contribution to profitability. Should the required return on earnings projects be increased to allow for this? A further question will be whether, and to what extent, the required return should be varied to reflect relative risk/uncertainty on individual projects.

11.5.2 All possible courses of action must be known.

The identification of possible future actions is dependent upon two things:

1 the recognition of a potential opportunity or problem;
2 the identification of possible ways of taking advantage of the opportunity or of solving the problem.

This also is no easy task. Decision situations do not begin life in a filing cabinet awaiting only the collection of information necessary for their evaluation. They must be created. If they do present themselves it is more likely to be a reaction to a problem rather than the awareness of an opportunity. Even then there is no guarantee that problems will be recognised; many situations may be allowed to continue because they are never questioned.

It is impractical to conduct a comprehensive search to identify all possible future actions. The firm will be in the position of trying to do its best to identify a reasonable range of possibilities that are open to it. The quality of investment decision-making is dependent not only upon the profitability of individual investments and upon the number of investments made, but also upon the mix of investments. In an ongoing business individual investments, even if profitable at the margin, may be insufficient collectively to provide for the total scale of resources required to operate the business.

Much depends upon how the process of identifying alternatives is undertaken. It is important that decisions regarding what resources should be acquired and how they should be used are not simply taken from time to time as and when the need arises. The emphasis should be on anticipating opportunities rather than reacting to problems. Whilst considerable difficulties will always be present in practice, the existence of a corporate planning framework should encourage and assist a firm to think ahead in order to identify problems and opportunities, and alternative ways of solving/taking advantage of them, but at the same time enable it to limit the range of possible alternative future courses of action for consideration.

Whether a sufficient number/mix of investments are made is not only dependent upon the number of investment proposals which are generated with profit potential but upon whether the profit potential of proposals is correctly identified, evaluated and realised.

11.5.3 Information concerning the effect of alternative courses of action must be available, identified, and expressed in a manner consistent with the means of expressing objectives.

Apart from a clear understanding of objectives, the assessment of viability is dependent upon the ability to identify the aspects of a business that will be affected by a decision, and to estimate what that effect will be. This involves not only correct forecasting but also the correct application of principles. Forecasting is not simply a question of estimating potential but of considering whether it is likely to be realised. The efficiency of management will make a considerable difference to the outcome of an investment, eg sales potential is not just dependent upon the potential size of the market and competition but on the ability of the firm to get a good product, set correct prices, at the right time, etc. This is very difficult to forecast.

Very often a special exercise will be required. The routine management accounting system, even if in the form of budgets and forecasts of the future, will often not provide information that is directly relevant to a particular decision, even if profit is the sole objective. The routine information system is based on certain general assumptions which may not be applicable in the specific case.

11.5.4 Information must be evaluated in such a way that a decision can be taken on the best alternative.

A model must be available for analysing the information relevant to a particular decision so that the expected outcome of alternatives can be assessed in relation to each other and in relation to the criterion of acceptability. The results of this evaluation must then be presented and communicated effectively to decision-takers.

Whilst certain general principles apply to all decision situations, the more complex the situation the more difficult they will be to apply. Also with capital investment decisions, further special aspects of evaluation apply and a variety of quantitative appraisal models are available and used. Their use should be determined by their appropriateness in relation to objectives sought. This in general should not present difficulties. However, a variety of different investment choice situations can arise, which dictate that a general model (eg: Discounted Cash Flow) should be used in a particular way in order that alternatives be correctly compared. This can cause difficulties. Indeed there has been, and continues to be, debate on the appropriate use of the discounted cash flow model in particular situations.

11.5.5 Decisions, once taken, must be successfully executed; potential must be realised.

Once a decision has been taken, management cannot simply sit back and expect things to turn out as planned. They must take active steps to try to ensure that events turn out as expected. Control needs to be exercised. Such control relates to the implementation and outcome of projects, and will endeavour to ensure as far as possible that targets are met in terms of events (ie things happen), timing (ie at the right time), and values (ie at the right cost or benefit).

Difficulty of application could be said to exist in as much as there are many different aspects to implementation and thus to control, especially in the larger and more complex projects. Some aspects are more controllable by the firm than others. It is not always possible to distinguish between errors of estimation that could have been avoided, (for example the overlooking or underestimating of critical variables), and less than expected results due to unforeseen environmental factors. Uncertainty is a fact of life; each project has a range of possible outcomes associated with it. Indeed if a range of possible outcomes is identified at the decision-making stage, even if subjective probabilities are attached to each, then any outcome within the (forecast) range is excused.

A further difficulty in exercising control over the outcome of projects is that it is sometimes difficult to separate out the effect of an investment. If a particular alternative course of action was chosen in preference to another, then despite the fact that it may be possible to identify the outcome of this course of action it cannot be known what would have happened if the other course of action had been taken instead. It may in any case be difficult to segregate operating costs and revenues associated with a particular investment.

There would thus appear to be significant difficulties in practice in carrying out the decision-making process suggested. Before reaching any firm conclusions it is appropriate to consider the nature of decisions.

11.6 THE NATURE OF DECISIONS

Decisions can be categorised in a number of different ways. For example in Chapter 8, the nature of decisions was looked at from the point of view of different events in relation to decision objects. Useful categories from the point of view of judging the relevance of the model (process) are:

1 According to the extent to which the decision situation is structured, which affects the ease with which alternatives and relevant variables can be identified.
2 According to the extent of choice that is available to the decision-taker, which affects the range and number of alternatives that need to be considered.
3 According to the extent to which relevant information for the decision can be quantified, which affects the nature of the analysis that will be carried out prior to making a decision.
4 According to the time period affected by the decision, which itself affects the other three categories above, viz structure, choice and quantification.

11.6.1 Structure

As far as structure is concerned, decision situations vary in the degree of difficulty of handling the choices. Simon suggested a distinction between 'programmed' and 'non-programmed' decisions, explaining this distinction as follows:

'Decisions are programmed to the extent that they are repetitive and routine, to the extent that a definite procedure has been worked out for handling them so that they don't have to be treated *de novo* each time they occur.... Decisions are non-programmed to the extent that they are novel, unstructured, and consequential. There is no cut-and-dried method of handling the problem because it hasn't arisen before, or because its precise nature and structure are elusive or complex, or because it is so important that it deserves a custom-tailored treatment.... By non-programmed I mean a response where the system has no specific procedure to deal with situations like the one at hand, but must fall back on whatever general capacity it has for intelligent, adaptive, problem-oriented action!'

The distinction between 'programmed' and 'non-programmed' or between 'structured' and 'unstructured' is not a simple dichotomy, but a whole continuum with highly structured decisions at one end and highly unstructured decisions at the other. The terms 'programmed' and 'non-programmed' are simply labels for the black and white of the range. In between the two extremes are decisions of all shades of grey.

The increasing availability of quantitative techniques has meant that more decisions have become structured. However, there is always a danger that the technique over-simplifies a situation, and thus it becomes unrealistic and leads to imperfect solutions. It is also possible that decisions can become more structured by breaking them down into separate parts and developing techniques for solving each part separately, eg the decision regarding the replenishment of stocks of raw materials involves questions of both when, and how many (and also from where) to buy. Given that cost minimisation is an important objective the question of when, and how many, can be answered separately on a regular basis by the use of quantitative models which provide a structure for the decision. The more a decision is structured the more that alternatives, and the type of information relevant to their analysis (ie the variables influencing it), will be clear.

11.6.2 Choice

Choice is a prerequisite of decision-making. However the nature of the choice and the extent of the alternatives available will depend upon the particular situation itself.

At one extreme a firm may have to decide whether to take action, if so how (there may be several alternative courses of action), and also when and where the decision is implemented eg the expansion of manufacturing capacity. At the other extreme the firm may have no choice as far as the 'whether' is concerned, eg given that a firm is manufacturing goods and selling from stock then it must have sufficient storage capacity. Also there may be no choice as to when and where, eg it may be required immediately at a particular location with no available outside storage as an alternative. The question may simply be as to how it is to be provided eg size and type of building.

A consideration of choice will lead to the identification of alternatives in a decision situation. The extent of the choice (and the ease of identification of alternatives, which is influenced by the structure of the decision) will influence the range and number of alternatives that have to be considered.

11.6.3 Quantification

As far as the information for the decision is concerned, while all decisions in business will have an impact on the business's future prosperity (however this is measured), situations vary in the extent to which the relevant variables are quantifiable.

Quantification will be possible where relevant variables in a decision situation impact fairly directly on some measurable unit. However, even then, much depends upon the uncertainty surrounding such a relationship and the ability to measure that uncertainty. Thus for example, it should be possible to estimate fairly reliably the cost of purchasing and installing a new machine, whereas it will be rather more difficult to estimate the increase in sales that may arise from a reduction in selling price. It will be impossible to quantify the effect of the appointment of a new managing director.

The extent to which reliable quantification is possible will affect the nature of the analysis that will be carried out prior to taking a decision. Reliability will depend upon the number of factors affected and the reliability of estimation of each. The ease of identification of relevant factors, which is affected by the structure of the decision will also be an influence.

11.6.4 Time period

Each of the above categories viz structure, choice, and quantification may be influenced by the time period affected by the decision.

The shorter the time period, the more repetitive and therefore more structured the situation is likely to be on average. This should lead to the easier identification of alternatives and of relevant information. The time period is also likely to influence the extent of the choice that is available, and both the number of variables affected by the decision and the extent to which they can be reasonably estimated. The shorter the time period the more limited the choice is likely to be, the fewer the variables affected, and the greater the degree of reliability in estimation. Evaluation will then be more straightforward, objectives more easily expressed in behavioural terms, and the solution will be more reliable. The reverse would be expected to be true of longer-term decisions. Short-term decisions will also be more easily implemented, in general, than longer-term decisions.

Thus some decisions are more structured than others, some with more choices than others, some more quantifiable than others, some shorter-term than others. If the result is that the necessary conditions for optimal decision-making can be achieved and thus a satisfactory analysis carried out, the decision becomes computational. The less these conditions can be met the more that judgement will be necessary. If, in addition, objectives are unclear, the decision becomes inspirational. Figure 11.1 shows the structure of decisions within the general model, summarising the factors considered in this section.

11.7 QUANTITATIVE DECISIONS AND THE ECONOMIC MODEL

Before passing further, and final, judgement on the prescriptive model it is important to recognise that the economic model as prescribed is designed for certain types of decision. The management accountant is essentially concerned with providing quantitative information to management. Thus he is concerned with the quantitative rather than the qualitative end of the decision continuum. Quantitative problems of choice include:

What to produce and sell	product mix adding/dropping products sell or process further
How much to produce and sell	quantity and pricing decisions economic batch/order quantities
Where/how to sell	selection of distribution channels selection of sales areas
Where/how to produce	optimal combination of men and machines machinery *v* labour choice between different machines flexible *v* specific equipment location of plant make or buy
Whether to produce and sell	suspending activities—closing down temporarily or permanently.

It is for these types of decision that the model may be prescribed. However, it is important to recognize that all decisions both quantitative and qualitative, will affect the achievement of profit objectives. The decision, for example, to appoint A or B as the next managing director is likely to have more far-reaching profit implications than the decision to produce or buy-in a particular component. Moreover, the quantitative and qualitative cannot be separated; they are interdependent. For example, the decision to appoint particular personnel may have a considerable influence on the potential and achievement on quantitative projects, and indeed on the quality of the information provided for quantitative decisions.

FIGURE 11.1 **The structure of a decision**

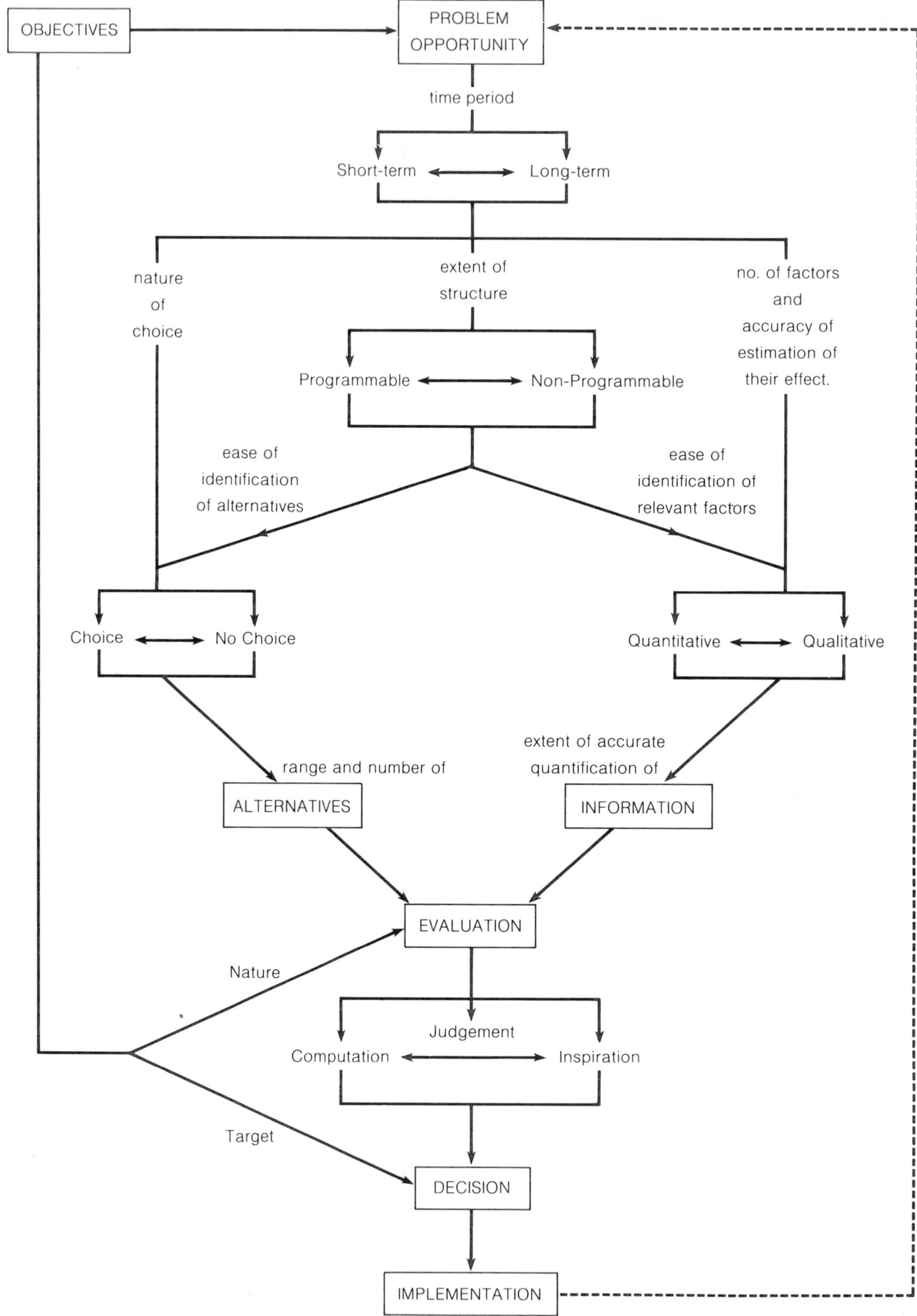

11.8 CONCLUSIONS

Despite narrowing the range of decisions for which the economic model prescribed may be suggested to be appropriate, all that has been said above would seem to call into question somewhat the usefulness (ie the descriptive validity) of the model.

However, the difficulties that exist do not invalidate the general model from the point of view of indicating the various elements of decisions. Rather they emphasise the importance of each stage of the model, the importance of behavioural factors in the process, and the need to exercise judgement in reaching a decision, rather than emphasis and reliance on computation alone. Thus recognition of the difficulties helps to emphasise the process of choosing, rather than simply the choice.

The process of choosing in practice (because of the difficulties that exist) has been described by Simon as one of 'bounded rationality' because in practice not only may objectives not be consistent (both corporate and individual) and thus trade-offs are involved, but also:

1. It is difficult to express objectives as behavioural goals.
2. Search tends to be problem orientated ie search takes place when a problem is recognised. If things are satisfactory there will be no search. In any case all possibilities cannot be known.
3. Individuals have limited capacity to identify and evaluate information, which is in any case not perfectly available. There is also a cost in gathering it which must be taken into account.
4. Once a choice is made successful implementation is never easy.

Whereas economic rationality has been based on a 'closed' decision model, 'bounded rationality' is more 'open'. The concept of bounded rationality, within which a decision-maker pursues satisficing choices in an open decision model is a more meaningful and useful perspective on the integrated process of decision-making.

However, the economic model is still valid as an ideal. None of the steps are completely invalidated in practice where bounded rationality will be the reality. It is important that judgement is exercised on the best possible information subject to possible constraints of time and cost in obtaining it. Trade-offs will often be required if more than one objective is pursued which make the decision-making process more complex. Bargaining and compromise take place and thus emphasis is placed on the social and political as well as the economic and technical. An awareness of the behavioural forces in an organisation become of consequence.

In a sense the importance of management accounting is lessened because computation is not supreme. In another sense it becomes especially important because figures should still be a primary motivator and there is particular scope for expertise in providing the best possible information (and guidance and interpretation) in order to prompt, make and control choices.

SUMMARY

A model of decision-making behaviour, which results in decisions by computation consistent with the business objective of long-term profit utility maximisation, was developed in the early part of this chapter. Whilst this provides a reasonable prescriptive model, if attention is focused on all stages of the process of choosing rather than simply the choice, it is important to recognise that other objectives may be valid, and that all stages of the process will be difficult in practice.

If an objective other than profit is pursued the nature of the computation will change but the general process should remain valid, as long as the objective is clear and measurable. If, however, objectives are unclear or conflicting, judgement and inspiration rather than computation are to the fore.

The degree of difficulty of the stages in the decision-making process will be influenced by the type of decision situation under consideration. Differences in the structure of decisions, in the extent of choice, in quantifiability, and in the time period affected will all impact on the process and the extent to which computation, and decisions based on such computation, is possible. As different stages of the process become difficult, computation again gives way to judgement and even inspiration. Simon's 'bounded rationality' applies. The process is constrained not only by the limited availability of information but by individual's experience, mental capacity and abilities.

Nevertheless, an attempt at computation should still be made wherever possible in order to provide a basis for exercising judgement. The fact that perfect information is not available does not invalidate the model; one can only do one's best with the information available. It is important that performance measurement systems do not get in the way; they should measure individual's performance in such a way that encourages decisions in the best interests of the business ie consistent with long-term objectives.

The Differential Costing Process

INTRODUCTION

Previous chapters have looked at decisions in different ways. Chapter 8 introduced the concept of different events in relation to decision objects and considered the influence that these events should have on routine information provision. Chapter 11 considered the nature of the evaluation that should be carried out depending upon structure, extent of choice, quantifiability and time period affected. This affects the extent and accuracy of computation, and is primarily influenced by the decision object itself. This chapter seeks to develop a framework for carrying out quantitative evaluation, whatever the object or event, and thus to provide computation. The extent to which computation can be carried out in practice, and the extent to which decisions can reasonably be based on computation, will vary. The context provided in the previous chapter should always be considered.

The emphasis in this chapter and in the rest of the section will be on the identification and evaluation of relevant information in decision-making situations. The other stages in the decision-making process, (ie, the identification of objectives and the establishment of criteria of acceptability; problem/opportunity generation with a range of alternatives; and the successful implementation of decisions), must also be borne in mind. It is assumed initially that information is available and that there are no obstacles to its identification, analysis and communication.

The chapter considers first the general principles governing relevant information for decision-making and then develops a framework for its analysis. The framework for analysis, and its illustration in the quantitative choice situations that follow, will concentrate on the measurement of the anticipated financial outcome of alternatives, with a view to selection of the most profitable. Although, as has been noted earlier, long-term profitability is unlikely to be the sole objective of a business, nevertheless it is likely to be very important, and therefore such measurement will always be necessary, even though it may not be the sole criterion of acceptability. Also, the general principles can be applied in the measurement of the effect of alternative courses of action on other objectives. Having developed a framework for analysis of decision-relevant information the chapter goes on to consider the difficulties associated with information availability, identification, analysis, and communication, and provides further illustrations of the concepts and difficulties.

12.1 DIFFERENTIAL COSTING

The process of identifying and evaluating relevant financial information for quantitative decision-making is called differential costing. The process is so named because it seeks to establish the difference in costs and revenues comparing one alternative with another. The underlying conceptual basis is the economic concept of marginal analysis, which is based upon the difference between one state of affairs against an alternative state of affairs.

Although it will be more difficult to identify and estimate relevant information in some situations than in others, there is no conceptual conflict between decisions which vary in this or any other respect. Thus despite the diversity of quantitative choice problems the basic approach is the same; the same general principles apply to the identification of relevant information. The test of relevance is that of avoidability. In making a choice between alternative courses of action, costs and benefits will be relevant if they are avoidable, depending upon which alternative is selected.

12.2 AVOIDABLE COSTS AND BENEFITS

In considering the relevance of information for decision-making, ie, its avoidability, the following distinctions are important:

1 It is necessary to look beyond the record of a business's past performance and to compare estimates of **future** costs and benefits. Whilst past performance may have some influence on future estimates, costs and benefits which have already occurred are not directly relevant as such; they are committed by past actions. The term 'sunk' has been applied by many to such costs. The term 'past' costs may also be used.

2 Estimates of future costs and benefits should be **economic** rather than accounting costs and benefits. Resources which have already been acquired, but not yet consumed, will be a future charge against profit from an accounting point of view. However, the amount paid for these resources is just as much a past cost from an economic point of view as is the cost of resources which have already been bought and consumed. Also, it is of no consequence whether or not the resources have been paid for or even yet received, as long as a contractual obligation exists. In all cases the cost is a past cost and, therefore, is irrelevant. However, the resources acquired may have a future value. The future economic cost of using such resources will depend upon what happens as a result, eg, if the resources would be replaced, then the replacement cost is the future economic cost.

3 Future economic costs and benefits will be relevant to a decision only to the extent to which they arise as a result of taking one of the courses of action under consideration. Such future costs and benefits are termed **uncommitted** as opposed to committed. Committed future economic costs and benefits are those that are totally unaffected by a particular decision, whichever alternative is chosen. This may be either because they will arise anyway as a result of other decisions concerning the future, or because they would not be incurred whichever alternative is accepted. This latter category would include, for example, the replacement cost of materials in stock in a situation where the usage of these materials would not lead to their replacement, (ie, only disposal alternatives are being considered), because no future use is anticipated which would justify incurring the replacement cost.

Thus relevant costs and benefits (the avoidable costs and benefits) for any decision are the **uncommitted future economic** costs and benefits.
Figure 12.1 demonstrates the concepts of costs and benefits.

FIGURE 12.1 **Concepts of costs and benefits for decision-making**

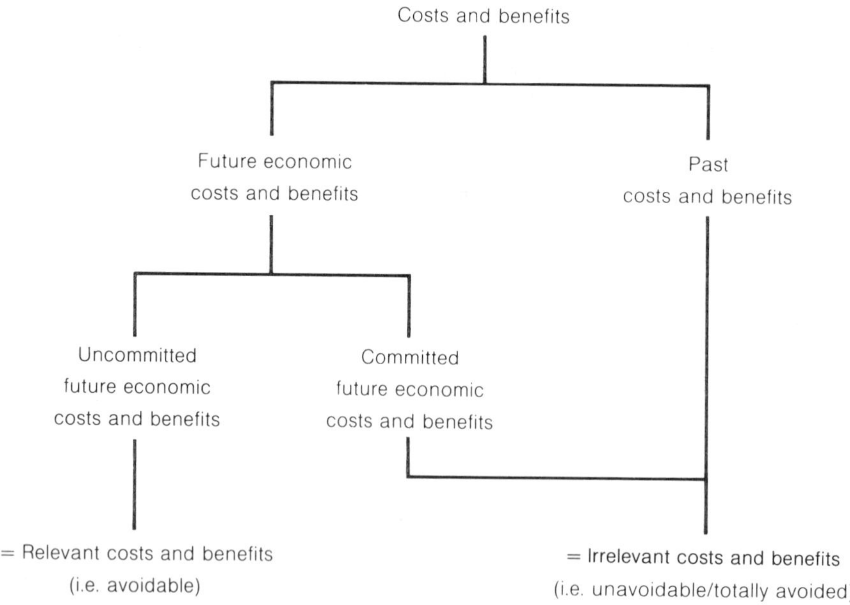

12.3 CONCEPTS IN ANALYSIS

Once avoidable costs and benefits have been identified in a decision situation, they need to be analysed in such a way that the result of taking particular courses of action can be correctly assessed and thus a choice made through comparison between alternatives. The avoidable costs and benefits that would arise as a result of taking a **particular** course of action can be termed **incremental** costs and benefits. In making a choice between alternatives, in addition to considering the costs and benefits which would arise from taking a particular course of action, one also has to consider those that would not now arise by not taking some other course of action. These become costs saved and benefits lost. Another term for such costs and benefits is **opportunity** costs and benefits. A cost saved is an opportunity benefit; a benefit lost is an opportunity cost.

Incremental and opportunity costs and benefits are thus two sides of the same coin, in that the incremental costs and benefits of selecting an alternative become the opportunity costs and benefits by not pursuing that alternative. It all depends on whether the alternative being considered is considered from the point of view of its selection or non-selection.

The comparison of one alternative with another identifies the **differential** costs and benefits. Figure 12.2 demonstrates the hierarchy of concepts in the analysis of relevant costs and benefits.

FIGURE 12.2 **Concepts in the analysis of decision-relevant costs and benefits**

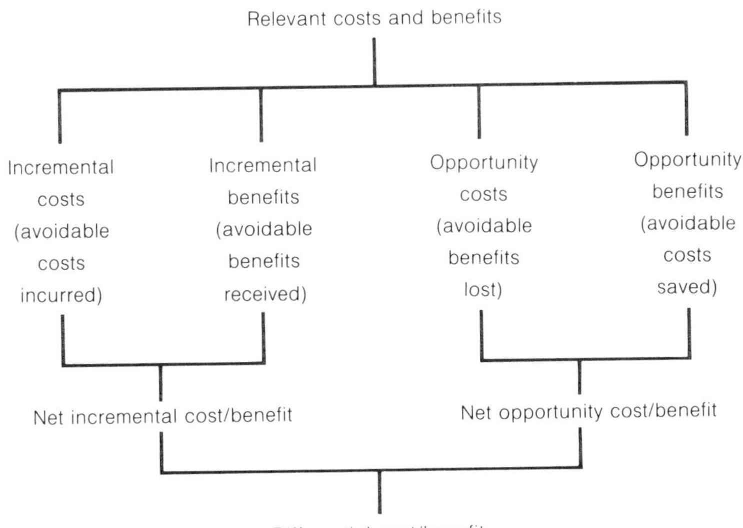

12.4 SUMMARY OF TERMS

The terms used in the identification and analysis of relevant costs and benefits are summarised as follows:

1 **Terminology of costs and benefits**

Past

Costs/benefits which have already occurred or where a contractual obligation exists, ie, committed by past actions (these are irrelevant, ie, **unavoidable**).

Future economic

Costs/benefits which have not yet occurred and where no contractual obligations exists.

Committed future economic

Future economic costs/benefits that would/would not occur, regardless of the decision under consideration (these are irrelevant, ie, **unavoidable/totally avoided**).

Uncommitted future economic

Future economic costs/benefits whose occurrence depends upon the choice of alternative in the situation under consideration (these are relevant, ie, **avoidable**).

2 **Terminology in analysis**

Incremental

Avoidable (ie, uncommitted future economic) costs/benefits that would be incurred/received by taking a particular course of action.

Opportunity

Avoidable (ie, uncommitted future economic) costs/benefits that would be saved/lost by not taking a particular course of action.

Differential
Incremental costs/benefits of taking a course of action, plus the opportunity cost (lost benefit)/ opportunity benefit (cost saved) of not taking an alternative course of action.

12.5 A FRAMEWORK FOR ANALYSIS

The first essential is to be clear about the decision alternatives; this will influence avoidable costs and benefits. It is then necessary to consider how the analysis of these alternatives is to be carried out. This requires the establishment of a base against which each alternative will be compared. The use of a consistent base is essential for correct evaluation. Finally, the avoidable costs and benefits are identified and analysed. This analysis is done in two stages: first, the avoidable costs and benefits of each alternative are compared with the base; second, alternatives are compared in order to identify differentials.

Thus there can be seen to be three major steps prior to the establishment of these differentials, which provide a useful framework for the analysis of all decision-making problems. These three steps can be called the ABC of decision-making as follows:

A is for Alternatives—clearly establish what the decision alternatives are;
B is for Base—select a suitable base against which each alternative is to be separately compared, ie, select the starting point for the analysis;
C is the Costs (and Benefits)—identify the avoidable costs and benefits, and for each alternative compare the incremental costs and benefits against the base;
D is for Differential—alternatives should be compared in order to identify the differential costs and benefits.

12.6 THE FRAMEWORK ILLUSTRATED

12.6.1 Problem

A company has some materials in stock which were bought for £350. Their current replacement cost is £400. However, their net saleable value would be only £200. The company has the opportunity to carry out a one-off job (Job 1), which would utilise these materials, yielding a revenue of £800. Additional costs (other than the cost of these materials) which would be charged to the job would be £710. This includes £190 apportionment of general administration overhead but all other additional costs are dependent upon fulfilling Job 1. Alternatively, the materials could be used as a substitute for other materials in another job (Job 2), which the company is carrying out. The materials replaced would have cost £300. These costs have been included in the evaluation of the viability of Job 2, which is expected to produce an additional net benefit of £550.

12.6.2 Alternatives

It must be assumed that all possible uses of the existing materials have been identified. There are therefore three alternatives:

1 Sell the existing materials and carry out Job 2, buying in the materials required.
2 Use the existing materials in Job 1 and carry out Job 2, buying in the materials required.
3 Use the existing materials in Job 2.

12.6.3 Base

There are several possible starting points for the analysis. The simplest may be to recognise the situation that exists, ie,

1 some materials already bought;
2 commitment to carry out Job 2 but it has to be decided which materials are to be used;
3 commitment to incur general administration costs.

This is the unavoidable position, as far as this decision is concerned.

12.6.4 Avoidable costs and benefits

It was established earlier that avoidable (and thus relevant) costs and benefits for decision-making are the uncommitted future economic costs and benefits. Past costs and benefits and committed future economic costs and benefits are irrelevant, as they are unavoidable or totally avoided. The relationships were demonstrated in Figure 12.1.

The £350 expenditure on the materials in stock is a past cost, because it has already been incurred and is thus irrelevant to the analysis. The £550 expected additional benefit is already committed, because the company has already undertaken to carry out the job, and is also therefore irrelevant. Whilst the precise amount of the benefit is uncertain until the job is completed, it is nevertheless irrelevant to the analysis. It is the cost of the materials to be used in the job which is avoidable.

All other costs and benefits are future economic costs and benefits if no other past commitments have already been made. This is arguable in the case of the £190 apportionment of general administration overhead. It could be that some or even all of this is a past cost, especially in the short-term. However, the argument is largely academic because, even if it is not yet a firm commitment, it could be regarded as a future cost which will occur in the future regardless of the decision at hand, ie, it will be committed by other decisions of the company.

The only remaining question concerns the £400 replacement cost of materials in stock. If there is no more than one opportunity to use these materials generating an incremental benefit (excluding any cost for the materials) in excess of £400, then the replacement cost is totally avoided, as replacement would not be considered. As alternatives 1 and 3 would not justify replacement, the cost is irrelevant. If more than one opportunity did exist to use these materials profitably, then the replacement cost would become an avoidable cost. However, the three possible courses of action in the above analysis would not then have been alternatives, ie, they would not have been mutually exclusive. Three quite separate decisions could be considered—the alternative in each case would be to do nothing (ie, not to replace the materials).

All other costs and benefits are uncommitted future economic costs and benefits, ie, they are all avoidable depending upon the alternative selected.

12.6.5 Analysis

The analysis of the avoidable costs and benefits would be carried out by comparing the incremental costs and benefits of each alternative against the base assumed earlier, as follows:

		Alternatives		
		1	2	3
Benefits				
	Sale of existing materials	£200	—	—
	Revenue from Job 1	—	£800	—
Costs				
	Costs of Job 1	—	(£520)	—
	Purchase of materials for Job 2	(£300)	(£300)	—
Net benefit/(cost)		(£100)	(£20)	—

The figures under each alternative are the incremental costs and benefits because the base simply recognises the situation that already exists. For example, if alternative 2 (using the existing materials on Job 1 and buying additional materials for Job 2) is being considered, then the £300 cost of materials for Job 2 is one of the incremental costs. The other incremental effects are the incremental benefit of £800 and the incremental cost of £520 of accepting Job 1. Compared with the base assumed (doing nothing) this is the effect of choosing this alternative. Benefits lost and costs saved, ie, opportunity costs and benefits, only arise when alternatives are compared with each other; it is only then that non-selection is considered.

On the face of it, it appears that no future action is worth while. However, it must be realised that something must be done; it is impossible to do nothing. The reason that none of the actions looks attractive is simply because a commitment has already been made to carry out Job 2, which will be profitable. The question is simply how to carry it out, which will influence what happens to the existing materials.

The comparison of one alternative with another identifies the differential costs and benefits. Alternative 3 is preferred because the cost saving from not having to purchase materials is greater than the net benefit that can be obtained from using the materials in the other alternatives.
Comparing alternative 3 with alternative 1:

Incremental costs and benefits	Nil	
Opportunity costs and benefits:		
Opportunity cost	£200	(Loss of revenue from not selling existing materials.)
Opportunity benefit	£300	(Cost saving from not having to purchase materials for Job 2.)
Net opportunity benefit	£100	
Differential benefit	£100	

Alternative 3 is preferred because the cost saving from not having to purchase materials is greater than the benefit that can be obtained from selling the existing materials. Compared with alternative 1, there is a differential benefit of £100 (no incremental cost or benefit, plus an opportunity benefit of £100), ie, the £300 cost saving is greater than the £200 that would be lost by not selling the existing materials.
Comparing alternative 3 with alternative 2:

Incremental costs and benefits	Nil	
Opportunity costs and benefits:		
Opportunity cost	£280	(Loss of net benefit from not carrying out Job 1 ie, £800–£520.)
Opportunity benefit	£300	(Cost saving from not having to purchase materials for Job 2.)
Net opportunity benefit	£20	
Differential benefit	£20	

Alternative 3 is again preferred because the cost saving from not having to purchase materials is greater than the net benefit from using the existing materials in Job 1. Compared with alternative 2, there is a differential benefit of £20 (no incremental cost or benefit, plus an opportunity benefit of £20).

Comparing alternatives 1 and 2, alternative 2 would be preferred. There is a differential benefit of £80 ie, the incremental benefit from carrying out Job 1, £280, exceeds the proceeds from selling the existing materials, £200. The cost of materials for Job 2 is common to both alternatives.

12.7 ALTERNATIVE ANALYSIS

Several alternative analyses are possible, depending upon the base chosen. Instead of simply recognising the situation that already exists, assumptions could be made in the base about future allocation of resources. This can be done as long as it is clear that the base adopted represents a viable course of action. This will usually mean that opportunity costs and benefits will be built into the initial analysis because incremental costs and benefits will generally be included in the base. These become opportunity costs and benefits when another course of action is considered instead.

What if one of the three alternatives is used as the base in our example? Alternative 3 could have become the base, as there is already a commitment to carry out Job 2; it is in any case profitable, and using the existing materials will involve no incremental cost. The initial analysis in fact would be identical to that already carried out, without a column for alternative 3, as no incremental costs and benefits arise by adopting this alternative and thus no opportunity costs and benefits arise when other alternatives are compared with it.

A further possibility would have been to use alternative 1 as the base, as this also is a worthwhile action per se. The base would now assume that Job 2 is carried out using materials costing £300 and that existing materials are sold. The analysis of other alternatives would be as follows:

	Alternative 2 (v Alternative 1)	Alternative 3 (v Alternative 1)
Incremental benefit:		
Revenue from Job 1	£800	—
Incremental cost:		
Costs for Job 1	(£520)	—
Opportunity benefit:		
Cost saving by not having to purchase materials for Job 2	—	£300
Opportunity cost:		
Loss of revenue from not selling existing materials	(£200)	(£200)
Net benefit	£80	£100

The figures in each column are the incremental costs and benefits of alternatives 2 and 3 respectively compared with the base (alternative 1). The analysis includes opportunity costs and benefits because assumptions have been made about future actions in the base. The result, in absolute terms, of adopting each alternative is thus changed because the base is changed.

If, for example, alternative 2 were selected, Job 1 would be undertaken, yielding an incremental benefit of £280. This, however, would be instead of selling the materials for £200. This is an opportunity cost. Job 2 would be unaffected. Net benefit would thus be £80. If alternative 3 were selected, £300 would be saved, an opportunity benefit, but £200 would again be lost by not now being able to sell the existing materials. Net benefit would thus be £100. The differential between alternatives is unchanged. Alternative 3 would be chosen, because it would produce a net benefit of £20, when compared with the next best alternative—alternative 2 (£100 compared with £80 from the above analysis).

12.8 OPPORTUNITY COSTS AND BENEFITS

It has been explained, and demonstrated, that opportunity costs and benefits arise from the comparison of alternatives. The opportunity cost (or benefit) of a particular course of action is the benefit that would be forgone (or the cost that would be saved) by not taking some alternative course of action. The opportunity costs or benefits of a particular course of action depend entirely upon what it is being compared against. Ultimately if the best alternative is selected there will be a net benefit.

In this example, however you look at it, using the existing materials in Job 2 is the best alternative, with a net benefit of £20. This can only be determined after the analysis has been carried out. It is the result of taking the best action compared with the next best alternative. If the possibility now arose of using the existing materials in yet another alternative way, what then would be the opportunity cost? Is it possible to specify the opportunity cost?

Following the analysis carried out already, it is certainly possible to specify the best alternative which would then become the next best alternative if a more attractive proposal appeared. But what is the opportunity cost if the alternative of using the existing materials in Job 2 is forgone? According to the first analysis the opportunity cost is zero but from the second analysis it is £100. Thus it depends on what is being used as the base point for the analysis. The opportunity cost of the existing materials on their own, ie, the incremental benefit required to justify a further potential use that may be found for the materials, is £300, ie, the cost saving by their use in Job 2. This would be shown by an analysis that starts from a base which not only recognises the situation that already exists but in addition assumes that materials costing £300 would be used in Job 2. This is summarised as follows:

	Alternative 1	Alternative 2	Alternative 3
Benefits	£200	£800	£300
Costs	—	(£520)	—
Net benefit	£200	£280	£300

Again differentials are unchanged.

The point being made is that great care needs to be exercised in the application of the concept of opportunity cost, as it is dependent upon the alternatives being considered and the base case.

A further point that should be noted is that, as opportunity costs and benefits arise from a comparison of alternatives, they are never recorded in the cost accounting system. The cost accounting system records events that occur; opportunity costs and benefits arise from a consideration of events that will not. Their inclusion in an exercise to establish 'cost' is an example of an 'inputed cost' (or benefit).

12.9 CHOICE OF BASE

It has been demonstrated that the base adopted has an important effect on the mechanics of the analysis but not on the alternative that should be chosen. If the situation as it exists is adopted, the initial analysis will be incremental. The differential analysis of alternatives incorporates the comparison of incremental and opportunity costs and benefits. If instead the base includes an avoidable future action, the initial analysis is not only incremental but also includes the opportunity costs and benefits of the base situation.

It must be stressed again that such a base should not be adopted unless it is, on the basis of the information available, a viable alternative. In any case it should be considered whether the base chosen affects the ease of analysis. In general the adoption of an uncommitted base—and thus the inclusion of only incremental costs and benefits in the initial analysis—is likely to be easier. No opportunity costs and benefits arise at this stage.

Whatever base is chosen it is vital for correct analysis that all alternatives are then compared consistently against this base. Again confusion and potential for error are likely to be lessened if such a base simply recognises the situation that already exists.

Self-assessment question 12.1

The Aldergrove Co Ltd has in stock some materials of type W which had cost £50,000 but are now obsolete and have a scrap value of only £14,000.

Apart from selling the materials for scrap there are only two alternative uses for them:

Alternative 1

Conversion and sale as specialist electronic equipment for the 'Do It Yourself' market. Details of the extra work and materials needed are:

Material X	400 units
Material Y	1,000 units
Direct labour	10,000 hours
Extra selling and delivery expenses	£18,000
Extra magazine advertising	£12,000

Conversion would produce 900 units of the saleable product and these would then be sold for £200 per unit.

Material X is already in stock and is widely used within the firm. Although present stocks, together with orders already planned, will be sufficient to facilitate normal activity, any extra usage by this alternative will require an immediate order for replacement of the materials used.

Material Y is also currently in stock and it is no longer possible to obtain any further supplies. Material Y is highly sought after, and at present it is used in an extremely popular combined cassette deck/tuner/amplifier made by Aldergrove and which has a sales price of £260 per unit and total variable costs (excluding material Y) of £140 per unit. Each model of the cassette deck/tuner/amplifier produced uses 4 units of material Y. Current stocks of Y are insufficient to meet in full the demand for the tuning device. The shortage of material Y is the only effective constraint on supplying the demand for the amplifier.

The various market and book values per unit of X and Y are:

	X	Y
	£	£
Book value—per unit	100	10
Realisable value—per unit	85	18
Replacement cost—per unit	90	—

Alternative II

Adaptation for use as a substitute for sub-assembly 149B which is regularly used within the firm. Details of the extra work and materials needed are:

Material Z	1,000 units
Direct labour	8,000 hours

Normally, 1,200 units of sub-assembly 149B are used per quarter at a price of £600 each. The adaptation of material W would reduce the quantity of 149B purchased outside the firm to 900 units for the next quarter only. However, due to the reduction in volume of the quantity purchased some discount would be lost and the price of those purchased from outside would increase to £700 per unit for that quarter.

Material Z is not available externally but is manufactured within Aldergrove Ltd. The 1,000 units required would be produced as extra production and are not available from stocks. The standard cost and normal book value of Z is:

Material Z—Standard cost

	Per unit
	£
Direct labour—3 hours	9.00
Raw materials	7.00
Variable overhead, 3 hours @ £2	6.00
Fixed overhead, 3 hours @ £3	9.00
	31.00

The standard cost excludes the overtime premium for labour and if produced in overtime the actual labour cost would, therefore, be £3 per unit higher.

Aldergrove Ltd have entered into a long-term contract and the raw material cost of £7.00 is the actual figure which would be paid for the materials required to produce one unit of Z.

In all cases the work required in Alternatives I and II would take place as additional work and hence will cause overtime to be worked.

The usual overhead recovery rates for production are

Variable overhead	£2 per direct labour hour
Fixed overhead	£3 per direct labour hour

These recovery rates are accurate and based on full normal capacity.

Labour costs are normally £3 per hour but the overtime premium is a further £1 per hour.

Required:

(a) Prepare suitable statements which indicate to Aldergrove Ltd whether the stocks of material W should be:

(i) sold;

(ii) converted—Alternative I; or

(iii) adapted—Alternative II.

State clearly which alternative is preferable.

(b) The production manager is confused by the figures of 'cost' attributed to materials X, Y, and Z in the statements you have produced in **(a)** above. Briefly explain why, for the purposes of the current decision, you have measured the cost or 'value' of materials X, Y and Z in the manner you have.

(*ACCA, Management Accounting, June 1979*)

Answers on p 534

Self-assessment question 12.2

(a) Write short notes on the uses of three of the following:
Marginal cost
Average variable cost
Imputed cost
Differential cost

(b) 'It is frequently claimed that opportunity cost is the relevant concept to employ for decision-making purposes and yet it seldom features in cost accounting systems.' Discuss.

(*ACCA, Management Accounting, December 1985*)

Answers on p 536

12.10 DIFFICULTIES AND LIMITATIONS OF ANALYSIS

The principles governing the identification of relevant information for decision-making, and the framework developed for its analysis, have so far been put forward on the assumption that information is available and that there are no barriers to its identification, analysis and communication. A clear understanding of principles is vital and the framework helps in information identification, analysis and communication, especially because the framework put forward encourages the clear identification of alternatives and the use of a consistent base which assists the application of principles.

Difficulties, however, remain. In Chapter 11 the problems at the 'information' stage of the decision-making process were outlined. These will now be considered further under four headings:

1 Availability of, and ability to identify and analyse, information.
2 Presentation and communication of information.
3 Conflict between decision data and control data.
4 Longer-term consequences.

12.10.1 Availability of, and ability to identify and analyse, information

Even if it is clear what the alternatives are, very often a special exercise will be required, involving additional work and calling for considerable powers of analysis and estimation. There may of course be situations where the information provided by the accounting system provides a reasonable basis for estimating relevant information for a particular decision, especially for certain short-term decisions where a marginal costing system is in operation. The distinguishing feature of marginal costing, that was noted in earlier chapters, is of course the classification of costs by behaviour, ie, fixed and variable costs.

However, it was recognised in Chapter 3 that the behaviour of costs as a result of changes in activity depends not only upon the nature of the expense but also upon such factors as:

the time period under consideration
the nature of the firm's activities
management policy
whether capacity remains fixed
the size of the increase/decrease in activity
the level of activity
efficiency, productivity, motivation, learning
economies of scale
the attributability of costs.

The concepts of fixed costs, and of variable costs which respond to changes in activity, as used in marginal costing, can only be sustained given assumptions about the above factors, particularly:

short-run time period, ie, one year
fixed capacity
limited range of activity levels
constant efficiency.

Even if the above conditions were valid in a particular situation it must still be recognised that cost behaviour is rather more subtle than the simple fixed/variable dichotomy. It is still an over-simplification of reality because:

1 Whilst some costs may be proportionately variable, it may not be directly in response to units of output but in response, for example, to number of salesmen's calls, number of purchase orders.
2 Product costs depend to some extent upon an arbitrary apportionment of overheads.
3 Some costs have both fixed and variable elements and thus accuracy depends upon the ability to identify the underlying behaviour patterns.

There is no doubt that management (including accounting management) approximate decision data by using information reported by the routine accounting information system, eg, for certain short-term decisions (and also some capital investment decisions) the incremental costs are based on the summation of average variable cost (assumed to be constant over the affected output range). However, this information should be used with caution. Information generated by the routine reporting system should only be used for decisions where the same conditions apply and where it is felt unnecessary and/or impossible to be more precise. It must always be remembered that they are general in nature, are based on an established situation, are frequently historic, and are not calculated to provide the information required for a particular decision. Very often, therefore, a special exercise should be undertaken. However, the requirements for special analysis should be reduced, the more flexible and comprehensive the routine information provision. Chapter 8 provided a framework for decision-centred routine information provision. Decisions should also be taken within an overall planning framework.

Thus, in decision making, there is no such thing as a fixed cost or a variable cost per se, but only in the context of a particular decision. One problem therefore is identifying those aspects of the business that will be affected; it is essential to consider all possible direct consequences of a decision, however remote.

Having determined those aspects of the business that will be affected by a decision, an equally important and difficult task is concerned with placing a value upon them. Unfortunately accountancy gives a spurious precision to decision data. Apart from the qualitative aspects of decisions (at times the effect of a decision, on a firm's workforce and customers particularly, will be impossible to quantify), it is important to recognise that uncertainty of quantitative estimates is a fact of business life. Accountants are increasingly becoming aware of the importance of and potential for introducing some form of risk analysis into the estimation of future events. If nothing else they should at least be mindful of the key variables and assumptions in a decision situation and be aware of the sensitivity of the analysis to changes in these variables and assumptions.

12.10.2 Presentation and communication of information

The results and conclusions of the exercise must be clearly presented and communicated to management so that they are in the best possible position to take a decision. In addition to providing figures it is important to ensure that the assumptions underlying the figures are known and clearly communicated and understood because, whatever the figures, judgement is always necessary. It will also have an influence on the identification of opportunities and problems. To quote from a publication of the Institute of Chartered Accountants over forty years ago ('Developments in Cost Accounting', 1947):

'A cost can only be a convention, and the expression 'an accurate cost' can have meaning only within the particular convention chosen as appropriate to the purpose for which the cost is required . . . If those whose task it is to prepare costs do so with a different notion as to the use to be made of them from those who in fact make use of them, then the costs may not only be useless but positively harmful'.

The lack of rules in cost and management accounting render communication essential.

12.10.3 Conflict between decision data and control data

The third problem is the potential conflict between decision data and control data. The cost accounting system analyses the acquisition and use of resources in detail and on a routine basis. Clearly the analysis is influenced by the decisions that are taken by the firm concerning the acquisition and allocation of resources. But equally, as has been noted in 12.10.1. above, decisions made about the acquisition and allocation of resources may be influenced by the analysis provided in the routine management accounts prior to the decision; the routine analysis provides a prompt, suggesting decisions that should be taken. Again it should be stressed that this analysis should only be used as a basis for the decision if considered relevant; it should never be automatically so.

However, further than this, it is important to recognise that decisions may be influenced by the way in which management anticipate that information will be provided in the routine information system as a consequence of the decision. The costs appropriate for a particular decision may not be reflected in subsequently reported results, particularly where absorption costing systems and performance measurement by profit or investment centre are employed. Managers will not be encouraged to take decisions the outcome of which is not reflected in the appraisal of their performance.

Thus it is important to recognise that the routine reporting system will influence:

(a) the information that *may* be used in making decisions;
(b) the information that *will* be provided once decisions have been taken.

It is possible of course that the routine information system provides the right information for a particular decision, that the correct decision is taken, and that the feedback provided is consistent with the basis for the decision. However, other situations are possible:

(i) Information may be inappropriate, but used for convenience, or through ignorance or misunderstanding.

(ii) Information may be inappropriate, but used because of the way the outcome will be measured. For example, a product line may be discontinued in order to avoid a fully absorbed loss, and thus improve return on capital employed (the measure used, let us assume, for judging managerial performance), despite the fact that the product was making a contribution to fixed costs. This can also occur in a negative way. For example, divisional management may not put forward proposals for modernisation of plant despite an anticipated discounted cash flow return in excess of the company's cost of capital, because average return on capital employed would be adversely affected. This may arise especially if existing plant is fully depreciated and does not appear in the capital base.

(iii) Information may be inappropriate, the decision taken correctly based on relevant costs, but lead to dissatisfaction when the outcome of the decision is reported on a different basis. For example, sales expansion which leads to increased contribution, but which causes greater apportionment of fixed overhead to be made against the particular product(s).

(i) and (ii) result in a lack of goal congruence ie, decisions taken which will not be in the best interests of the business. (iii) results in a lack of incentive with equally damaging consequences.

Whilst it is clearly impossible for the information system to be all things to all people, in all situations, it is vitally important that the above considerations are borne in mind when the design of information systems and performance appraisal methods is considered. Whilst differential costing should always be pursued, it cannot be divorced from the routine information system.

The task, therefore, is not simply to preach the doctrine of differential costing, but to encourage its usage by adopting reporting procedures which are as consistent as possible with economic reality. It is essential that decisions are taken in the best interests of the firm as a whole based on relevant costs.

12.10.4 Longer-term consequences

There is a danger of ignoring the longer-term consequences of decisions. Whilst the theory of differential costing should always be applied, it is easy to make the assumption that certain costs will be unaffected, even in capital investment decisions. This must always be seriously questioned. Whilst one decision may appear to have a very marginal effect, several such decisions can soon have a considerable cumulative effect. Also, if the situation is likely to be repeated, whilst not necessarily affecting the immediate decision the viability of taking on such business on a long-term basis is an important consideration. One possible result of considering longer-term consequences is that it may at least indicate other alternatives that should be considered in the long-term. The flexible and comprehensive framework suggested in Chapter 8 recognises such consequences.

12.11 THE DIFFICULTIES ILLUSTRATED

12.11.1 Problem

Polyplastics Ltd., maker of a variety of plastic products, has a large amount of unutilised facilities due to a decline in demand. It has been approached to see if it would be prepared to manufacture 300,000 serving trays for use in hospitals at a price of £1.20 per tray.

The variable cost of producing a tray is expected to be £1.30 but as the company's fixed costs, previously averaging £1.00 per unit, will now be spread over twice as much volume the managing director argues that the loss of 10p per tray on variable costs will be more than outweighed by the gain of 50p per unit from spreading the fixed costs. He therefore believes the order should be accepted.

12.11.2 Solution

There is undoubtedly a logic, albeit misguided, about the managing director's argument.

However, you explain to the managing director that it is important for him:

1 to distinguish clearly the alternatives open to him (ie, whether to carry on as at present with surplus capacity, or whether to take on additional business);
2 to decide on a suitable base against which to compare alternatives (ie, existing situation of surplus capacity);
3 to separate clearly those costs that will be affected by the decision (ie, those costs that will vary between alternatives and the base used) and decide what the effect will be.

The costs affected will be the variable costs of producing additional trays. The company's fixed costs, if they are genuinely fixed, will remain unchanged. The only effect of taking on additional business would be a transfer of fixed costs from one part of the information system to another. There certainly is no net gain. In fact if total (absorption) costing was adopted, a figure of £1.80 would be used (£1.30 + £0.50). This additional £0.50 is offset by the cost 'saving' of £0.50 elsewhere. The real increase in cost is, therefore, £1.30, which is £0.10 greater than the proposed selling price, clearly an uneconomic proposition.

However, is it as simple as that? Other questions that may be asked are:

Is the estimate of £1.30 based on routine classifications of cost or has a special exercise been undertaken?

Have the possible consequences of a doubling of output been properly considered?

Is this a one-off or will the order be repeated?

If the order will be repeated what effect will this have on capacity requirements and provision of back-up services?

Would this additional business have any effect on existing sales or is it entirely separate?

Are there alternative uses of the spare capacity?

12.11.3 Conclusions

1 It is important to establish the right approach to such situations, ie, consideration of alternatives, choice of base, identification of relevant costs.

2 In adopting such an approach:

(a) the relevance of existing reported data should always be questioned (whether produced by an absorption or a marginal costing system);

(b) it is important to consider how best to present information to management and to ensure that it is effectively communicated;

(c) one should consider whether the right approach is encouraged by the routine information system:

(i) by the information it provides prior to a decision;

(ii) by the feedback it provides after a decision. For example, if the price was £1.50 per tray, how would the product manager react if he knew that he would be charged £1.80 per tray.

(d) the potential longer-term consequences must be adequately considered.

Self-assessment question 12.3

(As with self-assessment question 12.1, the following is a past question from the ACCA Management Accounting examination paper and is again typical. Students should use the question as a basis for considering and applying all aspects covered in the chapter.)

The Anglia Company undertakes civil engineering contracts in East Anglia. Based upon Norwich, the basis of the organisation's operations is to send a project manager and plant to the site of the contracts. The manager recruits any labour required locally and arranges for Head Office to supply materials used in the contract.

Some time ago the company tendered successfully for two contracts which have now become mutually exclusive. It is currently considering which of these to accept. Both jobs would last for twelve months and there appears to be no possibility of any other suitable projects arising in the area.

The following information about the contracts is available:

	Job	
	Great Yarmouth	**Lowestoft**
	£'000s	*£'000s*
Contract price	85	90
Penalty payment (this is a condition of the tender, if offered the contract and not accepting it)	8	4
Materials Required		
In store (at cost)	10	12
Contracted for	—	18
To be ordered (at current cost)	20	17
Labour Required		
Project manager: salary	5	5
travel, lodgings, etc	2	2
Local recruitment	35	28
Head Office		
Plant depreciation	3	4
Interest on plant	1	1
General administration	4	4

Notes on this information are as follows:

1 The materials that would be used on the Great Yarmouth job have increased in money value from their purchase cost by 50%. Although the Anglia Company does not expect to be able to use these materials if they are not required for the Great Yarmouth contract, they are in common use in the industry and thus they could be resold. However, transportation and other selling costs would reduce the cash inflow from the sale of these materials by 20%.

The materials required for the Lowestoft job are fairly specific to the Anglia Company's uses. They have no resale value apart from scrap, which is 5% of their cost, costs of transport, etc being paid by the scrap merchant. However, it is probable that these materials could be used by the organisation next year in substitution for a different material normally costing the company 10% less than the cost of the materials to be used on the Lowestoft contract.

2 Local labour can be hired as and when required.

3 Plant is depreciated by Head Office on a straight line basis. The item of depreciation expense on plant used by the Great Yarmouth job is lower than on the Lowestoft contract as less plant would be used. Head Office would be able to sub-contract out the plant not required on the Great Yarmouth job for £1,000 per annum. The interest charged on the plant has been notionally calculated for book-keeping purposes.

4 Head Office expenses are expected to be fixed at £10,000 during the year whatever number of contracts are undertaken. These expenses do not include the cost of the organisation's project managers who were given five year contracts last year.

Required:

(a) Present the data to management in a form which will assist them in their decision as to which job to undertake. Provide notes to show the principles which you have used in the selection of your data and support any calculations made.

(b) Comment on the appropriateness of the approach used in your analysis.

(*ACCA, Management Accounting, June 1977*)

Answers on p 536

SUMMARY

The chapter provides a clear and logical framework of concepts which can be applied in the establishment of decision-relevant costs and benefits. The relationship between concepts has been put in a hierarchical structure and definitions have been presented. Decision relevant costs and benefits are those that may be avoided depending upon the course of action selected. Concepts of incremental costs and benefits, opportunity costs and benefits, and differential costs and benefits arise.

A framework has also been developed in this chapter for the analysis of decision relevant costs and benefits. Such a framework, and indeed structures of decision relevant costs and benefits also, are lacking in management accounting literature. Inconsistent, and as a result confusing, terminology also abounds.

A simple example was used to illustrate the concepts of avoidability and the framework for analysis. With such a straightforward example the approach may appear unnecessary. However, in situations with many alternatives and costs involved, a clear, logical and rigorous structure with precise terminology becomes critical. It is essential to clearly identify what the alternatives are. How one sees the alternatives influences relevant costs and benefits. Without a framework for analysis there may be inconsistencies.

However, various difficulties remain and have been identified in the chapter. It is important to recognise and as far as possible minimise such difficulties so that the best possible analysis can be carried out and thus better decisions taken.

No further exercises are provided for this chapter's material. Chapter 13 examines a series of different decision-making situations where the principles covered in this chapter will be applied.

Short-Term Decision-Making—Problem Situations

INTRODUCTION

Decisions fall into two basic categories: 'accept or reject' decisions and 'ranking' decisions. Accept or reject decisions arise when a firm is considering a particular opportunity, acceptance of which will not affect decisions on other projects that are expected to become available ie the alternative is to do nothing. Ranking decisions involve choosing between two or more competing opportunities, and generally result from either mutual exclusivity between opportunities which arise when different means of achieving the same or similar ends are being considered, or the existence of scarce resources where a business has insufficient supplies of one or more of its resources (eg labour, materials, space, machine capacity) to accept all available opportunities that are expected to be profitable. The former situation may be termed 'output mutual exclusivity', and the latter 'input mutual exclusivity.'

Simple accept/reject decisions are rare unless 'doing nothing' is interpreted to mean 'staying as you are.' In such situations the analysis may be relatively straightforward if the changes from the existing situation can be easily identified. A variety of short-term decision situations which fall into the 'accept/reject' or 'output mutual exclusivity' categories will be described and illustrated in this chapter. 'Input mutual exclusivity' situations, arising from the existence of scarce resources, will be considered in Chapter 14. The decision situations examined and illustrated will utilise the principles and framework established in the previous chapter.

13.1 PROBLEM SITUATIONS

In Chapter 11 the different types of quantitative decision-making situations were outlined. The different types are:

What to produce and sell	product mix
	adding/dropping products
	sell or process further
How much to produce and sell	quantity and pricing decisions
	economic batch/order quantities
Where/how to sell	selection of distribution channels
	selection of sales areas
Where/how to produce	optimal combination of men and machines
	machinery *v* labour
	choice between different machines
	flexible *v* specific equipment
	location of plant
	make or buy
Whether to produce and sell	suspending activities—closing
	down temporarily or permanently

The above groupings by type provide a structure for the consideration of decision-making situations that follow. Self-assessment questions are used to enable the reader to attempt to apply general principles to a variety of situations. The questions are predominantly taken from past ACCA Management Accounting examinations.

13.2 WHAT TO PRODUCE AND SELL

The choice between alternative products or activities, and the determination of the optimum product mix, will be considered in the context of a limitation of available resources, which is the subject of Chapter 14.

Many new products will involve capital expenditure, increased working capital requirements, and start-up and launch costs. Evaluation will be over a long-term horizon. At the other extreme the opportunity may occur to obtain additional one-off business which will utilise spare capacity in the short-term. Such a situation is a common examination question scenario requiring the identification of incremental revenue and operating costs. Self-assessment question 13.1 provides an illustration.

Self-assessment question 13.1

A small contractor has been asked to quote for a contract which is larger than he would normally consider. The contractor would like to obtain the job as he does have surplus capacity.

The estimating and design department has spent 200 hours in preparing drawings and the following cost estimate:

Cost Estimate			£
Direct materials:			
3,000 units of X at £10 (original cost)		—see note 1	30,000
100 units of Y (charged out using FIFO)		—see note 2	
50 units at £100	£5,000		
50 units at £125	£6,250		
			11,250
Direct material to be bought in:		—see note 3	12,000
Direct labour:			
—Skilled staff		—see note 4	
2,720 hours at £5 per hour			13,600
—Trainees		—see note 5	
1,250 hours at £2 per hour			2,500
Depreciation on curing press		—see note 6	
Annual depreciation (straight line) £12,000			
One month's depreciation			1,000
Subcontract work		—see note 7	20,000
Supervisory staff		—see note 8	6,150
Estimating and design department		—see note 9	
200 hours at £10 per hour	£2,000		
Overtime premium for 50 hours	£500		
			2,500
			99,000
Administration overhead at 5% of above costs		—see note 10	4,950
			£103,950

The following notes may be relevant:

(1) A sufficient stock of raw material X is held in the stores. It is the residue of a quantity bought some 10 years ago. If this stock is not used on the prospective contract it is unlikely that it will be used in the foreseeable future. The net resale value is thought to be £20,000.

(2) Material Y is regularly used by the contractor on a variety of jobs. The current replacement cost of the material is £130 per unit.

(3) This is the estimated cost of the required material.

(4) Staff are paid on a time basis for a 40 hour week. The labour hour rate includes a charge of 100% of the wage rate to cover labour related overhead costs. It is estimated that, at the current level of operations, 80% of the overheads are variable. It is considered that one extra worker will be required temporarily for 3 months if the contract is obtained. His salary of £100 per week (and the associated amount of labour related overhead expense) is included in the estimate of £13,600.

(5) No additional trainees would be taken on. The trainees' wage rate is £1 per hour but their time is charged out at £2 to allow for labour related overhead on the same basis as in note 4 above.

(6) The curing press is normally fully occupied. If it is not being used by the contractor's own workforce it is being hired out at £500 per week.

(7) This is the estimated cost for the work.

(8) It is not considered that it would be necessary to employ any additional supervisory staff. The estimated cost of £6,150 includes an allowance of £1,000 for overtime which it may be necessary to pay to the supervisors.

(9) The expense of this department is predominantly fixed but the overtime payments were specifically incurred to get the drawings and plans out in time.

(10) The administrative expense is a fixed cost. This is the established method of allocating the cost to specific contracts.

It is considered that any quotation higher than £100,000 will be unsuccessful. You are required to prepare a revised cost estimate using an opportunity cost approach. State whether you consider that the revised calculations can provide support for a quotation below £100,000.

(*ACCA, Management Accounting, June 1986 (part a)*)

Answers on p 542

In industries such as chemicals, petroleum, gas and meat processing, individual products are made simultaneously. They are neither identifiable as individual products until a certain stage of production known as the split-off point is reached, nor can any be produced without the others in the group. Products with significant worth in terms of sales value are joint products; those with insignificant sales value are by-products.

In some situations there may be a choice as to the depth of processing after split-off point of one or more of the products. The important thing to note is that all costs incurred prior to the split-off point, however apportioned to individual products, will be irrelevant to the 'sell or process further' decision. Indeed, in relation to individual products such joint costs are irrelevant to any decision taken. They are only relevant in their entirety in relation to decisions concerning the joint products as a whole.

For 'sell or process further' decisions relevant information comprises the extra revenue that may be obtained by further processing over and above that obtainable through sale at an earlier stage of processing, compared with the additional costs incurred in the further processing. Self-assessment question 13.2 provides an illustration. It also includes consideration of the mix of joint products and alternative use of limited capacity.

Self-assessment question 13.2

Furnival has a distillation plant that produces three joint products, P, Q and R, in the proportions, 10:5:5. After the split-off point the products can be sold for industrial use or they can be taken to the mixing plant for blending and refining. The latter procedure is normally followed.

For a typical week, in which all the output is processed in the mixing plant, the following Profit and Loss Account can be prepared:

	Product P	**Product Q**	**Product R**
Sales (volume)	1,000 gals	500 gals	500 gals
Price per gal	£12.50	£20	£10
Sales Revenue	£12,500	£10,000	£5,000
Joint Process Cost			
(apportioned using output volume)	£5,000	£2,500	£2,500

Mixing Plant			
Process Costs	£3,000	£3,000	£3,000
Other Separable Costs	£2,000	£500	£500
	£10,000	£6,000	£6,000
Profit/(Loss)	£2,500	£4,000	(£1,000)

The Joint Process Costs are 25% fixed and 75% variable, whereas the Mixing Plant Costs are 10% fixed and 90% variable and all the 'Other Separable Costs' are variable.

If the products had been sold at the split-off point the selling price per gallon would have been:

Product P	*Product Q*	*Product R*
£5.00	£6.00 .	£1.50

There are only 45 hours available per week in the mixing plant. Typically 30 hours are taken up with the processing of products P, Q and R (10 hours for each product line) and 15 hours are used for other work that generates (on average) a profit of £200 per hour after being charged with a proportionate share of the plant's costs (including fixed costs). The manager of the mixing plant considers that he could sell all the plant's processing time externally at a price that would provide this rate of profit.
It has been suggested:

(i) that, since product R regularly makes a loss, it should be sold off at the split-off point.
(ii) that it might be possible to advantageously change the mix of products achieved in the distillation plant. It is possible to change the output proportions to 7:8:5 at a cost of £1 for each additional gallon of Q produced by the distillation plant.

You are required to compare the costs and benefits for each of the above proposals. Use your analysis, to suggest any improvements that seem profitable and set out the weekly Profit and Loss Account for the improved plan, in a manner which you consider will assist the management with further problems of this type.

(*ACCA, Management Accounting, June 1985*)

Answers on p 543

13.3 HOW MUCH TO PRODUCE AND SELL

The selling price decision, and the related determination of the optimum level of output, is the subject of Chapter 15, as it forms an especially important, but also particularly difficult, decision for many businesses.

Another aspect of determining production requirements is how to schedule the production of different products so as to minimise costs. Determining economic batch quantities seeks to balance the costs of holding stocks, which increase with batch size, against the costs incurred in setting-up which are incurred once for each batch produced, and which therefore reduce in total for a period with increasing batch size. The batch size needs to be found which minimises the combined total of these costs.

The total costs for a period of holding stocks, (which includes the cost of funds tied up in stock and the cost of obsolescence, deterioration, insurance, handling, and space), which are relevant to the economic batch quantity decision, are those which are influenced by the batch quantity. There may in addition be buffer stocks which incur costs regardless of batch quantity. Holding costs resulting from batch quantity are:

$$\frac{\text{Batch quantity}}{2} \times \text{Holding cost per unit}$$

$$= \frac{QH}{2}, \text{ where Q is the batch quantity and H is the holding cost per unit}$$

Setting up costs for a period, (which include incremental labour, cost of down-time and any ancillary costs), depend upon the number of batches.
They may be expressed as:

$$\frac{\text{Total demand for period}}{\text{Batch Quantity}} \times \text{set-up cost per batch}$$

$$= \frac{DS}{Q}, \text{ where D is the total demand and S the set-up cost per batch.}$$

Total costs per period (TC), which are required to be minimised, can be expressed as:

$$TC = \frac{QH}{2} + \frac{DS}{Q}$$

Minimum cost can be determined by differentiating the above formula with respect to Q and setting the derivative equal to zero.

$$\frac{H}{2} - \frac{DS}{Q^2} = 0$$

$$\therefore \frac{H}{2} = \frac{DS}{Q^2}$$

$$\therefore Q^2 = \frac{2DS}{H}$$

$$Q = \sqrt{\frac{2DS}{H}}$$

A similar formula can be used to determine economic order quantities for materials/product purchased from suppliers. Set-up costs (S) are replaced by ordering costs (O), (consisting of the administration costs of preparing orders, receiving deliveries, and paying invoices), in the following formula:

$$Q = \sqrt{\frac{2DO}{H}}$$

Optimum production/purchase quantities obtained from the above formulae should be considered with care as they make simplifying assumptions about cost behaviour. Holding costs may not entirely vary with the number of units held; set-up/ordering costs may not vary with the number of batches/orders. Buffer stocks are likely to be influenced by the size of batch/order quantities. A further factor is whether the cost of the product itself is influenced by batch/order size. There may be economies of scale in production; quantity discounts may be available on purchase. A more complete analysis of holding, set-up/ordering, and production/purchase costs may be required over alternative production/purchase quantities. Self-assessment question 13.3 provides an illustration of the economic batch/order quantity decision.

Self-assessment question 13.3

Pink Ltd is experiencing some slight problems concerning two stock items sold by the company.
The first of these items is product Exe which is manufactured by Pink. The annual

demand for Exe of 4,000 units, which is evenly spread throughout the year, is usually met by production taking place four times per year in batches of 1,000 units. One of the raw material inputs to product Exe is product Dee which is also manufactured by Pink. Product Dee is the firm's major product and is produced in large quantities throughout the year. Production capacity is sufficient to meet in full *all* demands for the production of Dees.

The standard costs of products Exe and Dee are:

Standard Costs—per unit

	Product	
	Exe	*Dee*
	£	£
Raw materials—purchased from external suppliers	13	8
—Dee standard cost	22	—
Labour—unskilled	7	4
—skilled	9	5
Variable overheads	5	3
Fixed overheads	4	2
Standard cost	60	22

Included in the fixed overheads for Exe are the set up costs for each production run. The costs of each set up, which apply irrespective of the size of the production run, are:

Costs per Set Up

	£
(i) Labour costs—skilled labour	66
(ii) Machine parts	70
Total	136

The 'Machine parts' relate to the cost of parts required for modifications carried out to the machine on which Exe is produced. The parts can be used for only one run, irrespective of run length, and are destroyed by replacement on re-instatement of the machine. There are no set up costs associated with Dee.

The cost of financing stocks of Exe is 15% p.a. Each unit of Exe in stock requires 0.40 square metres of storage space and units *cannot* be stacked on top of each other to reduce costs. Warehouse rent is £20 p.a. per square metre and Pink is only required to pay for storage space actually used.

Pink is not working to full capacity and idle time payments are being made to all grades of labour except unskilled workers. Unskilled labour is not guaranteed a minimum weekly wage and is paid only for work carried out.

The second stock item causing concern is product Wye. Product Wye is purchased by Pink for resale and the 10,000 unit annual demand is again spread evenly throughout the year. Incremental ordering costs are £100 per order and the normal unit cost is £20. However the suppliers of Wye are now offering quantity discounts for large orders. The details of these are:

Quantity ordered	*Unit price*
	£
Up to 999	20.00
1,000 to 1,999	19.80
2,000 and over	19.60

The purchasing manager feels that full advantage should be taken of discounts and purchases should be made at £19.60 per unit using orders for 2,000 units or more. Holding costs for Wye are calculated at £8.00 per unit per year and this figure will not be altered by any change in the purchase price per unit.

Required:

(a) Show the optimum batch size for the production of Exes. If this differs from the present policy, calculate the annual savings to be made by Pink Ltd from pursuing the optimal policy. Briefly explain the figures incorporated in your calculations.
(The time taken to carry out a production run may be ignored.) (10 marks)

(b) Advise Pink Ltd on the correct size of order for the purchase of Wyes. (6 marks)

(c) Briefly describe two major limitations, or difficulties inherent in the practical application, of the model used in (a) to determine the optimum batch size.

(*ACCA, Management Accounting, June 1981*)

Answers on p 544

13.4 WHERE/HOW TO SELL

Decisions also arise regarding how best to distribute products/services and make them available to customers. This may involve determining geographical areas in which sales representation is justified; the optimum number of salespersons; whether to sell through agents, through wholesalers, to retailers, etc; or the optimum use of distribution facilities. This latter problem referred to as the 'transportation' problem, would be expected to be found in paper 2.6 'Quantitative Analysis', although students should always be prepared for such a problem in paper 2.4 also. Self-assessment question 13.4 provides an illustration of 'where/how to sell' decisions.

Self-assessment question 13.4

A Ltd markets its products through 900 retail outlets of which it supplies 400 directly while the remaining 500 are served by 25 wholesalers. The outlets served by wholesalers are those located in regions which are some distance from the company's factory. The average gross sales through retailers served by wholesalers are lower than those through retailers supplied directly and the management of A Ltd are studying a proposal to employ additional sales representatives so that all retailers could be supplied directly, replacing the wholesalers.

A normal year's activity for the purposes of this study has been agreed to be:

	Wholesale	**Retail**
Sales	£500,000	£700,000
Cost of Goods Sold	£420,000	£420,000
Number of sales representatives' calls	450	4,500
Number of invoice lines	45,000	255,000

Wholesalers are charged lower prices than retailers to compensate for the handling, distribution and selling costs which are borne by A Ltd on its direct sales to retail customers.

The company's six existing sales representatives, all salaried, currently cost £126,000 per year. This amount covers salaries, travel and samples. A representative working full time on retail sales can make 900 sales visits a year whereas one working full time on wholesale accounts can make only 450 as each visit takes longer and the wholesalers are farther apart.

The record keeping, order filling and document processing costs are currently £38,000 a year. These tend to increase in proportion to the number of invoice lines. Advertising expenditures of £62,000 a year are all devoted to advertising aimed at the final consumers of the company's products. Distribution costs on supplies to wholesalers are £15,000, and on supplies to retail outlets £85,000.

The company incurs £24,000 a year of warehouse rent for storage of goods held to service retailers. This rent is for the space occupied by the goods and has been found to change proportionately to changes in the cost of goods sold. Cost of goods sold is approximately 30% fixed and 70% variable.

The objective set for the study is to identify the channel of distribution that will maximise the profit of the company as a whole.

Required:

(a) Your calculation of the profit attributable to
 (i) the average wholesale customer and
 (ii) the average retail customer.

(b) Your reasoned views, supported by as much computation as possible, on whether the available information supports the proposals to deal directly with all retail outlets. Identify any further information you consider necessary to a final decision on this proposal.

Answers on p 547

13.5 WHERE/HOW TO PRODUCE

Each physical product in a manufacturing organisation results from the input particularly of:

1 Materials, which can require different sorts of storage and handling.
2 Time and skills of labour, carrying out various different operations.
3 Machinery which enable the materials to be converted into finished product.

The optimal combination of the above inputs, in order to achieve the required output as efficiently as possible, has to be decided. Because machinery is one of the necessary input elements, capital investment is frequently required and the decision needs to be taken over a long-term horizon. Once the investment commitment has been made there will be considerably less flexibility to change the mix of input resources.

Another decision that has to be made concerns the location of plant. This also is clearly of a long-term nature involving, in addition, investment in land and buildings.

One further decision which may be considered within this grouping is the decision whether to 'make or buy'. This also may involve capital investment, where no firm resource commitment has yet been made and the decision is being viewed as a long-term one. The 'make or buy' decision may also arise where capital investment has already been made, or equipment is rented with no long-term commitment, and the opportunity arises to buy from outside product which is currently made. The costs of buying-in need to be compared with the incremental costs that are/would be incurred as a result of manufacture. Self-assessment question 13.5 provides an illustration.

Self-assessment question 13.5

The production process of Lawson Ltd regularly produces 20,000 gallons per month of a highly toxic liquid waste product which needs to be neutralised before being discharged into the local river.

To neutralise each gallon of liquid requires the usage of:
2 grammes of A at a cost of £0.50 per gramme
4 fluid ozs. of B at a cost of £0.75 per fluid oz.
1 unit of C at a cost of £1.00 per unit.

The prices of A, B and C are fixed by long-term contracts.

The neutralising process is carried out on plant which is rented at a cost of £25,000 per month and needs to be in operation for only 100 hours per month to process the budgeted monthly volume of liquid. Factory overheads recovered per machine hour are:
variable overheads—£20 per machine hour.
fixed overheads —£50 per machine hour.

Fixed overheads recovered per machine hour are an apportionment of general factory overheads none of which will alter as a result of any changes in the activity of the neutralising plant.

The neutralising plant is operated by a single operative. This operator's labour costs Lawson £4.50 per hour (which includes all labour related overheads) and the operator is guaranteed payment for a minimum of 160 hours per month. Lawson has a policy of no redundancies—reductions in the workforce being caused only by natural wastage.

The long-term contracts which were entered into for the supply of materials A, B and C can be cancelled at Lawson's option by giving the following notice:

A 2 months
B 1 month
C 4 months

This means that Lawson is committed to paying for the normal monthly purchases during the notice period but can choose whether or not to take delivery. Any quantity of A, B or C surplus to requirements could be sold. Details of sales price and associated selling and delivery costs are:

Material	*Unit*	*Per Unit*		
		Sales Price	*Selling Cost*	*Delivery Cost*
		£	£	£
A	Gramme	0.40	0.25	0.25
B	Fluid oz.	0.60	0.15	0.20
C	Unit	0.90	0.20	0.25

The plant rental can be cancelled by giving 3 months' notice.

A contractor has offered to undertake the disposal of the toxic waste at a cost of £4.50 per gallon and Lawson's management team are uncertain whether they should enter into a long-term contract for the disposal of the waste or continue to undertake the neutralising process themselves.

Required:

(a) Advise Lawson of the long-term monthly saving or extra cost which would result from acceptance of the contractor's offer to dispose of the toxic waste. Show the effect that variation in the timing of acceptance of the contractor's offer has on its desirability. Specify precisely your advice on Lawson's best course of action.

(b) Explain how the decision reached, and the analysis pursued, in (a) above would have differed if—

(i) the plant was owned by Lawson and was depreciated at £25,000 per month. The plant has no alternative use and no scrap or disposal value;

(ii) Lawson operated a policy of not employing people when their job ceased to exist;

(iii) the contract for the supply of material A required four months' notice of cancellation and specified that Lawson had to accept delivery of the regular monthly quantities of the material during the cancellation period. Would the revised analysis be altered if delivery could be avoided by a penalty payment of

(1) £0.05 per unit
or (2) £0.15 per unit?

(*ACCA, Management Accounting, June 1980*)

Answers on p 549

13.6 WHETHER TO PRODUCE AND SELL

On occasion the question arises as to whether, and when, particular operations should be terminated. By 'operations' is meant more than simply the discontinuation of a particular product; rather, it is concerned with the possible closure of a whole department or even a factory. More costs are likely to be avoidable, and thus become relevant to the analysis. The following considerations may arise:

1 Redundancy payments to employees.
2 Effect on morale of remaining employees.
3 Redeployment opportunities.
4 Temporary staff costs to replace employees who have left.
5 Write-off, or reduced value, of remaining stocks.
6 Value of specialised buildings in a particular location.
7 Value of second-hand plant, machinery, vehicles, fixtures and fittings.
8 After-sales requirements for goods already sold.
9 Cost of terminating outstanding hire/lease commitments.
10 Making good any damage/deterioration to premises.

Self-assessment question 13.6 provides an illustration of departmental closure.

Self-assessment question 13.6

The original budget for the K department of Hilton Ltd for the forthcoming year was as follows:

Budget for Forthcoming year—K department
Budgeted Sales and Production—30,000 units

	Per unit of output	*Total for 30,000 units*
	(£)	(£'000s)
Sales revenue	10.0	300
Manufacturing costs		
Material A—one litre per unit	2.0	60
Material B—one kilo per unit	1.5	45
Production labour	2.0	60
Variable overhead	1.0	30
Fixed manufacturing overhead	2.0	60
	8.5	255
Non manufacturing costs	1.0	30
Total costs	9.5	285
Budgeted net profit for year	0.5	15

As part of Hilton's long-term strategic plan the K department was due to be closed at the end of the forthcoming year. However, rumours of the closure have resulted in the majority of K's labour force leaving the firm and this has forced the abandonment of the original budget for the department.

The managing director has suggested that the department could be closed down immediately or, by employing contract labour, could be operated to produce 10,000 or 20,000 units in the year. With the exception of the foreman (see Note (v)), the few remaining members of K's production labour force would then be redeployed within the firm.

The following further information is available:

(i) Each hour of contract labour will cost £3.00 and will produce one unit of the product. Contract labour would have to be trained at a fixed cost of £20,000.

(ii) There are 30,000 litres of material A in stock. This material has no other use and any of it not used in department K will have to be disposed of. Costs of disposal will be £2,000 plus £0.50 per litre disposed of.

(iii) There are 15,000 kilos of material B in stock. If the material is not used in department K then up to 10,000 kilos could be used in another department to substitute for an equivalent weight of a material which currently costs £1.80 per kilo. Material B originally cost £1.50 per kilo and its current market price (buying or selling) is £2.00 per kilo. Costs to Hilton of selling any surplus material B will amount to £1.00 per kilo sold.

(iv) Variable overheads will be 30% higher, per unit produced, than originally budgeted.

(v) Included in 'Fixed manufacturing overheads' are

(a) £6,000 salary of the departmental foreman,

(b) £7,000 depreciation of the machine used in the department.

If the department is closed immediately the foreman, who will otherwise retire at the end of the year, will be asked to retire early and paid £2,000 compensation for agreeing to this.

The only machine used in the department originally cost £70,000 and could currently be sold for £43,000. This sales value will reduce to £40,000 at the end of the year and, if used for any production during the year, will decrease by a further £500 per 1,000 units produced.

(vi) All other costs included in 'Fixed manufacturing overhead' and all 'Non manufacturing costs' are apportionments of general overheads none of which will be altered by any decision concerning the K department.

(vii) The sales manager suggests that a sales volume of 10,000 units could be achieved if the unit sales price were £9.00. A sales volume of 20,000 units would be achieved if the sales price per unit were reduced to £8.00 and an advertising campaign costing £15,000 were undertaken.

Required:

(a) Advise Hilton Ltd of its best course of action regarding department K, presenting any data in tabular form.

(b) For each of the following separate circumstances show how the advice given in (a) above is altered.

(i) Immediate closure of department K would enable its factory space to be rented out for one year at a rental of £8,000.

(ii) The quoted level of efficiency of the contract labour is the *average* for production of the first 5,000 units and any additional production would reflect the effects of the 90% learning curve which will be experienced. Show also the revised contract labour costs.

Ignore taxation and the time value of money.

(*ACCA, Management Accounting, June 1981*)

Answers on p 551

SUMMARY

This chapter has provided further illustration of the application of differential costing principles, and in a variety of different short-term decision-making situations. The principles remain the same; the applications vary according to situation. The six self-assessment questions provide a comprehensive illustration of the types of quantitative decision that arise. A limited number of end of chapter exercises are also provided.

EXERCISES

Exercise 13.1

The Singapore Stores imports dried milk from the UK which it markets under its own brand name, Klim.

Sales of the product show negligible seasonal variation and run at 12 million packets per annum. To ensure that there are no stock-outs the company always holds a base stock equal to one month's sales.

The company's Purchasing Officer orders in amounts equal to one month's sales paying S$1.0 per packet. The lead time between placing an order and delivery of the consignment to the Singapore Stores' warehouse is 37 days.

The supplying exporter has offered to reduce the price of Klim by 10% a packet if the Singapore Stores will treble the size of the orders that it places; however, it will also have to be prepared to accept twice the current lead time.

The Purchasing Officer discusses this with the company's Management Accountant. It is decided that if the change is made the same base stock as before could be held, but that the occupancy costs of the additional storage space associated with the increased stock holdings would cost S$72,000 per annum, and that there would also be an increase in handling costs of 8c per packet sold.

The Management Accountant also requires an opportunity cost to be imputed for the company's cost of capital at a rate of 1% per month on the value of average stocks, which is the same percentage as currently used.

Required:

(a) Your opinion as to whether the exporter's offer should be accepted based upon computations.
(b) Your views on any qualitative information which should be brought into the decision analysis.

(*ACCA, Management Accounting, December 1976*)

Answers in lecturer's manual

Exercise 13.2

Discuss the proposition that joint cost allocation procedures provide little useful information and none at all for decision-making purposes. Is there any justification for claiming further that they are not only useless but also positively harmful?

(*ACCA, Management Accounting, December 1982* (*part a*))

Answers in lecturer's manual

Exercise 13.3

Answer BOTH parts to this question

(a) A hospital operates a laundry which, just over one year ago, was re-equipped with machinery at a cost of £111,111. The current replacement cost of this machinery is £125,000. However, as it was specially built for the hospital's laundry, its highest resale value would be obtained from the manufacturer who guarantees to give back 10% of its initial cost at any time up to ten years in the future, for its scrap value.

The annual cost of running the laundry is:

	£
(1) Wages and salaries	25,000
(2) Maintenance contract for the equipment	15,000
(3) Depreciation on the equipment	10,000
(4) Soap powder	6,000
(5) Other direct costs	4,000
	£60,000

A new laundry has just been set up in the area by a firm specialising in commercial laundering. It has offered to launder the items that would be handled by the hospital's own laundry for £40,000 per annum for the next 9 years.

Notes

(1) Most of the staff could be redeployed. However, it is estimated that if the laundry was closed, redundancy payments would amount to £5,000.

(2) The second year's maintenance contract payment has just been made—this is non-refundable.

(3) The expected total life of the machinery is 10 years.

(4) There is a contract to obtain soap powder. This contract is renewable each year and has a cancellation clause in it which can be invoked by the hospital during any year at a cost of £1,000. However, the powder could be used by the hospital as a substitute for a floor cleaning liquid which currently costs it £5,400.

(5) The other direct costs for the current year have been incurred and paid.

(b) It is the year two thousand. K.U.'s reserves of South Ocean Gas have been exhausted for some years now and the K.U. Gas Corporation (KUG) has gone back to processing coal to enable it to obtain supplies of gas.

Currently KUG is producing coke and town gas, and the joint processing costs (including all material and manufacturing costs) per metric tonne input of coal cost $10 thousand. From this input gas and coke products, which have a sales value of $5 thousand and $7 thousand respectively, are produced.

For costing purposes KUG apportions all joint processing costs equally between the two products. Currently the production of town gas just breaks-even, and for some time KUG has been considering ways of improving the profitability of this product.

KUG has recently been approached by the Big Benne Motor Corporation (BBM) to ask whether it would be prepared to process the town gas further, by enriching and liquidising it for use in the Datota engine for cars that BBM is now making under licence. BBM guarantee that garages will take as much of this enriched liquidised gas as KUG can produce at a price of $9 thousand per metric tonne input of coal. In fact BBM are prepared to underwrite this guarantee, and also to pay any additional distribution costs incurred by KUG.

KUG's cost accountant states that the additional processing costs that would be incurred by enriching and liquidising the gas would be $6 thousand per metric tonne input of coal. He suggests that he should alter the costing system used to apportion joint costs, on to the basis of the heat output obtained from the final products, which in fact approximates to the ratio of the sales values of the products.

Required:
Your advice to—

(a) the hospital management committee;

(b) the K.U. Gas Corporation.

In both cases include a brief statement of the reasons for your suggestions.

(*ACCA, Management Accounting, December 1978*)

Answers in lecturer's manual

Exercise 13.4

Borealis p.l.c. produces a range of lamps, light fittings and lighting equipment. During 1982 there has been a fall off in demand and the management, at the end of that year, are reviewing the options open to them in 1983. As part of this reappraisal they are looking at the AS and ML departments.

The AS department makes automatic switches which sell at £4 each. The budgeted production and sales for 1982 were set, well below full capacity, at 100,000 units but the actual production has been 65,000 and only 50,000 were sold. The department is estimated to have incurred a loss of £61,600 for the year.

The ML department produces the Minicell Lamp which sells for £20. One of the lamp's components is a bought-in item called a link switch. Up to four years ago all link switches had been manufactured internally by the AS department but the cheap price quoted by an outside supplier and the fact that the AS department had, until recently, plenty of profitable outside work, had led to the use of the bought-in item. The production and sales budgets were set at 120,000 lamps for 1982 but actual production was 90,000 and only 80,000 were sold. Despite the serious fall in lamp sales, it is estimated that the ML department will make a profit over the year.

The budgeted and (estimated) actual profit and loss statements, on the conventional historical cost basis, are as follows:

Profit and Loss Statements—1982	*AS Department*		*ML Department*	
	Budget	*Actual (estimated)*	*Budget*	*Actual (estimated)*
	£	£	£	£
Sales Revenue	400,000	200,000	2,400,000	1,600,000
Production Costs				
Direct Material				
Raw Materials	45,760	30,320	449,280	343,440
Link Switches	—	—	334,290	255,540
Direct Labour	32,240	21,360	714,030	545,820
Other Expenses				
Salaries and General Production Expenses	179,220	171,540	299,500	267,100
Depreciation	30,880	30,880	30,600	30,600
Central Charges	60,000	60,000	80,000	80,000
Cost of Production	348,100	314,100	1,907,700	1,522,500
Add: Opening Stock	15,100	15,100	183,500	183,500
	363,200	329,200	2,091,200	1,706,000
Less: Closing Stock	16,300	67,600	198,200	342,500
Cost of Goods Sold	346,900	261,600	1,893,000	1,363,500
Profit/(Loss)	53,100	(61,600)	507,000	236,500
	£400,000	£200,000	£2,400,000	£1,600,000

In department AS the opening stock was 5,000 units. In department ML the opening stock was 15,000 Minicell Lamps. The budgets were constructed on the assumption that cost levels at the year end would be 8% higher than at the beginning of the year, and that this rise would occur evenly over the year. In fact the cost of inputs at the end of 1982 look like being 12% above their opening levels. It can be assumed that the actual level of operating efficiency for 1982 is in line with the budget so that all cost variances are price (inflation) variances. It is anticipated that cost levels at the end of 1983 will be 10% above the levels at the beginning of that year but it is intended to retain the selling prices for the company's products unchanged throughout 1983.

The company is considering two alternative plans, the details of which are as follows:

Plan 1 This plan would allow for the continued operation of the AS department at its current level of activity but the department would discontinue its manufacture of automatic switches for outside customers and would, instead, revert to making the link switches for the Minicell Lamp. No detailed costings for this have, as yet, been undertaken but it is considered that all the link switches required by the ML department during 1983 could be produced by the AS department with the same total input of resources as was used during 1982 and that the total 1983 expenses of the AS department would approximate the 1982 level, except for any increase caused by inflation. AS department would not hold any stock of link switches at the end of 1983, its existing stock of 20,000 automatic switches would be sold off at the current price of £4 and the reinstatement of their manufacture would be considered for 1984.

The ML department's production budget would be 80,000 lamps and its sales budget 100,000. The link switches required for this production would be transferred from the AS department to the ML department at the ruling outside price which currently (at the end of 1982) is £3 although it is anticipated that this will rise (in line with other prices) to £3.30 at the end of 1983. One link switch is required for each Minicell Lamp. Any unsold stock of lamps held at the year end would be valued at £15 each.

For 1983 Central Charges will be £62,000 for the AS department and £85,000 for the ML department. Depreciation for both departments will remain at the 1982 level.

Plan 2 This plan involves the closure of the AS department for 1983. The existing stock of automatic switches would be sold off (as in Plan 1) and the reinstatement of the production line would be considered for 1984. The closure would save all the department's variable expenses but this saving would be partially offset by redundancy payments of £15,000. Only 10% of the fixed expenses (excluding depreciation and central charges) would be avoided. The manager of the AS department would be seconded on full salary (£15,000 p.a.) to a post in the personnel office which is currently being advertised at £9,500. It would be possible for the ML department to use some of the freed space for storage purposes and this would save rent of £5,000 p.a. It is thought that some minimal maintenance of the AS department's plant would still be necessary—the estimated cost of this is £1,000.

The ML department's budget would be as for Plan 1 but it would purchase its supply of link switches from outside suppliers.

You are required:

(a) to advise the company on its choice between Plan 1 and Plan 2 and to calculate the net cost (or benefit) of adopting Plan 1

(b) to prepare the 1983 budget for the AS department under Plan 1 and to comment on whether this budget could be used as part of a cost/benefit analysis (as required in your answer to part (a)).

(*ACCA, Management Accounting, June 1983*)

Answers in lecturer's manual

Short-Term Decision-Making—Allocation of Scarce Resources

INTRODUCTION

In the introduction to the previous chapter, reference was made to ranking decisions where choices have to be made due to scarcity of resources. Such ranking decisions are the subject of this chapter.

Situations where there are scarce resources are also known as limiting factor problems. A business may not be able to obtain sufficient capital, labour, materials, machinery, or particular skills, especially in the short-term, to satisfy requirements. The resource in short supply becomes the limiting factor, ie it is this that puts the ceiling on a business's activity. The purpose of this chapter is to identify and illustrate a range of limiting factor problems.

14.1 LIMITING FACTOR SITUATIONS

Limiting factor situations arise because the demand for resources for use within a business exceeds the available supply. Availability is determined either by the external market or from within a business by management. Either way the situation is the same, except that it is more easily changed if imposed from within. Thus the decision is not simply for example 'should we produce and sell Product A'? but 'is it better to produce and sell Product A or Product B'? The opportunity cost of using a scarce resource is not just the cost of acquiring it but the profit foregone from not taking the opportunity of using the resource in some other way.

There is no one solution to the problem of determining the optimum allocation of resources in limiting factor situations. It is necessary first of all to identify what the precise problem is and then to consider what the alternatives are and what information is relevant to the necessary choice between alternatives.

Problem situations vary in respect of:

1. The number of constraints.
2. The number of alternative users of the resource(s).
3. The extent of divisibility of both the resource(s) and the user(s) of the resource(s). For example, raw materials may be infinitely divisible between users; other resources may not: a particular user may be able to adjust quantity utilised; another user may not.
4. The nature of the constraints. For example, the constraint may be an absolutely binding one; on the other hand it may be possible to overcome the constraint eg by sub-contracting work or by changing shift patterns.

14.2 LIMITING FACTOR ILLUSTRATION (SINGLE CONSTRAINT)

Initially the example will assume a situation where there is one constraint, two users of the scarce resource, a binding constraint on the number of working hours available, and divisibility of both resource and user.

14.2.1 Problem

N Ltd manufactures two products A & B which pass through the same two processes Y & Z during manufacture. Product A sells at £15 per unit and Product B at £20 per unit. Selling prices cannot be varied and annual sales potential at these prices is expected to be:

Product A—36,000 units
Product B—14,000 units

Variable costs (£ per unit) are:

	Product A	Product B
Direct material	4	7
Direct labour	5	8
Variable overhead	1	2

Processing hours per 100 units are:

	Product A	Product B
Process Y	6	8
Process Z	5	10

Operating hours are limited to a total of 2,400 per annum in Process Y.
N Ltd is seeking to determine the optimum allocation of its resources.

14.2.2 Solution

The first step is to identify the profitability of the two products and to establish whether the limit of processing hours available in Process Y provides a binding constraint on the activities of the company. It is assumed that N Ltd wishes to allocate its available resources in such a way as to maximise the contribution generated. It is also assumed that fixed costs, information on which is not included in the problem, will be unaffected in total by the resource allocation determined, and will be at a level which enables the company to make an adequate profit.

PROFITABILITY

	Product A £/unit	Product B £/unit
Selling price	12	20
Variable costs:		
Direct materials	4	7
Direct labour	5	8
Variable overhead	1	2
	10	17
Contribution	2	3
× Sales per annum	36,000 units	14,000 units
= Total contribution/annum	£72,000	£42,000
Contribution % of sales	16.6%	15%

It can be seen that both products are profitable in that both make a useful contribution which in the absence of any production constraint would total £114,000 per annum. In absolute profit terms Product A is better, heavily influenced by the higher units sold than Product B. In relative profit terms, measured as contribution per unit of sales, Product B is preferred to Product A. However if relative profitability is measured instead, on the basis of contribution as a percentage of sales, then Product A is again ranked higher.

In the absence of any limitation in resource availability, the relative ranking of the two products is unimportant as far as the allocation of resources is concerned. Sufficient resources would be available to meet sales potential for both products.

PRODUCTION POTENTIAL

However a question that arises in this problem is whether the limitation on the availability of operating hours in Process Y provides a constraint on activity ie does it limit production to a level below that which could be sold at the selling prices prevailing? This can be determined as follows:

		Process Y operating hours required
Product A	$\frac{36{,}000}{100} \times 6$	2,160
Product B	$\frac{14{,}000}{100} \times 8$	1,120
		3,280

It can be seen that there is a severe restriction on production capability in Process Y. Hours needed to meet sales requirements (3,280 operating hours) exceed production capability (2,400 operating hours) by 880 hours (36.6% of production capacity, or 26.83% of sales requirement).

ALLOCATION OF SCARCE RESOURCE

This is, therefore, a limiting factor problem. A choice between the allocation of Process Y resources to Product A or alternatively to Product B has to be made. As it has been assumed that operating hours are freely divisible between the two products and that any number of units of the two products could be sold within the maximum potential given ie the products are also freely divisible, then a very large number of production (and thus also sales) possibilities arise. At the extremes, ie, with Process Y resources devoted entirely to either Product A or Product B, the production possibilities are:

Product A $\frac{2{,}400}{6} \times 100 = 40{,}000$

Product B $\frac{2{,}400}{8} \times 100 = 30{,}000$

The two products, one limiting factor, situation can be demonstrated graphically in order to emphasise the production possibilities, subject to maximum sales (see Figure 14.1).

The shaded area includes all the production possibilities that are within the sales maxima. Those situated on the line CD fully utilise the available capacity (operating hours) in Process Y. The optimum solution will lie on this line as it would make no sense to leave capacity idle.

One possible solution would be to reduce sales, and thus production requirements, of both products by 26.83%. Thus:

		Production Units		Process Y Operating Hours
Product A	36,000 × 73.17% =	26,341	$\times \frac{6}{100}$	1,580
Product B	14,000 × 73.17% =	10,245	$\times \frac{8}{100}$	820
				2,400

FIGURE 14.1 **Production possibilities, process Y**

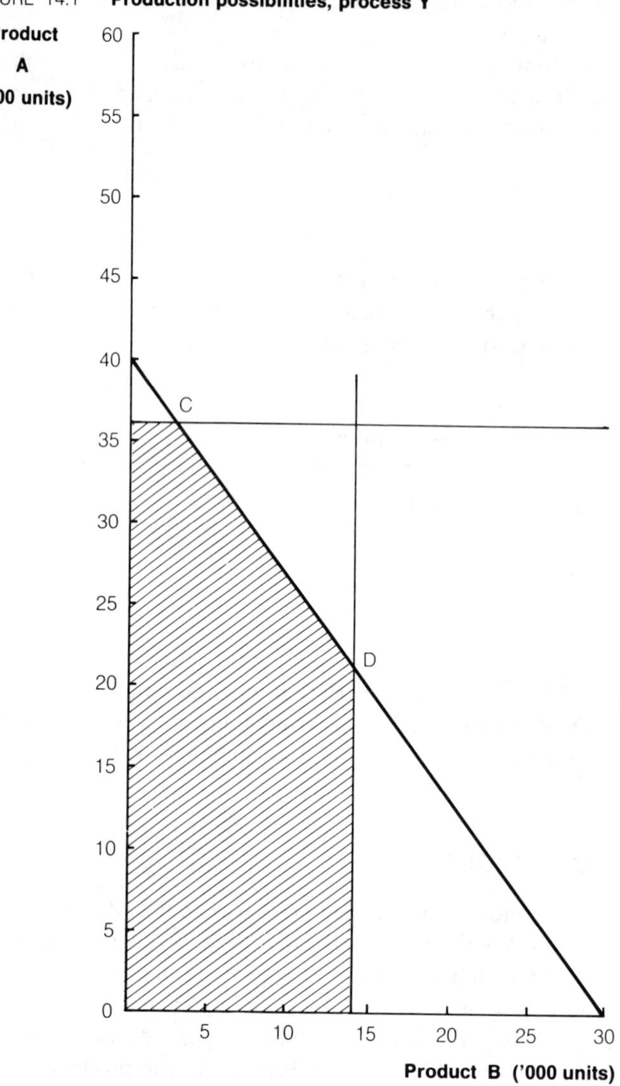

Contribution to fixed overhead and profit would become:

Product A	26,341 units at £2 per unit =	52,682
Product B	10,245 units at £3 per unit =	30,735
		£83,417

The above solution provides a combination of Products A and B which lies between the extremes on the production possibilities line for Process Y shown on Figure 14.1. Can the resulting contribution be improved upon?

There is no reason why the above allocation of resources should be optimal. Indeed there is a very good reason why it will not be so. Unless the profitability of the two products is identical it will always be preferable to move to one or other of the two extreme points on the production possibilities line. Thus, there are only two alternatives to consider:

1 Produce 36,000 units of Product A, with the balance of operating hours in Process Y on Product B

$$\left(\text{ie } (2{,}400\text{-}2{,}160) \times \frac{100}{8} = 3{,}000 \text{ units}\right) \text{ ie Point C}$$

2 Produce 14,000 units of Product B, with the balance of operating hours in Process Y on Product A

$$\left(\text{ie } (2{,}400\text{-}1{,}120) \times \frac{100}{6} = 21{,}333 \text{ units}\right) \text{ ie Point D}$$

Contribution to fixed overhead and profit provided by the two alternatives would be:

	Product A		Product B			
Alternative 1	36,000 × £2		3,000 × £3			
=	£72,000	=	£9,000	Total	=	£81,000
Alternative 2	21,333 × £2		14,000 × £3			
=	£42,667	=	£42,000	Total	=	£84,667

Thus Alternative 2 is preferred and also provides a higher contribution than the earlier allocation of resources (ie 26,341 units of Product A; 10,245 units of Product B).

Alternative 2 allocates resources to Product B in preference to Product A. Product B is at maximum sales with the balance of resources left for Product A. The reason is that Product B provides a greater relative contribution, not measured as the contribution per unit of product or the contribution relative to sales, but as the contribution generated per unit of the scarce resource. This is the relevant criterion in such limiting factor problems. Contribution per operating hour in Process Y is as follows:

Product A $\quad$ £2 per unit $\div \frac{6}{100}$ hours per unit = £33.$\dot{3}$

Product B $\quad$ £3 per unit $\div \frac{8}{100}$ hours per unit = £37.50

Product B generates more contribution per operating hour than Product A and thus is allocated as much of the scarce resource as possible. This can be demonstrated on the graph shown earlier by the plotting of a line of equal contribution (see Figure 14.2). For example in order to generate a contribution of £30,000 either 15,000 units of Product A or 10,000 units of Product B would have to be sold. If this line is extended outwards, each new line drawn parallel to the first will be a line of equal contribution greater than the previous one. Point D lies on the line of highest contribution that can be drawn without moving completely outside the production possibilities area.

The solution to the problem is most easily found from the outset by calculating the contribution that each product makes per unit of scarce resource and then by allocating resources according to the ranking that this produces. In this example resources are allocated first to Product B because contribution per operating hour is greater (£37.50 compared with £33.$\dot{3}$ for Product A). The contribution generated could be calculated as:

Product B	1,120 hours × £37.50	=	42,000
Product A	1,280 hours × £33.$\dot{3}$	=	42,667
	2,400		£84,667

The first solution suggested earlier produced a total contribution of £83,417 from the following resource allocation:

Product A	1,580 hours
Product B	820 hours

The reallocation of resources to provide the optimum contribution involved 300 additional operating hours on Product B (1,120 – 820) and 300 fewer hours on Product A (1,580 – 1,280). The extra contribution generated is the extra contribution of Product B per operating hour ie £4.1$\dot{6}$ (£37.50 – £33.$\dot{3}$) multiplied by the 300 hours. This provides an additional contribution of £1,250 (ie £84,667 – £83,417).

The opportunity cost of each operating hour in the example is £33.$\dot{3}$ extra above the normal cost ie it is the contribution that would be foregone if an hour was taken from Product A. Whether or not this is worthwhile will depend upon whether any other alternative can be found which offers an incremental contribution in excess of £33.$\dot{3}$ per operating hour. The opportunity cost could change to £37.50 per hour if more than 1,280 hours were lost. It also shows how much it would be worthwhile paying per hour in order to overcome the restriction. It should be noted that the optimum production

FIGURE 14.2 **Lines of equal contribution (— — —)**

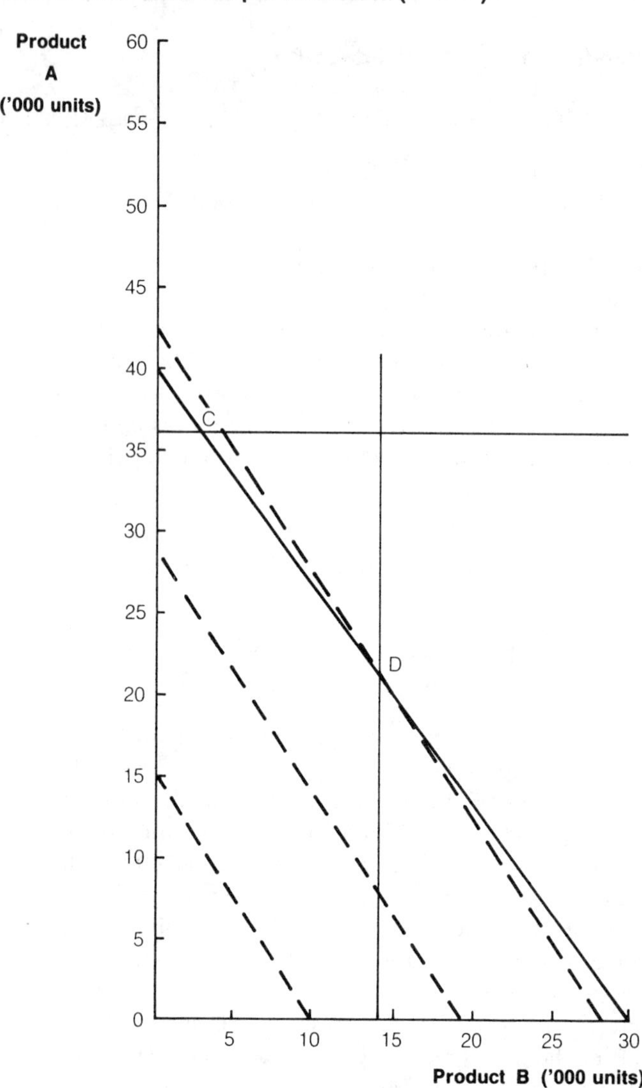

schedule is dependent upon relative contributions. Product B generates an additional contribution of £4.16 per hour, a premium of 12.5% over that of Product A. If A generated more contribution or Product B less such that the premium was removed the optimum production schedule would change.

Self-assessment question 14.1

Corpach Ltd manufactures three products for which the sales maxima, for the forthcoming year, are estimated to be:

Product 1	Product 2	Product 3
£57,500	£96,000	£125,000

Summarised unit cost data are as follows:

	Product 1	Product 2	Product 3
	£	£	£
Direct Material Cost	10.00	9.00	7.00
Variable Processing Costs	8.00	16.00	10.00
Fixed Processing Costs	2.50	5.00	4.00
	£20.50	£30.00	£21.00

The allocation of Fixed Processing Costs has been derived from last year's production levels and the figures may need revision if current output plans are different.
The established selling prices are:

Product 1	Product 2	Product 3
£23.00	£32.00	£25.00

The products are processed on machinery housed in three buildings:
Building A contains type A machines on which 9,800 machine hours are estimated to be available in the forthcoming year. The fixed overheads for this building are £9,800 p.a.
Building B1 contains type B machines on which 10,500 machine hours are estimated to be available in the forthcoming year.
Building B2 also contains type B machines and again 10,500 machine hours are estimated to be available in the forthcoming year.

The fixed overheads for the B1 and B2 buildings are, in total, £11,200 p.a. The times required for one unit of output for each product on each type of machine are as follows:

	Product 1	Product 2	Product 3
Type A Machines	1 hour	2 hours	3 hours
Type B Machines	1.5 hours	3 hours	1 hour

Assuming that Corpach Ltd wishes to maximise its profits for the ensuing year, you are required to determine the optimal production plan and the profit that this should produce.

(*ACCA, Management Accounting, June 1983 (part a)*)

Answers on p 553

14.2.3 Changed assumptions

Whilst continuing to maintain the initial assumption of a single resource limitation, how is the analysis changed if other assumptions are changed, or the limitation can be overcome? For example,

What if there are more than two users of the scarce resource?
What if resources and/or users are non divisible?
What if some other way can be found of obtaining additional product or resource?

Each of the above will be considered independently.

MORE USERS

If there are more than two users of the scarce resource the situation cannot be depicted on a two dimensional graph as before. However the approach to providing the optimal allocation of resources is unchanged with allocation based on the ranking of contribution per unit of scarce resource.

NON-DIVISIBILITY

Absolute non-divisibility of resources and/or product would mean that the requirements for each of the two products would either have to be met in full or not at all. The Anglia Company example (self-assessment question 12.3) was an example of such a situation. The company seemingly did not have the resources to take on both contracts. Thus the scarce resource had to be devoted to one or other contract. It would not have been feasible to devote any time left over to the other. In any case the customer would want the contract completed or not at all.

In the N Ltd example if we assume that absolute non-divisibility exists then the solution is on the basis of the absolute contribution generated. The choice is either generating £72,000 contribution from Product A, leaving 240 Process Y hours surplus, or £42,000 from Product B with 1,280 hours surplus, Product A would thus be chosen.

It may be that resources and/or products are to a certain extent divisible, but not infinitely so. Each situation would have to be resolved according to its particular characteristics. The solution could well be to assume divisibility and then to make adjustments to the solution to accommodate the extent of non-divisibility.

ADDITIONAL RESOURCE

Although there may initially be a limiting factor this may not be a binding constraint as additional product or resource may be obtainable. For example it may be possible to sub-contract work, or to change shift patterns in order to expand capacity.

Returning to the example of N Ltd it will now be assumed, in addition to the information provided earlier, that a quotation has been received from an outside supplier who is willing and able to manufacture N Ltd's requirements for additional product, at the following prices:

Product A	£11.00 per unit
Product B	£18.00 per unit

The situation has changed if it can be assumed that buying-in is considered worthwhile. It is now possible to meet sales requirements despite the restriction on N Ltd's own operating hours. The question now is how to allocate resources in order to meet sales requirements at minimum cost. The only variable is what additional cost will be incurred in buying-in product. The additional cost of buying-in, or the amount saved by producing, per unit of product is:

Product A	£1 per unit	(ie 11-10)
Product B	£1 per unit	(ie 18-17)

However the key question is 'what is the on-cost per operating hour saved by not producing'? For every 100 units of Product A that is bought-in, 6 fewer operating hours are required in Process Y; for every 100 units of Product B that is bought-in, 8 fewer operating hours are required in Process Y. The additional cost per equivalent operating hour is therefore:

Product A $\frac{100}{6} = £16.\dot{6}$ per hour

Product B $\frac{100}{8} = £12.50$ per hour

Alternatively this could be viewed as the amount saved for each operating hour in Process Y that is allocated to production of the products.

It is thus better to allocate production resources to Product A, a reversal of the previous situation. The production schedule would be:

	Process Y Operating Hours		Production Units
Product A	2,160	$\times \frac{100}{6}$	36,000
Product B	240	$\times \frac{100}{8}$	3,000
	2,400		

Eleven thousand units of Product B would be bought-in, representing 880 Process Y operating hours. The on-cost is £11,000 (ie 11,000 units × £1 per unit; or 880 hours × £12.50 per hour).

Total contribution is thus £103,000 (original contribution £114,000—on-cost £11,000). This can alternatively be shown as:

Product A	36,000 units at £2 per unit	£72,000
Product B	3,000 units at £3 per unit	£9,000
	11,000 units at £2 per unit	£22,000
		£103,000

If Product A was bought-in the on-cost would be £14,667 (880 hours × £16.$\dot{6}$ per hour.) Total contribution would be £99,333 (£114,000 – £14,667) or:

Product A	21,333 units at £2 per unit	£42,666
	14,667 units at £1 per unit	£14,667
Product B	14,000 units at £3 per unit	£42,000
		£99,333

It should be noted that the maximum on-cost that could have been considered would have been the equivalent of £33.$\dot{3}$ per hour. This is the opportunity cost identified earlier. If the 880 hours had been provided at such an on-cost the contribution would have remained at £84,667 ie

Basic contribution	£114,000
less on-cost (880 × £33.$\dot{3}$)	(£29,333)
	£84,667

This is equivalent to bought-in prices of:

Product A $\left(£33.\dot{3} \times \frac{6}{100}\right) + 10 = £12$

Product B $\left(£33.\dot{3} \times \frac{8}{100}\right) + 17 = £19.\dot{6}$

In conclusion, it can be stated that in situations where the production constraint can be overcome, contribution is no longer at risk through possible lost sales. Instead it is the amount of each unit's contribution that is at risk subject to possible on-cost from buying-in. Thus the criteria changes from being product contribution per unit of scarce resource to being the change in product contribution (as a result of on-cost) per unit of scarce resource.

Self-assessment question 14.2

A company manufactures four components, A, B, C & D. Budgeted production and standard costs for a period are as follows:

	Component			
	A	**B**	**C**	**D**
Budgeted production (units)	2,000	3,500	1,500	2,800
Standard costs per unit: (£)				
Variable costs:				
Direct materials	18.50	13.50	12.50	22.00
Direct labour	5.00	4.00	11.00	20.00
Direct expense	5.00	10.00	5.00	30.00
Fixed overhead	2.50	2.00	5.50	10.00

Direct expenses relate to the use of metal presses which cost £5 per machine hour to operate. Metal pressing capacity is limited to 20,000 hours in the period.

An outside supplier has quoted the following prices for manufacture and delivery of the components:

	£/unit
Component A	30.00
Component B	29.50
Component C	26.00
Component D	84.00

Flexible second shift working could be organised in order to increase metal pressing capacity. Second shift operations would increase direct labour costs by 25% over the normal shift, and fixed overhead by £250 for each 1,000 (or part thereof) second shift machine hours worked.

Required:

(a) Determine how the 20,000 hours of press time should be utilised in order to minimise costs.

(b) Establish whether the balance of components should be bought-in or manufactured on a second shift.

Answers on p 553

14.3 LIMITING FACTOR ILLUSTRATION (two or more constraints)

So far situations with one resource constraint only have been considered. There may, however, be more than one constraint. How does this affect the analysis? In order to provide illustration of such situations the original example of N Ltd will be used with the addition of a second resource constraint. It will be assumed initially, as was assumed when the example was first introduced, that there are two users of the scarce resources, a binding constraint on working hours available (now in both processes), and divisibility of both resource and user.

14.3.1 Problem

The problem will be repeated, to avoid any confusion and the need to refer back, with the addition of a second resource constraint.

N Ltd manufactures two products A and B which pass through two processes Y and Z during manufacture. Product A sells at £15 per unit and Product B at £20 per unit. Selling prices cannot be varied and sales potential at these prices is expected to be:

Product A	36,000 units
Product B	14,000 units

Variable costs (£ per unit) are:

	Product A	**Product B**
Direct material	4	7
Direct labour	5	8
Variable overhead	1	2

Processing hours per 100 units are:

	Product A	**Product B**
Process Y	6	8
Process Z	5	10

Operating hours are limited to a total of 2,400 per annum in each of the processes.
N Ltd is seeking to determine the optimum allocation of its resources.

14.3.2 Solution

As before, the first step is to calculate the profitability of the two products and to establish whether the resource availability provides binding constraints on activity. The additional restriction on Process Z may not change the situation in any way. This would be the case if any combination of production resources at the limit of Process Y's capacity can be fulfilled within Process Z. On the other hand it could totally replace Process Y as the binding constraint. Allocation of resources would then be simply on the basis of contribution per operating hour in Process Z. A third possibility is that both may be binding at different times depending upon the particular production schedule.

It is assumed again that N Ltd wishes to allocate its available resources in such a way as to maximise the contribution generated. It is also assumed, as before, that fixed costs will be unaffected and not relevant to the decision.

PROFITABILITY

The profitability of the two products remains as before, viz:

Product A contribution £2 per unit
Product B contribution £3 per unit

PRODUCTION POTENTIAL

The limit of 2,400 operating hours in Process Y remains a constraint. Whether it is a binding constraint depends upon whether the upper limit on operating hours in Process Z provides any further restriction on activity. It is useful to establish first of all whether the upper limit on operating hours in Process Z is a constraint on satisfying sales requirements, regardless of any restriction in Process Y. The Process Z operating hours requirement in order to satisfy demand can be calculated as follows:

			Process Z operating hours required
Product A	$\frac{36,000}{100} \times 5$	=	1,800
Product B	$\frac{14,000}{100} \times 10$	=	1,400
			3,200

This confirms that activity is constrained by Process Z capacity availability. Hours needed to meet sales requirements (3,200 operating hours) exceed production capability (2,400 operating hours) by 800 hours ($33.\dot{3}\%$ of production capacity; or 25% of sales requirement).

ALLOCATION OF SCARCE RESOURCES

The question, however, is whether it is Process Y or Process Z capacity which provides the greatest restriction.

On the face of it Process Y would seem to be the binding constraint as it can only meet 73.2 % of sales requirement, whereas Process Z can provide 75%. However, it is not as simple as that. This can be shown by considering whether Process Z can satisfy the extreme possibilities in Process Y, viz:

1 Produce 36,000 units of Product A, with the balance of operating hours producing 3,000 units of Product B.
2 Produce 14,000 units of Product B, with the balance of operating hours producing 21,333 units of Product A.

To satisfy the above production schedules, Process Z hours required would be:

1 Product A $\frac{36,000}{100} \times 5 = 1,800$

Product B $\frac{3,000}{100} \times 10 = 300$

2,100 (within capacity)

2 Product A $\frac{21,333}{100} \times 5 = 1,067$

Product B $\frac{14,000}{100} \times 10 = 1,400$

2,467 (above capacity)

This demonstrates that the restrictions in both Process Y and Process Z must be considered. There are a limited number of production possibilities in Process Y that could not be accommodated in Process Z. If resources in Process Z are devoted first to Product B, production of Product A is restricted to 20,000 units

$\left(\text{ie } (2,400 - 1,400) \div \frac{5}{100}\right)$

The production possibilities can be seen more clearly if presented graphically (see Figure 14.3).

FIGURE 14.3 **Production possibilities, processes Y and Z**

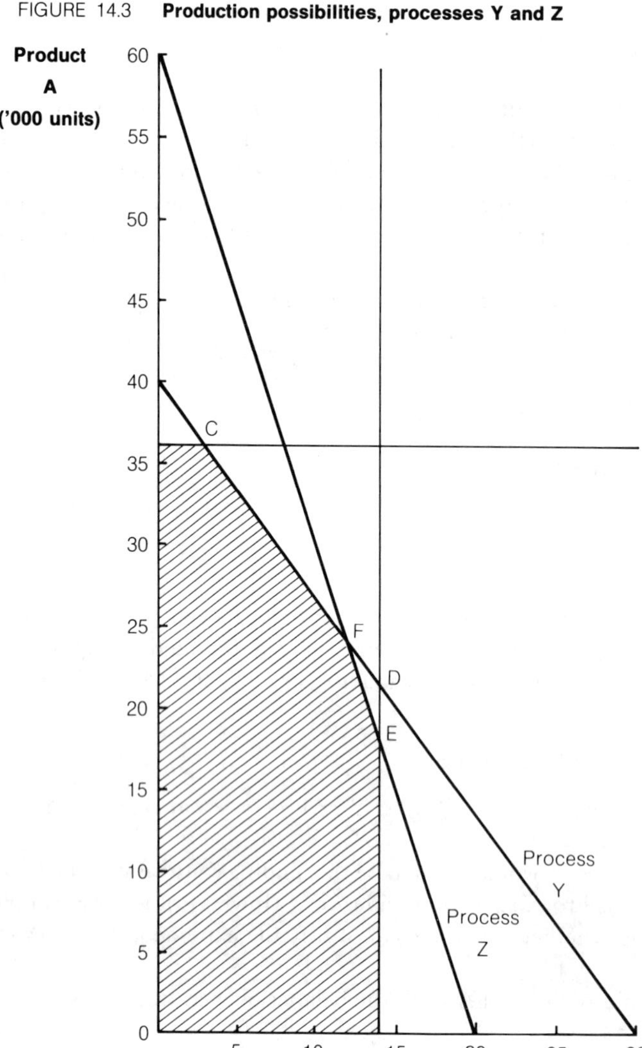

The shaded area includes all the production possibilities that can be accommodated by both processes and within the sales maxima. Those situated on the line CF fully utilise the available capacity in Process Y, with a surplus in Process Z. Those situated on the line FE fully utilise the available capacity in Process Z, with a surplus in Process Y. A change in the binding constraint is represented by turning a corner on the production possibilities area. Point F is the one production schedule which fully utilises capacity in both processes. It is not, however, necessarily the point of maximum contribution. There are three possible combinations of resources which could, on the face of it, provide maximum contribution (Points C, E and F).

The optimum combination (in the 2 resource constraint situation) can be determined in the same two main ways that were used in the single resource constraint situation:

1 Determine the production possibilities at each feasible point and find out the most profitable.
2 Carry out marginal analysis.

Each main method has a number of variants.

PRODUCTION POSSIBILITIES

The variants of this method reflect different ways of determining the production possibility at Point F, and different ways of determining the point of maximum contribution.

One way of determining the production schedule that fully utilises capacity in both processes (ie Point F) is to draw the graph (Figure 14.3) accurately and read off the production of the two products at that point. This could be checked for accuracy by confirming that the combination determined would utilise 2,400 operating hours in each process.

The other method of determining the production schedule at Point F (in the two products, two binding resource constraint situation) is by simultaneous equations. The equations for each process which express full utilisation of capacity are:

1 $6x + 8y = 2{,}400$ (Process Y)
2 $5x + 10y = 2{,}400$ (Process Z)

where:

x represents production in units of Product A (in hundreds)
and y represents production in units of Product B (in hundreds)

The two equations can be solved simultaneously as follows:

Equation 1 − Equation 2:

$x - 2y = 0$

$\therefore \quad x = 2y$

Substituting x for y in Equation 1:

$$6x + 4x = 2{,}400$$
$$10x = 2{,}400$$
$$x = 240$$ (Product A = 24,000 units)

From Equation 1:

$$1{,}440 + 8y = 2{,}400$$
$$8y = 960$$
$$y = 120$$ (Product B = 12,000 units)

Total contribution generated at the three feasible solution points is:

Point C:

Product A	36,000 × £2 =	£72,000
Product B	3,000 × £3 =	£9,000
		£81,000

Point E:

Product A	20,000 × £2 =	£40,000
Product B	14,000 × £3 =	£42,000
		£82,000

Point F:

Product A	24,000 × £2 =	£48,000
Product B	12,000 × £3 =	£36,000
		£84,000

The previous optimum solution, when there was only one constraint, favoured production of Product B in preference to Product A (Point D). The additional constraint on Process Z restricts the contribution to £82,000 (from £84,667) at Point E. The optimum solution now, however, is at Point F. The further restriction in Process Z reduces contribution by only £667 to £84,000.

An alternative to the above calculation of total contribution would have been to plot iso-contribution lines on the graph. The lines are unchanged from before and if plotted on Figure 14.3 and extended outwards would be seen to pass through the production possibilities area leaving at Point F.

MARGINAL ANALYSIS

The marginal analysis approach is based on the same principles as were applied in the single limiting factor situation, namely that contribution per unit of scarce resource should be the criterion. The difference is that this has to be calculated for each resource constraint and then applied in a more iterative fashion.

Contribution per unit of scarce resource is calculated as follows:

	Product A	**Product B**
Process Y (as before)	$£33.\dot{3}$	£37.50
Process Z	$\frac{200}{5}$	$\frac{300}{10}$
	= £40	= £30

This confirms what may have already been observed when Point F was previously determined as the optimum, namely that the ranking of products differs between the two processes. In Process Z, unlike Process Y, resources are better devoted to the production of Product A rather than Product B. This explains why Point F rather than Point E was determined as the optimum solution in the previous calculations.

It can be seen from looking at the contribution per unit of scarce resource figures in conjunction with the graph that Point F is preferable to both Points C and E. Moving from F towards C exchanges £37.50 per hour into $£33.\dot{3}$ per hour. Moving from F towards D exchanges £40 per hour into £30 per hour. If the same ranking had occurred in both Process Z and Process Y ie preference for Product B, then Point E would be preferred to Point F, which would be preferred to Point C.

How can the marginal analysis be used to determine the production schedule at Point F without resorting to simultaneous equations or to reading from a graph? The answer lies in starting from one of the feasible solutions that is known (ie Points C or E) and using information about the spare capacity at one or other of those points to calculate the change in production schedule required to eliminate that spare capacity.

For example, at Point E, spare capacity exists in Process Y. The use of capacity in Process Y is:

		Operating Hours in Process Y
Product A	$\frac{20{,}000}{100} \times 6 =$	1,200
Product B	$\frac{14{,}000}{100} \times 8 =$	1,120
		2,320

Space capacity in Process Y is thus 80 hours at Point E. If full capacity was maintained in Process Z, whilst at the same time substituting production of Product A for Product B, the production schedule would move along the line EF towards F and would gradually eliminate the spare capacity in Process Y. The effect on the spare capacity in Process Y, for every operating hour in Process Z that is transferred from production of B to production of A, would be as follows:

			Spare Capacity in Process Y
Product B	$-\frac{100}{10} = -10 \text{ units} \times \frac{8}{100}$	=	+ 0.8 hours
Product A	$+\frac{100}{5} = +20 \text{ units} \times \frac{6}{100}$	=	− 1.2 hours
			− 0.4 hours

Thus every hour substituted in Process Z would reduce spare capacity in Process Y by 0.4 hours. As spare capacity in Process Y at Point E is 80 hours, substitution of 200 hours (80 ÷ 0.4) in Process Z would eliminate the spare capacity in Process Y, and thus take the production schedule to Point F. The change in production schedule from E to F would be:

Product B −10 units × 200 hours = −2,000 units
Product A +20 units × 200 hours = +4,000 units

and thus the revised production schedule becomes:

Product A 20,000 + 4,000 = 24,000 units
Product B 14,000 − 2,000 = 12,000 units

Additional contribution generated from the change of 200 hours in Process Z (from Point E) would be £2,000, as each hour allocated to Product A in Process Z generates £40 contribution as opposed to £30 if allocated to Product B. Thus total contribution moves from £82,000 to £84,000.

Thus by marginal analysis, the optimum solution can be found. Exactly the same method could have been used from Point C to determine the optimum production schedule.

Self-assessment question 14.3

With reference to the situation of N Ltd, above, clearly demonstrate by marginal analysis if it is worthwhile moving production from Point C and if so by how much.

Answer on p 554

In the single resource constraint situation the opportunity cost of the scarce resource, over and above its basic cost, was identified. It is more complicated in the two resource constraint situation but the marginal analysis provides the basis for identifying such opportunity costs.

First, the resource constraint in Process Y. If say 10 hours are taken from their allocation to the production of Products A and B, capacity for these products would be reduced to 2,390 hours. Referring to Figure 14.3 a new production possibilities line could be drawn for Process Y to the left of, and parallel to, the original line. Production would move down FE towards Point E.

For every hour of Process Y lost, the hours substituted from Product A to Product B in Process Z would be 2.5 (ie based on the previously identified relationship of 1 hour substitution in Process Z = 0.4 hours of capacity in Process Y). The lost contribution would be £25 per hour of Process Y (ie 2.5 hours × £10 per hour difference in contribution between Product A at £40 per hour and Product B at £30 per hour). Alternatively this could be viewed as a reduction of Product A production of 50 units (2.5 hours × 20 units per hour) with a lost contribution of £100 and an increase of Product B production of 25 units (2.5 hours × 10 units per hour) with an increased contribution of £75.

The net £25 is the opportunity cost of capacity in Process Y, over and above its basic cost. Alternatively, it is the opportunity benefit if an additional unit of resource can be provided at the existing cost and is the on-cost that could be justified if additional capacity could be found. The opportunity cost of £25 per hour would remain for capacity reduction until Point E is reached (2,320 hours) after which the opportunity cost becomes the lost production of Product A at £33.$\dot{3}$ per hour. Spare capacity would be created in Process Z. For capacity expansion the opportunity benefit, or on-cost maximum, of £25 per hour would remain until 36,000 units of Product A are produced. No further expansion in Process Y could be justified without expansion in Process Z also.

Second, the resource constraint in Process Z can be considered. If say 10 hours are taken from their existing allocation, capacity available for production of Products A and B would be reduced to 2,390 hours. Referring again to Figure 14.3 a new production possibilities line could be drawn for Process Z to the left of, and parallel to, the original line. Production would move up FC towards Point C.

For every hour of Process Z lost, the hours substituted from Product B to Product A in Process Y would be 2.4 (ie based on the previously identified relationship of 1 hour substitution in Process Y = 0.41$\dot{6}$ hours of capacity in Process Z). The lost contribution would be £10 per hour of Process Z (ie 2.4 hours × £4.1$\dot{6}$ per hour difference in contribution between Product A at £33.$\dot{3}$ per hour and Product B at £37.50 per hour). Alternatively this could be viewed as a reduction of Product B production of 30 units (2.4 hours × 12.5 units per hour) with a lost contribution of £90 and an increase of Product A production of 40 units (2.4 hours × 16.$\dot{6}$ units per hour) with an increased contribution of £80. Opportunity costs and benefits can be viewed in a similar way to those in Process Y.

The net £10 is the opportunity cost of capacity in Process Z, over and above its basic cost. Alternatively, this could be viewed as the on-cost that could be justified if additional capacity could be found. This opportunity cost would remain for capacity reduction until Point C is reached (2,100 hours), after which the opportunity cost becomes the lost production of Product B at £30 per hour. Spare capacity would be created in Process Y. The situation would change again when a point is reached when only Product A is produced. A further reduction in capacity would have an opportunity cost of £40 per hour. For capacity expansion, the on-cost maximum of £10 per hour would remain until 14,000 units of Product B were produced. No further expansion in Process Z could be justified without expansion in Process Y also.

Expansion of both Process Y and Process Z at the same rate would generate additional contribution at £17.50 per hour (ie (25 + 10) ÷ 2). For example if capacity of both processes increases to 2,500 hours, the optimum production schedule becomes Product A 25,000 units, Product B 12,500 units. Total contribution becomes £87,500, an increase of £3,500 from 200 additional hours.

A further question is whether the optimum production schedule is sensitive to changes in unit contributions. A move to Point C would only be justified if the relative product contributions per hour of Process Y changed sufficiently to remove the current difference. If Product A contribution increased by more than 12.5% (to more than £2.25 per unit) or a similar reduction occurred in Product B contribution, a change in the production schedule would be justified. A move to Point E would only be justified if the relative product contributions per hour of Process Z changed sufficiently to remove the current difference. If Product B contribution increased by more than 33.3% (to more than £4 per unit) or a similar reduction occurred in Product A contribution, a change in the production schedule would be justified.

An alternative method of marginal analysis, based on the same principles as those applied above, is the simplex method of linear programming. The simplex method is a similar iterative process, analysing one solution after another until it automatically signals that the optimum solution has been reached. This is also done by starting with any feasible solution and then moving along the edges of the production possibilities area (referred to as the feasibility polygon) in an efficient manner until the optimum solution is found. The repetitive series of steps is called an algorithm. The simplex method is an extremely powerful tool of analysis and yields a considerable amount of information, apart from satisfying the objective of determining the optimum allocation of scarce resources.

Initially the bare bones are extracted and written down mathematically. There are four steps:

1 Assign symbols to the unknown quantities. As before in the use of simultaneous equations, x will be used to denote units of Product A (in hundreds) and y to denote units of Product B (in hundreds).

2 Express the restrictions in terms of inequalities on x and y. The capacity restrictions can be expressed as:

$6x + 8y \leq 2{,}400$
$5x + 10y \leq 2{,}400$
and the sales restrictions:
$x \leq 360$
$y \leq 140$
Also
$x \geq 0$
$y \geq 0$

3 Formulate the objective function, which is to maximise the total contribution expressed as:
$200x + 300y = \text{max.}$
The problem is thus to find values of x and y which meet the capacity and sales restrictions and which at the same time maximise the objective function.

4 Convert the linear inequalities into linear equations, through the insertion of slack variables (S_1,S_2, S_3 and S_4).
S_1 and S_2 represent the unutilised capacity (hours) in Processes Y and Z respectively.
S_3 and S_4 represent the unsatisfied demand (hundreds of units) for Products A and B respectively.
Thus:

$6x + 8y + S_1 = 2{,}400$
$5x + 10y + S_2 = 2{,}400$
$x + S_3 = 360$
$y + S_4 = 140$

The information can now be set up in a form suitable for the simplex algorithm. This form is:

Solution Variable	x	y	S_1	S_2	S_3	S_4	Solution Quantity
S_1	6	8	1	0	0	0	2,400
S_2	5	10	0	1	0	0	2,400
S_3	1	0	0	0	1	0	360
S_4	0	1	0	0	0	1	140
Opportunity (Cost) /Benefit per unit	(200)	(300)	0	0	0	0	0

It is assumed that students are familiar with the establishment and use of the simplex tableau and algorithm. The tableau starts from the point of zero production and shows the spare capacity, unsatisfied demand, unit profit forgone, and resources required. The opportunity cost, measuring the contribution forgone per unit of product by not using resources in another way, is sometimes alternatively expressed as the opportunity benefit, measuring the profit that could be obtained from an alternative use of resources. It simply changes the sign from negative to positive.

The solution for each variable can easily be seen. For example the spare capacity in Process Y (S_1) can be seen to be 2,400 hours, and in Process Z (S_2) also 2,400 hours. Unsatisfied demand for Product A (S_3) is 36,000 units (360 × 100) and for Product B (S_4) is 14,000 units (140 × 100). Products A and B (x and y) do not appear in the solution variable column as there is zero production. If the solution variable column was not shown in the tableau the variable associated with each solution figure can be found by finding a figure 1 in a column where all the other figures in the column are zero. For example, the 2,400 solution in the first row can be attributed to S_1 because a figure 1 appears in that column and all other figures in the column are zero.

The algorithm is repeated until there are no opportunity costs left (ie negative values on the bottom row). The final tableau is:

Solution Variable	x	y	S_1	S_2	S_3	S_4	Solution Quantity
x	1	0	$\frac{1}{2}$	$(\frac{4}{10})$	0	0	240
y	0	1	$(\frac{1}{4})$	$\frac{3}{10}$	0	0	120
S_3	0	0	$(\frac{1}{2})$	$\frac{4}{10}$	1	0	120
S_4	0	0	$\frac{1}{4}$	$(\frac{3}{10})$	0	1	20
Opportunity (Cost) /Benefit per unit	0	0	25	10	0	0	84,000

This indicates that production should be 24,000 units of Product A and 12,000 units of Product B generating a total contribution of £84,000. Unsatisfied demand for Products A and B is 12,000 units and 2,000 units respectively. There is no spare capacity in either process. This is consistent with the results of the other methods used earlier. The opportunity benefits that remain on the bottom row are also known as 'shadow prices' or 'dual prices'. They represent the increase in value of the objective function that would result from the availability of one more unit of the particular resource (or reduction if equivalent resource is lost). If one extra hour of Process Y time is made available there would be an increase in profits of £25. If one extra hour of Process Z time is made available there would be an increase in profits of £10. This is consistent with the opportunity benefits identified from the marginal analysis earlier. At the same time these become opportunity costs if process time is lost.

The increase in profits of £25 in Process Y would result from an increase of $\frac{1}{2}$ of x and a reduction of $\frac{1}{4}$ of y. Unsatisfied demand is correspondingly affected. These changes can be seen by looking at column S_1 in the tableau. $\frac{1}{2}$ of x represents 50 units of Product A with an increased contribution of £100 and $\frac{1}{4}$ of y represents 25 units of Product B, with a reduction in contribution of £75. The increase in profits of £10 in Process Z would result from a reduction of $\frac{4}{10}$ of x and an increase of $\frac{3}{10}$ of y. $\frac{4}{10}$ of x represents 40 units of Product A with a reduction in contribution of £80, and $\frac{3}{10}$ of y represents 30 units of Product B with an increased contribution of £90. The reverse applies if capacity is reduced. Again, this is entirely consistent with the results of the marginal analysis examined earlier.

Shadow prices can provide guidance on the maximum amount that is worth paying to relieve the capacity limitations. The shadow price remains valid only while a resource remains a binding constraint. This was explained and illustrated using the 'marginal analysis' approach earlier in the chapter. Using the simplex method, when the binding constraints change the solution should be reworked at which time new shadow prices (opportunity benefits) will result.

Self-assessment question 14.4

Refer back to Self-assessment question 14.1, which was part (a) of a question on the ACCA Management Accounting examination paper in June 1983. The following is parts (b) and (c) of that question.

(b) Assume that, before the plan that you have prepared in part (a) is implemented, Corpach Ltd suffers a major fire which completely destroys building B2. The fire thus reduces the availability of type B machine time to 10,500 hours p.a. and the estimated fixed overhead for such machines, to £8,200. In all other respects the conditions set out, in part (a) to this question, continue to apply.

In his efforts to obtain a revised production plan the company's accountant makes use of a linear programming computer package. This package produces the following optimal tableau:

Z	X1	X2	X3	S1	S2	S3	S4	S5	
0	0	0	0	0.5	1	0	0.143	−0.429	1,150
0	0	1	0	−0.5	0	0	−0.143	0.429	1,850
0	0	0	0	0	0	1	−0.429	0.286	3,800
0	0	0	1	0	0	0	0.429	−0.286	1,200
0	1	0	0	1	0	0	0	0	2,500
1	0	0	0	1.5	0	0	2.429	0.714	35,050

In the above: Z is the total contribution,
X1 is the budgeted output of product 1,
X2 is the budgeted output of product 2,
X3 is the budgeted output of product 3,
S1 is the unsatisfied demand for product 1,
S2 is the unsatisfied demand for product 2,
S3 is the unsatisfied demand for product 3,
S4 is the unutilised type A machine time
and S5 is the unutilised type B machine time.
The tableau is interpreted as follows:
Optimal Plan—Make 2,500 units of Product 1,
1,850 units of Product 2
and 1,200 units of Product 3.
Shadow Prices—Product 1 £1.50 per unit,
Type A Machine Time £2.429 per hour
Type B Machine Time £0.714 per hour.
Explain the meaning of the shadow prices and consider how the accountant might make use of them. Calculate the profit anticipated from the revised plan and comment on its variation from the profit that you calculated in your answer to part (a).

(c) Explain why linear programming was not necessary for the facts as set out in part (a) whereas it was required for part (b).

(*ACCA*, *Management Accounting*, *June 1983* (*parts b and c*))

Answers on p 555

14.3.3 Changed assumptions

Whilst continuing to maintain the initial assumption of a double resource limitation how is the analysis changed if other assumptions are changed, or the limitations can be overcome? For example:

What if there are more than two users of the resource?
What if resources and/or users are non-divisible?
What if some other way can be found of obtaining additional product or resource?

Each of the above will be considered independently.

MORE USERS

If there are more than two users of the scarce resources the situation cannot be depicted on a two dimensional graph as before and the optimal allocation of resources becomes more difficult to determine if both scarce resources provide a binding constraint dependent upon the particular production schedule. The simplex algorithm provides the only viable solution method as it provides a structural framework within which the marginal analysis can be carried out.

Solution calculations are not illustrated in this book, and would not be expected in Management Accounting examinations, beyond the two constraint/two user situation, although interpretation of the final simplex tableau in more complex situations may be required. Computer software is now widely available.

NON-DIVISIBILITY

The general approach would change and would be along the lines of that discussed in the single limiting factor situation.

ADDITIONAL RESOURCE

If the binding constraints can be overcome completely, such that they are no longer binding, then the criterion changes, as was illustrated earlier during the discussion of the single limiting factor situation. The selection would again be on the basis of on-cost in relation to the scarce resource, but with the complication that more than one scarce resource is involved.

SUMMARY

A variety of limiting factor situations have been illustrated in the chapter, as have various methods of determining the optimum allocation of scarce resources in such situations.

Limiting factor situations arise because an organisation's demand for one or more input resources exceeds their available supply. Situations vary in respect of the number of limitations; the number of alternative users of the limited resources; the extent of divisibility of both the resource(s) and the user(s) of the resource(s); and whether the limitation is binding.

In general terms, the contribution generated by the different users of scarce resources needs to be related to the quantity of scarce resource(s) utilised. Where there is a single limiting factor, and divisibility of both resource and users can be assumed, the allocation of the resource amongst users is on the basis of contribution per unit of limiting factor. The same principle is relevant where there is more than one binding factor; it becomes more difficult to apply, however. Where non-divisibility occurs, the solution is on the basis of the absolute contribution generated from alternative combinations of the limited resources.

EXERCISES

Exercise 14.1

The management of Alliance Engineering & Manufacturing Company Limited produce a range of components and products. They are considering next year's production, purchases and sales budgets. Shown below are the budgeted total unit costs for two of the components and two of the products manufactured by the company.

	Component 12 £ per unit	**Component** 14 £ per unit	**Product** VW £ per unit	**Product** XY £ per unit
Direct material	18	26	12	28
Direct labour	16	4	12	24
Variable overhead	8	2	6	12
Fixed overhead	20	5	15	30
	62	37	45	94

Components 12 and 14 are incorporated into other products manufactured and sold by the company, but they are not incorporated into the two products shown above.

It is possible to purchase components 12 and 14 from other companies for £60 per unit and £30 per unit respectively.

The current selling prices of products VW and XY are £33 and £85 respectively.

You are required to:

(a) Evaluate, clearly indicating all the assumptions you make, whether it would be profitable in the year ahead for the company to:
(i) purchase either of the components;
(ii) sell either of the above products.

(b) Prepare statements for management with supporting explanations as to how the following additional information would affect your evaluation in (a) above if next year's production requirements for the two components are 7,000 units of component 12 and 6,000 units of component 14 and the budgeted sales for the two products VW and XY are 5,000 units and 4,000 units respectively when a special machine, a MAC, is required.

The MAC machine is needed exclusively for these two components and two products because of specific customer requirements but for technical reasons the machine can only be used for a maximum of 80,000 hours in the year.

The budgeted MAC machine usage for any one year is 80,000 hours and requirements per unit for the various items are as follows:

Component 12	8 machine hours
Component 14	2 machine hours
Product VW	6 machine hours
Product XY	12 machine hours

The operating costs of the MAC machine have been included in the unit costs shown in (a) above.

(*ACCA*, *Management Accounting*, *June 1987*)

Answers on p 556

Exercise 14.2

A company manufactures a product which has three components, A, B and C. At present the company is working at full capacity producing the three components, and the final assembled product. All the machines are capable of making all the components. Current cost data concerning one hundred units of the product are as follows:

	Machine Hours	Cost (£)		
		Variable	*Fixed*	*Total*
Components—A	10	26	10	36
—B	16	32	12	44
—C	20	32	32	64
Assembly	—	52	22	74
	46	142	76	218
Selling Price (£)				250

The management is engaged in preparing next year's budget and an increase in sales is anticipated. No increase in the present machine capacity can be effected for over twelve months. The buying-in of components from outside suppliers is being considered.

The following quotations have been received per 100 components:

	£
Components—A	36
—B	46
—C	54

The sales manager feels that the minimum increase on existing sales and production that should be considered is 50% and that he could sell up to an increase of 80%.

Based on sales increases of 50% and 80% respectively, you are required to prepare a report for management giving your recommendations as to:

(a) which component should be ordered from outside suppliers for the coming year, if it is decided that the whole of the requirements of one component should be obtained in this way.

(b) how to best utilise production capacity if it is decided that buying-in part requirements of components is to be permitted.

As a start to your answer consider the following criteria and their relevance to solving the above.

	1	11	111
Component Bought-in	*Contribution per hundred units*	*Contribution per Prod. Hour*	*Extra cost per Prod. Hour Saved*
A	£98	£2.72	£1.00
B	£94	£3.13	£0.875
C	£86	£3.31	£1.10

Answers on p 558

Exercise 14.3

Rosehip has spare capacity in two of its manufacturing departments—Department 4 and Department 5. A five day week of 40 hours is worked but there is only enough internal work for three days per week so that two days per week (16 hours) could be available in each department. In recent months Rosehip has sold this time to another manufacturer but there is some concern about the profitability of this work.

The accountant has prepared a table giving the hourly operating costs in each department. The summarised figures are as follows:

	Department 4	**Department 5**
	£	£
Power Costs	40	60
Labour Costs	40	20
Overhead Costs	40	40
	120	120

The labour force is paid on a time basis and there is no change in the weekly wage bill whether or not the plant is working at full capacity. The overhead figures are taken from the firm's current overhead absorption rates. These rates are designed to absorb all budgeted overhead (fixed and variable) when the departments are operating at 90% of full capacity (assume a 50 week year). The budgeted fixed overhead attributed to Department 4 is £36,000 p.a. and that for Department 5 is £50,400 p.a.

As a short term expedient the company has been selling processing time to another manufacturer who has been paying £70 per hour for time in either department. This customer is very willing to continue this arrangement and to purchase any spare time available but Rosehip is considering the introduction of a new product on a minor scale to absorb the spare capacity.

Each unit of the new product would require 45 minutes in Department 4 and 20 minutes in Department 5. The variable cost of the required input material is £10 per unit. It is considered that:

with a selling price of £100 the demand would be 1,500 units p.a.;
with a selling price of £110 the demand would be 1,000 units p.a. and
with a selling price of £120 the demand would be 500 units p.a.

You are required to:

(a) Calculate the best weekly programme for the slack time in the two manufacturing departments, to determine the best price to charge for the new product and to quantify the weekly gain that this programme and this price should yield.

(b) Assume that the new product has been introduced successfully but that the demand for the established main products has now increased so that all available time could now be absorbed by Rosehip's main-line products. An optimal production plan for the main products has been obtained by linear programming and the optimal L.P. tableau shows a shadow price of £76 per hour in Department 4 and of £27 per hour in Department 5. The new product was not considered in this exercise. Discuss the viability of the new product under the new circumstances.

(c) Comment on the relationship between shadow prices and opportunity costs.

(*ACCA, Management Accounting, December 1984*)

Answers on p 560

Exercise 14.4

Following a fire at the factory of Elgar Ltd, the management team met to review the proposed operations for the next quarter. The fire had destroyed all the finished goods stock, some of the raw materials and about half of the machines in the forming shop.

At the meeting of the management team the following additional information was provided:

(i) Only 27,000 machine hours of forming capacity will be available in the forthcoming quarter. Although previously it was thought that sales demand would be the only binding limitation on production it has now become apparent that for the forthcoming quarter the forming capacity would be a limiting factor.

(ii) It will take about three months to re-instate the forming shop to its previous operational capacity. Hence the restriction on forming capacity is for the next quarter only.

(iii) Some details of the product range manufactured by Elgar are provided in the following table:

Per unit details of Elgar's product range

	Product				
	A	B	C	D	E
Sales price	£50	£60	£40	£50	£80
Units of special material required for production					
W or X	2	2	2	1	3
Y	—	—	—	—	6
Z	1	2	1	1	—
Other direct material costs	£6	£12	£6	£5	£13
Other variable production costs	£8	£4	£8	£4	£4
Fixed production costs (based on standard costs)	£6	£3	£6	£3	£3
Forming hours required	5	6	2	10	6

(iv) The forecasts of demand, in units, for the forthcoming quarter are:

Product	*A*	*B*	*C*	*D*	*E*
Units demanded	2,000	2,000	4,000	3,000	4,000

It was originally intended that the number of units produced would equal the units demanded for each product.

(v) Due to a purchasing error there is an excess of material W in stock. This has a book value of £6 per unit which is also its current replacement cost. This could be sold to realise £4 per unit after sales and transport costs. Material X could be used instead of material W; material X is not in stock and has a current replacement cost of £5 per unit.

(vi) Material Y was in stock at a book value of £2 per unit, which is its normal cost if ordered 3 months in advance, but the stocks of this material were entirely destroyed by the fire. In order to obtain the material quickly a price of £3 per unit will have to be paid for the first 3,000 units obtained in the quarter and any additional units required will cost £6 per unit. These special prices will apply only to this quarter's purchases.

(vii) Some of the stock of material Z was destroyed by the fire. The remaining stocks of 2,000 units have a book value of £7 per unit. The replacement price for Z is currently £8 per unit.

(viii) As a result of the fire it is estimated that the fixed production costs will be £42,000 for the next quarter and the administration and office overheads will amount to £11,500.

(ix) The demand figures shown in note (iv) include a regular order from a single customer for:

3,000 units of C, and
3,000 units of E.

This order is usually placed quarterly and the customer always specifies that the order be fulfilled in total or not at all.

Required:

(a) *Ignoring the information contained in note (ix) for this section of the question*, determine the optimum production plan for the forthcoming quarter and prepare a statement which indicates to the management of Elgar the estimated financial results of their planned production, in terms of total contribution, net current operating profit and financial accounting profit.

(b) Prepare a statement which clearly shows the management of Elgar Ltd. the financial consequences of both the acceptance and the rejection of the order mentioned in note (ix). Advise Elgar on the desirability of acceptance of the order in total. Indicate what further information would be useful in arriving at a decision whether to accept or reject the order.

(*ACCA, Management Accounting, December 1981*)

Answers in lecturer's manual

Pricing Decisions

INTRODUCTION

The determination of selling prices is an important and difficult decision in many businesses, and one to which the management accountant normally makes a significant contribution. For many products and services, selling price is a major determinant of demand as one of a number of variables in the marketing mix which together seek to gain a differential advantage. Other influential factors in the marketing mix include design, packaging, branding, quality, reliability, availability, delivery performance, after-sales service, advertising and sales promotion, credit terms, and selling effort and expertise. These factors have an effect on costs and also influence demand. At the same time they may permit some differentiation in price compared with competition and thus make the selling price decision even more difficult. For most products and services there are likely to be a range of prices which may be acceptable in the market place and the individual firm is likely to be in a position to determine for itself the price that it charges.

This chapter considers both theoretical and practical aspects of selling price decisions. The theoretical economic background to pricing known as marginal analysis is reviewed, together with the concept of price elasticity. In theory, price is a function of both demand and supply. In practice, pricing determined on the basis of 'cost plus' (ie supply factors), with seemingly little regard for demand conditions, is popular. Formula pricing methods based on 'cost plus' are described and their limitations discussed.

As with other chapters self-assessment questions and end-of-chapter exercises are included. Further pricing illustrations are provided in Chapter 18, 'Uncertainty in Decision-Making.'

15.1 THE ECONOMIC APPROACH TO PRICING

The economic approach shows how the firm should study demand as well as cost in an attempt to find the output level, and the corresponding selling price, at which profit will be maximised. Economic theory provides a summary explanation of profit maximising behaviour. Different market structures have implications for the ability of an individual supplier to decide selling price.

15.1.1 Market structures

In Chapter 4 the economist's and accountant's cost-volume-profit models were contrasted. The particular economic model presented in Chapter 4 was that portraying a situation of imperfect competition with differentiated products. In such a situation the individual firm is able to pursue an independent pricing policy. The model of an imperfectly competitive market is in contrast to that of a firm operating under conditions of perfect competition, where the selling price is determined by the market. In such a market there are a large number of buyers and sellers of an homogeneous product; the individual firm is a 'price-taker'. In practice even if there are a large number of sellers, the concept of a perfectly competitive market is unrealistic, as inevitably products may be differentiated in some way, or at least perceived to be so by consumers.

Other situations where firms will be prevented from determining, or will choose not to determine, selling price independently are where there is central price control by government or by a trade association, or where an oligopolistic market exists, (ie few sellers), and a firm either follows the price leader or there is price stability by tacit agreement between the few sellers.

Returning to the economic model of imperfect competition (and to the diagrammatic illustration provided in Chapter 4), where a firm is in a position to determine its own selling price, profit maximising output is where marginal revenue per unit is equal to marginal cost per unit (see

FIGURE 15.1 **The economic model of imperfect competition**

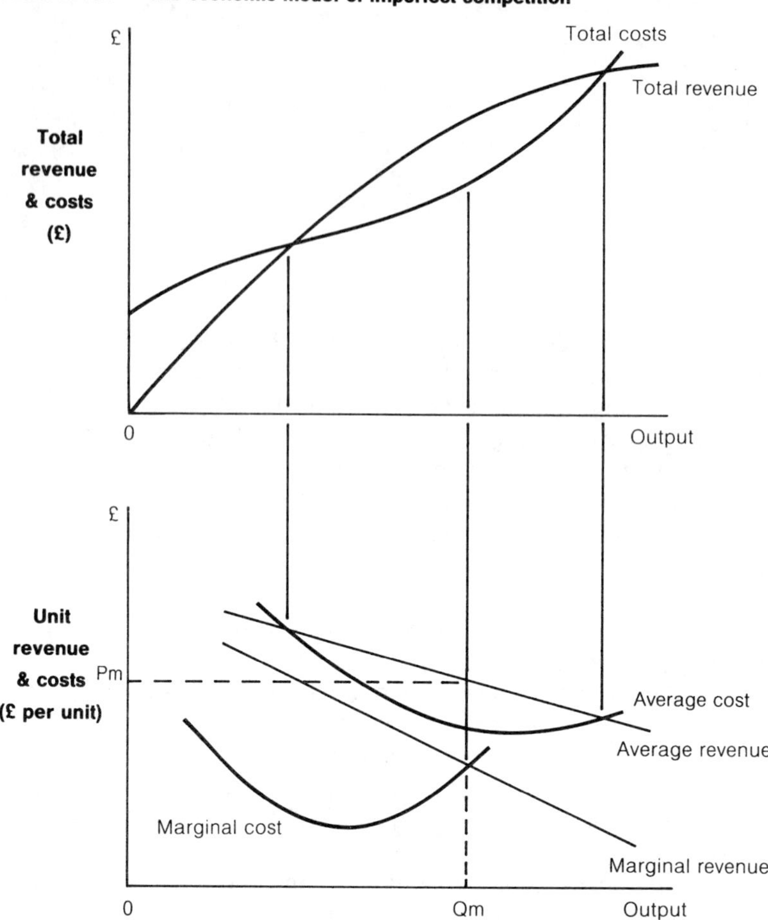

Figure 15.1 bottom). The gap between total revenue and total cost is widest at this point (see Figure 15.1 top). Profit maximising selling price is Pm and output Qm. To use the terminology of Chapter 12 it is the point at which future economic revenues (avoidable revenues) exceed future economic costs (avoidable costs) by the greatest amount.

15.1.2 Price elasticity of demand

In conditions of perfect competition, where the price charged by a business is dictated by the market, the revenue function will be a straight line, and the demand/price relationship is irrelevant to a business. Where imperfect competition exists, and the firm is a 'price maker', it is important to incorporate, in the revenue function, the degree of responsiveness of demand to changes in price.

The way in which demand for a product is affected by the selling price is explained by means of a demand function. There is likely to be an inverse relationship between demand and selling price, and thus a downward sloping demand function (see Figure 15.2). If selling price rises, demand falls; if selling price falls, demand rises.

The demand function may or may not be a straight line, and may alternatively be referred to as the demand curve. The concept of price elasticity of demand has been developed to provide a measure of the degree to which demand responds to a change in price.

The basic formula is:

$$\text{Price Elasticity of Demand} = \frac{\%\ \text{change in quantity demanded}}{\%\ \text{change in price}}$$

Because substitutes can be found for most products, and because individuals have many alternative ways of disposing of their incomes, there can be few products for which demand has no element of elasticity.

FIGURE 15.2 **Demand/price relationship under imperfect competition**

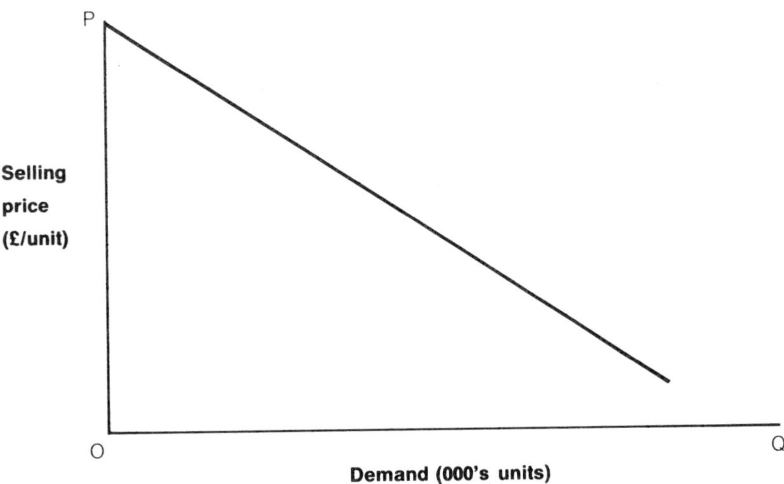

If the elasticity of demand, measured by the above formula, has a value between 0 and 1, demand is said to be 'inelastic'. This means that a change in selling price of a certain percentage results in a less than proportionate inverse change in demand. A price reduction causes total revenue to fall; a price increase causes total revenue to increase. Demand is said to be 'elastic' when the elasticity of demand is greater than 1. A change in selling price by a certain percentage results in a more than proportionate change in demand. A price reduction causes total revenue to increase; a price increase causes total revenue to fall. 'Unit elasticity' is where a percentage change in price is exactly matched by the percentage change in demand. Total revenue is unchanged.

The price elasticity of demand formula can be applied in two main ways. One application is called 'point elasticity'; the other 'arc (or range) elasticity'.

POINT ELASTICITY

The elasticity of demand at a particular point on the demand curve is calculated as:

$$\frac{Q_2 - Q_1}{Q_1} \div \frac{P_2 - P_1}{P_1}$$

Where $P_2 - P_1$ represents the change in selling price from P_1 to P_2, and $Q_2 - Q_1$ represents the resulting change in demand, going from output level Q_1 to output level Q_2.

For example, let us assume that a company can sell 3,000 units of a product in a period at a selling price of £70 per unit. If the selling price is reduced to £65 per unit, demand is expected to increase to 3,500 units per period.

$$\text{Point elasticity} = \frac{3{,}500 - 3{,}000}{3{,}000} \div \frac{65 - 70}{70}$$

$$= \frac{500}{3{,}000} \div \frac{-5}{70}$$

$$= -2.\dot{3}$$

For a downward sloping demand function, elasticity is always negative, but the minus sign is usually ignored. In the above example, demand is 'elastic' as the elasticity of demand is greater than 1. As explained earlier, total revenue increases in such a situation when price falls; demand changes by a greater proportion than price. The price reduction is 7.1%; the demand increase is $16.\dot{6}\%$.

$$\text{Elasticity} = \frac{16.\dot{6}}{7.1} = 2.\dot{3}$$

Total revenue at P_1 Q_1 = 3,000 × 70 = £210,000
Total revenue at P_2 Q_2 = 3,500 × 65 = £227,500

Whether profit increases depends upon the change in costs. In this example, if the increase in costs, as a result of the extra 500 units output, exceeds £17,500 (ie £35 per unit), then profit will be reduced, and vice versa.

If the above calculation of elasticity was repeated but this time for the reverse situation of an increase in selling price from £65 to £70 per unit and a reduction in demand from 3,500 units to 3,000 units, a different figure for the price elasticity of demand would result.

$$\text{Elasticity} = \frac{3{,}000 - 3{,}500}{3{,}500} \div \frac{70 - 65}{65}$$

$$= \frac{-500}{3{,}500} \div \frac{5}{65}$$

$$= 1.86$$

Although the absolute changes in price and demand are the same, the base point for each is changed and thus the relative values (the percentage changes) are different. The price increase is 7.7%; the demand decrease is 14.3%. Elasticity $= \frac{14.3}{7.7} = 1.86$

ARC ELASTICITY

The different value for the price elasticity of demand, depending upon whether one moves from P_1 to P_2 or from P_2 to P_1 is regarded as an unsatisfactory aspect of the point elasticity formula. The arc elasticity formula overcomes this problem by calculating the mid-point price and demand as the base points to be used. Elasticity is calculated as:

$$\frac{Q_2 - Q_1}{\frac{1}{2}(Q_2 + Q_1)} \div \frac{P_2 - P_1}{\frac{1}{2}(P_2 + P_1)}$$

Whether the price is reducing from £70 to £65 per unit, or increasing from £65 to £70 per unit, the arc elasticity is:

$$\frac{500}{3{,}250} \div \frac{5}{67.5} = 2.08$$

Difficulties remain however. There may be differing reactions to large price movements, as opposed to small price movements, in terms of the relative change in demand compared to the change in price. Connected with this is the fact that a demand curve is unlikely to have constant elasticity over the complete range of prices. Only if selling price and demand each change by a consistent percentage will elasticity remain the same. If both change consistently by the same percentage demand has unit price elasticity. If selling price changes by a larger percentage than demand, demand is price inelastic. If selling price changes by a smaller percentage than demand, demand is price elastic.

15.1.3 Profit elasticity

In the example used to illustrate point elasticity above, a selling price reduction of 7.1% (from £70 to £65 per unit) led to a demand increase of 16.6% (from 3,000 to 3,500 units.) If the contribution percentage of sales before the price change is 50%, total contribution would be the same for each selling price. Thus, in such a situation, an increase in demand of more than 16.6% would be required to justify the 7.1% price reduction. If the contribution percentage before the price change is less than

50%, total contribution would be reduced by the price reduction ie an even higher demand increase would be required. At a 40% contribution, for example, the demand increase required becomes 21.7%.

This effect on contribution is demonstrated by the following calculations:

		Selling Price £70 per unit	Selling Price £65 per unit
	Sales units	3,000	3,500
	Sales revenue	£210,000	£227,500
1	Contribution per unit	35	30
	Contribution % of sales	50%	46%
	Total contribution	£105,000	£105,000
2	Contribution per unit	28	23
	Contribution % of sales	40%	35%
	Total contribution	£84,000	£80,500

With a contribution of sales, before the price change, of 40%, the reduction in selling price of £5 per unit reduces unit contribution from £28 to £23. To maintain a total contribution of £84,000 (3,000 units × £28 per unit), sales units at the reduced selling price of £65 need to be 3,652 units, an increase of 21.7% $\left(\frac{652}{3{,}000} \times 100\%\right)$.

The effect on profit of price and volume relationships is easily misunderstood. For example, how many students, and indeed managers, would realise that for a product with a 30% contribution, a 10% increase in price coupled with a 25% volume decrease would be worthwhile? Total contribution would be the same with or without the price increase; the price increase would be justified by the reduced capital employed required on the lower volume. Equally, how many would realise that for the same product a more than 50% increase in demand would be required to justify a 10% price decrease?

The above situations are demonstrated by the following calculations based on a product with sales of 10,000 units at a selling price of £10 per unit:

Selling price per unit	£11	← +10% ←	£10	→ −10% →	£9
Sales units	7,500	← −25% ←	10,000	→ +50% →	15,000
Contribution per unit	4		3		2
Contribution % of sales	36%		30%		22%
Total contribution	£30,000		£30,000		£30,000

A more general picture of contribution sensitivity can be obtained from Tables 15.1 and 15.2. Table 15.1 shows the percentage volume increases required to maintain total contribution, at a range of contribution/sales ratios, and a range of selling price increases. Table 15.2 shows the percentage reductions in volume that can be afforded without reducing total contribution, where selling prices are increased.

		Contribution % of sales						
		20%	30%	40%	50%	60%	70%	80%
Selling price reduction	−5%	+33%	+20%	+14%	+11%	+9%	+8%	+7%
	−10%	+100%	+50%	+33%	+25%	+20%	+17%	+14%
	−15%	+300%	+100%	+60%	+43%	+33%	+27%	+23%

TABLE 15.1 **Volume increase to offset contribution effect of selling price reductions**

		Contribution % of sales						
		20%	30%	40%	50%	60%	70%	80%
Selling price increase	+5%	−20%	−14%	−11%	−9%	−8%	−7%	−6%
	+10%	−33%	−25%	−20%	−17%	−14%	−12%	−11%
	+15%	−43%	−33%	−27%	−23%	−20%	−18%	−16%

TABLE 15.2 **Volume decrease to offset contribution effect of selling price increases**

Thus, at the extremes of the information contained in the above tables, a product with a contribution/sales ratio of 20% for example would require a 300% increase in volume to justify a 15% reduction in selling price. That is without considering the cost of increased working capital requirements, and the implications for fixed costs. Against this there may be certain economies within variable costs as a result of the increased activity. Also, for some, the working capital implications may be positive. For example, a retailer buying on credit and selling for cash may gain from increased activity if the stock turnover ratio is high. At the other extreme, still considering the implications for volume of selling price reductions, a product with a contribution/sales ratio of 80% will only require a 7% increase in volume to justify a 5% price reduction.

Where price increases are being considered, for a product with a 20% contribution/sales ratio for example, a volume reduction of 43% would offset a selling price increase of 15%. For a product with an 80% contribution/sales ratio, a volume reduction of 6% would offset a 5% selling price increase.

From the information provided in Tables 15.1 and 15.2 it can be concluded that selling price reductions will never be justified if demand is inelastic. Point elasticity must always be greater than 1 (ie elastic) to justify a price reduction. In the extreme case in Table 15.1, (20% C/S ratio and 15% price reduction), point elasticity required is 20 (ie $\frac{300}{15}$).

Selling price increases will always be justified if point elasticity is less than 1 (ie inelastic). They may also be justified if point elasticity is greater than 1. This will depend upon the contribution/sales ratio and the percentage price increase. In the extreme case in Table 15.2, (20% C/S ratio and 5% price increase), point elasticity could be as high as 4 (ie $\frac{20}{5}$).

It is important that the effect of volume/price relationships on profit are understood when making selling price decisions, both as part of longer term pricing strategy and also for shorter term tactical decisions, for example deciding on price promotions.

Self-assessment question 15.1

The Holee College teaches wholly through the correspondence method. This is done by the production of self-study packs which enables students to prepare for professional qualifications.

Each course of study was sold at the price of £15 last year and a total of 10,000 units were produced and sold. The production costs of the various courses offered by the College are the same.

The variable cost of producing a study course last year was:

	£
Direct materials	5.00
Direct labour	6.00
Other direct costs (mainly postage)	0.60
Variable overhead	0.40
Total variable cost	£12.00

The fixed overhead for the Holee College during the year was £20,000. During the coming year the costs of the organisation are expected to increase by the following:

	%
Direct materials	20.00
Direct labour	16.67
Other direct costs	67.00
Variable overhead	25.00
Fixed overhead	5.00

Market research has shown that when the company increases the price of its courses to its students, as long as the increase is kept below 17.5% this is unlikely to have an effect on the number of units sold. However, for every 1% prices are raised above a 17.5% increase, the number of units sold can be expected to fall by 2%.

Required:
For the coming year:
(a) The selling price of the study courses if the number of study courses sold and the annual profits are to remain as before.
(b) The number of units that the organisation would have to sell if it did not change the price charged for these, but maintained the profit level attained in the previous year.
(c) A brief analysis of a situation where, when prices are changed the number of units sold is affected. The data provided in the above example can be used to illustrate your analysis.

(*ACCA, Management Accounting, June 1977*)

Answers on p 563

15.1.4 Establishing optimal price and output

COST AND REVENUE ANALYSIS

If both cost and revenue functions can be determined, profit maximising output and selling price can be calculated. For example, assume that the following information is available:
Fixed costs £80,000 per period; variable costs £30 per unit. At a selling price of £70 per unit, 3,000 units per period will be sold. For every £5 per unit that the selling price is increased, 500 fewer units will be sold; for every £5 per unit that the selling price is reduced, 500 more units will be sold.

The optimal activity level and selling price can be found by tabulating variable cost and revenue figures. Fixed costs are ignored on the assumption that they are unaffected by changes in the level of activity.

Variable Cost £/unit	Selling Price £/unit	Demand units	Total Variable Cost £	Total Revenue £	Contribution £
30	90	1,000	30,000	90,000	60,000
30	85	1,500	45,000	127,500	82,500
30	80	2,000	60,000	160,000	100,000
30	75	2,500	75,000	187,500	112,500
30	70	3,000	90,000	210,000	120,000
30	65	3,500	105,000	227,500	122,500
30	60	4,000	120,000	240,000	120,000
30	55	4,500	135,000	247,500	112,500
30	50	5,000	150,000	250,000	100,000
30	45	5,500	165,000	247,500	82,500
30	40	6,000	180,000	240,000	60,000

Profit maximisation is achieved at a selling price of £65 per unit, with demand of 3,500 units. Profit is £42,500 (£122,500 contribution less £80,000 fixed costs).

The range provided in the above table illustrates clearly the point of maximum profit and the response of revenue and contribution generally according to the demand/price relationship. Price elasticity is constantly changing in this example as, despite consistent changes in selling price and demand in absolute terms, the relative changes in price and demand, both separately and in relation to each other, depend upon the particular price. As a result, total revenue increases in response to price reductions, but by a smaller and smaller amount until, when price is reduced below £50 per unit, total revenue starts to fall. At a selling price of £50 per unit,

$$\text{Point elasticity} = \frac{500}{5{,}000} \div \frac{5}{50}$$
$$= 1$$

Arc elasticity (for price reduction)

$$= \frac{500}{5{,}250} \div \frac{5}{47.5}$$
$$= 0.9$$

and (for price increase)

$$= \frac{500}{4{,}750} \div \frac{5}{52.5}$$
$$= 1.1$$

indicating unit elasticity at that point, with demand becoming inelastic if price is reduced, and elastic if price is increased.

This can be contrasted with the situation at say a selling price of £85 per unit, where

$$\text{Point elasticity} = \frac{500}{1{,}500} \div \frac{5}{85}$$
$$= 5.7$$

Arc elasticity (for price reduction)

$$= \frac{500}{1{,}750} \div \frac{5}{82.5}$$
$$= 4.7$$

and (for price increase)

$$= \frac{500}{1{,}250} \div \frac{5}{87.5}$$
$$= 7.0$$

Demand is very elastic at this point. A selling price increase reduces revenue by a considerable amount; a selling price reduction increases revenue by a considerable amount.

The complete demand, revenue and cost, and profit functions are demonstrated in Figures 15.3, 15.4 and 15.5.

Figure 15.4 demonstrates that costs rise steadily. This is because of the cost function assumed. Revenues rise at first and then fall. At the extreme positions no sales would be made at a selling price of £100, whereas 10,000 units would be 'sold' if the product is given away. Sales revenue is maximised at output of 5,000 units, and profit at output of 3,500 units. (see Figures 15.4 and 15.5).

FIGURE 15.3 **Demand function**

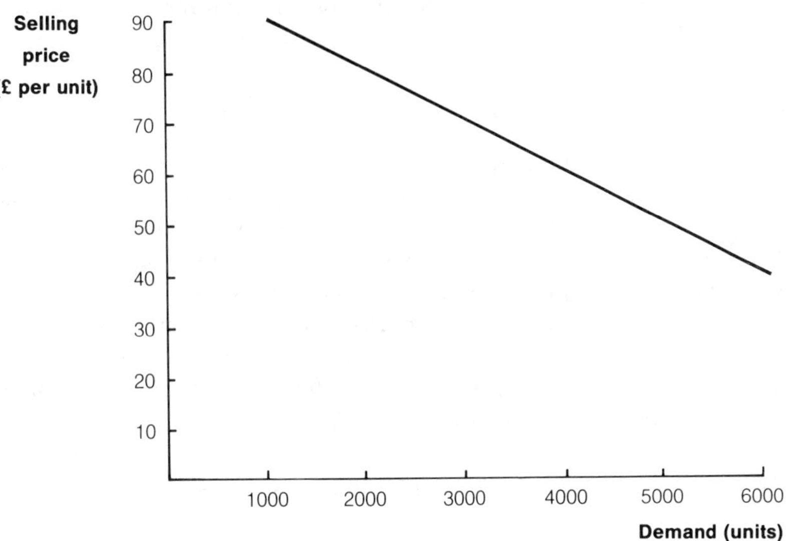

FIGURE 15.4 **Revenue and cost functions**

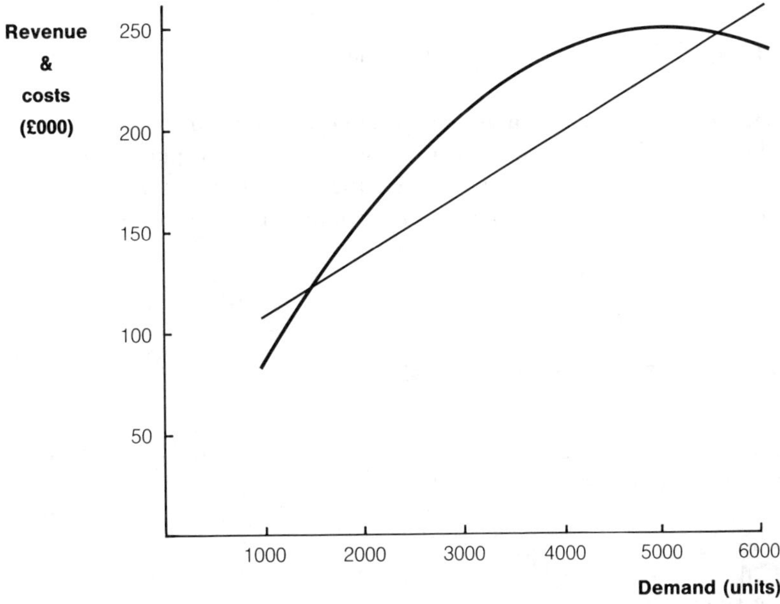

FIGURE 15.5 **Profit function**

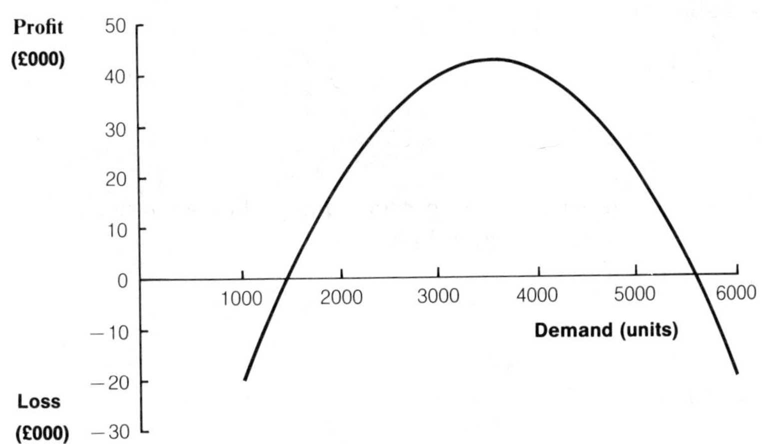

DIFFERENTIAL CALCULUS

Differential calculus can also be used to determine profit maximising selling price and output if equations can be derived for the revenue and cost functions as a whole. Using the example as above, an equation for the cost function is straight forward:

$TC = 30Q + 80{,}000$, where TC is the total cost, and Q is the number of units.

The revenue function is not quite so straightforward, but as noted before there is a consistent pattern, in absolute terms, of demand in relation to selling price. For every £5 change in price, demand changes by 500 units. To derive an equation for the revenue function in this example, the selling price is first expressed as a function of output. This is done by calculating the selling price at which output would be zero. The price would have to be increased by 6 times £5, to £100 per unit, before demand falls to zero. A reduction in selling price from £100 is then expressed in relation to the demand that would be generated. At a selling price of £90 for example, demand would be 1,000 units. The £10 reduction in selling price is 1% (0.01) of the 1,000 units output. At a selling price of £80 demand would be 2,000 units. The £20 reduction in selling price from £100 is again 1% of output, which is now 2,000 units.

The equation for the demand function, expressing price (P) as a function of output (Q) is:

$$P = 100 - 0.01Q$$

The equation for the revenue function is obtained by multiplying the equation for P by Q. Thus:

$TR = 100Q - 0.01Q^2$, where TR is the total revenue.

Using differential calculus, the marginal revenue and marginal cost can be determined by differentiating TC and TR with respect to Q. The marginal revenue is the additional revenue generated by increasing demand by one unit, and is the slope of the revenue curve. Marginal cost is the additional cost incurred by the production of one more unit, and is the slope of the cost curve.

$$\text{Marginal cost} = MC = \frac{dTC}{dQ} = 30$$

$$\text{Marginal revenue} = MR = \frac{dTR}{dQ} = 100 - 0.02Q$$

The output level, and selling price, to maximise profits is found at the point where marginal revenue per unit equals marginal cost per unit. Thus:

$$\begin{aligned} 100 - 0.02Q &= 30 \\ 0.02Q &= 70 \\ Q &= 3{,}500 \text{ units} \end{aligned}$$

To find the optimal selling price the value obtained for Q is substituted in the selling price equation derived above:

$$\begin{aligned} P &= 100 - (0.01 \times 3{,}500) \\ &= £65 \text{ per unit} \end{aligned}$$

Total sales revenue will be £227,500 (3,500 × 65)

Marginal revenue and marginal cost per unit, and profit maximising selling price and output (Pm and Qm) are demonstrated in Figure 15.6.

Total profit (TP) is TR – TC. Thus:

$$\begin{aligned} TP &= 100Q - 0.01Q^2 - 30Q - 80{,}000 \\ &= 350{,}000 - 122{,}500 - 105{,}000 - 80{,}000 \\ &= £42{,}500 \end{aligned}$$

Optimal output could have alternatively been calculated by differentiating TP with respect to Q.

$$\text{Marginal profit} = \text{MP} = \frac{\text{dTP}}{\text{dQ}} = 100 - 0.02\text{Q} - 30$$

At optimal output, MP = 0

$$\therefore \quad 0.02\text{Q} = 70$$
$$\text{Q} = 3{,}500 \text{ units}$$

FIGURE 15.6 **Profit maximisation**

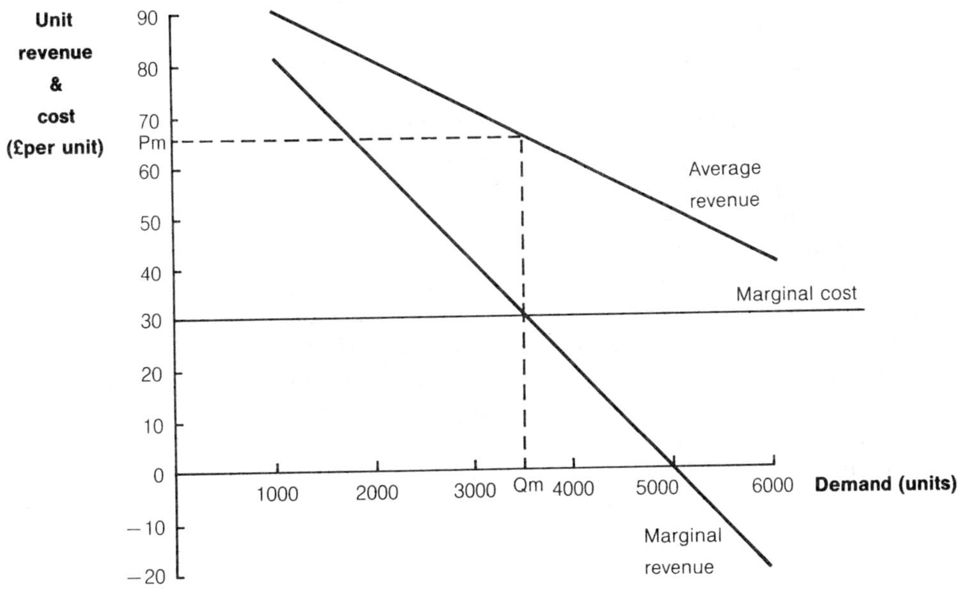

Self-assessment question 15.2

Refer back to the situation in Self-assessment question 15.1. Using the information provided, determine the selling price and output quantity that will maximise profits.

Answer on p 564

15.1.5 Limitations of economic theory

Whilst economic theory provides a useful starting point there are difficulties in applying it. Both the ends and the means rationality of the theory can be questioned.

ENDS RATIONALITY

First, the ends rationality. The discussion that prevails in economic theory assumes an objective of profit maximisation and rational behaviour. In practice, a business may not pursue such a clear-cut objective and the pricing policy which it implies. Objectives such as achieving a satisfactory profit/return on investment, in combination with earnings per share growth, and/or market share percentage, and/or sales growth targets may be pursued. If businesses do pursue other objectives, different pricing strategies and policies will be required and different pricing decisions are likely to result.

MEANS RATIONALITY

Second, the means rationality. Even if profit maximisation is the long-term objective the strategy for achieving it may result in short-term market-skimming, or alternatively market penetration, which may be detrimental to short-term profit. Market skimming is where a firm seeks to take the 'cream' off the top of the market by initially selling relatively low volumes at high prices before lowering price to attract volume business. Market penetration is the opposite policy. Low prices are charged initially in order to gain a sizeable share of a market. The aim would be to obtain product loyalty, followed by repeat purchase at higher prices. Another aim may be to eliminate competition.

A further aspect of means rationality may be that although profit maximisation could be the overall short-term objective, more flexible pricing strategies may be adopted on individual products in order to achieve the objective eg loss leader, diversionary pricing. Finally, the risk taking attitude of management may also be a factor. If the course of action which is expected to lead to profit maximisation is seen as a high risk alternative then another price may be selected.

Thus different pricing strategies may be pursued. These strategies may be influenced by the product portfolio, including the stage in the life cycle of different products, viz introduction, growth, maturity, saturation and decline, and by market share and market growth potential.

Further limitations of the means rationality revolve around the difficulty of obtaining the necessary information, particularly concerning price/demand relationships. Selling price is only one, albeit very important in many cases, of a number of factors in the marketing mix. In markets that are oligopolistic, or nearly so, non-price competition assumes tremendous importance. Advertising is often the largest item in selling costs. Together with other forms of selling cost, advertising seeks to shift the demand function to the right, with or without a change in its price elasticity.

Much depends also upon other features of the product itself, and upon competitors, consumers, and general economic aspects. The implications of all these factors for demand is difficult to quantify although surveys, market research, econometric analysis, test marketing, simulation models and feed back from salespersons can provide useful information and reduce uncertainty. Forecasting the cost function, and thus the marginal cost at different points, is also generally not easy.

The following provides a more complete list of considerations influencing demand in relation to price.

1 **Product**
- (a) Marketing mix and the relative importance of price and non-price competition.
- (b) Nature of the product eg luxury/necessity.
- (c) Closeness of substitutes.
- (d) Whether standard product or special line.
- (e) Relationship with other products.
- (f) Stage in product life cycle.

2 **Competition**
- (a) Market structure—number and size of competitors.
- (b) Likely behaviour of competitors.
- (c) New entrants to the market.

3 **Consumer**
- (a) Target market.
- (b) Consumer awareness of products/prices.
- (c) Income.
- (d) Income elasticity of demand—the effect on demand of a change in income.
- (e) Extent of differentiation of markets and thus the scope for discretionary pricing.

4 **General Economic**
- (a) State of national and international trade.
- (b) Employment.
- (c) State of the industry.
- (d) Government policy.
- (e) Legislation.
- (f) Inflation.

If an attempt can be made in practice to apply the principles of economic theory, the approach is likely to be iterative. A number of point estimates of demand may be made at a limited range of selling prices that are felt to be feasible, and from this information the optimal selling price determined. The sensitivity of the result to changes in assumptions can also be considered: the CVP model will be useful in this respect.

The iterative approach to establishing demand/price relationships may be the best that can be hoped for in practice because of the difficulty of forecasting, because of the need for sensitivity analysis, and because the demand function may not be constant and thus impossible to establish as an equation. Although the economic theory is appealing in its clarity it is, however, rather weak in its applicability to real life product pricing.

15.1.6 Sensitivity analysis

Cost-volume-profit sensitivity analysis may be useful as a complete substitute for precise demand forecasts. For example if a product's selling price is currently £10.00 per unit with a variable cost of £5.00 and with annual demand at 50,000 units, consideration may be given to a change in selling price to say either £11.00 or £9.00. Instead of requiring a forecast figure of demand at these revised prices an alternative approach is to calculate the reduction/increase in demand that would be required in order to leave profit unchanged. Judgement can be made according to whether expectations would be greater or less than the sensitivity figures calculated.

If selling price is increased to £11.00 per unit, contribution per unit becomes £6.00 per unit. Total contribution at existing selling price and demand is £250,000 (50,000 units × £5.00 per unit). The level of demand necessary at the increased price, in order to provide the same total contribution, would be £250,000 ÷ 6 = 41,667 units. A reduction in demand of $16.\dot{6}\%$ would offset the price increase of 10%. If point elasticity is less than $1.\dot{6}$, the price increase is justified.

If selling price is reduced to £9.00 per unit, contribution per unit becomes £4.00. The level of demand necessary at the reduced price, in order to leave contribution unchanged, would be £250,000 ÷ 4 = 62,500 units. An increase in demand of 25% would offset the price reduction of 10%. If point elasticity is greater than 2.5, the price reduction is justified.

15.2 COST BASED APPROACHES TO PRICING

If an organisation finds it very difficult, or impossible, to make an estimate of demand/price relationships it will frequently, and necessarily, resort to cost information as a primary basis for establishing selling price. Costs are more internal to an organisation and are, as a result, easier to forecast than demand, which is particularly dependent on a large number of factors external to, and thus outside the control of, the organisation. Also, as ultimately profit is important, costs cannot be ignored. Finally, it is important to recognise that in practice there are two problems, not one, in pricing. The question is not simply,

1 'What is the best price'?

but also,

2 'Is the price sufficient to justify the activity?

In judging sufficiency, a knowledge of cost to be recovered is necessary (ie 'what is the minimum acceptable price?')

However, even with costs, there are considerable difficulties of forecasting the general level of costs and how they change in response to changes in activity. Certain assumptions will be made about cost behaviour which may be an oversimplification of reality. Nevertheless, various pricing formulae based on cost are utilised. These have two components:

1 An estimate of cost
2 A mark-up on cost

In estimating costs, distinctions are made between long-run costs and short-run costs. There are two main formulae based on long-run costs: 'full cost plus' pricing and 'rate of return' pricing. The formula using short-run costs is 'marginal cost plus' pricing.

15.2.1 Long-run cost plus

The 'full cost plus' method establishes a unit cost based on full absorption costing principles and then applies a percentage mark-up to provide for the profit required. The total cost includes both variable costs and also fixed costs based on normal volumes. The mark-up to be applied to a particular product may take some account of market factors as well as profit targets.

The 'rate of return' method is simply a variant on 'full cost plus'. Unit cost is established in the same way; the difference with this method is that the mark-up is more firmly tied to profit requirements. This is done by setting a target return on capital employed and calculating the mark-up on total cost that is required to achieve it. For example, if a business has capital employed of £100m, total costs of £200m, and a target return on capital employed of 20%, the mark-up percentage on cost that is required in order to achieve such a return is:

$$\frac{100}{200} \times 20\% = 10\%$$

On the face of it the above pricing formulae based on total cost are attractive, because of their simplicity, because of the ability, as a result, to delegate pricing decisions whilst at the same time maintaining control, and because they recognise the requirement for a satisfactory profit. In the long-run each product/service should pay its way.

The full cost plus pricing methods have serious limitations however:

1 They do not take any account of whether the selling price determined is likely to be acceptable in the market place. They assume that selling price can be solely cost related.
2 Selling price is based on unit cost, which due to the incidence of fixed costs is influenced by volume, which is itself influenced by price. There is thus a circular problem which is always present when full cost plus pricing formulae are used. There can be no guarantee unfortunately that such methods will produce the desired profit.
3 Units costs are dependent, and in industries with a high indirect/direct cost ratio especially so, on the arbitrary apportionment and absorption of overhead. There can be no guarantee therefore that each product is providing the desired mark-up.
4 The determination of what is a desirable mark-up is arbitrary. This may, however, be seen as an advantage if it encourages, and enables, market factors to be considered. The mark-up is less arbitrary in the case of rate of return pricing in the sense of there being a clearer target for profit but as a result is more firmly based on cost, with the other limitations that follow from this. Also, the apparent reduced arbitrariness may be rather illusory. The required rate of return remains to some extent subjective, the necessary apportionment of capital employed will be arbitrary, and an additional circular problem ensues. Short-term capital employed will include stock and debtors, the level of which is influenced by volume, which is influenced by price. In the long-term, capacity requirements will also be influenced by the level of activity.
5 The pricing methods lack the flexibility required to deal with short-run situations, to incorporate other aspects of the marketing mix, and to pursue differing pricing strategies/policies.

The above limitations have led to fairly widespread condemnation in the academic literature of full cost plus pricing. Certainly it would be of particular concern if one or other method was used as *the* pricing formula. If instead they are simply used as a general guide to long-term pricing requirements, recognising in particular their inflexibility and circular reasoning, they may provide a useful start point for the pricing decision, whence market factors can also be considered. Management may vary the mark-up percentage, following consideration of demand, competition and available capacity, and consider the sensitivity of unit cost to changes in activity levels.

15.2.2 Short-run cost plus

In such a scenario 'marginal cost plus' pricing may also be found to be useful. Marginal costs were seen earlier to be a necessary component of the economic approach to pricing. In the absence of demand information, marginal cost establishes a minimum price that should be charged in the short-run. The minimum price may be especially useful where spare capacity exists and where price differentiation is possible, for example for pricing additional one-off business or for pricing off-peak in hotels, transport etc. It thus provides more flexibility than full cost pricing methods.

Marginal cost pricing may also be used as a substitute for full cost pricing by establishing a contribution mark-up required to generate adequate profits. Use of marginal cost pricing in this way provides much greater flexibility regarding mark-up on individual products, whilst at the same time recognising the long-term profit requirement, and recognises the arbitrary nature of overhead apportionment.

Marginal cost pricing, especially if used as a substitute for full cost pricing does however have several limitations:

1. It provides no indication of whether a particular product/service is paying its way in the long-run.
2. There may be a very large mark-up percentage applied because of a high ratio of fixed to variable costs. This may be just as inflexible as the mark-up using full cost pricing in the absence of demand information. If the same fixed percentage is applied to all products, the same contribution percentage will result and prices may not be in line with long-run cost. There will be little guidance as to how the flexibility should be applied, unless market information is available which will make the mark-up redundant anyway.
3. A business survives only if it earns, in total, a sufficient contribution to cover its fixed costs and make an acceptable profit. Contribution pricing should be used with caution. It may encourage price cutting, which if matched by competition, may not benefit any suppliers. Just as dangerous, however, can be a blind adherence to a full cost plus price if the result at the end of the day is no business.
4. The cost behaviour assumptions may be an over–simplification of short-term reality. Variable costs may not be proportionately variable. Even in the short term, fixed costs may creep upwards, especially as a result of combined activity changes on a number of products. These are limitations of the application of economic theory also.
5. The proportion of short-term fixed costs generally within business have been increasing and variable costs decreasing. Whilst providing more scope for marginal cost pricing, marginal costs on their own will be insufficient.

15.3 PRICING IN PRACTICE

Empirical evidence suggests that many firms do use 'cost plus' formulae, particularly full cost, as a basis for determining selling prices. The question is whether this is all that the firm does, or whether it adjusts the 'cost plus' price in a way which reflects its judgement as to what the market will bear, thus bringing in the demand side which is entirely unrepresented in the 'cost plus' formulae. Empirical evidence indicates that the 'cost plus' estimated selling price is used as a guide which is adjusted, as the firm considers appropriate, for market factors. Cost remains as an indicator as to whether the price so determined is sufficient to justify the product's existence. At any point in time the objective should be that cost reflects the true opportunity costs.

A recent study by Mills (Pricing Decisions in Practice: How are they made in Manufacturing and Service Companies? CIMA 1988), among 100 manufacturing and 100 service companies selected at random from the U.K.'s 7,500 largest companies, confirmed previous findings in both the U.K. and USA that cost based methods, usually reliant on full absorption costing principles, were the primary basis for determining prices under normal conditions. These cost-based prices were usually modified by non-cost considerations, of which reference to competitors' prices was the most important of a number used. In the case of a special order which could be met out of present capacity, the study revealed a marked increase in the use of marginal costing in comparison with its use under normal conditions.

Self-assessment question 15.3

Discuss the extent to which cost data is useful in the determination of pricing policy. Explain the advantages and disadvantages of presenting cost data for possible utilisation in pricing policy determination using an absorption, rather than a direct, costing basis.

(*ACCA, Management Accounting, June 1981*)

Answer on p 565

SUMMARY

Essentially the economic theory is common sense; the basic principles are valid. However, in considering their practical application, both the ends and means rationality of the economic model can be questioned. In practice, determination of selling price will depend upon:

1 Particular objectives and strategies pursued.
2 Relative importance of price/non-price competition.
3 Information available, which may depend fairly heavily upon cost factors because the demand factors are difficult to quantify.

Pricing formulae based on cost, especially full cost, are widely used in practice. The question is whether that is all that is done. In a jobbing engineering company for example, where jobs are undertaken on a regular basis to customers' specifications, a market price may be impossible to determine. The use of pricing formulae based on cost provides a means of delegating the frequent pricing decisions whilst at the same time maintaining control by top management. In other situations pricing formulae based on cost may well only provide an initial guide as to minimum and target prices that may be sought. Information on market factors is frequently used to refine the analysis. The use of loss-leader, diversionary, discretionary, penetration, and skimming pricing policies provides further indication that market factors are considered. Price and cost together will be used to judge the sufficiency of profit. In the short-term marginal cost provides an indication of the minimum price that may be charged.

A final aspect of cost-volume-profit relationships that should be noted is the use of 'backwards cost plus' pricing. When considering the introduction of a new product, estimates of selling price, volume, and desired cost mark-up may be used to arrive at an estimate of the maximum cost that would be acceptable for the product. The task then is to obtain the product at the cost allowed.

EXERCISES

Exercise 15.1

(a) Nantderyn Products has two main products, Exco and Wyeco, which have unit costs of £12 and £24 respectively. The company uses a mark-up of $33\frac{1}{3}\%$ in establishing its selling prices and the current prices are thus £16 and £32. With these prices, in the year which is just ending, the company expects to make a profit of £300,000 from having produced and sold 15,000 units of Exco and 30,000 units of Wyeco. This programme will have used all the available processing time in the finishing department. Each unit of Exco requires an hour of processing time in this department and every unit of Wyeco correspondingly requires half an hour.

Fixed overhead was £360,000 for the year and this has been charged to the products on the basis of the total processing hours used. All other costs may be assumed variable in relation to processing hours. In the current year it is estimated that £60,000 of the fixed overhead will be absorbed by Exco and £300,000 by Wyeco. With the existing selling prices it is considered that the potential annual demand for Exco is 20,000 units and that for Wyeco, 40,000 units.

You are required to comment critically on the product mix adopted by Nantderyn Products. Calculate what would have been the optimal plan given that there was no intention of changing the selling prices.

(b) For the forthcoming year increased capacity has been installed in the finishing department so that this will no longer be a constraint for any feasible sales programme. Annual fixed overhead will be increased to £400,000 as a consequence of this expansion of facilities, but variable costs per unit are unchanged.

A study commissioned by the Sales Director estimates the effect that alterations to the selling prices would have on the sales that could be achieved. The following table has been prepared:

	Exco		*Wyeco*	
Price	£13.50	£18.50	£29.00	£35.00
Demand in '000s	30	10	60	20

It is thought reasonable to assume that the price/demand relationship is linear. Assuming that the company is now willing to abandon its cost plus pricing practices, if these can be shown to be deficient, you are required to calculate the optimal selling price for each product and the optimal output levels for these prices. State clearly any assumptions that you find it necessary to make.

(c) 'The paradox is that, while cost plus pricing is devoid of any theoretical justification, it is widely used in practice.'

Discuss possible justifications for this use.

(*ACCA*, *Management Accounting*, *December 1983*)

Answers on p 566

Exercise 15.2

In the last quarter of 1985/86 it is estimated that YNQ will have produced and sold 20,000 units of their main product by the end of the year. At this level of activity it is estimated that the average unit cost will be:

	£
Direct material	30
Direct labour	10
Overhead: Fixed	10
Variable	10
	60

This is in line with the standards set at the start of the year. The management accountant of YNQ is now preparing the budget for 1986/87. He has incorporated into his preliminary calculations the following expected cost increases:

Raw material: price increase of	20%
Direct labour: wage rate increase of	5%
Variable overhead: increase of	5%
Fixed overhead: increase of	25%

The production manager believes that if a cheaper grade of raw material were to be used, this would enable the direct material cost per unit to be kept to £31.25 for 1986/87. The cheaper material would, however, lead to a reject rate estimated at 5% of the completed output and it would be necessary to introduce an inspection stage at the end of the manufacturing process to identify the faulty items. The cost of this inspection process would be £40,000 per year (including £10,000 allocation of existing factory overhead).

Established practice has been to reconsider the product's selling price at the time the budget is being prepared. The selling price is normally determined by adding a mark-up of 50% to unit cost. On this basis the product's selling price for 1985/86 has been £90 but the sales manager is worried about the implications of continuing the cost plus 50% rule for 1986/87. He estimates that demand for the product varies with price as follows:

Price:	£80	£84	£88	£90	£92	£96	£100
Demand in ('000s)	25	23	21	20	19	17	15

Required:

(a) Decide whether YNQ should use the regular or the cheaper grade of material and to calculate the best price for the product, the optimal level of production and the profit that this should yield. Comment briefly on the sensitivity of the solution to possible errors in the estimates.

(b) Indicate how one might obtain the answer to part (a) from an appropriately designed cost-volume-profit graph. You should design such a graph as part of your answer but the graph need not be drawn to scale providing that it demonstrates the main features of the approach that you would use.

(*ACCA, Management Accounting, December 1986*)

Answers on p 568

Exercise 15.3

A transport company has a monorail system which takes freight and tourists from the local town to a leisure complex in the nearby hills. On the return journeys to the town, products from craft workshops at the leisure complex and returning tourists are transported. Passengers may be assumed to return on the same train they used for the outward journey.

The mix of carriages between those for transporting freight or tourists can be adjusted as required. Each carriage has a capacity for 600 cubic metres of freight or 60 tourists.

The monorail will have 10 carriages linked together for each journey. It is budgeted to operate the monorail for two journeys in *each* direction on 200 days in the coming year. The freight/passenger carriage mix will be the same on inward journeys as for outward journeys to the leisure complex.

Market research has resulted in the following estimates for the coming year:

(i) Demand of 600 passengers per journey could be achieved where the adult fare for each journey is £9. For every 45p (5%) rise in adult fares above this level, demand would fall by 60 passengers.

(ii) The passenger mix will be 2/3 adult and 1/3 juvenile where the juvenile fare is 50% of the adult fare.

(iii) Freight would be available for transporting on the outward journeys to the leisure complex where the following pricing system is used:

Cubic metres	*Incremental revenue per cubic metre*
	£
1– 600	2.20
601–1,200	2.00
1,201–1,800	1.80
1,801–2,400	1.60
2,401–3,000	1.40
3,001–3,600	1.20

A minimum of 20% and a maximum of 60% of carriage capacity would be devoted to freight on the outward journeys.

(iv) On the inward journeys to the town, 20% of the carriages would be used to transport products from the craft workshops at a rate of £2 per cubic metre. No other freight business would be available.

(v) The passenger fare structure would be based on the outward journey capacity available (after freight utilisation) and would also be used for the inward journeys even though idle capacity may exist.

Other budgeted data for the coming year is as follows:

(i) Fuel costs per single journey: £500.

(ii) The total wage cost of the combined operation of loading and unloading each freight carriage is £300.

(iii) Miscellaneous other costs: £3,500,000.

Required:

(a) Determine the number of carriages which should be devoted to freight on the outward journeys in order to maximise profit and calculate the resulting profit for the coming year.

(b) Comment on any assumptions which are made in the information given in the question which could affect the accuracy of the answer in (a).

(c) The company is considering a two tier passenger fare system, whereby a passenger fare of £5 be set for all passengers (adult and juvenile) on inward journeys from the leisure complex to the town. The fares on outward journeys would remain as detailed in the market research estimates. In order to provide seating for the anticipated unlimited demand under this policy, empty freight carriages on the inward journey could be converted for temporary passenger use at a cost of £25 per carriage per journey.

Calculate the choice of freight/passenger carriage mix on the outward journeys which would now maximise profit. Advise the company on whether this two tiered fare system should be adopted.

(*ACCA, Management Accounting, December 1988*)

Answers on p 569

Exercise 15.4

French Ltd is about to commence operations utilising a simple production process to produce two products, *X* and *Y*. It is the policy of French to operate the new factory at its maximum output in the first year of operations. Cost and production details estimated for the first year's operations are:

Product	*Production resources per unit*		*Variable cost per unit*		*Fixed production overheads directly attributable to product*	*Maximum production —units*
	Labour hours	*Machine hours*	*Direct labour*	*Direct materials*	(£'000s)	('000s)
			(£)	(£)		
X	1	4	5	6	120	40
Y	8	2	28	16	280	10

There are also general fixed production overheads concerned in the manufacture of both products but which cannot be directly attributed to either. This general fixed production overhead is estimated at £720,000 for the first year of operations. It is thought that the cost structures of the first year will also be operative in the second year.

Both products are new and French is one of the first firms to produce them. Hence in the first year of operations the sales price can be set by French. In the second and subsequent years it is felt that the market for *X* and *Y* will have become more settled and French will largely conform to the competitive market prices that will become established. The sales manager has researched the first year's market potential and has estimated sales volumes for various ranges of selling price. The details are:

Product X		*Product Y*	
Range of per unit sales prices	*Sales volume*	*Range of per unit sales prices*	*Sales volume*
£ £	('000s)	£ £	('000s)
Up to 24.00	36	Up to 96.00	11
24.01 to 30.00	32	96.01 to 108.00	10
30.01 to 36.00	18	108.01 to 120.00	9
36.01 to 42.00*	8	120.01 to 132.00	8
		132.01 to 144.00	7
		144.01 to 156.00*	5

*Maximum price.

The managing director of French wishes to ascertain the total production cost of *X* and *Y* as, he says, 'Until we know the per unit cost of production we cannot properly determine the first year's sales price. Price must always ensure that total cost is covered and there is an element of profit—therefore I feel that the price should be total cost plus 20%. The determination of cost is fairly simple as most costs are clearly attributable to either *X* or *Y*. The general factory overhead will probably be allocated to the products in accordance with some measure of usage of factory resources such as labour or machine hours. The choice between labour and machine hours is the only problem in determining the cost of each product—but the problem is minor and so, therefore, is the problem of pricing.'

Required:

(a) Produce statements showing the effect the cost allocation and pricing methods mentioned by the managing director will have on
 (i) unit costs,
 (ii) closing stock values, and
 (iii) disclosed profit for the first year of operations.

(b) Briefly comment on the results in (a) above and advise the managing director on the validity of using the per unit cost figures produced for pricing decisions.

(c) Provide appropriate statements to the management of French Ltd. which will be of direct relevance in assisting the determination of the optimum prices of *X* and *Y* for the first year of operations. The statements should be designed to provide assistance in each of the following, separate, cases:
 (i) year II demand will be below productive capacity;
 (ii) year II demand will be substantially in excess of productive capacity.
 In both cases the competitive market sales prices per unit for year II are expected to be

 X—£30 per unit
 Y—£130 per unit

Clearly specify, and explain, your advice to French for each of the cases described. (Ignore taxation and the time value of money.)

(*ACCA, Management Accounting, June 1980*)

Answers in lecturer's manual

Exercise 15.5

'The transition from minimum price setting requires one crucial ingredient: information about demand conditions.'
(*From Pricing and Output Decisions by John Arnold*).

Required:
Discuss the short–run situation for both:

(a) the factors which affect the minimum price that could be charged for a product or service; and

(b) the influence that information about demand conditions has on the optimal price set for a product or service.

(*ACCA, Management Accounting, June 1977*)

Answers in lecturer's manual

Capital Investment Decision-Making: Appraisal Techniques

INTRODUCTION

There are two features which distinguish capital investment from other quantitative decisions. These are:

1 Whilst virtually all decisions involve forgoing present consumption in the hope of receiving some increased future consumption (ie, they are rarely self-financing), with capital investment the time lag between investment and return will be years rather than months or weeks.

2 Many capital investment decisions involve the acquisition of fixed assets which will lose value as they are used in the business. Shorter-term decisions invariably involve investment in working capital but this would generally be expected to maintain its value over time. Investment in working capital arises simply from the need to pay out money for resources before it can be recovered from sales of finished product/service, rather than from the acquisition of resources which are going to be used on a continuing basis within the business.

The result is that, in considering the model used for analysing the information relevant to an investment decision, consideration needs to be given in analysis to the way in which these costs and benefits are to be compared over time. The purpose of this chapter is to describe and critically examine the methods in use.

16.1 METHODS OF ANALYSIS

There are three main methods of analysis of capital investment projects (commonly referred to as investment appraisal techniques), namely:

1 Accounting Rate of Return
2 Discounted Cash Flow
3 Payback.

The objective of these methods is the assessment of the economic viability of investment projects (once relevant information has been identified and correctly sorted). Some investments must be made without recourse to the above criteria, because they have no monetary return as such, eg offices, car parking, recreational and canteen facilities, boiler-houses. They are non-earnings, or 'must' investments.

Example:

The following example will be used to illustrate the various investment appraisal methods:

Capital investment in new machinery—(£25,000)

Project life—10 years

Terminal value of investment—nil

Annual profits/(losses) (based on straight-line depreciation of machinery) commencing 1 year after investment:

Year 1	(£1,500)
2	500
3	2,500
4	4,500
5	6,500
6	8,500
7	6,500
8	(500)
9	(500)
10	(1,500)
Total net profit over 10 years	£25,000

16.1.1 Accounting Rate of Return

The Accounting Rate of Return methods employ the normal accounting technique to measure the increase in profit expected to result from an investment by expressing the net accounting profit arising from the investment as a % of that capital investment, viz:

$$\frac{\text{Profit}}{\text{Investment}} \times 100\% = \text{Accounting Rate of Return (ARR)}$$

(also called Return on Capital Employed (ROCE) or Return on Investment (ROI).

There are different ways of calculating the percentage return in common use. Some calculate it on initial capital, some on average capital, some using total profits, some using average annual profits, and some on average profits once the project has built up. The treatment of taxation is also subject to some variation. The test of profitability for a project would be whether the percentage ARR meets the criterion established for acceptability. This would be based on the returns required to satisfy the providers of capital to the business.

The two most common methods of calculating the ARR are:

1 $$\frac{\text{Average Annual Profit}}{\text{Gross Investment}} \times 100\%$$

2 $$\frac{\text{Average Annual Profit}}{\text{Average Net Investment (reduced by depreciation)}} \times 100\%$$

In the example, the average annual profit of the project is

$$\frac{£25{,}000}{10 \text{ years}} = £2{,}500$$

The average net investment (ie the net book value of the machinery half way through the project) is

$$\frac{£25{,}000 + £0}{2} = £12{,}500$$

The machinery will have a nil terminal value (and therefore nil net book value) at the end of the project.

Thus, using method 1:

$$\text{ARR} = \frac{2{,}500}{25{,}000} \times 100\% = 10\%$$

and using method 2:

$$\text{ARR} = \frac{2{,}500}{12{,}500} \times 100\% = 20\%$$

16.1.2 Discounted Cash Flow

The objective in using Discounted Cash Flow (DCF) techniques is to relate the cash flows (rather than accounting profit) arising from a project to a base year, by means of discount factors, on the basis that £1 today is worth more than £1 at some future time because of its earning potential. The earlier that cash is received the greater the return on investment. The DCF techniques take account of both the size and timing of returns by taking account of cash flows when they take place.

Discounting is the opposite of compounding with which the reader is likely to be more familiar. In compounding:

$$\text{Future value} = \text{present value} \times (1 + i)^t$$

where i is the rate of interest per time period and t is a future time period.
For example, £1 invested at 10% per annum compound

$$= 1 \times (1 + 0.1)^1 \text{ after 1 year} = £1.1$$
$$= 1 \times (1 + 0.1)^2 \text{ after 2 years} = £1.21$$
$$\text{or } (1.1 \times (1 + 0.1))$$

In discounting:

$$\text{Present value} = \frac{\text{future value}}{(1 + i)^t}$$

£1.21 to be received in 2 years' time at 10% per annum

$$= \frac{1.21}{(1 + 0.1)^2} \quad \text{present value} = \frac{1.21}{1.21} = £1$$

Thus £1 to be received in 2 years' time at 10% per annum

$$= \frac{1}{1.21} \quad \text{present value} = £0.8264.$$

This is referred to as a discount factor and is available from discount factor tables. A discount factor table is provided on page 645 shows the present value of £1 at different rates of interest and received at different time periods in the future.

It is important to recognise that in the long run (ie over the life of a capital investment project), the net cash flow will be exactly equal to the net profit arising from a project. Accrual accounting methods are employed because of the desire (and requirement) to measure performance over shorter time periods (eg annually). The difference between accounting rate of return and discounted cash flow methods is not the size of the returns but the treatment of the timing of those returns, and how they are related to the original investment.

Using the example as before, it is necessary to convert the net profit figures into annual cash flows. In this example, it will be assumed that the only difference between the timing of net profit and cash flow is the incidence of depreciation. In assessing the DCF return the investment is included as an outflow at the commencement of the project, and any terminal value brought in at the end. The total depreciation will be the difference between the two. In practice, there will be numerous reasons for slight differences between net profit and cash flow from period to period (although not in total for a project over its life), due to the accrual method of accounting (eg accrued and prepaid expenses,

TABLE 16.1 **Calculation of the IRR**

Time (year)	Cash Flow In/(Out) (1)	Discount Rate					
		15%		14.6%		14.5%	
		Discount Factor (2)	Net Present Value (3) = (1) × (2)	Discount Factor	Net Present Value	Discount Factor	Net Present Value
0	£(25,000)	1.000	£(25,000)	1.0000	£(25,000)	1.0000	£(25,000)
1	1,000	$\frac{1}{1.15} = 0.8696$	870	$\frac{1}{1.146} = 0.8726$	873	$\frac{1}{1.145} = 0.8734$	873
2	3,000	$\frac{1}{(1.15)^2} = 0.7561$	2,268	$\frac{1}{(1.146)^2} = 0.7614$	2,284	$\frac{1}{(1.145)^2} = 0.7628$	2,288
3	5,000	$\frac{1}{(1.15)^3} = 0.6575$	3,288	$\frac{1}{(1.146)^3} = 0.6644$	3,322	$\frac{1}{(1.145)^3} = 0.6662$	3,331
4	7,000	$\frac{1}{(1.15)^4} = 0.5718$	4,003	$\frac{1}{(1.146)^4} = 0.5798$	4,059	$\frac{1}{(1.145)^4} = 0.5818$	4,073
5	9,000	$\frac{1}{(1.15)^5} = 0.4972$	4,474	$\frac{1}{(1.146)^5} = 0.5059$	4,553	$\frac{1}{(1.145)^5} = 0.5081$	4,573
6	11,000	$\frac{1}{(1.15)^6} = 0.4323$	4,755	$\frac{1}{(1.146)^6} = 0.4415$	4,856	$\frac{1}{(1.145)^6} = 0.4438$	4,832
7	9,000	$\frac{1}{(1.15)^7} = 0.3759$	3,383	$\frac{1}{(1.146)^7} = 0.3852$	3,467	$\frac{1}{(1.145)^7} = 0.3876$	3,488
8	2,000	$\frac{1}{(1.15)^8} = 0.3269$	653	$\frac{1}{(1.146)^8} = 0.3361$	672	$\frac{1}{(1.145)^8} = 0.3385$	677
9	2,000	$\frac{1}{(1.15)^9} = 0.2843$	569	$\frac{1}{(1.146)^9} = 0.2933$	586	$\frac{1}{(1.145)^9} = 0.2956$	591
10	1,000	$\frac{1}{(1.15)^{10}} = 0.2472$	247	$\frac{1}{(1.146)^{10}} = 0.2559$	256	$\frac{1}{(1.145)^{10}} = 0.2582$	258
Total	£25,000		£ (490)		£ (72)		£ 34

stock, debtors, creditors). Thus £2,500 (the annual depreciation) is added to each year's profit in order to arrive at the following cash flows:

Year	
0	(25,000)
1	1,000
2	3,000
3	5,000
4	7,000
5	9,000
6	11,000
7	9,000
8	2,000
9	2,000
10	1,000
	25,000

Total net cash flow over the whole project is £25,000 (£50,000 inflow–£25,000 investment), the same as the total net profit.

INTERNAL RATE OF RETURN (IRR)

One method of using Discounted Cash Flow is known as the 'Internal Rate of Return' (IRR) method, which involves calculating the rate of return it is estimated will be earned on the amount of capital invested over its life. This is achieved by finding the percentage rate of discount that will reduce the present values of the sequence of inward cash flows to the same value as the present value of the cash invested in the project. Thus the IRR, like the ARR, provides a relative profitability measure (ie the return is expressed as a percentage of the investment).
The IRR, r, as a decimal, can be expressed as where:

$$\sum_{t=0}^{t=n} \frac{Ct}{(1+r)^t} = 0$$

where t is a future time period
n is the number of time periods
C is the net cash flow in a time period
and r is obtained by trial and error to achieve the equation.

The test of profitability of a project is the relationship between the internal rate of return (%) of the project and the minimum acceptable rate of return (%). The decision rule is:

Invest if $r > i$ where i is the minimum acceptable rate of return.

The calculation of the project IRR is illustrated in Table 16.1

As can be seen, the higher the percentage used to discount (and thus the smaller the discount factors, ie $\frac{1}{(1+r)^t}$), the lower will be the net present value. At 0% (ie undiscounted), the net present value is £25,000, ie it is the total net cash flow. The object is to increase the discount percentage until the £25,000 surplus is reduced to zero. Several trial calculations may be required in order to get close to the IRR. At a discount rate of 15%, the net present value is negative, which means that the cash inflows have been discounted at too high a rate (although only just). The calculation at discount rates of 14.6% and 14.5% indicates (because both a negative and a positive net present value occur) that the IRR % is between these two rates.

In practice, calculation of the IRR to the nearest per cent would be sufficiently accurate. Calculation of the return to decimal places of a per cent gives a spurious precision to the data. The IRR of this project is acceptable if the required return on investment is 14% or less.

NET PRESENT VALUE (NPV)

An alternative to the 'Internal Rate of Return' is the 'Net Present Value' (NPV) method in which the minimum acceptable rate of return is used as the discount rate in order to calculate the net present value of the future cash flows at this rate.
Thus:

$$NPV = \sum_{t=0}^{t=n} \frac{Ct}{(1+i)^t}$$

where t is a future time period
n is the number of time periods
C is the net cash flow in a time period
and i is the minimum acceptable rate of return, expressed as a decimal.

The test of profitability of a project is the relationship between the total of the positive cash flows that will be arising in the future at their base year values, when discounted at the minimum acceptable rate of return, and the total of the negative cash flows similarly discounted (where necessary). The decision rule is:

Invest if Net Present Value > 0 (ie positive).

Unlike the IRR and the ARR, the NPV provides an absolute (rather than a relative) measure of profitability. It measures the cash surplus (in present value terms) arising from a project over and above the required return on investment.

In order to calculate the net present value, it is necessary to establish the required return on investment (the criterion for acceptability). Let us assume that the required return is 10%. A discount

TABLE 16.2 **Calculation of the NPV**

Time (year)	Cash Flow In/(Out) (1)	Discount Rate 10%	
		Discount Factor (2)	Present Value of Cash Flow (3) = (1) × (2)
0	£(25,000)	1.000	£(25,000)
1	1,000	$\frac{1}{1.1} = 0.9091$	909
2	3,000	$\frac{1}{(1.1)^2} = 0.8264$	2,479
3	5,000	$\frac{1}{(1.1)^3} = 0.7513$	3,757
4	7,000	$\frac{1}{(1.1)^4} = 0.6830$	4,781
5	9,000	$\frac{1}{(1.1)^5} = 0.6209$	5,588
6	11,000	$\frac{1}{(1.1)^6} = 0.5645$	6,209
7	9,000	$\frac{1}{(1.1)^7} = 0.5132$	4,618
8	2,000	$\frac{1}{(1.1)^8} = 0.4665$	933
9	2,000	$\frac{1}{(1.1)^9} = 0.4241$	848
10	1,000	$\frac{1}{(1.1)^{10}} = 0.3855$	386
Total	£25,000		£5,508

rate of 10% would thus be used in the calculation of the NPV (see Table 16.2). The calculation of the NPV is more straightforward than the calculation of the IRR. The project is acceptable because the NPV is positive (a surplus remains after having charged 10% to any outstanding investment during the project).

16.1.3 Payback

The payback method recognises that the recovery of the original capital invested in a project is an important element in appraisal. The basic element of this method is a calculation of this recovery time, by the accumulation of the cash flows (not net profit, as the inclusion of depreciation would double-count the cost of the investment), year by year, until they equal the amount of the original investment. The length of time this process takes gives the 'payback period' for the project. This method makes no attempt to measure a percentage return on the capital invested and is often used in conjunction with other methods. The assumption is that, on average, projects with a short payback are better investment propositions than those with long payback periods.

A variation of this method, which can be used if DCF methods are employed, is the calculation of a 'discounted payback period'. This is calculated in much the same way as the payback, except that the cash flows accumulated are the base year value cash flows which have been discounted at the discount rate used in the NPV method (ie, the required return on investment). Thus, in addition to the recovery of the cash investment, the cost of financing the investment during the time that part of the investment remains unrecovered is also provided for. It thus, (unlike the ordinary payback method), ensures the achievement of at least the minimum required return, as long as nothing untoward happens after the payback period is reached.

Thus using the same example as before:

Payback period = 5 years (ie accumulated cash inflows for first five years = £25,000, exactly equal to the investment).

Discounted payback period = 6.3 years (ie accumulated discounted cash flows (at 10%) for first 6 years = £23,723. Thus £1,277 is required out of the year 7 present value of £4,618 (approx. 0.3) in order to accumulate to £25,000).

The calculation of both payback periods depends upon when cash flows take place during each year. For convenience, in the calculation of DCF returns, it was assumed that cash inflows would arise at yearly intervals commencing one year after the investment. This would be equivalent to assuming that these yearly intervals are mid-points of a year with cash flows arising six months either side. The calculation of the payback period has not been entirely consistent with this, eg the payback period would be $5\frac{1}{2}$ years not 5 years, using that assumption.

16.2 APPRAISAL TECHNIQUES AND DIFFERING PROJECTS

Before critically examining and comparing the various appraisal techniques a further illustration will be provided of the results of using the different methods for similar types of investment (ie plant and machinery with no terminal value at the end of its useful life), but differing project lives and cash flow patterns. Four projects will be considered (see Table 16.3) (Project B is the example already used to illustrate the various techniques).

A further factor which has an important effect on the viability of capital investment projects is taxation. It is an important variable, not just because of its incidence, but because it has differing consequences depending upon the nature of the investment. Expenditure on fixed assets is generally an allowable expense for tax purposes, as is most revenue expenditure (eg expenditure on raw materials, wages, etc). The important question is when. The availability and timing of tax allowances, and the rate of corporation tax, are subject to change from time to time by Government. Consideration of the effect of taxation on capital investment project viability is outside the scope of this book.

TABLE 16.3 **Differing project lives and cash flow patterns**

	Project A	**Project B**	**Project C**	**Project D**
	£	**£**	**£**	**£**
Initial Capital Outlay	(25,000)	(25,000)	(25,000)	(25,000)
Cash Inflow—Year 1	5,000	1,000	—	1,000
2	5,000	3,000	—	3,000
3	5,000	5,000	—	5,000
4	5,000	7,000	10,000	7,000
5	5,000	9,000	15,000	9,000
6	—	11,000	5,000	11,000
7	—	9,000	5,000	9,000
8	—	2,000	5,000	2,000
9	—	2,000	5,000	2,000
10	—	1,000	5,000	1,000
11	—	—	—	2,500
12	—	—	—	2,500
13	—	—	—	2,500
14	—	—	—	2,500
15	—	—	—	2,500
Net Cash Flow	—	£25,000	£25,000	£37,500
Project Life	5yrs.	10yrs.	10yrs.	15yrs.
Alternative criteria:				
ARR				
% on Gross Cap. Employed	—	10%	10%	10%
% on Av. Net Cap. Employed	—	20%	20%	20%
DCF				
DCF Internal rate of return	—	14.5%	12.1%	16.1%
NPV at 10%	(£6,046)	£5,508	£2,912	£9,161
Payback				
Payback	5yrs.	5yrs.	5yrs.	5yrs.
Discounted Payback	—	6.3yrs.	8.6yrs.	6.3yrs.

As can be seen, rather different results are obtained (both absolute and relative) depending upon which appraisal technique is used.

16.3 TECHNIQUES COMPARED

The techniques will be compared and judged according to their efficiency in measuring the economic viability of capital investment projects over their life.

16.3.1 Accounting rate of return

Whilst the Accounting Rate of Return is relatively easy to calculate and is based on profits, a concept readily understood by most managers, there are limitations to this appraisal method which centre around its failure to recognise correctly the timing of returns (ie cash flows) and their relationship with the investment. Because of this failure the method:

1 fails to measure properly the rate of return on a project even if the cash flows are even over the project life. It also, therefore, fails to take account of fluctuations in the level of earnings from year to year, both in assessing the profitability of a project and in making comparisons between projects, eg Project B v Project C;

2 is not comparable to cost of capital;

3 cannot cope adequately with disparities of length of life between projects, eg Project B or C v D;

4 is particularly vulnerable to errors in estimation of project life;

5 cannot effectively take account of taxation, a very important factor in investment decisions;
6 provides a distorted picture of the relationship between different sorts of projects.

Thus overall it is economically unrealistic in concentrating on accrual accounting rather than cash flows.

In comparing the two main methods of calculating the ARR, (one based on gross investment, the other on average net book value), the use of the original outlay (ie gross investment) may have practical advantages on the grounds that it does not change over the life of the investment and, therefore, follow-up and comparison of actual rates of return with those predicted is made easier. On the other hand the average method (ie average net book value of investment over the project life) recognises that depreciable assets do not have a permanent investment of the original amount. The funds are gradually recovered as the earnings are achieved. This, at least, is closer to economic reality, but may not provide a more accurate solution.

As can be seen from the four-project example, the ARR will tend to understate the true return where gross assets are used, because no allowance is made in the investment base for the return of capital, although depreciation is deducted from profits. Where net assets are used, the ARR tends to overstate the return because, while allowance is made in the investment base for the return of capital, the returns do not allow for their declining present value over time. However the treatment of taxation will also be an important influence. In all cases this will understate the return if it is applied to profits but not to investment (unless the investment is not allowable against tax). The extent of the understatement depends upon the tax rules applying at the time. For example, the significant changes in tax allowances and corporation tax rates in the 1984 Finance Act reduced the extent of the understatement.

16.3.2 Discounted cash flow

The DCF techniques are economically realistic in confining the analysis to cash flows and forgetting about customary book allocations. By taking account of the fact that money has a value over time:

1 They weigh the time pattern of the investment outlay and the cash earnings from the outlay in such a way as to reflect real and important differences in the value of near and distant cash flows. They therefore take full account of fluctuations in earnings from year to year.
2 The method is strictly comparable to cost of capital ratios so that decisions can be made quickly and safely on the basis of the relationships between indicated rate of return and the value of money to the company.
3 They cope adequately with disparities of length of life between projects.
4 Errors in estimating the project life have a far less dramatic impact on project profitability.
5 They correctly take account of the timing of tax cash flows.
6 The relationships between different types of projects are clear.

16.3.3 Payback

The payback method has severe limitations as a technique for measuring the economic viability of projects. These are its failure to take account of the timing of returns and the cost of capital, and its failure to consider the whole lifetime of a project.

Because the timing of the cash flows and the cost of capital are ignored there is no basis for judging whether a project is acceptable. This, coupled with the fact that the method takes no account at all of cash flows arising after the payback period has been reached, means that projects cannot be compared. Projects with the same payback period may have differing lives, differing total cash flows, and differing patterns of cash flows (see earlier example).

Compared with the basic payback method, the discounted payback at least takes account of the timing of cash flows and the cost of capital, although it continues to ignore cash flows after the payback period has been reached. It therefore at least ensures that the cost of capital is reached, provided that the cash flows thereafter are positive. In this sense it provides a measure of profitability.

16.4 APPRAISAL TECHNIQUES IN PRACTICE

The discounting of future cash flows as a tool for evaluating the viability of capital investment projects was not used in commerce and industry until the 1950's. Even then it emerged predominantly in the United States and it was not until the 1960's that any significant usage was evidenced in the United Kingdom.

Much empirical research has been conducted since, into the techniques that are used in practice to evaluate the worth of capital investment projects. The results of such research can be summarised as follows (as far as recent practice in the United Kingdom is concerned):

1 The use of DCF techniques, even in larger companies, is far from universal. For example, Pike's survey in the early 1980's (Capital Budgeting in the 1980's) of the 208 largest UK manufacturing and retail companies in terms of market capitalisation (150 usable responses were received), revealed that 70% of these firms used DCF methods of appraisal.
2 Instead of a movement toward one theoretically correct criterion, there has been a trend toward multiple criteria, especially in larger companies. It appears that whilst the usage of DCF techniques has increased, the older methods have not been abandoned, and indeed in some cases usage has also increased. The survey referred to above found that 79% of companies were using the payback method and 51% the ARR.
3 Considerable emphasis is placed, in the investment decision, on the results revealed by payback and ARR analysis. Using the results of the same survey (which it must be recognised are only an indication and not entirely consistent with the results of other surveys—if nothing else there are inevitably changes over time) of the different quantitative methods, DCF methods were preferred by 48%, payback by 26% and ARR by 26%.

16.5 DCF IN PERSPECTIVE

One could conclude, from the evidence provided and from the earlier consideration of techniques, that the emphasis placed on the use of the traditional investment appraisal methods (ie payback and accounting rate of return) in practice, both in terms of general usage and of their part in the final decision, is seriously misplaced.

However, it is important to recognise that the traditional techniques have shown a tremendous capacity for survival in the face of such criticism for some considerable time. One should perhaps look more closely therefore at the continued use of the traditional techniques, before reaching final conclusions about the place of DCF techniques, and in order to judge the seriousness of any misapplication.

The case for DCF may be influenced by several factors:

1 Ease of use and extent of understanding of different appraisal techniques.
2 Closeness of substitutes.
3 Difficulties or misapplication in appraisal.
4 Part played by computation in decision-making.
5 Objectives other than long-term profit.

16.5.1 Ease of use and extent of understanding of different appraisal techniques

Research evidence shows that these are important factors in the continued use of traditional techniques. There is a general reluctance to change to new techniques, especially when the existing ones are familiar and accepted and the new ones appear rather daunting. This certainly helps to explain the very gradual acceptance of DCF. However, although there is undoubtedly a clear general understanding of both payback and accounting rate of return, it is perhaps doubtful whether there is sufficient understanding of how they are actually calculated and of the significance of the result.

It is likely that payback is interpreted to mean that the investment is recovered in a certain time, without appreciating that this does not provide for any return on capital outstanding over this time. Also, what payback criteria should be adopted?

With accounting rate of return it is likely that the result is interpreted to be consistent with the calculation of the cost of capital, without appreciating the serious overstatement or understatement that can arise (depending upon which ARR method is used).

If traditional techniques are theoretically unsound, mere familiarity cannot justify their continued use, unless there are insurmountable difficulties in using and understanding the newer methods. This surely is not the case.

16.5.2 Closeness of substitutes

However, justification for continued use of the traditional techniques would be much greater if, despite their theoretical shortcomings, they are likely to lead to the same decisions being made as would be made with DCF.

In certain situations it is possible to establish specific relationships between the traditional methods and the DCF internal rate of return. If the cash inflows from an investment project are the same in each year of the project's life, then:

$$R = Rp - Rp\left(\frac{1}{1+R}\right)^n$$

$$R = \left(Rt + \frac{1}{n}\right)\left(1 - \left(\frac{1}{1+R}\right)^n\right)$$

$$R = \frac{\left(Ra + \frac{1}{n}\right)\left(1 - \left(\frac{1}{1+R}\right)^n\right)}{2}$$

where:
R is the DCF internal rate of return
Rp is the reciprocal of the payback period
Rt is the ARR on gross investment
Ra is the ARR on average net investment
n is the project life in years.

However, the extent of the difference between the IRR on the one hand and the payback reciprocal or the ARR on the other, depends upon the size of the return and the length of project life. This is demonstrated in the following tables:

TABLE 16.4 **Extent of the *overstatement* of the payback reciprocal (as a %) compared with the DCF internal rate of return %**

	Project Life in Years					
% IRR	*2*	*5*	*8*	*10*	*15*	*20*
5	49	18	11	8	5	3
10	48	16	9	6	3	2
15	47	15	7	5	2	1
20	45	13	6	4	1	1
30	44	11	4	2	1	0
40	42	9	3	1	0	0

TABLE 16.5 **Extent of the *understatement* of the ARR% of gross investment compared with the DCF internal rate of return %**

% IRR	*Project Life in Years* 2	5	8	10	15	20
5	1	2	2	2	2	2
10	2	4	4	4	4	3
15	4	5	5	5	5	4
20	5	7	6	6	5	5
30	7	9	8	8	6	5
40	8	11	10	9	6	5

TABLE 16.6 **Extent of the *overstatement* of the ARR% of average net investment compared with the DCF internal rate of return %**

% IRR	*Project Life in Years* 2	5	8	10	15	20
5	3	1	1	1	1	1
10	5	3	3	3	3	4
15	10	5	5	5	6	7
20	11	7	7	8	9	11
30	17	12	13	15	18	20
40	23	18	20	23	27	30

Thus the extent of the percentage points under/overstatement varies considerably depending upon the size of the return and the length of project life, even if it is reasonable to assume that cash inflows from a project will be a constant annual amount.

Nevertheless, the systematic nature of the relationships demonstrated above, and the range over which the deviations remain relatively small, have been held to be very relevant for the positive theory of investment. Levy and Sarnat (Capital Investment and Financial Decisions) claim that

'. . . they can help to account for the fact that most successful business firms used short-cut rules of thumb* in the past and explain why many still persist in their use today, even in the face of the overwhelming theoretical arguments in favour of time discounting.'

However, there seems little justification for this view. Using the ARR method, even if cash flows are expected to be the same each year, and projects are long life and target returns low (one implication of constant cash flows is that the appraisal is being carried out on cash flows expressed in real terms, as opposed to money terms, and thus target returns will be relatively low), the size of the deviation in relation to the size of the returns is significant in most cases. In the instance of the payback reciprocal, in all cases the overstatement is particularly large for low return projects.

In any event, the assumption of constant annual cash flows would seem unreasonable. Factors such as product life cycles, patterns of maintenance expenditure, incidence of taxation, working capital requirements, effect of inflation, would all suggest the need for a more rigorous analysis and the unreasonableness of assumptions of constant annual cash flows. In this case relationships between the results of traditional and DCF appraisal methods would vary tremendously.

Much also depends upon how the traditional methods are used. Firstly, in the case of the ARR methods, a further important factor is the question of how taxation is accounted for. It is possible, as suggested earlier, that the way that tax is treated leads to an understatement of the return for both ARR methods. Secondly, with the payback method, survey evidence reveals that the criteria of acceptability frequently adopted in practice is a required payback of five years at most, and in some cases one as low as two years. Adopting such criteria would seem to demonstrate clearly a complete lack of awareness of the possibility of any such relationship. For example, a project with constant cash

(*ie payback and accounting rate of return)

flows, a life of ten years, and a required return in real terms (ie over and above maintaining the real value of capital) of as much as 10%, would only need to payback within 6.2 years.

Thus the traditional methods are not sufficiently close substitutes even if used correctly. The evidence available of how they are used would seem to indicate an understatement of the worth of projects and, consequently, underinvestment. On the assumption that information used in the appraisal is accurate, whether the extent of the underinvestment is serious depends upon the proportion of projects where conclusions regarding viability, and thus decisions taken, would be reversed. If a high proportion of projects show returns near the margin, then the use of appraisal methods which understate the return (especially if significantly so) may have serious implications for the level of investment. If, on the other hand, most projects tend to be highly profitable then it is likely that they will be approved anyway.

Carsberg and Hope ('Business Investment Decisions under Inflation') found some evidence that traditional techniques are used only as a first appraisal method, or only for small projects, or only for projects with even cash flows. If this is the case, then in such situations any bias associated with the use of non-discounting methods is reduced. This, however, would be expected to influence the weighting attached by respondents to particular methods, and thus already influence indications about the emphasis placed upon different techniques provided by the survey evidence.

16.5.3 Difficulties or misapplication in appraisal

One objection sometimes raised to the use of DCF techniques is that, because the future is so uncertain and estimates are therefore unreliable, there is little point in applying economically realistic criteria to them. The answer to this objection is that there is surely less point in compounding estimating error by using crude investment criteria. Nevertheless, it is important to recognise that the best of the appraisal methods cannot do better than the predictions that go into the appraisal. Sophisticated manipulation of erroneous data may be worse than a waste of time.

The more difficult that information becomes to identify, the more bias may creep in. Such bias may be demonstrated by an over-optimism as to what management are capable of achieving. It has certainly been found by many companies, as illustrated by Unilever in their submission to the Wilson Committee, that project profitability obtained in the event is significant below that estimated in advance. Thus, if most projects put forward appear highly profitable (where it would appear not to matter which appraisal technique is used), one should perhaps question the reasonableness of the estimates made. The use of appraisal methods which understate the return could even be claimed to help avoid overinvestment!

Another important influence on the level of investment is the criterion that is used for judging the acceptability of project returns. The establishment of a hurdle rate is also no easy task. However, misapplication has also been shown to exist in this aspect of appraisal. Carsberg and Hope found in their survey that many firms had misunderstood the relationship between returns and the cost of capital in an inflationary situation. The cost of capital was being seriously overstated, through its measurement in money terms, which was leading companies to reject projects that were economically worthwhile, which in turn led to underinvestment. In this situation, however, the use of accounting rate of return, rather than DCF, would be likely to lead to even more serious underinvestment.

16.5.4 Part played by computation in decision-making

Chapter 11 considered the stages in the decision-making process and the difficulties at each stage. It should certainly be the case that the more these difficulties exist the less the decision will be taken on the basis of computation, and the less important therefore will be the quantitative evaluation. However, whilst it is important to recognise this, it is in itself no justification for using anything less than the best available techniques of appraisal. Survey evidence tends to indicate that in practice the rate of project acceptance at the final approval stage is extremely high (ie if the figures look good it is approved). Nevertheless, it could be the case that the decision is made earlier and more qualitatively, and that figures are then provided to support such judgement.

16.5.5 Objectives other than long-term profit

Although long-term profit must be an important motive of business, this may not be the sole objective in the long run, and in any case should never be so to the total disregard of shorter-term profit and liquidity requirements. In this respect, for certain projects the traditional methods may have some part to play, albeit only in a secondary role and not in fact in the way that the methods have been shown to be used earlier as appraisal devices.

For example, the effect of major investment decisions on annual profits from year to year must be considered. Major projects may well take some time to realise their full potential, with a possible adverse effect on reported profits in early years. Also, if at a particular time, projects are being financed by increased borrowing rather than, for example, from retained profits, then the requirement to pay high interest charges to finance the capital investment in early years may have a particularly damaging effect on the profit remaining for shareholders in those years. However, it is the effect of a project on, for example, the return on capital employed in particular years that is important, not the average ARR over the life of the project. Equally, in considering the effect of major projects on liquidity it is not simply the payback period but the precise pattern of anticipated cash flows over the payback period that is important.

16.5.6 Conclusions

It should be recognised that only the DCF methods of investment appraisal provide a theoretically sound evaluation of project worth against an objective of long-term profit maximisation. However, much depends upon whether the objective can be clearly and correctly expressed in terms of a criterion of acceptability, whether adequate information relevant for a particular evaluation can be, and is, identified, and correctly used, and whether projects are successfully implemented. Even then there will be no guarantee of adequate profits. Projects must first be spotted. However, this should not be used as justification for using inferior methods. They may have a secondary role to play for certain major projects but they do not justify themselves on the grounds of simplicity or sufficient similarity of result.

Thus DCF techniques are not a panacea but nevertheless have an important part to play in capital investment decision-making. At times, however, this part has been rather overplayed in the academic literature. The difficulties must be sufficiently recognised. Certainly judgement or inspiration should have a part to play and survey evidence suggests that they do.

It is difficult to weigh up the implications of using the traditional techniques. If they are used for economic appraisal, as evidence suggests, then whether underinvestment results, and how seriously, depends not only upon how many projects are affected but also upon the extent and effect of other misapplications in appraisal, and upon the part that computation plays in the investment decision.

16.6 CALCULATION OF THE IRR—INTERPOLATION AND EXTRAPOLATION

As was noted earlier, if the NPV method is used, a decision is made in favour of a project if the NPV is a positive amount when discounted at the minimum acceptable rate of return. The IRR method on the other hand requires the calculation of a rate of interest which when used in discounting will reduce the NPV of a project to zero. This enables comparison of the IRR with the minimum acceptable rate of return.

Of the two (NPV and IRR) the NPV calculation is the easier to make. With IRR the usual approach is to proceed in an iterative fashion, guessing at the likely rate, entering further values for r (on the basis of the previous result) and then approximating between two values to obtain the value of r that reduces the NPV to zero.

In order to demonstrate further the calculation of the IRR, it is useful to plot on a chart the impact on the net present value of changes in the discount rate. Using the same example as was used earlier in the chapter to demonstrate the use of the different appraisal techniques, a range of NPVs at varying discount rates are as follows:

Discount rate	*NPV (£)*
0%	25,000
5%	13,664
10%	5,508
12%	2,886
14%	564
14.5%	34
14.6%	(72)
15%	(490)
17%	(2,440)
20%	(4,987)

When the discount rate is zero (ie undiscounted) the NPV is simply the sum of the cash inflows and outflows over the life of the project. As the discount rate is increased, the NPV decreases as future cash flows have a smaller present value due to their increased lost earnings potential.

This relationship between NPV and discount rate is demonstrated in Figure 16.1. It can be seen that the response of NPV to changes in discount rate is represented by a curve. This demonstrates that the NPV reduces by an increasingly smaller absolute amount as the discount rate is increased, ie as i (the discount rate) is increased the discount factor

$$\frac{1}{(1+i)^t}$$

reduces by a smaller and smaller amount for each one per cent change in i. This is due to the fact that although $(1 + i)$ is increasing by the same absolute amount (ie 0.01), this is an increasingly smaller amount relative to the previous $(1 + i)$.

The curve cuts the discount rate axis at the project's IRR, ie this is the point at which NPV is zero. This is the break-even discount rate for the project (the highest possible minimum acceptable rate of return). The various NPVs that would be generated at varying discount rates around the break-even can be read from the chart.

The IRR of 14.5% was obtained earlier by a trial and error process, which culminated in the calculation of the NPV of the project at 14.5% and 14.6%. It has already been stressed that, in practice, calculation of the IRR to the nearest % would be sufficient and, therefore, calculation of the

FIGURE 16.1 **NPV Profile**

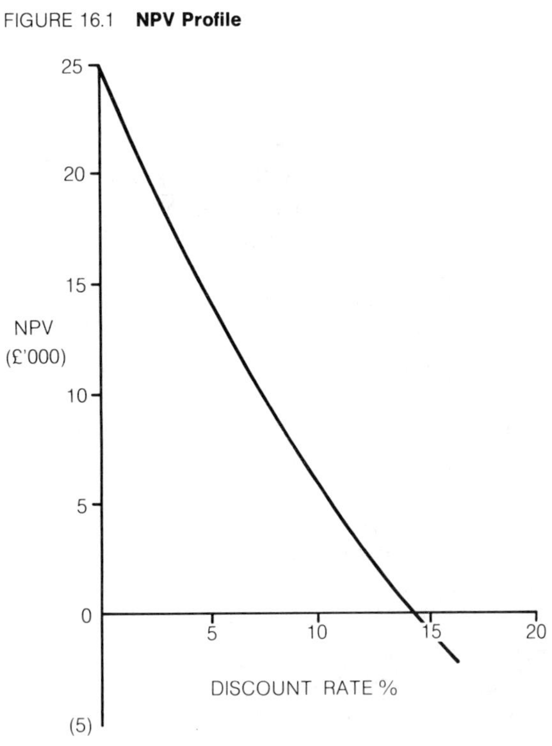

NPV at discount rates of 14% and 15% would have produced the desired result. In fact, the IRR % can be approximated from any two points by assuming that the NPV is a linear function of the discount rate (rather than the actual curvi-linear function). The important question is 'When is it reasonable to approximate?'

In order both to demonstrate the calculation of an approximate IRR and also to consider when such approximation can reasonably be made, the NPV values obtained at 14% and 15% discount rates will be used. Using round percentages, this will provide the best approximation to the real return, and thus a basis for comparison with other approximations.

The change in NPV from £564 at a discount rate of 14% to (£490) at a discount rate of 15% is assumed to be a linear function of the 1% change in discount rate. The approximate IRR is obtained by calculating what proportion of the total NPV change of £1,054 (ie 564 + 490) is required to reach zero NPV. Using 14% as a base it is

$$14\% + \frac{564}{1{,}054} \times 1\% = +0.54\%$$

Thus the IRR is 14% + 0.54% = 14.54%. Equally it could have been worked backwards from 15% as

$$15\% - \frac{490}{1{,}054} \times 1\% = -0.46\%$$

and the IRR is 15% – 0.46% = 14.54%.

As was stated above, this approximation of the IRR can be calculated from any two points. If the two points used lie either side of the IRR (ie one rate of interest higher than the IRR with a negative NPV and one lower with a positive NPV), as demonstrated above, then such an approximation is called interpolation (the calculation of an intermediate term).

Extrapolation (the calculation of a term outside the known range) is equally valid using either two positive NPV values or two negatives. For example, the NPVs at 12% and 14% could have been used as follows:

$$\text{Approximate IRR} = 12\% + \left[(14 - 12) \times \frac{2{,}886}{2{,}886 - 564}\right]\%$$

$$= 12\% + 2.49\%$$

$$= 14.49\%.$$

The general formula can be stated as:

$$\text{Approximate IRR} = \text{Base point discount rate (\%)} \pm{}^{*} \left(\text{change in discount rate (\%) between base point and other point used} \times \frac{\textit{NPV at base point}}{\text{Change in NPV between the two points used}}\right)$$

*This will be + if the base point has a positive NPV
This will be – if the base point has a negative NPV

If interpolating, the factor $\dfrac{\textit{NPV at base point}}{\text{Change in NPV between the two points used}} < 1$

If extrapolating, the factor $\dfrac{\textit{NPV at base point}}{\text{Change in NPV between the two points used}} > 1$

Interpolation will always overstate the return and thus would lead if anything to a rounding downwards. Conversely, extrapolation will always understate the return and thus would lead, if anything, to a rounding upwards. The true IRR, therefore, lies between 14.49% and 14.54%.

As a general rule of thumb, two particular NPV values can be used to estimate the IRR of a project, given that *either* one of the NPV values is within 1/10th of the NPV for the project at 0%, or alternatively that *both* NPV values are within 1/5th of the NPV for the project at 0%, and given sensible rounding.

16.7 CALCULATION OF THE INTERNAL RATE OF RETURN—SHORT CUTS

It is possible to make a reasonable estimate of the IRR having made only one NPV calculation (apart from the value undiscounted, ie at 0%, which is easily determined). Consideration will now be given to whether, and if so how, it can be ensured that this is the case, ie is it possible to find as a first approximation a rate of interest which produces an NPV within 1/10th of the NPV value at 0%?

There are two methods of approximation, which will be demonstrated using the same project example as previously. The task is to provide as a first estimate a reasonable approximation of the rate of interest which will discount total cash inflows over 10 years of £50,000 to a present value of £25,000.

16.7.1 Average discount factor

The first method of approximation involves the calculation of the *average discount factor* required to reduce the £50,000 cash inflows down to the present value of £25,000, ie it is

$$\frac{25{,}000}{50{,}000} = 0.5$$

Whilst the discount factors will vary according to the year, on average a discount factor of 0.5 is required. If the cash inflows were the same in each year of the project then each year's discount factor will be given the same weighting (ie multiplied by the same cash flow), and thus it would be possible to estimate the IRR by finding that rate of interest having a discount factor of 0.5 half way through this project (ie between years 5 and 6). This would not be exactly right because the discount factors do not change by a constant amount from one year to another, but it would be a very reasonable approximation.

Another difficulty, however, is that the cash flows may fluctuate from year to year. Obviously, if in a particular project the majority of the cash inflows occur in the early years then the return will be considerably higher than in a project of the same life and same total cash inflows where the majority of the cash inflows occur in the later years. Nevertheless, both projects would have the same average discount factor, calculated as above. Thus adjustments may be required to reflect the particular pattern of earnings. If, for example, the majority of the cash inflows are in the early stages of the project then the average discount factor would need to be looked for earlier than the half-way stage of the project because of the increased weighting of the earlier years. The reverse would be true if the majority of the cash *flows* occurred in the *later* years of the project.

In our example, despite the uneven cash flows from year to year, they nevertheless display a pattern which gives approximately equal weighting to cash inflows in each of the two halves of the project (ie years 1–5 and years 6–10). The total cash inflows are £25,000 in each half, and the weighting of cash inflows in the latter part of the first five years is compensated for by early cash flows in the second five years. Thus, it would seem reasonable to look for a discount factor of 0.5 between years 5 and 6 (ie the half-way stage) of the project. The present values of £1 occurring in 5 and 6 years' time are:

	13%	*14%*
At Year 5	£0.5428	£0.5194
Year 6	£0.4803	£0.4556

Thus, if no previous calculations had been carried out, the NPV would have been calculated at 13 or 14%. This clearly would be satisfactory as a first approximation. An extrapolation using 0% and 13 or 14% could be rapidly performed.

16.7.2 Cumulative discount factor

The second method of approximation, in order to provide a first estimate of the IRR, involves the calculation of the *cumulative discount factor* (over 10 years in this example) which, when multiplied by the average annual cash inflow, produces a total present value of £25,000, ie the average annual cash inflow

$$= \frac{£50,000}{10 \text{ years}} = £5,000$$

and therefore, the required cumulative discount factor over 10 years is

$$\frac{£25,000}{£5,000} = 5$$

This method will be more accurate than the first method considered, in that it does not suffer from one of the potential limitations of that method, namely that it used an oversimplified average of the required discount factor. Using the cumulative discount factor method, the discount factors over the whole life of the project are correctly considered. Thus, if the project has the same cash inflows in each year, then this method will calculate correctly the IRR.

However, this second method also has to overcome the potential difficulty caused by fluctuations in cash inflows from year to year. The average cash flows may not be sufficiently representative of average timing. If the majority of the cash flows occur in the early stages of the project then the IRR will be higher (ie the weighted average cash flow will be higher, producing a lower cumulative discount factor required) and vice versa.

As noted before in the particular project under consideration, despite the fluctuations from year to year, the average annual cash flow of £5,000 is fairly representative of their timing. This time, tables for the present value of an annuity of £1 are used.

Using these tables the cumulative discount factor over 10 years is:

At	*14%*	*15%*	*16%*
	5.2161	5.0188	4.8332

Thus, a discount rate of 15% would be used in the calculation of the NPV for the project. This time, interpolation between 0% and 15% would provide a rapid solution to the IRR.

Self-assessment question 16.1

A company is considering several possible capital investment opportunities:

(a) A new machine costing £114,000 could be purchased so as to save manual operations costing £27,000 per annum. The machine would last 8 years and have no residual value at the end of its useful life.

You are required to calculate:

(i) the IRR of the project;
(ii) the level of annual saving required in order to provide a 12% IRR;
(iii) the NPV if the cost of capital is 10%.

(b) The chief engineer of the company has been considering another cost–saving project and has justified the project as follows:
'The cost of the machine is £120,000. It will last for 6 years and will reduce costs by £35,000 net of machine operating costs, excluding depreciation. After allowing for depreciation of £20,000 per annum, extra profit of £15,000 per annum will result. This assumes that there will be no scrap value at the end of the machine's life. £15,000 profit on an average investment of £60,000 provides a return of 25% which is almost double bank

overdraft rate, and as the investment pays for itself in just over 3 years we are not at risk for very long. I don't see what there is to discuss with the management accountant.'

You, as the management accountant, are required to respond to the engineer's comments.

(c) Three further projects are being considered. In each case the investment sum is the same and for each project even annual cash inflows will result. Payback periods and economic lives of the three projects are as follows:

	Project		
	A	**B**	**C**
Payback	3.3 years	4.0 years	4.2 years
Project life	5 years	15 years	4 years

Required:
Without the use of present value tables or equations:

(i) state which project, if any, can be rejected without further analysis.
(ii) determine the approximate IRR of the projects.
(iii) state which project promises the highest rate of return.

(d) Project A, in (c) above, would provide facilities to manufacture a new product which has a contribution/sales ratio of 40%. Investment would be £200,000 in new equipment. Straight-line depreciation would be charged over the five-year life; no scrap value is expected after 5 years. Costs, normally classified as fixed (excluding depreciation), will increase by £48,000 per annum. It is expected that annual sales will be the same each year.

Required:
Determine the annual sales required in order to provide a DCF return of 20%.

Answers on p 571

16.8 RELATIVE RANKING OF PROJECTS: IRR v NPV

The relative ranking of projects, using the different DCF methods, will be considered initially in simple accept/reject situations (ie where the alternative for all projects is to do nothing). This will be extended later to an assessment of situations where a choice has to be made between two or more alternatives other than doing nothing (eg a choice between one machine and another to carry out a particular operation).

In simple accept/reject situations a firm is able to implement all projects showing a return at or above the firm's cost of capital. Both methods (NPV and IRR) would appear to be equally valid in the sense that they will both lead to the acceptance (and, therefore, rejection) of the same projects. Using NPV, all projects with a positive net present value, when discounted at the firm's cost of capital, will be accepted. Using IRR, all projects which yield an internal rate of return in excess of the firm's cost of capital will be chosen. However, although both IRR and NPV lead to the same conclusion regarding project acceptability, the ranking of a set of projects obtained from IRR does not necessarily agree with that produced using NPV, since, in the latter case, the ranking may vary according to the particular discount rate used.

It can be seen from the chart (Figure 16.2) showing the NPV profiles of two different projects, that the NPV ranking, as well as project acceptability, depends upon the cost of capital. At cost of capital rates below approximately 11% Project 2 will be ranked higher. Above 11% Project 1 is preferred, a ranking consistent with that produced under IRR. Ranking differences exist wherever the NPV profiles of investment opportunities intersect at a positive amount, and at a discount rate which is above the cost of capital.

FIGURE 16.2 **NPV Profiles**

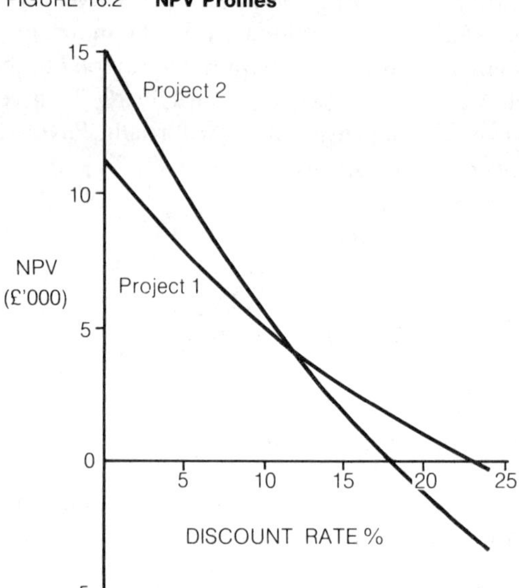

Argument about the merits of the relative rankings in simple accept/reject situations is thus concerned with the question of value. It is argued that the IRR measures only the quality of the investment, while NPV takes into account both the quality and the scale. This is because the IRR provides a relative measure of value (% IRR) while the NPV provides an absolute measure (£ surplus). Thus the IRR would rank, for example, a 100% return on an investment of £1 considerably higher than a 20% return on an investment of £1 million, whereas the reverse would be true using NPV (as long as the cost of capital is below 20%). While one project may have a higher rate of profit per unit of capital invested than another, if it has fewer units of capital invested in it, it may make a smaller contribution to the wealth of the firm. Thus, if the objective is to maximise the firm's wealth, then the ranking of project NPVs provides the correct measure; if the objective is to maximise the rate of profitability per unit of capital invested, then IRR would provide the correct ranking of projects, but this objective could be achieved by rejecting all but the most highly profitable projects. This is clearly unrealistic and, therefore, one would conclude that NPV ranking is correct and IRR unsatisfactory as a measure of relative project value.

Thus, possible differences in ranking of projects by IRR and NPV is caused by differences in the scale of projects. Where projects have differing outlays, the difference in scale is established at the outset and is increased or decreased by the subsequent pattern of cash flows. Where different projects have the same investment sum, the difference in scale is determined by the pattern of subsequent cash flows only, but is no less significant for that fact. In defence of IRR in such situations, the argument would appear to be academic in that decisions on which projects to accept would not be altered.

The situation is of course different where a choice needs to be made between two or more operational alternatives as the possibility of different rankings provided by IRR and NPV would appear to take on greater significance. Table 16.7 shows the two projects whose NPV profiles were demonstrated in Figure 16.2, and assumes that the cost of capital (the minimum acceptable rate of return) is 10%. If a choice has to be made between Project 1 and Project 2 because they are operationally mutually exclusive, the project chosen will depend upon the appraisal method used, because conflicting rankings occur.

TABLE 16.7 **Project Rankings**

	Project 1	*Project 2*
Yr 0	(£14,000)	(£25,000)
Yrs 1–5	£5,000 per annum	£8,000 per annum
IRR	23%	18%
NPV at 10% cost of capital	£4,950	£5,320
Ranking: Using IRR	1	2
Using NPV	2	1

It has been argued already that the NPV method is preferable because it provides a better measure of the value to be derived from an investment. Thus alternative 2 would be preferred because, despite offering a lower percentage return on average, it involves investment of an extra £11,000—the return on which is sufficient to generate a further profit surplus (ie an increase in the NPV) when discounted at 10%.

The apparent potential conflict between NPV and IRR methods in such situations arises, not because of the use of the IRR method itself, but because of its misuse. If the IRR method is to be used in such alternative choice situations, the correct choice can only be ensured by calculating the internal rate of return on the differential investment, if the smaller-scale alternative has already been found to be worthwhile. In this way the IRR on the difference in scale between alternatives can be found. As alternative 1 (Project 1) is worthwhile, we have the situation shown in Table 16.8.

TABLE 16.8 **Project Choice**

		Alternative 2 v *Alternative 1*
Yr 0	Differential investment	(£11,000)
Yrs 1-5	Differential cash inflow	£3,000 per annum
	IRR	11%
	NPV at 10%	£370 (ie £5,320–£4,950)

Thus, using IRR, alternative 2 (Project 2) would be chosen because it provides a differential return in excess of the minimum required return. If used in this way the IRR method will always produce results consistent with those using the NPV method. Indeed, it could be argued that it is useful to know the quality of the differential investment, which is much more difficult to judge using the NPV method, because the differential NPV is dependent upon both quality and scale. The IRR percentage, when compared with the cost of capital, provides a general indication of the margin of safety. Also, the establishment of a minimum acceptable rate of return, especially difficult when risk is taken into account, comes later in the evaluation process. These may be reasons why, in contradiction of the normative preference for NPV, the IRR method is more popular in practice. Pike found this especially to be the case in larger companies. Another reason for the preference for IRR is that the investment return is expressed as a familiar percentage, rather than an absolute £ surplus.

Self-assessment question 16.2

A company is considering four capital investment projects, with the following cash flows:

(£000)	**Project**			
	A	B	C	D
Capital Investment:				
Year 0	(250)	(100)	(100)	(200)
Cash Inflows:				
Year 1	115	10	80	—
Year 2	115	140	60	—
Year 3	115	—	—	250

Required:

(a) On the assumption that the four projects are independent of each other, and that funds are freely available at the company's cost of capital of 10%, indicate which projects should be accepted.

(b) Calculate the IRRs of projects B and C, and on the assumption that they are mutually exclusive, determine which project should be selected.

Answers on p 572

SUMMARY

Despite the clear normative preference for the use of discounted cash flow methods of capital investment appraisal the more traditional methods of accounting rate of return and payback remain popular in practice. This chapter has sought to explain the mechanics of each method and to critically examine the extent to which the different methods provide a measurement of investment potential.

Also in contradiction of the normative preference, the IRR method of discounted cash flow is more popular in practice than NPV. There appear to be practical advantages with IRR. Whichever DCF method is used it is important that these techniques of appraisal are understood and used correctly in different situations. However, even if these requirements are fulfilled, it cannot guarantee that the right decisions are made. The other necessary conditions for optimal decision-making, which were identified in Chapter 11, must also be satisfied; for example information relevant to the decision must be gathered, and arranged correctly, prior to the application of DCF appraisal techniques. The identification, analysis and use of information in the appraisal is considered in Chapter 17.

EXERCISES

Exercise 16.1

A company is considering a capital investment proposal where two alternatives, involving differing degrees of mechanisation, are being considered. Both investments would have a five-year life.

In Option 1 new machinery would cost £278,000, and in Option 2, £805,000. Anticipated scrap values after 5 years are £28,000 and £150,000 respectively. Depreciation is provided on a straight line basis. Option 1 would generate annual cash inflows of £100,000, and Option 2, £250,000. The cost of capital is 15%.

Required:

(a) Calculate for each option

- **(i)** the payback period
- **(ii)** the accounting rate of return, based on average book value
- **(iii)** the net present value
- **(iv)** the internal rate of return.

(b) Identify the preferred option, giving reasons for your choice.

Answers on p 573

Exercise 16.2

Using the Discounted Cash Flow Yield (Internal Rate of Return) for evaluating investment opportunities has the basic weakness that it does not give attention to the amount of the capital investment, in that a return of 20% on an investment of £1,000 may be given a higher ranking than a return of 15% on an investment of £10,000.

Comment in general on the above statement referring in particular to the problem of giving priorities to (ranking) investment proposals.

Your answers should make use of the following information.

	Project A Cash Flow £	*Project B Cash Flow* £
Y 0 Capital Investment	(1,000)	(10,000)
Y 1 Cash Flows	240	2,300
Y 2 "	288	2,640
Y 3 "	346	3,040
Y 4 "	414	3,500
Y 5 "	498	4,020
Cost of Capital	10%	10%

Answers on p 575

Exercise 16.3

Two investment projects are being considered with the following cash flow projections:

	Project 1 £000	**Project 2** £000
Initial outlay	(200)	(200)
Cash inflows:		
Year 1	10	120
Year 2	30	90
Year 3	210	50
Year 4	50	10

Required:

(a) Prepare, on a single graph, present value profiles for each project. Use interest rates from 0% to 20% at 5% intervals.

(b) Using the graph paper determine the IRR for each of the projects.

(c) State for which range of costs of capital Project 1 would be preferred to Project 2.

Answers on p 577

Exercise 16.4

The traditional methods of capital investment appraisal have been shown by surveys to remain popular in practice, despite the clear normative preference for discounted cash flow methods. Comment.

Answer in lecturer's manual

Capital Investment Decision-Making: Identification, Analysis and Presentation of Information

INTRODUCTION

Capital investment projects need to be assessed, in terms of the information that is relevant, in exactly the same way in principle as the shorter-term quantitative decisions examined in previous chapters. There is no conceptual conflict between them; the essence of the distinction is time. Cash flows will be relevant if they are avoidable depending upon the alternative selected. The longer the time period under consideration the more costs, in general, become at least to some extent avoidable.

This chapter considers the identification of information relevant in capital investment decisions and the analysis and presentation of such information using discounted cash flow methods of appraisal. The cash flows that must be quantified are the net cash investment, which is a measure of the cost in terms of cash resources to the business of a new investment, the annual cash flows which represent the cash arising from operating the investment or from its alternatives, and the net residual value, which is the net cash flow arising at the end of the investment life. The costs and benefits to be included depend upon the nature of the decision under consideration. Different types of capital investment decision are considered and the general principles regarding the relevance of information illustrated in each. The effect of inflation on the appraisal of investment decisions is then explained and illustrated. Finally, the difficulties and limitations of the analysis are considered.

In practice, the effect of taxation, through the incidence of corporation tax and the availability and timing of tax allowances, is an important factor which must be considered. Tax implications are outside the scope of this book.

17.1 TYPES OF DECISIONS

A variety of decision situations has been considered and illustrated in earlier chapters. Quantitative problems of choice involving investment in fixed assets can be classified at a summary level as:

1. Expansion
2. Modernisation
3. Replacement

In addition, the possibility of divestment may have to be considered from time to time, when the question of dropping products or suspending activities arises.

17.2 EXPANSION

Expansion situations occur when new activities/products are being considered. Such situations may require investment in additional fixed assets. At the same time choice may have to be made between different machines, which may vary in terms of capacity, in terms of flexibility, and in their degree of automation. A further source of choice may be regarding the location of plant. Thus situations vary as does the information potentially relevant to making the choice. The principles established in Chapter 12, and illustrated in the varied short-term decision-making situations in Chapters 12 and 13, should be applied equally to capital investment situations.

In expansion situations it is necessary to consider particularly the cost of purchasing, installing and commissioning new fixed assets; the contribution that will be generated from new activities; the additional 'fixed' costs that will be incurred and how these are affected if different investment options are available; and the working capital implications of the business expansion.

Example 17.1

A company is considering the introduction of a new product. A feasibility study has been carried out, at a cost of £60,000, which suggests that the selling price of the product should be £22.50 per unit. Demand is expected to be 20,000 units per annum for five years.

Units costs are estimated as follows:

	£/unit
Direct materials	4.50
Direct labour	5.00
Variable overheads	2.50
Fixed overheads	9.90
	21.90

Fixed overheads include:

1. Factory rent of £20,000 per annum. The new product would be manufactured in a factory rented specially for the purpose.
2. Depreciation of plant and machinery which would be purchased at a cost of £500,000. The plant and machinery would have no residual value when the manufacture of the new product ceased after five years, and is depreciated on the straight line basis.
3. Factory manager's salary of £18,000 per annum. The manager is at present employed by the company, but is due to retire in the near future on an annual pension, payable by the company, of £6,000. If the manager continued to be employed, the pension would not be paid during this period. Subsequent pension rights would not be affected.
4. Head office costs charged at the rate of £2.00 per unit of product. Total head office costs would not be expected to be affected by the introduction of the new product.

In the appraisal of the viability of introducing the new product, head office costs should be ignored as they are unaffected by the decision. Also £6,000 of the factory manager's salary is unavoidable. Depreciation is not relevant as an annual cost; it is included as a total investment cash outflow at the commencement of the project. The cost of the feasibility study is a past cost and, therefore, not relevant to the decision.

It is useful to clearly separate those elements of the project which vary with the number of units produced and sold, and those which are a fixed annual incremental cost regardless of the level of activity. Thus:

	£/Unit	**Annual Activity (units)**	**Annual Cash Flow (£)**
Selling price	22.50		
Variable costs:			
Direct materials	(4.50)		
Direct labour	(5.00)		
Variable overhead	(2.50)		
	(12.00)		
Contribution	10.50	× 20,000	= 210,000
Factory rent			(20,000)
Factory manager's salary			(12,000)
			(32,000)
Incremental profit			178,000

The IRR of the project can be calculated as:

$$\frac{500,000}{178,000} = 2.8090 \text{ (cumulative discount factor over 5 years)}$$

From the annuity tables this can be determined as an IRR of just below 23%. The project is acceptable if the required return is less than 23%.
If, say, the required return is 12%, the NPV can be calculated as:

178,000 × 3.6048 (cumulative discount factor over 5 years at 12%)
= 641,654
(500,000)
£141,654

17.2.1 Sensitivity analysis

CVP analysis principles can be applied to capital investment decisions so as to indicate the sensitivity of the return to changed assumptions regarding the variables in the project. For example if other variables are assumed unchanged the annual contribution required to provide a 12% DCF return can be calculated as follows:

$$\frac{500{,}000}{3.6048} = £138{,}700$$

+ 32,000
£170,700

This is 81.3% of the annual contribution forecast. Thus annual activity could be as low as 16,260 units, for example, if all other factors are as forecast. If the volume estimate remains at 20,000 units per annum the unit contribution required to provide a 12% return is £8.54, approximately £2 per unit below that forecast.

17.2.2 Working capital

An important aspect of expansion projects, which has not been considered in the above example, is the impact of such projects on working capital requirements. It has been assumed in the calculations that the cash inflow from sales is instantaneous with the cash outflow for resources utilised in the manufacture and sale of the product. In most situations working capital will be required to finance production as cash outflows for resources will be incurred in advance of cash inflows from credit sales.

Working capital requirements can be incorporated into the appraisal either by identifying separately the cash outflows for different resources and the cash inflow from sales, or by making the net contribution calculations as previously with a separate adjustment to reflect cash flow timing due to working capital. The latter is preferred and will be illustrated.

The following assumptions will be made about working capital requirements for the introduction of the new product in the example above:

Production would be 22,000 units in year 1
20,000 units in years 2, 3 and 4
18,000 units in year 5

Debtors at the end of each year would be 20% of sales.
Creditors would be 10% of materials and variable overheads.
Adjustment to the annual cash flows previously calculated would be:

Stock:	Year 1	2,000 units × £12.00 per unit
		= (£24,000)
	Year 5	£24,000

Debtors:	Year 1	20,000 units × £22.50 per unit × 20%
		= (£90,000)
	Year 5	= £90,000
Creditors:	Year 1	22,000 units × £7.00 per unit × 10%
		= (£15,400)
	Year 2	(2,000) units × £7.00 per unit × 10%
		= £1,400
	Year 5	= £14,000

The NPV of the project, at the required return of 12%, becomes:

			£141,654 (as before)
+ Year 1	(129,400)	× 0.8929	= (115,541)
Year 2	1,400	× 0.7972	= 1,116
Year 5	128,000	× 0.5674	= 72,627
			£99,856

The IRR is just over 18%. Discounting at 18% produces present values as follows:

	£'000
Year 0	(500)
Year 1–5 £178,000 × 3.1272	556.6
Year 1 (£129,400) × 0.8475	(109.7)
Year 2 £1,400 × 0.7182	1.0
Year 5 £128,000 × 0.4371	55.9
	3.8

The incidence of working capital, based on the particular assumptions made in this example, reduces the IRR by almost 5%. It should be noted also that the cash flow timing assumed in the above calculations is slightly generous towards the project as it assumes that working capital build-up occurs during Year 1, with release during Year 5. In practice, the build-up is at the beginning of Year 1, with release at the end of Year 5, extending into Year 6. The release of working capital could alternatively be assumed in Year 6. This would then be rather harsh and thus would understate the true return. The IRR calculated in this way becomes just under, rather than just over, 18%.

17.3 MODERNISATION

The motivation to invest in more modern fixed assets may be to achieve cost savings. Another reason for modernisation investment may be to better satisfy customer requirements, by providing more reliable product or more flexible and speedy service. The cost savings, or better satisfaction of customer requirements, may enable a business to obtain competitive advantage or at least to remain competitive.

Modernisation investment may involve the mechanisation/automation of previously manual operations. Alternatively it may involve the replacement of existing fixed assets with more modern fixed assets. Investment in advanced manufacturing technology (AMT), which was described in Chapter 2, provides an example of modernisation investment. Such investment will not generally be justified on what may be referred to as 'conventional' financial terms, which have frequently looked for cost savings alone to justify investment. A wider view of potential benefits is required but these are very often more difficult to recognise and quantify. A recent NEDO publication expressed the view that 'although the general level of awareness of AMT is high, credibility is still a problem with many companies uncertain of the likely costs and benefits to them'. The ACARD report expressed the view that 'the principle cause of failure to invest is the lack of conviction of the vital importance of doing so'.

17.3.1 Benefits from new technology

Potential benefits vary with the particular applications of new technology and concepts, the number of departments that use computer aids, the extent to which databases are a shared resource, and the particular characteristics of the individual firm. The integration of systems can provide further benefits. However, it is possible to generalise about expected benefits which may arise in five main areas: operating cost savings, reduced stockholding, increased flexibility, better quality product, and improved delivery performance.

17.3.2 Operating cost savings

Material cost savings may result from a change in product design, which may itself result from consideration of the suitability of the product's design for production based on the new technology. The greater reliability of product quality that may be expected from using advanced manufacturing methods may be a further source of material cost saving. As a result of reduced human involvement with simplified tooling and setting up, and thus a reduction of potential human error, and with the ability to produce tight tolerances, fewer material rejects could be expected. The use of automatic testing also enables rejects to be identified earlier and thus at reduced cost. Other benefits that result may be reduced rework costs, reduced warranty and service costs, and increased customer satisfaction. Material costs may also be reduced by CAD-based component standardisation.

Labour savings may arise in various areas, and will depend upon the extent and nature of the investment. With CAD systems, savings can be expected in the number of drawing office personnel employed. In the production area, savings may result in both direct and indirect personnel, not only from the replacement of manual tasks, but also from increased productivity. Reductions in set-up costs, tooling, rework, material handling, idle time and supervision should result with, in addition, avoidance of other consequences of labour employment and the division of labour.

Benefits are likely to be increased by investment in flexible manufacturing systems but of course at considerably increased capital cost. Payroll savings of salary, overtime, national insurance and pension contributions are not the only considerations as shop floor personnel incur overhead costs and other expense elements such as overalls, shoes, safety glasses, etc, and canteen and welfare costs. Savings in indirect labour may also result in other areas eg warehouse labour, clerical labour. Projected labour savings built into an investment appraisal should be increased to the extent that increases in labour costs in real terms (ie above average inflation) would have been anticipated over time. A largely qualitative factor is the general effect on morale of the changed nature of work and the work environment.

Savings in numbers of staff and their associated cost may be partly offset, not only by initial redundancy and training costs, but also by a requirement for higher-grade staff and the possible need to pay shift premiums. Achievement of the required labour savings, compared with conventional methods, will be particularly dependent on achieving adequate capacity utilisation, as labour costs become far more fixed in nature, especially in the short run. Profit per unit becomes highly sensitive to total production volume because fixed costs approach 100% of all added value costs.

In addition to savings in material and labour (both direct and indirect), reductions in other indirect expenses may also be achieved. These will largely derive from the smaller labour force, and the reduced requirement for space, especially storage, but may also include energy savings and reduced warranty costs, service costs, insurance and stock write-off. What should also result is a better utilisation of existing overheads through increased output.

A further important area for attention, where potential for improvement may only partially be realised by new technology, is the number of activities which do not add value. In many industries value-added activities are less than 20% of the total activities in the production operation.

17.3.3 Reduced stockholding

Various different aspects of AMT may give rise to savings in stock investment and thus reduced interest cost as well as operating cost savings. First the automation of manufacturing allows work output to be precisely estimated and planned. This means that inventory at all stages can be cut or introduced on a 'Just in Time' basis. Secondly, greater production speeds result in shorter production cycle times and thus reductions in work-in-progress. Thirdly, changes in the economics of production mean shorter production runs and thus reduced stocks of both work-in-progress and finished product.

The economic batch quantity approaches one because changeover costs and time are minimal, and thus minimisation of inventory holding costs is all-important. A fourth advantage of the new technology, impacting on working capital requirements, is the greater ability to adjust to unpredictable sales. This reduces the requirement to keep safety stocks of finished products, and should reduce the likelihood of stock build-up on slow moving lines. Finally, a reduction in downtime (and reduced queues) should also lead to a reduction in work-in-progress.

17.3.4 Flexibility

It is somewhat difficult to determine whether changes in the market place are consumer led or come about because manufacturers themselves create market needs which they are then able to satisfy. Whatever, consumers today are more sophisticated and demand greater variety and/or custom products and services. Thus products need to be more varied, display increasing complexity, and have shorter life cycles in virtually all markets. As a result, faster product innovation is also important, both proactive and reactive.

Investment in AMT provides a new flexibility which is of strategic importance. Such systems enable a rapid shift, with minimal disruption, from one product to another, and thus reduce significantly the cost penalty of product diversity. AMT also enables new products and modifications to be introduced more quickly. The traditional conflict between marketing, which wants to offer customers more choice, and production, which has wanted to limit product line variety for the sake of production efficiency, is becoming a thing of the past. Companies with high variety and small market share may no longer suffer cost penalty. The economics of volume versus variety can be radically shifted.

17.3.5 Quality

Quality will be improved by the use of new machine tools with strict tolerances in manufacturing, and through automated inspection, not only of the finished product but also of the component parts, and at each stage throughout the manufacturing cycle. In-process gauging allows errors to be detected as soon as they occur, stopping the continued manufacture of defective parts. In some cases, defects can be found, where detection was not previously possible eg the use of machine vision. Non quality has both marketing and cost penalties. AMT can produce better quality product, fewer rejects, and reduced cost of rework and warranty claims.

17.3.6 Delivery

A recent survey by the British Institute of Management revealed poor delivery performance despite the fact that delivery was generally recognised as being an important competitive factor. Less than half the firms surveyed managed to deliver 75% of their orders on time whilst almost the same proportion had no formal procedure for checking actual deliveries against promised.

The significant reductions in lead times which may result from improvements in design and estimation as a result of CAD, from speedier production, smaller batch sizes, increased production flexibility, and less downtime and queuing should improve delivery times and the certainty that delivery promises can be met.

Poor delivery performance should be of great concern, and certainly contributed to the demise of UK manufacturing industry in the late 1970s. With the introduction by customers of concepts such as JIT, delivery performance is vital, and will be an even greater influence in obtaining and maintaining business.

17.3.7 Investment and alternatives

The full cost of investment in new manufacturing technology is the cost of planning, purchasing, installing and commissioning the new machinery and the related computer hardware and software.

This is frequently a considerable investment, though reduced by tax relief, and in some situations by Government grants. Even at the planning stage expenditure may be significant, and may be incurred in training, in consultancy fees and in establishing an in-house project team. It is therefore vital that investment is tailored to a particular company's needs and that alternatives both as to the extent of investment in new technology and its phasing, are very carefully considered. Expenditure incurred in commissioning new systems may also include the cost of disrupting production, and the cost of running old and new systems in parallel where this is possible. Expenditure may thus continue for a considerable period. Where large capital investment is not required considerable investment in revenue costs may nevertheless be necessary in order to achieve the new factory organisation and environment. Some of the running costs incurred in using the new facilities may be expected to reduce, as outlined above. However, other costs may be expected to increase. Power, insurance and maintenance costs need to be carefully considered.

It is important to recognise that the investment should be seen as a strategic one, and that some factors may be particularly difficult to quantify. Nevertheless, this should never be an excuse for non-quantification. A value can always be placed on factors if they can be identified. It is also important to think very seriously about what the real alternative is. The ACARD report expressed the view that 'those firms which do not make use of these technologies risk being overtaken by competitors achieving superior quality at lower cost . . . too many companies have not yet applied advanced manufacturing technology to their manufacturing process . . . those companies will become progressively less competitive and many will not survive the next ten years'. This both expresses the view that investment in the new technology is essential for survival, and also demonstrates the fact that the justification for investment may not necessarily be found in benefits in comparison with the existing situation, but because of the decline in relative competitive position that would result from non investment. The question then becomes 'can we afford not to invest?' rather than 'can we afford to invest?'

At the same time however, one should not get carried away by the benefits in market factors (eg flexibility, quality and reliability) as a justification for new investment. An important question that must be asked is whether it is reasonable to assume that any long-term competitive advantage would be gained by investment in new technology. For this to be the case, presumably one must assume that competition will not also invest on the same timescale. Is this likely? In many cases, especially in markets where there is considerable competition from overseas manufacturing, or from foreign companies manufacturing in the UK, competitive investment may have already taken place. It may not be a question of trying to gain a competitive advantage but of trying to maintain competitive position.

A further factor to consider is that any reduced requirement for space, both manufacturing and storage, would lead in the long-term to less requirement for infrastructure investment. This could be a significant factor in the long-term and is quite opposite to the normal situation regarding manufacturing investment justification. Projects are normally evaluated on a marginal basis, without any, or with at least a less than full, requirement for investment in service facilities, buildings, etc. This is one reason why a premium return is often required, over and above the basic cost of capital, as evidenced by surveys of appraisal methods used in practice. A reduced target return or some reduction in investment costs may be justified with AMT.

However, AMT on its own is not enough for profitable manufacture, even where it has relevance. There must be the necessary management and organisation to make it work. Nor is investment in AMT necessarily essential in order to remain competitive. Improvements in competitive position in manufacturing may be possible without such investment. Management style and labour relations appear to be at least as important in raising efficiency as is technology. Greater attention to quality and inventory could bring savings. Principles of JIT may be capable of application without major capital investment.

17.4 REPLACEMENT

The essential difference between replacement decisions and modernisation decisions is that whereas the focus of modernisation investment is on the advances that the new asset offers, the focus of replacement investment is on the declining performance and economy of the old asset. The plant replacement decision should be made with care and should consider whether to replace, if so when to replace, and what to replace existing assets with.

The approach to determining whether to replace, where there is a choice, depends upon whether the existing asset is capable of continued operation. If the asset is no longer operational and continuation of the operation is not essential, the cost of the replacement asset can be justified by the total earnings generated by the asset use. There may, however, be no choice as to 'whether' if the asset itself is an essential part of a business's infrastructure. If continued operation of the existing asset is possible, replacement justification is dependent upon the relative performance and economy expected from the new asset in comparison with the old asset.

The timing of replacement, (where existing assets are still operational and where there are no external factors like safety of operation, or risk to the environment from pollution), will also depend upon relative performance and economy. The determination of the optimum replacement cycle of assets that are continually replaced, for example motor vehicles, is outside the scope of this book. Many assets will not be subject to continual replacement. They may be subject to technological progress such that an element of modernisation also enters into the decision. Changed capacity requirements may also be a consideration. Fixed assets are thus rarely replaced by identical assets; replacement assets are likely to be more modern and of different capacity. A number of factors, therefore, enter into their evaluation.

One aspect of performance is reliability. If a machine is subject to breakdown, and the frequency of breakdown increases, production will be lost with possible adverse consequences for business. Economy will also suffer with idle labour costs, ever increasing maintenance costs, the cost associated with lost production, the cost of carrying higher stocks to offset the uncertainty of output, and increases in other operating costs such as setting up and cleaning.

Another aspect of reliability is product quality which is also likely to fall as machine parts become worn and less accurate, with increased costs of quality control, more defects and an effect on customer acceptability. A second aspect of performance is technological development; a replacement machine is likely, as already noted, to be more advanced technologically. It will, as a result, probably be more reliable and also, as noted above, be more cost efficient and capable of higher outputs.

A point is reached where the capital costs of replacing the asset are lower than the current costs of operating and maintaining it. This is the point when replacement should take place. Once the replacement timing has been established it is necessary to decide which piece of plant should be acquired. This will depend upon the relative capability, reliability, ease of maintenance, ease of operation and economy that is anticipated from the alternatives.

Economy is dependent upon the life cycle cost of assets ie the total cost of owning a physical asset during its economic life. This will include: the initial purchase and installation cost; maintenance cost over asset life; operating costs; cost of lost production; terminal value. It is the monitoring of life cycle costs of assets which will be an important influence on asset replacement decisions. Accounting involvement is required from the design stage to final disposal. The initial cost of the asset is only one aspect.

The following example provides an illustration of the decision whether to replace assets, where continued operation has already been established as being worthwhile. In principle the example covers both replacement and modernisation situations.

Example 17.2

Two options are being considered by a company for replacement of existing machinery used to manufacture components. Component manufacture is currently in three stages with a separate machine at each stage. The two options consist of replacement of existing machines with either new individual machines or with a single multi-purpose machine capable of performing all three operations.

Operating expenses of the existing machines and those anticipated for the new machines are as follows:

	Existing machines	**New machines**
Operation 1	£50,000	£17,500
Operation 2	£52,500	£20,000
Operation 3	£30,000	£15,000
Multi-purpose		£42,500

The economic life of the new machines is expected to be eight years. The existing machines could continue to be used for that period.

Capital cost of new machinery is as follows:

Operation 1	£125,000
Operation 2	£132,500
Operation 3	£ 77,500
Multi-purpose	£365,000

The new machines would have no value after eight years. The existing machines currently have no disposal value, but the book value is:

Operation 1	£4,000
Operation 2	£4,500
Operation 3	£3,000

The cost of capital is 14%.

There are three alternatives:

1 Continue with the existing machines.
2 Purchase the individual machines.
3 Purchase the combined special purpose machine.

If continued use of the existing machines is assumed in the base, appraisal of new machine purchase will be through comparison with this existing situation as follows:

£000	Alternative 2 versus 1				Alternative 3 versus 1
	Operation 1	Operation 2	Operation 3	Total	
Investment yr 0	(125)	(132.5)	(77.5)	(335)	(365)
Cost savings yrs 1–8	32.5	32.5	15	80	90
Present value of cost savings (annual saving × 4.6389*)	150.8	150.8	69.5	371.1	417.5
Net present value	25.8	18.3	(8.0)	36.1	52.5

* Cumulative Discount Factors for 8 years at 14%.

It should be noted that the book value of existing machines is irrelevant.

Purchase of the combined special purpose machine is worthwhile and offers the highest expected NPV, which is £16.4K greater than the next best alternative which is to replace each of the existing machines with new individual machines. However, it should be noted that replacement of the Operation 3 machine does not seem justified on its own. It may be feasible to replace the Operation 1 and 2 machines whilst continuing to use the existing machine for Operation 3. This possibility does not alter the preferred situation, however; the special purpose machine has projected NPV £8.4K greater than that offered by replacement of the machines for Operations 1 and 2 only.

17.5 INFLATION

Cash flows, arising from given events, change over time due to the existence of inflation. Comparisons of monetary values can become difficult because they may be measured in different purchasing power terms at different times. This should be a consideration whenever information is being identified and analysed for decision-making purposes, but is a particular problem in capital investment decision-making because of the time period affected.

When inflation occurs future cash flows will increase over what they would otherwise have been, while at the same time the purchasing power of the cash flows is decreased. Since rational decision-makers are presumably interested in real returns, (ie at least maintaining the ability to purchase the same amount of goods and services in the future), higher monetary returns will be required to compensate for inflation. The existence of inflation will thus have an influence on both aspects of the evaluation process, namely the monetary returns, and the criterion for establishing the acceptability of such returns.

It is essential, when evaluating projects under inflation, to ensure that like is compared with like (ie cash flows and cost of capital must both be measured either in 'money' terms or in 'real' terms). 'Money' terms involves the estimation of what the cash flows will actually be when they occur at some future time, which are then discounted by a cost of capital based on rates of return including inflation. 'Real' terms involves the estimation of future cash flows expressed in terms of prices prevailing at the time the investment is being appraised. Future cash flows are thus expressed in terms of a common purchasing power rather than changing purchasing power as with the estimation in money terms. Cash flows in real terms are then discounted at a cost of capital which is net of inflation.

It may on the face of it seem possible, and reasonable in view of the difficulty of forecasting inflation and its effect, to take current costs and revenues (on the basis that these represent real cash flows for a project over its life), and to evaluate these cash flows using the current cost of capital. However, such evaluation would be seriously deficient because:

1 It would not be comparing like with like. Current costs of capital are in money terms and thus must be reduced by an inflation factor to be comparable. Alternatively cash flows may be expressed in money terms.

2 The incidence of taxation means that cash flows (and the cost of capital), even if eventually appraised in real terms, must first be estimated in money terms and then reduced by an inflation factor. Net of tax flows are affected by the availability of capital allowances on money values and upon time lags in liability/relief.

In order to reduce the cost of capital in money terms to the cost of capital in real terms the following relationships apply:

$$\frac{(1 + m)}{(1 + i)} = (1 + r)$$

where:
m is the money cost of capital rate
i is the inflation rate
r is the real cost of capital rate

If, for example, the money cost of capital is 15% and inflation is 8%, the cost of capital in real terms is:

$$\frac{1.15}{1.08} - 1 = 0.0648$$
$$= 6.48\%$$

In a similar way cash flows in money terms can be reduced to real terms. A money cash flow of £10,000 estimated in two years' time at an annual inflation rate of 8% can be reduced to an estimate in real terms of:

$$\frac{10{,}000}{1.08^2} = £8{,}573$$

It would then need to be further discounted by the cost of capital in real terms in order to convert the cash flow to a present value. If the cost of capital in real terms is as the above illustration, ie 6.48%, the present value is:

$$\frac{8{,}573}{1.0648^2} = £7{,}561$$

Exactly the same result would be achieved by discounting the money cash flow by the money cost of capital. Thus

$$\frac{10{,}000}{1.15^2} = £7{,}561$$

The present value is in current terms. It thus makes no difference whether 'money' cash flows or 'real' cash flows are being discounted as long as the appropriate cost of capital is used. However, whilst the final assessment of a project's worth can be made in real terms, this can only be after cash flows and the cost of capital have been established in money terms. If taxation is ignored (which in practice it should not be), the relationships are more straightforward and cash flows estimated directly in real terms may be justified.

A further factor to consider is whether there may be differential inflation between the different cash flow items in a project. For example labour costs may rise faster than other costs and selling prices.

Example 17.3

A company has developed a new product which will require investment in machinery costing £700,000 if it is to be produced and sold. Annual sales are expected to be 27,000 units at a selling price of £25 per unit. Incremental production costs include new materials of £7 per unit and labour of £8 per unit. Other incremental costs are expected to be £5 per unit. The above selling prices and costs are at current prices. The life of the investment is expected to be eight years. The realisable value of the machine after eight years, measured in current prices, is expected to be £60,000. All prices are expected to increase at the rate of 7% per annum, and the cost of capital in money terms is 18%.

In appraising the viability of the project it is essential to compare like with like. In practice, if the final appraisal is in real terms, cash flows must first be projected in money terms. In this example this is not necessary due to the absence of taxation. Thus instead of determining money cash flows at a compound rate forward of 7% and then discounting the money cash flows by 18%, the cash flows in real terms (ie current terms) can simply be discounted by $\left(\frac{1.18}{1.07} - 1\right) \times 100\% + 10.3\%$. Avoiding more complicated calculations the annuity factor for 8 years at 10.3% can be calculated from the factors at 10% and 11% as:

$$5.3349 - [(5.3349 - 5.1461) \times 0.3] = 5.278$$

Project viability can be assessed as:

				Present value
Yr 0	(£700,000)	x	1.000	(700,000)
Yrs 1–8	£135,000*	x	5.278	712,530
Yr 8	£60,000	x	0.457	27,420
				£39,950

*Annual cash inflow is:

	£/unit		
Selling price	25		
Less			
Materials	7		
Labour	8		
Other costs	5		
	20		
Incremental profit	5	×	27,000 units
		=	£135,000

Investment in machinery is just worthwhile on the basis of the estimates provided.

Self-assessment question 17.1

A company has a machine which is used exclusively for the manufacture of one of its products. Variable product costs are currently £68 per unit. Investment in a replacement machine is being considered. Greater efficiency in using materials and labour with the new machine would be expected to reduce variable product costs to £53 per unit. The new machine would also enable output to be increased from the current level of 5,000 units per annum, sold at £88 per unit. If selling price is reduced to £79 per unit annual sales are expected to increase to 7,000 units. The new machine would cost £300,000 and the existing machine could be sold now for £40,000. The product is expected to be sold for five more years. The existing machine could continue to be used for five more years at its current level of efficiency with no disposal value in five years time. The new machine if purchased would be expected to continue at the same level of efficiency for five years and have a disposal value of £50,000 at that time (at current price).

The company requires a rate of return on investment of 16% in money terms. Selling prices and all costs other than labour are expected to increase at 6% per annum. Labour costs are expected to increase at 10% per annum. Labour costs per unit, at current prices, for the existing and new machine are £30 and £20 respectively.

Required:
Calculate whether purchase of the replacement machine is worthwhile.

Answer on p 580

17.6 DIFFICULTIES AND LIMITATIONS OF ANALYSIS

It has been seen that in determining whether or not a proposed investment in fixed assets is worthwhile, a clearly established principle is that a business should consider the incremental effect that such an investment will have and compare this with the incremental effect of other alternatives open to it. Only those costs and benefits that are expected to arise as a result of taking one or other alternative, which would not otherwise arise, are relevant to the analysis. The principle has been applied in the examples of capital investment decisions considered earlier in the chapter, and has been applied equally to a wide range of short-term decision-making problems in previous chapters.

However, whilst the principle is clear, the application in practice is difficult. The main areas of difficulty were considered in Chapter 12 under the following four headings:

1 Availability of, and ability to identify and analyse, information.
2 Presentation and communication of information.
3 Conflict between decision data and control data.
4 Longer-term consequences.

As far as the availability and identification of information is concerned, capital investment decisions are likely to be even more difficult than shorter-term decisions because of the need to forecast over a longer period. A special exercise will always be required. As with shorter-term decisions emphasis needs to be placed on analysis, presentation and communication of information. The final two areas of difficulty noted above require more detailed consideration.

17.6.1 Conflict between decision data and control data

Potential conflict between decision data and control data was recognised as a problem in Chapter 12 and illustrated in a short-term decision-making situation. Potential conflict also exists with capital investment decisions, but more so. If DCF appraisal techniques are used there will be greater potential disparity between decision and feedback measures. Also, whatever measure is used for appraising the viability of the investment project over its expected life, feedback of information for intermediate periods will emphasise only a relatively small part of the project's life. As a result, decisions may be influenced by the conventions of routine reporting which will also not provide the feedback required to monitor project progress.

However, it should also be recognised that investment performance is likely to be measured at investment centre rather than project level and thus separate feedback on the outcome of individual projects is required anyway. Cash flows arising from individual projects should be identified where possible and compared with expectations. In many projects full re-appraisal, referred to as post-audit, may be difficult as it cannot be known what would have happened if the investment had not taken place.

The possibility remains, however, that investment decisions will be influenced by the way in which their expected outcome will affect performance as indicated by investment centre (and also profit centre) measures. Whether or not a project is likely to increase the average percentage return on capital employed, and particularly in the short-term, may be a significant factor affecting the decision process. Whilst this may be avoided by the use of residual income as the investment centre performance measure, the measure remains inconsistent with DCF and is still likely to be influenced by the effect of a project on the measure in the short-term.

Great care needs to be taken in using measures of investment performance in the short-term. Investment decisions can only be effectively planned and controlled over a long-term cycle by:

1 The use of DCF techniques for measuring the economic viability of capital investment profits.
2 Post-audit of investment projects.
3 Measurement of centre performance over a long-term cycle.

17.6.2 Longer-term consequences

In applying incremental principles to the appraisal of a particular capital investment opportunity, a number of expense and fixed asset types may be regarded as totally unaffected, or at least relatively little affected, by whichever alternative is selected. These are likely to be expenses and fixed assets which result from infrastructure investment. However, even if an investment project on its own may have little incremental impact on general facilities (eg warehouse, canteen, office block, size of factory, general administration) collectively investment projects are likely, over time, to have an effect. There is, therefore, the possibility of creeping incrementality. Even if this is recognised, it very often cannot be tied to a particular project, and thus may not appear in the incremental evaluation. There is also the possibility of creeping incrementality on an individual project which may go unrecognised.

The question arises as to whether capital investment projects should be made to bear a proportion of apparently non-incremental assets and expenses. The general question is similar to that which may be asked in short-term decisions as to whether a full absorption cost, or at least some absorption, of apparently non-incremental costs may be useful as an indicator of project viability. It is not just a question of whether additional resources will be required, but also whether replacement of existing assets will be hastened. The use of existing resources for a project could alternatively be regarded as utilising capacity which would otherwise be available for some other project. Apportionment of a share of their associated expenses may be a proxy for opportunity cost.

In any case, in the long-run, all costs have to be recovered if the firm is to make a profit. It is especially important to be aware of this in capital investment decisions because they are of a long-term nature. Apportionment of a share of all costs and assets would provide an approximate view of whether individual investments are likely to pay their way in the long-term which may be useful in exercising judgment.

Evidence from a number of surveys of capital investment evaluation in practice indicates that some firms make an adjustment to the incremental evaluation of profit earning projects in order to incorporate a provision for apparently non-incremental assets and expenses. It may not be the case that there is any fundamental disagreement with incremental principles, but simply a recognition that such principles are difficult to apply. The important thing is to provide a range of information to management so that judgment can be exercised on individual projects.

It is suggested that supplementary analysis of the full potential longer-term repercussions of investment in marginal projects should be provided. This would provide a broad indication, albeit very approximate, of:

1 The return on the project if it had to pay its share of all the resources that it utilises.
2 The extent to which the project is being evaluated marginally (ie the difference between the incremental return in the main analysis and that provided in the supplementary analysis) which will depend upon both the extent to which the initial analysis includes incremental infrastructure assets and overheads, and also the extent to which the project is likely to have an impact upon such resources in the long run.

It may lead to further analysis between the two extremes of full cost allocation and incremental. An adjusted incremental analysis for aspects of the business which are more likely to be affected eg share of warehouse costs, rather than share of managing director's salary, could be carried out. At times no further analysis may be required. This may be because:

1 Other resources which the project utilises have no opportunity cost, or
2 other resources are not involved. For example, in a decision to replace labour by machinery there may be no additional space, administration, or distribution requirements.

As a result of the above, more extensive information would be provided on which to exercise judgment in the final decision. It is not that projects should not be accepted on a marginal basis, but simply that they may not. The analysis should encourage questions such as:

Is there space capacity in service facilities?

What demands will a project make on service facilities?

What other projects are coming along which collectively may exert pressure on infrastructure assets and expenses?

The supplementary analysis becomes a form of sensitivity analysis—an extension of that normally carried out—on the basis of which final judgment can be exercised. Although the decision computationally will be less clear-cut, it should be more informed.

SUMMARY

This chapter has considered further the evaluation of capital investment projects using discounted cash flow methods. Information relevant to a variety of capital investment decision situations has been discussed and illustrated. Decision situations involving investment in fixed assets have been classified as either expansion, modernisation or replacement projects. Different information will be relevant to the justification of investment depending upon the nature of the project.

All capital investment projects will be affected by inflation. It is essential in investment evaluation to compare like with like; cash flows and the cost of capital must both be expressed in either 'money' terms or 'real' terms. In practice, because of the effect of taxation, even if the final evaluation is carried out in real terms, cash flows must first be assessed in money terms, ie inclusive of the effect of inflation, before being reduced to real terms. As taxation is not considered in this book, and is not part of the ACCA Paper 2.4 syllabus, evaluation of the problems provided does not require cash flows to be identified in money terms. This in no way alters the requirement to consider the effect of inflation on projects.

The final section of the chapter raises again areas of difficulty in encouraging and achieving reliable evaluation of decision-making situations. A particular difficulty considered in relation to capital investment decisions has been the relationship between information relevant to the investment evaluation and the information provided as a measure of performance after a decision has been taken and implemented. It is important that investment feedback is consistent in principle with the basis for the investment evaluation.

A second area of difficulty concerns the identification of what is truly incremental to an investment project. There is always a danger of creeping incrementality. In the long run all assets and expenses have to be recovered if a business is to make a profit. It is suggested that supplementary evaluation of capital investment projects is carried out, to include a share of apparently non-incremental assets and expenses, as an aid in decision-making.

EXERCISES

Exercise 17.1

The sales of Greenfingers Ltd., manufacturers of garden tools, have been declining for some years. The marketing director of the company, who along with the rest of the Board recognizes that the company needs to critically review its product range, has put forward proposals for the launch of a new product. Whilst some of the existing manufacturing facilities could be utilised, a considerable investment in new facilities would need to be made. The required funds could be provided at a cost to the company of 15% per annum.

The following forecasts have been collected by the management accountant:

Sales £100,000 in year 1, increasing at the rate of £8,000 per annum.
Variable costs £50,000 in year 1, increasing in proportion with sales.
Additions to costs normally regarded as fixed are expected to be £33,000 per annum (including depreciation of £28,000 per annum).
The product life cycle is estimated at 5 years.
Investment in plant and machinery £140,000.
Residual value of investment at end of year 5—Nil.

The existing manufacturing facilities which the new product would utilise are currently being used for the manufacture of products yielding a contribution of £2,000 per annum. These facilities currently have a disposal value of £4,000 and a book value of £10,000 (depreciating at the rate of £2,000 per annum). The facilities are expected to have a further five years of useful life with a disposal value of £1,000 in five years time.

In addition, it is estimated that sales demand for other existing products will be affected by the launch, causing a loss of contribution of £9,000 per annum. However, the manufacturing facilities released could be utilised for some of the time to yield an additional contribution of £3,000 per annum. Whilst fixed costs saved through the reduced manufacture of existing products would be £1,000 per annum, it is anticipated that if fixed overhead absorption rates remain unchanged, an under-absorption of £3,000 per annum will result.

The marketing director concedes that despite extensive research which has been undertaken at a cost of £10,000 the pattern of future demand is difficult to forecast.

Required:

(a) Prepare calculations based on the above estimates to show whether it is worthwhile launching the new product.

(b) Show the sensitivity of the net present value to the following alternative sales forecasts:
  (i) Sales years 1–5 £100,000 per annum.
  (ii) Sales year 1 £120,000 increasing at the rate of £14,000 per annum.

Answers on p 581

Exercise 17.2

Smith and Jones own an engineering firm. They have asked your financial advice regarding the replacement of their existing equipment for the manufacture of flibbets.

Smith explains:

'I am not keen on the idea. The new equipment would cost £250,000, but it will be worthwhile using for only 5 years. It should yield a net revenue (after all costs except depreciation) of £250,000 in the first year, declining by £50,000 per year thereafter. We would have to keep higher stocks of raw materials and finance more debtors, so about £60,000 additional working capital would be needed above the present level of £40,000 required with our existing equipment.

If we bought the new equipment we could sell the existing equipment for only £50,000 although it has a written down value of £150,000 in the firm's books. It is still serviceable and would yield a net revenue (after all costs except depreciation) of £50,000 per year if we did not replace. After 5 years the market for flibbets will almost certainly be negligible, and whatever equipment we have then will not be worth anything, even as scrap.

Taking the current realisable value of the existing equipment as the basis for depreciation, the status quo offers us a net profit of £40,000 per year:

	£
Net revenue before depreciation	50,000
Depreciation (straight line)	10,000
Net profit	40,000

As a return on capital that is pretty good; £40,000 per year on the current realisable value of £50,000 is 80 per cent.

Compare the new equipment. That will involve a £100,000 loss on the sale of the old equipment, which we cannot charge in our accounts against reserves because we have no reserves. So £20,000 per year will have to be charged against future profits, which added to straight line depreciation of £50,000 per year on the new equipment, gives an outlay cost equivalent to £70,000 per year.

Thus:			(£'000)		
End of year:	1	2	3	4	5
Net revenue before depreciation	250	200	150	100	50
Less: 'outlay cost'	70	70	70	70	70
	180	130	80	30	(20)
Less: annual profit foregone on existing equipment	40	40	40	40	40
Net profit/(loss)	140	90	40	(10)	(60)

Averaged over the five years those net profit figures come to £40,000 per year. On an investment of £310,000 (new equipment £250,000 plus working capital £60,000) that yields a return of about 13 per cent. We have access to ample funds, but we estimate our cost of capital at 14 per cent per annum, so the new equipment is unattractive. In any case it is well below the 80% return on existing equipment.'

Jones objects:

'Although I agree with Smith's basic figures and forecasts, I cannot accept his juggling. The new equipment will pay for itself in the first year; that is good enough for me, and I want to go ahead.'

Assume that the working capital levels mentioned by Smith would apply throughout the five years, that the cash outlay on the new equipment (less the amount received for the existing equipment) would occur immediately, and that all other receipts and payments would occur end-year.

Required:

(a) Your own numerical analysis of the alternatives (calculate to the nearest £100).

(b) Comments on your results in relation to the views expressed by Smith and Jones.

Answers on p 582

Exercise 17.3

(a) A business may invest in capital projects of differing types. Describe the cash flow information that will be relevant to the appraisal of:

(i) a machine replacement

(ii) investment required for an addition to the product range.

(b) A business is considering two proposals for capital investment as follows:

Proposal 1: to purchase electrostatic spray painting plant at a cost of £80,000 in order to provide painting facilities for new product XX.

Justification: (i) existing hand spray equipment has insufficient capacity to handle the increased volume of expected production.

(ii) hand spraying would be uneconomical.

Proposal 2: to purchase a high-speed threading machine at a cost of £45,000 in order to provide facilities for threading components hitherto profile turned on copy lathes.

Justification: (i) cost savings are estimated at £9,720 per annum as follows:

	£
Labour: 1,800 hours at £3.00 hr =	5,400
Overhead: 80% of labour cost =	4,320
	9,720

(ii) The existing equipment does not produce components of acceptable accuracy.

Required:
Comment on the adequacy of the information provided in the justification of the two proposals above, as a basis for appraising the viability of the investments.

Answer in lecturer's manual

Exercise 17.4

A company is considering the introduction of a new product which would require investment in additional manufacturing facilities. Investment cost would be £600,000 and the project would have a ten year life with no terminal value.

100,000 units of the product would be produced and sold each year. Selling price would be £7.50 per unit at current prices.

Materials A and B are used in the manufacture of the product. Current purchase price of the materials is £1.00 per kilo and £2.20 per kilo respectively. Material A is used regularly by the company. 50,000 kilos of Material B are in stock but the material is not currently used by the company. If the new product is not introduced the existing stock of Material B would be sold for £1.00 per kilo. Usage of the two materials in the new product would be 1 kilo of Material A and 1/2 kilo of Material B per unit of product.

Each unit of the product requires 1/4 hour of skilled labour and 1/4 hour of unskilled labour. Current wage rates are £6.00 per hour for skilled labour and £4.00 per hour for unskilled labour.

It is the policy of the company to apportion all overhead costs to its various products. The overhead cost per unit for the new product, at current prices, is:

	£/Unit
Variable overheads	0.50
Depreciation of new machinery	0.60
Share of depreciation of other fixed assets utilised	0.45
Other apportioned production fixed costs	0.60
Apportioned administration costs	0.55
	2.70

Selling price, materials costs and overheads are expected to increase in price at a rate of 10% per annum. Labour costs are expected to increase at an annual rate of 15%. The cost of capital in money terms is 20%.

Required:
Determine whether the new product should be introduced.

Answer on p 584

Uncertainty and Decision-Making

INTRODUCTION

It is possible to predict the outcome of some decisions with complete certainty because only one outcome can arise. However, there are many occasions when a decision can lead to more than one possible outcome. Such situations are beset with uncertainty. The decision to carry an umbrella in case of rain is commonly used as an example of decision-making and can illustrate both certainty and uncertainty. In some countries, lack of rainfall can be predicted with total certainty and there are many days when carrying an umbrella would be foolish. In the United Kingdom, on the other hand, it is difficult or impossible to predict rainfall even on days when the skies are full of clouds. The decision to carry an umbrella can lead either to the use of the umbrella to avoid a drenching or to the inconvenience of carrying an unnecessary burden. At the time of making the decision to take the umbrella, it is impossible to predict with absolute certainty whether the umbrella would be used or not. This latter class of problem, decision-making under uncertainty, is the subject of this chapter.

Topics within the chapter consider the difference between risk and uncertainty, techniques for establishing decision rules, ways in which data can be collected from managers and the value of knowledge which reduces uncertainty.

18.1 RISK AND UNCERTAINTY

The traditional definition of the difference between risk and uncertainty has been that uncertainty cannot be quantified whilst risk can. In this sense, the chapter which follows is concerned with risk since it is concerned with the use of quantifications of the likelihood of future outcomes. However, it is customary to use the terms to some extent interchangeably and this book will share with other books of its kind the use of the word uncertainty to cover all future outcomes which cannot be predicted with accuracy.

People have different attitudes towards the future. Some welcome the opportunity to take chances and may be called risk takers or risk seekers. Others are risk averse. Consider the project shown in Figure 18.1. The x axis shows outcomes, from a loss making situation at one extreme to a

FIGURE 18.1

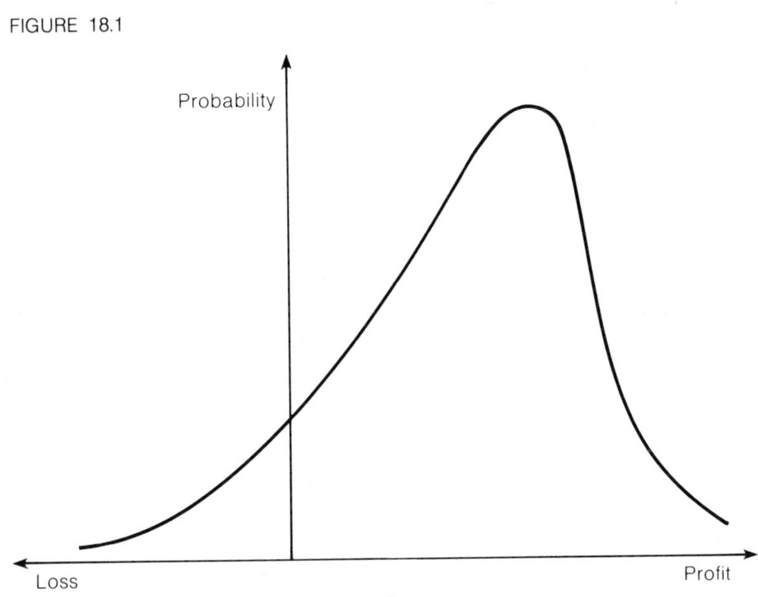

high profit at the other extreme. The y axis provides a visual representation of the likelihood of a particular outcome. There is seen to be little chance of either a high profit or a loss, with a good chance of a reasonable level of profit. Figure 18.2 shows a different project, with a very good chance of making low profits but no chance of making either high profits or losses. A risk taker would by definition prefer the project shown in Figure 18.1 because of the opportunity of high profits. A person who is risk averse would prefer the project shown in Figure 18.2 because of the desire to avoid a potential loss making situation. A satisfactory mean value coupled with a low standard deviation has some considerable appeal for the person who is risk averse. Returning to the umbrella example, someone who is excessively risk averse would always carry an umbrella in the United Kingdom. A risk taker would tend to leave the umbrella at home to avoid inconvenience.

FIGURE 18.2

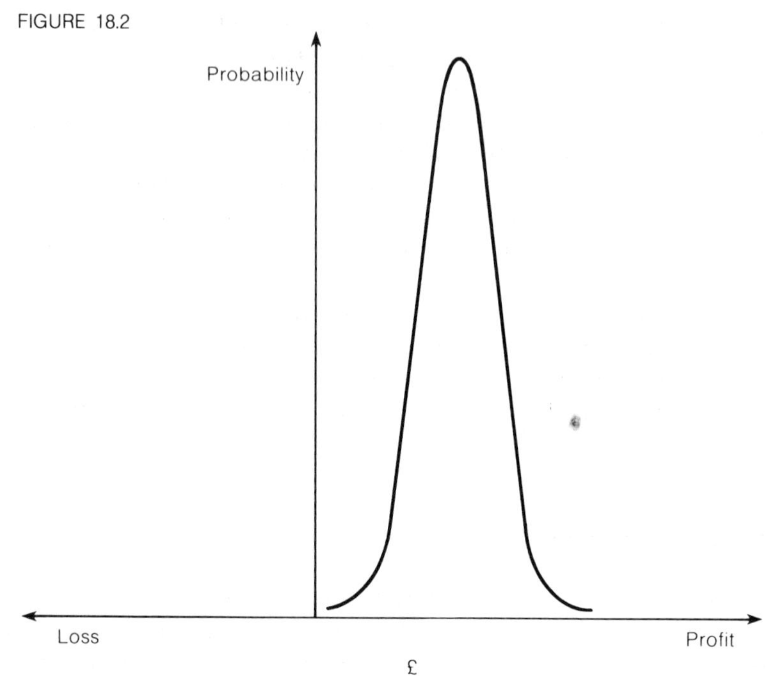

18.2 STATING THE PROBLEM

There are two possible actions for the umbrella example; to take the umbrella or to leave it at home. There are also two possible outcomes; it might rain or it might not rain. These actions and outcomes can be summarised into a table as follows:

TABLE 18.1 **Statement of the umbrella problem**

Action	Take umbrella	Leave umbrella at home
Outcome		
Rain	Use umbrella	Inconvenience of getting wet
No rain	Inconvenience of carrying umbrella unnecessarily	No unnecessary burden

The table can be interpreted in terms of costs and benefits. If the umbrella is carried and it does not rain, there is a cost associated with the inconvenience of carrying the umbrella. If the umbrella is left at home and it rains, there is the inconvenience of feeling uncomfortable and needing to dry upon arrival at home. If an umbrella is carried and it rains, the benefit is that the umbrella can be used to avoid the rain. If the umbrella is left at home and it does not rain, then the inconvenience of unnecessarily carrying the umbrella has been avoided. The table ensures a systematic evaluation of all of the alternatives in terms of costs and benefits and may thus aid the decision maker in reaching a rational decision. If it were possible to quantify the costs and benefits there would be mathematical approaches available to make an objective assessment of the available choices. Since such costs and benefits are not easily quantifiable for the umbrella example, a second situation will now be considered.

Example 18.1

The Ruddle Co Ltd has planned to install and, with effect from next April, commence operating sophisticated machinery for the production of a new product—product Zed. However, the supplier of the machinery has just announced that delivery of the machinery will be delayed by six months and this will mean that Ruddle will not now be able to undertake production using that machinery until October.

'The first six months of production' stated the commercial manager of Ruddle 'is particularly crucial as we have already contracted to supply several national supermarket groups with whatever quantities of Zed they require during that period at a price of £40 per unit. Their demand is, at this stage, uncertain but would have been well within the capacity of the permanent machinery we were to have installed. The best estimates for the first period are thought to be:

Estimated demand—first 6 months

Quantity—units (000s)	Probability
10	0.5
14	0.3
16	0.2

'Whatever the level of demand, we are going to meet it in full even if it means operating at a loss for the first half year. Therefore I suggest we consider the possibility of hiring equipment on which temporary production can take place. Details of the only machines which could be hired are:

	Machine		
	A	**B**	**C**
Productive capacity per six month period—units	10,000	12,000	16,000
Variable production cost for each unit produced	£6.5	£6	£5
Other 'fixed' costs—total for six months	£320,000	£350,000	£400,000

'In addition to the above costs there will be a variable material cost of £5 per unit. For purchases greater than 10,000 units a discount of 20% per unit will be given, but this only applies to the excess over 10,000 units.

'Should production capacity be less than demand then Ruddle could sub-contract production of up to 6,000 units but would be required to supply raw materials. Subcontracting costs are:
up to 4,000 units subcontracted—£30 per unit
any excess over 4,000 units subcontracted—£35 per unit

'These subcontracting costs relate only to the work carried out by the subcontractor and exclude the costs of raw materials.'

The commercial manager makes the following further points. 'Due to the lead time required for setting up production, the choice of which machine to hire must be made before the precise demand is known. However, demand will be known in time for production to be scheduled so that an equal number of units can be produced each month. We will, of course, only produce sufficient to meet demand.

'We need to decide which machine to hire. However, I wonder whether it would be worthwhile seeking the assistance of a firm of market researchers? Their reputation suggests that they are very accurate and they may be able to inform us whether demand is to be 10, 14 or 16 thousand units.'

(*ACCA, Management Accounting*)

Self-assessment question 18.1

Before a decision can be taken, it is necessary to clearly state the problem and to consider the possible alternatives. Before reading on, re-state Example 18.1 into a format similar to that given in Table 18.1 for the umbrella problem. DO NOT quantify the problem at this initial stage.

A solution is provided below.

The table might look like the following:

TABLE 18.2 **Statement of the machine hire problem**

Action	Hire Machine A	Hire Machine B	Hire Machine C
Outcome			
Demand:			
10,000 units	Demand is met exactly	Surplus capacity of 2,000 units	Surplus capacity of 6,000 units
14,000 units	Subcontract 4,000 units	Subcontract 2,000 units	Surplus capacity of 2,000 units
16,000 units	Subcontract 6,000 units	Subcontract 4,000 units	Demand is met exactly

The problem has now been translated into a form which is structured and which is amenable to analysis. The second stage is to quantify the costs of hiring each machine, taking into account the different effects of subcontracting.

There are a variety of ways in which the quantification of Table 18.2 can proceed. Table 18.3 is a payoff table which shows the outcomes as measured by sales less material, hire and subcontracting costs. These figures will be used for the next stage in the discussion of the decision making process but this is one of the least efficient means of quantifying the decision. Detailed workings, which are time consuming but not difficult, are therefore not shown. Table 18.5 will later present a more efficient means of quantification which produces the same conclusions as Table 18.3.

TABLE 18.3 **Profits and (losses) for the machine hire problem**

Action	Hire Machine A	Hire Machine B	Hire Machine C
Outcome			
Demand:			
10,000 units	(£35,000)	(£60,000)	(£100,000)
14,000 units	(£11,000)	£12,000	£24,000
16,000 units	(£ 9,000)	£24,000	£86,000

The result of hiring machine A is a loss of between £9,000 and £35,000. At the other extreme, hiring machine C results in a loss of £100,000, a profit of £24,000 or a profit of £86,000.

An alternative way of presenting problems is in the form of a decision tree. Figure 18.3 illustrates the presentation of a tree based on the data contained in Table 18.3.

Having now stated the problem, the next section shows ways in which the decision can be resolved.

18.3 RESOLVING DECISION-MAKING PROBLEMS

18.3.1 The maximin criterion

An intuitive assessment of Table 18.3 might conclude that either machine A or machine B would appeal to the risk averse. A systematic way of looking at the problem in these terms is provided by the maximin criterion. This provides a decision rule which can be stated as follows:

The maximin payoff act chooses the option with the highest minimum payoff.

From Table 18.3, it can be seen that the minimum payoffs for machines A, B and C are £35,000 loss, £60,000 loss and £100,000 loss respectively. The highest payoff is a £35,000 loss and therefore the decision to hire machine A would be taken.

FIGURE 18.3

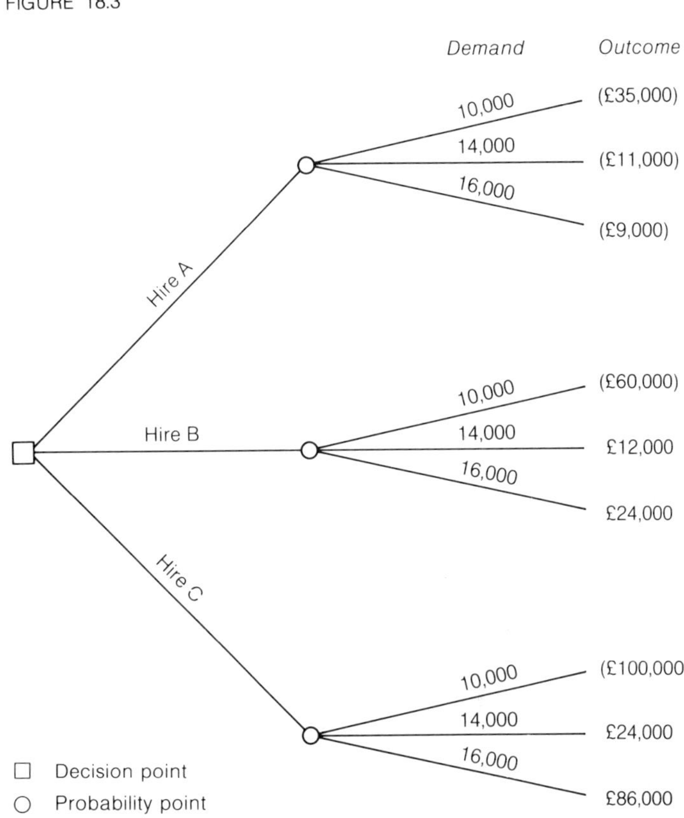

The maximin criterion is suitable for situations where there is no information on likely outcomes. It reflects a pessimistic view of the world, based on cutting losses where they arise. Since Example 18.1 provides information on likely outcomes, the maximin criterion does not necessarily provide the most reliable answer.

18.3.2 Simulation

Under simulation, the events of the real world are mirrored by a model. A flight simulator, for instance, mirrors the way in which an aeroplane operates under different conditions. A pilot can practise manoeuvres with no personal risk and acquire the necessary skills to be used in actual flying. The simulator incorporates knowledge of the cause and effect relationships which determine the operation of an aircraft in flight. It cannot fly but it can give the impression of flight. Similarly, a financial simulation does not provide the results which are to be reported but does incorporate knowledge of cause and effect relationships. Running a financial simulation improves knowledge of likely outcomes.

Imagine a decision about the manning levels for a raw materials store. It may be known that personnel spend some of their time doing nothing whilst at other times production may be held up, or lorries kept waiting, because manning levels are inadequate to meet demands. Information can be gathered on a variety of factors, such as the time to unload a lorry, place raw materials in store and make an issue to production, the time between deliveries and the number of issues. This information can be programmed into a computer together with information on how the store is managed. A series of simulations can then be run, say for a year, with different manning levels. The computer programme would monitor the simulated stores activity and report on down time and waiting times for various staff levels with the result that decisions could be taken on the basis of the simulation exercise.

For Example 18.1, most of the necessary information is provided in Table 18.3. The major unknown factor is the level of demand for Zed. A random number can be linked to the probabilities of estimated demand to create a single enactment of the future. From this, a decision can be taken which is consistent with the outcome of the simulation.

The author has run a simulation of Example 18.1 using a spreadsheet. The random number 35.35 was generated by the software. This can be related to the following table constructed from the probabilities produced by the management of Ruddle Co Ltd:

Quantity—units	Probability	Cumulative probability	Random numbers
10,000	0.5 (50%)	0.5 (50%)	0.01— 50
14,000	0.3 (30%)	0.8 (80%)	50.01— 80
16,000	0.2 (20%)	1.0 (100%)	80.01—100

35.35 falls in the range 0.01 to 50 and so for this simulation a demand of 10,000 is experienced. The management of Ruddle Co Ltd should choose to hire machine A based on this outcome because A minimises the costs at a demand of 10,000.

Management may understandably be concerned about following the advice provided by a single simulation. In situations such as the one illustrated by Example 18.1, it is useful to repeat the simulation a number of times and then to evaluate the results of the simulation, perhaps using suitable measures of dispersion. Table 18.4 provides data arising from a simulation comprising 30 and 100

TABLE 18.4 **Illustrative simulation for Example 18.1**

Payoff table

Random number	**Hire A**	**Hire B**	**Hire C**
0.01 – 50	– 35000.00	– 60000.00	– 100000.00
50.01 – 80	– 11000.00	12000.00	24000.00
80.01 – 100	– 9000.00	24000.00	86000.00

Simulation

Random number	Outcomes based on action of hiring: A	B	C
35.35	–35000.00	–60000.00	–100000.00
74.63	–11000.00	12000.00	24000.00
14.66	–35000.00	–60000.00	–100000.00
18.41	–35000.00	–60000.00	–100000.00
52.91	–11000.00	12000.00	24000.00
74.58	–11000.00	12000.00	24000.00
77.71	–11000.00	12000.00	24000.00
82.52	–9000.00	24000.00	86000.00
93.86	–9000.00	24000.00	86000.00
47.60	–35000.00	–60000.00	–100000.00
30.15	–35000.00	–60000.00	–100000.00
98.09	–9000.00	24000.00	86000.00
57.88	–11000.00	12000.00	24000.00
89.96	–9000.00	24000.00	86000.00
56.52	–11000.00	12000.00	24000.00
65.24	–11000.00	12000.00	24000.00
8.75	–35000.00	–60000.00	–100000.00
87.91	–9000.00	24000.00	86000.00
15.79	–35000.00	–60000.00	–100000.00
83.98	–9000.00	24000.00	86000.00
96.48	–9000.00	24000.00	86000.00
71.23	–11000.00	12000.00	24000.00
4.73	–35000.00	–60000.00	–100000.00
3.56	–35000.00	–60000.00	–100000.00
31.63	–35000.00	–60000.00	–100000.00
76.49	–11000.00	12000.00	24000.00
68.57	–11000.00	12000.00	24000.00
43.77	–35000.00	–60000.00	–100000.00
66.65	–11000.00	12000.00	24000.00
42.76	–35000.00	–60000.00	–100000.00
30 trials mean	–20133.33	–14000.00	–11133.33
100 trials mean	–22320.00	–20640.00	–23120.00

trials. Results are shown in detail for 30 trials and the mean is given for the trial as a whole. For the 100 trial simulation, the mean alone is given. Based on the 30 trial simulation, machine C should be hired because it minimises average loss.

Interestingly, a different conclusion arises from the 100 trial simulation; machine B minimises the cost after 100 trials. The larger the number of simulations, the closer the average cost approaches the expected loss values of £22,600, £21,600 and £25,600 for the three machines. Expected value is explained in the next section.

18.3.3 Expected value and decision trees

The commercial manager of Ruddle Co Ltd has assessed the probabilities of the various estimated demand levels. In general, there are two ways in which this sort of information could have been generated: on the basis of prior experience or according to the subjective opinions of the managers. Since the situation presented is original, the opinions of managers must have been used and the probabilities can be referred to as the subjective probabilities. These subjective probabilities can be used to produce an expected value for each of the machine hire options.

Figure 18.4 shows the expected value for the machine hire problem. The three actions of hiring A, B or C have the differential costs as listed in the cost column. Differential cost calculations are shown in Table 18.5 below. The probabilities of each cost arising are given in the column next to the costs. Expected value is the weighted average of costs, the weighting being the subjective probabilities. It can be seen that hiring machine B gives the lowest expected value of differential cost and this is the option which management should select, based on a rational, economic evaluation.

FIGURE 18.4

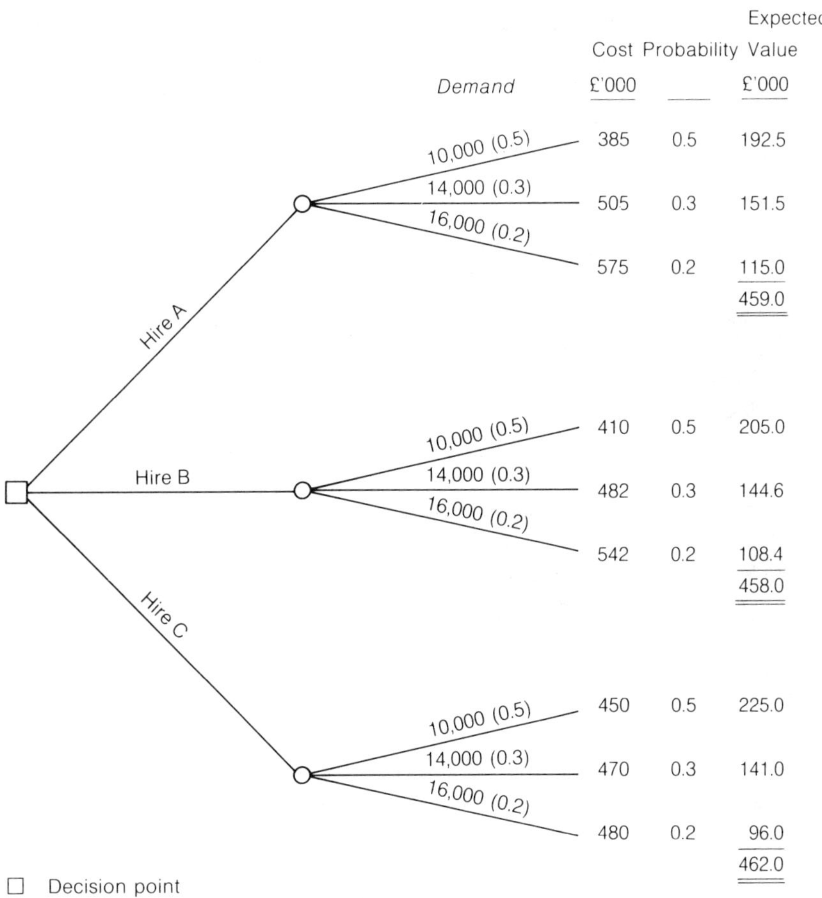

Differential costs have been calculated as follows:

TABLE 18.5 **Differential costs for the machine hire example**

Action	**Hire Machine A**	**Hire Machine B**	**Hire Machine C**
Outcome Demand:			
10,000 units	Hire costs: 10000 @ £6.5 +£320000 £385,000	Hire costs: 10000 @ £6 +£350000 £410,000	Hire costs: 10000 @ £5 +£400000 £450,000
14,000 units	Hire costs: 10000 @ £6.5 +£320000 Subcontracting: 4000 @ 30 £505,000	Hire costs: 12000 @ £6 +£350000 Subcontracting: 2000 @ £30 £482,000	Hire costs: 14000 @ £5 +£400000 £470,000
16,000 units	Hire costs: 10000 @ £6.5 +£320000 Subcontracting: 4000 @ £30 2000 @ £35 £575,000	Hire costs: 12000 @ £6 +£350000 Subcontracting: 4000 @ £30 £542,000	Hire costs: 16000 @ 5 +£400000 £480,000

Selection of options by means of the maximum expected payoff is sometimes known as the Bayes decision rule after the eighteenth century mathematician who first proposed this means of assessing decisions under uncertainty. It has the advantage over the minimax criterion of utilising all of the available data. Lapin illustrates an example where its advice can be unhelpful, however. Assume that one option has outcomes of a £1,000,000 loss and a £2,000,000 profit. A second option has outcomes of £250,000 profit and £750,000 profit. If the actions or events which cause these outcomes are felt to be equally likely, an expected value of £500,000 is calculated for both options. The two options do not appear to be equally suitable, in reality, but would hold different values depending on whether the decision maker is a risk taker or risk averse. Bayes decision rule does not account for the attitude to risk of the decision maker.

18.3.4 Minimax opportunity loss

The opportunity loss of an event is the amount foregone by taking a non-optimal decision. For Example 18.1, for a demand of 10,000 units, the best decision is to choose machine A. The opportunity losses for the decisions to hire machines B and C are £25,000 (£385,000 less £410,000) and £65,000 (£385,000 less £450,000) respectively. These are the values foregone by not choosing the best alternative. Applying this principle to all of the possible outcomes produces the figures in Table 18.6.

TABLE 18.6 **Opportunity losses for the machine hire example**

Action	**Hire Machine A**	**Hire Machine B**	**Hire Machine C**
Outcome Demand:			
10,000 units	385000-385000 £nil	385000-410000 £25,000	385000-450000 £65,000
14,000 units	470000-505000 £35,000	470000-482000 £12,000	470000-470000 £nil
16,000 units	480000-575000 £95,000	480000-542000 £62,000	480000-480000 £nil

The minimax decision rule selects the option which shows the minimum amount of maximum loss.

The maximum losses for machines A, B and C are £95,000, £62,000 and £65,000 respectively and so machine B would be hired to minimise the opportunity loss under the most pessimistic outlook.

Examiners and some authorities prefer the Bayes rule to the maximin and minimax approaches because it makes use of all of the available information. However, where subjective probabilities are not available, the minimax rule should share with the maximin rule an appeal for the risk averse. It does, however, provide different advice to that given by the maximin decision rule for the machine hire problem. Both approaches are pessimistic and yet can provide different advice to the decision maker. No single best way of looking at the future is available simply because the future is uncertain.

A second use of the opportunity loss table is the ability to provide information on the theoretical value of perfect information.

18.4 THE VALUE OF PERFECT INFORMATION

In certain situations, it is possible to incur costs to secure more information about a particular decision. Market research services may be bought to discover more about the operation of a particular market, cost investigations may be instigated to ascertain future cost levels to a greater degree of accuracy or work study exercises may be set up to investigate the impact of the learning curve, for instance. The availability of more information will itself reduce the uncertainty of a particular decision, but information costs money and the question of the amount of money to be incurred becomes important.

Applying the Bayes decision rule to the opportunity loss table produces not only a decision recommendation but also reveals the value of perfect information. The value of the decision which minimises the expected opportunity losses shows which decision should be taken. The expected opportunity loss for the most attractive option is the value of perfect information. This represents the amount of money foregone by not having perfect information.

Self-assessment question 18.2

Prepare a decision tree for Example 18.1. Calculate the expected value of the opportunity losses for the decision using the figures from Table 18.6. Which decision would you recommend and what is the maximum amount of money that you would recommend should be paid by the company to secure perfect information?

Answers on page 587

This particular decision tree, together with the accompanying calculations in Tables 18.5 and 18.6 provide one of the most efficient ways of answering the question set in Example 18.1.

An alternative way of looking at the value of perfect information is to ask the question 'what would we have done if we had known the outcome with certainty?' For Example 18.1, the answer to this question for each of the three levels of estimated demand is tabulated in Table 18.7. Computing the expected value of the payoffs under certainty and comparing this value with expected values confirms the value of perfect information.

The value of perfect information is the expected value under certainty, or with perfect information, less the expected value of the optimum solution under the Bayes rule. In this example, the value of perfect information is given by £429,500 less £458,000. This confirms the answer to self-assessment question 18.2 and the relationships between expected value under certainty, expected opportunity losses and expected values under uncertainty are shown in Table 18.7.

18.5 DISCRETE AND CONTINUOUS DISTRIBUTIONS

Section 3 of this book is concerned with the processing of information for decision-making. Whilst other chapters have shown calculations with single outcome values, this chapter has described

TABLE 18.7 **Calculating the value of perfect information**

Action:	Hire Machine			
	A	**B**	**C**	With perfect information select:
Demand:				£'000
10,000 units	£385,000	£410,000	£450,000	A: cost 385
14,000 units	£505,000	£482,000	£470,000	C: cost 470
16,000 units	£575,000	£542,000	£480,000	C: cost 480

Expected value under certainty:

Demand:	Cost with perfect information	Probability	Expected Value
	£		£
10,000	385,000	0.5	192,500
14,000	470,000	0.3	141,000
16,000	480,000	0.2	96,000
			429,500

	A	**B**	**C**
Expected values under uncertainty:	£459,000	£458,000	£462,000
Expected opportunity losses:	£29,500	£28,500	£32,500
Expected value under certainty	£429,500	£429,500	£429,500

alternative means by which decision rules can incorporate a range of values. This range is necessary because of the lack of realism resulting from processing single figure values where outcomes from a decision are uncertain. This section considers alternative ways of looking at distributions of outcomes and discusses some of the problems to arise from the analysis of multiple outcomes.

Data is provided as discrete values for Example 18.1. Demand is estimated as being either 10,000 units, 14,000 units or 16,000 units. These values, together with the associated probabilities can be plotted as shown in Figure 18.5. A moment's consideration raises the question about the intermediary values: 'What is the probability of a demand of, say, 12,000 units, or 15,000 units, or 10,997 units?'. It could be argued that a more realistic distribution of probabilities would be as shown in Figure 18.6. Such a distribution can be mathematically manipulated using integration. A third way of looking at possible outcomes is to ask managers for estimates of ranges rather than estimates of discrete values. It could be argued that it is more natural to think of uncertain situations as a range of outcomes than as a single outcome. For the machine hire problem, managers may estimate demand at, say, between 7,000 and 13,000 units, with a probability of 50%, between 13,000 and 15,000 units, with a probability of 30% and between 15,000 and 17,000 units, with a probability of 20%. Such a distribution is represented by Figure 18.7. To calculate expected values, the mid points of each of the ranges are used in calculations, to give the same results as previously, in this particular example. Taking mid points uses the assumption that any outcome within each range is equally possible. This is another way of saying that the probability of individual outcomes within each range is unknown.

The shape of a particular distribution is, in part, given by the way that the management accountant decides to collect data for the decision analysis. Where the accountant collects information for a single figure outcome, there ensues a relatively straightforward calculation, the result of which advises management according to a relatively simple success/fail. For example, where variable production costs of, say, £3 are produced, as the result of a cost investigation, and compared with a component buy in price of £4, the management accountant responds by advising that the component

FIGURE 18.5

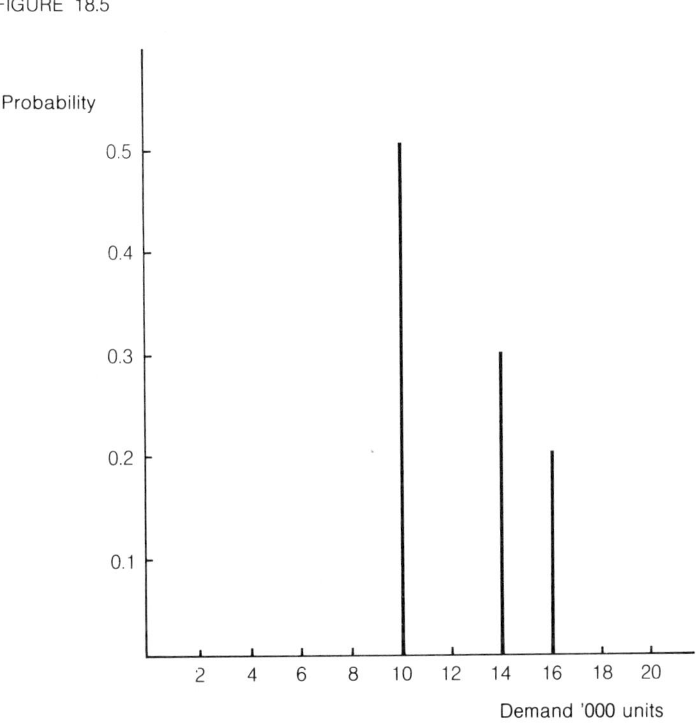

FIGURE 18.6

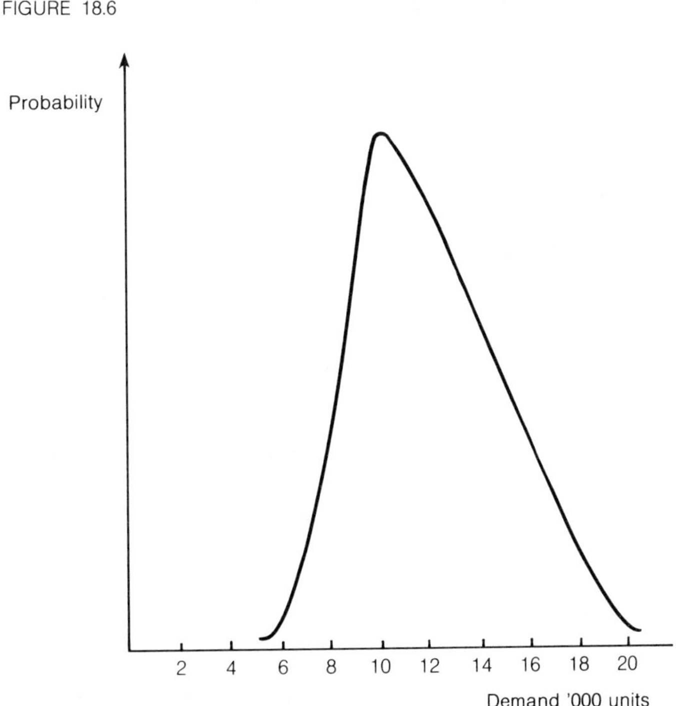

should not be bought in. £3 may be the mean of expected future variable costs or the most likely level of cost or the best cost that is available from existing records. It is unlikely that future costs will turn out to be £3, but the single figure does have advantages in terms of cost collection and the simplicity of decision taking. Collecting data for the analysis according to a distribution of likely outcomes should be more realistic but is beset with practical problems:

1 The providers of information may be unaccustomed to providing a range of possible information and education may be required to ensure the provision of reliable information.

FIGURE 18.7 **Calculation of Joint Probabilities**

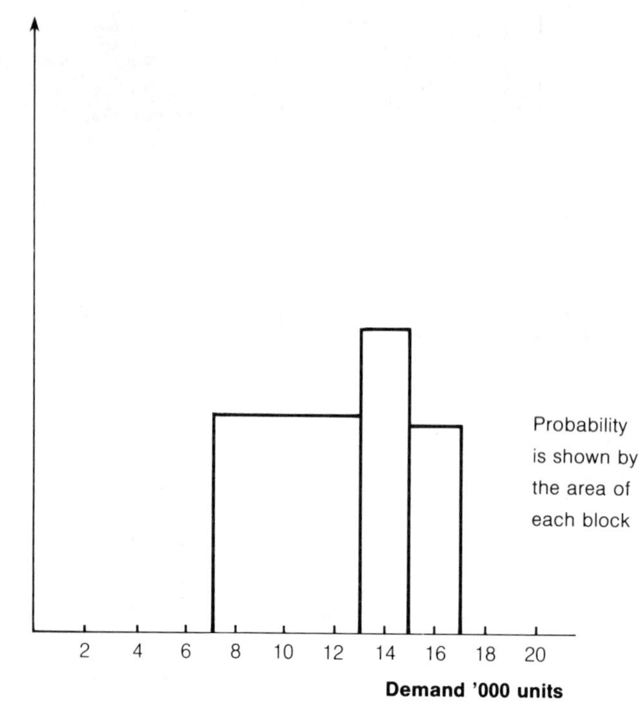

FIGURE 18.8 **Calculation of Joint Probabilities**

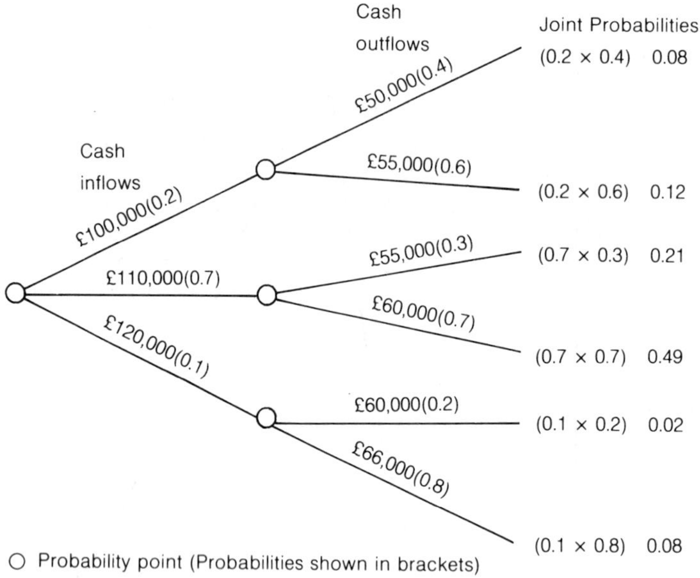

2 Many engineers are accustomed to thinking in terms of tolerances, where it is acknowledged that scientific data conforms to a range rather than an absolute figure, but some managers may take the inability of the accountant to arrive at the 'single correct answer' as an adverse comment on the credibility of 'accurate' accounting.

3 It is known that there are problems in extracting subjective probabilities from people, in particular:

(a) low probabilities may be overstated. An event or action which is highly unlikely may attract a subjective probability greater than anticipated;

(b) high probabilities may be understated. An event or action which is highly likely may attract a subjective probability lower than anticipated;

(c) probabilities may not sum up to 1, or 100%.

Uncertainty poses the accountant with the problem that simple assumptions and discrete values may not adequately reflect the way in which the world is operating, but do provide clear cut decisions and relatively easy calculations and explanations of decision choice. Earlier sections of this chapter show that calculations under uncertainty provide alternative answers, even where a risk averse posture is adopted consistently. Not a single illustration provided a solution of intuitive attraction to the risk taker. The adoption of an approach to decision making under uncertainty requires that the management accountant use judgment in the selection of a technique and in the evaluation of analysis. Once an analysis has been completed, the decision may have to be explained to management who have little grasp of the implications of calculations incorporating uncertainty considerations.

Explaining the results of uncertainty calculations can be challenging, even where the data collection problems have been overcome. The author was once involved in a company which was making a decision about the launch of a new product. The management accountant advised the Board of Directors that the launch should proceed if there was better than a one in ten chance, or better than a 10% probability of success. The management accountant used expected values to calculate a break-even in terms of probabilities. The Board of Directors received this advice with great confusion and the Marketing Director pursued the matter with particular concern. Finally, the following dialogue was initiated by the management accountant:

'Do you believe that there is better than a 1 in 10 chance of success?'

'Yes, of course.'

'Then the product should be launched.'

'But how can you make a statement like that. Other accountants just say whether a proposal will be successful or not.'

'It's just another way of working the figures. There is some risk in most things to do with the future and I thought it may be helpful to state the amount of risk involved. After all, you would have to be very unlucky not to succeed with this launch, but there is a chance.'

'Yes, but I still don't see how you can make a statement like that when other accountants just say whether to go ahead or not.'

The Marketing Director finally went ahead with the product launch. The particular product is still advertised on national television in the United Kingdom, some ten years after the decision was taken. Although the Marketing Director was clearly confused, a suitable decision was taken.

18.6 JOINT PROBABILITIES

In some situations, the probability of one outcome leads to probabilities of other outcomes occurring. Consider the decision to invest in a new machine. It could be expected that the new machine would generate a range of possible cash inflows from sales. For each level of sales, there could be a range of possible cash outflows for cost of sales. A decision tree for such an example is illustrated by Figure 18.8. For decision trees such as these, a calculation based on the subjective probability associated with combinations of branches of the tree has to be made. Such a calculation involves joint probability.

Taking the top most series of branches, the probability of a cash inflow from sales of £100,000 per annum is 0.2. The probability of a cash outflow of £50,000 for sales of £100,000 is 0.4. The chance of both a sales inflow of £100,000 and a cash outflow of £50,000 is given by multiplying the probabilities together to give 0.08.

Self-assessment question 18.3

The Riddle Company Limited is considering a decision to invest in a new building in order to expand capacity. At present, the business is limited by the availability of production capacity and it is believed that the market will bear some increase in supply, although the exact amount is difficult to determine. Two options are currently being considered and information for each option is provided below. Neither building is yet available but the Riddle directors are certain that negotiations for either building could proceed successfully. If the directors bid for both buildings at the same time, it is considered that the market values for both buildings would be set at the highest level possible. The directors are therefore most concerned to make the correct decision as to which building to expand into.

	Building Wye		Building Zed	
	Probability	*£'000*	*Probability*	*£'000*
Initial cost	0.2	1,000–1,100	0.3	2,100–2,400
	0.25	1,100–1,300	0.3	2,400–2,800
	0.35	1,300–1,400	0.3	2,800–3,000
	0.2	1,400–1,500	0.1	3,000–3,500
Fixed cost/year	0.3	500– 700	0.4	500– 700
	0.7	700– 900	0.6	700– 900
		000 units/ year		000 units/ year
At a fixed cost of £500,000 to £700,000 per year:				
Capacity	0.5	500– 750	0.6	1,200–1,400
	0.5	750– 900	0.4	1,400–1,600
At a fixed cost of £700,000 to £900,000 per year:				
Capacity	0.2	500– 750	0.5	1,200–1,400
	0.8	750– 900	0.5	1,400–1,600

It is anticipated that the average sales price for items produced from either building will be somewhere between £6 and £7 and variable costs will be somewhere between £4.50 and £5.50. There is no information on the likely probabilities of selling price or variable cost levels and it is thought that an average based on the range of possible values should be built into the calculations.

The company's cost of capital is 20%. Long-term projects are usually appraised over a ten year period.

You are required to make a recommendation to management on the best course of action, supporting your recommendation with appropriate calculations and comments. State any assumptions which you make in preparing your analysis and ignore taxation.

Answers on page 587

18.7 REDUCING UNCERTAINTY

The value of perfect information is important in providing a means by which the cost of reducing uncertainty can be analysed formally. Unfortunately, perfect information may not be available in many practical decision-making situations because decisions relate to future outcomes and the future is often uncertain by nature. Information may be imperfect because it is not available, because it is irrelevant due to weaknesses in the process of collecting information, or because it is biased. Section 4 discusses various aspects of biased information. Steps may be taken by management to reduce the uncertainty affecting their decision-making processes in other ways than through the purchase of perfect information, including:

1. Selection of projects with low payback periods to reflect the fact that uncertainty increases the longer the time horizon under consideration.
2. Use of a high discounting rate to reflect risk. The longer it takes for a cash flow to arise, the lower effect it has on the decision, if a high discounting rate is applied.
3. The application of prudence and the building in of slack, or overly pessimistic estimates, to ensure that future events are no worse than predicted.
4. The selection of projects with acceptable average predicted outcomes and low standard deviations.
5. The use of sensitivity analysis to determine the critical factors within the decision-making process. Management effort can be directed to those factors which are critical to the success of a particular decision.

Self-assessment question 18.4

To illustrate the process of sensitivity analysis, recalculate the results of your calculation for self-assessment question 18.3 increasing the cost of capital by 10% (ie 2% in absolute terms) and reducing the selling price by 10%. Compare the original analysis with the revised figures for higher cost of capital and compare the original analysis with the lower selling price figure and then answer the following questions:

(a) Which is the most critical factor, cost of capital or selling price?

(b) Does changing cost of capital or selling price affect your advice about the choice of building?

(c) How is uncertainty reduced by using sensitivity analysis?

Answers on page 591

SUMMARY

Decisions are beset with uncertainty because it is difficult to predict a single outcome in many decision-making situations. It is possible to build decision rules which take account of uncertainty. These rules supplement, but do not replace, judgment and evaluation in the decision-making process. Most rules reflect a pessimitic attitude towards the results of decisions and may thus appeal rather more to the risk averse than to risk takers. In general, the Bayes decision rule is to be preferred to minimax or maximin approaches because it takes into account the maximum amount of information available. The implementation of systems which take explicit account of uncertainty may be difficult to explain to a management which is unfamiliar with uncertainty analysis. It may also be difficult to secure useful subjective probabilities and other necessary information from managers. A range of approaches is available to managers to reduce uncertainty in the decision-making process, including the use of sensitivity analysis.

EXERCISES

Exercise 18.1

QRS Ltd is reviewing the price that it charges for a major product line. Over the past three years the product has had sales averaging 48,000 units per year at a standard selling price of £5.25. Costs have been rising steadily over the past year and the company is considering raising this price to £5.75 or £6.25. The sales manager has produced the following schedule to assist with the decision.

Price		£5.75	£6.25
Estimates of demand:			
Pessimistic estimate	(Probability 0.25)	35,000	10,000
Most likely estimate	(Probability 0.60)	40,000	20,000
Optimistic estimate	(Probability 0.15)	50,000	40,000

Currently the unit cost is estimated at £5, analysed as follows:

Variable costs:	
Direct material	£2.50
Direct labour	£1.00
Overhead	£1.00
Fixed costs:	
Overhead	£0.50
	£5.00

The cost accountant considers that the most likely value for unit variable cost over the next year is £4.90 (subjective probability 0.75) but that it could be as high as £5.20 (probability 0.15) and it might even be as low as £4.75 (probability 0.10). Total fixed costs are currently £24,000 per annum but it is estimated that the corresponding total for the ensuing year will be:

£25,000 with a probability of 0.2
£27,000 with a probability of 0.6
£30,000 with a probability of 0.2

(Demand quantities, unit costs and fixed costs can be assumed to be statistically independent.)

(a) Analyse the foregoing information in a way which you consider will assist management with the problem, give your views on the situation and advise on the new selling price. Calculate the expected level of profit that would follow from the selling price that you recommend.

(b) It can be argued that the use of point estimate probabilities (as above) can be dangerous because it unrealistically constrains the demand and cost variables to taking just one of three possible values. Comment on the criticism and suggest how this problem might be cured.

(*ACCA, Management Accounting, June 1985*)

Answers on page 592

Exercise 18.2

'A fundamental characteristic of all decision problems is that the outcome is uncertain. Since the data are estimates of future events, it is not possible to predict decision outcomes with perfect accuracy . . .' (from *Management Accounting: A conceptual approach*, by L R Amey and D A Eggington).

(a) Describe the problems which the existence of uncertainty poses the preparer of statements for decision-making purposes.

(b) Explain three ways in which uncertainty may be incorporated into the data presented for decision-making purposes and discuss the extent to which each is effective.

(c) Specify and explain the objective which should be pursued by the preparer of data for decision-making under uncertainty.

(*ACCA, Management Accounting, June 1980*)

Answers on page 593

Exercise 18.3

Describe some of the approaches that have been suggested for incorporating risk and uncertainty into management accounting calculations. Illustrate your answer by reference to cost-volume-profit analysis.

(*ACCA, Management Accounting, December 1985, adapted.*)

Answers not provided.

Exercise 18.4

Makeit plc is considering the decision whether to tender for a one-off order for a batch of plastic overalls for a local hospital. The order will be given to the company quoting the lowest price. The Board of Directors has produced the following figures, based on its best estimates:

Selling price tender for the complete batch	Probability of success in securing the order
£2,000	0.8
£3,000	0.4
£4,000	0.2
£5,000	0.05

The manufacturing manager believes that the batch could be produced for a cost of between £1,900 and £2,800 but cannot predict the exact figure with any accuracy without spending £200 on a trial exercise. The best guess is that there is an even chance of the cost falling in the ranges £1,900 to £2,000, £2,000 to £2,600 and £2,600 to £2,800. The manufacturing director also believes that it would be possible to pay £300 to find out the exact value of the quotations to be made by competitors.

The Board of Directors is known to be risk averse.

You have been called upon to provide advice in your capacity as management accountant. In particular, you are required to:

(a) suggest a selling price to be quoted for the tender;

(b) advise on the desirability of paying £200 for the trial exercise and £300 for the information on competitors' quotations.

Answers not provided.

Section 4

PLANNING AND CONTROL

Planning is concerned with many things: with predicting the future, with ensuring that adequate resources exist, with making decisions on how to allocate resources for the future, with motivating people to achieve outcomes which are necessary to continued existence or prosperity. Planning takes place at all levels in society: at a global level in deciding appropriate action to safeguard the world and its inhabitants, at a national level in ensuring the well-being of individuals and countries as a whole, at company level in furthering corporate objectives and at a personal level in seeking to make the most of the opportunities and threats which beset everyday living. The accountant undertaking accounting studies probably planned a career path before opening the covers of this book. The company for which the student works probably has some form of budgeting system in operation. The country within which the student lives probably has some form of national budgeting. Section 4 shows how planning and control are inextricably linked and explains the role of the management accountant in implementing organisational planning and control systems.

This section begins with three chapters which discuss the framework within which planning and control systems operate. Chapter 19 provides an outline of planning and control and relates evaluation to these two functions. Chapter 20 discusses information used in long- and short-term planning. Chapter 21 presents material on the effects of control systems on organisational behaviour, the reactions of human beings to the kinds of systems which accountants commonly implement. The ensuing chapters build on material studied at an introductory level and illustrate the principles established in Chapters 19 to 21. Illustrations of calculations and procedures are provided which are typical of standard costing and budgeting systems. The aim is to develop the necessary degree of flexibility and knowledge commensurate with an advanced study of these topics. The final chapter is appropriately concerned with performance evaluation since planning, control and decision-making can all be influenced by management accounting systems which measure the performance of products, projects, departments and managers.

Planning, Control and Evaluation: An Outline

INTRODUCTION

The purpose of this chapter is to discuss various definitions and ideas related to planning, control and evaluation and to show how these three aspects of management activity are inter-related. It will be seen that planning is concerned with future events and their implications. Control is concerned with the day to day operations within organisations. Control may be influenced by planning and could affect the decisions which are taken about the future. The evaluation of both plans and controls is explained. The exercises which are set throughout the chapter are designed to be thought provoking and to provide practice in writing about aspects of the management acccountant's work for which there are no clear right or wrong answers. Future chapters will apply the ideas raised in the chapter to the budgeting and standard costing areas.

It is assumed that students are fully familiar with material and labour control systems and are aware of the importance of budgeting in planning and control. A basic knowledge of auditing and standard costing is assumed.

19.1 DEFINITIONS

19.1.1 Planning

The Oxford English Dictionary provides two meanings which help in understanding the significance of planning to management. The first is associated with design; for instance, in the sense of designing a floorplan. The second is concerned with "devising, contriving, scheming, projecting and arranging beforehand". Combining these brief definitions, two important threads of meaning can be discerned; the idea of projecting forward and the idea of designing to meet future eventualities.

1 Projecting forward in order to determine what will happen in the future. For the purpose of this book, this will be termed the forecasting function. Forecasting is concerned with looking forward in time in order to understand the implications of possible future outcomes. If it were possible to forecast ahead with complete accuracy, appropriate responses could be initiated in advance. For instance, imagine it is known that the overall market for a particular commodity will double in the next five years. This information could be used by a particular company to justify investment in increased capacity. To take a slightly different example, current forecasts on the effects of some company products on the world's ozone layer are leading to some major producers increasing spending on research and development. This can have two effects; one ecological, the other competitive. Competitive advantage may be gained from research and development spending. Responses to the impact of future opportunities and challenges need to be laid out or made in the present.

2 Devising, scheming and arranging so that the future follows patterns which individuals and organisations establish rather than waiting for the future to create its own effects. For the purpose of this book, this will be termed the strategic function. A company may plan to expand and take steps to ensure that expansion occurs, such as lowering selling prices in competitive markets or increasing its spending on marketing and research and development. This aspect of planning can be compared with designing a floorplan for a building. A floorplan shows where each of the rooms in a building should go, given constraints on the size of the building, the availability of the resources, forecasts of how the building will be used and the objectives or goals

of putting up the building. Budgeting can be seen as a system concerned with designing for the future. It can be based on constraints, forecasts and objectives. In the sense of the meaning of the word used here, planning is concerned with ensuring that an organisation achieves the targets which it sets for itself and takes the greatest advantage of future opportunities. It could be said that information about the future provides the power to dominate the future.

These two descriptions suggest reactive and proactive aspects to planning. A reactive approach is concerned with reacting to events as they arise. A reactive company might plan by taking the present year's results and making an adjustment for known future changes. British Petroleum's Robert Horton has stated that '95 per cent of human beings are short-term, extrapolative forecasters . . . following the disasters they see at the moment extrapolated, or the triumph they see at the moment extrapolated.' It appears that in Horton's view, the majority of organisations are reactive. A proactive approach is concerned with taking steps to create the changes which are beneficial to the individual or organisation. A proactive approach needs both objectives or goals for the future, commitment to achieve those goals and forecasts to assess how quickly the goals can be achieved. A proactive company takes steps to shape the future so that its aims and objectives are achieved.

19.1.2 Control

The Oxford English Dictionary provides two explanations of the use of the term control:

1 checking and directing action; the function or power of directing and regulating; domination
2 restraint, check.

John Sizer sums up the implications of restraining current actions whilst dominating future outcomes in a succinct and clear manner:
'Control is concerned not with correcting past mistakes, but directing future actions. Thus management control consists, in part, of inducing people in an organisation to do certain things and to refrain from doing other things.'

Charles Handy makes the same basic point in defining the purpose of control systems as:
'Information that is required to monitor the work of the organisation, to point out requirements for corrective action or opportunities for improvement.'

The essence of control would thus appear to be that checks on current situations are carried out, in order to ensure compliance in the present and to provide direction for the future. An analogy is provided by a ship's rudder. This controls a voyage by ensuring that present hazards such as rocks are avoided and that the eventual goal of arriving at the required destination is met. The ship complies with the present requirement that it should not sink and is directed to its future goal or destination. A stock control system involving the use of maximum, minimum and re-order levels provides an example from the area of management accounting. A perpetual inventory system ensures that stock does not run out in the present and that future decisions regarding when to order will be taken at the appropriate time.

John Sizer's comments on control also reveal the importance of people. A budgetary control system, in the form of a mass of paper comprising a routine report, does not ensure that present actions comply with requirements or that future actions will lead to the goals of an organisation. For these eventualities to arise, people must use the information provided by the budgetary control system. The sheets of paper which comprise a monthly statement of management accounts will not cause materials wastage to improve or sales levels to change, without people to convert the information provided by the accounts into positive actions.

Organisational factors, such as the ways in which individuals use information, are a central consideration in determining ways of controlling organisations.

On the other hand, some systems can operate reasonably autonomously if the potential of computers and information technology is realised. A computerised stock system can operate with a reducing intervention from people as technology is increasingly exploited:

1 A perpetual inventory system keeps a track on the stock on hand. People make out documents and enter data from documents into the computer. With the use of bar codes, the importance of people is declining from the days when bin cards were written out by hand and manual operations such as additions needed to be double-checked.

2 When a re-order level is reached, a purchase order is automatically created in accordance with economic order quantity model calculations. People are needed to switch on the printer and to post the order. There are developments which may lead to computers placing orders with each other through communication systems, thus avoiding the postal system and the need for people to carry out mundane tasks.

3 People deliver the goods and load the goods into stock. Issues are made by people to people.

This example shows the relationship between people and the technical system in trying to meet the requirement of maintaining stock levels to avoid disruption to production.

Control systems design is concerned with both the technical aspects of implementing sound ways of processing information and with the behavioural aspects of implementing tasks in suitable ways for people, taking advantage of the available technology. Computers can reduce the mundane, routine work necessary to the operation of some control systems.

Self-assessment question 19.1

Design an information technology system for the control of labour which you imagine could be in operation in the year 2000. What do you think are the technical (eg ensuring that people are only paid for work that contributes to meeting the organisation's objectives) and organisational (eg the effect of the system on the people's attitudes to the organisation) considerations which will result from the system you outline; will your system be more efficient, economic and effective than today's systems? Will the people like the system better than clock cards and time-sheets and thus have a more positive attitude to the organisation?

Answers on page 593

Self-assessment question 19.2

The following definitions of control as a restraining mechanism are taken from the *Oxford English Dictionary*:

1 Check or verify and hence to regulate.
2 Check by comparison and test the accuracy of.
3 Take to task, call to account, rebuke, reprove.
4 Exercise restraint over, exercise power of authority over, to dominate or command.

Which of these four definitions are important to each of the following accounting systems:

1 Budgeting
2 Standard costing
3 Responsibility accounting
4 Auditing

Answers on page 593

19.1.3 Evaluation

The term evaluation is used by management accounting text books in relation to performance evaluation, in particular. The same term is used in the systems approach to audit, where the concern is to evaluate a system's controls. This section provides a definition of the term which is common to both of these applications and describes one approach to evaluation. Auditing will be considered first and then the implications for management accounting will be addressed.

The *Oxford English Dictionary* provides the following definition:

1 The action of appraising or valuing (goods, etc).
2 The action of evaluating or determining the value of (a mathematical expression, a physical quantity, etc), or of estimating the force of (probabilities, evidence).

The auditor collects evidence in order to form a judgment about a set of published accounts in relation to the true and fair view concept. Evaluation is part of that process. Measurement, through analytical review, for instance, and the application of judgment based on the collected evidence appear to be essential features of evaluation.

The systems audit process can be described as comprising the following stages:

1 Plan the audit. Determine audit objectives.
2 Ascertain, record and confirm the accounting system.
3 Evaluate the controls and weaknesses of the system.
4 Test the system.
5 Review and express an opinion.

The controls and weaknesses of a system can be evaluated against criteria established through each of the following means, amongst others:

1 Standard Statements of Accounting Practice and other forms of Generally Accepted Accounting Practice.
2 Standard Statements of Audit Practice and other forms of Generally Accepted Auditing Practice.
3 The auditor's experience.
4 The auditor's expertise.
5 The objectives of the system being evaluated; if a system is designed to report a debtors' figure for inclusion in a balance sheet, it would be inappropriate to criticise the system for failing to give a geographical analysis of customers' addresses (which may be important for a system of personalised debt collection).

The management accountant does not have such a degree of formalisation of procedures as the auditor. One explanation for this is that the management accountant is faced with the need to design systems for organisations which may differ. Attempts to formalise practice for all organisations must therefore fail. However, it is possible to consider some of the ways which the management accountant may use to consider performance, once measurements have been taken:

1 Literature may provide some insight into acceptable levels of performance. Trade literature may provide guidance on acceptable profit results. Text books provide advice on how to calculate measurements and the limitations of some of the measurements.
2 The management accountant can use experience either gained personally (possibly for other organisations in the same type of industry or business) or by comparing results with previous periods.
3 The management accountant can apply personal expertise in determining the significance of evaluation results.

Seen in these terms, the process of evaluation appears to be remarkably similar in both auditing and management accounting. A general approach is suggested in Figure 19.1. Given a plan or objectives, a set of criteria is established based on available written sources, experience or expertise. Systems or measurements and judgments are assessed in relation to the criteria.

Evaluation can be applied to both organisational plans and controls. Once the budget has been completed, for instance, the management accountant may carry out an evaluation to consider whether the planned results meet performance criteria; questions such as the following may be asked:

1 Does the planned profit meet the objectives laid down by the organisation?
2 Is the organisation going to be financially sound at the end of the budgeted period?
3 Does the cashflow forecast reveal any problems?

FIGURE 19.1

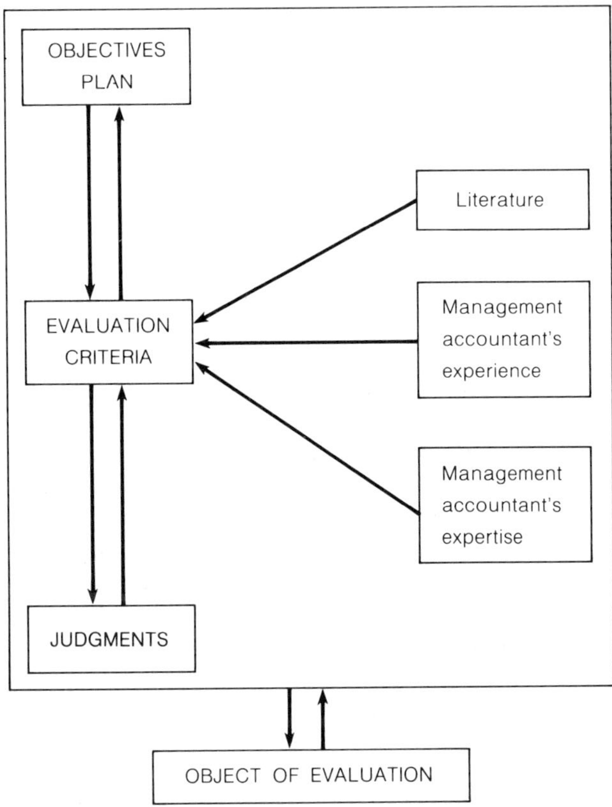

Performance measurements can be applied to budget statements to provide answers to questions such as these. The management accountant may also be given the role of evaluating an organisation's controls. Procedures similar to those outlined above for audit may be used. Where evaluation of controls is carried out on a formal and extensive basis, an internal audit function may be established. Internal audit may have similar detailed objectives as external audit, including the objective of reviewing internal controls, but may also be concerned with broader objectives such as management and operational audits.

19.2 FORMAL ACCOUNTING CONTROL MECHANISMS

Two forms of control are described in this section. One is primarily based on management and administrative procedures, the other on a mechanism suggested by a formal study of systems. Both of these forms of control influence the way in which budgeting and standard costing systems are implemented.

19.2.1 Internal control

Internal controls are established within organisations to safeguard assets, check the accuracy and reliability of accounting data, to promote operational effectiveness, efficiency and economy and to encourage individuals within the organisation to work towards organisational objectives. Some of the mechanisms by which internal control operates can be found throughout this book, such as responsibility accounting. For the sake of completeness, commonly found internal control mechanisms are listed here as follows:

1 Control systems are reviewed by management on a regular basis. In a court case in the early 1980s, involving the pilferage of stock by employees, the judge held that management were partially culpable for failing to ensure the operation of adequate stock control systems. Management have a clear responsibility for reviewing organisational controls.

2. Global accounting controls are applied to monitor the operation of specific systems. A common accounting control may be to test the discrepancy:

   opening stock
   plus inputs to stock such as purchases
   less outputs from stock such as issues
   equals a theoretical stock in hand.

   The theoretical stock is compared with a physical count, such as that provided by continuous stocktaking or an annual stocktake. The difference can be established and investigated if necessary.
3. Management ensure that staff and resources are adequate to fulfil the requirements laid down for each system operated.
4. Where necessary, assets are protected by physical security methods such as closed stores.
5. An organisational structure may be established to specify the authority and responsibilities of individuals. Where a system of budgeting is operated, budget centres can be used to apply the principle of responsibility accounting. A budget centre may be a department or a division for which the budget centre manager assumes responsibility.
6. A system of segregation of duties may be used to ensure that inputs and outputs of individual systems can be compared with corresponding figures from other departments. For example, the total cost of labour posted to jobs by one accounting section may be checked against a payroll cost analysis produced by another accounting section.

19.2.2 Cybernetic control

Cybernetic control is concerned with the automatic regulation of systems by the systems themselves. So far in this book, the word 'system' has been used without explaining its meaning or its importance to management accounting. In this section, systems will be explained, a mechanism by which systems can be self-regulating will be described and the difficulties of applying cybernetic control to management situations will be explored.

SYSTEMS

A system is an orderly, interconnected arrangement of parts which may be complex. Examples of systems are biological systems (people, animals, birds, plants, for instance), mechanical systems (a room thermostat, for instance), organisational systems (for example, industrial companies, hospitals or accountancy practices and possibly departments and divisions within organisations) and information systems (such as standard costing or budgeting systems). These apparently different examples of things we may see in our everyday lives have the following characteristics in common:

1. They all need inputs. People need food, organisations need raw materials, a room thermostat makes measurements of room temperature, information systems all take in documents such as goods received notes.
2. They all process inputs in order to create outputs. Food creates energy which allows people to walk or carry objects or conduct their everyday jobs. Manufacturing organisations convert raw material into finished goods which are sold. Thermostats convert a measurement into a flow of electricity if the room is below the required temperature. Information systems produce reports.
3. They all have objectives. People have goals such as the desire to be adequately fed or to have a good circle of friends or to become wealthy or to pass a professional accounting examination. Whether organisations can have objectives is debated, but for this book we will accept the assumption that organisations can have objectives associated with matters such as profit, survival, expansion or behaving responsibly to the community through policies on employment or ecology. The goal of a thermostat is to regulate a room temperature; to maintain the temperature at 20 degrees centigrade, for instance. The objectives of information systems may be to inform or to direct attention or to promote beneficial actions by individuals within organisations. Two objectives of accounting information are to keep a record of events as they occur, the scorekeeping function, or to direct accounting users' attentions to areas of significance, the attention directing function.

Common systems attributes are:

1 Systems have boundaries between themselves and the environment within which they operate. Organisations work within an environment which has competitors, suppliers, government policies and social attitudes on matters such as fashion.
2 Systems can be broken down into sub-systems. An organisation can be broken down into functions such as manufacturing, administration and marketing and into departments such as quality control or accounting.
3 Systems may relate to other systems within their environment. Organisations may form important working relationships with suppliers. Actions by competitors may cause reactions such as price changes, the development of new products or spending on public relations or advertising.
4 Systems may be deterministic/mechanistic or probabilistic/stochastic. Deterministic or mechanistic systems are those for which a given input will give rise to a known output, for instance in a room with a temperature of 15 degrees centigrade, there is little doubt that a thermostat set at 20 degrees centigrade will continue to allow the room to be heated. Probabilistic or stochastic systems are those systems beset by uncertainty for which a given input is capable of creating a range of outputs. An advertising campaign can be expected to create a range of possible effects on sales performance.

The management accountant operates information systems which provide an analysis of the workings of organisational systems. The ways in which information systems are designed may imply something about the way in which the organisation is operating. Let us take the example of budgeting. Where a management accountant produces a single figure of budgeted profit, it is implied that the organisation is a deterministic system; that its efforts will result in one outcome. When management react to a failure to meet budgeted profitability by determining responsibility for the failure, they are continuing to assume that the organisation is deterministic. This assumption may or may not be valid, given the degree of uncertainty facing the company. An extreme case may be where a company cannot influence suppliers' prices or its own market share or the prices charged for finished goods. Its results will reflect actions in the environment by competitors, suppliers and customers.

In this case, any action by the company can give rise to a range of profit outcomes, depending on the actions of suppliers or competitors or customers. It would seem harsh in these circumstances for the management to fix blame for shortfalls of profit with responsible budget centre managers. The process of planning may still be important to allow management to consider alternative reactions to events which may arise. The process of control is still important so that management can take essential actions to constrain present actions and direct future outcomes. The problem arises in the evaluation of the situation, where the assumptions about the ways in which the information and organisational systems work in relation to each other are crucially important.

Self-assessment question 19.3

Outline any differences which you can see between a standard costing system for a milk bottling plant which has served a constant number of customers for the past five years and a budgetary control system for a company which repairs a range of one thousand motors when customers' machines break down. The milk bottling plant has no competitors. The motor repair company has five competitors each making similar charges for work carried out.

Both companies operate similar budgetary control systems. The purchases cost variance for both companies is identical, as measured in terms of the size of the variance and its relationship to sales value. Do you think that the management accountants in each company should evaluate the variance in an identical manner?

Answers on page 596

SELF REGULATING SYSTEMS

Cybernetic systems adapt to their environment through a process by which inputs are changed when outputs are not in line with objectives. The overall approach is illustrated in Figure 19.2. Inputs are

FIGURE 19.2

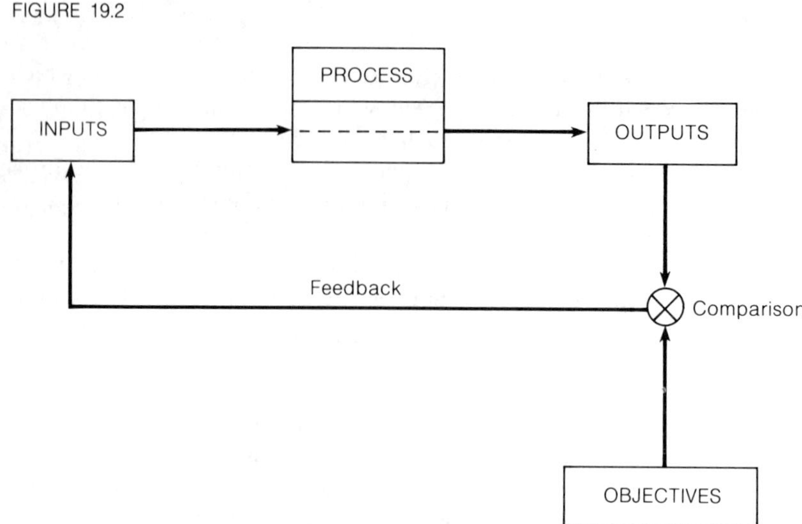

processed to create outputs. Outputs are compared with objectives and any necessary actions result in changes to future inputs, by a process termed feedback.

Feedback can take two forms: negative feedback and positive feedback. Negative feedback creates actions which result in future outcomes complying with objectives. If the objective is to control the cost of wastage, and a target of 3% wastage has been set, for example, action is directed to ensuring that wastage levels comply with the target. A recorded level of 4% for any month will result in action to find the cause of the excess wastage so that corrective action can be taken. The following month may see a figure of 5%, showing that the corrective action was ineffective. Further corrective action may bring wastage down to 2% in the next month. Positive feedback, on the other hand, reinforces the trend which the process is taking. An example is provided by a bank account which pays interest. Imagine that £100 is invested and no money is drawn from the account. At the end of the first year, the amount invested would rise to £110 if interest at 10% is credited. At the end of the second year, the balance would be £121 and at the end of the third year, the balance would be £133.10. The measured output from the input of £100 is £110; £121; £133.10 with a continuing trend upwards. Feedback in this case results in the output increasingly deviating from the initial input. Figures 19.3 and 19.4 show negative and positive feedback for these two examples in graphical form.

Self-assessment question 19.4

For the company with wastage problems, described in the previous section, what action would be taken once the wastage figure of 2% is achieved, assuming that the management accountant:

1 continues to operate the control system on a negative feedback basis,

2 decides to change the way in which the system operates so that positive feedback operates.

Answers on page 596

Systems may be considered to be closed or open. An open system is one which interacts with its environment. In systems such as these, it may be appropriate to amend objectives in the light of information relating to the environment, rather than to amend inputs. If a supplier increases a price as a result of a general price change in the market, buying less expensive goods as a result of negative feedback would tend to cause quality problems. Rather than buy sub-standard goods to meet a cost target, it may be more appropriate to change the cost target to reflect the uncontrollable price change. A double loop system can be operated, as illustrated by Figure 19.5. Either inputs or the objective can be changed. In contrast, a closed system is one which carries out its processes irrespective of the effect of the environment. A thermostat typically operates on a closed systems basis. A target temperature for the room is set. Once the target temperature is reached, the thermostat ensures that no more heat comes into the room. Once the temperature drops below the target, the

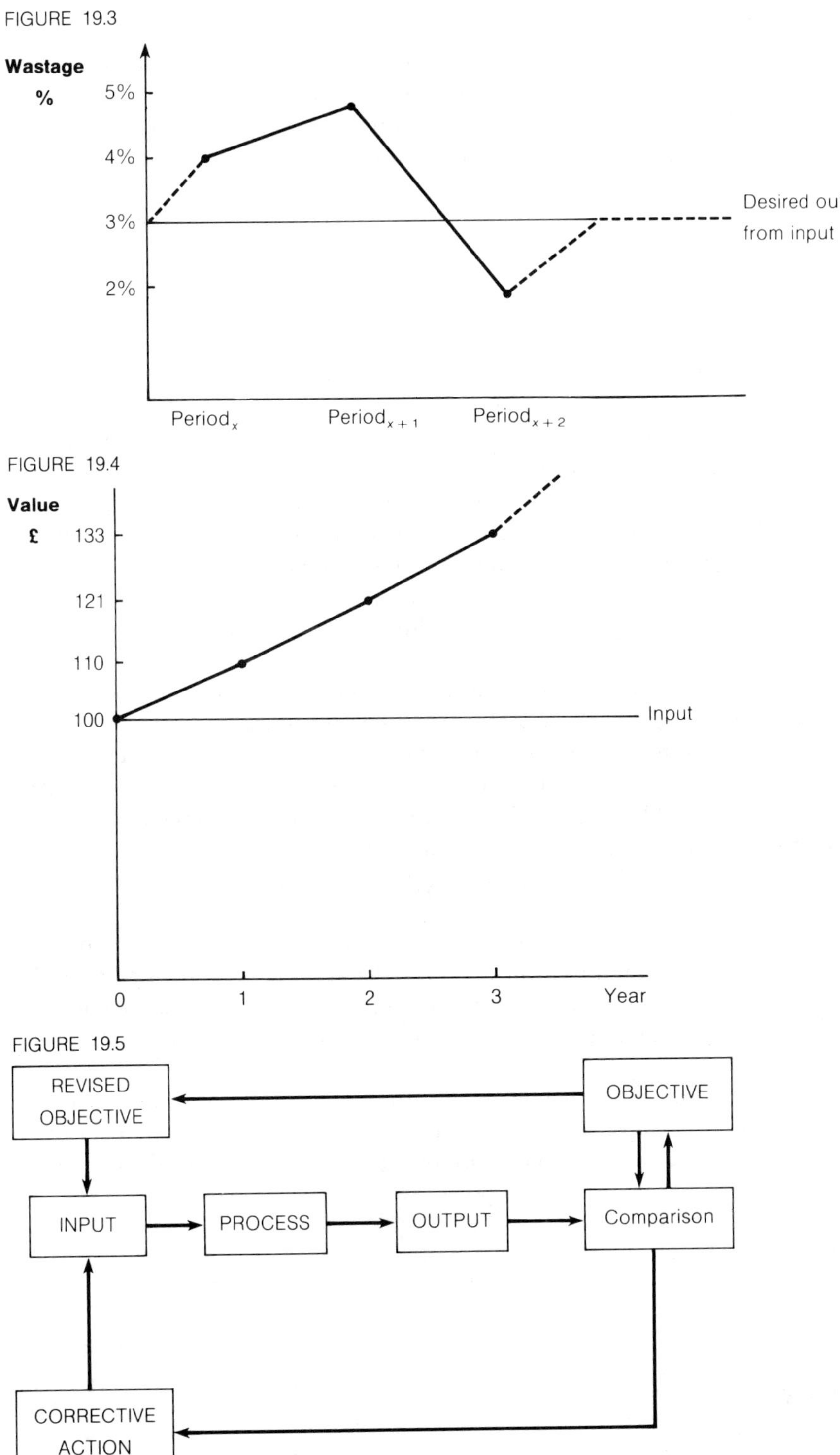

thermostat automatically switches the heating back on. This happens irrespective of the environment; it does not matter who owns the building, how big the room is, whether it is night or day.

Self-assessment question 19.5

Would you operate a budgetary control system on a closed system or an open systems basis that is operating a double loop system to respond to changes in the environment?

Answer on page 596

ORGANISATIONAL CONTROL SYSTEMS

The theory of cybernetic control systems has been successfully applied to mechanistic systems such as thermostats. Unfortunately, organisational systems do not always behave in the same way as thermostats. This has caused some writers to list the requirements to be met for a cybernetic system's approach to be effective. The requirements, with comments, are as follows:

1 Objectives must be clear. In Chapter 23, we will consider the problems which can arise from the fact that budgetary control systems are sometimes implemented with multiple, conflicting objectives in mind. Problems also arise where sub-systems do not share the same goals, as we shall discuss in Chapter 21 under the topic of goal congruence.
2 Inputs must be accurate. It is known that some errors occur in making out documents such as materials requisitions, labour time sheets or goods received notes. Some of these errors may be fraudulent, where an employee attempts to claim more than the entitled payment for wages, or careless, where a stores keeper enters a receipt of 419 nails as 491 in the stores system. Errors such as these detract from the effectiveness of a cybernetic control approach.
3 Outputs must be clear and unambiguous. If a report can be interpreted in more than one way, feedback may be incorrect or confused. For example, if a particular adverse materials usage variance can be considered either the responsibility of purchasing (through poor quality materials leading to wastage) or production (the process is operated inefficiently), and there is no way of establishing clear accountability, then in which department can corrective action be effectively instigated?
4 There must be a clearly understood model of the way in which a system is operating. A model is a simplification of the real world which allows us to reach an understanding of a system and which allows us to make predictions. The learning curve is a model which allows us to predict labour costs. The linear assumption behind the accountant's understanding of cost behaviour is a simplification of how costs behave in the real world. If the accountant's cost behaviour model is inappropriate, cybernetic control can result in misleading control signals. An example could be where action to increase output to increase profit leads to a reduction in profit due to diseconomies of scale.
5 Feedback should ideally be frequent and timely. If feedback is delayed or infrequent, corrective actions may have an impact on factors which are no longer important to the operation of the system. A temporary price increase picked up either too late or as part of the average price for a long time span may not give rise to appropriate control action.

In addition to the above points, some authorities question whether organisations, comprised of people rather than machines, can be controlled in a way which is effective for machines. Chapter 21 discusses the organisational implications of control systems and deals with this matter more fully.

SUMMARY

Planning, control and evaluation are an essential part of the life of any organisation. Management accountants design systems such as standard costing and budgetary control in order to provide information to aid management in carrying out these three functions. Planning is concerned with the future and can be used in different ways, depending, for instance, on whether an organisation is reactive or proactive. Control is concerned with present actions but provides direction to influence future outcomes. Evaluation requires judgment and can be applied to plans or controls. Formal accounting control systems can work at the level of procedures, as illustrated by internal control, or through cybernetic control. Cybernetic control illustrates one way in which plans and control are linked; a situation is thought to be under control where results coincide with plans. Cybernetic control is effective when applied to mechanised systems and there are possible limitations to its use in the control of people. The management accountant has the responsibility to design systems which are effective in both technical and organisational terms.

EXERCISES

Exercise 19.1

Prepare a diagram to show the operation of a budgetary control costing system by means of cybernetic control. Under which circumstances do you think the system could be expected to operate effectively?

Answer on page 597

Exercise 19.2

What role do you think that self-control by individuals within companies contributes to meeting organisational objectives?

Answer on page 597

Exercise 19.3

Comment on the problems of designing management accounting systems for the type of organisation described in the following quotation from Charles Handy:
'A power culture is frequently found in small entrepreneurial organisations, . . . occasionally found in some property, trading and finance companies . . . . This organisation works on precedent, on anticipating the wishes and decisions of the central power source. There are few rules and bureaucracy. Control is exercised by the centre largely through the selection of key individuals . . . . It is a political organisation, in that decisions are taken very largely on the outcome of a balance of influence rather than on procedural or purely logical grounds.'

Answer on page 598

Exercise 19.4

Explain the importance and implications of applying internal control and cybernetic control approaches to the control of business organisations.

Answer in lecturer's manual.

Exercise 19.5

Consider ways in which a standard costing system could be designed as:

1 an internal control system
2 a cybernetic control system

Discuss the relative merits of adopting each approach.

Answers in lecturer's manual.

Information for long- and short-term Planning and Control

INTRODUCTION

Management can make plans for the immediate or for the long-term future of their enterprises. Information is required in order to do this. This chapter will discuss a framework for considering management's information needs in both the long- and short-term. The framework provides a complementary view of the relationship between planning and control to that provided in the last chapter and rounds off the material which is necessary to explain the management role of budgets and standards. Strategic planning, management control and operational control are explained, some useful concepts from communication theory are explored and a way of using budgets for short- and long-term planning is described. The end of chapter exercises illustrate ways in which material from this chapter and the previous chapter have been examined for professional accounting purposes in recent years.

20.1 A FRAMEWORK FOR LONG- AND SHORT-TERM INFORMATION NEEDS

Some years ago, Anthony suggested a framework from which the information needs of management could be understood. The framework has survived the test of time and is still useful today. Management's planning and control activities are categorised into three headings: strategic planning, management control and operational control. Simon explains the contrast between strategic planning and operational control and it is perhaps easiest to begin by looking at these two extremes before fitting management control into the picture.

20.1.1 Strategic planning

Strategy is concerned with asking questions such as 'what business should we be in?', 'which product range fits the business as we see it?' or 'where will we be ten years from now?' Strategic planning is concerned with establishing, reviewing and changing objectives and strategies and may be expressed formally in terms of a long-term plan. Strategic information is predominantly judgmental, is broad in scope, is inexact, is related to future periods of time rather than with the present and may be concerned with several years into the future. Strategic planning is carried out by senior management. Decisions are non-programmed; the prediction of the likely outcomes is beset by great uncertainty.

Strategy can be contrasted with tactical planning. Tactical planning is concerned with short-term opportunities or threats. Where strategy may be broad in scope, tactics relate to particular opportunities and threats which arise. Where strategy is concerned with uncertainty, the outcomes of tactical decisions can often be predicted with certainty. Where strategy is judgmental, the outcomes of tactical decisions can often be subjected to detailed analysis and calculation. The short-term budget may be an expression of tactical planning where uncertainty over the budgeting period is low. The long-term budget should normally be a quantification of strategic planning.

To use the analogy of a board game such as chess or draughts, a strategy may be concerned with establishing a dominating position or with creating the kind of position with which the player feels comfortable. Some players prefer certain opening moves to others purely because experience shows that such opening moves tend to create particular kinds of position; closed positions, where few pieces are removed from the board in the opening phase of the game, suit the temperament of certain types of player, open positions suit others. Tactics arise when one player makes a mistake or drifts into an inferior position. The game may be won within a few moves or a combination of moves may give one player an advantage in terms of the number or strength or pieces held. The strong player applies sound strategies and takes advantage of tactical opportunities.

Management strategies are concerned with determining ways in which an organisation can move from its present position to the position it would like to be in. If a company were merely playing a board game, management would consider the best ways of converting an opening position, or arrangement of pieces, into a won position. A game is similar to a model in that it simplifies real world situations. In the real world, management can apply the same principles if they define in exact terms the opening position and won position for their organisations. They also need to consider the rules of the game; the allowable changes to the position of pieces as the game progresses, and the pieces with which the game is played; the variables which management must manipulate.

A statement of opening position can be determined by means of a position audit. A position audit is concerned with an assessment of the organisation's present state of affairs in terms of markets, production facilities, finance, people and products. A particular company can analyse its customer base, determine its production capacity and the availability of fixed assets. It can assess its financial position through balance sheets, profit and loss statements and cash flow statements. It can consider the talents of its managers and the skills of its workforce. It can analyse its products in terms of the product life cycle, market share or market growth. The product life cycle is concerned with the way that products develop, mature and fall out of fashion as time passes. Market share and growth have been categorised according to a well-known approach referred to as the Boston classification. Combinations of share and growth are classified. In conducting an analysis of opening position, management are answering the question 'where are we now?'

The won position is difficult to determine. Real life does not come to end for the successful organisation in quite the same way that a board game comes to an end for the successful player. The nearest an organsiation comes to winning is when it achieves its objectives. It is possible for a particular organisation to be following one or more of a range of possible objectives. Some objectives are listed below:

1 maximise profit, return on capital employed or profit margin;
2 maximise earning per share;
3 maximise dividend per share;
4 expand markets or sales of individual products;
5 maximise product quality;
6 maximise employee satisfaction;
7 improve the national economic position through maximising exports;
8 improve the world's ecology;
9 survival.

It should be noted that a conflict situation may arise where an organisation pursues more than one objective. A company which increases salaries by twice the rate of national inflation may improve employee satisfaction but may or may not simultaneously improve profit; the outcome depends on the effect of salary changes on productivity. A company which maximises dividends per share may not retain sufficient funds in the business to ensure that future earnings are maximised; the outcome may depend on the costs of financing future investment.

It should also be noted that organisations are collections of people; shareholders, managers, employees, working in a world of people. Objectives which are acceptable to one group of people may not be acceptable to another. Expenditure on the world's ecology may be seen as beneficial to the world at large but not to shareholders if profits are reduced. Groups of people may come into conflict in determining organisational objectives. Additionally, since shareholders are also a part of the world at large, an individual may need to resolve a conflict of priorities; is ecology sufficiently important to warrant a loss in individual wealth? Setting objectives includes a process of evaluation.

The rules of the game can be seen in terms of the relationships between people; acceptable behaviour between groups of people, power positions and procedural regulations such as legislation, for example. To return to the example of the product life cycle, a major management decision may concern the timing of the release of new products or the updating of old products in response to decline. Customer and competitor behaviour influence these considerations. Legal considerations may govern the acceptability of certain products; no law abiding company would develop and market products such as illegal drugs. Power positions are illustrated by industrial relations. Where trades unions hold significant power, this power may be translated into large pay rises for employees, which may not be seen to be beneficial to other groups such as shareholders. Where management hold the balance of power in industrial relations, they may control pay rises effectively, from the point of view of the organisation as a whole. Alternatively, management may hold down pay rises to maximise profits where the position of shareholders is dominant. Attitudes to acceptable behaviour provide the rules of the game and depend largely on organisational factors in its widest meaning.

A number of the variables which management manipulates in strategic planning have already been referred to in the preceding examples. In general, these variables will be concerned with the organisation, as a system, adapting to its environment. Management will be concerned with customers, competition, new technology and political, economic and social forces. Such considerations can formally be translated into an analysis which considers the organisation and its environment now and in the future. An analysis of the present can be conducted through a position audit. An analysis of the future may be conducted through an environmental analysis which aims to consider the environment within which the organisation's objectives should be achieved. Forecasting market growth and market share provides an example of the use of forecasting in environmental analysis.

The process of formally setting down strategies is concerned with establishing means by which the organisation as it now stands, described by the position audit, can move towards its objectives, within its environment as described by the environmental analysis. Before strategy is formalised, it may be appropriate to combine the three elements of objectives, position audit and environmental analysis into a statement of organisational strengths and weaknesses, and opportunities and threats. Where such a statement is developed to the point of analysing the difference between an extrapolation of the present situation and organisational objectives, a process known as gap analysis may be implemented. The gap between projected outputs and objectives can be analysed in terms of strengths, weaknesses, opportunities and threats. Information for this process can be gathered via feedforward mechanisms. Feedforward is concerned with comparing predictions of outputs with plan. Where feedback is concerned with changing inputs based on differences between objectives and outputs, feedforward is concerned with anticipating the implications of future deviations in order to take strategic action.

In summary, strategy provides a means by which objectives can be achieved. Given the diversity of objectives, the many different states an organisation may find itself in and the many environmental differences which can arise, there may be numerous strategies available. Typical strategies may be to expand existing market share, to move into new markets, to acquire new companies, to exploit technological opportunities, to develop new products or to eliminate organisational weaknesses. Carrying out a successful strategy involves ensuring that adequate resources are available and that people within the organisation are motivated to meet organisational goals.

Self-assessment question 20.1

Develop a formal strategy for your accounting studies.

Answer on page 599

20.1.2 Operational control

Operational control focuses on a single task or transaction. Its scope is precise and narrow. Decisions taken within operational control systems are not judgmental and may be guided by pre-established procedures or decision rules, many of which can be developed in terms of mathematical models. The short-term is predominant; data is captured real-time. Control is repetitive, stable, predictable and exact. Systems generate large volumes of data. Decisions are programmed; predictions of the outcomes of decisions can be made reliably and with a high degree of certainty. Higher management involvement should be low.

Raw material stock control systems provide a good example of operational control. Typical decisions concern when to order goods and the quantity of raw materials to order and to issue. The issuing of raw materials is largely controlled procedurally. A requisition note is authorised by a responsible person and is presented to the storekeeper. If the goods are in stock, the quantity requested is issued. Records reflect the reduction in stock which occurs. Quantities are measured in physical terms such as kilograms or metres or numbers of units. Differences between records and a physical count of stock can be classified according to a list which is given in many first stage cost and management accounting text books, including clerical error or computer typing error, pilferage and losses occurring as bulk orders are broken down. Ordering may be implemented by means of one or more models which are commonly referred to by the terms 'economic order quantity' and 'minimum, maximum and re-order levels'. These models provide information on quantities to be ordered and the time to re-order, which is governed by stock level. Operational control has been able to provide mathematical analysis to improve the effectiveness of ordering by means of models described in first stage cost and management accounting texts. Stores decision-making can be computerised; the rules which govern ordering can be defined with sufficient clarity that computer programmes can be written.

Self-assessment question 20.2

Classify each of the following systems under the headings of 'strategy' or 'operational control'.

1 A labour control system where each employee uses a clock card to record attendance time and a time sheet to record work on individual jobs. At the end of the week, the clock cards and time sheets are compared to determine the non-productive time of each employee.

2 A pricing system where managers change selling prices in order to gain a competitive advantage.

3 A pricing system where accounting staff calculate the standard cost of a new product, add a percentage for profit and notify the marketing director of the selling price. This price is then charged to customers.

4 A system of planning where the present year's results are increased by a fixed percentage to allow for inflation. Negative feedback is then implemented in order to control costs during the year.

5 A capital investment appraisal system which is used as the basis for investment decisions. All projects showing a positive DCF result are accepted.

6 A capital investment appraisal system, based on the intuition and entrepreneurial capabilities of its senior managers, which does not use any formal screening method such as DCF.

Answers on page 599

20.1.3 Management control

Emmanuel and Otley see management control as:

'The mediating activity between strategic planning (the setting of objectives) and operational control (the carrying out of specific tasks). It is integrative because it involves the whole organisation and is concerned with the effective management of the inter-relationships between disparate parts. Unlike strategic management and operational control, management control is an essentially routine affair, reporting on the performance of all aspects of an organisation's activity on a regular basis, so that all areas are systematically reviewed. Defined in this way, the major tool for achieving management control is thus seen to be management accounting information.'

Management control from the point of view of the management accountant involves collecting, analysing and summarising data from operational control systems. The aim is to supply management with key information on the day to day running of the organisation. On a daily or weekly basis, this information may be concerned with production levels achieved, sales orders received, productive and non-productive hours worked by employees and cash received from debtors, for example. On a monthly basis, routine management accounts can be expected to monitor areas such as profit earned, contribution to sales ratios by groups of products, markets or geographical locations. Variances from plan or standard, financial position such as number of days debtors or aged debtors lists, and cash flow position.

Summary management control information, in the form of statements of profit and loss, financial position, cash flow and funds flow can be incorporated into the position audit so that strategy can address key financial considerations. Strategic statements such as long-term plans can then include clear financial objectives such as planned earnings per share, return on capital employed, profit margins, debtors payment days, investment strategies and financing arrangements, as appropriate to each organisation. It could be expected that these statements would be co-ordinated with objectives for the marketing, production and research and development areas.

The aged debtors list provides an interesting case of information which can be used for both operational control and management control purposes and also shows how information can be summarised for strategic purposes. The task of collecting debts can be facilitated by using the aged debtors list in procedures which ensure a hierarchy of warnings, from a gentle reminder, within a few days of the normal due date, to letters from solicitors, where the number of days credit taken becomes excessive. These procedures could be carried out at the operational control level by a credit controller, or could be semi-automated by using computers. The aged debtors list could be reviewed weekly or monthly by management in order to monitor the debtors position for management control purposes. The debtors ratio may also be incorporated as a means to summarise the debtors situation. A large number of old debts may imply poor debt collection and/or an unsatisfactory incidence of bad debts. A large number of days debtors may imply poor debt collection implementation. Feedback principles could be applied; an objective of number of days debts or bad debts as a percentage of sales can be set and management action could be triggered upon actual results exceeding objective. Finally, at the strategic level, decisions would be taken to balance a possible loss of customers, through tight credit controls, and a possible loss of profits through bad debts. The marketing and financial implications would be co-ordinated at the strategic level.

Figure 20.1 portrays a model which shows the relationships between strategy, management control and operational control. Strategies are determined by senior management. The management controls which are implemented reflect control conditions necessary to implement strategy. The second law of cybernetics (the first is said to be feedback) is given by Ashby's law of requisite variety; there should be enough control actions to match all possible control conditions. Those controls which are significant influence the reporting of key management information. The requirements of providing information for management control influences the design of tasks at the operational control level. Operational control data then feeds back into management information and influences future strategy in the way illustrated for the debtors example. It is important to appreciate that this is a model which may be descriptive of some organisational practices or alternatively a prescription for how some managers may feel that planning and control systems should be conducted. The author's experiences of planning and control systems in a wide variety of organisations suggest that a range of variations on this basic model are to be found in practice.

FIGURE 20.1

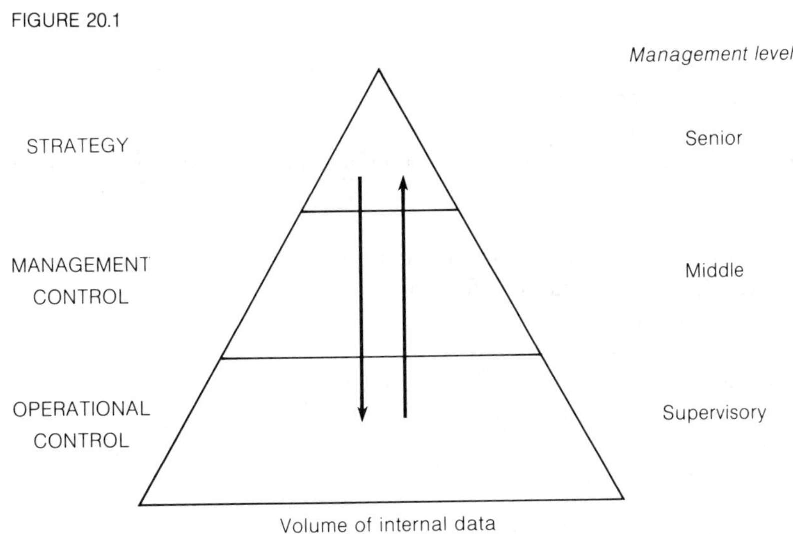

Self-assessment question 20.3

Classify each of the following systems into the categories 'strategy', 'management control' and 'operational control'. Use a fourth category for systems which you cannot classify from the information provided.

1 A budgeting system which brings together managers from all parts of an organisation to talk about their plans, co-ordinate their activities and quantify their ideas in terms of objectives for the year ahead, measured in £ terms.
2 A budgetary control system which monitors monthly results and reports variances so that management can initiate corrective action.
3 A standard costing system which reports purchase price and material usage variances as part of a responsibility accounting system for purchasing and production departments.
4 A standard costing system which values labour down-time as it arises so that supervisors can keep an account of labour utilisation on an hour by hour basis.
5 A computerised manufacturing system which controls the flow of raw material fluids and powder through to production processes and reports the standard cost of issues from stock on a second to second basis.
6 A budgeting system which incorporates standard costs in the planning process.

Answers on page 600

20.2 INFORMATION

It is possible to discover a range of different types of information system in operation within organisations. Information may be informal; discussions between people on a staircase or in a corridor, about family and friends or about the future plans of the managing director. Information may be formal; memorandums from heads of responsibility centres, monthly accounting reports, financial statements issued to shareholders. Within these headings of formal and informal information, quantitative and qualitative information may be communicated. Quantitative information may be in the form of production targets and results, sales turnover figures, or management accounting reports. Qualitative information may be concerned with an evaluation of an organisation's quality or customer relations performance, or statements regarding its strengths and weaknesses. A final classification of information commonly met concerns whether information is routinely produced or reported only when required, on an ad hoc basis. A weekly discussion between students about a particular television or radio programme could be described as routine, informal, qualitative information.

Self-assessment question 20.4

For an organisation with which you are familiar, list examples for each of the following categories of information:

1 routine, formal, quantitative information;
2 routine, informal, qualitative information;
3 ad hoc, formal quantitative information;
4 ad hoc, formal, qualitative information;
5 ad hoc, informal, quantitative information;
6 routine, formal, qualitative information.

Answers on page 600

The above leads to a consideration of the meaning of the word information. Is it usual to think of a discussion of matters such as television programmes as 'information'? Taking another example, operational control systems generate enormous quantities of data; can that data convey information? Does a set of monthly management accounts produced three months after the period to which the accounts relate constitute information? Answers to these questions have been the subject of considerable debate. Responses of importance to accountants can be formalised under two headings; data/information and communication theory.

20.2.1 Data and information

Data comprises symbols such as words and numbers. To provide examples from operational control systems, data is the dates, descriptions, signatures and quantities which appear on goods received notes, invoices or labour reports.

By themselves, these numbers and words do not convey meaning.

Information does convey meaning. Generally speaking, information is formed from data. Throughout this book, there are many examples of techniques of manipulating data so that reliable information can be produced. The process of filtering, or selecting certain data, is a process which helps data to become information. Information from an operational control system can become the data for a management accounting system. Information from a management control system can become the data for the strategic planning process. 'Meaning' in relation to information must be judged in terms of the purpose of the reporting system and the knowledge of the user of the information. Technical descriptions of parts may not convey meaning at a strategic level but may be critical to the operation of operational control systems. Knowledge of five hundred issues of six inch Spencer Wells Artery Forceps may be essential information in a stores ordering system but is unlikely to convey meaning to a government official determining a strategy for the National Health Service.

20.2.2 Communications theory

Communications theory has generated ideas which have influenced accounting thought in recent years. It deals with the processing of signals in telecommunications and similar systems.

It is important to understand the concepts of information measurement, distortion and noise, filtering and information measurement, although the mathematics of these areas will not be covered to any depth. An additional aspect, associated with more general communications theory, is also discussed; the relative merits of one and two way communications systems.

DISTORTION AND NOISE

A communication system is conceived as a transmitter connected to a receiver by a wire or, more correctly, by a sub-system comprising a communications channel. In the channel, the signal which originated at the transmitter is subject to change so that the signal arriving at the receiver may not coincide exactly with the signal leaving the transmitter. The two major causes for the change are distortion and noise.

Distortion can be illustrated by a classroom example commonly called 'Chinese Whispers'. One person in the class is given a message, without anyone else being able to know what the message is. That person has to whisper the message to a neighbour, without anyone else being able to hear. The neighbour cannot ask for the message to be repeated but must immediately pass the message to another neighbour, and so on, until all members of the class have heard the message. The final person in the chain then speaks the message out loud. A good example is given by the initial military message:

'Send reinforcements, we are going to advance.'

being converted into the final message:

'Send three and four pence, we are going to a dance.'

If the exercise is repeated in a classroom where everyone is shouting, the effects of noise can also be established.

Distortion changes the form of the message. Bias, discussed in the next chapter, is an example of a way in which information can be distorted. A manager may increase a planned cost budget by 10%, say, so that apparently good results will be shown by budgetary control reports. Noise is random and can obliterate the message entirely, in extreme circumstances. In Chapter 26, the investigation of variances will be considered. The problems of accounting for the effects of random deviations from standard or budget will be discussed; in other words, the problems facing the management accountant when faced with noisy data will be recognised. Noisy data includes incorrect entries on operational control documents such as goods received notes. Communications theory states that noise is unavoidable. Distortion can be countered if the effects that the communications channel creates are sufficiently well understood. For instance, good quality hi-fi does not distort input signals significantly. Less good quality hi-fi can distort input signals but the distortion can be corrected by means of graphic equalisers. In management accounting systems, if the effects of distortion can be corrected by equal and opposite corrections, the signal can be received in its proper form. If it is known that a manager regularly increases budgeted cost levels by 10%, the management accountant can reduce the final budgeted level by 10% to compensate.

FILTERING

Filtering is concerned with the selection of certain information and the rejection of other information available on a communications channel. It can be used to reduce the quantity of data transmitted, whilst still meeting the objectives of the communications system. Earlier in this chapter, the process of summarising information for management control and strategic planning was explained. More correctly, operational control is filtered for management control purposes and management control information is filtered into strategic planning. Possible advantages of filtering are as follows:

1 Communications channels may not have the capacity to process all the data available; taking unessential data out of a channel through filtering may enable the communications system to function more effectively. A telephone system does not allow all of the frequencies present in the voice to pass down the telephone line and yet the objective of allowing people to talk is met. A management accounting reporting system does not need to report every detail available within an operational control system in order to meet management's needs for information. The manager may not be able to absorb an excessively detailed set of reports. A more effective report might summarise essential matters.

2 Filters discriminate in favour of one type of information; tuning a radio ensures that the message sent out at a particular frequency is accepted whilst all other messages are rejected. Management accountants design systems to discriminate the significant from the insignificant. An example is given by the application of ABC theory or Pareto analysis to stores control. The stores ledger system only receives detailed information on the significant items in stock; detailed information on insignificant items is filtered out in order to operate stores more effectively. Exception reporting can be explained in similar terms.

The importance of filtering to the strategic management, management control and operational control framework is illustrated earlier by Figure 20.1. From the mass of data processed by operational control systems in the form of goods received notes, invoices and timesheets, for example, summarisation and the rejection of information considered insignificant to management leads to management control reports. A further process of summarisation and filtering yields reports from which strategies can be formed.

A short-term budget can be used in budgetary control to monitor results as they arise and thus provide valuable management control information. The results reported would summarise more detailed information available in operational control systems such as stores ledgers and labour records. A number of apparently insignificant considerations, such as details of the temperature inside the factory building or of the relationships between employees would not be reported. These sort of considerations may be of fundamental importance and may be the subject of intense informal communications. The management accountant, however, might decide that such information is irrelevant to the purpose of financial reporting. The judgment of the management accountant is used to make decisions about the significance of information available on communications channels.

A long-term budget would probably be produced in considerably less detail than a short-term budget. One reason for this is that detailed plans in quantitative terms contain much detail whilst the long-term future is viewed in general terms. Detailed implications, whilst necessary at a tactical level for taking advantage of short-term advantages, are not appropriate at the strategic level.

INFORMATION MEASUREMENT

Formally speaking, a bit is not an abbreviation of the words 'binary digit' but is a measurement of information. The information, measured in bits, conveyed by a message, x, is equal to log, base 2, of the inverse of the chance that the next message will indeed be x. In a computer system, for example, it is assumed that there is a 50:50 (0.5) chance that the next signal to be transmitted will be a '0'. There is also a 50:50 (0.5) chance that the next signal to be transmitted will be a '1'. Information is measured as:

$$\begin{aligned}\text{Information transmitted} &= \log_2 \text{ of } 1/0.5\\ &= \log_2 \text{ of } 2\\ &= 1 \text{ bit.}\end{aligned}$$

If there is a 100% (1.0) chance that the next signal will be a 0, the information conveyed by the 0 will be:

$$\begin{aligned}\text{Information transmitted} &= \log_2 \text{ of } 1/1.0\\ &= \log_2 \text{ of } 1\\ &= 0 \text{ bits.}\end{aligned}$$

In other words, if the message in a signal is known in advance, the signal carries no information.

It is worth pointing out the significance of the basic idea of information value to the management accountant:

1 Information which is already known will be of relatively low value. A management accounting report which reports information which is already known will be of relative unimportance or will at least not cause much interest within an organisation. Reporting over sufficiently short periods and producing reports shortly after the end of a period would appear to increase the potential impact of management accounting information.

2 The more uncertain the events to be described, the more valuable will be information produced. Information systems designers are unlikely to produce valuable information if their systems report on certain events.

ONE AND TWO WAY COMMUNICATIONS

An example of one way communication is given by the television. The receiver is not allowed to communicate with the transmitter. All signals pass from the transmitter to the receiver. Some management accounting systems may also provide examples, where the management accountant prepares reports, dispatches them to appropriate recipients as listed on a distribution list and does not seek reactions. The recipient simply considers the report and the reporting cycle begins again, with the management accountant working to produce the next set of reports.

Two way communication allows both ends of a communication channel to pass signals to each other. An example is the telephone. Management accounting reporting may also provide an example. The management accountant prepares a report and issues it to a suitable audience. Formal or informal meetings are then set up so that the results and implications of the report can be discussed. The management accountant and the recipients of information talk to each other and can thus resolve any points of interest in a two way discussion.

It has been clearly established that two way systems are more effective forms of communication than one way systems. To prove this, try the Chinese Whispers experiment that was used to explain distortion, but allow neighbours to discuss quietly before the message is passed to the next neighbour. By establishing a contact between neighbours and by allowing questions to be asked, less distortion should arise.

SUMMARY

Planning and control can be important to management as short-term, or tactical, mechanisms and long-term, or strategic, mechanisms to ensure that the objectives of a particular organisation are met. Strategy is a formal mechanism whereby objectives are set and the means by which objectives are to be met are resolved, possibly through a position audit, an environment analysis and gap analysis. Management controls can be established to ensure that the process of meeting strategic goals is met satisfactorily. Operational controls affect the real time management of everyday tasks from which data can be collected to provide information for management control. In recent years, communications theory has had an increasing influence on the ways in which management accountants think about their reporting systems and terms such as distortion have entered the language of the management accountant.

EXERCISES

Exercise 20.1

In the context of budgeting, describe the meaning of and write notes on four of the following terms:
Feedback control;
Feedforward control;
Noise;
Distortion;
Short-term plan;
Long-term plan.

(*ACCA, Management Accounting, December 1986, adapted*)

Answers on page 601

Exercise 20.2

Explain the specific roles of planning, control and evaluation in a system of budgeting and budgetary control.

(*ACCA, Management Accounting, June 1987, adapted*)

Answers on page 601

Exercise 20.3

Explain the operation of a formal system of planning and control involving the routine use of short- and long-term budgeting. Assess the advantages of such a system over an informal or ad hoc system of planning and control.

Answer in lecturer's manual.

Organisational Implications of Management Accounting Systems

INTRODUCTION

The influence of management accounting systems on organisations, in particular on the behaviour of individuals in organisations, has been the subject of considerable research in the last thirty-five years. This research has provided a substantial volume of evidence about the impacts of control and evaluation on the organisations for which management accountants work. With a knowledge of this evidence, it can be expected that management accountants of the future will be able to design and implement their systems in a way which ensures that systems create beneficial rather than damaging effects.

The structure of the chapter is as follows:

1 A background section provides one explanation for the differences in research findings and opinion which contribute to the wealth of contemporary knowledge about the organisational implications of management accounting systems (Section 21.1).

2 The scene is set by showing ways in which accounting systems do not achieve the outcomes intended by accountants because of their impacts on people (Section 21.2).

3 Examples taken from the substantial literature on the topic are used to raise some of the more important issues. The framework used to assemble these examples is illustrated in Figure 21.1. Organisational structure and management style influence the operation of groups which themselves have an impact on the individual (Sections 21.3, 21.4 and 21.5 respectively).

4 Three general approaches to the design of technical systems are described. The student is recommended to design management accounting systems which consider the wider context of the organisation, its groups and individuals, working in its environment. Information systems require the accountant to deal with the social aspects as well as the technical aspects of their systems (Section 21.6).

The interested student will want to read further in this substantial area of management accounting. Two books are particularly recommended: Emmanuel and Otley, *Accounting for management control;* Macintosh, *The social software of accounting and information systems.* These were both published in the mid 1980s. For the latest research findings, students are referred to the journal *Accounting, Organisations and Society.* Articles from this journal provide detailed accounts of the latest thoughts on many of the issues raised in this chapter.

By the end of the chapter, the student should be able to discuss the various factors which have been seen to affect the operation of management accounting systems from an organisational point of view. This is an area of study which has been popular with professional accounting examiners. The student should be able to clearly explain key terms and be able to debate issues where there are no clear right or wrong answers.

21.1 THE DEBATE ON ORGANISATIONAL THEORY

Astley and Van de Ven provide a concise summary of the debate on organisational theory. The debate exists because a number of the issues pertaining to human behaviour have existed throughout the recorded history of mankind, without being satisfactorily resolved for all cultures at all time. One of these fundamental issues is the extent to which mankind is self determining; are individuals free to determine their own future or is the whole of experience determined in advance? Astley and Van de Ven refer to the former view as representing a voluntarist orientation and the latter as a deterministic orientation.

A voluntarist orientation provides the strategic choice view. Managers can be proactive and can determine their own futures and the futures of their organisations with a reasonable expectation of achieving the objectives which are established. A free choice in planning and decision-making is possible and managers can shape their worlds through political and social actions. Strategic management is associated with this school of thought; organisations are challenged to develop long-term plans, to determine their own destiny and to monitor events as they arise so that objectives can be achieved. Plans can be created and plans can be changed to meet the needs of members of the organisation.

A deterministic orientation sees behaviour as constrained by external or environmental mechanisms which act upon the organisation and determine its future. This is essentially the systems theory perspective; an organisation is seen as adapting to meet changes in the environment through a process of feedback. The management role is to be reactive; as events arise which differ from expectations, corrective action results in the organisation adapting to meet the demands of its environment. Relationships between people are not so much determined by social or political forces but by their roles and hierarchy. People work to ensure that the organisation functions effectively, efficiently and economically in the face of a hostile environment. For instance, a managing director directs the overall operations of a particular company, the financial director, marketing director and technical director each have their own specific roles which they play for the benefit of the organisation as a whole.

Within these broad categories, a number of schools have developed. The contribution of the individual schools to research on the impacts of management accounting will not be spelt out in the chapter which follows, but the discerning reader may be able to spot the general orientation of individual contributions. One school of thought will need to be considered in its own section, however. This is that associated with the term contingency theory, considered by Astley and Van de Ven to represent a deterministic orientation.

Since this most fundamental debate on the nature of mankind has not been resolved and yet influences attitudes to the impacts of management accounting information, it is essential for students to state references to authorities in answers presented to examiners. For this reason, this chapter contains many more references than does any other in the book.

FIGURE 21.1

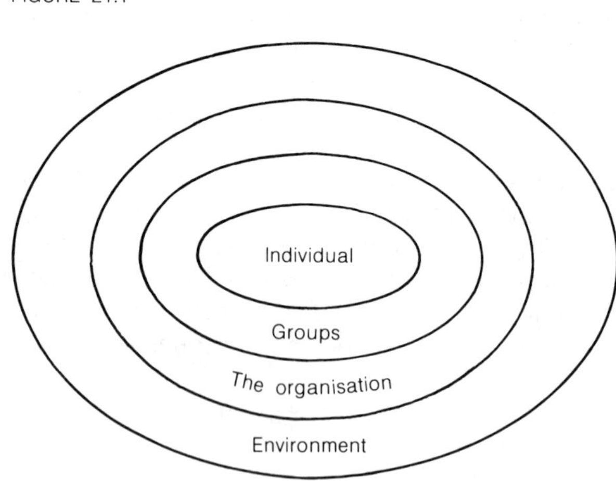

21.2 THE NEGATIVE IMPACTS OF CONTROLS

21.2.1 The contribution of Argyris

In 1952, Argyris investigated the use of budgets by going inside an organisation to collect evidence. He found that the accountant's point of view towards budgets differed somewhat from that held by budget centre managers. In particular, from the accountant's point of view:

1 Budgetary control was concerned with uncovering errors and mistakes so that corrective action could lead to improved efficiency. Where no negative variances arose, the accountant found it difficult to quantify the benefits of accountancy. Where correcting negative variances resulted in increased profits, the accountant could point to a measurable benefit to management of investing in an accounting function. Success for the accountant was seen in terms of exposing the failures of managers and supervisors.

2 Budgets were seen as a powerful force to motivate employees. Managers were considered to be motivated to achieve organisational objectives if a budget communicated those objectives down through the organisation. The accountant did not acknowledge that the manager may have personal goals which may have been in conflict with the goals of the organisation. Goal congruence, the situation where all members of the organisation work towards the same goals, which coincide with organisational objectives, is not seen to be a consideration in the design of budgeting systems. In reality, individuals may pursue their own goals to the detriment of the organisation and a lack of goal congruence may become significant. Accountants believe that the budget centre manager would react unselfishly and rationally to the challenge presented by a budget so as to meet planned targets.

Unfortunately, managers did not necessarily share the accountants' views:

1 Budgets were used frequently and strongly as a pressure device to maintain the authority of senior managers. Middle managers rarely used budgets to control subordinates because production workers would respond with resentment, hostility and aggression towards the company with a consequent loss of production.

2 Budgets were used to apply pressure to improve efficiency and effectiveness but insulted personal dignity rather than creating the motivation to improve performance. Budgets were commonly felt to contain unrealistic goals.

That success for the accountant resulted in failure for the manager created a potential for conflict. The impact of the budget was dysfunctional; it did not create the results it was designed to create. Budget centre managers could respond to the pressure exerted by senior management by forming groups to combat pressure rather than by being motivated to improve performance. Budgets had little effect at the operational level of the organisation.

Argyris suggested solutions to the problems of budgeting: human relations training for accountants, group discussions to promote more positive responses to budgets and a participative management style. This final point, in particular, has proved to be the subject of substantial research in the years which have followed.

21.2.2 Other contributions

Since the Argyris study, a number of authors have discovered a number of failings in budgeting, performance evaluation and control systems in general. The following list provides an insight into the issues raised:

1 Internal control and evaluation targets may aim to establish conformity to laid down procedures and rules. Since managers are rewarded for conforming, they need only learn how to follow procedures and to play the game well. The rules of the game are laid down by targets such as Return on Capital Employed which are measured through accounting conventions and can be distorted by shrewd managers. Typical devices are depreciating fixed assets in a way which ensure good performance results and depleting stock levels at period ends.

Merton found that in these conditions, management behaves in a simplistic, rigid and defensive manner. This impairs the effectiveness of an organisation which is undergoing change. Senior management may attempt to improve effectiveness by implementing even more controls.

2 Selznick studied decentralisation. The effect of decentralising may be that individuals acquire loyalties to their divisions and become motivated to improve local performance, even where this is to the detriment of the organisation as a whole. This phenomenon is normally termed sub-optimisation. The organisation as a whole fails to achieve optimum results due to individual segments optimising their own results. Chapter 10 showed that residual income approaches can

be used by management accountants to reduce sub-optimisation as measured by the routine, formal, quantified reporting of information.

3 Emmanuel and Otley provide numerous references to studies which show that distortion of budgeting and performance evaluation can result from behavioural causes. Managers may see advantages in setting themselves easy targets by building slack into their budgets. A cost budget can be overstated so that reported results appear to be favourable. Plans might be biased rather than objective. Profits may be stated incorrectly in one year so that favourable impressions are gained in following years.

Such bias can have a harmful effect on the organisation in the long-term, as illustrated by Dopuch, Birnberg and Demski. They give a time sheet example. Workers may report that they are spending the majority of their time on productive activity rather than non-productive activity to make their performance appear to be efficient even though this is not the case. Knowing that data is being biased, management may apply an adjustment to compensate for the distortion, but it is difficult to be certain that the adjustment is reasonable. Additionally, the adjustment can be a source of conflict between manager and worker and the worker may respond by reporting even less non-productive time. Lower productivity may result from increased conflict. Evaluation thus becomes difficult and performance may deteriorate. Perhaps even more importantly, according to Dopuch, Birnberg and Demski, the quality of management decision-making can be affected. How can management use accounting data as the basis for decision-making when the data is unreliable?

Self-assessment question 21.1

Write brief notes for each of the following negative results of the implementation of controls:

1 lack of goal congruence;
2 the budget is taken to be a pressure device;
3 conflict;
4 simplistic, rigid and defensive management;
5 sub-optimisation;
6 dysfunctional decision-making;
7 bias or budget slack.

Answers on page 603

Given the existence of a range of negative results of control systems, research in the years following Argyris' contribution has explored his suggestions for improvement and raised other issues of importance to the design and implementation of management accounting systems. The sections which follow discuss some of these issues.

21.3 ORGANISATIONAL STRUCTURE AND MANAGEMENT STYLE

21.3.1 Organisational structure, the environment and accounting systems design

Small organisations can be managed without undue difficulty on a centralised basis. As growth and complexity increase, centralised managers find it increasingly difficult to maintain the local knowledge to make effective day to day decisions and the social contacts with workers to be able to motivate effectively. If the organisation remains centralised, it may need to establish uniform procedures and policies which are implemented by local managers who are allowed little discretion or autonomy. In behavioural terms, this may undermine the authority of the manager and cause a lack of respect from subordinates. Divisionalisation has the effect of splitting large and complex organisations into small businesses again. Responsibility is given to divisional heads to manage their division with authority and thus to make decisions from the basis of local knowledge and to motivate individuals with whom personal contact can be maintained.

Emmanuel and Otley bring together material from different sources to support their views on organisational design. They see appropriate control being influenced by the environment within which the organisation operates, including the degree of uncertainty experienced. The following specific points, raised by Emmanuel and Otley, can have an important influence on the way in which management accountants design systems:

1 Control over the behaviour of individuals can be exercised personally, as when a manager gives direct commands to subordinates, or through a hierarchy. Organisational charts will normally show the formal hierarchy, with, for example, the board of directors at the top of the chart, linked to managers responsible to individual board directors, supervisors responsible to managers and production workers responsible to supervisors. If the production director wishes to control the behaviour of an individual production worker, indirect commands can be sent through the appropriate manager and supervisor. As uncertainty increases, control can become less personal, moving towards control over outputs through production and sales reports, or control over inputs, the resources used by an organisation in meeting its objectives. Reward systems such as bonuses may become important impersonal devices for motivating managers.

2 For a centralised structure, increasing the number of levels or complexity in the hierarchy may lead to the need to re-design communications channels. As each new layer is added to the hierarchy, so information goes through further filtering processes before arriving at the top management level. If managers bias information, by suppressing information which is detrimental to their personal futures, control loss results. This may make it difficult to co-ordinate the separate parts of the organisation effectively. Information passes both upwards and downwards in organisations and distortion of strategic information can lead to the inappropriate definition of operational control tasks. Divisional heads may be in competition with each other for the scarce resources of the organisation and deficiencies in communication effectiveness can result in opportunist behaviour, where one manager can pass distorted information to senior management in order to gain a competitive advantage over other divisional managers.

3 Organisations are made up of individuals. These individuals have their own objectives and it may not be possible to ensure that these objectives can be made congruent with organisational objectives, particularly in non-programmed situations. In these circumstances, behaviour which is acceptable to top management as a means by which the organisation can develop in a positive manner is of paramount importance. Behaviour congruence replaces goal congruence. Emmanuel and Otley argue that non-programmed decisions are dominant in organisations of any reasonable complexity, facing uncertainty.

4 The major theoretical basis for the views presented by Emmanuel and Otley is contingency theory. This theory argues that there is not a single rule of organisation or management which is best for all organisations, but that particular factors or variables are important in particular circumstances. These are called contingent factors; the design of organisations is contingent upon certain critical factors. Such factors include technology, the market environment, competition and the nature of the product. Theoretically, there is an optimum form of organisation and management for combinations and characteristics of contingent factors. Unfortunately, the combinations and characteristics are so complex that there is no systematic statement of optimum organisation and management form which has proved acceptable to all.

5 Different organisations have different cultures. Different cultures may be found in the same organisation. The role culture and the existential culture are central to the arguments put forward by Emmanuel and Otley. The role culture seeks to define responsibilities and jobs in a clear, precise and unambiguous manner. The organisational assumption of internal control is that such a culture is the predominant means by which organisational effectiveness, efficiency and economy can be achieved. The existential culture is based on individuals meeting their own personal needs. Numerous organisations, including universities, polytechnics, colleges and schools, are designed to allow individuals, such as students, as members of those organisations, to meet their personal needs of self-development.

Self-assessment question 21.2

The following table is a summary of views about the implications of organisational design on the design of management accounting systems.

	Conditions of certainty	Conditions of uncertainty
Contingent factors		
Rate of change	Low	High
Predictability	High	Low
Competitive hostility	Low	High
Product range	Homogeneous	Heterogeneous
Corporate responses		
Organisational design	Centralisation	De-centralisation
Control system assumptions		
Congruence	Goals	Behaviours
Culture	Role	Existential
Systems aims	Functional efficiency	Divisional effectiveness
Accounting information system characteristics		
Participation	No participation	Divisional managers participate in planning
Rewards	Linked to financial performance measures	Not linked to financial performance
Evaluation criterion	Short-term, budget constraints	Long-term trend, including non-financial and qualitative measures

(*Emmanuel and Otley, adapted*)

Explain as many of the ideas presented in the above table as you can and relate them to your understanding of contingency theory.

Answers on page 603

21.3.2 Management style

CLASSIFICATION OF MANAGEMENT STYLE: LIKERT

The following quotation comes from Likert's book, New Patterns of Management:

'The supervisors and managers in American industry and government who are achieving the highest productivity, lowest costs, least [labour] turnover and absence, and the highest levels of employee motivation and satisfaction display, on the average, a different pattern of leadership from those managers who are achieving less impressive results.'

If these aims can be achieved by management style, perhaps accountants should be aware of the different types of style and tailor management accounting systems accordingly.

Likert classified managers into three groups: the highest-producing managers, the mediocre-producing managers and the low-producing managers. His research then led him to consider the characteristics of the highest-producing managers. For these managers, he found:

1 Favourable attitudes amongst members of the organisation, towards each other, towards superiors, towards the work and towards the organisation. There was a high commitment to the achievement of organisational objectives, expressed through high performance goals and great dissatisfaction when results fell short of objectives.

2 Motivation was not concerned with the economic motive alone (rewarding through increased salaries or bonuses, for example), but with a range of motivations:
   (a) The ego motive; recognition was given to the need of the individual to achieve personal development and to achieve personal goals such as 'self-fulfilment, . . . status, recognition, approval, acceptance and power and the desire to undertake significant and important tasks.'
   (b) The security motive; the individual may need to feel secure about the organisation and the individual's position in the future of that organisation, rather than feel the insecurity which comes from threats such as redundancy.
   (c) Curiosity, creativity, and the desire for new experiences.
   (d) The economic motive.

3 The organisation is seen as a closely knit, effective social system. The system is made up of a number of sub-systems or groups of individuals with a high degree of group loyalty.

4 Performance measurement is used for self-guidance and not for control purposes. Participation and involvement are essential parts of the leadership process and information is fully shared. Part of the information process is concerned with realising that additional information is required and being able to take steps to make that additional information available.

The following quotation is revealing of Likert's view, especially in the light of the ideas that were required to be explained for self-assessment question 21.2:

'The low-producing managers, in keeping with traditional practice, feel that the way to motivate and direct behaviour is to exercise control through authority. Jobs are organised, methods are prescribed, standards are set, performance goals and budgets are established. Compliance with them is sought through the use of hierarchical and economic pressures.'

There are numerous ways in which management accounting systems can be designed and used within organisations. Likert's high-producing management use accounting data to provide information and information becomes a thing of value within the organisation. New information is requested as it becomes necessary, and new information is provided in response to managers' requests. Low-producing managers, in Likert's view, work through a hierarchical organisation structure to impose compliance to accounting and other control data.

CLASSIFICATION OF MANAGEMENT STYLE: McGREGOR

McGregor classified management styles according to assumptions about human behaviour. There are two extremes; theory X, referred to as the traditional view of direction and control, and theory Y, the integration of individual and organisational goals. Theory X managers make the following assumptions about human behaviour:

1 'The average human being has an inherent dislike of work and will avoid it if he can';

2 'because of this human characteristic of dislike of work, most people must be coerced, controlled, directed, threatened with punishment to get them to put forth adequate effort towards the achievement of organisational objectives';

3 'the average human being prefers to be directed, wishes to avoid responsibility, has relatively little ambition, wants security above all'.

Theory Y managers have quite a different view:

1 'The expenditure of physical and mental effort in work is as natural as play or rest. The average human being does not inherently dislike work';

2 'external control and the threat of punishment are not the only means for bringing about effort toward organisational objectives. Man will exercise self-direction and self-control in the service of objectives to which he is committed';

3 'commitment to objectives is a function of the rewards associated with their achievement'. Such rewards include the satisfaction of ego, as in Likert's views.

4 'the average human being learns, under proper conditions, not only to accept but to seek responsibility';

5 'the capacity to exercise a relatively high degree of imagination, ingenuity and creativity in the solution of organisational problems is widely, not narrowly, distributed in the population';

6 'under the conditions of modern industrial life, the intellectual potentialities of the average human being are only partially utilised.'

McGregor feels that these assumptions are important determinants of the ability of organisations to change and to innovate. Changes of the kind brought about by technology are unlikely to be managed successfully if organisations are managed and controlled in the theory X manner. McGregor concludes:

'Genuine innovation, in contrast to a re-furbishing and patching of present managerial strategies, requires first the acceptance of less limiting assumptions about the nature of the human resources we seek to control [ie theory X assumptions], and second the readiness to adapt selectively to the implications contained in those new assumptions [ie theory Y assumptions]. Theory Y is an invitation to innovation.'

Management accounting systems can either reflect theory X or theory Y assumptions. The decision to investigate only adverse variances may presume that unfavourable situations will continue unless the accountant intervenes. It may be as important to meet ego needs by pointing out favourable variances. Monitoring performance measures and formally reporting deficiencies may presume that managers need external stimulus to improve results; that self-motivation will not lead to the manager taking necessary action upon the receipt of suitable information.

CLASSIFICATION OF MANAGEMENT STYLE: HOPWOOD

Hopwood classified managers into three categories: budget-constrained, profit-conscious and non-accounting.

Budget-constrained managers are evaluated according to their ability to comply with budgeted targets. Such managers are highly cost conscious but tend to have poor relations with other people in the organisation and experience a high degree of tension in their working lives. There is every reason for budget-constrained managers to manipulate accounting information in order to bias reported results in their favour.

Profit-conscious managers are evaluated on the basis of their ability to generate profits. Budgets may still be employed, but these are used as a tool to guide performance rather than as a strait-jacket to enforce compliance with pre-set targets. Such managers enjoy good relationships with others. They are motivated to achieve the economic objectives of the organisation and convert such motivation into profit-related actions. There is little manipulation of accounting information.

Non-accounting managers make little use of accounting information. This results in little cost consciousness, against which can be set good working relationships.

From the accountant's point of view, the implementation of systems which promote profit consciousness would appear to be best, within the confines of this model of management style.

21.4 GROUPS, PARTICIPATION AND BARGAINING

21.4.1 Becker and Green

Argyris suggested that one of the responses to the problems of budgetary control might be to promote participation. Becker and Green found that participation alone could not guarantee the success of budgets but that the attitudes of the group involved in the participative process were important. The following table summarises their view.

Group cohesiveness	Attitude to budget	Outcome
High	Positive	Maximum motivation and efficiency
Low	Positive	Efficient performance
Low	Negative	Depressed production results
High	Negative	Production slow down

Maximum motivation and efficiency resulted from high group cohesiveness and a positive attitude to budgeting. This supported the work of other authorities in showing the importance of the group as a basic unit to be managed. It also reveals that participation can be a force for good or bad.

21.4.2 Hofstede

Hofstede considered the traditional view of participation. This suggests that participation in the setting of standards, such as those contained in budgets and standard costing systems, leads to higher performance because involvement brings advantages of better communication and motivation. He found that the reality of participation is not quite this simple. This led him to suggest an improved model of participation, as follows:

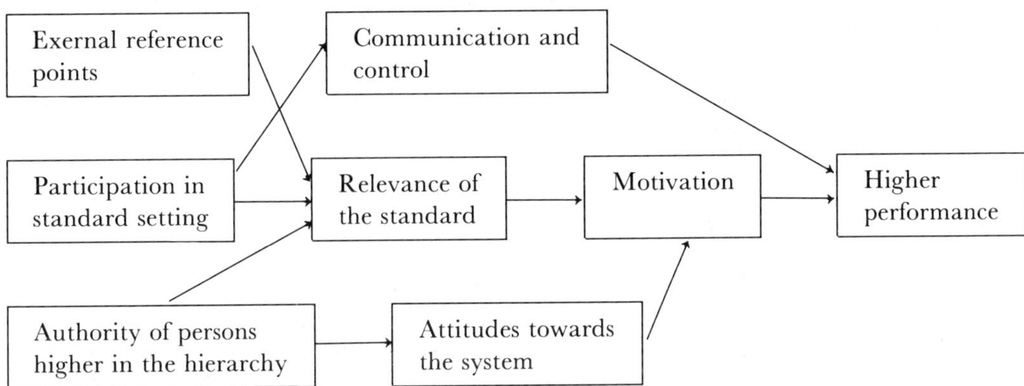

Higher performance was found to be a function of motivation, communication and control. Motivation, itself, depended upon the relevance of the standard and attitudes towards the system, which in turn were governed by external reference points, participation in standard setting and the authority of senior managers. A standard price might be assessed against the reference point of the price charged by suppliers, and if the standard proved to be unreasonable and this shortcoming was not overcome by positive attitudes to the system, then managers would not be motivated by the accounting system. Communication and control depend upon the level of participation, which can also help to improve the relevance of the standard.

Hofstede contributed the idea that accountants and top management should instil a game spirit into the budgeting process. A well-played game is one where involvement, co-operation and a positive contribution from people within the organisation results. By providing rules of the game in the form of performance targets, the budget becomes a way of shaping behaviours. Previous sections have already suggested some of the negative consequences of the game, notably the distortion of information by the manipulation of accounting data; changing figures in reports in order to give the appearance of good performance, for instance. A range of permissible accounting outcomes is more commonly applicable to business situations. In such circumstances, a poorly played game may be one where a divisional manager wins by biasing results towards the favourable end of the spectrum of acceptable accounting figures.

21.4.3 Schiff and Lewin

Schiff and Lewin found that participation allowed managers to build slack into their budgets at the planning stage. Examples might include:

1. Stating cost standard at levels which did not take into account known planned improvements;
2. allowing budgets for discretionary costs such as advertising to become a 'permission to spend' rather than a guarantee that benefits would be achieved to more than cover costs;
3. increased personnel levels were planned and then recruitment deferred to provide a tolerance between budget and reported results.

The result of this could be bargained budgets, where the amount of bias can easily become unknown. A process called pseudo-participation may arise;

1. Middle managers are asked for budget targets, which they provide;
2. senior managers suspect that slack has been built into the targets which managers have set for themselves and so tighter targets are recommended for adoption by middle management;

3 a final budget may result from bargaining, where middle managers seek to slacken targets whilst senior managers seek to tighten targets. In some cases, budgets are simply finalised by senior management and middle managers are called upon to meet targets over which they had little real influence;

4 at the next budget cycle, the skilled middle manager either starts to build in slack or increases the level of slack previously built in. It is anticipated that senior management will tighten budgets irrespective of the levels managers set.

Slack is a form of bias and has the harmful effects discussed earlier. However, Onsi points out that slack can have a beneficial effect by reducing the harmful effects of personal stress and uncertainty. A slack budget may be beneficial to an organisation facing an uncertain future. Where budgets suggest cash flow deficiencies, for example, action can be taken in advance to ensure that funds will be made available should the worst situation arise.

21.5 MOTIVATION AND THE INDIVIDUAL

There are numerous theories about motivation. Two examples of these theories come from the writings and research of Maslow and Herzberg. Maslow argued that people are motivated to meet their needs. These can range from satisfying basic physical needs for food to the ego needs described by Likert; the need for personal growth. Herzberg divided the factors which provide job satisfaction into motivators and hygiene factors. Motivators increase the motivation to improve performance. A deficiency in hygiene factors can lead to job dissatisfaction, because of the need to avoid unpleasantness, but an abundance of these factors does not necessarily improve motivation. Hygiene factors include company policy and administration, supervision, salary, inter-personal relationships and working conditions. Motivators include the nature of work itself, achievement, recognition, responsibility and advancement. The remainder of this section concentrates on the notion of achievement and relates achievement to motivation within the confines of budgeting situations.

21.5.1 Expectancy theory

This theory suggests that motivation results from two influences:

1 The likelihood that a particular outcome will arise;
2 the value of the outcome to a particular individual.

This could be applied to an example of a budgeting situation as illustrated by the small case study which follows. Fictional names have been used because the events actually occurred within a company with international standing.

Example

Joe Soap had progressed successfully through a large multi-divisional organisation by means of a succession of promotions. His latest appointment was in a loss-making division of a struggling subsidiary company, the Cut and Paste Division. There was every expectation that Joe would turn the division into a success, despite problems caused by inexpensive imports which had undermined the market for the particular product marketed by Cut and Paste. One dominant customer had developed the power to restrict prices so that Joe had no choice but to follow a high quality and low pricing strategy. This resulted in low margins for the majority of the product range.

Past success had led Joe to the belief that he could be successful in creating profits for the division and he devoted fourteen hours a day to enthusiastic management. The following devices reveal the methods he used to promote profitability:

1 A strategy of expansion was implemented. Decisions were taken within the divison to purchase additional premises in order to expand output. Funds were required for this purpose and the division approached the group company with a proposal. Group Head Office insisted on a DCF calculation. First estimates revealed an IRR of 28% and Joe approached Group officials on an informal basis with this information. Group officials stated that their experience had shown that proposals showing less than 30% turned out to be unsuccessful and that they would not recommend purchase of the premises. Joe discussed the matter with his Divisional Accountant and formally submitted a proposal showing an IRR of 34%. It was accepted.

2 Every item which could conceivably be described as capital expenditure was capitalised. The amount of work this created was immense; invoiced items of less than £1 were taken into the capital expenditure system. Eventually, company accountants called a halt to this process because their already stretched plant register section could not cope with the volume of data coming from the Cut and Paste division.

3 A major task for the divisional accountant was the production of "debit notes" for claims against suppliers. The organisation was vertically integrated, with group divisions providing the input to other group divisions. The majority of these claims were therefore internal to the group. Joe developed the reputation of being an aggressive negotiator and all claims were quickly settled. Joe included every consequential loss arising from problems of supply; downtime was measured in terms of lost contribution, the cost of the other raw materials which had been used before the supply problem became apparent were claimed, all labour costs were included and an allowance was made for overhead based on absorption costing principles.

4 Transfers between divisions were charged on a rate agreed with Group Head Office by a means of three way negotiation between Head Office, supplier divisions and customer divisions. Supplier divisions happened to be politically strong and so Joe could do nothing about raw material prices. However, some ad hoc transfers between divisions occurred from time to time. These were always settled by local negotiation, avoiding head office involvement. Joe had the reputation for being tough but fair and usually came out of negotiations with transfer prices which were advantageous to the Cut and Paste Division.

At the end of his first, full year in charge of Cut and Paste, the division showed a profit for the first time in some years.

This case study illustrates a number of the ideas covered in this chapter, but in particular the ability to explain motivation in terms of expectancy theory. The divisional director strongly believed that the division could become profitable. Otherwise, it would have made little sense for him to work as long and hard as he did and to go to virtually any length to achieve his purpose. Previous directors had believed that profitability constituted an impossible aim due to factors beyond their control; particularly the impact of imports and the dominant position of one customer able to force a price-taking situation on the division. These previous directors had been unable to find the motivation to improve performance and had been eventually demoted to other positions or asked to leave the Group of Companies. The Divisional Director also had reason to believe that the effort of achieving a profitable situation would be valuable to him on a personal basis since previous successes had furthered his own goals of promotion. It was widely accepted that he aimed for eventual promotion to the Group Board of Directors.

The value of the outcome to the individual is combined with two likelihoods associated with outcome. The first is that some form of effort is able to produce an acceptable level of performance. The divisional director did not expend effort in lobbying Parliament to control imports or in negotiating higher prices with the dominant customer because these were not felt to be means which would positively lead to profit. The second likelihood is that the performance would lead to the desired outcome or reward. The director valued promotion and felt that profit would result in promotion. The motivation to improve performance would not have arisen for an individual who believed that effort would not have resulted in profit or who could see no form of reward resulting from the achievement of profit.

21.5.2 Aspiration levels

A budget provides a target toward which managers may or may not aim. It has been argued by Kay and Meyer that improvements in performance only result from situations where specific objectives have been set and agreed in time and measurement terms. A problem may arise from the agreement of objectives; what happens, for instance, where a manager is forced by an imposed budget to meet a target which is not perceived by the manager to be feasible? Expectancy theory suggests that no motivation would result from this situation. In exploring this particular situation, it is useful to differentiate the budget as a target and the target which a manager believes to be attainable. This latter target can replace the budget as a personal target or aspiration level.

STEDRY

Stedry conducted an experiment where participants were given different types of budget, relating to specific tasks, and their later performance monitored. They were asked to state their aspiration levels, or the performance they hoped to achieve. Four types of budget were used with different groups:

1 A high or challenging budget;
2 A medium budget;
3 A low budget;
4 Participants were not provided with goals.

Participants provided information on their aspiration levels.

The following results were revealing:

1 Low budgets were associated with low performance.
2 Performance declined where high budgets were provided which were above aspiration levels previously stated;
3 The best performance was in groups which received high budgets and set their aspiration levels after seeing the budget target.

This suggests that managers may perform best where they are provided with a challenge which they can then internalise or accept at a personal level. If managers have already formed opinions on performance levels and these opinions conflict with imposed budgets, then performance will suffer, but will not be worse than where low budgets have been set.

HOFSTEDE

Hofstede proposed the framework shown in Figure 21.2.

It is assumed that if a normal expense level arises from setting no budget, actual results will vary about the norm as a function of performance. Improved performance will provide a result lower than the normal level of cost and deteriorations in performance will lead to costs exceeding the norm. The budget line sloping downwards from left to right represents an ever greater challenge to the manager.

A loose or low budget, in terms of the challenged presented to the manager, results in actual costs exceeding the norm, as results reflect aspiration levels set for a poor level of performance. Favourable variances are shown even though performance is worse than the norm. As the budget becomes tighter, or more challenging, so aspiration levels and performance improve. Results better than the norm occur even though adverse variances are reported. There will be some effort to minimise the adverse variances and so aspiration levels will be set for better and better levels of

FIGURE 21.2

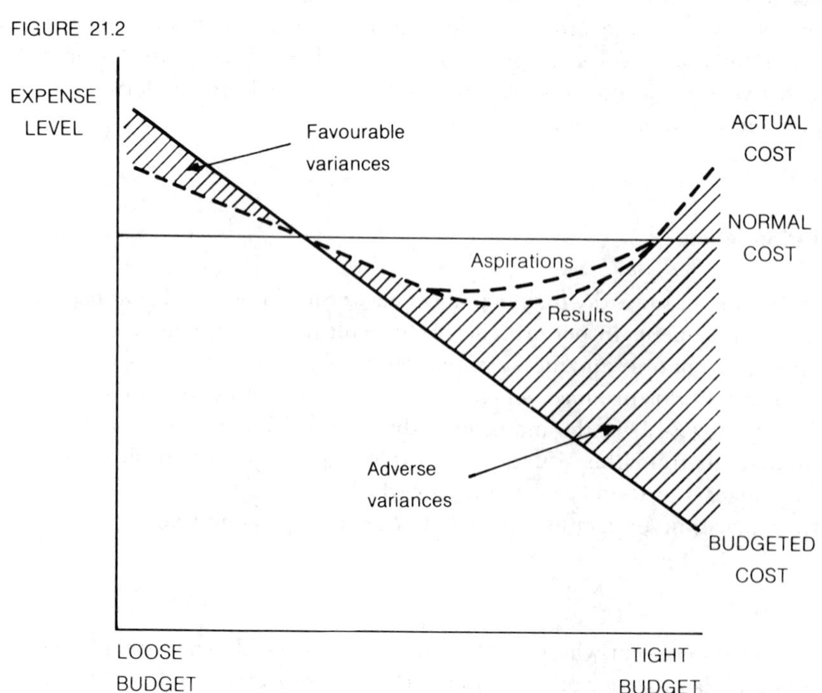

performance. At some stage, the aspiration levels will cease to be attainable and results will not match personal targets. As budgets become increasingly impossible to meet, results and aspiration levels will deteriorate. Eventually, budgets become so impossible that aspiration levels are no longer set and performance deteriorates to the poor level similar to setting low budgets.

This point of view argues that up to a certain point, challenging budgets motivate and result in improved performance. Budgets, aspiration levels and performance are related through impacts on motivation. Excessively challenging budgets have negative impacts on motivation to improve performance.

Atkinson made similar points, relating these to success and failure as represented by favourable and adverse variance outcomes:

1. Where a manager prefers to achieve success rather than avoid failure, medium budgets are best. Low or high budgets demotivate.
2. Where a manager prefers to avoid failure rather than achieve success, managers are demotivated by medium budgets because adverse variances are reported. Better results are gained by setting low budgets and even high budgets were better for such management's performance than medium budgets.

Hopwood suggested that the solution to budgeting problems might be to set two budgets: an expectations budget and an aspirations budget. An expectations budget provides a plan based on reasonable predictions of the future and strategic considerations. An aspirations budget provides a target which will promote motivation.

21.6 DESIGN OF ACCOUNTING INFORMATION SYSTEMS

Figures 21.3, 21.4 and 21.5 provide three different views on design for the workplace.

Figure 21.3 suggests that design need only be concerned with technical aspects. Applying this to accountancy, this is the view that the accountant need only concentrate on producing numbers and reports which add up and balance and are appropriate to particular circumstances. Argyris provides evidence that this view can lead to dysfunctional consequences.

Figure 21.4 is associated with the Tavistock Institute and, for instance, the work of Trist and Bamforth in the coal mining industry. They found that effective management involved considering technical and social implicatons of designing tasks such as coal mining. Social and technical factors need to be co-optimised; it is not sufficient merely to have the best technical system available if the aim is to maximise performance. Social factors such as relationships between people are as important as technical factors. Applying this principle to the design of Accounting Information Systems such as budgeting, the accountant must consider the effects of accounting systems on managers as well as the technical problems of calculating financial figures. This leads to budgets which allow an appropriate level of participation and which motivate managers through the impact on aspiration levels. Different forms of organisation, from fully centralised at one extreme, to fully de-centralised at the other extreme should also be considered as a means of achieving management accounting objectives.

Figure 21.5 is normally associated with ergonomics. Ergonomics is concerned with how machines can be designed with optimum effects when they come to be used with people. Car seat designs, computer video display screens and forms and layout of machine monitoring gauges are amongst the subjects of interest to the ergonomist. The implication of the ergonomics approach to the accountant is that it stresses that people must be at the centre of the design of technical systems and

FIGURE 21.3

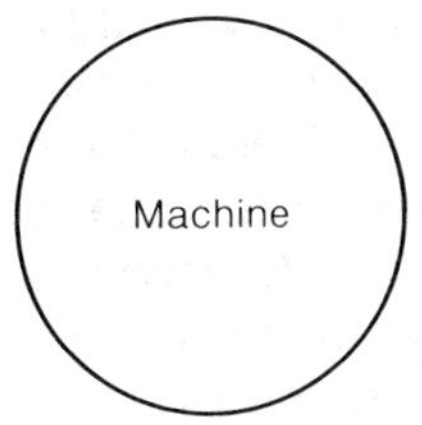

Technical optimisation

FIGURE 21.4

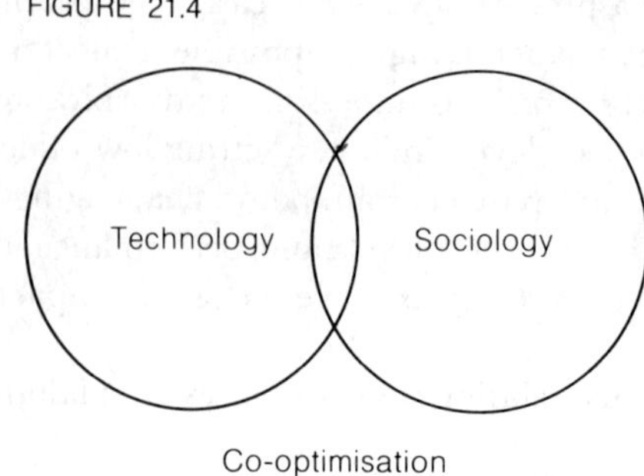

Co-optimisation

FIGURE 21.5

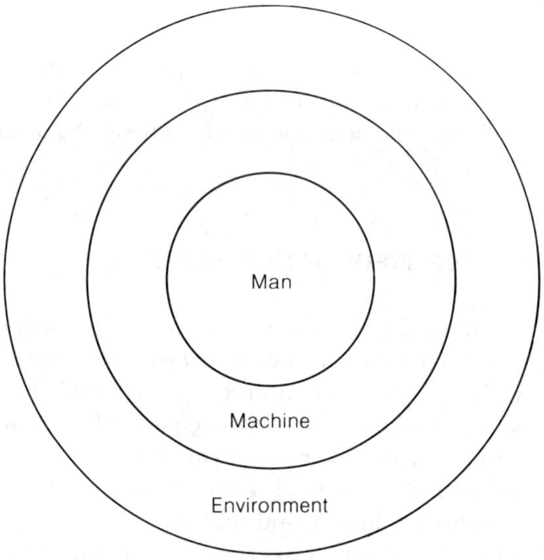

Man

Machine

Environment

the environmental factors should also be taken into account. Contingency theory suggests that there is no single accounting system specification which will be optimum for all circumstances. Good accounting systems design derives from an appropriate design response to the factors impinging on a particular organisation at a particular time or phase in its development.

SUMMARY

It can be argued that organisational studies, including the study of the behaviour of people in organisations, are essential to the development of the management accountant. Accountants design systems for people. Accountants' systems affect the level of motivation and conflict which can arise in groupings of people. Accountants affect the lives of people by measuring their performance and providing an evaluation of the success and failures of individuals and groups.

Unlike the balancing of a balance sheet, where one set of figures will give rise to success, there is no single answer to how accountants should produce accounts which have a beneficial effect on the people around them. At an academic level, this can be explained in terms of debates which go back to the dawn of civilisation. There are numerous views about how people behave. This chapter provides a summary of views about the organisational considerations which have been influential in shaping current attitudes to accountancy and people. These attitudes can be broadly placed into three groups; environmental factors and the organisation, groups within organisations and the individual within organisations.

EXERCISES

Exercise 21.1

(a) In the context of budgeting, provide definitions for four of the following terms:
aspiration level;
budgetary slack;
feedback;
contingency theory;
responsibility accounting.

(b) Discuss the motivational implications of the level of efficiency assumed in establishing a budget.

(*ACCA, June 1986, slightly adapted*)

Answers in lecturer's manual.

Exercise 21.2

In the context of budgeting, describe the meaning of and write notes on four of the following terms:
feedback control;
feedforward control;
budgetary slack;
aspiration levels;
control limits;
noise.

(*ACCA, December 1986*)

Answers in lecturer's manual.

Exercise 21.3

Contingency theory states that there are no universally valid rules of organisation and management but that both are dependent on circumstances. Discuss the implications of this theory for management accounting systems.

(*ACCA, December 1986*)

Answers on page 604

Exercise 21.4

Explain the specific roles of planning, motivation and evaluation in a system of budgetary control.

(*ACCA, June 1987*)

Answers in lecturer's manual.

Exercise 21.5

(a) 'Excessive reliance on budgetary control of business and management can have dysfunctional consequences.'

Comment on the relevance of the above statement in relation to each of the following:
(i) Budgetary slack;
(ii) Budget standard setting;
(iii) Short-term versus long-term objectives.

(b) Itemise and comment on the physical and behavioural costs and benefits which could arise from the operation of a standard cost system.

(*ACCA, December 1987*)

Answers on page 604

Exercise 21.6

(a) Discuss the behavioural arguments for and against involving those members of management who are responsible for the implementation of the budget in the annual budget setting process.

(b) Explain how the methods by which annual budgets are formulated might help to overcome behavioural factors likely to limit the efficiency and effectiveness of the budget.

(*ACCA, June 1988*)

Answers in lecturer's manual.

Variance Data for Planning and Control

INTRODUCTION

This chapter is concerned with variance analysis in its most general form. The general term 'variance' is explained and its importance to management is considered. Because variance analysis is not being linked to a specific application, such as standard costing, a general terminology is used and this terminology is explained. A variety of forms of variance is illustrated by means of examples, which are used to show the choice facing the management accountant in designing systems to report variances.

The aims of the chapter are to:

1. Discuss the nature of variance analysis as it relates to the presentation of information to management;
2. Apply variance analysis to non-complex but varied situations;
3. Show that variance analysis can be carried out in different ways and show the importance of objectives, conventions and organisational factors in the design of variance reporting.

It is assumed that the student has a basic knowledge of budgeting, flexible budgets and standard costing but it is advisable that little attempt is initially made to relate the variances shown here to standard costing variance analysis. The framework provided by this chapter is consistent with standard costing variances but is also applicable to any situation where the use of variance reporting may be valuable to management. This chapter aims to develop a degree of flexibility in approaching variances which is necessary at this level of study.

22.1 VARIANCE ANALYSIS

22.1.1 Variance analysis definition

'Variance' means difference. The difference between a budget and an actual result is referred to as a budget variance. In standard costing systems, it is customary to check on the difference between the results of a period and the results that would have been achieved under standard conditions. A variance may be broken down or analysed into further variances by means of 'variance analysis'.

Variances and variance analysis may be useful in situations outside budgeting and standard costing. For this reason, we will not use the terms 'actual', 'budget' and 'standard' but instead talk of 'result' and 'reference data'. The result represents the data management is monitoring, perhaps the historically produced accounting figures for a particular period. The reference data represents the data against which the result is compared. Reference data may take a number of forms:

1. An objective.
2. A budget or flexible budget.
3. A standard.
4. An assessment of the results which should have arisen, prepared after the end of a period.
5. A set of accounts for the previous period.
6. A set of accounts for the same period in the previous year.
7. Data for other divisions or departments within the same group of companies.
8. Data provided by other organisations in the same type of manufacturing or service industry.

A compelling reason for using 'result' and 'reference data', even in standard costing systems, is that words like 'actual' and 'standard' can become misleading. An accountant working in a large UK company once said that 'the problem with standard costing is not calculating the variances but deciding what the 'actual' and 'standard' figures are'. In complex systems, an 'actual' figure can be based on a standard cost valuation.

22.1.2 Implications for management information

There is choice as to how information can be presented and used. Consideration will be given to the ways in which variance data can be presented to provide useful management information and ways in which it can be used to create actions within an organisation. Ultimately, the value of information can be assessed by its effect on the actions which it creates. Information which is presented well creates beneficial actions which contribute to the organisation meeting its objectives. Contingency theory would argue that there is no single way in which variance analysis should be applied in all situations. It should be adapted to meet the needs of individual circumstances.

Management information can take a variety of forms. Financial information such as profit and loss accounts and balance sheets, detailed information on revenues and costs and quantitative data on departmental throughputs are all examples of the types of quantitative data which can be used to provide information for management control. Each of the figures arising from these types of data can be presented:

1 On its own; for example, a sales figure for a period or a profit figure. These are examples of absolute measures.
2 In relation to an equivalent figure; for example, a sales figure can be compared with earlier periods to determine trend. Profit figures can be considered over a period of years in order to assess the success of the company in recent times. Published financial accounts often provide information for a number of years to aid shareholders. These are examples of information on trend.
3 In relation to other figures; for example, profit as a percentage of sales or cost per unit as calculated by process accounts. Interpretation of accounts or analytical review techniques use the relationship between figures, especially in relation to corresponding relationships from previous periods, to form a more complete understanding of a business situation. These are examples of relative measures.
4 As a difference between two figures. This is a measure of variance.

In order to present useful information to management, it is possible that one or more of these approaches will be adopted. For the purpose of our discussion on variances, it is useful to consider the effect of combining the approaches; for instance, variance data can be presented in absolute terms, as a trend, or in relative terms. Considerations which may be borne in mind by the designer of management accounting systems when deciding how to present variance information include:

1 The absolute measure (£s for instance) may show whether or not the company has performed better than expected and by how much. This may be a method for assessing whether or not the company is under control; a zero variance implies that the organisation is performing according to expectations and is thus under control. The existence of a variance may signal to management that an unexpected situation has arisen and that the organisation may have gone out of control.
2 In some circumstances, though not all, the absolute variance will be the amount of profit directly affected by the cause of the variance, as in the example of a standard cost variance. If an adverse standard cost variance of £20,000 arises, a return to standard performance or zero variance will increase profits by £20,000. Where the objective of management is to maximise profits such variances may be particularly important to management.

The drawback to a single absolute measure is that it may not be typical of the way in which the business is operating; the variance may have arisen from chance circumstances which will not repeat in future periods. For this reason, it may be appropriate to consider the trend of the variance.

3 The trend shows how results are performing in relation to reference data over a period of time. Where, for example, a £20,000 adverse standard cost variance has occurred for each of the last six accounting periods the implication is that a permanent change has occurred in the way in which the company is operating. If corrective action has been attempted during the six periods, it may be necessary to revise expectations, as in the case of a supplier's price increase on raw materials, where there are no suitable substitutes. If the variance is reducing, this suggests that the situation is coming under control. If a management accountant can see that a situation is being brought under control, the possibly expensive cost of investigation and correcting the processes which have caused the variance can be avoided.

The drawback to absolute trend information is that the level of activity may vary from period to period; £20,000 may be 20% of cost in one period or 10% in another, if the production doubles.

4 A relative measure such as 20% or 10% of cost shows the materiality of the variance in relation to a relevant base. Consider the following example:

Sales:	£100,000;	£140,000;	£200,000;	£150,000;	£90,000.
Variance:	£10,000;	£14,000;	£20,000;	£15,000;	£9,000.

By considering the separate variances in £ terms, little information is conveyed about the materiality of the variances; for a company with £100 million sales, variances in the range of £9,000 to £20,000 would seem to be insignificant. It is by relating the variance to a base that its significance is more fully understood. Also note how the knowledge that the variance is 10% in all cases increases the information which can be conveyed. Knowledge of the trend of the relative measure allows us to see whether a process is constant, which may help to show that a process is under control.

The problem of determining whether a situation is under control is not resolved in any simple way, as this and other chapters should illustrate. When thinking about examples and when attempting self-questions and exercises, think about the need to consider each of the different ways of presenting information itemised above. Variance data is also limited to those aspects of organisations which can be described in quantitative terms so that the impact of non-quantifiable factors will affect the quality of the information which the management accountant can provide for management use.

It may be possible to automate, or semi-automate control systems through negative feedback or feedforward systems approaches. Under negative feedback systems, the existence of a variance may result in corrective action so that future results become closer to the reference data. This will be discussed in further detail in Chapter 26, 'Interpreting and Investigating Variances'.

Under feedforward systems, the existence of a variance will lead to an analysis of the implications of the variance for the future. A number of situations can arise, for instance:

1 Positive feedback may be an appropriate way of managing a situation. For example, where a favourable sales situation arises, management may seek to encourage the improved trend so that results in the future diverge from the reference data in a way which is advantageous to the organisation.
2 It may be necessary to adopt an open loop approach so that management action is concerned with the revision of expectations or plans. This situation may arise because of a decision significant variance, which is explained in Chapter 26. Alternatively, an unsatisfactory variance may require significant action by creating change in other parts of the business. For example, if an adverse interest cost variance arises because interest rates in a country's economy rise and appear to be set to rise or remain high for the foreseeable future, an organisation may need to reduce costs, improve short-term cash flow, renegotiate loans to a fixed interest basis or, in drastic situations, perhaps sell assets or move to another country where interest rates are acceptable and stable.

The existence of a significant variance is the automatic mechanism which causes action to be taken. An acceptable level of variance results in no action. Management by exception is the name given to this general approach. A clear advantage of applying management by exception is that management does not have to consider every control situation which could arise on a regular basis; the task involved may be too great for even firms of medium complexity. Only exceptional circumstances are managed.

22.2 ONE FACTOR ANALYSIS

22.2.1 Calculation

One factor analysis produces a single variance between two numbers. If a company plans a profit of £100,000 for a particular period and achieves a profit of £90,000, a variance of £10,000 arises. If we assume that the objective of the company is concerned with profitability, the variance is adverse because a lower profit occurs in the result than was expected in the reference data. Generally speaking, the material in this book will show a variance as favourable or adverse because of its effect on profit rather than because deducting one figure from another gives a plus or a minus figure. Hence,

£100,000-£90,000 = £10,000 adverse,

because the result is worse than the reference data in profit terms, not because the difference is plus £10,000.

22.2.2 Examples

The following examples illustrate the use of one-factor analysis and apply some of the ideas raised in Section 22.1.

Example 22.1

Oldcastle Wholesale PLC produces detailed monthly management accounts together with a summary statement. Budgets are prepared for planning purposes and the managing director believes that the company is under control if the actual and budget figures coincide. The company buys finished items which are packaged by means of a recently purchased machine. The latest set of results for Oldcastle Wholesale PLC are provided below:

Management Accounts for March 19×8

	Actual	*Budget*	*Variance*
	£'000	*£'000*	*£'000*
Sales	3255.0	3500.0	245.0 Adv.
Purchases	1714.3	1750.0	35.7 Fav.
Labour	108.0	100.0	8.0 Adv.
Overheads	654.0	650.0	4.0 Adv.
Cost of sales	2476.3	2500.0	23.7 Fav.
Gross Profit	778.7	1000.0	221.3 Adv.
Expenses	659.0	650.0	9.0 Adv.
Net Profit	119.7	350.0	230.3 Adv.

Comment

The variance column provides information on the difference between the actual results and the budget, which provides the reference data because the management of the company have decided that the plan is a good way of checking that the company is in control.

Each separate variance provides little information. However, by considering variances in relation to each other, the conclusion can be formed that the company's inability to meet budgeted profit is due to sales levels. In absolute terms, the variances for sales and profit are similar. Beyond this, the absolute measures do not of themselves say much about the materiality of a particular variance; it is helpful to have a relative measure for this purpose:

Management Accounts for March 19x8

	Actual	*Budget*	*Variance*	
	£'000	*£'000*	*£'000*	%
Sales	3255.0	3500.0	245.0 Adv.	7.0 Adv.
Purchases	1714.3	1750.0	35.7 Fav.	2.0 Fav.
Labour	108.0	100.0	8.0 Adv.	8.0 Adv.
Overheads	654.0	650.0	4.0 Adv.	0.6 Adv.
Cost of sales	2476.3	2500.0	23.7 Fav.	0.9 Fav.
Gross Profit	778.7	1000.0	221.3 Adv.	22.1 Adv.
Expenses	659.0	650.0	9.0 Adv.	1.3 Adv.
Net Profit	119.7	350.0	230.3 Adv.	65.8 Adv.

Percentages are based on budgeted values.

If it assumed for the moment that a variance of 5% or more is significant, sales, labour, gross profit and net profit need to be brought under control. The analysis suggests that the labour costs are out of control; an interpretation which was not easy to make from the absolute values alone. However, whilst this information may prove valuable, little additional information on the cause of the profitability problem has been provided. Additionally, the percentage figures taken on their own suggest that the labour variance is more important than the sales variance. A combination of absolute and relative variance information appears to be helpful.

Example 22.2

Oldcastle's management accountant is currently studying for the examinations of one of the professional accounting bodies and has just studied flexible budgeting. Flexible budgeting adjusts (or flexes) budgeted data to reflect knowledge of cost behaviour and the actual level of activity. Regression analysis of past records suggests that purchases vary largely in proportion to sales turnover (R squared = 0.92), whilst labour, overheads and expenses behave as fixed costs.

Flexible budget statement for March 19x8

	Actual	*Flexed Budget*	*Variance*	
	£'000	*£'000*	*£'000*	%
Sales	3255.0	3255.0	nil	—
Purchases	1714.3	1627.5	86.8 Adv.	5.3 Adv.
Labour	108.0	100.0	8.0 Adv.	8.0 Adv.
Overheads	654.0	650.0	4.0 Adv.	0.6 Adv.
Cost of sales	2476.3	2377.5	98.8 Adv.	4.2 Adv
Gross Profit	778.7	877.5	98.8 Adv.	11.3 Adv.
Expenses	659.0	650.0	9.0 Adv.	1.3 Adv.
Net Profit	119.7	227.5	107.8 Adv.	47.4 Adv.

Percentages are based on flexed budget values.

The flexed budget for purchases is calculated:

Budgeted cost (£1,750,000), divided by Budgeted activity (£3,500,000), multiplied by Actual activity (£3,255,000).

Comment

Although this statement still applies one-factor variance analysis, since a single figure is given as the difference between the actual and flexed budget figures, the conclusions to be drawn differ significantly from the initial statement of actual and budgeted costs. Materials are now shown to be materially out of control and to be the most significant reason for the shortfall in profits in absolute terms. Flexible budgets serve a different purpose to fixed budgets (which may be described as static, in comparison with flexible budgets). Fixed budget variances reflect changes in output between the result and the reference data as well as changes in costs and revenues: flexible budgets only reflect differences in costs and revenues. Additionally, the sales value does not entirely explain all of the relationship between purchases and sales values (R squared appears to be good but is not 1). There may be a better measure of activity for the company than sales value in assessing cost behaviour implications.

If one-factor variance analysis is to be used for control, the purposes, assumptions and limitations of the reference data must be taken into account.

22.3 TWO FACTOR ANALYSIS

22.3.1 Calculation

Two factor analysis produces two variances for the difference between two numbers, where each variance can be related to a separate cause of factor or variable. If a company plans to sell 50,000 units at a profit of £2 per unit and achieves a profit for a period by selling 36,000 units for a profit of £2.50 each, two variances arise: one because of the difference in quantity (14,000 units adverse or 28% of plan) and one because of the difference in the value or profit per unit (£0.50 favourable or 25% of plan). If the company wishes to relate these variances to the effect on profit, the raw variances must be converted into £ values in a way which allows an assessment of the relative materiality of the variances to be gained. This creates the problem that different combinations of numbers provide a satisfactory breakdown of the total difference of £10,000. Multiplying combinations of 36,000, 50,000, £2 and £2.50 provides two methods of agreeing back to a total of £10,000:

Value variance	**Quantity variance**	**Total**
Method 1		
36,000 units @ £0.50	£2.00 for 14,000 units	
£18,000 favourable	£28,000 adverse	£10,000 Adv.
Method 2		
50,000 units @ £0.50	£2.50 for 14,000 units	
£25,000 favourable	£35,000 adverse	£10,000 Adv.

An alternative way of looking at the problem is by means of Figure 22.1. This seems to confirm the results of method 1. Does this mean that method 1 is correct? For an answer to this question, we need to look at the problem a little more closely. First, let us look at the situation where two adverse variances occur; for instance where the profit per unit becomes £1.50 for the example we are using. Figure 22.2 provides a way of looking at this problem and shows that there are now three ways of carrying out the variance analysis.

FIGURE 22.1

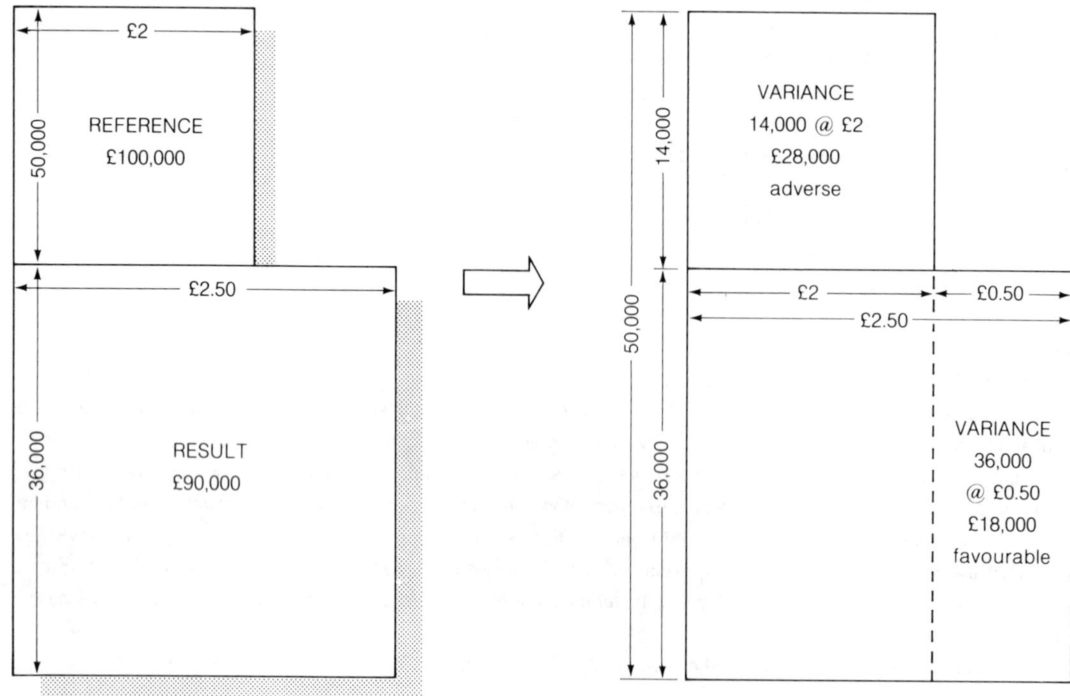

FIGURE 22.2

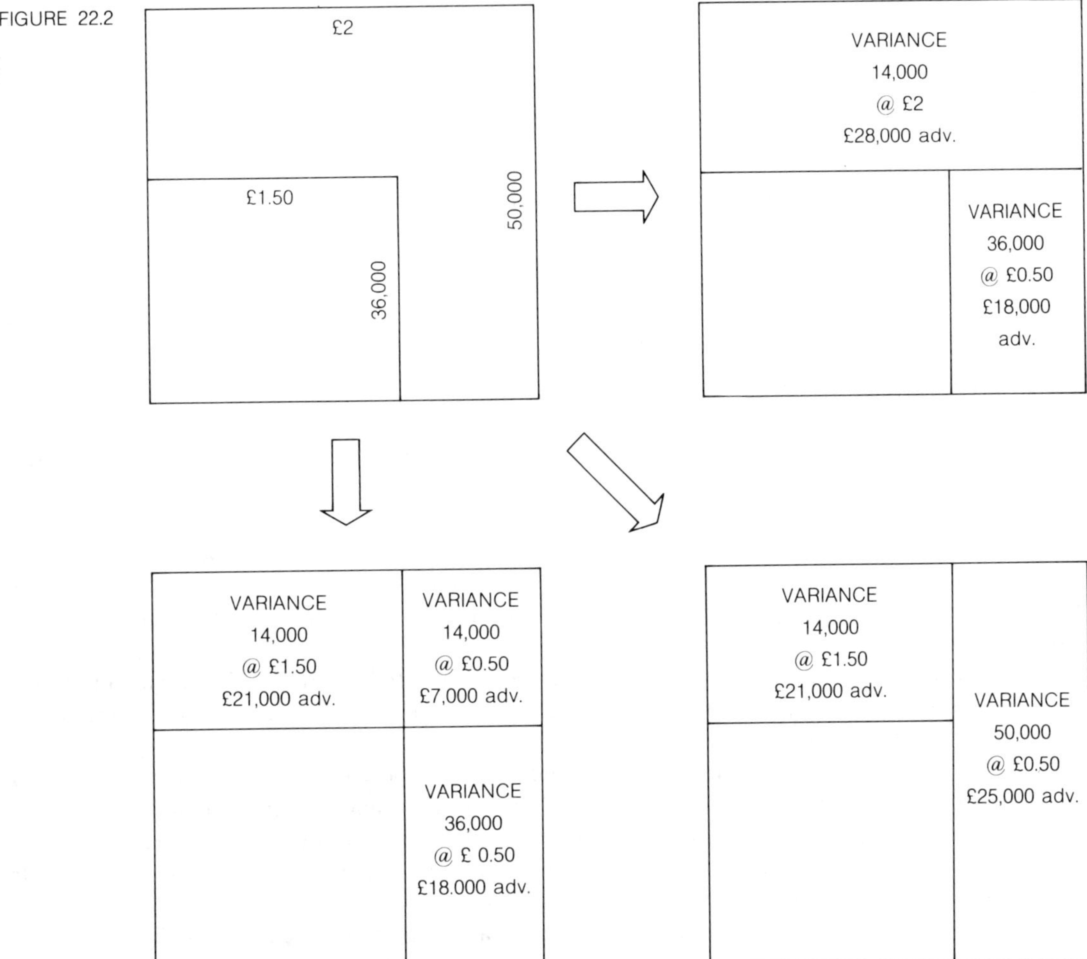

These can be calculated as follows:

Value variance	**Quantity variance**	**Total**
Method 1		
36,000 units @ £0.50	£2.00 for 14,000 units	
£18,000 adverse	£28,000 adverse	£46,000 Adv.
Method 2		
50,000 units @ £0.50	£1.50 for 14,000 units	
£25,000 adverse	£21,000 adverse	£46,000 Adv.
Method 3		
36,000 units @ £0.50	£1.50 for 14,000 units	
£18,000 adverse	£21,000 adverse	
	Joint value-quantity variance	
	14,000 units @ £0.50	
	£7,000 adverse	£46,000 Adv.

Having seen the possibility of calculating variances in different ways for two factor analysis, we will now consider the convention adopted by management accountants throughout the world. This convention will be explained by means of a further example, which will initially take the form of a self-assessment question.

Self-assessment question 22.1

The management accountant of Oldcastle Wholesalers PLC investigated the materials variance for March 19x8 and discovered that there was a better correlation between units sold and materials cost (R squared = 0.95). The following data is therefore to be incorporated into the analysis of Oldcastle's results as presented in Examples 22.1 and 22.2.

	Actual	*Budget*
Number of units sold	2,170,000	2,500,000

Required:

1 Prepare a flexible budget statement, flexing revenues and costs on the basis of units sold.
2 Prepare a statement showing the difference between the fixed budget and actual purchase costs, calculating value and quantity variances in as many different ways as possible.
3 Comment on your two statements.

Answers on page 607

22.3.2 Conventional two factor analysis

Method 1 is the conventional two factor approach to variance analysis. The joint value-quantity variance is included in the value variance. Drury gives the following explanation for the treatment of two factor variance analysis for material costs:

'. . . conventional variance analysis includes this joint [value]-[quantity] variance as part of the [value] variance. . . . the [quantity] variance is considered to be far more important than the [value] variance because management can exert a more direct influence over the [quantity] variance.'

Another explanation for the same accounting treatment is to be found in Horngren and Foster: '. . . the responsibility of the purchasing manager is usually deemed to include buying for all needs regardless of whether the materials are used efficiently.'

These explanations differ from each other and may not apply to the circumstances of the self-assessment question but both Drury's statement and Horngren and Foster's statement reveal the importance of justifying our treatment of variances in terms of organisational factors. These are seen to be important to the justification of the management accountant's approach to designing a suitable means by which information can be reported to management.

There are advantages to be gained from adopting a consistent approach to two factor analysis; for instance, the management accountant ensures a certain degree of standardisation in information produced around the world. The additional advantage of a consistent approach may be that information could be thought to be more credible if all expert management accountants agree on basic approaches.

There are advantages to be gained from consistency and organisational considerations which leads the management accountant to apply the following rule or convention:

Value variances are based on result quantities:
Quantity variances are based on reference values.

This rule allows variances to be calculated using either a procedure or a pre-set formula. The procedure and formula approaches will be explained in the next sections. The general procedure (Section 22.3.3) can be relatively easily applied to all situations and will form the basis for variance material presented in the remainder of the book. One advantage of using a formula approach (Section 22.3.4) is the ease with which computers can be programmed. There would thus appear to be good reasons for being able to approach variance analysis in different ways and with a certain degree of flexibility. In all cases, the calculations provide identical answers if the rule stated above is applied.

22.3.3 A procedure for two factor variance analysis

Each of the two factors or variables which create or cause the result are itemised. Each factor is then varied in turn to reflect the reference data. Horngren describes this procedure as the general approach. We can illustrate the general method as follows:

A. Result = Result Quantity × Result Value
B. Result Quantity × Reference Value
C. Reference data = Reference Quantity × Reference Value

Between lines A and B, the result value is changed to the reference value. The value variance therefore results.

Between lines B and C, the result quantity is compared with the reference quantity. The quantity variance therefore results. Using the example of purchases from self-assessment question 22.1, the answer could be shown as follows:

Actual = 2,170,000 × £0.79 = £1,714,300
↓
2,170,000 × £0.70 = £1,519,000
↓
Budget = 2,500,000 × £0.70 = £1,750,000

The value variance is £195,300 (£1,714,300 less £1,519,000).

This is adverse because the price paid for purchases was greater than budgeted and the resulting profit is therefore reduced.

The quantity variance is £231,000 (£1,519,000 – £1,750,000).

This is favourable because fewer purchases were made in comparison with the budget. This has the effect of improving profit.

22.3.4 Two factor variance formulae

From the general procedure in Section 22.3.3, the value variance is:

Result quantity × Result value – Result quantity × Reference value

This simplifies to the formula:

Result quantity (Result value—Reference value)

Similarly, the general procedure provides the following formula for the quantity variance:

Reference value (Result quantity—Reference quantity)

Applying the formula to self-assessment question 22.1 gives:

Value variance = 2,170,000 (£0.79 – £0.70) = £195,300
Quantity variance = £0.70 (2,170,000 – 2,500,000) = £231,000

The normal convention of checking the effect of the variance on the profit implications gives the same favourable and adverse categorisation as in Section 22.3.3.

SELF-TEST QUESTIONS

22.1 A variance is:

1 an alternative term for standard costing
2 the difference between two numbers
3 an analysis of budget failures
4 information on company performance

22.2 ABC Company uses standard costing. Last month, its single product used 5 units of raw material costing £10/unit. The standard is 6 units of raw materials costing £11/unit. 30,000 units of raw material were purchased and used. No stocks are held. The value variance for purchases was:

1 £1 favourable
2 £1 adverse
3 £30,000 favourable
4 £30,000 adverse

22.3 The quantity variance for ABC was:

1 1 unit favourable
2 £66,000 favourable
3 £60,000 favourable
4 £60,000 adverse

22.4 The ABC Company has a flexed budget, flexed on the basis of units. From the data provided, the flexed budget variance was:

1 Impossible to calculate without more information
2 £96,000 favourable
3 £90,000 favourable
4 £96,000 adverse

Answers on page 611

22.4 THREE FACTOR ANALYSIS

22.4.1 A statement of the basic problem

Three factor analysis produces three variances to explain the difference between two numbers, where both numbers can be explained by three factors or variables. A common situation might arise from a plan to sell 25,000 units of one product, which we might call X, at a profit of £3 per unit and 25,000 units of another product, Y, at a profit of £1 per unit. Differences between the planned profit of £100,000 and any result can arise because:

1 The profit earned on each of the products may differ; let us assume that £3.50 profit on X and £1.50 profit on Y arise for a particular period. This would be a value variance.
2 The quantity sold can differ; let us assume that instead of selling a total of 50,000 units as planned, a total of 36,000 units are sold for a particular period. This would be a quantity variance.
3 The proportion of sales of X to Y can differ from the 1:1 proportion planned. Let us assume that for a particular period the proportion of X:Y is 3:1. This is called a mix variance.

A summary of the result and reference data is provided below:

Reference data (*plan*)				Result (*actual figures for a period*)			
Mix	Quantity	Value	Total	Mix	Quantity	Value	Total
50%	25,000	£3.00	£75,000	75%	27,000	£3.50	£94,500
50%	25,000	£1.00	£25,000	25%	9,000	£1.50	£13,500
100%	50,000	£2.00	£100,000	100%	36,000	£3.00	£108,000

The total result of £108,000 and the planned profit of £100,000 differ because of mix, quantity and value factors. From our discussion of two factor analysis, it should be clear that there are a number of ways in which three factor analysis could be calculated in general. The equivalent diagram to the rectangles used to illustrate two factor analysis would be three dimensional blocks resembling cubes. The differing ways of calculating variances for three factor analysis are much debated and the value of the mix variance is a contentious issue. However, this book will confine itself to applying the rules that were stated for two factor analysis in the way normally shown in text books.

22.4.2 A three factor analysis

An approach using our general procedure from Section 22.3.3 would be as follows:

A. Resulting Quantity × Resulting Mix × Resulting Value

↓

B. Resulting Quantity × Resulting Mix × Reference Value

↓

C. Resulting Quantity × Reference Mix × Reference Value

↓

D. Reference Quantity × Reference Mix × Reference Value

A − B gives a Value variance
B − C gives a Mix variance
C − D gives a Quantity variance

Applying this to the example provides the following analysis:
A: Result, as given earlier:

27,000	@	£3.50	£94,500
9,000	@	£1.50	£13,500
36,000	@	£3.00	£108,000

B Restate result values to reference values:

27,000	@	£3.00	£81,000
9,000	@	£1.00	£9,000
36,000	@	£2.50	£90,000

C Restating the result quantity of 36,000 to the reference proportions gives quantities of 18,000 and 18,000 for each of the products, that is, a 50:50 or 1:1 mix:

18,000	@	£3.00	£54,000
18,000	@	£1.00	£18,000
36,000	@	£2.00	£72,000

D Reference data, as stated earlier:

25,000	@	£3.00	£75,000
25,000	@	£1.00	£25,000
50,000	@	£2.00	£100,000

The value variance is the difference between A and B, which can be provided for each of the two products X and Y separately, or in total. The value variance is £18,000 favourable.

The mix variance is the difference between B and C, £18,000 favourable. The figures can be shown for each product separately, if required.

The quantity variance is the difference between C and D, £28,000 adverse. The figures can be shown for each product, separately, if required.

The mix and quantity variances can be calculated by using approaches based on the total quantities of 36,000 and 50,000 and the weighted average values, £2.50 and £2.00. In order to arrive at these weighted average values, tables such as those given for B, C and D above are produced. From each table, the weighted average is calculated by taking the total value and dividing by the total quantity.

The mix variance is given by the difference in the weighted average value for the result mix and for the reference mix. In this case, £2.50 less £2.00 equals £0.50, which multiplied by the result quantity, 36,000, gives £18,000 favourable, as calculated earlier.

The quantity variance is given by the difference in the result and reference quantities, 14,000 units. This is multiplied by the reference weighted average of £2 per unit to give £28,000 adverse, as shown earlier.

The mix variance is thought by some authorities to be difficult to explain to managers. Approaches based on the weighted average calculation given above have been established so that information can be provided to managers in a form which allows them to more easily see where the variance comes from. Two forms will be considered:

1 The mix variance could be seen to arise because the expected value of a particular product varies from the expected weighted average:

	Reference value	*Weighted average*	*Result quantity*	*Variance*	
				£/unit	*£*
Product X	£3	£2	27,000	1 fav	27,000
Product Y	£1	£2	9,000	1 adv	9,000
					18,000

The favourable variance of £18,000 arises because more is sold of the product which has a favourable value in comparison with the average. This suggests that profit would result from selling more of Product X. Unfortunately, this is not necessarily true since the mix variance might deteriorate if more of Product Y were sold at the same time that more of Product X were sold. The important factor is the proportion of one product to the other.

The quantity variance would be calculated as 14,000 units @ £2 favourable.

2 To overcome the drawback to 1, the following statement could be used. This shows that the mix variance arises because reference and result quantities differ and individual product values differ from the weighted average.

	Result quantity	*Result quantity, Reference mix*	*Reference value*	*Weighted average*	*Variance*
X	27,000	18,000	£3	£2	9,000 fav @ £1 fav.
Y	9,000	18,000	£1	£2	9,000 adv @ £1 adv.

A £9,000 favourable variance arises for each product.

The quantity variance is 14,000 units @ £2, as for **1**.

This shows that a greater than expected proportion of product X, whose value is favourable in comparison with the average for all products, was sold. For Y, a lower proportion of units were sold than expected. This is favourable for the company because product X provides a lower than average value when it is sold.

This analysis shows the importance of not only calculating the variance, but also the desirability of presenting information to management in a form which shows the meaning and implications of the calculation. Calculations of variances can be made in a variety of forms; the best form for a particular organisation may be the form of calculation which carries most information for the organisation's particular management team.

This second method is specifically mentioned by the syllabus of the ACCA. It is described as the 'use of weighted average vs individual standards as the base for mix calculations.'

Self-assessment question 22.2

Newlyformed Retailers PLC have been in business for five years, selling three products through three separate divisions. Each division sells to a different area of the country. The management of Newlyformed Retailers are particularly concerned about the sales for the Northern Division, although its profit performance is comparable to the other divisions. No system of budgetary control or standard costing is in operation but divisions are regularly compared in order to assess performance. The management accounts for last month showed the following:

Sales turnover analysis for June 19×8

	Southern division			Central division			Northern division		
Product	Units		Value	Units		Value	Units		Value
			£			£			£
L	30,000	£4	120,000	60,000	£4.50	270,000	50,000	£4	200,000
M	30,000	£5	150,000	30,000	£5.50	165,000	25,000	£5	125,000
N	40,000	£6	240,000	30,000	£6.50	195,000	25,000	£6	150,000
			510,000			630,000			475,000

You are required to produce useful management information to analyse the situation provided, including explanations and comments which may be useful to the management of Newlyformed Retailers PLC.

Answers on page 608

SUMMARY

Variances are differences between results or actual figures and reference data, which can take a variety of forms, including budgets and standards. Variance analysis breaks down variances into separate factors, variables or causes in such a way as to provide useful information for management purposes. There is a choice as to how a variance is broken down in general but management accountants have a convention which permits variance analysis to be provided in a standardised form around the world. A variety of reasons are given to support the convention when applied to two factor analysis, primarily of an organisational behaviour nature. In the case of three factor analysis, the conventional approach is debated. The convention establishes the rule:

Value variances are based on result quantities:
Quantity variances are based on reference values.

When providing information for management, the form of calculation may help to explain the implications of the variance. This is particularly true of the mix variance, where a weighted average calculation may convey greater information than other approaches. Variances are data which can convey information if organisational and information issues are suitably resolved by the person designing the variance reporting system.

EXERCISES

Exercise 22.1

The OPQ Company produces quarterly management accounts, from its financial accounting records, in the following form:

OPQ Company Management Accounts for Quarter 2 19×8

	This year	Last Year	Variance
Sales	£6,800,000	£5,500,000	£1,300,000 fav.
Cost of goods sold	£4,100,000	£3,000,000	£1,100,000 adv.
Gross Profit	£2,700,000	£2,500,000	£ 200,000 fav.
General expenses	£2,000,000	£1,900,000	£ 100,000 adv.
Net Profit	£ 700,000	£ 600,000	£ 100,000 fav.

Budgets are produced for planning purposes but are not incorporated into the quarterly management accounting reports because management feel that trends over time, as shown by comparisons of one year to the next, are more helpful than comparisons with plan. The budget for quarter 2 showed:

Sales	£6,000,000
Cost of goods sold	£3,500,000
Gross Profit	£2,500,000
General expenses	£1,900,000
Net Profit	£ 600,000

The fixed cost element in cost of goods sold comes mainly from decisions taken in the past (depreciation, rent and rates, for instance). It has been approximately £1,000,000 per quarter for the past four years. This figure has been incorporated into the budget.

The selling price last year was £5 per unit. This price was used in preparing the budget but the price in quarter 2 was £5.44 due to a general increase in prices in the market in which OPQ trades.

You are required to produce information for management, assuming that:

1 variable costs respond to sales value;
2 variable costs respond to the number of units sold.

Answers on page 609

Exercise 22.2

The marketing department of OPQ Company (for which data is provided in Exercise 22.1) pays each sales executive a sales commission of 10% of contribution earned above £500,000 in each quarter of the year. Last year, it paid 8% of contribution earned above £480,000 in each quarter. Each of the seven sales executives employed by OPQ received commission in each of the two years. Produce an analysis which will be helpful to management.

Answers on page 610

Exercise 22.3

The purchasing department of OPQ Company (for which data is provided in Exercise 22.1) imports its major raw material from Germany. The budget was prepared on the basis of an average raw material price for this particular item of £20 and an exchange rate of 3 DM to the £. During the year, £540,000 was spent on purchasing the raw material. The accounts show that an average of £18 per unit was spent on the raw material and the exchange rate averaged 3.1 DM to the £. Provide an analysis which will be helpful to management.

Answers on page 610

Exercise 22.4

Wedgegrow Ltd specialises in growing young plants for sale to both commercialised and retail outlets. The plants are grown from seed pellets which are sown in a compost mix in a box of 40 plants in an automatic sowing department. Once germinated, seeds are transferred to a growing house and are dispatched when the plants have reached a suitable size and condition. Twenty-eight per cent of all plants sown, irrespective of variety, are lost in germination or growing. Plants are organised in such a way that boxes always contain 40 plants when moved from each department.

Budgeted/standard data is as follows:

Automatic sowing department
Monthly production: 125,000 boxes (Variety A 60,000 boxes, Variety B 45,000 boxes, Variety C 20,000 boxes).

Dispatch department
Monthly dispatches to customers: 90,000 boxes.

Standard Cost per box dispatched: £2.75.

Selling prices: Variety A £3.10, Variety B £3.20, Variety C £3.70.

Actual data for February, 19×8 was as follows:

	Variety A	*Variety B*	*Variety C*
Sales units	46,000	30,000	10,000
Sales £ per unit	3.00	3.30	3.50

Prepare an analysis of the sales performance for the period, using the standard weighted average margin (sales less standard cost of sales) as the variance valuation basis. Comment on the arguments which may be given in favour of the weighted average approach for sales variance calculations.

(*ACCA, December 1988, adapted*)

Answers in lecturer's manual.

Exercise 22.5

Explain why variance trend and materiality data in percentage terms may provide useful information for management.

(ACCA, June 1988, adapted)

Answers in lecturer's manual.

Budgets: Preparation, Procedures and Purposes

INTRODUCTION

This chapter is concerned with advanced aspects of the preparation of budgets. Within a framework of the annual budget as a short-term expression of long-term planning, the purposes of budgeting are listed in terms of budgetary objectives and the problem of conflicting objectives is noted. The preparation of budgets is described as an iterative process involving the formulation of subsidiary and master budgets. Procedures are described in terms of individual techniques such as Cash Budgeting, Flexible Budgeting and Zero Based Budgeting. Some of these are basically administrative procedures for the allocation of scarce resources, such as the case of Zero Based Budgeting, and some are techniques involving the manipulation of financial figures, as in the case of Cash Budgeting. Where financial figures are involved, both cost and financial accounting skills need to be brought to bear by the accountant in producing information for management. A section on the application of forecasting techniques is provided, giving brief descriptions of procedures and statistical approaches which have been suggested. This section also reports on some firm evidence on the non-use by practising accountants of 'sophisticated' techniques. Budgeting is finally seen as a model which is amenable to analysis by means of financial modelling languages and spreadsheets.

By the end of the chapter, the student should be able to:

1 Prepare budgets for a variety of situations;
2 explain the objectives of budgeting and budgetary control;
3 critically examine the applicability of a variety of procedures to the formulation of budgets.

23.1 OBJECTIVES

23.1.1 Statement of objectives

David Otley, in an article in *Management Accounting* in May 1987, suggested that a budget serves three functions:

1 The budget is a quantification in financial terms of organisational plans;
2 The budget ensures that the plan can be financed. The cash budget is a means by which the effects on the liquid resources of an organisation can be predetermined;
3 The budget is a control device.

Two major aspects of budgeting are evident: planning and control. Budgets aim to convert a range of possible input information concerning the immediate or tactical future of the organisation into output information or reports for management use. Table 23.1 provides a list of possible inputs and outputs for the budget as a planning device and the budget as a control device.

TABLE 23.1 **The inputs and outputs of a typical system of budgeting**

	Plan	Control
Inputs	—Forecasts	—Actual sales and costs
	—Extant data on capacities, stocks, cost behaviour	
	—Policies	
	—Objectives	—'The Budget'
Outputs	—'The Budget'	—Actual: budget comparisons
		—Variance reports

The budget as a plan may be built up from forecasts and data on such variables as capacities, stocks and cost behaviour. These can be quantified as financial information in the form of profit and loss statements, balance sheets, cash flow forecasts and funds flow statements. The results, as finalised in financial statement form, should be consistent with company policies and company objectives. The budget is therefore a statement, in financial form, of the plans of an organisation which are consistent with long-term plans of that organisation.

Once formulated, the budget is compared with results in order to generate financial statements commonly termed management accounts. The aim is to control through a feedback process, where the budget assumes the role of objective within the feedback cycle.

Budgets are a form of management control. Their preparation is concerned with the uncertainty of future events. A typical time horizon for the budget is a single year. A degree of judgment is necessary in both formulating budgets and in interpreting the difference between budgeted figures and actual results for control purposes. Budgets are concerned with the effective, efficient and economic use of resources.

Long-term budgets may be formed with a time horizon of, say, three to ten years. These budgets will be in a generalised, summarised form and will have a strategic intent. In some cases, they may be an extrapolation of the annual, or short-term budget. In other cases, the long-term budget will form the basis for the short-term budget. In either case, it is logical for the budget process to be consistent with long-term plans. This may overcome the deficiency that short-term budgeting can place an emphasis on short-term achievements with dysfunctional consequences for the long-term.

Simon suggested that accounting in general fulfils three functions: attention directing, problem solving and scorecard keeping. Budget objectives can be consistent with this framework. Attention directing may be concerned with directing management's attention to deviations from plan, perhaps through exception reporting. Problem solving is concerned with identifying problems and seeking solutions, including the evaluation of alternative courses of action. This is an essential part of budget preparation. Scorecard keeping is concerned with keeping a record of management performance, perhaps through the preparation of monthly management accounts.

Specific objectives of budgeting are:

1 **Planning**. Budgeting is a formal means by which investigation leads to a financial statement of future intent. This can be a means by which the operational and management consequences of objectives and policies can be expressed and communicated throughout an organisation. The formal aspect of budgeting through a budget committee can be a means by which participation in planning can be encouraged.

2 **Co-ordination**. Organisations are complex arrangements of separate parts whose co-ordination is necessary to achieve the best results for the organisation as a whole. Sales and production efforts must be co-ordinated to avoid supply or overstocking problems, for instance. The budget can act as a form of co-ordination of human effort by allowing the separate divisions of an organisation to work together to form plans and monitor results. In another sense, the budget also allows an organisation to co-ordinate its response to economic trends and challenges posed by the environment within which it operates.

3 **Communication**. The budget can be used to communicate plans and control information. Once formulated, the aspects of the plan having a bearing on a particular division of the organisation can be communicated to that division. Monthly management accounts can be circulated to responsibility departments, or budget centre managers.

4 **Motivation**. A budget provides a target which can influence aspiration levels and increase motivation within organisations. The chapter on the behavioural consequences of control systems showed that budgets can be implemented as a force to promote motivation but that dysfunctional consequences can arise.

5 **Control**. A budget serves to control specific operations, processes or departments and to prevent wastage and inefficiency. These objectives must be achieved through the actions of people and so the control aspects of budgets are closely related to motivation. A budget seeks to motivate managers to achieve objectives in a goal congruent manner and thereby to establish control within the organisation.

6 **Performance evaluation**. The budget can be used to measure the performance of individual managers or departments by monitoring the ability to achieve targets. Good performance is normally associated with achieving or bettering performance targets set in cost, profit or investment centre terms.

7 **Authorisation**. The budget can be used to authorise expenditure or the pursuit of certain initiatives. Once the budget has been approved, it can become a permission to spend, an acceptance that senior management have allowed a new project to be commenced or an instruction to recruit new members of staff, for instance.

23.1.2 Discussion: the conflicting nature of objectives

The previous section provided a broad review of the objectives of budgeting. This section provides a limited assessment of the extent to which these objectives cannot be fully achieved because they are inherently self-contradictory and conflict with each other. This assessment will be provided by means of examples.

Starting with the theories of motivation and aspiration, it can be shown that the same budget cannot both motivate and be a plan. Imagine that the board of directors has established that its company can sell, say, 100,000 motor bikes in the year ahead, based on forecasts of market share and market size. The capacity of the factory is 150,000 under normal circumstances and the factory manager believes that 160,000 bikes might be produced under exceptional circumstances. A budget set to motivate the factory manager would use the aspiration level of 160,000 output. This budget is unrealistic as a plan because achievement of the plan would lead to overstocking. The planning and motivational objectives of budgeting conflict with each other in this situation. Which level should be incorporated into the budget? 100,000 would seem to be the most sensible solution, since the alternative would lead to increases in stocks and problems in financing working capital. The budget cannot then be expected to motivate the production manager to maximise output. A hierarchy of objectives is necessary because of the impracticability of pursuing two objectives at the same time.

The objectives of planning and performance evaluation may be in conflict as a result of giving the factory manager the target of 100,000 bikes. Performance evaluation does not measure the ability of the manager in this situation, except in so far as the manager is asked to conform. There is little incentive for the manager to create improved performance by applying imagination and initiative because the essential task is to conform to the requirements of the market acting as a limiting factor. If the manager achieves an output of 98,000 bikes, but this is the production necessary to meet the marketing needs, the manager has performed well in terms of the underlying objectives of the budget, but poorly in terms of the absolute measures provided by the budget. A mechanism for planning and co-ordination cannot necessarily meet the simultaneous objective of providing performance evaluation measures. Again, a hierarchy arises within which one budgeting objective dominates.

Accounting for the processes of accounting, the alternative layer of meta accounting, would suggest that two levels of objectives are necessary to the effective use of budgets:

1 The objectives of the company must be clearly stated and communicated. These objectives should be reflected in the formulation of budgets.
2 The objectives of the budget must be clearly stated and conflicts between objectives resolved to avoid establishing unrealistic aspirations for the effects of budgetary impacts. These objectives should be reflected in the implementation of budgeting.

23.2 PREPARATION

23.2.1 The iterative nature of budget preparation

Figure 23.1 provides a model used by the ACCA examiner in the December 1986 examination to illustrate an iterative approach to the preparation of budgets.

This is a bottom-up approach to budget preparation whereby budget centre managers prepare their own plans and budgets within corporate objectives, policies and constraints. These budgets are passed to senior management who may call upon budget centre managers to revise budgets to conform to organisational requirements. The process can become a bargained means by which budgets are prepared. Senior managers and budget centre managers bargain towards budgets which are mutually acceptable. This can represent the ideal. Unfortunately, the process can also become a form of 'pseudo participation', where authoritarian senior managers ultimately provide targets for budget centre managers to meet irrespective of budgets submitted from below. The allocation of budget targets to budget centre managers without any form of consultation is termed a top-down approach.

FIGURE 23.1

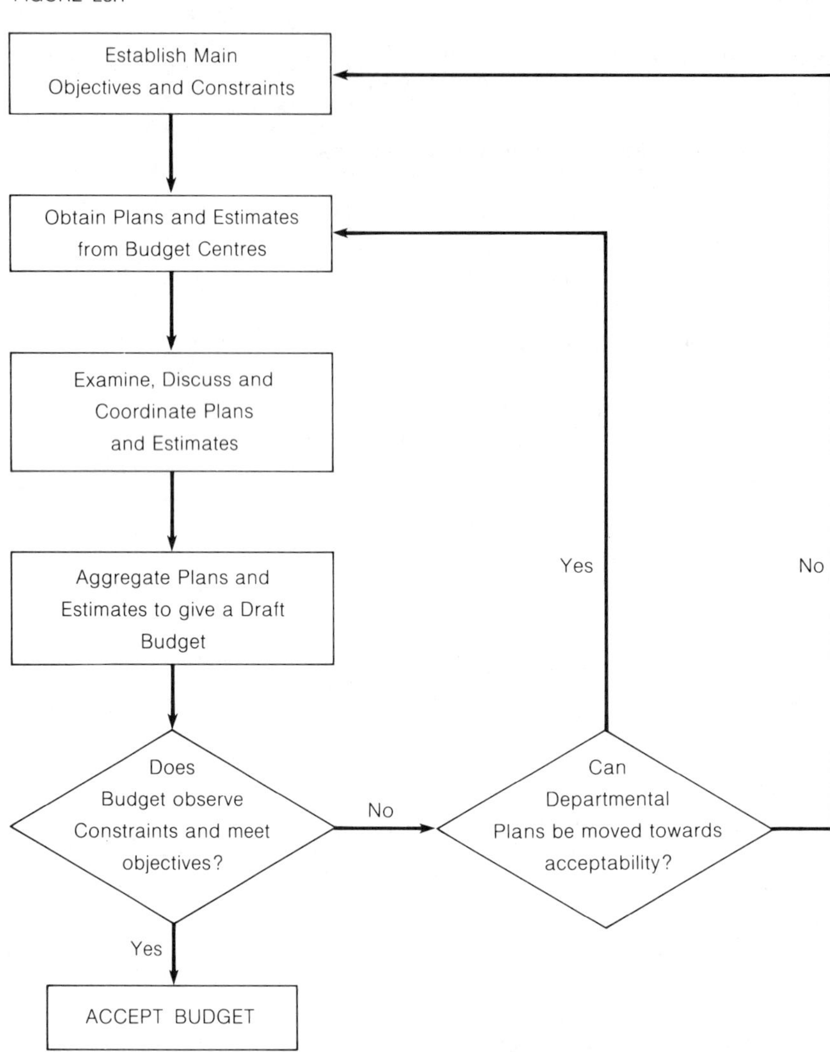

A complementary model is provided by Drury. It illustrates the significance of feedback in the process of budgeting. Figure 23.2 illustrates how the strategic and management control aspects of budgeting can be combined within a single formal process. Feedback based on divergences from expectation leads to a further search for alternative means of achieving corporate objectives at the strategic level or changes to the way in which the budget is implemented at the tactical level. The model operates as an open system with double loop feedback. Feedback loops in this case provide a form of iteration on a longer time horizon than that implied by the model of the budget as a bargaining process.

23.2.2 Subsidiary and master budget formulation

Figure 23.3 (see page 384) illustrates a general process by which subsidiary budgets are inter-related and contribute to the formation of the master budget.

The limiting factor, or principal budget factor, or key factor, is the variable which acts as a constraint on the organisation. Linear programming is a technique for optimising decisions under multiple constraints and its relevance to budgeting will be mentioned later; Figure 23.3 assumes a single constraint. Either the market place or production capacity, expressed as a number of machine hours, labour hours or the availability of materials, determine the limiting factor. Where sales are the limiting factor, the budgeted sales level will be initially established. Where production capacity in terms of hours is the limiting factor, production quantities will be budgeted first. Where raw materials constitute the limiting factor, purchase quantities will be budgeted first. Remaining quantities can be ascertained on the basis of the budgeted level for the limiting factor subject to working capital policy.

FIGURE 23.2

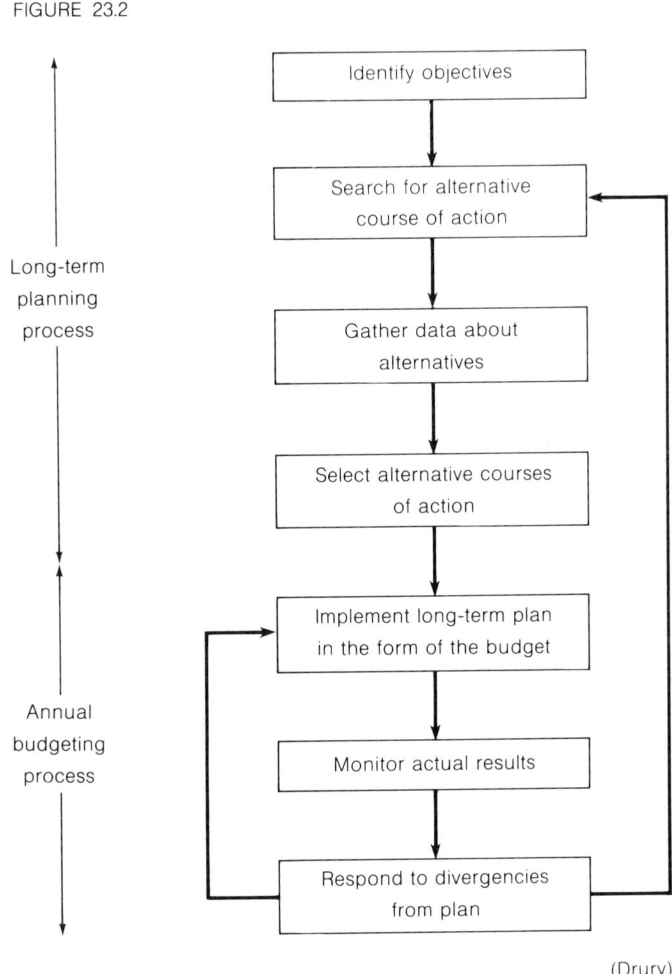

(Drury)

This may call for an increase or a decrease in stocks. Other management policy changes, such as adopting JIT measures, would also have an important influence at this stage. The simplest model of the relationships between quantity budgets and stocks is as follows:

Opening stock of raw materials
plus **Purchases**
less **Issues**
equals **Closing stock of raw materials**

Opening stock of work-in-progress
plus **Inputs**
less **Production**
equals **Closing stock of work-in-progress**

Opening stock of finished goods
plus **Production**
less **Sales**
equals **Closing stock of finished goods**

This basic model, which is the same model used for accounting control, must be adapted to meet individual circumstances. This is adequately tested at earlier stages of management accounting studies; revision is provided by means of the self-assessment question which follows.

Self-assessment question 23.1

Factors Limited are preparing a budget for the year ended 19×0. The production manager has reported a capacity of 150,000 units of production for the single product, known locally as Esse, but has stated that a level of 160,000 units could be attained under exceptional circumstances. The sales manager has held a conference for the sales force at a hotel in Basingstoke and has provided a sales forecast of 100,000 units for the year ahead. The financial director has called for a reduction in all stocks of 10% to ease cash flow problems and to reduce interest payments on a bank overdraft. According to the cost accountant's standard costing information, each unit of Esse requires 10kg of raw materials. Stocks at the beginning of the budget year are expected to be as follows:

Raw materials 50,000 kilograms

Work-in-progress stocks (60% complete for material content and conversion) 4,000 units

Finished goods stocks 10,000 units

You are required to produce quantity budgets for Factors Limited, stating any assumptions which are necessary to complete the exercise.

Answer on page 612

Once the quantity budget has been finalised, revenues and costs can be determined according to the customary linear cost assumption of valuation. Sales quantities are multiplied by a pre-determined sales value per unit. Costs are determined according to the general cost function:

Cost = No units x Variable cost per unit plus fixed cost

FIGURE 23.3

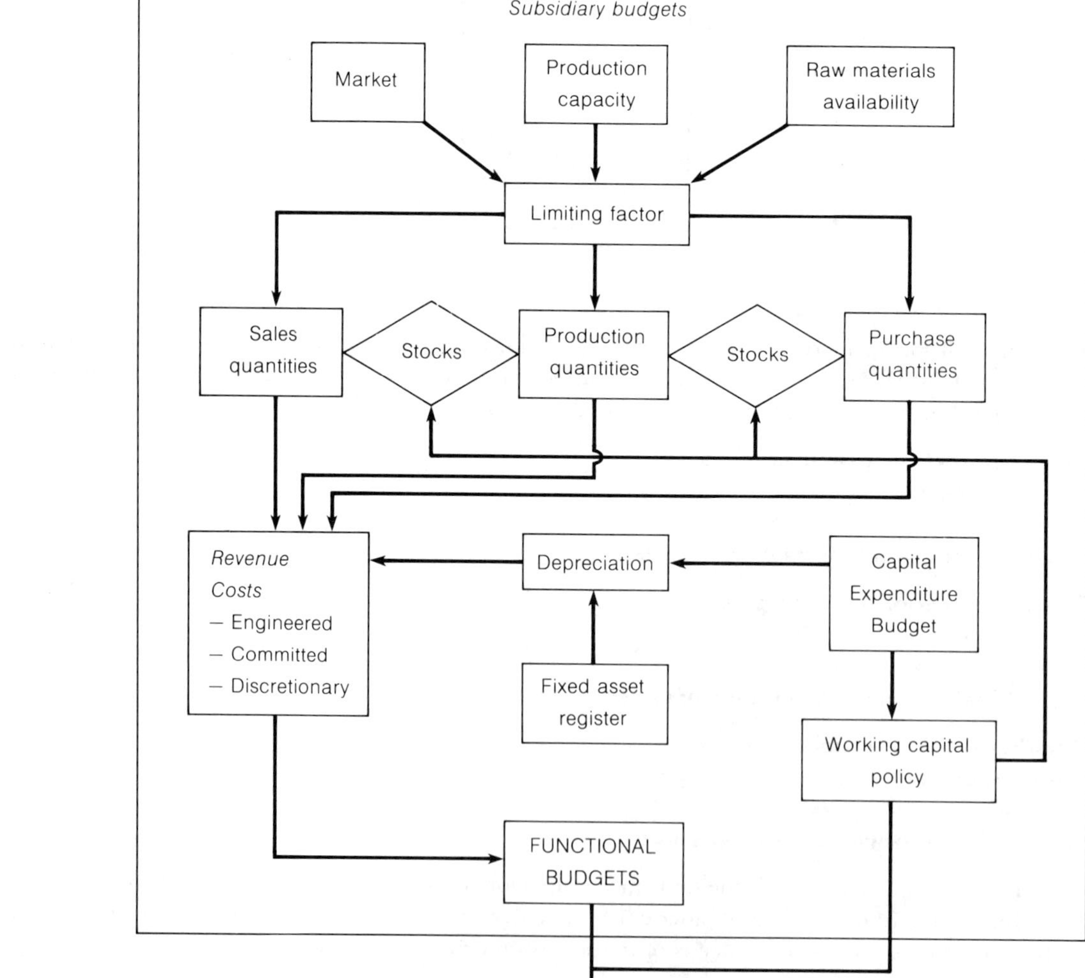

Less scientific methods of determining costs and revenues may be encountered in practice. Incremental budgeting describes the process where budgets are fixed by taking the present year's budgeted or actual level of expenditure or revenues and building increases for inflation, expansion or other known factors. This appears to be a common form of budgeting for government managed operations such as health or education. Alternatively, where a sales forecast is expressed in £ terms, costs may be determined as a percentage of turnover. This has the drawback that all costs are treated by the accounting system as though they are variable costs. Organisations adopting this approach appear to come from a variety of industries and until research can ascertain fully the reasons for such budgeting, a justification can only be the subject of conjecture. A speculative conjecture is given by the cost benefit model; the costs of simple techniques are low and may easily exceed benefits measured intuitively. The preparation model described in Figure 23.3 can be costly to operate on a manual basis.

It is important to differentiate engineered, committed and discretionary costs at a practical level. Information on committed costs will certainly be available within the organisation, because of the nature of such costs. Depreciation on existing assets can be calculated for the year ahead on the basis of plant register data. Rents and rates can be based on the present year's levels, with due regard for increases caused by factors such as inflation. There is little reason to bargain for committed costs; indeed, for senior management to suggest alterations to carefully calculated committed costs may undermine the respect of budget centre managers for the process of budget preparation since little control or responsibility can be allocated at the management control level. Engineered costs, such as material and some types of labour cost, may be calculated on a per unit basis and related to budgeted quantities. There may be reason to bargain for wastage or productivity or pricing levels, and such bargaining will affect motivation. Setting too tight a target and then using the target in performance measurement may lead to reduced motivation and performance as shown by the research into the effects of budget targets on aspiration levels. Discretionary costs, such as marketing, research and development or management accounting services present a problem of allocating remaining resources once committed and engineered costs have been accounted for. These are most amenable to bargaining and procedures have been developed to formalise the bargaining and ultimate allocation of resources. These procedures are described in the Zero Based Budgeting section (23.3.4).

Costs and revenues can be summarised into functional budgets; budgets for each department within the organisation. This leads to administration budgets, production budgets and marketing budgets, for example.

Functional budgets are summarised into the form of a master budget. This may be presented in the form of profit and loss accounts, balance sheets, cash flow forecasts and funds flow statements.

The preparation of the budget is managed by the budget committee within policies, procedures and practices which may be detailed within a budget manual. In a bottom-up system, the budget committee might have the responsibility to decide on a timetable for budget preparation, will communicate objectives, policies and information on constraints, will co-ordinate the separate budget centre submissions, suggest revisions, bargain and decide upon the stage at which to finalise the budget preparation. The budget committee may be given responsibility for monitoring results and suggesting interpretations and recommendations for action to investigate individual variances. The budget manual may contain information on corporate objectives and policies. It may state how individual variables such as inflation are to be accounted for. It may contain a recommended approach to budget preparation.

Figure 23.3 provides a systematic approach to the preparation of budgets which has been proven in practical application and which is broadly in agreement with material in text books for the area. However, it would be a mistake to imply that this is the only model for the preparation of budgets. The actual form of preparation is likely to reflect the objectives of the organisation or the objectives of budgeting or a host of other factors such as the prior experience and expertise of management.

Self-assessment question 23.2

Factors Limited have now successfully completed their quantity budgets and confirmed the answers to self-assessment question 23.1. The following additional targets have now been provided:

Selling price: £50 per unit;
Engineered costs: Materials £2 per kilogram;
Committed costs: Production overhead £1,000,000;
Discretionary costs: Non-production overhead: 30% of turnover
Debtors: 30 days sales;
Creditors: 30 days engineered and discretionary costs and 30 days for 50% of the committed costs;
Fixed assets: £5,000,000;
Bank overdraft: £100,000.

You are required to produce a budgeted profit and loss and balance sheet for Factors Ltd in as much detail as the above information allows. Use material from the self-assessment question 23.1 and its answer as necessary.
Ignore taxation implications.

Answer on page 613

23.3 PROCEDURES

Within the general framework of budget preparation described in the previous section, there are detailed procedures worthy of more detailed consideration. This section considers some such procedures.

23.3.1 Cash budgeting

A cash budget provides information on the cash implications of the budget. It is useful in determining in advance the need to negotiate for additional long- or short-term funds, in order to overcome cash deficiencies, or the advantage to be gained from investing funds, where cash surpluses are indicated. The cash budget is a fundamental tool for use in managing an organisation's liquidity. A bank manager normally requests a cash flow forecast before extending overdraft facilities or providing business loans. In this case, the cash flow forecast would be taken as evidence of the ability to pay interest charges and repay a loan at a particular time.

The calculation of a cash budget follows usual financial accounting procedures, with particular emphasis on the following points:

1 The form of layout is essentially a summarised receipts and payments account. There is some discretion over the detailed method of presentation, but the following pro-forma layout illustrates the general principles to be followed:

Cash flow forecast for the year ending . . .

	Total	*Period 1*	*Period 2 . . .*
Receipts			
Sales			
Share issue			
etc			
Total receipts			
Payments			
Materials			
Wages			
Capital expenditure			
etc			
Total payments			
Net cash flow			
brought forward			
carried forward			

Net cash flow is the difference between total receipts and total payments for each period. It may provide useful information from one year to the next on the cash flow cycle; the pattern over time of surpluses and deficiencies which may show a seasonal consistency. Each year, cash may flow out during a certain period of the year but flow in during another period. By adding the net cash flow to the balance of cash at the beginning of the period, the cash balance at the end of the period is calculated. The balance at the end of the period becomes the balance brought forward at the beginning of the following period.

2 Non-cash items should be appropriately treated. Depreciation will appear in budgeted profit and loss accounts but not in cash flow budgets. Capital expenditure will appear as a payment in the cash flow budget for the period in which payments are anticipated to be made, taking into account credit arrangements.

3 Timing adjustments other than for non-cash situations, must be made according to the information provided by working capital policy. If timing adjustments, such as the number of days stock or the number of days of creditors, are not stated explicitly as working capital policy, balance sheets for past periods may be analysed to determine normal stock and payment periods.

4 A funds flow statement, whilst not strictly representing cash flow, may be advantageously used to present liquidity information. The form of the statement can follow normal company practice, perhaps consistent with the layouts illustrated in SSAP 10; sources and applications of funds statements.

Self-assessment question 23.3

Silveryseas plc is a wholesale business with small warehouses throughout Northern Europe. Sales for the first six months of the coming financial year are as follows:

	Sept	**Oct**	**Nov**	**Dec**	**Jan**	**Feb**
	£'000	*£'000*	*£'000*	*£'000*	*£'000*	*£'000*
Sales	540	540	705	1,275	890	440

An average of 25% gross margin on selling price is normally expected. 60% of sales are made for cash and 40% of sales are made to customers who are allowed to take two months' credit. In preparing the cash budget, it is normal to assume that all credit customers will take the full credit period before paying. An allowance for bad debts of 1% of total sales is to be made. Sales in August are £390,000.

Stocks at the end of each month are sufficient to meet 20% of the following month's sales. Suppliers allow one month's credit. Sales in March are expected to be £300,000.

Operating costs normally amount to £100,000 per month, including depreciation of £10,000. Payments are made during the month in which they are incurred. Because of the increased business and necessity to make overtime payments before Christmas, operating costs are expected to increase to £130,000 for December.

A long-term loan has to be repaid in January. The loan was initially for £120,000 but £132,000 is to be repaid because of interest charges. An overdraft facility has been negotiated. A charge is to be made of 2% per month on balances overdrawn at the end of each month, the charge to be added to the overdraft before the start of the following month.

The balance sheet as at 31 August shows:

Fixed assets	£1,500,000
Stocks	£ 81,000
Debtors	£ 207,000
Cash	£ 30,000
Shareholders capital	£1,383,000
Long-term debt	£ 120,000
Creditors	£ 315,000

Required:
Use the information provided above to calculate a master budget for the first six months of the budget period. Show, month by month, the profit and loss budget, the budgeted balance sheet,

the budgeted cash flow statement and the budgeted funds flow statement in as much detail as possible.

Answers on page 615

23.3.2 Standard costing and budget formulation

A budget is a financial quantification of plans whilst a standard cost is a predetermined statement of the intended cost of a product. Both systems therefore relate to future periods. The objectives of the two systems may coincide in motivational terms since each may intend to provide targets for managers to meet. Both systems may incorporate feedback to achieve organisational control. Each system may also influence the other. Standards for material and, in some cases, labour, may be incorporated into budgets. Budgeted overhead expenditure may be incorporated into standard costs. Standard costing variances may be used to reconcile budgeted and actual profit levels. Whilst these systems may overlap, the relationship should be viewed as complementary. Fundamentally, standard costing and budgeting are different systems, with different purposes and a range of different potential applications. Standards may not be applicable to organisations with no measurable output but such organisations may still advantageously apply budgeting. Budgeting may not be useful to organisations facing uncertainty, but in some situations, standard costs may still be useful. Small businesses with erratic order books for constant product ranges may find the task of budgeting unhelpful but may still benefit from knowledge of standards and standard cost variances. A small business with a regular cash flow cycle, experiencing rapid expansion, may monitor product profitability month by month by comparing revenues by individual products with standard costs but be happy to plan only in an informal, general manner.

23.3.3 Fixed and flexible budgets and standard costs

Fixed budgets are prepared for a single level of output and are compared with actual results without account being taken of the differences between budgeted and actual output levels. Flexible budgets can be produced for a range of different output levels, or as a statement of budgeted cost allowance, and compared with actual results for the actual level of output experienced. It has been argued that since flexible budgeting takes into account cost behaviour and output levels, it is more useful for control purposes. It could be argued that because fixed budgets are prepared at a single level of output, they are less confusing as statements of plans. It seeems that both fixed and flexible budgets may have their places in the planning and control cycle. In addition, it has been noted by some authorities that standard costing systems and flexible budgeting systems report the same variance under certain circumstances. The extent to which these systems are complementary will depend upon the basis for analysis of cost behaviour.

1. Standard costs of output are always calculated on the basis of actual levels of output in product terms (units sold or units produced, for example).
2. Flexible budgets should be flexed on the basis upon which information on cost behaviour rests. If cost behaviour information suggests that costs respond to product output, flexible budgets and standard costs will report the same total variances. If cost behaviour information suggests that costs respond to factors other than product output, perhaps the hours worked for labour costs, or the level of investment for some overhead costs such as depreciation, or to more than one variable, as in the case where multiple regression provides reliable cost behaviour information, then the flexed budget will differ from the level of standard cost of output.

Fixed budgets do not account for changes in output levels; flexible budgets incorporate cost behaviour information to provide reliable cost targets for actual levels of activity; standard costs are product based.

23.3.4 Zero based budgeting

A definition of zero based budgeting (ZBB), consistent with a famous paper by Pyrrh, is provided by Cheek:

'An operating, planning and budgeting process which requires each manager to justify his entire budget request in detail from scratch (zero) and shifts the burden of proof to each manager to justify why he should spend any money at all. This . . . requires that all activities be identified in "decision packages" which will be evaluated by systematic analysis and ranked in order of importance.'

Decision packages represent units of intended activity, such as the intention to carry out an advertising campaign, or to set up a system for the regular reporting of standard costing variances, or a research and development project. Each decision package can be related to organisational objectives and justified in cost benefit terms so that the organisation can receive assurance that its limited resources are being used effectively. At the outset, there is the presumption that the organisation will spend nothing on decision packages. The procedure may not be useful for committed or engineered costs. Only by making a suitable case to the budget committee can a manager be expected to be allocated a share of the resources of the organisation representing discretionary spending.

The primary rationale for ZBB is to overcome the defects of incremental budgeting, whereby the budget is adding an amount to existing resource allocations. These defects can be listed as follows:

1 There is no guarantee that budget allocations of resources will reflect organisational objectives, especially where these need to change in response to a changing environment.

2 Planning and budgeting may become separate activities in some organisations. The budget procedure may concentrate on taking the present situation and adjusting for inflation and other obvious changes. Planning may be an informal process not incorporated into budgeting for the lack of an obvious procedure or the lack of any knowledge of the relationship between plans and financial implications. This situation can be experienced by organisations with weak management information systems or organisations so constrained by cash or other resource limits that the budget becomes a strait-jacket and plans attempt to reduce the damage caused by inadequate financing. Imagine attempts to plan when information on the availability of funds is made available on an annual basis, based on spending in the previous year, one or two months before the beginning of the financial year.

3 Functional cost effectiveness is not assessed. The existing level of expenditure is simply perpetuated with no review of the contribution of a particular function to the corporate objectives.

4 There is no need to justify the resources requirements for new and existing activities. The rich departments are able to maintain their riches and have the ability to take new initiatives. The poor departments may merely survive from year to year because at the time the budgeting system was set up, the department happened to spend at a low level. In one situation known to the author, an incremental budgeting system led to one department owning numerous computers, few of which were actively used, whilst another department was forced to beg for a single computer when there was an established need for many computers. Incremental budgeting does not lead to the reallocation of resources to meet changing needs.

5 The lack of any justification for levels of spending does not allow fair quantitative or qualitative measurement of the achievements of departments. As long as departments spend at the level permitted by the budget, departmental performance gives the appearance of being satisfactory, irrespective of departmental achievements.

6 The process of considering alternative ways of committing resources in order to meet organisational objectives is not pursued. There is a possibly incorrect assumption that by continuing established patterns of expenditure, the objectives of the organisation will be met.

ZBB may be implemented in the following way:

1 Decision units are defined;
2 Alternative means by which organisational objectives can be met are formally considered;
3 Clear objectives for each decision unit are defined;
4 Cost benefit analysis is applied;
5 Decision units are submitted to the budget committee or equivalent filtering mechanism;

6 Decision units are ranked;
7 A process of bargaining proceeds through discussion and negotiation between the budget committee and the individuals responsible for submitting decision units;
8 A final list of approved decision units is communicated to budget centre managers. This list acts as permission to proceed with the decision units listed.

The decision units must be clearly defined in terms of description and objectives. Without a clear understanding of the causal links between decision units, activities anticipated and levels of resource allocation, the process of filtering decision units may not result in a list which benefits the organisation. There is a danger that those individuals skilled in the preparation of proposals will gain a larger share of the available scarce resource at the expense of possibly more worthy submissions which failed to persuade the budget committee because of the quality of the proposal rather than the quality of the decision unit.

Decision unit ranking can be a challenging process, especially where the budget committee comprises members with budget centre interests and, therefore, vested interests in the final listing. Where the budget committee comprises an unacceptable mixture of people to take a decision in the interests of the company as a whole, it may be possible to establish a special committee, budget staff may assume responsibility for filtering or the budget manager may take decisions. The opportunity for conflict to arise out of a process which allocates relative wealth should be clear to the reader. To minimise conflict, it may be possible to develop techniques so that the filtering process can be verified and so that the decision takers can be made accountable to the organisation as a whole. Techniques include:

1 **A single criterion**. The capital investment decision is a specialised example of a ZBB type of system, where individual projects may be subjected to NPV or IRR as a single criterion for acceptance. Other economic criteria may include the ability of the decision unit to create expansion, or cost reduction, or a suitable level of profitability.
2 **Multiple criteria**. Some decision units may be necessary to improve economic performance, others may meet legislative requirements, such as the provision of financial accounting information for published accounts purposes. In some circumstances both economic and legal requirements will need to be met and a single criterion will not satisfy the need to accept a portfolio of alternative decision units. In such circumstances, multiple criteria may be necessary, with considerable loss in the simplicity of operation of the filtering process.
3 **Voting**. Where a committee comprises members with the ability to take decisions to the benefit of the organisation as a whole, even where this implies some personal loss, a voting system may be effective.

A major problem in the implementation of ZBB, even where the screening process is sound, is associated with the time and quality of information which the process demands. Preparation of decision units, assessment of costs and benefits and committee meetings require time, commitment and a not insubstantial amount of effort. Different budget centre managers may have different understandings of the nature of decision units and may be advantaged or disadvantaged by their perceptions. Some decision units may cross budget centre boundaries and require the time of more than one manager (although the ability of ZBB to cross boundaries may also be seen as an advantage, in comparison to incremental budgeting). Decision units with a high degree of uncertainty, perhaps because of new technology implications, may be at a disadvantage in comparison with decision units which can show clear, short-term economic advantages.

Program planning and budgeting systems (PPBS) and Priority based budgeting (PBB) share some commonalty with ZBB. PPBS establishes programs (as opposed to decision units) which must be justified before acceptance. The term program may relate to an educational program such as the integration of technology into schools and colleges, or a local authority program, say to improve safety on the roads by spending money on traffic control. PBB demands that activities be prioritised in order that the relative merits and costs of those activities can be assessed. Prioritisation can be linked with cost reduction; low priority activities cease to be operated with a commensurate saving in resources. Both of these schemes employ a fairly high degree of judgment, either in assessing costs and benefits under PPBS, or in assessing priorities under PBB. Both seek to make explicit the rational basis for committing resources, through a process which is intended to be both scientific and objective.

As a postscript, it is interesting to note a finding made by Novick. Apparently the General Motors' Budget and Finance procedures, dated 1924, contained the following stages in budget preparation:

1 Major objectives should be defined;
2 Define the programs which are essential to meet those objectives;
3 Identify resources against specific objectives;
4 Systematically analyse alternatives.

The ideas which underpin ZBB, PPBS and PBB seem to go back a long way in time.

Self-assessment question 23.4

To what extent do you believe that ZBB meets the requirements of budget preparation as laid down by the General Motors' Budget and Finance procedures, 1924?

Answer on page 617

23.3.5 Management by objectives

Where plans cannot be quantified or expressed in financial terms and there is still a need for objective measurement of achievement, Management By Objectives MBO can be applied. This technique has much in common with budgeting whilst not providing a financial quantified statement of plans. An individual meets a senior manager in order to discuss future plans. A process of bargaining leads to a formal statement of plans in the form of a list of objectives, together with clear statements of timing. For example, a management accountant may agree to develop a formal capital investment appraisal system, incorporating DCF techniques, by June 19×0. The financial director may then arrange a meeting in June 19×0 to assess progress and hopefully to receive a report detailing the system to be implemented. Management by objectives is particularly suitable to those areas of performance where qualitative approaches pertain.

23.3.6 Management audits

The term management audit enjoys a range of meanings. For the purpose of this brief introduction, the definition provided by the Chartered Institute of Management Accountants will be adopted:

'An objective and independent appraisal of the effectiveness of managers and the effectiveness of the corporate structure in the achievement of company objectives and policies.

Its aim is to identify existing and potential management weaknesses within an organisation and to recommend ways to rectify these weaknesses.'

The audit will consider management systems, perhaps by attending management meetings or by reviewing formal communication systems, for instance. Evidence of the existence of long-term planning procedures will be expected. Strategic, management control and operational control links will be explored to determine the extent to which objectives and long term plans are capable of being converted into goal congruent action at appropriate organisational levels. An assessment of effectiveness, efficiency and economy will be made.

Where budgets represent a planning and control device for the financial aspects of an organisation and Management By Objectives may provide a planning and control device for the qualitative aspects of an organisation, management audit is concerned with control of the strategic and management control processes themselves. Corrective action results from evaluation against criteria which the auditors must judge to be appropriate for the organisation within which the audit proceeds. Where the budget must rely for its scientific and objectivity bases on the quality of the process by which the budget is produced, and Management By Objectives must rely on the quality of the bargaining process between manager and subordinate, the management audit relies on the judgment, integrity, experience and expertise of the person or team conducting the audit. Planning and control is a multi-faceted activity calling for a range of approaches and a range of judgments.

23.3.7 Forecasting

In an article published in March 1983 in Management Accounting, McHugh and Sparkes provided a substantial amount of evidence concerning forecasting in theory and in practice. Much of this section is based on their article because of the importance of the material to a fuller understanding of both budgeting itself and to the reasons for differences between the subject of text books and the practice of accountants.

Before discussing forecasting in more depth it is appropriate to establish the difference between forecasting and budgeting and the role which forecasting may play in the budgeting process. Budgeting is a formal process, necessitating the involvement and co-ordination of all aspects of the business. Forecasting may be formal or informal and may only involve one aspect of the business, as in the sales forecast, or a summary of the main financial variables, as in the case of the profit forecast. Potentially, the budget has many objectives. The forecast is primarily concerned with predicting future outcomes. The budget may take a number of months to produce because of its iterative nature and the need for communication and co-ordination. The forecast may be a morning's exercise for the sales director or the financial director. The budget may be expressed as a single target. The forecast may be expressed as a range of possible outcomes. 'We expect a profit of between £1.0 million and £1.3 million' may be a respectable expression of forecast. A budget may be produced once a year. Forecasts may be updated monthly or at more regular intervals, as circumstances change. Despite these differences, forecasts may be incorporated into budgets where this meets the objectives laid down. A sales forecast may form the basis for targets appearing in the budget. A profit forecast for the company as a whole may be used by senior management in the review of budget centre submissions.

McHugh and Sparkes divide forecasting techniques into three broad categories: subjective, statistical and causal model building. Subjective approaches include the following:

1 **Individual assessments**. The sales director assesses the sales forecast based on personal experience, contacts with the sales force, contacts with customers and trends. The financial director applies financial models, including knowledge of cost behaviour, to extrapolate forward on the basis of sales forecasts and known changes in circumstance. A summarised profit and loss account may be produced.
2 **Team assessments**. The board of directors may meet and agree on sales and profit forecasts by a process of discussion and informal and formal calculations. Perhaps the financial director will have produced a spreadsheet model of the profit and loss account and will try different figures in the model, as the meeting progresses.
3 **Delphi method**. Individual assessments are made on an independent basis. The results of these assessments are then summarised and fed back to the individuals, who can reassess their forecasts on the basis of knowledge of the opinions of others. The process is iterative to a point at which a consensus emerges or no further useful progress can be made.

Statistical approaches include:

1 **Moving averages**. Moving averages are calculated and used to extrapolate results into the future.
2 **Exponential smoothing**. An example of exponential smoothing follows.

Example 23.1

Foresee plc uses exponential smoothing to predict its sales for the following period. The first period that Foresee started in business, sales of £100,000 were achieved. Since no further information was available, £100,000 was predicted as the sales for the second period. In fact, the sales for the second period turned out to be £90,000. The forecast for the third period was calculated as follows:

Present result	× 0.3	90,000 × 0.3 = £27,000
Previous forecast	× 0.7	100,000 × 0.7 = £70,000
		£97,000

The figure of 0.3 is determined from experience. It could be referred to as "alpha". The figure applied to the previous forecast is (1 – alpha) or 0.7. Where alpha is 1, the forecast is the same as the present result. Where alpha is 0, the forecast is the same as the previous forecast. It is normal for alpha to be somewhere between 0 and 1, therefore.

The result for period 3 was £103,000. The forecast for period 4 would be:

Present result	× 0.3	103,000 × 0.3 = £30,900
Previous forecast	× 0.7	97,000 × 0.7 = £67,900
		£98,800

Once several periods' forecasts and results have been collected, it may be appropriate to check whether other values of alpha would have given forecasts closer to the results. If so, the revised figure of alpha could be applied to future forecasting. The suitability of statistical approaches can be tested on past data and only used for forecasting purposes where a good fit between forecasted and reported values occurs. Statistical approaches are least easily applied where past conditions are not a fair reflection of future events.

Causal model building includes:

1 **Regression.** This can be particularly applied to the forecasting of costs by means illustrated in the section on cost behaviour earlier in the book. If regression analysis shows that the total cost of output is given by, for instance:

£2.50 × output + £600,000,

a forecast of output can be used to generate the cost forecast. For example if an output of 100,000 units is predicted, the cost forecast would be £850,000 (£2.50 × 100,000 + £600,000).

2 **Econometric.** This model building process is normally associated with economic forecasting. A series of variables is defined in relation to the object to be forecasted. Constants, or parameters are determined for each of the variables in order to provide predictive capability. Once the model has been constructed and tested, inputting values for each variable results in a forecast through a process by which values are evaluated according to parameter values.

Example 23.2

An example of using model building to forecast a sales value can be shown by the following variables and parameters:

Variables	Parameter
Market size	0.2
Average selling price	0.9
Inflation	1.0

If the company can now gain access to national information on anticipated inflation and trade information on market size and average selling price, the forecast could be produced as follows:

Market size	1,000,000
Average selling price	£2
Inflation	5%

Forecast: (1,000,000 × 0.2) × (0.9 × 2) × (1 × 1.05)
£378,000

The process of using models and statistics can be summarised as follows:

1 Determine the variables of relevance to the forecast;
2 Conduct analysis to determine the impact of variables on the forecast;

3 Select an appropriate model from the various modelling approaches available. Perhaps a forecasting expert could be consulted at this stage;
4 Test the model on existing data in order to assess the degree of error caused by the selection of an inappropriate model or caused by random variations (noise) in the historical data;
5 Use the chosen model to provide a forecast. If the model proves to be unreliable, begin the process again, at 1 above, or perhaps use a judgmental approach if more scientific means cannot be established.

McHugh and Sparkes found the following causes for the non-use of formal techniques of forecasting:

1 Practitioners lacked knowledge, expertise or confidence in formal techniques;
2 Insufficient past data was available to apply particular techniques;
3 Time was not available to develop and apply formal techniques;
4 Practitioners considered that formal techniques cannot make a useful contribution to forecasting.

Equally interesting are the factors considered to limit the accuracy of forecasting techniques in general:

1 Instability in the world and national economy;
2 The impact of unknown factors;
3 The impact of inflation;
4 Inadequate market knowledge;
5 Lack of internal and external data, including lack of suitable government and trade association data;
6 Lack of knowledge and expertise in individual forecasting techniques.

A number of these points can be not only related to forecasting in particular but also to budgeting as a planning device, if the objective is to make assessments about the likely impact of future events. Chapter 27 provides some responses to the problem of budgeting in times of uncertainty.

23.3.8 Financial models

Extending the ideas presented in the forecasting section, it is possible to express budgets in terms of financial models. The following examples provide examples of models which may be relevant to budgeting:

1 Purchases = (Sales + increase in finished goods stock + increase in work-in-progress stock) × (raw material usage per unit of production + increase in raw material stock) × price per unit of raw materials.
The basic formula would be summed for all raw materials.
2 Total cost = Sales £ × present total cost/present sales £.
3 Total cost = Variable cost per unit × output units + fixed cost per unit.
4 Labour cost = number of labour hours for the first unit × cumulative number of units, to the power of the learning coefficient × wages rate per hour.

The final model is the learning curve model.

The budget as a whole can be expressed as a series of formulae suitable to the company. Relations between limiting factors, quantity budgets, values, capital expenditure and working capital can be expressed so that the budget is seen as a series of mathematical formulae rather than as a set of steps or procedures for the accountant to follow. The advantage of expressing the budget as a formal model is provided by the capacity of the computer to take over the routine processing of numbers once a model has been developed.

Two types of model are relevant to budgeting:

1 **Descriptive models**. Perhaps a spreadsheet or modelling language such as FCS can be used to describe the budget so that numbers can be input to the model for processing. Processing results would be assessed in the iterative manner associated with the budgeting process.
2 **Optimising models.** Linear programming techniques could be applied to the basic budget data in order to provide information on the optimum levels of activity. Where this procedure is followed and results are translated into organisation planning, care needs to be taken in relation to the decision significant variance explained in Chapter 26.

It has been argued that budgeting is a financial model irrespective of the way that figures are processed. The time consuming process of developing the model to a formal level by employing technology can save time in the long-term and thus achieve good cost benefit outcomes.

SUMMARY

Budgeting is a process by which planning and control can be effected. Its objectives are varied, at a detailed level, and encompass co-ordination, communication, motivation and performance evaluation. The procedures adopted may vary from organisation to organisation but are likely to be iterative in nature. Within a general framework of procedures, it is likely that a variety of detailed processes may be employed, including modelling, forecasting, management audit, management by objectives, zero based budgeting and cash budgeting. Each process has potential advantages and suitable areas of application and each process has inherent weaknesses. Research has shown a variety of reasons for the use of relatively simple techniques in practice despite the existence of more sophisticated approaches.

EXERCISES

Exercise 23.1

(a) 'The linear cost model is basic to conventional budgeting systems'. Explain and discuss.
(b) 'The linear cost model is an unsatisfactory approximation to reality'. Explain and discuss.

(*ACCA, Management Accounting, December 1986, slightly adapted*)

Answers in lecturer's manual.

Exercise 23.2

Tomm Ltd has three manufacturing departments. One of these is regarded, for responsibility accounting purposes, as a cost centre whereas the other two are classified as profit centres. Cost centre 1 (CC1) produces two joint products, P12 and P13. P12 is processed further in profit centre 2 (PC2) to yield P2. P13 is processed further in profit centre 3 (PC3) to yield P3.

The draft budgets for the three departments are as follows:

Department	CC1	PC2	PC3
Budgeted output	20,000kg of P12 40,000 kg of P13	40,000 units	20,000 units
	£'000	£'000	£'000
Budgeted sales revenue	—	1,600	800
Cost of goods sold			
Bought in material	100	20	30
Internal transfers	(600)	200	400
Direct labour	120	150	110

Department	CC1	PC2	PC3
	£'000	£'000	£'000
Processing cost	150	115	145
Administrative salaries	55	135	150
General overhead allocation	175	30	15
		650	850
Budgeted profit (loss)		950	(50)

The processing costs can be analysed as follows:

Department	CC1	PC2	PC3
Variable			
Identifiable with individual departments and varying with output	120	20	5
Fixed			
Identifiable with individual departments and controllable by departmental management	25	90	130
Central computer services not controllable by departmental management—allocated on basis of floor area	5	5	10

If the centrally provided computer facilities were obtained from outside the organisation on an individual basis by the individual departments, it is estimated that this would cost:

CC1	PC2	PC3
£'000	£'000	£'000
25	20	5

The costs of CC1 have been allocated to PC2 and PC3 on the basis of the weight of material transferred during the period. This basis has been used in the past but is now being questioned as it seems to bias the figures in favour of PC2. An investigation of this, and other aspects of the budgeting system, has been undertaken and the following recommendations have been made:

1 Fixed and variable costs should be separated in the budgets.
2 Controllable and uncontrollable costs should be clearly distinguished.
3 Joint costs (both fixed and variable) should be allocated so that both profit centres show the same profit rate (as a percentage of sales value).
4 Central computer costs should be allocated in a manner which recognises the cost savings achieved by using a central facility.

You are required to redraft the budget in a way that conforms to these recommendations. Make (and state) any assumptions that you consider necessary or appropriate. Provide a report for management on the implications of the changes for the budgeting process in general.

(*ACCA, December 1986, Management Accounting, slightly extended*)

Answers in lecturer's manual.

Exercise 23.3

Prepare a flow chart to explain the statement that budgeting is an iterative process.

(*ACCA, Management Accounting, December 1986*)

Answer in lecturer's manual.

Exercise 23.4

'Developments in information technology have significant effects on the accountant's use of mathematical modelling.'

Describe five areas in which the use of mathematical modelling using computers might benefit management accounting.

(*ACCA, June 1987*)

Answers on page 617

Exercise 23.5

Use the tables which appear at the end of this exercise to answer the following question.

Narud plc is nearing the end of year 7 and has prepared summary profit and loss account data for year 6 (actual) and year 7 (projected annual) as shown in Table 1. Table 1 also shows the bank overdraft at the end of year 6 and the projected bank overdraft at the end of year 7. Sales and production mix may be taken as constant from year 6 to year 9, with all production being sold in the year of production.

Budgeted direct material cost is variable with output volume but budgeted direct labour cost contains a fixed element of £50,000 in year 6 with the remainder varying with production volume and used in the calculation of the labour efficiency index in Table 2.

Production overhead contains a fixed element of £150,000 (at year 6 price levels). Included within this fixed element is a depreciation charge of £30,000 which will remain unaltered irrespective of price level changes.

Variable production overhead varies in proportion to units produced.

Budgeted administrative/selling overhead is wholly fixed, whilst distribution expense should vary with sales volume.

The financial charges figure for each year is calculated as the average borrowing for the year times the borrowing rate (taken as 20%)
ie Financial charges per year = $((2x\text{-}y) \times 0.2)/2$
where x = previous year end overdraft and y = net profit for current year before financial charges and depreciation.

Narud plc are concerned about the level of borrowing and high financial charges. A number of changes are planned in order to attempt to eliminate the overdraft by the end of year 9, eg:

(i) Change the type of material used from year 8 onwards as a means of reducing scrap and hence improving efficiency.
(ii) It is anticipated that the material change per (i) above together with extra training of operatives in each of years 8 and 9 will improve labour efficiency.
(iii) Selling prices will be cut in years 8 and 9 in order to stimulate demand.

Tables 2 and 3 show cost indices for performance and price respectively which show the projected changes from a year 6 base 100. The performance indices show the cost effect of performance changes, eg material usage in year 8 indicates a 5% cost reduction from the base year level because of the reduced level of material per product unit referred to in (i) above.

Table 4 shows the sales volume and price movements from a year 6 base of 100.

Required:
(a) Give detailed working calculations which show how the year 7 projected figures (per Table 1) have been arrived at for (i) labour cost (ii) production overhead and (iii) financial charges, using the year 6 data per Table 1 as the starting point and using indices from Tables 2, 3 and 4 as necessary.
(b) Prepare forecast profit and loss accounts for years 8 and 9 and calculate the forecast bank balance or overdraft at the end of years 8 and 9, assuming that the overdraft is affected only by the net profit adjusted for the non-cash effect of the depreciation charge.
(c) Enumerate THREE items not incorporated in the profit and loss account which may affect cash flow.

(d) Explain how the calculations in (b) above demonstrate the use of a feed-forward control model.

(*ACCA, Management Accounting, June 1988*)

Answers on page 618

TABLE 1 **Narud plc**

Summary Profit and Loss Account

	Year 6	Year 7
	£	£
Sales revenue	2,000,000	2,310,000
Less cost of sales:		
Direct material cost	1,000,000	1,201,200
Direct labour cost	150,000	163,300
Production overhead	310,000	350,124
Admin/selling overhead	100,000	115,500
Distribution overhead	140,000	158,466
Financial charges	130,000	124,859
	1,830,000	2,113,449
Net profit	170,000	196,551
Bank overdraft	800,000	573,449

TABLE 2 **Indices reflecting the cost effect of changes in performance level from year 6**

Year	Material usage	Labour efficiency	Production overhead utilisation (fixed and variable)	Selling overhead utilisation	Distribution overhead utilisation
6	100	100	100	100	100
7	104	103	103	110	98
8	95	99	99	105	95
9	85	97	97	100	95

TABLE 3 **Indices reflecting the cost effect of price level changes from year 6**

Year	Material price	Labour rate	All overheads expenditure
6	100	100	100
7	105	100	105
8	120	110	112
9	125	115	118

TABLE 4 **Indices for sales/production volume changes and sales price changes from year 6**

Year	Sales volume	Sales price
6	100	100
7	110	105
8	120	103
9	130	101

Exercise 23.6

Discuss the importance of FOUR of the following items to the formulation of fixed or flexible budgets:

(i) learning curve
(ii) cash budget
(iii) zero based budgeting
(iv) standard costing
(v) management by objectives
(vi) forecasting.

Answers in lecturer's manual.

Exercise 23.7

In the third week of April the accountant of the SW division of Jackson Brothers plc* is reviewing the division's Cash Budget up to the end of the company's financial year (31 August). Each of the company's divisions has its own bank account but arrangements are made centrally for transfers among these as a need or opportunity arises. Interest is charged (or allowed) on such intra company transfers at a market related rate.

The three months of May, June and July are the SW division's busiest months, providing two-thirds of its annual profit, but there is always a cash flow problem in this period. In anticipation of a cash shortage, arrangements have been made to borrow (internally) £100,000 over the busy period at an annual interest rate of 15% (chargeable monthly). The agreed borrowing and repayment schedule is as follows:

1 May borrowing of £30,000
1 June borrowing of £70,000
1 July repayment of £20,000
1 August repayment of £60,000
1 September repayment of £20,000

The accountant has in front of him the budgeted divisional profit and loss account figures for the four months to 31 August and the profit and loss accounts for March and April—the latter being an estimated statement. These documents can be summarised as follows:

	March	*April*	*May*	*June*	*July*	*August*
	£	£	£	£	£	£
Sales revenue	120,000	120,000	230,000	250,000	300,000	160,000
Factory cost of goods sold	100,000	100,000	182,500	197,500	235,000	130,000
Selling and distribution costs	4,200	4,200	6,400	6,800	7,800	5,000
Administrative costs and interest charges	7,000	7,000	7,375	8,250	8,000	7,250
	111,200	111,200	196,275	212,550	250,800	142,250
Divisional Profit	8,800	8,800	33,725	37,450	49,200	17,750
	£120,000	£120,000	£230,000	£250,000	£300,000	£160,000

The accountant is using the following assumptions:

1 Each factory cost of goods sold figure includes a fixed cost element of £10,000 of which £2,000 is depreciation. The remaining fixed factory cost can reasonably be assumed to be paid as it is charged.

2 Direct material cost is approximately 75% of the variable factory cost of the firm's products.

* *In Great Britain, the Companies Act 1980 requires public limited companies to use Public Limited Company or the abbreviation p.l.c., as part of their names.*

The suppliers of this direct material are paid in the month following its purchase. Other variable factory costs of production are paid in the month that the production takes place.

3 Half of the fixed selling and distribution cost is a depreciation charge for motor vehicles. The remaining cost under this heading is paid in the month in which it is charged.

4 A monthly Central Administration charge of £1,000 and interest on any borrowings are charged to Administrative Costs and Interest Charges and credited to a Head Office Current Account. Other administrative costs of approximately £6,000 per month are paid monthly.

5 The following policies are followed by the division:

(a) the target month end stock level for finished goods is £10,000 plus 25% of the variable cost of next month's budgeted sales—finished goods are valued at variable cost for accounting purposes;

(b) the target month end stock level for direct materials is £10,000 plus 25% of the material required for next month's budgeted production.

6 All sales are on credit terms. 20% of the cash from customers is received in the month following that in which the sales were made, the remainder is received in the next month.

7 The cash at bank and in hand at the end of April is expected to be approximately £10,000.

(a) You are required to prepare the division's cash budget for the months of May and June. Each cash figure should be rounded to the nearest £1,000.

(b) The accountant has been experimenting with the use of the following formula for predicting month end cash holdings:

$$\text{CB} = \text{OB} + 0.8S_{i-2} - 0.12S_{i-1} - 0.37S_i - 0.08S_{i+1} - 15$$

where CB is the predicted closing cash balance in £'000 for month i;
OB is the (estimated) opening cash balance in £'000 for month i;
and S_i is the sales figure for month i in £'000, actual or budgeted as appropriate.

Assuming that this formula is appropriate, comment on the effect on the division's cash holding at the end of May, of deviations of ±10% in the May sales figure from the budgeted figure.
(*Note*: Do not use the formula in part (a) to this question)

(c) Consider the possibility of introducing a discount scheme to encourage customers to pay promptly. How would you judge the worthwhileness of such a scheme?

(d) The Finance Director of Jackson Brothers plc is considering a change in the procedures for evaluating divisional performance. Instead of merely charging interest on intra company cash borrowing, he is considering the charging of interest on the company's total investment in each division. Comment on this proposal and discuss the difficulties and advantages of such a system.

(*ACCA, Management Accounting, December 1982*)

Answers in lecturer's manual.

Exercise 23.8

ZBB Ltd has two service departments—material handling and maintenance, which are in competition for budget funds which must not exceed £925,000 in the coming year. A zero base budgeting approach will be used whereby each department is to be treated as a decision package and will submit a number of levels of operation showing the minimum level at which its service could be offered and two additional levels which would improve the quality of the service from the minimum level.

The following data have been prepared for each department showing the three possible operating levels for each:

Material handling department

Level 1. A squad of 30 labourers would work 40 hours per week for 48 weeks of the year. Each labourer would be paid a basic rate of £4 per hour for a 35 hour week. Overtime hours would attract a premium of 50% on the basic rate per hour. In addition, the company anticipates payments of 20% of gross wages in respect of employee benefits. Directly attributable variable overheads would be incurred at the rate of 12p per man hour. The squad would move 600,000 kilos per week to a warehouse at the end of the production process.

Level 2. In addition to the level 1 operation, the company would lease 10 fork lift trucks at a cost of £2,000 per truck per annum. This would provide a better service by enabling the same volume of output as for level 1 to be moved to a customer collection point which would be 400 metres closer to the main factory gate. Each truck would be manned by a driver working a 48 week year. Each driver would receive a fixed weekly wage of £155.

Directly attributable overheads of £150 per truck per week would be incurred.

Level 3. A computer could be leased to plan the work of the squad of labourers in order to reduce their total work hours. The main benefit would be improvement in safety through reduction in the time that work in progress would lie unattended. The computer leasing costs would be £20,000 for the first quarter (three months), reducing by 10% per quarter cumulatively thereafter.

The computer data would result in a 10% reduction in labourer hours, half of this reduction being a saving in overtime hours.

Maintenance department

Level 1. Two engineers would each be paid a salary of £18,000 per annum and would arrange for repairs to be carried out by outside contractors at an annual cost of £250,000.

Level 2. The company would employ a squad of 10 fitters who would carry out breakdown repairs and routine maintenance as required by the engineers. The fitters would each be paid a salary of £11,000 per annum.

Maintenance materials would cost £48,000 per annum and would be used at a constant rate throughout the year. The purchases could be made in batches of £4,000, £8,000, £12,000 or £16,000. Ordering costs would be £100 per order irrespective of order size and stock holding costs would be 15% per annum. *The minimum cost order size would be implemented.*

Overheads directly related to the maintenance operation would be a fixed amount of £50,000 per annum.

In addition to the maintenance squad it is estimated that £160,000 of outside contractor work would still have to be paid for.

Level 3. The company could increase its maintenance squad to 16 fitters which would enable the service to be extended to include a series of major overhauls of machinery. The additional fitters would be paid at the same salary as the existing squad members.

Maintenance materials would now cost £96,000 per annum and would be used at a constant rate throughout the year. Purchases could be made in batches of £8,000, £12,000 or £16,000. Ordering costs would be £100 per order (irrespective of order size) and stock holding costs would now be 13.33% per annum. In addition, suppliers would now offer discounts of 2% of purchase price for orders of £16,000. The minimum cost order size would be implemented.

Overheads directly related to the maintenance operation would increase by £20,000 from the level 2 figure.

It is estimated that £90,000 of outside contractor work would still have to be paid for.

Required:

(a) Determine the incremental cost for each of levels 1, 2 and 3 in each department.

(b) In order to choose which of the incremental levels of operation should be allocated the limited budgeted funds available, management have estimated a 'desirability factor' which should be applied to each increment. The ranking of the increments is then based on the 'incremental cost × desirability factor' score, whereby a high score is deemed more desirable than a low score. The desirability factors are estimated as:

	Material handling	*Maintenance*
Level 1	1.00	1.00
Level 2 (incremental)	0.60	0.80
Level 3 (incremental)	0.50	0.20

Use the above ranking process to calculate which of the levels of operation should be implemented in order that the budget of £925,000 is not exceeded.

(c) Comment on factors which should be taken into account in practice in arriving at the decision as to the ranking of the various levels of operation.

(*ACCA, Management Accounting, December 1988*)

Answers in lecturer's manual.

Exercise 23.9

(a) At the end of December the management accountant has in front of him the company's budgeted profit and loss account figures for each of the months from the following January to June. The July and August budgets follow the same pattern as that for June. The budgets can be summarised as follows:

	January	*February*	*March*	*April*	*May*	*June*
Sales quantity	2,500	2,500	3,500	5,000	7,500	4,000
Production quantity	3,000	3,500	4,500	5,000	5,000	4,000
	£	£	£	£	£	£
Sales revenue	30,000	30,000	42,000	60,000	90,000	48,000
Factory						
Cost of production	28,500	33,250	42,750	47,500	47,500	38,000
Stock adjustment	(4,750)	(9,500)	(9,500)		23,750	
Factory						
Cost of goods sold	23,750	23,750	33,250	47,500	71,250	38,000
Selling and distribution						
Costs	2,250	2,250	2,350	2,500	2,750	2,400
Administration costs	3,000	3,000	3,000	3,000	3,000	3,000
Profit	1,000	1,000	3,400	7,000	13,000	4,600
	30,000	30,000	42,000	60,000	90,000	48,000

The budgeted factory fixed overhead for the year is £140,000 and this is absorbed into the factory cost of production at the rate of £3.50 per unit. £32,000 of this overhead is depreciation of machinery and buildings, the remainder arises evenly throughout the year and is paid as it arises. Month end balances representing budgeted under or over absorbed overhead are carried forward and for the year as a whole the budgeted overhead is fully absorbed by the budgeted production. One quarter of the variable factory cost of production is direct material cost and the balance is predominantly manufacturing labour and similar services that are paid for as they arise. The planned direct material purchases of one month are determined by the planned production of the subsequent month. Suppliers are normally paid 30 days after the receipt of goods but it is possible to delay payment in some cases for another month. This course of action is only resorted to sparingly as the company does not wish to spoil its credit standing. 20% of the purchases attract a 5% discount for prompt (ie immediate) settlement. 75% of customers settle their accounts in the month following the sale, 20% take another month's credit and the remaining 5% pay in the third month following the sale.

The company normally pays an interim dividend at the end of June and it is anticipated that the net payment to be made in the forthcoming June will be £30,000.

You are required to prepare the company's Cash Budget for the months of April, May and June assuming that the cash balance at the start of April is estimated at £5,000 and the company's policy is to maintain a month end cash balance no lower than £4,000 and no higher than £10,000. Surplus cash can be invested on a short-term basis at 10% p.a. interest. No recognition has been given in the budgeted profit and loss accounts to any discount receivable or short-term loan interest.

(b) Discuss and describe the possible use of a spread sheet computer package in the development of an organisation's cash budgets.

(*ACCA, Management Accounting, June 1985*)

Answers in lecturer's manual.

Exercise 23.10

A company has two machines – A and B – each of which may be used to produce Products X and Y. The products are fabric, made in a number of widths by passing untreated fabric across one of the machines and then adding a colour dye.
Budget/Forecast data for 1988 are as follows:

(i) Stocks at 1 January 1988:

Product X	30,000 metres at 120 cm width
Product Y	5,000 metres at 200 cm width
Untreated fabric	25,000 sq metres
Fabric dye	25 kilos

(ii) The closing stock of untreated fabric is budgeted at 10% of the required input to production during 1988. No closing stocks of X or Y are budgeted.

(iii) Fabric yield is budgeted at 90% of input for Machine A and 80% of input for Machine B, due to processing losses.

(iv) Fabric dye is used at the rate of 1 kilo per 500 square metres of *output* for both Products X and Y. The maximum quantity available from suppliers during 1988 is 520 kilos. If there is insufficient dye to meet production requirements, the output of the narrowest product would be reduced as required.

(v) The budgeted rates of good output for Machines A and B are the same and vary with the width of products according to the following table:

Product width (*cm*)	*Good output per machine hour* (*metres*)
100	120
120	100
140	90
160	80
180	70
200	50
240	40

(vi) The maximum output width of product from each machine is Machine A: 140 cm, Machine B: 240 cm.
It is company policy not to use Machine B for product widths less than 125 cm.

(vii) Each machine is manned for 35 hours per week for 46 weeks in the year. Part of this is budgeted to be lost as idle time as follows: Machine A: 20% of manned hours; Machine B: 30% of manned hours. This idle time does not include any idle time caused by a shortage of fabric dye.

(viii) The sales forecast for 1988 is as follows:

Product X	90,000 metres at 120 cm width
	70,000 metres at 160 cm width
Product Y	30,000 metres at 200 cm width
	100,000 metres at 100 cm width

(ix) If production capacity is not sufficient to allow the sales forecast to be achieved, the budgets for production on each machine will be set by limiting the quantity of the narrowest product on that machine.

Required:

(a) Prepare budgets for 1988 analysed by product type and width for (i) production quantities and (ii) sales quantities. The budgets should make maximum use of the available resources.

(b) Prepare a purchases budget for untreated fabric. Express the budget in terms of square metres purchased.

(c) Suggest ways in which the company might attempt to overcome any inability to meet the sales forecast. Comment on any problems likely to arise in the implementation of each of these ways.

(*ACCA, Management Accounting, December 1987*)

Answers in lecturer's manual.

Standards: Preparation, Procedures and Purposes

INTRODUCTION

Chapter 22 explained that a range of sources of reference data is available from which variances can be calculated. In the next chapter, the specific variances commonly associated with standard costing are examined and their meaning explained. This chapter is concerned with reviewing standard costing systems themselves, largely in isolation from variance analysis. Standard costing approaches can be used for a variety of purposes. These purposes are discussed. Since standard costing and variance analysis are often closely associated, the meaning of the term standard is closely considered and the relationship with variance analysis is explained.

At the end of the chapter, the student should be able to:

1 Calculate a standard product cost and appreciate the alternative bases for such a calculation;
2 Design a standard costing system from basic principles of systems operation;
3 Explain the interaction between standards and budgets and be able to define the meaning of standard;
4 Discuss the purposes of standard costing systems and explain the role of variance analysis in feedback.

24.1 PREPARING STANDARD COSTS

24.1.1 The meaning of standard cost

CIMA define a standard cost as a:
'predetermined calculation of how much costs should be under specified working conditions.'

A dictionary provides a less specialised, but no less useful, series of definitions. Here are some of the many definitions:

1 'The authorised exemplar of a unit of measure or weight; eg a measuring rod of unit length; a vessel of unit capacity, or a mass of unit weight, preserved in the custody of public officers as a permanent evidence of the legally prescribed magnitude of the unit.'
2 'A normal uniform size or amount; a prescribed minimum size or amount.'
3 'An authoritative or recognised exemplar of correctness, perfection, or some definite degree of any quality.'
4 'A rule, principle, or means of judgment or estimation; a criterion, measure.'
5 'A definite level of excellence, attainment, wealth or the like, or a definite degree of any quality, viewed as a prescribed object of endeavour or as the measure of what is adequate for some purpose.'

A summary of these definitions leads to the following definition of standard as it applies in accounting situations:

1 A standard applies to a future period (it is predetermined);
2 A standard is a measure of quality. Since an accepted definition of quality is 'conformance or

fitness for purpose', it is necessary to link the definition of standard with its purpose;

3 A standard is used as a yardstick against which other measures can be related. In this regard, the standard carries a prescribed element arising from a level of authority.

Unfortunately, these aspects of the term standard can easily conflict with each other when applied to real world accounting problems. In an uncertain world, a predetermined measure can lose its relevance as events and circumstances arise which could not be foreseen. Previous study of organisational implications should suggest that standards which are no longer relevant will not carry the same authority, or ability to act as a yardstick to motivate managers, as a relevant standard. Consider the example of a company which develops a standard for material prices based on present prices and an assessment of future price increases. Unexpected changes in the market place can quickly invalidate the use of the standard as a yardstick. Similarly, a predetermined value may cease to be a relevant measure of quality, subject to the purpose of the standard.

Emmanuel and Otley relate standards to the scientific management principles associated with Taylorism. This implies the yardstick definition of standard. A particular aspect of Taylorism which is known to be problematic is the application of workstudy. Examples of difficulties which are known to arise from the timings of direct workers, one aspect of the work of the workstudy expert, is the building in of slack by workers who know that loose timings can result in increased wage payments. A worker may decide to work at a low level of productivity when being timed and return to a normal level of productivity once the particular operation becomes part of normal production. This can lead to the kinds of bargaining noted for the management of slack in budgeting. Management may assess the timing in terms of a particular level of performance and this level can become a subject of negotiation with union officials. If results are perceived to be unfavourable from the point of view of the workforce, the next workstudy timing may be further biased. It is thus difficult to divorce standards from the people to whom the standards will apply, when the yardstick element is present.

Some authorities differentiate estimates and standards, even though the definitions above could embrace both terms. A standard is seen by these authorities as being a scientific, pre-determined measure where an estimate is merely pre-determined. In practice, the distinction may be one of usage rather than absolute difference in meaning. An estimate may be used for a variety of purposes; as a rough forecast of future costs and revenues or as a quotation provided to customers. In situations where a quotation becomes a fixed contract price, the estimate must be more than a loose prediction of future outcomes; it becomes in effect a standard which a company must match in order to meet target profitability; any deviation from estimate has a direct consequence for profitability. The estimate must be at least as scientifically derived as a standard. The author is aware of companies which use the same product cost as an estimate in dealings with customers and as a standard in motivating the workforce. In such situations, the difference becomes one of semantics rather than accounting significance. The importance of the purpose of the estimate and the standard explains any differences which arise.

Standards are thus seen as future values which have connotations of quality and/or control, through usage as yardsticks. Standards introduce organisational implications and necessitate comparison with other values used by the organisation, such as estimates. Standards can be applied to costs and revenue values. We can thus talk about standard selling prices, standard costs and standard profits, each of which may convey slightly different meanings in different organisations, depending on the purposes to which standards are used.

The importance of standards is summarised well by a quotation from a Rolls Royce consultant, given in Sizer and Coulthurst's case study book:

'All business activities are undertaken with the primary purpose of making profits. Profits represent the main-spring of industry and a cost system, like any other business instrument, must be regarded solely from the standpoint of the extent to which it directly or indirectly aids in the making or safeguarding of profits.

'Prospective or standard systems of cost accounting which are based on the underlying idea that cost information to be of constructive value must be shown in relation to standard and not confined merely to records of actual costs expressed without relation to what costs should be.'

For the remainder of the chapter, standard will be taken to mean 'what costs should be'. The purpose of this opening section is to point out that it is impossible to consider 'what costs should be' in isolation from organisational implications and particular purposes to which standard costing is applied.

24.1.2 Approaches to establishing standards; engineered costs

MATERIALS

Materials standards are of three types: quantity standards, value standards and mix standards. From the point of view of developing standards, mix standards arise from the preparation of quantity standards and so will not be considered separately.

Quantity standards for materials are concerned with establishing the categories and quantities of materials used in producing finished output. There are four ways in which categories and quantities can be determined:

1 **By stripping a finished product to its basic components.**
This may be an appropriate method for small or non-complex finished items such as furniture or textile products. A jumper can be cut up into panels, each panel weighed and the yarn forming each panel determined. In an extreme case, each panel can be unravelled so that individual yarns can be weighed. This extreme will not be necessary where designers or production management are in a position to state the proportions or mix of yarns for each type of panel in the completed jumper. A sample approach is likely to be necessary since one jumper may not be representative of all jumpers produced; it may be at one extreme of the tolerances which are inevitable and permitted by quality control. For example, the lengths of sleeves may vary by small amounts which are not significant in market terms but which may cause problems when the weight of an individual garment is multiplied by the total production for a period of time. An allowance for wastage needs to be added on to the quantities calculated in this fashion.

This aproach is time consuming and therefore relatively expensive. Where a company has a wide product range, with variations in sizings for each product, this method is particularly expensive. Variations between production runs, even where output is within tolerances, can lead to distortions in results unless very careful sampling procedures are followed.

2 **By ad hoc trials.**
Inputs to a particular process are carefully measured and outputs are counted for a particular period of time. The standard is determined by dividing the separate categories of input materials by the number of output units. A suitable example may be provided by the biscuit industry. A batch of dough can be mixed from known raw materials. The number of units of finished biscuits can then be physically counted for the batch. For each raw material, sugar, flour and so on, the quantity required per unit of output can then be determined.

The major drawback to this approach is that the ad hoc trial may not provide normal production conditions. Some years ago, researchers noted the 'Hawthorne effect' which resulted in improved performance from the presence of interested third parties. The research was concerned with the effects of lighting on productivity. As changes were made, productivity improved. The researchers returned lighting to its original levels to validate their findings but were amazed to find yet a further improvement in performance. Ad hoc trials may suffer from the same phenomenon; performance during the trial in terms of wastage and general quality performance may be better than normal and thus the standard may be distorted.

3 **By investigation of specifications.**
Some industries, for example the motor car industry, create detailed specifications in order to convert design prototypes into production goods. These specifications can be used by buyers to ensure an adequate supply of raw materials, by quality control to ensure compliance or fitness for purpose, and by management accounting departments to provide information on the commodities and quantities necessary to produce a finished item. Where the specification stipulates waste factors, the standard can apply these. In other situations, as assessment of waste will need to be made.

4 **By interview and/or observation.**
Knowledge of how materials are built into a particular product or service must be present at some level within an organisation. Production directors or managers or employees must know how a particular product is manufactured or else it would be impossible for an end product to arise. In some cases, it is most appropriate to tap that knowledge directly, possibly in conjunction with one of the other methods given above. Formal or informal interviews with members of staff, or actually observing employees assemble raw materials can be an interesting and important process in forming an understanding of a particular product or service. In

organisations which have a predisposition towards informal forms of information, the interview or observation may provide a means by which specifications can be formally established.

This approach would appear to be applicable to a range of organisations, from a single adviser to a complex manufacturing company operating JIT and FMS systems. The range of interviewing and observation approaches is likely to be similarly wide and to require the exercise of judgment and interpersonal skills on the part of the person carrying out the costing. In fact, knowledge in general of the problems of writing expert systems, in particular, reveals just how difficult it is to extract reliable information from experts, including those working directly on production and other processes. Interviewing and observing must be seen as tasks requiring not insubstantial levels of skill.

Price standards could be determined from existing suppliers' invoices, information from future contracts, especially where materials are purchased through annual agreements, purchasing department experience and expertise and by direct contact with suppliers. Where evidence is not collected from a documentary source, as in the case of invoices or contracts, the procedure is largely one of interview. This can be difficult in the case of contacting suppliers, where there may be sensitivity about communicating future price information. However, the technique has been used with good results, where the supplier is made aware that information provided is not of a contractual nature. Suppliers may have more up-to-date information than buyers.

A range of approaches is thus possible. Whichever approach, or combination of approaches is to be applied, may depend upon individual circumstances. There may also be other sensible approaches which have not been described. The objective of the section is to provide a range of possibilities, which have been successfully tested in practical situations, as an illustration of the types of approach to be adopted in developing material standards.

DIRECT LABOUR

The basic approaches outlined for materials may be applicable to labour situations, with suitable adjustment to suit the particular differences between labour and material situations. Breaking down the finished product in order to ascertain and weigh basic inputs is more appropriate to materials than labour, but it is possible for experts, particularly work study officers, to provide timing estimates for finished items by inspecting the finished items themselves. Ad hoc trials, specification details and interviews and observations may be equally well applied to labour as to materials.

Where work study is practised, the task of establishing standards may be linked to payment systems if piece rate methods are applied. For continuing products, standard times may be based on existing timing information, suitably amended if necessary to reflect the differing aims of work study and standards, where such a difference exists. For example, piece rate systems may be based on productivity levels of, say, 90% and may result in favourable payments to the workforce who regularly achieve 95%. This apparent 'overpayment' may be viewed by management as an important means to gain acceptance of a piece rate system with the workforce. For the standard costing system, a standard equivalent to, say, 96% may be set for the departmental manager in order to motivate the manager in accordance with the aspiration level principles discussed in Chapter 21.

Work study is not only concerned with piece rate systems and timings and is a significant area of study in its own right. Where work study departments exist, if the complete expertise of the work study officer is utilised, it can be expected that substantial direct labour information can be provided.

Where a day rate is paid, perhaps in the form of a salary, factors other than production may affect the time spent on an individual product; the availability of work may well affect time taken, for example. A trivial example of this is given by a visit to a hair dresser. During busy periods, it has been known for a hair dresser to cut a man's hair at the rate of five minutes per customer. At less busy times, the same haircut may take twenty minutes. Such examples exist in other services and in manufacturing industry. How can a time standard be established in these circumstances? Work study methods may be applied but how useful is the information derived?

In high technology and generally capital intensive plants, labour timings may be governed by the speed of plant and equipment. In some plants, robots may dominate the production line. In service industries such as leisure parks, high technology rides may dictate the productivity of labour. In these situations, timings may become machine timings rather than labour timings. Sizer and Coulthurst report that Rolls–Royce have changed to machine cycles rather than time based methods of costing. It is difficult to see how labour standards can have the same significance in such environments as in labour intensive conditions. Labour costs may take on the characteristics of overhead.

Wages rates can typically be determined from existing personnel records, from wages system records, from discussions with the personnel director or manager or from discussions with front line management.

24.1.3 Overheads

Although standard costs provide information on the standard cost of overhead per unit, the information on overhead is most unlikely to arise directly within the standard costing system. Overhead treatment in establishing standard costs is exactly the same as for any pre-determined overhead approach. The basis of accounting for overheads within standard systems will be given by pre-determined overhead absorption procedures. Budgeted costs will be apportioned to departments, where departmental rates of overhead are appropriate, absorption rates for each department will be calculated and the cost of an individual product will be made by taking the standard unit measure, in terms of machine hour, labour hour or labour cost, for example, and multiplying by the absorption rate.

Self-assessment question 24.1

In broad terms, suggest appropriate methods of producing standards for the following situations:

(a) A manufacturing company, producing large engines by means of Flexible Manufacturing Systems, wishing to use the standards to quote contract prices to customers;
(b) An institution of higher education, wishing to calculate the viability of its accountancy courses;
(c) A manufacturer of biscuits, with a diverse product range and a capital intensive policy.

Answers on page 621

24.1.4 Wastage, scrap and by-products

An assessment of the quantity of substandard goods to be produced must be made and included in a standard product cost. The assessment is going to be governed by factors such as individual judgment, past experience, policies for the future or organisational objectives. The accounting treatment then follows process costing principles, as illustrated by the following example.

Example 24.1

Based on an investigation of materials, labour and overheads, the Standard Flag Company has produced the following standard cost for its major product.

Materials	£1.00
Labour	£0.40
Overhead	£0.60

The standard product cost for material is based on breaking the finished item into its component parts and costing each component individually. No allowance has been made for wastage, scrap or by-products, which all arise during the production process.

Labour and overheads standards are based on estimating the time taken to complete one unit.

Near to the start of the process, 10% of all components initially bought in to produce the finished item are wasted. When the product is half complete in labour and overhead cost terms, a quality inspection occurs and 5% of all units inspected are rejected. These can be sold for £0.30 each and are treated as a by-product of the production process. All finished items are inspected and marketing policy dictates that all rejects, which amount to 2% of those inspected, are scrapped at a value of £0.05 each.

The easiest way of seeing what is happening to the costs in this situation is to design a simulation where, say, 100 units are introduced at the beginning of the process. The normal process costing principles are then applied:

Wastage is 10% of 100: 10 units.

By-product is 5% of 100 less wastage of 10 ie 5% of 90 is 4.5, leaving 85.5 in every 100 units introduced to the process.

Scrap is 2% of the units remaining after the by-product has been extracted:

2% of 85.5 is 1.71, leaving 83.79 in every 100 units to be transferred to finished goods.

Costs at first inspection stage:	
Materials:	£100 (100 @ £1)
Labour and overheads (50%)	£ 45 (100 less 10% waste @ 1/2 (£0.40 + £0.60))
less value of by-product (4.5 @ £0.30)	£ 1.35
	£143.65
Cost per unit: £143.65 / 85.5 units	£1.6801169
Cost of finished items:	
Cost at first inspection stage:	£143.65
Labour and overheads (50%)	£ 42.75 (85.5 @ 1/2 (£0.40 + £0.60))
less value of scrap (1.71 @ £0.05)	£ 0.0855
	£186.3145
Cost per unit: £186.3145 / 83.79	£2.2235887

Notice that a number of decimal places is being carried. In practical situations, the standard will be multipled by substantial volumes, for instance to calculate the cost of goods sold, and showing standards to a limited number of decimal places can lead to important distortions in results.

The figure of £2.2235887 can be arrived at in the following manner:

	Cost per unit
Input cost: Materials:	£1.00
add increase due to wastage:	
loss on wastage: £1.00 per unit lost on 10/90 of output	£0.1111111
add labour and overhead element up to by-product stage	£0.50
sub-total	£1.6111111
add increase due to by-product:	
loss on by-product: £1.6111111—£0.30 lost on 5/95 of output	£0.0690058
sub-total	£1.6801169
add labour and overhead element between by-product and final inspection stages	£0.50
sub-total	£2.1801169
add increase due to scrap:	
loss on scrap: £2.1801169—£0.05 lost on 2/98 of output	£0.0434717
	£2.2235886

Note that the adjustment for wastage, scrap and by-products is identical. The value per unit which is lost, the difference between sales or net residual value and the process cost, is multipled by the percentage of substandard goods and the resulting cost is recovered over the percentage of good units produced. This is the fundamental process costing approach; the cost of normal, substandard items is recovered into the cost of good items so that the cost of the finished item incorporates the cost of quality. The same calculation is applied to by-products where they arise in a comparable fashion to joint products, that is, as perfect goods as an unavoidable part of the process.

Where a series of operations is involved, and wastage alone arises, it is useful to apply this latter principle in order to arrive at a composite wastage figure. For this situation, it is helpful to show the alternative treatments where wastage is measured in relation to input, as in the Example 24.1, or in relation to output.

Example 24.2

The Easypass College has calculated its basic cost per annum accounting student starting the course at £2,000. Courses run over four years. Failure rates for each year are:

Year 1	25%
Year 2	28%
Year 3	30%
Year 4	15%

Calculate the total cost per successful student, assuming that:

1 Failure rates are based on the numbers of students starting each year's course (ie wastage is based on input);

2 Failure rates are based on the numbers of students successfully completing each course (ie wastage is based on output).

A simulation will be given, followed by a method for reducing the workload necessary for the simulation. Simulations are useful in original situations, as sometimes posed by examiners and found in practice.

Assuming that 100 students begin the first year course, the numbers remaining at the end of each year are as follows:

	1		**2**	
Year 1	(100 – 25% × 100)	75	(100/1.25)	80
Year 2	(75 – 28% × 75)	54	(80/1.28)	62.5
Year 3	(54 – 30% × 54)	37.8	(62.5/1.3)	48.076923
Year 4	(37.8 – 15% × 37.8)	32.13	(48.077/1.15)	41.80602

Costs in both cases would be £8,000 (2,000 per annum × 4 years) for each student, £800,000 in total for 100 students. This gives costs per unit of:

1	(800,000/32.13)	£24,899
2	(800,000/41.80602)	£19,136

A more direct way of calculating these results, using the method which underpinned Example 24.1, is as follows:

1 Wastage for year 1 is 25/75, or 33.33333% of output.
year 2 is 28/72, or 38.88888% of output.
year 3 is 30/70, or 42.85714% of output.
year 4 is 15/85, or 17.64705% of output.
Output percentage can be combined as follows, to give a cost:

$$£8{,}000 \times 1.333333 \times 1.388888 \times 1.4285714 \times 1.1764705 = £24{,}899$$

2 Output percentages can be combined, to give a cost:

$$£8{,}000 \times 1.25 \times 1.28 \times 1.3 \times 1.15 = £19{,}136$$

In both Examples 24.1 and 24.2, simulations are useful to understand the effects of wastage, scrap or by-products. The more efficient ways of combining percentages provide a suitable means by which these procedures can be computerised.

24.1.5 Types of standard

CIMA defines four types of standard, as follows:

1. **Basic standard:** 'a standard established for use over a long period of time from which a current standard can be developed.' Whilst such standards may quickly become out of date during times of uncertainty and change, by valuing output at standard over a period of time, a basis for comparing results can be established.
2. **Current standard:** 'a standard established for use over a short period of time, related to current conditions.' A current standard may be developed from a basic standard by updating prices, perhaps by means of price indices, and by making changes for known quantity factors.

These may include changing technology. Where a basic standard is not available, the current standard would be re-assessed periodically.

3 **Attainable standard:** 'a standard which can be attained if a standard of unit of work is carried out efficiently, a machine properly operated or material properly used. Allowances are made for normal shrinkage, waste and machine breakdowns. The standard represents future performance and objectives which are reasonably attainable. Besides having a desirable motivational impact on employees, attainable standards serve other purposes, eg cash budgeting, inventory valuation and budgeting departmental performance.' Note that the attainable standard can be related to both basic and current standards. The attainable current standard is the one which is likely to achieve the results defined by CIMA. Note also that the attainable standard should be presumably set to take into account aspiration levels in order to motivate.

4 **Ideal standard:** 'a standard which can be attained under the most favourable conditions. No provision is made, eg for shrinkage, spoilage or machine breakdowns. Users believe that the resulting unfavourable variances will remind management of the need for improvement in all phases of operations. Ideal standards are not widely used in practice because they may influence employee motivation adversely.' Again, as with the attainable standard, the ideal standard may be linked to basic or current standards. The quality implications of using the ideal standard are significant. The Japanese are associated with the zero defects assumption. This implies that wastage will be zero, or ideal. Under standard costing systems which operate under ideal standards, any wastage is costed at full standard cost value and the organisation's attention is continually drawn to the full cost of quality. It has been claimed that quality orientated strategies are successful in reducing the cost of quality. An ideal standard could form a good basis for quality costing in such circumstances.

24.1.6 Inflation

There are two approaches to accounting for the uncertainty associated with inflation which will be considered here. The problems of uncertainty in general are covered in Chapter 27.

1 No allowance is made for inflation in the standard, but where standards are incorporated into budgets, an unfavourable price variance is budgeted. This approach has the advantage of administrative ease, whilst maintaining the capability to monitor the general effects of inflation on the organisation. The inflationary impact is measured by dividing the adverse price variance into the total value of materials purchased or used.

2 Inflation is estimated in advance and standards are inflated with the aim that a favourable variance is reported in the first half of the year and an adverse variance, equal to the favourable variance, is reported for the second half of the year. It may be considered that this has advantages over the first method because of the motivational reasons of avoiding an inevitable adverse variance. Where individual prices are increased in line with anticipated inflation, it may be difficult to monitor the general effects of inflation.

24.1.7 Product and service costs

Whilst much of the terminology of standard costing arises from manufacturing situations, examples given above should alert readers to the potential of operating standard costing systems in service situations, such as education. Limitations to the use of standard costing are given by the existence of a measurable output, which may not always be obviously present in services. Where services can be measured in terms of an output, be it hours for a personal adviser, or patients in terms of the Health Service, for example, the potential to use standard costing will be present. Experience has shown that the process of developing standard costs for patients, for example, is complex, but other approaches appear to be no less difficult.

Self-assessment question 24.2

The Drinkit Company manufactures porcelain cups for sale to the retail industry. The managing director has decided to improve financial controls and a firm of consultants has recommended the application of standard costing principles. The production director has carried out some trials to establish the standard cost of the one product manufactured and has provided the following data:

Weight of clay used in trials:	2476 kg.
Weight of cups produced:	2302 kg.
Number of cups produced:	8063

In discussions with the production director, it becomes apparent that the production director normally expects 6% of clay to be wasted.

The sales director points out that 10% of finished cups fail quality control checks and are sold as seconds in the company shop. Seconds prices have been set at half the price of perfect quality goods.

The managing director has called upon you, as the management accountant, to produce a report on the preparation of standard costs, assuming:

(a) the preparation of current, attainable standards;
(b) a zero defect principle.

Include in your report a consideration of all factors which could influence the preparation of standards in the two situations presented.

Answers on page 622

24.2 OPERATING STANDARD COSTING SYSTEMS

24.2.1 Cost recording systems

Once the standard has been prepared, it can be used in cost recording systems. Figure 24.1 shows a representation of the flow of costs through a recording system. For such systems, standard costing can be viewed as an input-output system. Inputs and outputs are valued in relation to historic or standard costs as appropriate. Differences between inputs and outputs represent differences or single factor variances. Interpretation of variances depends upon individual circumstances and the decisions on input-output valuation. In many circumstances, the single factor variance can be sub-divided to provide multiple factor variances. Again, individual circumstances and decisions will affect the ability to sub-divide variances. Further details are provided in the next chapter.

The valuation of inputs and outputs on a basis related to standard will lead to systems carrying stocks on a standard cost valuation basis. Where attempts are made to value stocks on an actual basis, for purposes of audit, for example, a stock variance arises. Example 24.3 illustrates:

Example 24.3

During 19×9, the Standard Flag Company operates a standard costing system, valuing purchases and issues for the single raw material at a standard value. The standard price in operation for the year was £2. A price increase in the middle of the year took the actual price paid for the raw material to £2.10. Auditors insist that an actual basis for stock valuation operates and recommend the use of a FIFO policy. A summary of the raw materials stock for 19×9 is as follows:

Opening stock, at 1 January	57,213 kg
Purchases	659,845 kg
Issues	657,912 kg
Closing stock, at 31 December, as counted	54,184 kg

An assessment of the stock situation, in standard costing terms, would be as follows:

	kg	£
Opening stock	57213	114426
Purchases	659845	1319690
Issues	657912	1315824
Stock loss	4962	9924
Closing stock	54184	108368

Note that in standard costing terms, the internal control check 'balances' in that:

Opening stock plus purchases, less issues and losses, gives closing stock.

The closing stock would be valued at £113,786.40 (54,184 kg at £2.10), on a FIFO basis. This gives a stock variance of £5,418.40 favourable (£113,786.40 less £108,368). The opening stock would also carry a variance and the net effect of opening and closing stock variances could be taken to the profit and loss account. Where separate cost and financial systems are in operation, this variance is considered as a reconciliation factor rather than a variance per se.

FIGURE 24.1

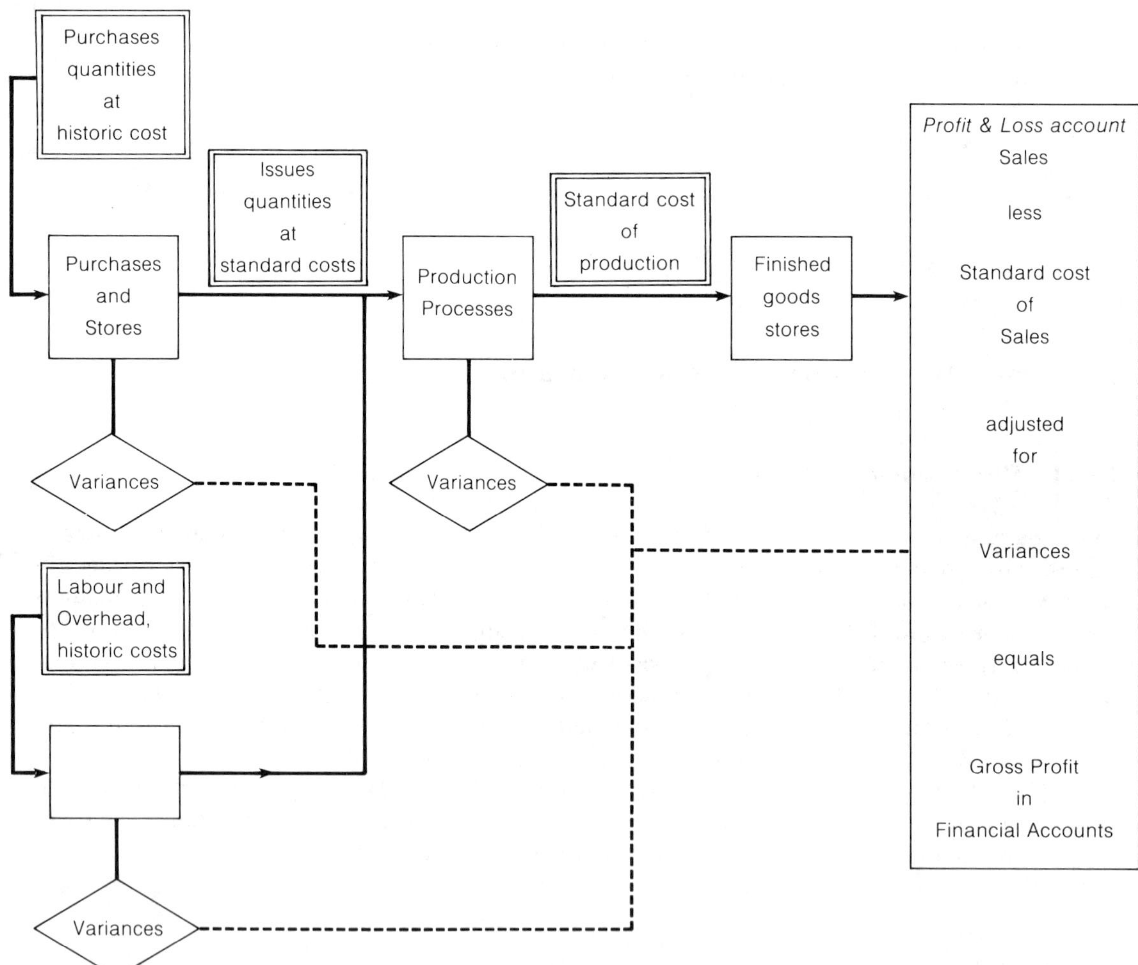

24.2.2 Feedback and efficiency for responsibility centres

Given that the system of recording as outlined in Section 24.2.1 measures inputs and outputs, standard costing can be used as a direct measure of efficiency. Efficiency is concerned with input-output relationships. The greater the output in relation to input, the greater the efficiency. Output values can be compared with input values in absolute or relative measures. These can then be used to test the efficiency of responsibility centres. If standard costing systems are to be used in this way, the definition of systems and sub-systems as part of the process of developing the standard costing system takes on a central importance. Each system or sub-system for which inputs and outputs are measured on a basis of standard costs becomes a responsibility centre.

The decision to take the price variance at the purchases stage presumes that the purchasing function will be responsible for prices. Figure 24.2 illustrates this point, using figures from Example 24.3. Each unit of input to the purchasing department is valued at £2.10 in the second part of the year. Each output, which becomes the input to the stock system, is valued at £2.00. The variance of £0.10 becomes the responsibility of the purchasing department and becomes a measure of the department's efficiency in purchasing units from suppliers.

A complementary view of the purchasing situation is that the standard is equivalent to an objective. In this circumstance, the output of £2.10 becomes feedback against the objective of £2.00 and the effectiveness rather than the efficiency of the purchasing department is measured. Not for the first time, it can be seen that the management accounting system can be designed to serve more than one purpose and that the way in which the system is specified can be crucial to the way in which results are evaluated.

FIGURE 24.2

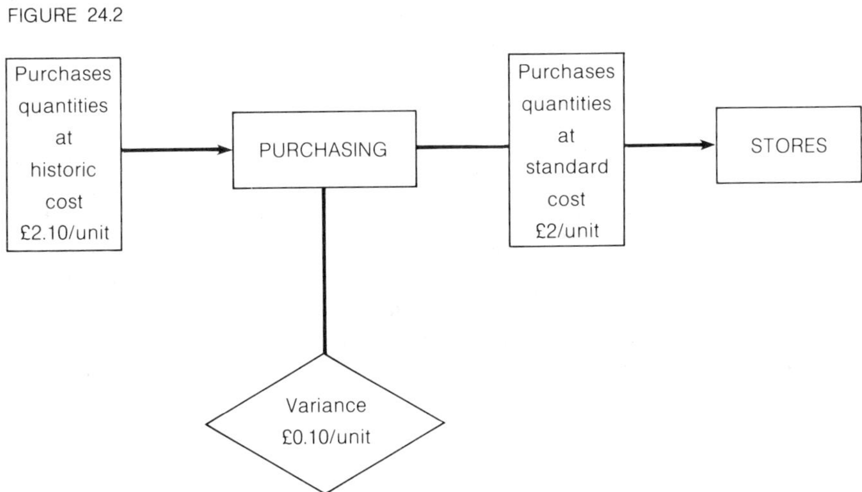

24.2.3 Investigations

Once inputs and outputs have been measured in terms of the operation of the standard costing system, and variances have been appropriately calculated, the process of standard costing can be completed by investigating significant variances. Chapter 26 provides a full discussion on the meaning of significance.

Since sub-systems are inter-related, the investigation of variances faces the problem that variances may arise from a common cause and be inter-related in a complex manner. Where sub-systems are linked to responsibility accounting and systems boundaries are considered in a rigid manner, the possibility of unfair evaluation of variances can become a reality. Investigation is the major means by which such unfairness can be overcome, but is sometimes beset with the problem of buck passing. This organisational problem of investigation can be most simply illustrated by means of an example.

Example 24.4

A variance arises in a production department. Investigations reveal that the variance is attributable to the fact that wastage exceeds standard significantly. Unfortunately, the cause of the problem is difficult to determine as the following views show:

Production Director: 'We knew about the wastage problem and told Alice, the Purchasing Manager about it. She insists on buying sub-standard goods because she reckons that a favourable price variance is to her credit.'

Purchasing Manager: 'I didn't say anything to George, the Production Director, about favourable price variances. The truth is that Jo, the Quality Control Manager, reckons that the substitute I've been buying is cheaper and better. Jo does have a staff problem, though. There is talk that some good production is sent off as wastage because her new staff don't know what they are doing.'

Quality Control Manager: 'My staff are fully trained and there is no question about their competence. If you want to know the truth, Sally, the Marketing Director is insisting on quality improvements as part of a long-term strategy. There are bound to be quality problems until the production work force can improve its standard of work.'

Two outcomes can arise from investigation. If the standard costing system can be operated on a closed systems basis, investigations will lead to corrective action and negative feedback. In situations such as Example 24.4, an open systems basis would appear to be more appropriate. Depending on the type of standard which is in operation, the standard may be amended to reflect present situations or aspirations. In this case, investigation is a means by which the standard cost can be refined in order to reflect current circumstances. Investigation almost becomes a means by which the standard cost is updated.

24.3 PURPOSES OF STANDARD COSTING

The suitability of a standard cost for a particular purpose depends upon the type of standard developed. In general terms, however, standards may be used for decision making, planning, control, evaluation and financial accounting purposes.

24.3.1 Decision-making

Decisions relate to future periods of time. A decision taken today will affect future outcomes. Standards are pre-determined costs. They are designed to reflect the future. Standard costs are thus suitable for use in decision-making calculations where they reflect future expectations. Short-term decisions could use standard marginal cost. Long-term decisions could take the cash flow implications of the engineered costs associated with a particular investment proposal. Selling price decisions may use standard marginal cost or standard absorption cost, where prices are formed on a cost-plus basis.

24.3.2 Planning

Plans relate to future periods of time. Standards are pre-determined. Standard engineered costs may thus be used in the preparation of budgets. Where selling prices are determined on a cost-plus basis, standard selling prices may be incorporated into sales forecasting. Standards relate to individual products and services and can thus be used to later break down budgetary variances into greater detail.

24.3.3 Control

Standards are yardsticks or measures of quality and show how much values or other quantitative data should be. They can therefore be used to control organisations by providing a base or criterion against which results can be evaluated. Feedback is possible where the standard is used as a target or objective. Efficiency measures are possible because inputs and outputs can be measured on a basis of standard costing values. Accounting control, as part of internal control, can be achieved because disparate units can be valued at standard cost and relationships tested. Consider a finished goods stock comprising ten thousand different items. Were these to be valued at standard cost, and the cost of production and cost of sales also to be valued at standard cost, probably on a computerised basis, the following relationship can be tested:

Opening stock of finished goods
plus Standard cost of goods produced
less Standard cost of sales
would equal Closing stock of finished goods, but for stock losses, which can be determined in terms of standard values.

This relationship can be tested for the stock as a whole and if the stock losses, in relative or absolute terms, are considered unacceptable, investigation into individual product losses would be initiated.

24.3.4 Performance evaluation

Where responsibility centres have been established, the effectiveness or efficiency of centre managers can be established through the use of standards. In multi-divisional organisations, where inter-departmental trading occurs, and managers are evaluated on a profit or investment centre basis, transfer prices may replace standard costs as the relevant output measure. Chapter 28 contains a detailed consideration of transfer pricing and shows that standard costs are one of the bases for the determination of transfer price.

24.3.5 Financial accounting

Standard costs can be used as the basis for stock valuations for inclusion in financial accounts, where the auditors consider standards to be a fair reflection of the SSAP 9 concept of cost.

In other situations, it may be necessary to re-value stocks or to add back into stock valuations variances which have arisen during the current period. Where standard costing systems are in operation, the auditor will need to have a good understanding of the preparation of standards and of the operation of standard costing systems in order to conduct the audit; including audit of stock values and evaluation of internal controls.

SUMMARY

Standards are pre-determined and provide a measure of quality which can be used by manufacturing and service organisations to make decisions, to plan, to control and to discharge financial accounting duties. There is a variety of means by which standards can be developed. Once a standard has been developed, inputs and outputs can be valued on a standard basis. The cost recording system can assume standard values rather than actual values. Differences between inputs and outputs, or variances, create variances which can be investigated in order to initiate corrective action or to improve the reliability of the standard costs themselves. A choice of types of standard is available to the systems designer. Each type of standard has its own uses and advantages and the systems designer would need to consider the effect of the standard on the organisation. The purpose of the standard costing system is of prime importance; there are various ways in which a particular system can be designed to have alternative impacts on the organisation.

EXERCISES

Exercise 24.1

You are auditor of M Ltd; a company which manufactures three basic products, all of which are components for the electronics industry. The company sells to three major customers who account for 90% of the company's turnover, the remaining 10% of sales being to overseas customers. The company's year-end is 31 December and for stock valuation purposes all completed components in stock at that date are valued using their standard costs.

(Note: There is no work-in-progress and no production takes place on the last day of the year.)

The standard costs are revised quarterly and those set at 1 October are used for year-end valuation purposes. Details of stock for the year ended 31 December 1984 are as follows:

	Component			Total value of stock at 31 Dec 1984
	A	**B**	**C**	
Number in stock at 31 December 1984	25,200	8,150	17,700	
Standard cost at 1 October 1984	£0.73	£2.16	£1.85	
Value at 31 Dec 84 (@ 1 Oct standards)	£18,396	£17,604	£32,745	£68,745
Number of components sold in year	55,420	48,900	92,400	
Standard cost of sales for year	£39,600	£100,245	£166,320	
Total variances for the year	£750 A	£40,100 A	£15,470F	
Revised standards for the quarter commencing 1 Jan 85	£0.74	£2.20	£1.55	

Required:

(a) Explain under what conditions standard costs may be used for year-end stock valuation purposes.

(b) Using the figures given above, carry out a review to determine the areas that do not appear to make sense and thus the areas on which the auditor would concentrate when substantiating the stock valued at £68,745 in the financial statements as at 31 December 1984.

(c) State the TWO critical matters to be considered when auditing the standard labour cost.

(*ACCA Level 2 Auditing, slightly adapted, December 1985*)

Answers on page 622

Exercise 24.2

Wedgerow Ltd specialises in growing young plants for sale to both commercial and retail outlets. The plants are grown from seed pellets which are sown in a compost mix in boxes of 40 plants in an automatic sowing department. The boxes are then transferred into a germinating room. Any seed which does not germinate is removed before the boxes of germinated seed are transferred into growing houses. Any diseased or damaged plants are removed before the young plants are then transferred to the dispatch department for delivery to customers.

Wedgerow Ltd keeps accounting records for each process. Each process is charged with the actual costs directly incurred, but transfers between processes are made at standard cost per box of plants. Any difference between the total costs incurred by the process and the standard cost transferred from each process is simply shown as a variance which is transferred to profit and loss account.

Budgeted/standard data based on the maximum capacity of the premises are as follows:

Automatic sowing department

Monthly production: 125,000 boxes each containing 40 seed pellets. (Variety A 60,000 boxes; Variety B 45,000 boxes; Variety C 20,000 boxes)

	Costs	Losses as a percentage of good output
Seed pellets	1p each	2%
Compost mix (3 kilos per output box)	20p per kilo	2.5%
Boxes	10p each	1%
Operating costs	£30,000 per month	

(There are assumed to be no losses of complete boxes in the automatic sowing department.)

Germination room
Operating costs per month: £50,000
Normal loss: 20% of input

Growing houses
Operational costs per month: £27,000
Normal loss: 10% of input

Actual usage, cost and output data for the month of May are as follows:
Automatic sowing department
Seed pellets: 5,200,000 pellets costing £52,000
Compost: 370,000 kilos at 21p per kilo
Boxes: 129,000 boxes costing £14,190
Operating costs: £29,800
125,000 boxes of sown pellets were transferred to the germinating room.

Germination room
Operating costs: £50,000
Transfers to growing houses: 100,000 boxes of plants

Growing houses
Operating costs: £30,000
Transfers to dispatch department: 86,000 boxes of plants
There is no opening or closing work-in-progress in any of the processes.

Required:
(a) Calculate the standard cost per box of plants at the end of each of the three processes.
(b) Show the entries you would expect to find in the accounting records maintained by Wedgerow Ltd.
(c) Comment on the results shown in your answer to (b).

(ACCA, Management Accounting, December 1988, adapted)

Answers on page 623

Exercise 24.3

Discuss the advantages and disadvantages of operating a standard costing system, in comparison with the historical cost based systems usually associated with job and process costing.

State the situations which are necessary for the successful operation of a standard costing system.

Answers in lecturer's manual.

Exercise 24.4

Discuss the matters which should be borne in mind by the designer of a standard costing system.

Answers in lecturer's manual.

Exercise 24.5

'To establish standard costs for a product it is necessary to determine the costs which will be incurred for labour, materials and overheads. Consequently, a detailed study of the operations which are involved in the manufacture of each product should be undertaken. The standard costs for labour, materials and overheads are then added together to establish the product standard cost.'

Colin Drury

Discuss the above statement in relation to the following types of organisational setting:

(a) a manufacturer using FMS;
(b) a research and development department within a large, multinational organisation;
(c) a long-term contractor in the ship building industry, required to quote a contract price in advance of securing each order;
(d) a milk bottling plant.

Answers in lecturer's manual.

Standard Costing Variance Analysis

INTRODUCTION

The principles underpinning standard costing variance analysis were explained in Chapter 22. Standard costing provides a suitable set of reference data against which variances can be extracted. The basic rationale for extracting variances against standard is the provision of information for management on efficiency or effectiveness, for implementation through negative feedback systems, although management will always have the discretion to use information in a manner which most closely suits their organisation. A number of alternative approaches to the extraction of variances need to be understood, including the implications of marginal and absorption cost based variances. In order to explain standard costing variance analysis, this chapter analyses a single example and provides a detailed analysis and exposition of the variances which can arise. At the end of the chapter, the student should be able to carry out variance analysis for complex situations. Exercises at the end of the chapter provide practice to reinforce the principles illustrated.

The chapter has been planned to include the following elements:

1 An initial statement of the problem is stated by means of an example. This example is based on a simplification of a practical standard costing system which was operated in the floorcovering industry. Some of the simplifications include:
   (a) reducing the number of products;
   (b) considering work-in-progress in terms of equivalent units. In the actual system which was operated, some twenty production stages were in operation and work-in-progress was accounted for according to the actual stage reached in the production cycle;
   (c) reducing the number of raw materials involved. In the actual situation, there were over one hundred separate raw materials to be accounted for.

2 Absorption costing variances are presented, broken down into raw materials, labour, overheads, sales and quality cost variances. Each type of variance is explained in turn and illustrated by using data from the example.

3 Variances for overheads are calculated in terms of a relative basis, as opposed to an absolute £ basis.

4 Differences between absorption costing and marginal costing are discussed and variance analysis according to marginal principles is presented.

5 The significance of considering variances in terms of quantities rather than values is explored.

Each of the separate variances can be advantageously studied in isolation before a full understanding of the complexity of the example is appreciated.

Example 25.1

In December 19×8, Quill plc prepared their budget for 19×9. The Marketing Director prepared the following sales forecast:

	Units	£/unit	£'000
Alpha	50,000	8.00	400
Beta perfects	40,000	10.00	400
Beta seconds	8,000	2.00	16
			816

The sales forecast for Beta seconds was based on the fact that the production manager predicted a seconds level of 1/6th of production. The Production Manager budgeted machine hours to be 40,000, although the plant was capable of 50,000 machine hours under normal conditions. In practice, due to machine down-time, a loss of $7\frac{1}{2}\%$ of machine hours had been incurred for some years and this loss was allowed in arriving at the budgeted standard hours available. It was discovered that the budgeted capacity allowed the sales forecast to be achieved. The Financial Director was satisfied that all stocks should be budgeted to remain at a constant level, although he expressed concern at the existing level of stock of Beta seconds. A budget of £296,000 for production overheads was also agreed between the Financial Director and the Production Manager, based on the following analysis of cost behaviour produced by the Cost Accountant:

Output, machine hours:	30,000	40,000	50,000
Production overheads:			
Rent and rates	50,000	50,000	50,000
Plant and machinery costs	126,000	126,000	126,000
Power	65,000	70,000	75,000
Salaries	45,750	50,000	54,250

The Cost Accountant also prepared the product cost. Marketing, Research and Development and Administrative overheads, which were budgeted at £20,000, £11,000 and £5,450 respectively, are absorbed into the product cost for perfect quality goods at 5% of production cost, after allowance is made for the cost of seconds. Machine time required for Alpha and Beta is 30 minutes and 15 minutes respectively and labour time required is 30 minutes of grade I labour for Alpha and 30 minutes of grade II labour for Beta. Grade I labour is paid at £2 per hour whilst grade II labour is paid at £2.50 per hour. Raw materials details are provided below:

Usage, grams per unit

	standard price	**Alpha**	**Beta**
Raw material A	£2 kg	300	800
B	£6 kg	300	500

The Financial Accountant produced the following accounts at the beginning of 19×0:

Manufacturing, Trading and Profit and Loss Account for the year ended 31 December 19×9

	£	£
Raw material consumed		346,000
Direct labour		109,000
Production overheads:		
Rent and rates	52,500	
Plant and machinery	126,000	
Power	68,000	
Salaries	47,500	
		294,000
		749,000
add: decrease in w.i.p. stocks		(27,500)
		721,500
Sales		799,000
Cost of goods sold		728,660
Gross Profit		70,340
Marketing	20,000	
Research and development	10,000	
Administration	10,000	
		40,000
Net Profit		30,340

The following working papers were produced during the process of drawing up final accounts:

Raw material stock:

	A		B	
Opening stock	10,000kg.	£20,000	5,000kg.	£30,000
Purchases	60,000kg.	£126,000	40,000kg.	£248,000
	70,000kg.	£146,000	45,000kg.	£278,000
Closing stock	15,000kg.	£30,000	8,000kg.	£48,000
	55,000kg.	£116,000	37,000kg.	£230,000

Work-in-progress stock:

	Alpha			Beta		
	Units	Degree of completion		Units	Degree of completion	
		Materials	Conversion		Materials	Conversion
Opening stock	5,000	100%	50%	8,000	50%	40%
Closing stock	10,000	50%	25%	10,000	80%	60%

Finished goods stock:

	Alpha		Beta Perfects		Beta Seconds	
	Units	£	Units	£	Units	£
Opening stock	6,000	7.40	5,000	9.02	25,000	2.00
Production	50,000		40,000		10,000	
Closing stock	8,000	7.40	7,000	9.02	5,000	2.00

Sales analysis:

Alpha	48,000 units @ £8.50	£408,000
Beta Perfects	38,000 units @ £9.50	£361,000
Beta Seconds	30,000 units @ £1.00	£ 30,000

Direct labour analysis:

Grade I	26,000 hours	£49,400
Grade II	23,000 hours	£59,600

Overhead details:

Machine hours worked:		39,000 hours
Variable costs:	Power	£ 19,500
Fixed costs:	Rent and rates	£ 52,500
	Plant and machinery	£126,000
	Power	£ 48,500
	Salaries	£ 47,500

The example requires a thorough analysis of the variance implications of the financial accounting results together with a statement of findings.

It is important for students to work through the material in this chapter in a systematic way. In order to assist in this process, answers are given in the text but detailed workings are relegated to the suggested answers section, on page 625. Text answers should be considered very carefully and detailed workings should only be considered as a last resort. Self-assessment questions ask students to explain variances in ways which would be helpful to management. This cannot be successfully carried out unless the variance calculations are carefully considered.

The starting point for an exercise of this kind is to draw up a standard product cost for each product, as shown below. The exercise of preparing a product cost provides revision of cost behaviour, in order to split variable and fixed overheads, overhead absorption rates and the treatment of losses in process costing situations. The loss in value caused by goods being classified as seconds is treated in the same way as illustrated in the previous chapter, for by-products, scrap and wastage. The resultant cost is termed by CIMA as the quality cost allowance.

	Alpha		Beta
	£		£
Direct materials:			
A: 300gm @ £2/kg.	0.60	(800gm)	1.60
B: 300gm @ £6/kg.	1.80	(500gm)	3.00
Direct labour:			
Grade I 30 min @ £2/hr	1.00		
Grade II 30 min @ £2.50/hr			1.25
Variable production overhead:			
30 min @ £1/hr	0.50	(15 min)	0.25
Fixed production overhead:			
30 min @ £7/hr	3.50	(15min)	1.75
	7.40		7.85
Quality cost allowance	–		1.17
	7.40		9.02
Marketing, Research and development, Administration	0.37		0.451
Total cost	7.77		9.471
Net profit	0.23		0.529
Selling price	8.00		10.000

25.1 ABSORPTION COSTING

25.1.1 Raw materials

Three variances can be extracted from raw material situations. The alternative permutations, together with names and relationship to the value, quantity and mix variances, as calculated in Chapter 22, are as follows:

	Value	Quantity	Mix
Price variance taken at the purchases stage:			
One factor analysis of purchases:	Price	—	—
One factor analysis of issues:	—	Usage	—
Three factor analysis of issues:	nil	Yield	Mix

Price variance taken at the issues stage:

	Value	Quantity	Mix
One factor analysis:	Total variance is termed 'cost'		
Two factor analysis:	Price	Usage	—
Three factor analysis:	Price	Yield	Mix

A diagrammatic representation is provided in Figures 25.1 and 25.2, using a simple illustration. This representation makes the organisational assumption that variances occurring at the purchase stage will be attributed to the purchasing function and those occurring at the issues stage will be attributed to production.

Where the price variance is taken at the purchase stage, the input to the purchase system is measured at prices paid. The output will be valued at standard and the purchasing function assumes responsibility for differences, for which the manager will be asked to account. Price variances can be traced back to individual raw materials. Computerised bought ledgers can report the price variance as a by-product of bought ledger invoice processing, where a file is created of standard prices for each raw material. Input to production systems is at standard values and variances arising in production will be attributable only to quantity and mix factors. The price variance in the three factor case is zero because the prices paid by production are valued on a standard basis. The production function is

FIGURE 25.1 **Price variance taken at the purchases stage**

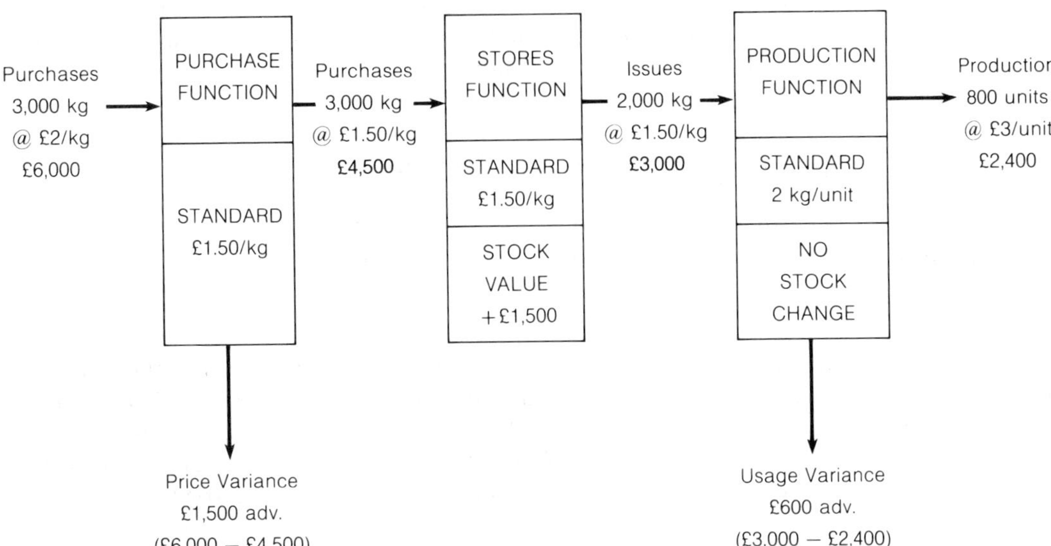

therefore not made accountable for price variances. Stocks are most easily valued on a standard costing basis, from an administrative point of view. Stocks can be maintained on an 'actual' basis, such as weighted average or first in first out but stock variances will arise, as described in the last chapter.

Where the price variance is taken at the issues stage, the production function assumes responsibility for all variances. This case may be pertinent where purchasing is seen as a sub-system of production. The production manager would presumably hold the purchasing manager responsible for price variances. Under this system, the price variance arises when issues are made and this will create a delay in reporting upon supplier's prices where stocks are held. This may create confusion where significant time delays are involved or where weighted average systems of stock issue are employed. Price variances reported in one month will reflect purchasing in previous months. Stocks of raw materials will be maintained on an 'actual' basis using a weighted average, first in first out, or similar convention.

FIGURE 25.2 **Price variance taken at the issues stage**

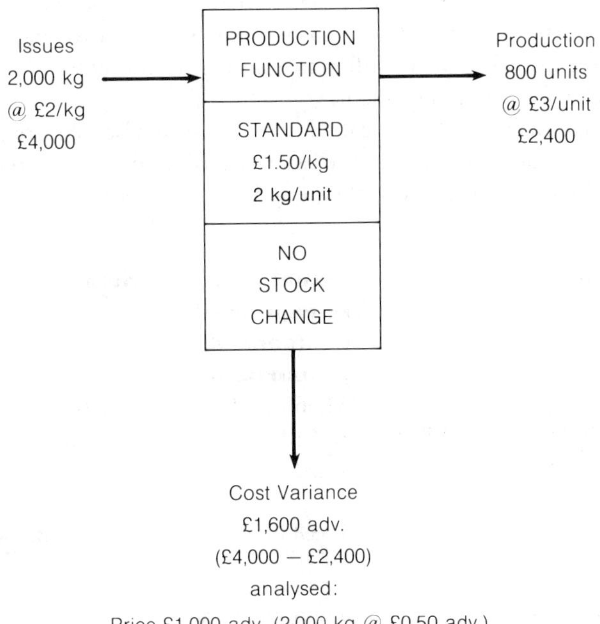

For Example 25.1, investigation of the basis for stock valuation, as revealed in the financial accounts, shows that stocks are valued at standard. This implies that the price variance was extracted at the purchases stage. Materials price variances must be calculated based upon purchase quantities and mix and yield variances based upon issues quantities.
At the purchase stage:

	Quantity	**Actual price**	**Standard price**
		£	£
Raw material A	60,000	126,000	120,000
Raw material B	40,000	248,000	240,000
		374,000	360,000

The price variance is £14,000 adverse (£374,000-£360,000) At the issues stage, the price variance is nil because materials are input to production at standard values. Mix and yield variances arise because of the existence of two materials and because of the nature of the process.

To calculate the mix variance, the issues of 92,000kg are expressed at a standard mix of 58:42, calculated from the standard cost quantity of materials required for the work carried out in the period as follows:

	Alpha	**Beta**
Work done in period, equivalent units:		
Production	50,000	50,000
less: completed in previous period	(5,000)	(4,000)
Work carried out in current period on items produced	45,000	46,000
Work carried out in current period on closing stock	5,000	8,000
	50,000	54,000

Standard usage of materials, based on work done during the period:

	Total		**Alpha**		**Beta**	
			50,000		54,000	
	kg		kg		kg	
Raw material A	58,200	(58%)	15,000	(300gm)	43,200	(800gm)
B	42,000	(42%)	15,000	(300gm)	27,000	(500gm)

58:42 is the approximate mix. At the end of the exercise, it may be interesting to recalculate the results using exact proportions of material A to material B. In presenting the answer in the way suggested here, it is being argued that the difference arising from greater accuracy is immaterial and therefore of little consequence to management.

The standard usage of materials, as calculated above, is also required to calculate the yield variance. Sufficient is now known to analyse the issues situation in relation to the usage which should have been required for work carried out in the period:

Issues:	**Actual issues**		**Actual issues re-expressed to standard proportions**	**Standard issues**
A	55,000 @ £2	(58%)	53,360 @ £2	58,200 @ £2
B	37,000 @ £6	(42%)	38,640 @ £6	42,000 @ £6
	92,000	(100%)	92,000	
Value	£332,000		£338,560	£368,400

Mix variance is £6,560 favourable (£332,000-£338,560).
Yield variance is £29,840 favourable (£338,560-£368,400).

Self-assessment question 25.1

Using the different approaches to three factor analysis explained in Chapter 22, provide explanations for the mix and yield variances shown above.

Answers on page 626

Self-assessment question 25.2

Assume that the senior management have decided that the Production Manager should be responsible for all aspects of materials. Recalculate materials variances for Example 25.1 to show materials cost, price, mix and yield variances based on taking the price variance at the issues stage. State the nature of any implications which this may cause from the technical accounting point of view and comment on the results of your calculations.

Answers on page 627

25.1.2 Direct labour

Although three factor analysis of direct labour is possible for example 25.1, since two types of labour are involved, it is appropriate for this example to apply two factor analysis. General terminology is as follows:

	Value	**Quantity**	**Mix**
One factor analysis:	Total variance is termed 'cost'		
Two factor analysis:	Rate	Efficiency	
Three factor analysis:	Rate	Productivity	Mix

For Example 25.1, the actual expenditure of £109,000 is compared with the labour cost expected for the equivalent amount of output.

Standard hours produced, based on the amount of work carried out by the workforce, must be calculated before calculating variances.

Standard hours:

	Alpha	**Beta**
Work done in period, equivalent units:		
Production	50,000	50,000
less: completed in previous period	(2,500)	(3,200)
Work carried out in current period on items produced	47,500	46,800
Work carried out in current period on closing stock	2,500	6,000
	50,000	52,800
Standard hours per unit	0.5	0.5
Standard hours produced: total 51,400	25,000	26,400

Variances:

	Actual	Actual hours, standard rate	Standard
I	£49,400	26,000 @ £2	25,000 @ £2
II	£59,600	23,000 @ £2.50	26,400 @ £2.50
Values	£109,000	£109,500	£116,000

Rate variance is £500 favourable (£109,000 – £109,500)
Efficiency variance is £6,500 favourable (£109,500 – £116,000)

Self-assessment question 25.3

Provide a statement commenting on the variances shown above, in a form which is useful for management. To what extent do you believe that management would benefit from information related to the mix and productivity variances?

Answers on page 627

25.1.3 Variable overheads

Variable overhead analysis has much in common with labour variance analysis, in a general sense as well as in the case of Example 25.1. A summary of the analysis is as follows:

	Value	Quantity
One factor analysis:	Total variance is termed 'cost'	
Two factor analysis:	Expenditure	Efficiency

In Example 25.1, the amount of work carried out in terms of variable overheads is the same as that for labour.

In general, calculation of standard hours can be based on either labour hours, where the variable overhead efficiency variance would convey the same underlying information as the labour efficiency variance, or machine hours. In the case of Example 25.1 machine hours provide a more suitable basis than labour hours; a consideration of the relative size of production overheads and labour costs suggest that the company is machine intensive. In fact, the company upon which the case study was based amalgamated labour with overheads because labour production and productivity was governed by machine speeds. The separation in Example 25.1 arises from the need to provide a comprehensive illustration of variance calculations applicable to a variety of businesses.

The following variance analysis results:

Variances:

	Actual	Actual hours, standard rate	Standard
	£19,500	39,000 @ £1	38,200 @ £1
Values	£19,500	£39,000	£38,200

Expenditure variance is £19,500 favourable (£19,500 – £39,000)
Efficiency variance is £800 adverse (£39,000 – £38,200)

Self-assessment question 25.4

Provide a statement for management explaining the variances given above. In providing your explanation, include a consideration of the following questions.

Can you see the essential difference between explaining the labour rate variance and the variable overhead expenditure variance?

A particular problem of categorisation between fixed and variable overheads applies to this case study. Can you see a way of resolving the problem?

Answers on page 628

25.1.4 Fixed overheads

Variances will be initially analysed in the same way as for variable overheads.

Variances:

	Actual	**Actual hours, standard rate**	**Standard**
	£274,500	39,000 @ £7	38,200 @ £7
Values	£274,500	£273,000	£267,400

Expenditure variance is £1,500 adverse (£274,500 – £273,000)
Efficiency variance is £5,600 adverse (£273,000 – £267,400)

Interpreting these results in reverse order, the efficiency variance adds little to existing knowledge about the efficiency of the company: the underlying efficiency in machine usage is adverse in comparison with standard as shown by the variable overhead analysis. The fixed overhead efficiency variance simply increases the cost associated with machine inefficiency. This measures the fact that additional output would have allowed the company to produce more units of output and thus improve its overhead absorption.

The expenditure variance as it stands defies sensible attempts at interpretation.

Fixed overhead, by its nature, does not vary with changes in output. This implies that expenditure should be constant over a range of output levels. Budgeted expenditure for the number of hours worked does not provide a reasonable reference point from which to measure the amount of fixed overheads spent. A more suitable reference point is the budgeted level of expenditure. A reasonable measure of expenditure performance is therefore given by a comparison of actual expenditure with budget. To be more accurate, and in an attempt to unify the approaches adopted for fixed and variable overheads, it could be said that overhead expenditure variances measure the difference between actual expenditure and the flexible budget. In the case of variable overheads, the expenditure variance was calculated as the difference between actual expenditure and flexed budget, flexing the budget on the basis of machine hours worked. This reasoning provides a fixed overhead expenditure variance as follows:

Fixed overhead expenditure variance:

Actual expenditure:	£274,500
Budgeted expenditure:	£259,000
Variance:	£15,500 adverse.

Comparing this with the earlier, incorrect figure of expenditure variance (£1,500 adverse) reveals a difference of £14,000 favourable. This can be sensibly explained. Taking the difference between planned activity (37,000 hours in this example) and the hours that the plant was operated for (39,000 hours), explains this difference (2,000 hours favourable @ £7 per hour). This is termed the capacity variance because it measures the extent to which an organisation uses its plant capacity as intended. In Example 25.1, had management been able to operate for a further 2,000 hours, an additional £14,000 of fixed overheads would have been absorbed.

The complete analysis of fixed overhead variances is as follows:

Fixed overhead variances:

Acutal expenditure	£274,500
Flexed budget (budgeted hours × absorption rate)	£259,000
(actual hours × absorption rate)	£273,000
Standard cost (standard hours × absorption rate)	£267,400

Expenditure variance is £15,500 adverse (£274,500 – £259,000)
Capacity variance is £14,000 favourable (£259,000 – £273,000)
Efficiency variance is £5,600 adverse (£273,000 – £267,400)

Together, the capacity and efficiency variances comprise a volume variance. This reflects the under or over absorption of overheads; improvements in either capacity utilisation or efficiency would automatically result in a higher level of absorbed overhead.

The treatment of variances is known to cause confusion and difficulty for students and managers alike. This has resulted in some authorities calling for the variance to be shown as a single variance, without further analysis. Contingency theory would suggest that the wisdom of this approach depends upon the particular characteristics of the company being analysed. How useful do you think is the information which has been produced in this section for Quill plc?

Self-assessment question 25.5

Provide a report for the management of Quill plc discussing the fixed overhead variances for the year ending 31 December 19×8.

Answers on page 629

25.1.5 Sales variances

Sales variances can be summarised as follows:

	Value	Quantity	Mix
One factor analysis:	Total variance is termed 'sales profit'		
Two factor analysis:	Price	Volume	—
Three factor analysis:	Price	Volume	Mix

The choice of valuation base for variances depends on particular circumstances. Increasing or decreasing sales volumes in mix or quantity terms affects both total sales value and total cost of sales. A higher level of sales output in quantity terms leads to higher total sales value at higher costs. Where the intention is to use variances to provide a reconciliation of budgeted and actual profit results, it is necessary to value sales variances on a profit value basis rather than a sales value basis for this reason. Where the intention is to use variances to motivate a salesforce, sales variances based on a profit value may tend to motivate individual sales personnel to sell more highly profitable products, where discretion allows. Use of sales value for variance calculation purposes may motivate sales personnel to sell high sales value items, which may not be consonant with selling high profit items.

For Example 25.1, a reconciliation of budgeted and actual profit will be provided in a later section. Variances will be based on a valuation base reflecting the impact of sales on profit. Since absorption costing is adopted in the financial accounts and this part of the chapter illustrates absorption costing variances, gross profit is the measure to apply. Were net profit to be applied, a volume variance would arise on marketing, administration and research and development costs. Applying a gross profit approach leads to profit and loss items being measured for variance terms in relation to a comparison of budget and actual.

For the purpose of calculating the 'actual standard gross profit' standard cost per unit is deducted from actual sales profit per unit. The reason for using standard cost per unit is that the difference between actual and standard costs per unit are taken out in the cost variance analysis illustrated above. To consider cost variances through the sales variance calculations would lead to double counting and difficulties of reconciliation.

'Actual standard gross profit' is calculated as follows:

	Alpha	**Beta Perfects**	**Beta Seconds**
Sales units	48,000	38,000	30,000
Standard cost per unit	£7.40	£9.02	£2.00
Standard cost of sales	£355,200	£342,760	£60,000

	£	£	£
Sales	408,000	361,000	30,000
Standard cost of sales	355,200	342,760	60,000
Standard gross profit	52,800	18,240	(30,000)

Adjusting the total standard gross profit for cost variances gives the actual gross profit. If you wish to try this reconciliation, a difference of £11,700 will result. This is explained in the next section. It is important to include all of the cost variances shown in previous sections.

A statement showing the calculation of actual gross profit is provided on page *629*.

It is also necessary to consider 'budgeted standard gross profit'. On a per unit basis, this is £0.60 for Alpha, £0.98 for Beta perfects and nil for Beta seconds. Beta seconds have a notional cost equal to sales value because of the treatment provided by the calculation of the product cost. It is permissible to provide a notional profit, in order to motivate sales personnel to sell substandard items, by writing down the notional cost to below selling prices.

Three factors are present in the analysis because more than one product is sold and because it is being assumed that a calculation of mix variance will be helpful to management. Variance analysis proceeds along identical lines to any three factor analysis.

Sales variances:

	Actual sales, actual standard profit	**Actual sales, budgeted standard profit**	**Actual sales, budgeted mix, budgeted standard profit**	**Budget**
Alpha	£52,800	48,000 @ 0.60	59,184 @ 0.60	50,000 @ 0.60
Beta	£18,240	38,000 @ 0.98	47,347 @ 0.98	40,000 @ 0.98
	(£30,000)	30,000 @ nil	9,469 @ nil	8,000 @ nil
	£41,040	£66,040	£81,910	£69,200

Price variance £25,000 adverse (£41,040 – £66,040)
Mix variance £15,870 adverse (£66,040 – £81,910)
Volume variance £12,710 favourable (£81,910 – £69,200)

Self-assessment question 25.6

Provide a statement commenting on the results of the sales variance analysis for Quill PLC and providing your opinion of the value of the information conveyed, particularly the large adverse mix variance.

Answers on page 629

25.1.6 Quality cost variance

This final variance illustrates a single factor variance which arises whenever substandard goods are produced. Its inclusion illustrates an implication of process costing raised in previous chapters. Along with the stock variance, it is not to be found in the main body of management accounting theory. Practical design of systems may call for systems' designers to apply text book principles and illustrations in a way which is relevant to the particular organisation. There is not normally space in text books to supply answers for all practical situations, although the student can expect to have met all the principles necessary to the practising accountant before successful completion of studies. The quality cost variance can be considered as an example of a variance to be found in practice, if not widespread practice, which illustrates principles to be found in management accounting theory.

The output value of production is:

Alpha	50,000 units @ £7.40	£370,000
Beta	50,000 units @ £7.85	£392,500
		£762,500

The input value to finished goods stock is:

Alpha	50,000 units @ £7.40	£370,000
Beta perfects	40,000 units @ £9.02	£360,800
Beta seconds	10,000 units @ £2.00	£ 20,000
		£750,800

The quality cost variance is £11,700 adverse (£762,500 – £750,800).

If standard quality of output had been achieved, seconds of $16\frac{2}{3}\%$ would have resulted. This would have given an input to finished goods value of:

Alpha	50,000 units @ £7.40	£370,000
Beta perfects	41,666 units @ £9.02	£375,833
Beta seconds	8,333 units @ £2.00	£ 16,667
		£762,500

This is identical to the output value of production, giving rise to a variance of £nil. The quality cost variance measures the difference between perfect/substandard production mixes set as the standard and achieved during a particular period. A higher proportion of substandard output than standard is reflected in an adverse quality cost variance.

There is good reason to believe that the variance does not adequately reflect the importance of quality to a company. Note how it reduces in size when recalculated on a marginal costing basis in Section 25.2.

25.1.7 Profit or Operating statement

The variances can be summarised into the form of a profit or operating statement.

Operating statement for the year ending 31.12.19×8

	£ favourable	£ adverse	£
Budgeted profit			32,660
Variances:			
Raw materials price		14,000	
mix	6,560		
yield	29,840		
Direct labour rate	500		
efficiency	6,500		
Variable overhead rate	19,500		
efficiency		800	
Fixed overhead expenditure		15,500	
capacity	14,000		
efficiency		5,600	
Quality cost		11,700	
Marketing	nil		
Research and development	1,000		
Administration		4,460	
Sales price		25,000	
mix		15,870	
volume	12,710		
	75,110	77,430	(2,320)
Actual profit			£30,340

Additional detail can be provided in the form of percentages or ratios. Ratios to complement fixed overhead variances can be presented through the following calculations, for instance:

Capacity utilisation ratio	(39,000/37,000)	105%
Efficiency or productivity	(38,200/39,000)	101%
Production volume ratio	(38,200/37,000)	103%

Ratios such as these are intended to measure the same variables as the complementary variances. Capacity utilisation, for instance, is concerned with the difference between planned and actual usage of the capacity of the organisation's plant and machinery. In variance terms, the difference as measured in hours is valued at an absorption rate. The ratio expresses the actual hours used as a percentage of planned hours. Both measures attempt to motivate managers to use facilities to the level planned, when the management accounting system is designed to operate through a negative feedback mechanism.

25.2 MARGINAL COSTING

Under the marginal costing principle, the product cost incorporates only variable costs. The product cost for Example 25.1 would be produced as follows:

	Alpha £		Beta £
Direct materials:			
A: 300gm @ £2/kg	0.60	(800gm)	1.60
B: 300gm @ £6/kg	1.80	(500gm)	3.00
Direct labour:			
Grade I 30min @ £2/hr	1.00		
Grade II 30min @ £2.50/hr			1.25
Variable production overhead:			
30min @ £1/hr	0.50	(15min)	0.25
	3.90		6.10
Quality cost allowance	–		0.82
	3.90		6.92

	Alpha	Beta
	£	£
Contribution	4.10	3.08
Selling price	8.00	9.82

Work-in-progress and finished goods are valued upon the basis of the product cost. The management accounting profit under the marginal principle would be revised as follows, starting with the financial profit as a base:

Financial accounting profit		£30,340
add: effect of revaluing opening finished goods stock		£31,500
		£61,840
less: effect of revaluing work-in-progress	£ 4,900	
closing finished goods stock	£42,700	
		£47,600
Marginal costing profit		£14,240

The principles of variance calculation do not change as a result of producing marginal costing statements. Valuation bases do change. Sales variances are based on contribution rather than gross profit. The quality cost variance is valued at variable cost rather than total production cost.

Since fixed production overheads are no longer included in stock valuations, they are treated in exactly the same way as marketing, administrative and research and development overheads were treated under absorption costing principles.

The revised operating statement would be presented as follows:

Operating statement for the year ending 31.12.19×8

	£ favourable	£ adverse	£
Budgeted profit			32,660
Variances:			
Raw materials price		14,000	
mix	6,560		
yield	29,840		
Direct labour rate	500		
efficiency	6,500		
Variable overhead rate	19,500		
efficiency		800	
Quality cost		8,200	
Fixed production overhead		15,500	
Marketing	nil		
Research and development	1,000		
Administration		4,460	
Sales price		25,000	
mix		74,640	
volume	60,280		
	124,180	142,600	(18,420)
Actual profit			14,240

Self-assessment question 25.7

Provide an interpretation of the operating statements for Quill plc:

(a) for the absorption costing statement;
(b) for the marginal costing statement;
(c) from a comparison of absorption and marginal presentations.

Answers on page 632

SUMMARY

This chapter has presented a single complex example to illustrate the best known variances which are associated with standard costing. Principles from process costing were revised. Variances were interpreted to provide information from which management could take action to control materials, labour or overheads, as illustrated in answers to the self-assessment questions. Example 25.1 is a simplification of a real world situation, the simplifications reflecting the need to condense knowledge of an organisation into a single chapter. In considering a realistic situation, a little known variance occurred, the quality cost variance. In practice, it can be anticipated that individual companies will develop their own idiosyncratic variances where necessary. A student at this level needs to develop the ability to adapt the principles explained in this book in a flexible manner if a good contribution is to be made to the operation and understanding of management accounting systems. The exercises which follow reflect the variety of situations created by the ACCA examiner to test the student's knowledge of standard costing variance analysis.

EXERCISES

Exercise 25.1

The budgeted income statement of one of the products of Derwen plc for the month of May 1986 was as follows:

Budgeted Income Statement—May 1986

		£	£
Sales revenue			
10,000 units at £5			50,000
Production costs			
Budgeted production 10,000 units			
Direct materials:			
Material A 5,000kg. at £0.30	£1,500		
B 5,000kg. at £0.70	£3,500	5,000	
Direct labour:			
Skilled 4,500hrs. at £3.00	£13,500		
Unskilled 2,600hrs. at £2.50	£6,500	20,000	
Overhead cost:			
Fixed		10,000	
Variable 10,000 units at £0.50		5,000	
		40,000	
Add Opening stock			
1,000 units at £4		4,000	
		44,000	
Deduct Closing stock			
1,000 units at £4		4,000	
Cost of goods sold			40,000
Budgeted profit			10,000

During May 1986 production and sales were both above budget and the following income statement was prepared:

Income statement—May 1986

	£	£
Sales revenue		
7,000 units at £5		35,000
4,000 units at £4.75		19,000
		54,000

		£	£
Production costs			
Actual production 12,000 units			
Direct materials:			
Material A 8,000kg. at £0.20	£ 1,600		
B 5,000kg. at £0.80	£ 4,000	5,600	
Direct labour:			
Skilled 6,000hrs. at £2.95	£17,700		
Unskilled 3,150hrs. at £2.60	£ 8,190	25,890	
Overhead cost:			
Fixed		9,010	
Variable 12,000 units at £0.625		7,500	
		48,000	
Add Opening stock			
1,000 units at £4		4,000	
		52,000	
Deduct Closing stock			
2,000 units at £4		8,000	
Cost of goods sold			44,000
Profit			10,000

In the above statement stock is valued at the standard cost of £4 per unit.

There is general satisfaction because the budgeted profit level has been achieved but you have been asked to prepare a standard costing statement analysing the differences between the budget and the actual performance. In your analysis, include calculations of the sales volume and sales price variances and the following cost variances: direct material price, mix, yield and usage variances; direct labour rate, mix, productivity and efficiency variances; and the overhead spending and volume variances.

Provide a commentary on the variances and give your views on their usefulness.

(*ACCA, Management Accounting, December 1986*)

Answers on page 633

Exercise 25.2

Bamfram plc is a well-established manufacturer of a specialised product, a Wallop, which has the following specifications for production:

Components	Standard Quantity	Standard Price
WALS	15	60
LOPS	8	75

The standard direct labour hours to produce a Wallop at the standard wage rate of £10.50 per hour has been established at 60 hours per Wallop.

The annual fixed overhead budget is divided into calendar months with equal production per month. The budgeted annual fixed overheads are £504,000 for the budgeted output of 2,400 Wallops per annum.

Mr. Jones, a marketing person, is now the managing director of Bamfram plc and must report to the board of directors later this day and he seeks your advice in respect of the following operating information for the month of May:

	£	£
Sales		504,000
Cost of sales:		
Direct materials	281,520	
Direct labour	112,320	
	393,840	
Fixed production overheads	42,600	
		436,440
Gross profit		67,560
Administration expenses		11,150
Selling and distribution expenses		17,290
Net profit		£39,120

The sales manager informs Mr Jones that despite adverse trading conditions his sales staff have been able to sell 180 Wallops at the expected standard selling price.

The production manager along with the purchasing manager are also pleased that prices for components have been stable for the whole of the current year and they are able to produce the following information:

Stocks for May are as follows:

	1 May	31 May
Component WALS	600	750
Component LOPS	920	450

The actual number of direct labour hours worked in May was 11,700, considerably less than the production manager has budgeted. Further, the purchasing manager advised that WALS had cost £171,000 at a price of £57 per unit in the month of May and 1,000 LOPS had been acquired for £81,000.

Mr Jones, eager to please the board of directors, requests you, as the newly appointed management accountant, to prepare appropriate statements to highlight the following information which is to be presented to the board:

(a) The standard product cost of Wallop.
(b) **(i)** The direct material variances for both price and usage for each component used in the month of May assuming that prices were stable throughout the relevant period.
(ii) The direct labour efficiency and wage rate variances for the month of May.
(iii) The fixed production overhead expenditure and volume variances.

Note: You may assume that during the month of May there is no change in the level of finished goods stocks.

(c) A detailed reconciliation statement of the standard gross profit with the actual gross profit for the month of May.
(d) Draft a brief report for Mr Jones that he could present to the board of directors on the usefulness, or otherwise, of the statement you have prepared in your answer to **(c)** above.

(*ACCA, Management Accounting, June 1987*)

Answers in lecturer's manual.

Helpful definition: The examiner uses the term 'standard gross profit' to mean 'actual standard gross profit' rather than 'budgeted standard gross profit', in this instance.

Exercise 25.3

When an absorption cost approach is adopted for fixed production overheads, the budgeted idle capacity cost could arise. Explain briefly how this could happen and comment on the relevance of this to management.

(*ACCA, Management Accounting, December 1987*)

Answers in lecturer's manual.

Helpful comment: There are two allied interpretations of this question. One is provided by the capacity variance explained in the chapter. The examiner takes a slightly different stance by suggesting that the standard might be based on an SSAP 9 principle, creating a budgeted idle capacity variance which would be shown in the budgeted profit and loss statement and which would be additional to the customary capacity variance.

Exercise 25.4

A company has an inspection department in which operatives examine fruit in order to extract blemished input before the fruit is transferred to a processing department.

The input to the inspection department comes from a preparation department where fruit is washed and trimmed.

A standard output rate in kilos per hour from the inspection process has been agreed as the target to be aimed for in return for wages paid at a fixed rate per hour irrespective of the actual level of idle time.

The standard data for the inspection department are as follows:

(i) standard idle time: as a percentage of total hours paid for: 20%
(ii) standard wage rate per hour: £3.00
(iii) standard output efficiency is 100%, ie one standard hour of work is expected in each hour excluding idle time hours.
(iv) wages are charged to production at a rate per standard hour sufficient to absorb the standard level of idle time.

The labour variance analysis for November for the inspection department was as follows:

	£	**Expressed in % terms**
Variances		
Productivity	525 (F)	2.2 (F)
Excess idle time	150 (A)	2.5 (A)
Wage rate	800 (A)	3.3 (A)

The actual data for the inspection department for the three months December to February are as follows:

	Dec	Jan	Feb
Standard hours of output achieved	6,600	6,700	6,800
Labour time paid for	8,600	8,400	8,900
Idle time hours incurred	1,700	1,200	1,400
Actual wages earned	£26,660	£27,300	£28,925

The labour variances to be calculated in the operation of a standard cost system are as follows:

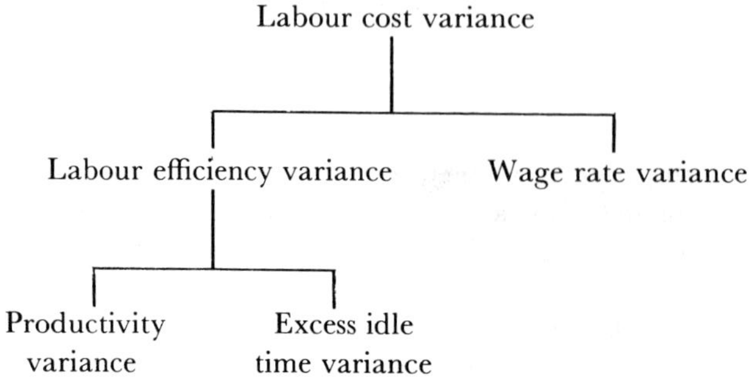

Required:

(a) Calculate the labour variances for productivity, excess idle time and rate of pay for each of the months December to February.

(b) In order to highlight the trend and materiality of variances calculated in **(a)** above, express them as percentages as follows:

Productivity variance: as a percentage of standard cost of production achieved;
Excess idle time variance; as a percentage of expected idle time;
Wage rate variances: as a percentage of hours paid for at a standard rate of pay.

(c) Comment on the data given for November and calculated for December to February, giving possible explanations for the figures produced.

(*ACCA, Management Accounting, June 1988, slightly adapted*)

Answers in lecturer's manual.

Interpreting and Investigating Variances

INTRODUCTION

Interpretation is a necessary forerunner to the decision to investigate variances. Investigating variances is a necessary forerunner to the decision to take corrective action. Evidence gained in interpreting and investigating is used to motivate people to control the aspects of the organisation over which they have responsibility. This chapter is concerned with the factors which impinge on interpretation and the investigation decision. The first section summarises the processes which were necessary to formulate the suggested answers to the self-assessment questions posed in the previous chapter. The second section considers the formal techniques proposed for the investigation decision and assesses the importance of those techniques to the practising accountant.

26.1 INTERPRETING VARIANCES

Variances may be interpreted in isolation from each other. If the aim is to apply negative feedback concepts, then taking each variance individually, any variance could be taken to be evidence that a process is out of control. Both favourable and adverse variances could be taken to be undesirable from the point of view of mechanical systems control. However, it is difficult to separate the interpretation of variances from the behavioural consequences arising from target setting and measurement procedures. Rightly or wrongly, value judgements are applied to variance interpretation. An interpretation of an adverse raw material usage variance, reflecting the amount of abnormal wastage, might be that the standard could have incorporated a tight measurement of normal waste in order to provide motivation commensurate with our knowledge of the influence of aspiration levels. In other words, the adverse variance may be acceptable in terms of what the standard is intending to achieve. An alternative reponse to the adverse raw material usage variance is to assume that the manager has in some way failed and fairness demands that the reward/punishment structure should be brought to bear. Interpretation by people about people may vary and differ from interpretation of mechanical consequences of the operation of formal systems. Organisational interpretation may imply political, social and personal consequences.

Variances may be interpreted in relation to each other. A 'big' variance may receive more attention than a 'small' variance. The quality cost variance in the last chapter did not assume major importance because other variances were of greater magnitude. A marginal costing analysis showed that sales was the vital problem. An absorption costing analysis split concern between sales and production functions. Here, the interpretation was governed by technical accounting principles and approaches to measurement. It is difficult to see from the case study which measurement or accounting principles would have most usefully contributed to the furthering of organisational objectives. However, it should be clear from the case study that accounting approaches affect the magnitude of variances in relation to each other in ways which may not reflect the importance of the different organisational variables to management. If managers wish to follow a quality objective, the quality cost variance in the form illustrated in the last chapter would not have reflected the importance of quality, in relation to other variances. Interpretation must take into account the advantages and limitations of accounting models in relation to the organisation and its objectives.

Variances can arise from a common cause. A fixed overhead efficiency variance is likely to be based on the same number of hours as the variable overhead efficiency variance. Where labour hours are used to absorb overheads, both fixed and variable overhead efficiency variances are based on the number of hours used in the labour efficiency variance. Instead of interpreting the variances in isolation by reporting to management that 'the labour efficiency is good/bad/as expected, and so is the variable overhead efficiency and so is the fixed overhead efficiency', it makes some sense to report 'the cost of efficiency was £x in total different to targets', totalling the variances which measure the same underlying reality. Such an approach requires flexibility and imagination on the part of the management accountant.

A slightly different case is given by variances which are interrelated. A poor wages rate variance, indicating that workers received a higher wage than expected, can imply a more skilled or a more satisfied workforce. This may have a good influence on labour productivity and materials usage. Paying for higher-quality materials may have a positive influence on materials usage and labour productivity. Again, a good measurement system will pool together variances which are related to the same underlying cause so that instead of separate variances, management are shown the total variance attributable to employee skill and motivation or the total variance attributable to good-quality materials.

The ideas above make good sense on paper. In practice, they may reflect sound principles which are simply not practicable. Take the case of a company which is processing two hundred different raw materials through thirty different processes using FMS. The possible number of variance permutations is immense. In an uncertain world, the task of assessing the implication of a single higher-quality raw material in a complex mix of products is not easy. Routine processing of variances may more conveniently produce reports which are interpreted in an *ad hoc* manner through investigations of individual variances. Investigating one variance should have implications for other variances in a real world where results measure interrelationships and interactions but considering variance in isolation makes a complex problem solvable.

26.2 INVESTIGATING VARIANCES

The topic of investigating variances is concerned with looking at individual variances in isolation from each other and coming to a decision whether to investigate or to ignore the information provided. In an ideal world, all variances, including zero variances, would be investigated to ensure that managers have all matters of importance brought to their attention. In a less than ideal world, zero variances are not investigated because there is no time to look at matters which are proceeding as expected. Managers have time only to consider matters of significance. In practice, zero variances rarely occur and decisions have to be taken as to which of many variables should be investigated. There is scope to debate how matters of significance are assessed.

Measurements make sense only within tolerances. An engineer cutting a metal bar to a length of 5.5 metres may be satisfied with a cut which actually measures 5.501 metres. The instruments which are used to measure are accurate only within tolerances, and hence the need for standard measures against which measures used in everyday life can be checked and revised where necessary. Imagine catching a bus or train. A timetable provides a standard measurement. A train is given as leaving London at 9.30. An exact person might arrive at 9.30, expect to walk on to the train and expect the train to leave immediately. A more realistic approach would be to arrive between 9.15 and 9.25 and not object to the train leaving at any time between 9.30 and 9.32. In everyday life people become accustomed to managing their affairs within tolerances. So it is with variances. 'Small' variances are expected and are therefore ignored. They may be immaterial or due to random factors. Noise is random and all systems are said to be affected by noise. There is little to be gained from investigating random factors or noise since they may not continue and are difficult to control. It is only the significant variance which causes concern. But what is meant by the term significant? This chapter suggests different means by which systems can be set up to investigate significant variances.

The act of investigating variances costs money. Time is spent in deciding the cause of the variance. Interpretation may suggest possible cause of variances but investigation must arrive at definite conclusions about the cause of the variance so that action to correct the variance can be effective. Corrective action may be expensive. Machinery may need to be modified, a new processing method may be necessary to overcome a change in unavoidable raw material changes, labour relations may be affected by attempts to correct the behaviour of a member of staff who is working below an acceptable level of performance. Benefits from incurring the costs of investigation should ideally be considered; this is meta-accounting or accounting for the results of accounting; accounting for accounting. This chapter suggests approaches and discusses the problems of meta-accounting for the investigation of variances decision.

There are behavioural as well as technical consequences to the decision to investigate variances. If no variances are ever investigated, the cost of investigation in money terms is slight but managers may begin to ask questions on the effect of variances on their everyday lives and may cease to be motivated by the systems which produce the variances. Investigating favourable and adverse variances may create positive behavioural reinforcements, with implications for motivation, aspiration levels and interdepartmental relationships. Drury states that 'the application of statistical techniques to determine the probability of variances being and due to random uncontrollable factors should result in a number of improvements in the behavioural consequence of variance analysis'. This aspect will not be further developed in this chapter but it is important that material on the behavioural consequences of control systems, as discussed in Chapter 21, should be related to the investigation of variances decision.

The remainder of this chapter is organised into sections each representing a different technique either used in practice or suggested by theory.

26.2.1 Heuristics

A heuristic is a rule of thumb. It has come to be associated in recent years with expert systems and ways in which experts take decisions. Experts, including management accountants, are faced with enormously complex problems for which the current trend of thought suggests that optimal resolution is not practicable. Experts reduce unmanageable problems to manageable proportions by using rules of thumb.

A typical rule of thumb may be: 'investigate all adverse variances over 5% or £10,000, whichever is the smaller'. 5% and £10,000 are numbers determined by the management accountant, possibly based on experience. The author once asked a Financial Director the reason for selecting 3% as a level at which variances should be investigated. The answer was that experience over a number of years had shown a level of 3% to be effective.

A decision rule which states 'investigate all adverse variances over 5% or £10,000, whichever is the smaller' enjoys some clear advantages. The rule is clear and unambiguous. It is easily understood. It can be built into accounting procedures so that the system of investigating variances can be enacted at the operational level, at a reduction in cost from avoiding the use of expensive middle manager and senior manager time. As a measure of materiality, some percentage or absolute measure may be effective in reducing the number of insignificant or randomly occurring variances which are investigated. Studies of materiality in auditing reveal the existence of percentage guidelines or rules of thumb which have been suggested by authorities as being applicable in various situations.

Drawbacks to the use of heuristics include the subjective nature of the numbers which are used and the fact that the heuristic does not guarantee that a variance is worth investigating. Is 3% or 5% the most appropriate measure of materiality. Are there other percentages which are just as good or better? Is there any point in investigating a 6% variance costing £15,000 per month if the cost of correcting the variance is £16,000 per month? Some retailers are reputed to allow pilferage because the costs of security measures easily exceed the cost of pilferage encountered. It may be better to monitor some variances to ensure that they stay within certain tolerances rather than to instigate expensive investigation and correction procedures. Heuristics are based on expert behaviour which is practicable but known to exhibit significant weaknesses. In particular, experts are known to use preconceptions which are biased and potentially flawed. The more scientific approaches, described in some of the following sections, overcome the problems of expert behaviour but may be considered less practicable.

26.2.2 Trends

Where the trend of a variance is consistent, it may be concluded that the process is under control. If a variance is significant but following a trend, the implication may be that the standard is not consistent with current circumstances, perhaps because an ideal standard is in use or that the cost of correcting the underlying problem is prohibitive.

Why should it be necessary to monitor a variance trend when a cost trend may be just as useful and less expensive to administer? The first self-assessment question in this chapter helps to answer this question.

Self-assessment question 26.1

Trendyco plc uses a standard costing system. The following cost of material details relate to the most immediate months.

Materials usage: kg	100,000	100,000	100,000	100,000
£	500,000	500,000	500,000	500,000
Output	50,000	45,000	52,000	55,000

The standard product cost shows that materials should cost £3 per kilogram and that each unit of output should use 2kg.

Calculate variances and state which variances should have been investigated by the company.

Answers on page 637

26.2.3 Control charts

Past data can be used to measure the variation of results as measured in standard deviation terms. The point of this is to provide information on the extent to which results vary due to random factors or noise. Assuming that past results are normally distributed about the mean, random results may fall outside, say, two standard deviations of the mean. If analysis can show the equivalent variance in terms of standard deviations, charts can be constructed on to which variance results can be plotted. Figure 26.1 illustrates the appearance of a control chart once some variances have been entered. In this example, the one standard deviation level is treated as a warning; a note may be sent to the responsible individual pointing out a processing problem. At two standard deviations, action is taken

FIGURE 26.1

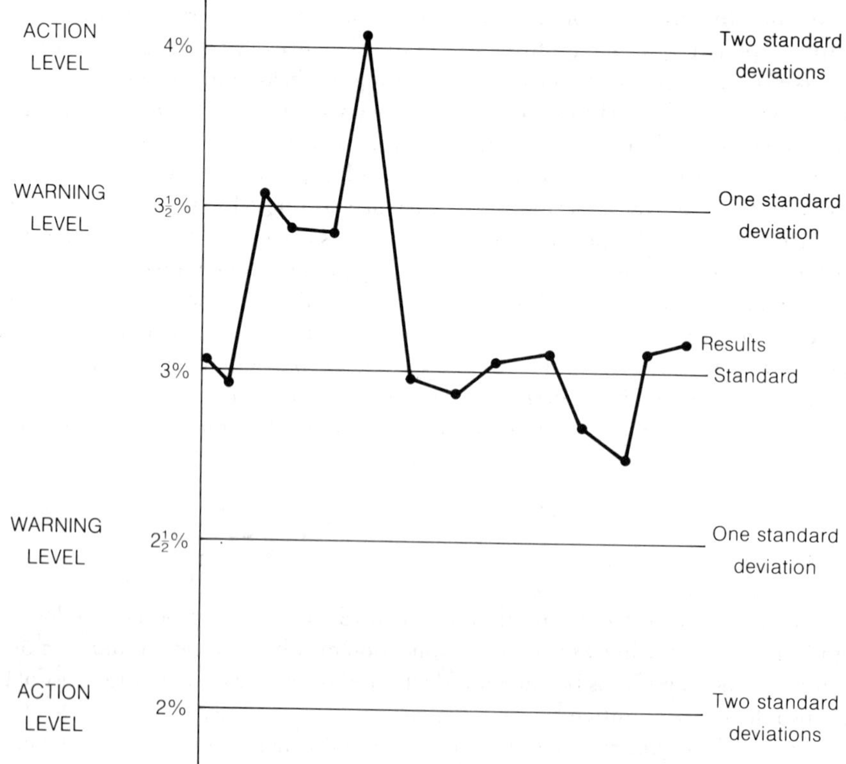

Control chart: Wastage levels in production of N

to investigate the variance. 1.96 standard deviations is sometimes thought to be more suitable since 95% of all observations should fall within this level; the heuristic of 5% appears to enjoy popularity as a determining factor in setting levels, even where statistical approaches are followed.

The control chart approach has the advantage of ensuring that random variances are not investigated. These can be thought to be non-controllable and self-correcting. Once the statistical analysis has been completed and the chart drawn up, the procedure is easily implemented at the operational control level. Variances can be regularly entered on to the chart. The disadvantages include problems over the availability and relevance of past data in relation to current variances and the lack of consideration of costs of investigation. An additional important consideration concerns the extent to which costs are normally distributed in practice.

Self-assessment question 26.2

The cost of supervisory salaries for Chartrend plc has been budgeted at £12,500 per annum. Analysis of past cost behaviour records show that this is a fixed cost for which the standard deviation is £550, per annum adjusted for the effects of inflation. A control chart is operated with a control limit set at the 2% level (98% of all observations occur within 2.33 standard deviations either side of the mean, if the data is normally distributed). Salary costs for the first six months of the year are as follows:

Period 1 £1,050
Period 2 £1,110
Period 3 £1,190
Period 4 £1,010
Period 5 £1,000
Period 6 £1,100

Produce a control chart for Chartrend plc and comment on the results.

Answers on page 637

26.2.4 Decision tree approach

In advance of the decision to investigate or not to investigate all variances, an assessment of costs and benefits arising from investigating or not investigating can be made. The assessment can be expressed in the form of a decision tree. Probabilities of the effectiveness of investigation can be applied to the decision tree in order to determine whether an economic advantage would arise.
Figure 26.2 illustrates a simple form of decision tree.

FIGURE 26.2

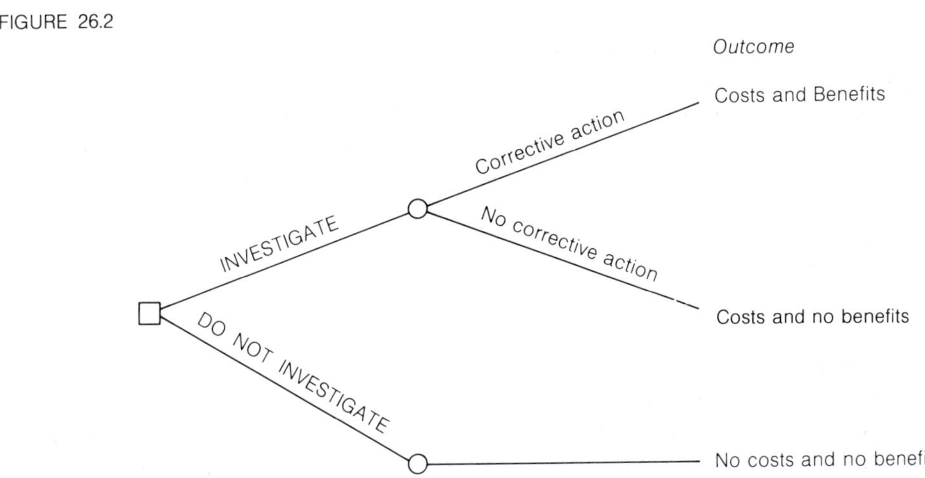

If all variances are investigated, some lead to corrective action whilst for others no action results. If corrective action occurs, some form of benefit can be anticipated but investigation costs money. If no action results, the cost of the investigation has been suffered but no benefits occur. Prior knowledge of the results of investigation, expressed as subjective probabilities, can be applied. If no variances are investigated, neither benefits nor costs arise.

Costs can be broken into two parts: the time involved in conducting the investigation and the cost of taking corrective action. The benefits can be considered under three distinct headings:

1 The avoidance of future adverse variances. This is problematic in that there is no academic agreement about the time horizon over which the continuance of the variance can be assumed to continue. A problem arises from the fact that even without variance investigation, there may come a time when lack of process control becomes so obvious that the manager notices the problem without accounting information and is forced into taking corrective action. There is agreement that where adverse variances are expected to continue well into the future the cash flows should be discounted. Additionally, there does not yet appear to be a sensible treatment of favourable variances under conditions of negative feedback.
2 The perpetuation of favourable variances. Where investigation leads to reinforcement of behaviours leading to favourable variances, perhaps coupled with encouragement through positive feedback, the amount of the benefit could be given by the discounted value of future cash flows to perpetuity. This assumes that the variances would tend to reduce to zero without the process of reinforcement and encouragement. This is a questionable assumption.
3 Decision significant variances are those variances which have an impact on decisions taken by an organisation. Standard product costs can be used in optimisation models at the budgeting stage. A certain level of standard cost will drive a particular decision on product mix. If an unavoidable variance leads to a change in the standard product cost, this could change the optimum mix. Feeding the revised standard into a linear programme, for example, may result in a decision to change the production mix. The benefit from the investigation of the variance is given by the opportunity cost associated with producing a non-optimal mix. This is illustrated by Example 26.1.

Example 26.1

The product costs for the two products sold by Bestdecide PLC are give below:

	Product Kue	Product Arr
Materials	£2.50	£3.00
Labour (£6 per hour)	£6.00	£9.00
Contribution	£1.50	£3.00
Selling price	£10.00	£15.00

Bestdecide follow a policy of diversification, producing at least 30,000 units each year of each product, but concentrate remaining resources on producing the product or mix of products which provides the maximum profit in the short term. For the year ahead, there are only sufficient skilled workers to allow 120,000 labour hours (10,000 hours per period) to be worked.

An investigation of variances in period 6 shows that the time taken to produce Kue can be halved because of a decision taken in a factory quality circle meeting.

At the start of the year, a decision would be taken to maximise the production of Arr because it shows a contribution per unit of limiting factor of £2 per hour, as opposed to £1.50 for Kue. Assuming that the company takes its mix decision on an annual basis, at the time that standards and budgets are produced, the production for the year would be:

Kue 30,000 units (30,000 hours)
Arr 60,000 units (90,000 hours)
Budgeted contribution: £225,000

At the end of period 6, investigation of variances suggest that the contribution from Kue becomes £4.50 and the contribution per limiting factor becomes £9 per hour. The results for the second half of the year, assuming that output results coincide with budget, would give a contribution of £315,000, an impressive improvement on the £112,500 anticipated. However, by transferring capacity from Arr to Kue, a contribution of £470,000 is possible, showing an opportunity cost of

£155,000 associated with the value of the decision significant variance. By investigating the variance and then changing the decision made at the beginning of the year, an extra contribution of £155,000 could be earned.

The decision tree method has the advantage of providing a model which includes the costs and benefits of investigation. Random variations are accounted for through an assessment as to whether the process is in or out of control. The decision rule is simple to operate since the intention is to determine the economic implication of investigating all or none of the variances. Practical problems include the determination of values, as explained above, and the determination of probabilities. The manager must be able to provide reliable cost and benefit data and an estimate of the probability of the process being in or out of control. Where probabilities can be determined on the basis of past experience, there is no assurance that past conditions would be relevant to future events. Where probabilities are subjective, there is the practical problem of systematically securing information from managers and gaining a consensus amongst managers on the size of the probabilities.

26.2.5 Decision theory approach (game theory)

A game theory approach has been suggested which has the advantage of recognising that the process may be under control even though a variance is reported. Coupling this idea to the decision tree ideas provides the following tableau:

States	In control	Out of control
Actions		
Investigate	C	C + M
Do not investigate	£0	L

C—cost of an investigation
M—cost of correction
L—present value of future cash flows from the benefit gained by investigating

Given that P_1 is the probability that the process is under control and P_2 is the probability that the process in out of control, the expected costs are:

$$\text{cost of investigation} = CP_1 + (C + M)P_2$$
$$= C(P_1 + P_2) + MP_2$$
$$= C + MP_2$$

Cost of not investigating $= LP_2$

The decision rule is:

Investigate where

$$C + MP_2 < LP_2$$

$$\text{or } C - (L - M)P_2 < 0$$

This means that an investigation should occur where the cost, less the difference between costs and benefits of correcting an out of control process, multiplied by the probability of the process being out of control, shows a saving.

The decision rule is reasonably clear and intuitively sensible. In practice, there may be difficulty finding out the level of probabilities in much the same way as for the decision tree approach.

26.3 DISCUSSION

The previous section provided a survey of existing approaches to the investigation of variances decision. The survey was not intended to be complete and omitted some important contributions to the area. For instance, the application of Bayes theorem is not included but has been suggested as a suitable way of taking account of the in/out of control situation. Additionally, Drury provides an approach which combines a standard deviation approach with a cost/benefit assessment. The theory of the investigation of variances decision is not insubstantial.

Whilst the survey of techniques is not complete, every effort has been made to ensure a reasonable coverage of the considerations to be borne in mind by the accountant interpreting variances and instigating investigations. These can be listed as:

1 **Materiality.** How material, or significant, is the variance?
2 **Trend.** Is the trend of the variance consistent with past experience and knowledge of the process?
3 **Random non-controllable variations.** Are variances within tolerances that can be expected?
4 **Cost-benefit considerations.** Do the benefits arising from investigating variances exceed the cost incurred in investigation and in taking corrective action?
5 **Controllability.** Is the process in control despite the variance reported? If the process is under control, the variance will be corrected without the need for investigation.
6 **Ease of implementation.** Can the decision rule be stated clearly and be implemented effectively at a suitable level within the organisation?
7 **Availability and relevance of data.** Is data available for the operation of a particular technique? Is the available data relevant to the future operation of a particular process?

The investigation of variance decision is a notable example of an area where the academic literature discusses techniques and approaches which are apparently little used by practising accountants. The practicality of decision theory or decision tree approaches, for instance, is therefore an issue. Reasons for accountants to use heuristics or trend information in preference to techniques which appear to show clear answers to the drawbacks of these 'simple' approaches is a matter for conjecture until evidence of the kind given in Section 23.3.7 in relation to forecasting is collected.

SUMMARY

Interpretation is the process of analysing variance information in order to form an understanding of the information conveyed. Interrelationships and interactions between variances could be considered as part of a process which ultimately leads to a suggestion that certain variances should be further investigated. This is usually associated with the process of interpreting variances. It is convenient to consider variances in isolation from each other but in relation to a number of factors, including materiality and trend. This is associated with the decision to investigate a variance. Benefits arise from action to correct out-of-control processes. In earning these benefits, costs are incurred in investigation and in correction. A variety of techniques for taking decisions has been suggested.

EXERCISES

Exercise 26.1

Explain why the cause, trend, materiality and controllability should be considered when assessing the relevance of variances from budget.

(*ACCA, Management Accounting, December 1988*)

Answers in lecturer's manual.

Exercise 26.2

Branchtree plc is considering whether it should investigate standard costing variances on a routine basis. For the past six months, the Management Accountant, Lynne Smith, has investigated variances on a sampled basis and has compiled the following information:

Proportions of variances where:

No action resulted from the investigation because the variances were found to arise from random causes:	29%
Corrective action was taken, but the variance continued. The standard was eventually changed, with no benefit to Branchtree plc:	9%
Corrective action was taken and adverse variances ceased:	31%
No corrective action was taken, but favourable variances continued:	18%
No corrective action was taken and favourable variances ceased:	13%
The average of adverse variances, other than those arising from random causes:	£8,990/month
The average of favourable variances, other than those arising from random causes:	£9,320/month
The average cost of an investigation:	£890
The average cost of corrective action:	£3,020

The management accountant can see no reason for the incidence of causes of variance changing in the future. It has been decided that a reasonable assumption about the impact of investigating variances is to predict that, without a procedure for investigation:

(a) adverse variances would continue for six months before action would be taken to change the standard.

(b) favourable variances would not continue.

The company usually plans long term over a five-year period and has a cost of capital of 13%. It does not project accounting figures beyond five years because of its attitudes to uncertainty.

You are required to recommend to the Management Accountant whether it is advantageous to investigate variances on a routine basis. Clearly state any assumptions you make.

Answers on page 638

Exercise 26.3

'Modern management can take all necessary decisions on whether or not to investigate variances by considering variance levels in absolute and relative terms alone.'

Discuss the above statement, supporting your arguments by explaining examples of techniques for the investigation of variances decision.

Answer in lecturer's manual.

Uncertainty: Impact and Responses in Budgets and Standards

INTRODUCTION

This chapter describes a range of techniques for responding to the problems associated with uncertainty. The first group of techniques briefly applies the ideas from the uncertainty and decision-making chapter. The second group illustrates approaches based on the common idea that as events and outcomes become known, then budgets and standards should be updated to reflect known changes from the assumptions that were originally formulated. These revisions are made before the coming period, as reflected in the term ex ante. The final group of technique revises standards at the end of a particular period. With the benefit of hindsight, variances are divided into two components; the variance due to operational causes and the variance arising from uncertainty in the planning process. These revisions are sometimes associated with the terms ex post, indicating that the revision takes place 'after the event'. It seems that however good the process of formulating budgets and standards, some difference between plans and events will naturally arise because of the impossibility of looking forward with absolute certainty.

At the end of the chapter, the student will have been exposed to a range of ideas which have been proven to be useful in solving practical problems arising from uncertainty. It is anticipated that the student will be able to describe these techniques and assess their relevance in meeting real world problems.

27.1 PROBABILITY, SIMULATION AND SENSITIVITY ANALYSIS

The chapter entitled uncertainty and decision making considered a range of techniques in detail and provided practice in answering problems related to decision making. This chapter will recall some of these techniques in a budgeting context.

27.1.1 Three-tier budgeting

A single, deterministic statement of planned outcomes appears to be at odds with approaches which people take when managing their everyday lives. Instead of planning for, say, a single profit, it could be argued, a range of profits may be a more realistic means by which the future can be assessed. The rationale behind three-tier budgeting is to consider three levels of outcome: the most likely outcome, the most pessimistic outcome and the most optimistic outcome. A sales director, for instance, could be asked for a personal assessment of sales for the coming year based on these three levels. Consider the fictional responses to this question from two different sales directors:

	Sales director A	Sales director B
Most pessimistic	1,000,000 units	550,000 units
Most likely	2,000,000 units	600,000 units
Most optimistic	2.500,000 units	650,000 units

One advantage of this approach is that an informal measure of risk is provided by means of the spread of anticipated outcomes. Sales director A would appear to be in a higher-risk business than sales director B. The three-tier budgeting approach provides information on levels of activity, in the same way as does a traditional, deterministic budget. Sales director B has significantly lower sales levels than does sales director A.

Two approaches to processing this kind of data present themselves. The first approach is to build computer models so that a range of possible outcomes can be explored. By stating most pessimistic, most likely and most optimistic expectations for all variables within the model, a range of outcomes results from a combination of all variables combined at their most pessimistic figures to all variables combined at their most optimistic figures. This range can be used to assess risk and to make contingency plans. A contingency plan may take the form of 'what action shall we take if the worst situation arises?' or 'how can we best take advantage of the best situation?' Where the cost of building an appropriate model is unlikely to provide commensurate benefits, risk assessment and contingency planning may be applied to each variable in isolation and a single budget constructed by applying the following formula to each variable.

$$\text{Budgeted figure} = \frac{p + 4m + o}{6}$$

where p is the most pessimistic value,
m is the most likely value,
o is the most optimistic value.

This applies a weighting of 4 to the most likely value but retains some reflection of the most pessimistic and most optimistic values predicted. Applying this formula to the sales director example given above, director A would incorporate 1,916,667 units into the sales budget.

27.1.2 Decision trees and joint probabilities

Three-tier budgeting restricts the budget committee to information on three levels and a fixed weighting where a single budget is required. Decision trees can theoretically develop a large number of levels of prediction and apply subjective probabilities considered to be appropriate to particular managers for particular situations. Figure 27.1 provides an example of a decision tree.

An assessment of market share by the sales director has suggested that four possibilities for output level could arise. Subjective probabilities have been provided by the director. For each level of output, a different variable cost level might apply because of economies of scale. Costs may be at two levels and the production director and cost accountant have assessed both costs and subjective probabilites. The tree shows all of the possible outcomes in terms of total cost and joint probability and shows the figure which would be used to provide a single plan for the year ahead.

This example has been simplified and yet eight different outcomes arise. Stocks have been excluded. Costs have not been broken down into the separate elements of materials, labour and overheads. A larger range of possible outcomes could have arisen. It is unlikely that the decision tree approach could be developed into a practicable tool without the use of computing. Even then, there is some doubt about the ability of people to provide logical subjective probabilities. The technique has the advantage of explicitly and scientifically accounting for a range of possible outcomes but has the drawback that it requires great skill and time to implement.

27.1.3 Simulation

Simulation may overcome the problems of drawing up substantial decision trees in order to consider the range of possible results. It also introduces the element of chance which could be considered to be a part of the real world. Once a budget model has been established as a range of possible outcomes, with probabilities or measures of dispersion such as standard deviation attached, input figures to the model are determined on a random basis and the model produces a result. By iterating the process, a number of possible master budgets are produced. Risk and contingency planning may be based on the simulation exercise.

FIGURE 27.1

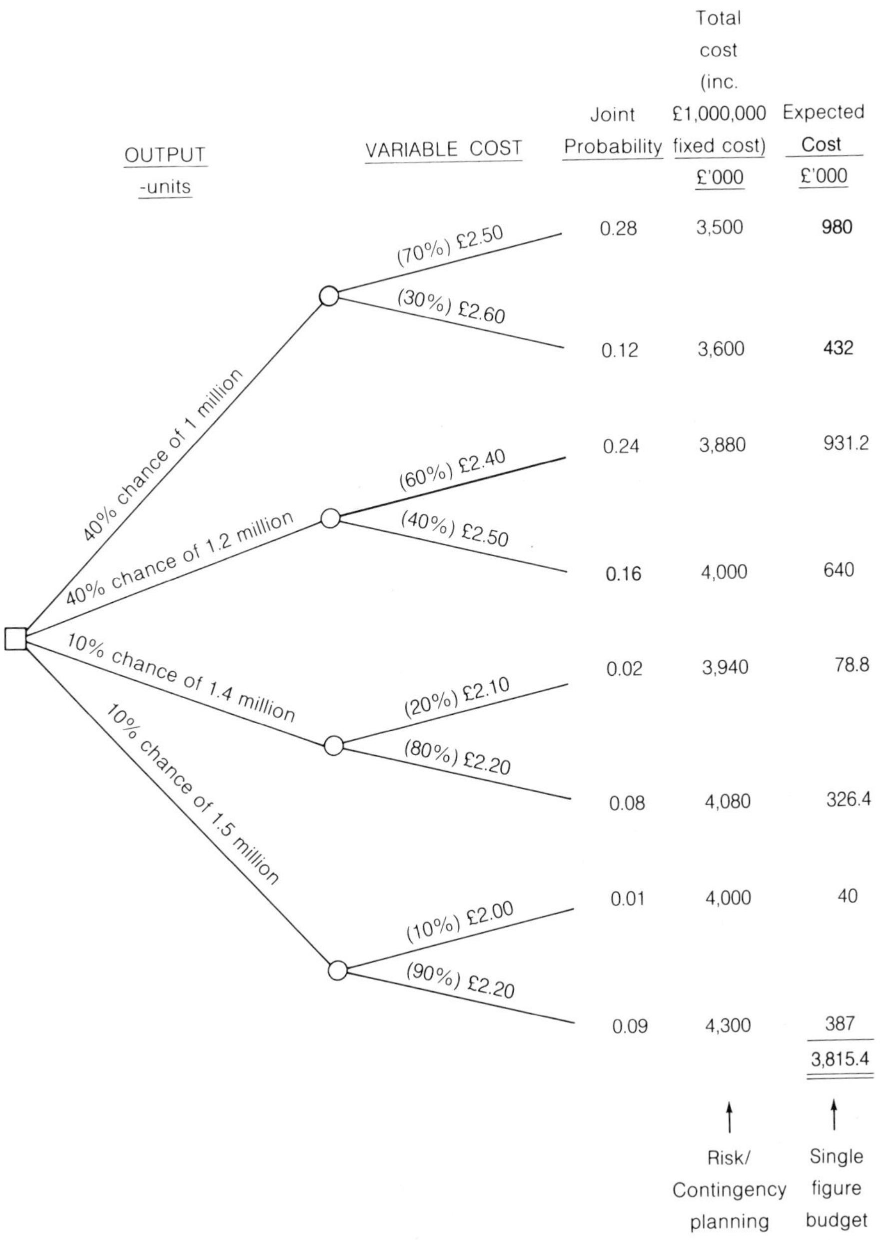

OUTPUT -units	VARIABLE COST	Joint Probability	Total cost (inc. £1,000,000 fixed cost) £'000	Expected Cost £'000
40% chance of 1 million	(70%) £2.50	0.28	3,500	980
	(30%) £2.60	0.12	3,600	432
40% chance of 1.2 million	(60%) £2.40	0.24	3,880	931.2
	(40%) £2.50	0.16	4,000	640
10% chance of 1.4 million	(20%) £2.10	0.02	3,940	78.8
	(80%) £2.20	0.08	4,080	326.4
10% chance of 1.5 million	(10%) £2.00	0.01	4,000	40
	(90%) £2.20	0.09	4,300	387
				3,815.4
			↑ Risk/ Contingency planning	↑ Single figure budget

27.1.4 Sensitivity analysis

Sensitivity analysis involves changing variables by a set amount in order to assess the importance of each variable to the model and hence to the organisation's planning and control process. Where a variable has a significant impact on an organisation's results, greater care can be expended at the planning stage and more emphasis can be placed on control for the particular variable. An example, applicable to a budgeting situation is provided below. Given the use of computers, the technique is relatively simple and appears to be easily understood by managers. There is evidence that this technique is more used in practice to make an assessment about the range of possible outcomes than are probabilistic and simulation problems.

Example 27.1

The following profit and loss account is the final budget for Sensitine plc.

		£
Sales (100,000 units @ £5)		500,000
Cost of goods sold		300,000
Gross Profit		200,000
Administrative costs	50,000	
Marketing costs	100,000	150,000
Net Profit		50,000

The Board of Directors of Sensitine plc are concerned about the amount of uncertainty facing the company and are particularly concerned about the following matters:

(a) Variable costs, which amount to two-thirds of the budgeted cost of goods sold, may increase due to a shortage of raw materials in the market;

(b) Sales prices may need to be decreased in response to competitors' activities. If sales prices are not reduced, the management anticipate a 3% loss in market share for every 10% reduction in competitors' prices. Sensitine currently holds a 12% market share;

(c) A reduction in wastage is anticipated as part of a quality control scheme which is to be set up early in the coming year. A level of 5% wastage has currently been built into the cost of goods sold figure.

A sensitivity analysis of the above situation requires that each of the factors under consideration should be adjusted by a fixed percentage, say 10%. The following questions and answers can then be framed:

(a) What if variable costs increase by 10%?
The cost of goods sold figure would increase:
Current variable cost of goods sold: £200,000
Loss in profit from an increase of 10% = £20,000

(b) What if competitors decrease sales prices by 10%?
(i) If Sensitine reduce its selling prices,
The sales figure would decrease:
Current sales turnover: £500,000
Loss in profit from a decrease of 10% = £50,000
(ii) If Sensitine maintains its current selling prices,
The sales volume would decrease by one-quarter (3%/12%):
Current contribution: (£500,000-£200,000) £300,000
Loss in profit from a decrease of one-quarter = £75,000

(c) What if a saving of 10% is achieved?
The wastage level would reduce, thus reducing variable cost.
The current cost of wastage is (5/105 × £200,000) £9,520.
Gain in profit from a saving of 10% = £952

This is only one way of looking at the wastage situation; other assumptions are available which would produce other answers.

It can be seen that Sensitine plc is most sensitive to competitors' actions. Further management effort could be most usefully expended in the marketing area.

A variation on this theme becomes possible by using the goal seek function offered by some modelling and spreadsheet software. If a high degree of uncertainty is known to be associated with a particular variable, it is possible to calculate the level of that variable in terms of an acceptable result. The following example illustrates:

Example 27.2

Sensitine plc believes that it can survive the short-term effects of competition as long as its profit figure does not fall below £30,000. At this level, it is believed that the owners of the business would sell the company to the competitors because of the opportunity to earn greater returns on investment in a bank.

In this situation, it is useful to calculate the reduction in competitors' prices which will be necessary to cause a profit reduction of £20,000. For the output level of 100,000 units, a sales value of £480,000 gives a reduction in profit of £20,000. This is equivalent to a selling price of £4.80 per unit. The reduction in selling price necessary to create this selling price is 4% (£0.20/£5.00). Goal seeking would thus alert management to the fact that the business would not continue in its present form if competitors reduce their prices by more than 4%. Management may then speculate about the chances of such a price reduction occurring. At the control level, management may monitor prices and consider drastic action if price reductions approach the 4% level.

27.2 EX ANTE REVISION OF BUDGETS AND STANDARDS

These techniques have in common the revision of budgets or standards in advance of the period to which the targets will relate. Revisions will be made in the light of knowledge which has been gained since the original target was set. There is an acceptance that uncertainty will cause change and that sound planning should respond to known changes.

27.2.1 Continuous budgeting and rolling forecasts

Under this technique, a budget or forecast would be established at the beginning of a particular period of time, perhaps a year. As time passes, perhaps on a monthly basis, the budget or forecast is compared with actual results. A process of double loop feedback is applied. Where differences between plans and results come from an uncertain knowledge of the future, perhaps because of changes in the marketplace affecting sales and purchases costs, or changes in the economic environment such as interest rates or exchange rates, adjustments are made to future plans. An additional feature of this approach is that the planning horizon does not change. At the end of the first month, changes will be made to the following eleven periods' plans or predictions and an additional month will be added to the plan. There will always be budgets or forecasts available for a year.

Figure 27.2 illustrates an example where a company is using continuous budgeting to produce annual budgets within a feedback period of one month. At the end of January 19×0, budgets for February to December of 19×0 are revised if necessary, and a budget for January 19×1 is produced. At the end of February, budgets for March to the end of the following January are prepared by considering differences between February's budget and results achieved. Amendments for variances which can be corrected are not made. The system can apply the feedforward mechanism. By budgeting for February 19×1, a budget for one year ahead is always available. This budget can continually be compared with objectives and long-term plans.

Continuous budgeting provides the benefit of creating plans which are up to date. The budget does not cease to be relevant because the assumptions which were used to formulate the budget cease to be useful. A major drawback to practical use is the cost, especially time, required for their effective implementation. A combination of a static budget and rolling forecasting seems to have a popularity in some companies because forecasting is by definition less time-consuming than budgeting. At one stage accountants in a certain company known to the author were assessed on the accuracy of their forecasts; the degree to which rolling forecasts coincided with results was used as a performance measure by which accountants were rewarded or punished. In some cases, manipulation of profit results was practised to ensure that performance appeared to be good. This may be an extreme case, but illustrates the importance to organisations of both formal plans and a means to predict and assess the future.

Sizer has suggested that there is value in comparing forecasts with each other to provide information about the planning process. A company preparing a budget and then forecasting periodically to update its planning information can be envisaged. Results can be compared with latest forecasts to assess the extent to which performance conforms to plan. The latest forecast can be compared with previous forecasts. Forecasts can be compared with budget. Comparisons can be quantified by means of variance analysis. This provides information on the implications of changes thought to be important to planning as well as information on the extent to which the organisation is under control, as measured by the variance between the latest result and the latest forecast.

FIGURE 27.2

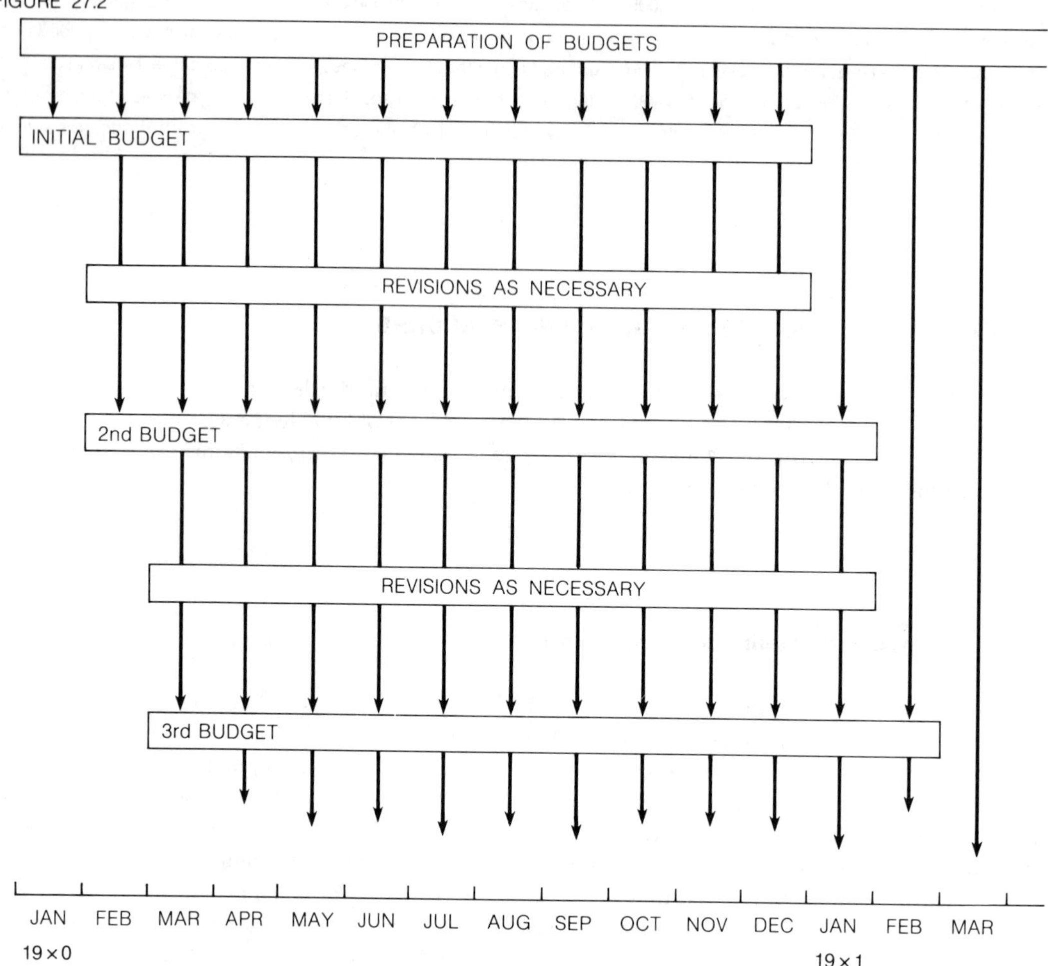

27.2.2 Revision of standards

Where significant uncontrollable variances arise it may be appropriate to reformulate standard product costs to ensure their relevance to the control process. Some text books debate the frequency with which standards should be updated. Part of the reason for this debate is that the revision of standards for manually operated systems can be a time-consuming and expensive process. The situation for computerised systems seems to be unclear and may depend upon individual companies and the manner by which standard costs are prepared. A traditional view is that standards should be reviewed annually in advance of the finalisation of budgets, where standard costing information is to be incorporated into and to reflect the budget. Where standards are revised more regularly than once a year, because of uncertainty, and where management receive operating statements reconciling budgeted and actual results, a revision variance results, as illustrated in Example 27.3.

Example 27.3

The Revisit Manufacturing Company plc operates standard costing and budgetary control systems in an extremely uncertain environment. For the current year, the budget was produced on the basis of the following product costing for the single product processed:

	£
Direct materials (5 kg. @ £5/kg.)	25
Variable Production Overhead	5
Contribution	20
Selling price	50

Sales of 250,000 units were budgeted, giving a net profit of £1,250,000. Fixed overheads of £3,750,000 are expected to be incurred evenly throughout the year.

After three periods of the twelve-period year, it became clear that raw materials would cost at least £6 for the remainder of the year. The standard cost was revised.

Results for the fifth period of the year, when the budgeted sales were anticipated to be 20,000, were as follows:

	£	£
Sales (19,000 units @ £51)		969,000
less: Variable cost of sales:		
Direct materials (93,100 kg. @ £6.50)	605,150	
Variable production overheads	91,200	696,350
		272,650
less: Fixed costs		270,000
		£ 2,650

A statement comparing results with budget might be presented as follows:

Operating Statement

	Favourable £	Adverse £	£
Budgeted Profit			87,500
Variances:			
Revision		95,000	
Materials price		46,550	
usage	11,400		
Variable overhead	3,800		
Fixed overhead	42,500		
Sales price	19,000		
volume		20,000	
	76,700	161,550	84,850
Profit for the period			£ 2,650

The revision variance is found by taking the difference between the original product costing and the revised product costing. In this example, the difference is £5 because the increase in raw materials of £1 per kilogram is applied to the 5 kilograms of raw material used in each unit of product. The basic rule of variance analysis is then applied:

Value variances are based on result quantities:

Quantity variances are based on reference values.

The £5 revision in product cost is multiplied by the 19,000 units of output in the result to give £95,000.

Self-assessment question 27.1

Provide working papers to show the calculations of variances shown in Example 27.3.

Answers on page 639

27.3 EX POST REVISION OF BUDGETS AND STANDARDS

The previous section covered techniques which revised budgets, forecasts and standards in advance of a control period. This section is concerned with the revision of the standard at the end of the period. With the benefit of hindsight, an assessment is made of the target which would have been appropriate for the period in question. This attempts to overcome the criticism that information which is relevant for planning purposes may not be useful for control because planning cannot be accurate under conditions of uncertainty. If salaries are planned to be £15,000 per annum on average but are actually £14,000 because of lower than anticipated inflation, the level of £15,000 is inappropriate to control. The control level should take into account those factors over which management can exercise genuine control. An ex post revision of budgets or standards would use an assessment of the realistic level of salaries, bearing in mind the conditions prevailing under the period to be controlled. A budget of £14,000 may be considered appropriate, although judgment may dictate that management could have negotiated a higher or lower level to achieve effectiveness.

27.3.1 Planning and operating variances

Planning variances are those which arise because there is uncertainty at the stage of preparing a standard cost. With hindsight, the standard cost would have been different to that implemented for a particular period because situations change with the passage of time. Planning variances are inevitable in an uncertain world and cannot be controlled by management. Operating variances are those variances which arise from operational efficiency and economy and are controllable by managers. A system of planning and operating variances would hold responsible individuals accountable only for operating variances. Example 27.4 shows the calculations necessary to operate such systems.

Example 27.4

Planop plc operates a standard costing system in an uncertain environment. For one of its two hundred and twenty different products, Operplan, it produces the following materials standard:

Material Aye	4kg per unit @ £3 per kilogram
Bee	4kg per unit @ £6 per kilogram
Cee	8kg per unit @ £2 per kilogram
Dee	4kg per unit @ £5 per kilogram

This standard operates throughout the year but management review standard costs at the end of each month. A management meeting held on February 2nd. witnessed the following discussion:

Purchasing manager: 'It was a good month for purchasing. We underspent by £0.10 on all materials used in Operplan except for Cee, which we bought for £2.50'.

Production manager: 'I don't think that is quite right. According to my information, Cee should have been purchased at £2.30 because all of our competitors paid that price. Indeed, the price that was paid for the other materials was the same paid by everybody else. It was a good month for production, though, because we used 5% less materials in production than expected'.

Quality control manager: 'That may be so, but we doubled the proportion of Bee in the mix to comply with new government restrictions. The proportions of the other materials were held constant in relation to each other. The aim was to reduce the amount of toxic waste created. We held some trial runs for the new mix and achieved a 10% saving in the quantity of materials used'.

Assuming that 100,000 units of Operplan were produced in January and that the comments made by the managers were reliable, variances would be based on the following table:

Result	Ex post Standard	Standard
285,000 @ £2.90	270,000 @ £2.90	400,000 @ £3
760,000 @ £5.90	720,000 @ £5.90	400,000 @ £6
570,000 @ £2.50	540,000 @ £2.30	800,000 @ £2
285,000 @ £4.90	270,000 @ £4.90	400,000 @ £5
£8,132,000	£7,596,000	£7,200,000

The planning variance is the difference between the standard and the ex post standard, £396,000. The operating variance is the difference between the ex post standard and the result, £536,000.

Each of these variances can be subdivided according to the principles explained earlier in the book. In analysing the planning variance, the result measured in terms of the ex post standard is compared with reference data given by the standard. In analysing the operating variance, the result is compared with the reference data given by the ex post standard.

Only two operating variances arise:

Materials price variance	
(Cee, 570,000 kg @ £0.20 adv.)	£114,000
Materials yield variance	
(100,000 kilograms @ £4.22)	£422,000
	£536,000

Self-assessment question 27.2

Prepare full working papers to show the calculations and full variance analysis for Example 27.4.

Answers on page 639

Whilst reflecting the effects of uncertainty on standard costing systems with the benefit of hindsight, planning and operating variance systems suffer from two major drawbacks. Time and costs need to be extended in gathering information from which the decision to divide the total variance between planning and operating causes is taken. At a behavioural level, there is every incentive for managers to claim that all variances are due to planning causes. This is especially the case where standard costing is linked to performance measurement systems. Imagine the purchasing manager whose bonus system is linked to the level of variance. Such a manager may be motivated to provide biased purchasing information to the budgeting committee in order to ensure that purchasing variances are seen in the best possible light. Planning and operating variances provide a suitable response to the problem of uncertainty when objective information at a suitable price is available to form the basis of the analysis.

SUMMARY

This chapter extended the principles discussed in the uncertainty and decision-making chapter to include planning and control situations. A variety of responses to the treatment of uncertainty have been suggested and these have been described and illustrated in this chapter. There are question marks over the practicality of individual techniques, especially with regard to the time taken for implementation, and each section makes an assessment concerning the appropriate circumstances where each approach might be useful. The techniques include probabilistic and simulation approaches and ex post and ex ante revisions of planning or predicative information.

EXERCISES

Exercise 27.1

The manual for a computerised financial planning package includes sections on:

(i) sensitivity analysis and
(ii) probabilistic simulation.

Describe the techniques that you might expect to be explained under each of these headings and discuss the relevance of these techniques to financial planning.

(*ACCA, Management Accounting, December 1986*)

Answers in lecturer's manual.

Exercise 27.2

Explain the use of FOUR of the following approaches to budgeting in uncertain environments:

Three-tier budgeting.
Decision trees and joint probabilities.
Simulation.
Sensitivity analysis.
Continuous budgeting.

Answers in lecturer's manual.

Exercise 27.3

Update plc prepares a budget once each year and applies a system of rolling forecasts. The following table summarises information taken from the budget, the available forecasts and the results for period 6. Assume a constant level of stocks and an average selling price of £2 per unit.

	Sales £'000	Materials £'000	Labour £'000	Overheads £'000
Budget	2,500	1,250	250	500
Forecast 1	2,550	1,147.5	250	500
Forecast 2	2,525	1,212	250	500
Result	2,607	1,227	255	505

Prepare an analysis of variances to provide information suitable for management, including a comment on the results of your analysis.

Answer on page 640

Exercise 27.4

Simplo Ltd make and sell a single product. A standard marginal cost system is in operation. Feedback reporting takes planning and operational variances into consideration. It is implemented as follows:

1 Permanent non-controllable changes from the original standard are incorporated into a revised standard.
2 The budgeted effect of the standard revision is reported for each variance type.
3 The sales volume variance is valued at the revised standard contribution and is analysed to show the gain or loss in contribution arising from a range of contributory factors.
4 The remaining operational variances are then calculated.

Information relating to Period 6 is as follows:

(i) A summary of the operating statement for Period 6 using the variance analysis approach detailed above shows:

	£
Original budgeted contribution	51,200
Budget revision variances (net)	13,120 (F)
Revised budgeted contribution	64,320
Sales volume variance	16,080 (F)
Revised standard contribution for sales achieved	80,400
Other variances (net)	8,200 (A)
Actual contribution	72,200

(F) = Favourable, (A) = Adverse.

(ii) Original standard cost data per product unit:

	£	£
Selling price		100
Less: Direct material 5 kilos @ £10	50	
Direct labour 3 hours @ £6	18	
		68
Contribution		32

(iii) The current market price is £110 per unit. Simplo Ltd sold at £106 per unit in an attempt to stimulate demand.

(iv) Actual direct material used was 12,060 kilos at £10 per kilo. Any related variances are due to operational problems.

(v) The original standard wage rate excluded an increase of £0.60 per hour subsequently agreed with the trade unions. Simplo Ltd made a short–term operational decision to employ a slightly lower grade of labour, who were paid £6.20 per hour. The total hours paid were 7,600. These included 200 hours of idle time, of which 40% was due to a machine breakdown and the remainder to a power failure.

(vi)

Budgeted production and sales quantity	1,600 units
Actual sales quantity	2,000 units
Actual production quantity	2,400 units.

Required:

(a) Prepare a single operating statement for Period 6 which expands the summary statement shown in **(i)** above.
This single operating statement should clearly show:
(i) The basis of calculation of the contribution figures for original budget, revised budget and revised standard for sales achieved;
(ii) The analysis of the budget revision variance by variance type;
(iii) The analysis of the sales volume variance showing the quantity and value of the gain or loss arising from each of the following factors:
Additional capacity available;
Productivity reduction;
Idle time;
Stock increase not yet translated into sales;
(iv) The analysis of the 'other variances' by variance type.

(b) Prepare a brief report to the management of Simplo on the performance in Period 6 making full use of the information contained in the operating statement prepared in **(a)**. Your report should indicate the relevance of the analysis utilised in the operating statement.

(*ACCA, Management Accounting, December 1987*)

Answers in lecturer's manual.

Exercise 27.5

The accountant of Laburnum Ltd is preparing documents for a forthcoming meeting of the budget committee. Currently, variable cost is 40% of selling price and total fixed costs are £40,000 per year.

The company uses an historical cost accounting system. There is concern that the level of costs may rise during the ensuing year and the chairman of the budget committee has expressed interest in a probabilistic approach to an investigation of the effect that this will have on historic cost profits. The accountant is attempting to prepare the documents in a way which will be most helpful to the committee members. He has obtained the following estimates from his colleagues:

Average Inflation Rate over ensuing year		*Probability*
Pessimistic	10%	0.4
Most likely	5%	0.5
Optimistic	1%	0.1
		1.0

Demand at Current Selling Prices		
Pessimistic	£50,000	0.3
Most likely	£75,000	0.6
Optimistic	£100,000	0.1
		1.0

The demand figures are given in terms of sales value at the current level of selling prices but it is considered that the company could adjust its selling prices in line with the inflation rate without affecting customer demand in real terms.

Some of the company's fixed costs are contractually fixed and some are apportionments of past costs; of the total fixed costs, an estimated 85% will remain constant irrespective of the inflation rate.

Required:
Analyse the foregoing information in a way which you consider will assist management with its budgeting problem. Although you should assume that the directors of Laburnum Ltd are solely interested in the effect of inflation on historic cost profits, you should comment on the validity of the accountant's intended approach. As part of your analysis you are required to calculate:

(i) The probability of at least breaking even, and
(ii) the probability of achieving a profit of at least £20,000.

It can be argued that the use of point estimate probabilities (as above) is too unrealistic because it constrains the demand and cost variables to relatively few values. Briefly describe an alternative simulation approach which might meet this objection.

(*ACCA, Management Accounting, June 1986*)

Answers in lecturer's manual.

Transfer Pricing and Performance Evaluation

INTRODUCTION

Transfer pricing is simple in concept and yet complex in implementation. It provides a divisional output valuation where output from one division becomes the input of another division within the same organisation. This is often necessary to the operation of profit or investment centres. Complexity in implementation arises from the availability of a number of valuation bases, each with their own implications for the ways in which an organisation is to be managed. This chapter provides a description of the major valuation bases found in practice and in theory. Transfer prices are necessary to the operation of performance measurement based on profit and investment centres and the chapter includes a critical appraisal of performance measurement in general.

The chapter is divided into three. The first section describes the purpose of transfer pricing. In the second section, methods of transfer pricing are described and briefly evaluated. In the final section, a critical appraisal of performance measurement in general and transfer pricing in particular is provided.

28.1 TRANSFER PRICING: PURPOSES

Transfer pricing can contribute directly to the process of departmental performance measurement and indirectly to the measurement of product performance.

A transfer price is a value attached to the output of a department in order to measure the value of its trade with other departments inside the organisation. The transfer price of the supplying division is charged to the receiving division. Transfer prices do not affect overall organisational profit results but do affect the profits reported by divisions. Example 28.1 illustrates this point.

Example 28.1

Profitcentre inc. plc. sells a single product at £5 per unit. The product is manufactured by passing raw materials through two departments, A and B, at costs of £1.50 and £2.50 respectively. A transfer price of £2 has been established to measure the profit achieved by department A.

Department A:		
Transfer price per unit		£2.00
Cost per unit		£1.50
Profit		£0.50
Department B:		
Selling price per unit		£5.00
Transfer price	£2.00	
Other costs	£2.50	£4.50
Profit		£0.50
Profitcentre inc.		
Selling price per unit		£5.00
Cost per unit:		
Department A	£1.50	
Department B	£2.50	£4.00
Profit		£1.00

The total cost of the product is £4 per unit providing a profit to the company of £1 per unit. Department A has costs, or inputs, of £1.50 per unit and a transfer price of £2 per unit as a measure of output value. It thus shows a profit of £0.50 per unit. Department B has input costs of £2.50 per unit, plus a transfer price of £2 per unit, and an output value of £5. Department B also shows a profit of £0.50 per unit, therefore. The profit of both departments together is £1 per unit (£0.50 plus £0.50). The organisation's profit of £1 per unit is unaffected by the transfer price because the output value attached to department A's production becomes an input value for department B.

If a transfer price of £1.50 per unit is used in this situation, department A appears to show £nil as a profit. The costs to department B are £1.50 plus £2.50, giving a £1 profit per unit for a selling price of £5 per unit. This transfer price ensures that department A's costs are transferred to department B but does not offer a profit motivation to department A's manager. Department A is unlikely to take action to improve performance if all credit for such effort is shown under department B's results. Different transfer prices allocate profit in different ways between divisions and it should be clear that:

1 Transfer pricing shares profits between divisions but does not, on its own, affect total profits;
2 Transfer pricing can motivate managers to take actions to improve profits for their divisions and for the organisation as a whole. The transfer price should allow the opportunity for effort to be translated into a positive measurement of performance.

Transfer pricing is similar to cost apportionment and allocation in that values of one department are passed to another. For cost apportionment and allocation systems, costs of one department are passed to another with the objective of accumulating costs for product cost information purposes. In a sense, apportionment and allocation provides a mechanism of transfer pricing primarily based on input measures such as floor area or direct labour hours. Under transfer pricing arrangements, values of one department are also passed to another. Output measures of activity are used to charge departmental costs and allowable profits to other departments. The information produced can be used to accumulate product costs. Where transfer prices are cost based and make no allowance for profits, the results would differ from apportionment and allocation systems only with regard to the basis for transferring costs between departments.

Where performance measurement is linked to rewards such as promotion or salary, the method of transfer price can have a direct impact on the motivation of the divisional manager. For example, a divisional manager appraised on a profit centre basis will be in a position of advantage where high transfer prices are established for the particular division. The effect of motivating managers to improve profits may lead to bargaining for transfer pricing methods which provide the highest transfer prices for their particular divisions. In a transfer pricing situation, as in a number of accounting situations, there will inevitably be winners and losers. The challenge to the accountant is to devise a transfer pricing methodology which ensures that the winners are those who will benefit the organisation most in the long term.

Some multinational companies are in a position to use transfer pricing to reduce total taxation costs. This can be achieved by establishing transfer prices towards the higher end of the spectrum of allowable values in countries with low taxation. This would tend to lead to high profits in countries with low taxation and lower profits in countries with higher taxation. Governments in some countries take steps from time to time to regulate the operation of transfer pricing systems for this reason.

28.2 TRANSFER PRICING METHODS

Transfer pricing methods are concerned with the alternative means by which a transfer price can be set and its impact on organisations gauged. Emmanuel and Otley bring together a number of reviews of transfer pricing methods in practice. Essentially, they report that there are three categories of transfer price: cost based, market based and negotiated. Within the surveys reported, in terms of very rough approximations, about 20% of companies used negotiated prices, about 30% of companies used market values and about half used cost based prices. For each category, a good degree of discretion existed to develop alternative bases at a detailed level. For market based prices, for instance, competitors' prices, list prices, most recent bid and values adjusted by a discount provided alternative bases. The description which follows does not go to such a level of detail but concentrates on four main approaches: absorption cost bases, variable cost bases, market value bases and negotiated value bases. A final section describes the use of linear programming.

28.2.1 Absorption cost based transfer prices

Absorption, or full cost systems, transfer the full cost of the supplying department to the receiving department. Where a profit is to be allowed to the supplying division, it is necessary to determine a policy which can be consistently applied. Typical systems may allow a profit based on cost, sales or investment, as shown in Example 28.2

Example 28.2

A division has a product costing £5 which is transferred within a group of companies. Calculate a transfer price for the division for each of the following mutually exclusive divisional targets:

1 a net profit margin of 10%;
2 a mark-up on cost of 10%;
3 a net assets turnover rate of 5 and an ROCE of 30%.
4 an output of 1,000,000 units, a capital employed of £2,000,000, and an ROCE of 20%.

Solutions:

1 A net profit margin of 10% is the same as a mark-up on cost of 10/90. The selling price is 100/90. Using a cost of £5, the transfer price should be:

£5 × 100/90,
or £5 /0.9,
which is £5.56, a profit of £0.56

2 The transfer price would be £5.50.
3 Using the relationship:

$$\text{Return on capital employed} = \frac{\text{Net profit}}{\text{Capital employed}} = \frac{\text{Net profit}}{\text{Sales}} \times \frac{\text{Sales}}{\text{Capital employed}}$$

The figures for the division would be:

30% = Net profit margin × 5
Net profit margin = 6% (30%/5)
Transfer price = £5.32 (£5 / 0.94)

This example illustrates a general procedure applicable in other situations. Section 28.3 contains an example which applies the same approach to a situation with an ROCE target alone.

4 Each unit of output utilises £2 of capital employed (£2,000,000/1,000,000). The required return is 20% and this gives a proft per unit of £0.40. The required transfer price is therefore £5.40.

The two major drawbacks to the full cost approach concern its inability to motivate the supplying division's manager to improve performance and the danger of making incorrect decisions. Since all costs are passed on, irrespective of economy or efficiency in the supplying division, there is little incentive for managers of supplying divisions to cut costs or to operate more efficiently. Once costs are passed on, fixed costs of the supplying division are interpreted as variable costs of the receiving division and it is therefore possible for divisions to make short-term decisions which are suboptimal for the organisation as a whole. Consider a make or buy decision for which divisional variable costs are £2, including £0.30 fixed cost included in a transfer price, and the external supplier's costs are £1.90. The division would buy in the product, despite the fact that the company's variable costs, at £1.70, are lower than the buy-in price. The company would wish the division to continue to make, but can only do so by centralisation of the decisions rule, with a loss of autonomy at the divisional level.

In order to ensure that inefficiencies are not passed on by suppliers, it has been suggested that standard absorption costing can produce reliable results. Underutilisation of plant capacity, inefficiencies and lack of price control remain in the division in which they occurred and are reported through the calculation of standard costing variances. However, the problem of suboptimisation would not be overcome by standard absorption costing transfer prices.

28.2.2 Variable cost based transfer prices

Variable cost based systems overcome the decision-making problem of full cost systems. Transfers from one division to another are made at variable cost. Standard variable cost overcomes the problem of passing on inefficiences and diseconomies from division to division.

There are two ways by which profits can be created at a divisional level. The first approach is to apply the principles illustrated in Example 28.2 to marginal costing. Transfer pricing schemes would allow a suitable level of contribution, as measured in terms of contribution to sales ratio. An alternative approach is to create a two-part charging system. One part of the scheme would transfer a lump sum, representing an allowance for divisional fixed cost once a year to allow each division the chance of creating a final profit. The second part of the scheme would value transfers at variable cost.

28.2.3 Market value based transfer prices

There is universal agreement that in competitive markets a market value based transfer price should achieve optimal results. In this circumstance, it can be expected that:

1. The autonomy of the division is not undermined because markets determine the value of outputs, not centralised departments or divisional costs. Market prices would be seen to be objective and fair to all. The aim of creating an organisational structure where each division operates as an organisation in its own right can be achieved. Ideally, suppliers should be permitted to sell to external customers and receivers should be allowed to buy from external producers;
2. Managers' performance reflect their ability to compete with external companies in a free market. This may be a fair indication of the manager's ability and potential to perform at higher levels within the organisation and thus forms a fair basis for promotion and salary decisions;
3. From 2, it can be expected that the transfer pricing mechanism will be neutral in motivating managers to perform in accordance with organisational goals; that is, the transfer pricing mechanism will not be biased in any manner other than that created by market forces. Performance measurement schemes can thus be established to motivate managers to act in a goal congruent manner;
4. Reliable decisions would arise at divisional level. For instance, in a joint product situation, products which should be sold at the split-off point would not be processed further since the post split-off processing division would show a loss based on the transfer price.

Unfortunately, two problems illustrate that market based prices may not be able to achieve these aims in all circumstances. The first problem arises because transfer pricing situations are not simply selling situations. The supplying division, for instance, does not have to incur the costs of selling normally associated with selling to external customers. The receiving division may be in a position to influence quality and delivery because it is in the interests of both divisions that the company as a whole prospers. It is sometimes desirable to adjust the market price to reflect such factors, with a commensurate loss in the objectivity which market prices can bring. The second problem is more fundamental; there may simply not be a perfect market in operation. A vertically integrated company, for instance, may not possess a market for its intermediary products. In this case, there is no market from which to establish market values. Other market imperfections would produce bias which would work to the benefit of either the supplying or the receiving division.

28.2.4 Negotiated prices

Where market based prices are not applicable, it has been argued that allowing managers to bargain with each other in order to establish transfer prices develops the kind of management skills which are necessary to the future of the enterprise. Managers would need to have detailed knowledge of their own resources and costs and would need to apply their inter-personal skills of communication, persuasiveness and bargaining in order to show a profit. Negotiated prices thus stress the human behavioural aspects of the organisation. Social and political skill can be translated into good divisional performance, as measured by the accounting system.

Unfortunately, negotiated prices can also lead to conflict, especially where two managers cannot agree on a transfer price. In such circumstances, a mechanism for resolving the dispute is required at a central level. The intervention of central authority to resolve conflicts clearly results in a loss of autonomy with dysfunctional consequences. A system which aims to reveal the behavioural skills of managers can as easily reward those who can manipulate the inherent tensions between centre and divisions to their best advantage.

28.2.5 Linear programming based transfers

Consider the following example:

Example 28.3

Two products, Exe and Wye, are produced by Hifi, an electronics company which operates two departments. Both departments are limited to working a maximum of 10 hours per day per machine and both departments utilise 10 machines. A five-day week is in operation. Product cost information for Exe and Wye is as follows:

	Exe	**Wye**
	£	£
Selling price	9.50	8.50
Materials cost	1.00	1.00
Variable overheads cost:		
Department 1		
2 hours @ £1.50	3.00	
1 hour @ £1.50		1.50
Department 2		
1.25 hours @ £2	2.50	
2 hours @ £2		4.00
Contribution	3.00	2.00

Processing this example through a linear programming computer package reveals a total contribution of £818.18 from a production of 181.8 units of Exe and 136.4 units of Wye, with shadow prices for departments 1 and 2 of £1.2727 and £0.3636 respectively. Were the centralised management accounting department to run this package, they would instruct both departments to produce 182 units of Exe and 136 units of Wye. The transfer price would be calculated as the total of variable cost and opportunity cost. The opportunity cost of each product is given by the shadow price; in the case of Exe, calculated as follows:

Department 1	2 hours @ £1.2727	£2.545
Department 2	1.25 hours @ £0.3636	£0.455
		£3.000

There is no coincidence that this is the product contribution in this case. Transfer prices of £7 for Exe and £4.50 for Wye would be established. This implies that department 2 would not be able to show a profit.

Drury illustrates a situation where the constraints of the linear programming model lead to the supplying division's manager being motivated to achieve optimum levels of production through the transfer price. In this case, the transfer price can itself motivate the achievement of optimum levels of output for both the supplying division and the organisation as a whole, where all output from one division is processed by the next. The supplying division is not allowed a profit and must be given production instructions from the centre, with loss of divisional autonomy.

28.3 CRITIQUE OF PERFORMANCE MEASUREMENT

This section brings together material from the first two parts of this chapter and from other parts of the book in order to provide a critical appraisal of performance measurement. In a sense, all of the material in the book can be related to the measurement of performance; good managers make good decisions, form good plans, establish good control practices and this should be reflected in measures of performance. An alternative view is that performance measurement drives the decision making, planning and control functions of management; managers manipulate performance results so that they can appear to be performing well. This provides an explanation for ROI approaches to the capital investment decision; managers are more concerned to appear to be making the right decision than to be making the right decision in reality. Whatever the view, transfer pricing and performance measurement provides good material for assessing the problems facing the management accountant who is trying to devise systems which will benefit organisations. The critique which follows provides a summary of the problems of ensuring that performance measurement systems achieve the purposes for which they are designed. The list which is provided can be considered as a coverage of some of the themes which influence management accounting as a whole.

1 Transfer pricing and performance measurement relies upon the judgement of the management accountant to make a suitable choice of approach and to calculate suitable values where appropriate.

Example 28.4

Alton division (A) and Birmingham division (B) are two manufacturing divisions of Conglom plc. Both of these divisions make a single standardised product; A makes product I and B makes product J. Every unit of J requires one unit of I. The required input of I is normally purchased from division A but sometimes it is purchased from an outside source.

The following table gives details of selling price and costs for each product:

	Product I	Product J
	£	£
Established selling price	30	50
Variable costs		
Direct material	8	5
Transfers from A	—	30
Direct labour	5	3
Variable overhead	2	2
	15	40
Divisional fixed cost (per annum)	£500,000	£225,000
Annual outside demand with current selling prices (units)	100,000	25,000
Capacity of plant (units)	130,000	30,000
Investment in division	£6,625,000	£1,250,000

Division B is currently achieving a rate of return well below the target set by the central office. Its manager blames this situation on the high transfer price of product I. Division A charges division B for the transfers of I at the outside supply price of £30. The manager of division A claims that this is the price 'determined by market forces'. The manager of B has consistently argued that intra group transfers should be charged at a lower price based on the costs of the producing division plus a 'reasonable' mark-up.

The board of Conglom plc is concerned about B's low rate of return and the divisional manager has been asked to submit proposals for improving the situation. The board has now received a report from B's manager in which he asks the board to intervene to reduce the transfer price charged for product I. The manager of B also informs the board that he is considering the possibility of opening a branch office in rented premises in a nearby town, which should enlarge the market for product J by 5,000 units per year at the existing price. He estimates that the branch office establishment costs would be £50,000 per annum.

You have been asked to write a report advising the board on the response that it should make to the plans and proposals put forward by the manager of division B. Incorporate in your report a calculation in the rates of return currently being earned on the capital employed by each division and the changes to these that should follow from an implementation of any proposals that you would recommend.

(*ACCA, Management Accounting, December 1986*)

An answer to this question would be provided in report style for examination purposes. The discussion which follows shows the influence of management accounting judgement rather than providing an ideal examination answer. It is anticipated that students will have the necessary skill to convert the points of discussion into an answer suitable for examination conditions.

If I and J are traded in a perfect market and both divisions are given complete autonomy, the present transfer price is optimal. Any increase in transfer price would lead to B purchasing from external sources, which would not be in the interests of the organisation. Any decrease in transfer price would lead to A selling to external customers, which would again not be in the best interests of the organisation.

It could be argued that A does not have to find the resources to market I and that some reduction from the external price is appropriate in setting the transfer price. The amount of the reduction could be a matter of negotiation between the managers of A and B or could be established through the judgment of the management accountant, bearing in mind any information available on competitors' selling costs.

If the market is imperfect then negotiated or cost based prices should be considered. It is a matter of judgment to determine whether negotiated prices would provide a suitable resolution to the problem, taking into account the personalities of the managers of A and B. Although the managers appear to be entrenched in their respective points of view, management training and/or an explanation of the purpose of transfer pricing may improve relations between the managers, lead to an acceptable transfer price and improve the future prospects for Conglom as a whole. Divisional autonomy would be maintained. Negotiated prices are thus to be recommended to the board of directors as a suitable alternative. The management accountant would have a role to play in educating managers in the purposes, benefits and limitations of management accounting systems. Cost based prices would require a degree of intervention from the centre, the part of the organisation where it could be expected that the necessary information is available.

Division A can meet B's demand for 25,000 units and the outside demand for 100,000 units, within its capacity of 130,000 units. Division B would meet the external demand. This would lead to the following financial statement under the present transfer price:

	Division A £'000	Division B £'000
Sales revenue (external customers)	3,000	1,250
Transfers	750	(750)
	3,750	500
Variable cost (excluding transfers)	1,875	250
Contribution	1,875	250
Fixed cost	500	225
Profit	1,375	25
Investment	6,625	1,250
Return on investment	20.8%	2.0%

If autonomy is maintained, division A could make a decision on whether to sell to division B or not, and at what price, on a short-term basis. The existence of surplus capacity should lead to any price in excess of variable cost being acceptable. Using variable cost as the transfer price would lead to the following results:

	Division A £'000	Division B £'000
Sales revenue (external customers)	3,000	1,250
Transfers (at A's variable cost of £15 per unit)	375	(375)
	3,375	875
Variable cost (excluding transfers)	1,875	250
Contribution	1,500	625
Fixed cost	500	225
Profit	1,000	400
Investment	6,625	1,250
Return on investment	15.1%	32.0%

Any cost based price between £15 and £30 would appear to be acceptable and the management accountant could apply judgment to decide on appropriate levels of profitability for each of the divisions.

If it is judged that an equal opportunity to achieve profit returns should be given, then the transfer price could be calculated as follows:

Total profit involved: £1,400,000
Total investment involved: £7,875,000
Average return on investment: 17.8%
Total costs in department A are: (1875 + 500) = £2,375,000
Applying the relationship:

$$\text{ROI} = \text{Net profit/Investment}$$
$$= \frac{\text{Net profit}}{\text{Total costs}} \times \frac{\text{Total cost}}{\text{Investment}}$$

provides: 17.8 = Net profit mark-up × 2,375/6,625
Net profit mark-up = 49.7%

Cost per unit in A is (2375/125)	£19
Average selling price is (19 × 1.497)	£28.44
Total sales: 125,000 @ £28.44	£3,555,000
less external sales:	£3,000,000
Transfer value:	£ 555,000
Transfer price (555/25)	£22.20

The reported financial statements would be as follows:

	Division A	Division B
	£'000	£'000
Sales revenue (external customers)	3,000	1,250
Transfers (at £22.20 per unit)	555	(555)
	3,555	695
Variable cost (excluding transfers)	1,875	250
Contribution	1,680	445
Fixed cost	500	225
Profit	1,180	220
Investment	6,625	1,250
Return on investment	17.8%	17.6%

There are two aspects to the behavioural aspects of this situation which will be discussed. The first concerns the extent to which the managers of A and B would find the transfer price 'fair'. Any attempt by the management accountant to impose a transfer price would be perceived to be an infringement of autonomy and may lead to dysfunctional consequences. Wherever possible, if the autonomy of the division is to be guarded and an imperfect market operates, negotiated prices appear to offer most prospects of optimising the behavioural implications. The second behavioural implication concerns the motivation of managers to accept worthwhile projects. If it is accepted that managers are motivated to improve their reported performance, performance measures which lead to managers rejecting profitable projects are dysfunctional. This particular idea can be explored in relation to Exercise 28.1.

At the existing transfer price of £30, the manager of B would produce the following calculation of the value of opening the branch office:

Additional sales 5,000 @ £50		£250,000
Additional variable costs:		
Transfer price	£150,000	
Other variable costs	£ 50,000	
Fixed costs	£ 50,000	£250,000
Net profit		£ nil

On behavioural grounds, the project would be rejected by the manager because performance does not improve as a result of the effort necessary to open the branch. However, from Conglom plc's point of view, the calculation would appear as follows:

Additional sales 5,000 @ £50		£250,000
Additional variable costs:		
Transfer price	£ nil	
Other variable costs	£125,000	
Fixed costs	£ 50,000	£175,000
Net profit		£ 75,000

It is advantageous to the company as a whole for the branch office to be opened. Since A has spare capacity sufficient to meet the additional requirement, a transfer price equal to the variable costs incurred in division A would lead to the manager of department B making the correct decision. A transfer price between £15 and £30 would lead to the branch being opened but a transfer price of £15 alone would ensure that all future decisions were evaluated correctly at divisional level. This leads to the second point in the critique of performance measurement.

2 Values which are suitable for performance measurement purposes are not necessarily suitable for decision making, planning and control purposes. Example 28.4 illustrated the problem of meeting both performance measurement and decision-making requirements. In the chapter on budgeting, the problems of conflicting objectives were discussed. For planning purposes, reasonable future forecasts or targets which meet long-term planning requirements present two acceptable approaches and incremental budgeting offers a third means by which values can be established in practice. For control purposes, values should ideally be set just above aspiration levels. For performance measurement purposes, values should be set which avoid sub-optimisation and dysfunctional behaviour and which further the objectives of the performance measurement scheme and of the company in general. It is unlikely that a single value can meet all requirements.

In some circumstances, multiple values can be established. In overcoming the problem of setting up reliable and valid values for planning, control, decision making and performance measurement needs, however, further problems may arise. Imagine that a company establishes one target for performance measurement purposes and another, lower value, for planning purposes. The planning value must be kept secret from the divisional manager if it is to motivate since some types of manager may lower aspiration levels to the planned target. Secrecy can have detrimental effects to the coordination and communication objectives of budgeting. Again, the behavioural consequences of establishing values are of paramount importance and the management accountant finds that effective accounting is partly based on setting up sound systems at the technical level and partly based on setting up systems which work for the people within the organisation.

3 Emphasis on cost, profit and investment centre performance in the short term can have detrimental effects on the organisation in the long term. Example 28.5 is taken from a situation which has occurred in practice.

Example 28.5

A company found it necessary for cash flow purposes to close one of its divisions. Two divisions were prime contenders for closure. Each would have brought in roughly equal amounts of cash and the amounts involved would have been sufficient to solve the cash flow crisis. Division A was set up ten years earlier and its assets were almost fully depreciated. Division B was set up two years earlier, incorporating the latest technology and had substantial balance sheet values because its assets were depreciated over a ten-year period. In the previous financial year, division A showed a 30% ROCE whilst division B showed a 20% ROCE. Which division should have been closed?

The company closed division B, because division A showed the best performance, as measured by ROCE. However, it found two years later that it needed to invest substantially in division A because of obsolete assets. A further cash flow crisis ensued.

This dysfunctional decision could have been avoided by applying a more appropriate valuation base for the assets than that provided by historic values derived from balance sheets designed primarily for financial accounting purposes.

Original cost, replacement value or an SSAP 16 philosophy have all been suggested as means by which ROCE can more reliably measure performance. The selection of asset valuation base is a matter of judgment.

Further examples of dysfunctional decisions arising from the need to meet short-term goals in terms of performance and/or budgetary control include postponing vital expenditure or investment. Postponent has the effect of ensuring that short-term goals are met but can disadvantage organisations in comparison with competitors who pursue long-term optimisation at some slight loss of optimisation in the short term.

4 Accounting figures can provide distorted information. Where a company imposes a cost based transfer price, results may be biased in favour of certain divisions at the expense of others, as Example 28.4 illustrated. Where a company uses ROCE as a performance measure, performance appears to improve as assets age because the effect of depreciation is to reduce the asset base in the ROCE calculation. The accountant's figures on performance do not necessarily measure the *true* improvement or deterioration in divisional performance.

5 Financial measures of performance can give insufficient emphasis to non-financial and qualitative aspects of organisational management.

6 It is difficult to determine whether the manager's performance or the department's performance is being measured in some circumstances. This is important where an organisation wishes to promote its most able managers to ensure the long-term successful management of the enterprise.

7 Independence and interdependence factors can lead to pseudo-profit and investment centres, where the accounting system treats divisions as autonomous despite the reality that autonomy cannot be achieved without detriment to the organisation as a whole. A transfer price which requires a decision from head office is likely to infringe divisional autonomy. Any system which requires a central accounting function to calculate a transfer price is therefore likely to lead to a loss of independence at divisional level.

8 The accounting models available to management accountants appear to create a potentially spurious sense of accuracy, reliability and validity. A budgeted target appears to have validity because it is visible and appears to be certain. In an uncertain world, deterministic targets may be invalid and probabilistic approaches may be more valid, but are unfortunately beset by problems, particularly the difficulty of establishing subjective probabilities. The section on forecasting suggested a number of reasons why managers tend to rely on relatively simple forecasting models in order to predict the workings of a complex world.

The problem facing the practical management accountant is to select an accounting model which most closely matches the reality of the situation faced by an organisation and for which data capture is feasible.

SUMMARY

Where performance measurement is based on profit centres and divisions trade with each other, a transfer price mechanism needs to be installed by the management accountant. Transfer prices charge values from one division to another. Product costs are thereby accumulated and divisions can be motivated to achieve corporate goals through decision making, planning and control at the divisional level. Ideally, divisions should be autonomous and there should be an objective means by which the values of transfer prices can be determined. The ideal is attainable through the use of market values for perfect markets. Where the market is imperfect, accounting judgements and behavioural consequences arise from the need to choose between cost and negotiation based transfer prices. The degree of choice in such situations is typical of management accounting in general, where the management accountant is faced with selecting a technique or model which best fits a particular organisation. Where there is a poor fit between the accountant's model and the real world, numerous consequences can arise, as illustrated by the final section of the book. This provided a critique of performance measurement systems.

EXERCISES

Exercise 28.1

Two of the divisions of Sanco are the Intermediate division and the Final division.

The Intermediate division produces three products, A, B and C. The products are sold to overseas specialist producers as well as to the Final division at the same prices. The Final division uses products A, B and C. Consequently, the Intermediate division has been instructed by the board of directors to sell all its products to the Final division.

The price and cost data is as follows:

Intermediate division			
Product	A	B	C
	£	£	£
Transfer price	20	20	30
Variable manufacturing cost per unit	7	12	10
Fixed costs	50,000	100,000	75,000

The Intermediate division has a maximum monthly capacity of 50,000 units. The processing constraints are such that capacity production can only be maintained by producing at least 10,000 units of each product. The remaining capacity can be used to produce 20,000 units of any combination of the three products.

Final division			
Product	X	Y	Z
	£	£	£
Final selling price	56	60	60
Variable costs per unit:			
Internal purchase	20	20	30
Processing in final division	10	10	16
Fixed costs	100,000	100,000	200,000

The Final division has sufficient capacity to produce up to 20,000 units more than it is now producing, but, because of the lack of products A, B and C, is limiting production. Further, the Final division is able to sell all the products that it can produce at the final selling prices.

Required:

(a) From the viewpoint of the Intermediate division, compute the products which would maximise its divisional profits and to calculate the total company profit, given that all Intermediate's production is transferred internally.

(b) From the viewpoint of the Final division, compute the products and quantities purchased from the Intermediate division which would maximise its divisional profits and indicate the effect on the total company profits.

(c) Compute the product mix which would maximise the total company profits assuming all transfers were internal.

(d) If there were no transaction costs involved for either division in buying or selling A, B or C outside the company, what, if anything, is lost by the policy of internal transfers only?

(e) Discuss the effectiveness or otherwise of the transfer pricing system currently used at Sanco Limited.

(*ACCA, Management Accounting, June 1987*)

Answers on page 642

Exercise 28.2

CB Division of the Meldon Group manufactures a single component which it sells externally and can also transfer to other divisions within the group.

CB Division has been set the performance target of a budgeted residual income of £300,000 for the coming year.

The following additional budgeted information relating to CB Division has been prepared for the coming year:

(i) Maximum production/sales capacity: 120,000 components;
(ii) Sales to external customers: 80,000 components at £20 each;
(iii) Variable cost per component: £14;
(iv) Fixed costs directly attributable to the division: £60,000;
(v) Capital employed: £1,600,000 with a cost of capital of 15%.

The XY Division of the Meldon Group has asked CB Division to quote a transfer price for 40,000 components.

(a) Calculate the transfer price per component which CB Division should quote to XY Division in order that its budgeted residual income target will be achieved.

(b) Explain why the transfer price calculated in **(a)** may lead to suboptimal decision making from a group viewpoint.

(c) XY Division now establishes that it requires 50,000 components. External Company L is willing to supply 50,000 components at £15.50 each but is not willing to quote for only part of the requirement of XY Division. External Company M is willing to supply any number of components at £18 each.

For each of the cases below (taken separately), calculate the transfer price applicable to 50,000 components. State the source or sources from which XY Division should purchase the components in order to maximise its own net profit and explain why the particular source or sources have been chosen, assuming that CB Division is willing to supply the components to XY Division:

(i) at an average price per component for the quantity required, such that the budget residual income of CB Division will still be achieved,

(ii) at an average price per component which reflects the opportunity cost of components transferred,

(iii) at prices per component which reflect the opportunity cost of each component.

(d) State which of the bases for transfer prices in **(c)** should lead to group profit maximisation and calculate the reduction in group profit which should arise from the operation of each of the other transfer prices in comparison.

(ACCA, Management Accounting, December 1987)

Answers on page 643

Exercise 28.3

(a) Transfers between processes in a manufacturing company can be made at (i) cost or (ii) sales value at the point of transfer.

Discuss how each of the above methods might be compatible with the operation of a responsibility accounting system.

(b) Shadow prices (net opportunity costs or dual prices) may be used in the setting of transfer prices between divisions in a group of companies, where the intermediate products being transferred are in short supply.

Explain why the transfer prices thus calculated are more likely to be favoured by the management of the divisions supplying the intermediate products rather than the management of the divisions receiving the intermediate products.

(*ACCA, Management Accounting, June 1988*)

Answers in lecturer's manual.

Exercise 28.4

Black and Brown are two divisions in a group of companies and both require intermediate products Alpha and Beta which are available from divisions A and B respectively. Black and Brown divisions convert the intermediate products into products Blackalls and Brownalls respectively. The market demand for Blackalls and Brownalls considerably exceeds the production possible, because of the limited availability of intermediate products Alpha and Beta. No external market exists for Alpha and Beta and no other intermediate product market is available to Black and Brown divisions.

Other data are as follows:

Black division
Blackalls: Selling price per unit £45
Processing cost per unit £12
Intermediate products required per unit:
Alpha: 3 units
Beta: 2 units

Brown division
Brownalls: Selling price per unit £54
Processing cost per unit £14
Intermediate products required per unit:
Alpha: 2 units
Beta: 4 units

A division
Alpha: Variable cost per unit £6
Maximum production capacity 1,200 units

B division
Beta: Variable cost per unit £4
Maximum production capacity 1,600 units

The solution to a linear programming model of the situation shows that the imputed scarcity value (shadow price) of Alpha and Beta is £0.50 and £2.75 per unit respectively and indicates that the intermediate products should be transferred such that 200 units of Blackalls and 300 units of Brownalls are produced and sold.

Required:

(a) Calculate the contribution earned by the group if the sales pattern indicated by the linear programming model is implemented.

(b) Where the transfer prices are set on the basis of variable cost plus shadow price, show detailed calculations for:

- **(i)** the contribution per unit of intermediate product earned by divisions A and B and
- **(ii)** the contribution per unit of final product earned by Black and Brown divisions.

(c) Comment on the results derived in **(b)** and on the possible attitude of management of the various divisions to the proposed transfer pricing and product deployment policy.

(d) In the following year the capacities of divisions A and B have each doubled and the following changes have taken place:

1 Alpha: There is still no external market for this product, but A division has a large demand for other products which could use the capacity and earn a contribution of 5% over cost. Variable cost per unit for the other products would be the same as for Alpha and such products would use the capacity at the same rate as Alpha.
2 Beta: An intermediate market for this product now exists and Beta can be bought and sold in unlimited amounts at £7.50 per unit. External sales of Beta would incur additional transport costs of 50p per unit which are not incurred in interdivisional transfers.

The market demand for Blackalls and Brownalls will still exceed the production availability for Alpha and Beta.

(i) Calculate the transfer prices at which Alpha and Beta should now be offered to Black and Brown divisions in order that the transfer policy implemented will lead to the maximisation of group profit.
(ii) Determine the production and sales pattern for Alpha, Beta, Blackalls and Brownalls which will now maximise group contribution and calculate the group contribution thus achieved. It may be assumed that divisions will make decisions consistent with the financial data available.

(*ACCA, Management Accounting, December 1988*)

Answers in lecturer's manual.

Solutions to questions

Solutions to Chapter 1 questions

ANSWERS TO SELF-ASSESSMENT QUESTIONS

1.1 **(a)** **(i)** **Main points:**

Whilst profit in absolute terms has increased compared with the previous year, this does not take account of the amount of capital employed in the business in each of those years. The ultimate test of the profitability of a business in the long-run is whether a satisfactory return on capital is earned. A popular measure of return on capital is to provide a relative measure, ie: to calculate the profit as a percentage of capital employed.

Return (profit before interest and tax) as a percentage of capital employed (share capital plus reserves, plus long-term loans) in the two years is:

Year just ended	*Previous year*
$\frac{13{,}740}{94{,}470} = 14.5\%$	$\frac{12{,}500}{77{,}800} = 16.0\%$

Whilst it is useful to provide a measure of return on long-term funds invested, ultimately it is the return on share capital that is critical. This is measured by the ratio of profit after tax as a percentage of share capital plus reserves. Thus:

Year just ended	*Previous year*
$\frac{5{,}670}{74{,}470} = 7.6\%$	$\frac{5{,}500}{62{,}800} = 8.7\%$

Thus percentage returns on capital have decreased, but appear at least to be greater than cost of bank loan (6% after tax).

(Students should also consider problems caused by inflation in looking at returns on historic cost assets and in making comparisons with previous years.)

Further analysis of the change in profitability over the two years, through additional ratio analysis would be useful eg

$$\frac{\text{Profit before interest and tax}}{\text{Sales}}$$

$$\frac{\text{Sales}}{\text{Share capital + reserves + long-term loans}}$$

NB: The product of these two secondary ratios = % return on capital employed.

(Students should recognise expansion in sales at reduced margins; probably replacement of lorry; lack of control over debtors.)

(a) **(ii)** **Main points:**

Advisability of distributing profits as dividends depends upon:

1 Cash availability

2 Future plans—even if cash is currently available if the business is expanding further, finance will inevitably be required. Retained profits will be an important source of funds, especially for the smaller business.

Cash availability can be usefully demonstrated by the preparation of a funds flow statement as follows:

	£	£
Sources of Funds		
Profit before tax	11,340	
Add back: Depreciation	10,310	
Funds generated from operations		21,650
Issue of shares		8,000
Bank loan		5,000
		34,650
Uses of Funds		
Net increase in vehicles	13,000	
Purchase of office equipment	600	
Tax paid	5,500	
Dividend paid	2,000	21,100
Increase in Working Capital		13,550
Increase in stock	120	
Increase in debtors	12,100	
Increase in prepaid expenses	160	
Increase in creditors	(110)	
Reduction in accrued expenses	190	12,460
Reduction in Bank Overdraft		1,090

This helps to explain why the balance sheet still shows an overdraft, but reduced compared with the end of the previous year. Even if cash was seemingly currently available, one would need to have regard to major liabilities pending (eg tax, repayment of loans).

Students may also consider the limitations of historic cost accounting (ie that distribution of all profits measured on an historic cost basis may dilute capital in real terms).

(a) (iii) Main points:

The purpose of depreciation should be considered. It is certainly not the purpose of depreciation to provide funds for replacement. In any case, accounts prepared under the historic cost convention would make inadequate provisions.

(b)

	Increases Bank Balance/Reduces Overdraft	Increases Profit Before Tax	Decreases Bank Balance/Increases Overdraft	Decreases Profit Before Tax
(b) (i)			1,760	
(b) (ii)			100	100
(b) (iii)	5,000			
(b) (iv)				300
(b) (v)		40		
(b) (vi)			1,000	50

Solutions to Chapter 3 questions

ANSWERS TO SELF-ASSESSMENT QUESTIONS

3.1 (**a**)

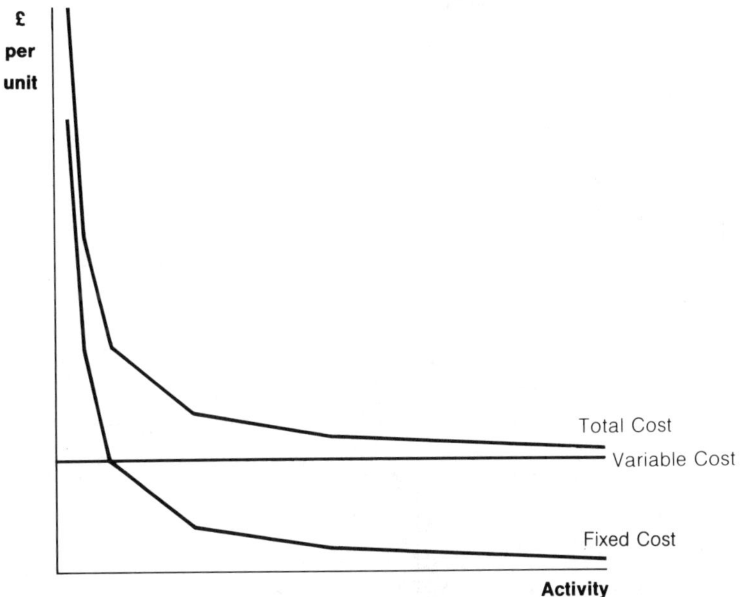

(**b**) The comment 'fixed costs are really variable: the more you produce the less they become', refers to the pattern of behaviour demonstrated in the above chart which reflects costs per unit at varying levels of activity. Fixed costs are variable in the sense that fixed costs per unit change as activity changes. Every additional unit produced has the effect of reducing unit costs for a particular period.

(**c**) (**i**)

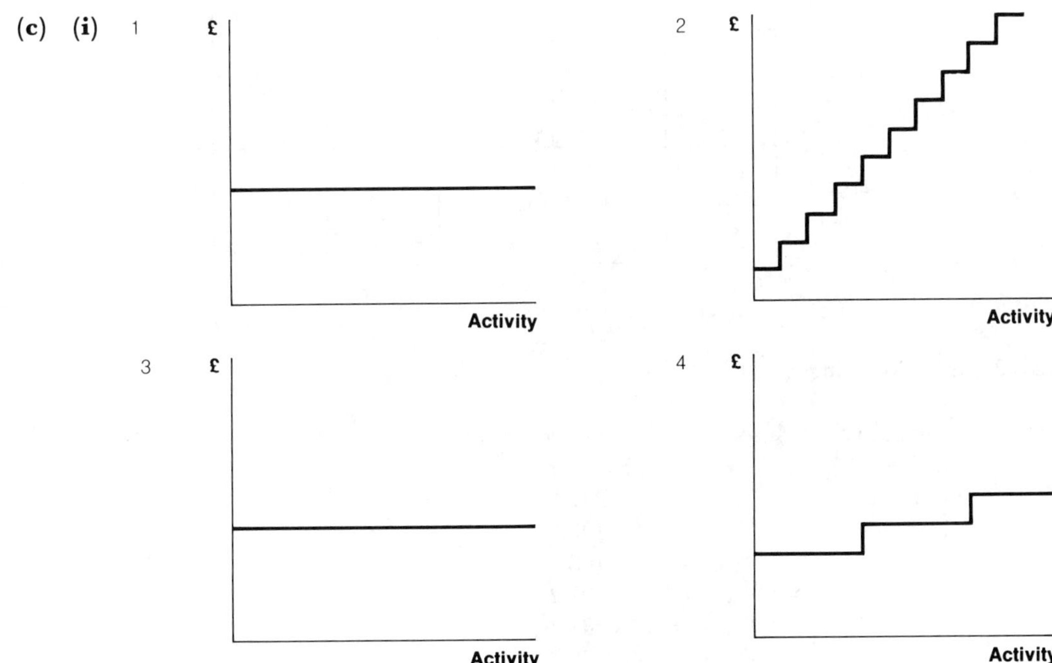

(continued)

(continued)

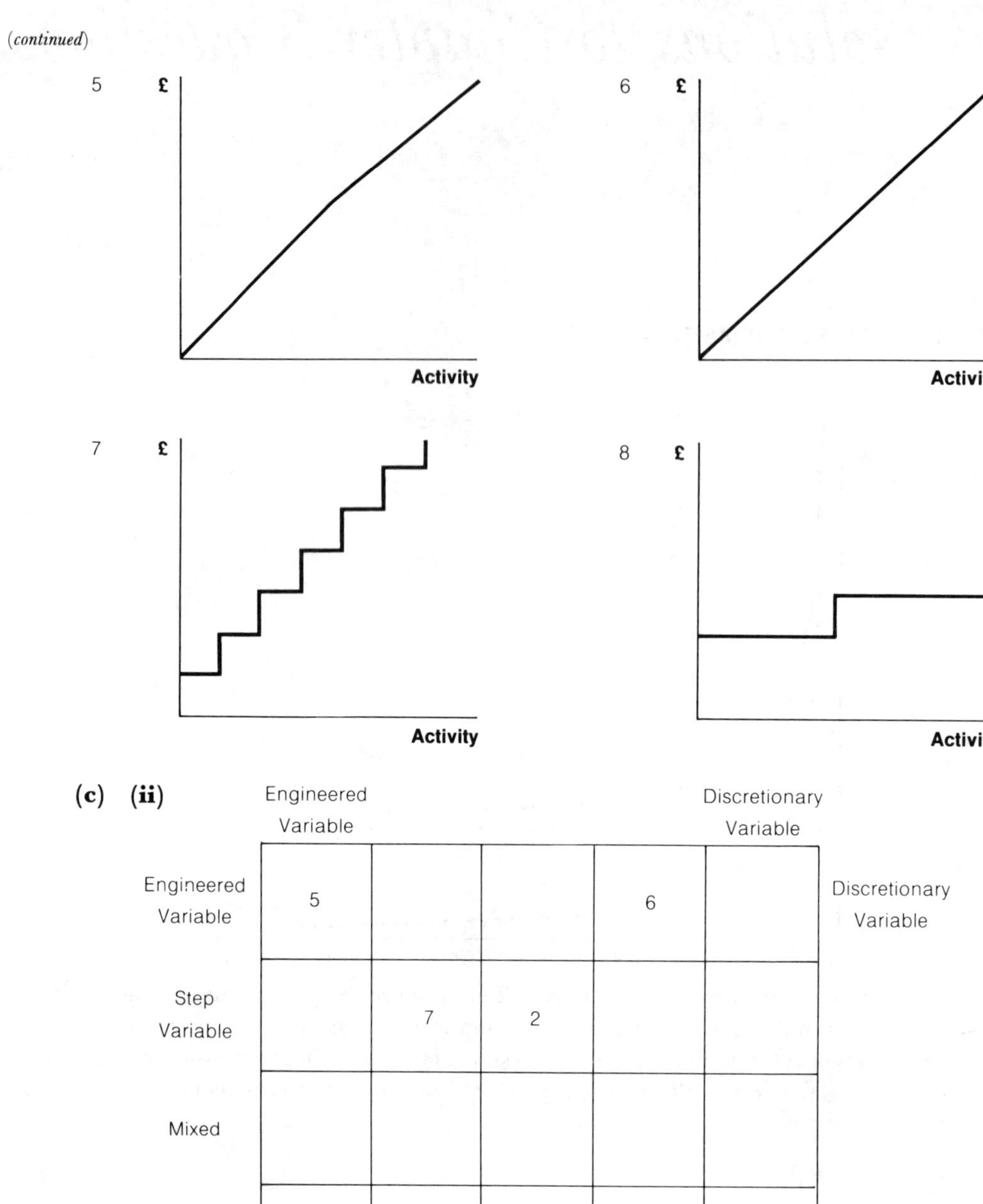

(c) (ii)

	Engineered Variable				Discretionary Variable	
Engineered Variable	5			6		Discretionary Variable
Step Variable		7	2			
Mixed						
Step Fixed	4				8	
Capacity Fixed	1	3				Discretionary Fixed
	Capacity Fixed				Discretionary Fixed	

3.2 **(a)** Workings:

Cumulative Batches Produced			Average Hours per Batch
1			120
2	× 90%	=	108
4	× 90%	=	97.2
8	× 90%	=	87.5
16	× 90%	=	78.7

(see graph)

(b) Let y_1 = cumulative average hours per batch

$$y_1 = 120\,x^{-0.152}$$
$$\log y_1 = \log 120 - 0.15202 \log x$$
$$= 2.07920 - 0.15202 \log x$$

where $x = 10$

$$\log x = 1$$
$$\log y_1 = 1.92718$$
$$y_1 = 84.56 \text{ hours per batch (see graph)}$$

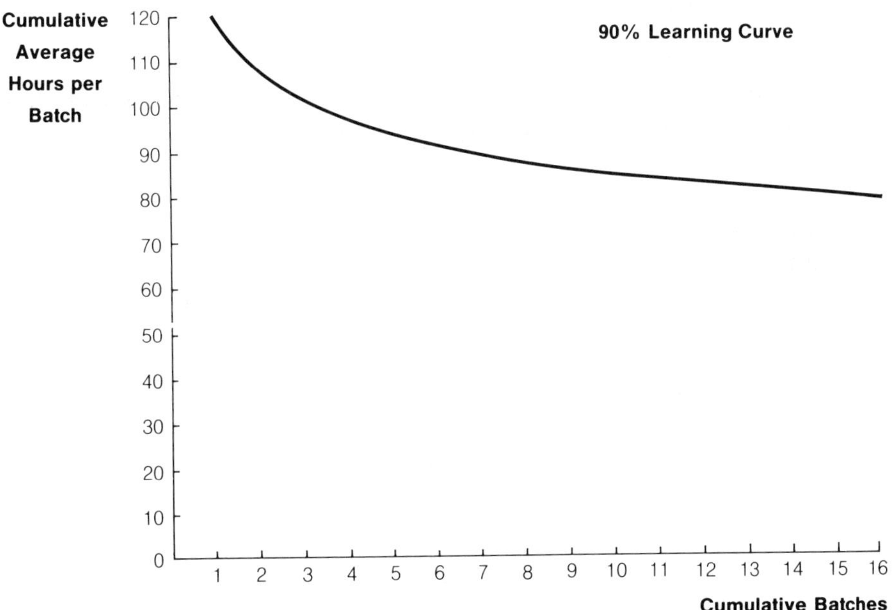

where $x = 20$

$$\log x = 1.30103$$
$$\log y_1 = 1.88142$$
$$y_1 = 76.11 \text{ hours per batch}$$

It should be noted that average hours for 20 batches are 90% of average hours for 10 batches (ie on a doubling of output).

(c) Let y_2 = total cumulative hours

$$y_2 = 120 \times 10^{0.84798}$$
$$\log y_2 = \log 120 + 0.84798 \log 10$$
$$= 2.07920 + 0.84798$$
$$= 2.92718$$
$$y = 845.6$$

(ie 10×84.56)

(d) Additional hours to double output $= 84.56 \times 80\% \times 10$
$= 676.5$ hours

Alternatively it can be calculated as

$(76.11 \times 20) - (84.56 \times 10) = 676.5$ hours

3.3 A scattergraph can be drawn to provide a better indication of the reasonableness of assuming a linear relationship between activity and cost (see Graph 1).

An approximate linear relationship exists. Using the high low method, total fixed costs and unit variable costs can be estimated, as follows:

$$\text{unit variable cost} = \frac{1{,}110 - 855}{30 - 15}$$
$$= \frac{255}{15}$$
$$= £17.00 \text{ per unit}$$
$$\text{fixed cost} = 1{,}110 - (30 \times 17)$$
$$= £600$$

The cost line, y = 17x + 600 does not use representative values and thus does not provide an adequate fit, (as can be seen on the graph (see Graph 2)).

GRAPH 1

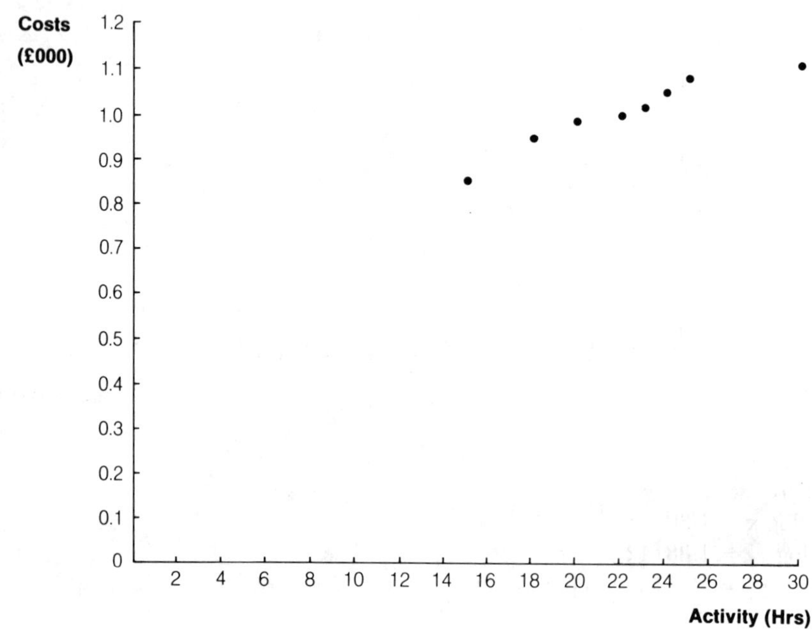

GRAPH 2

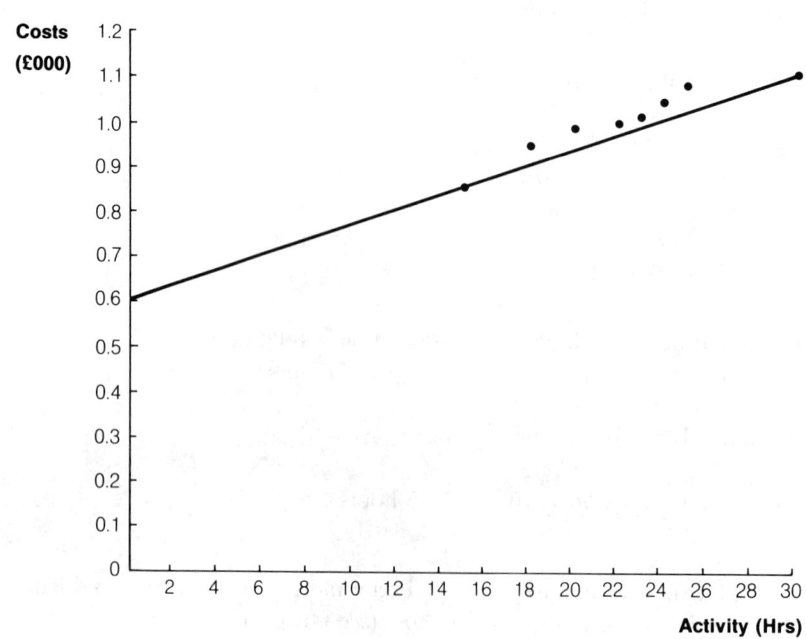

Least squares regression can also be used to estimate activity/cost relationships.

Workings:

x	y	xy	x^2	y^2
20	990	19,800	400	980,100
24	1,050	25,200	576	1,102,500
18	950	17,100	324	902,500
22	1,005	22,110	484	1,010,025
30	1,110	33,300	900	1,232,100
25	1,080	27,000	625	1,166,400
15	855	12,825	225	731,025
23	1,020	23,460	529	1,040,400
177	8,060	180,795	4,063	8,165,050

Using the normal equations:

$$8{,}060 = 177a + 8b \qquad (1)$$
$$180{,}795 = 4{,}063a + 177b \qquad (2)$$

Multiplying equation (1) by 22.9548:

$$185{,}016 = 4{,}063a + 183.638b \qquad (3)$$

Deducting equation (2) from equation (3):

$$4{,}221 = 6.638b$$
$$b = £635.9$$

Substituting for b in equation (1):

$$a = \frac{8{,}060 - (8 \times 635.9)}{177}$$
$$a = £16.80 \text{ per hour}$$

The cost line, $y = 16.8x + 635.9$, can also be plotted on the scattergraph (see Graph 3).

GRAPH 3

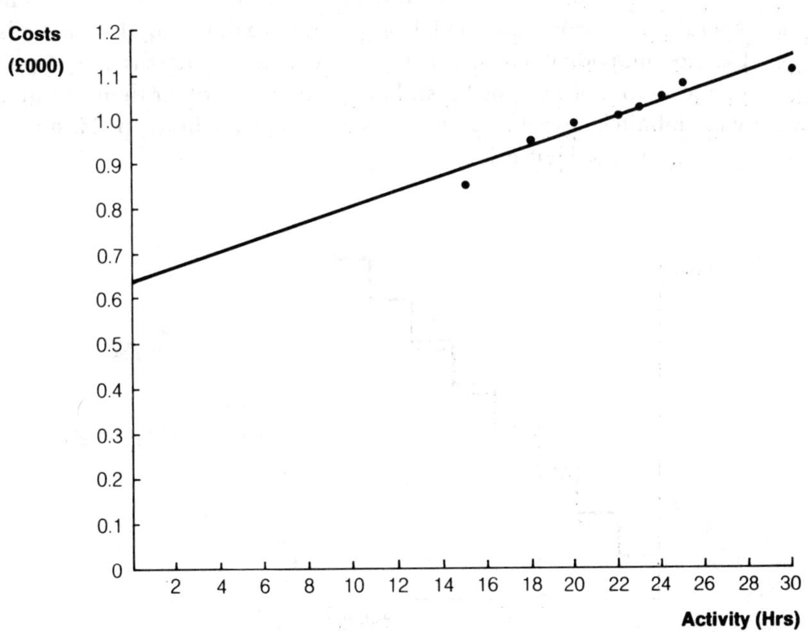

The cost function determined by regression analysis can be tested to establish how well the estimated relationship explains the variation in the observations. The coefficient of correlation measures the extent to which changes in activity in this situation explain the changes in costs, calculated as follows:

$$\frac{(8 \times 180{,}795) - (177 \times 8{,}060)}{\sqrt{(4{,}063 \times 8) - 31{,}329}\sqrt{(8 \times 8{,}165{,}050) - 64{,}963{,}600}} = 0.964$$

This suggests a strong linear relationship between activity and cost.

The coefficient of determination, which is the square of the coefficient of correlation, indicates to what extent the variation in costs may be predicted by changes in activity. 92.9% (ie $0.964^2 \times 100\%$) of the variation in costs in this situation may be predicted by changes in the activity level.

The advice to sales and marketing management would be that, in the short-term and whilst spare capacity remains, the cost per hour of taking on additional work is approximately £16.80. There is a high level of fixed cost, however. Management should be mindful that at current average levels of activity, total cost is £45.54 per hour.

ANSWERS TO EXERCISES

3.1 The term 'cost behaviour' is commonly used to describe the way in which costs vary as an organisation's activity level changes.

The conventional cost accounting model assumes that total cost is a linear function of activity, $y = ax + b$, where 'y' is the total period cost, 'a' is the variable cost per unit of activity, 'b' is the level of fixed cost, and 'x' is the level of activity.

Costs are thus assumed in the model to be at the extremes of cost variability. At one extreme costs may be expected to vary in proportion to activity. At the other extreme costs are assumed to be fixed regardless of activity. Mixed costs are recognised but it is usually argued that these can be split into fixed and variable component parts.

It should be recognised that the model is assumed to apply to short-term activity, a period during which the basic framework of an organisation's facilities cannot easily be changed. In the long-run all costs become subject to change according to activity level.

Whilst the linear cost model may provide a reasonable approximation of short-term reality in general and a workable model of an organisation's total costs, it is important to recognise that, for individual costs, other cost behaviour patterns may apply. A common pattern in practice is that of a stepped cost. For variable costs other than raw materials, because resources are not infinitely divisible, costs are likely to increase in stepped fashion, rather than in proportion to activity (see Figure 1).

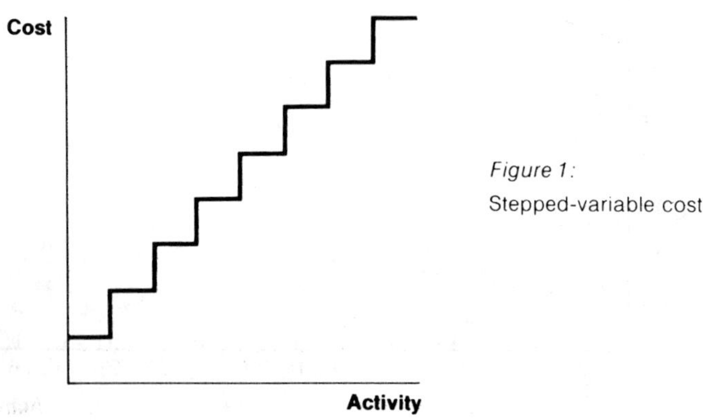

Figure 1:
Stepped-variable cost

At the other extreme fixed costs will only remain absolutely fixed within a particular range of activity. Over time, and given a sufficient change in activity, a change in the level of resources may be required and possible (see Figure 2).

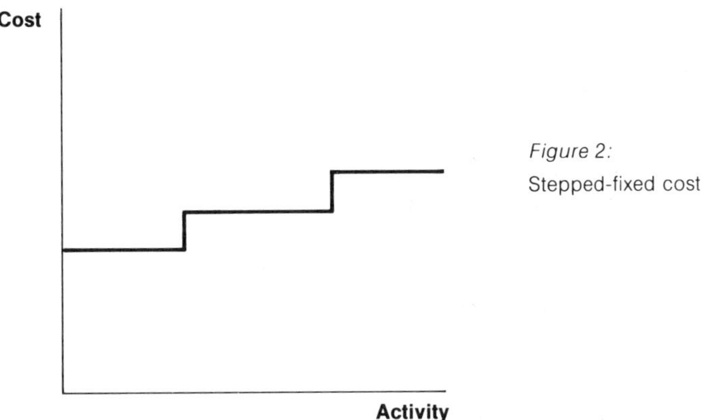

Figure 2:
Stepped-fixed cost

Various other patterns of cost behaviour are possible, between the two extremes, due to changes in input prices in relation to quantity, to changes in efficiency including the effect of learning, and to management policy and control. These may approximate to a curvi-linear, rather than a linear, cost function eg the learning curve.

The short-run cost function of standard economic theory is non-linear (see Figure 3).

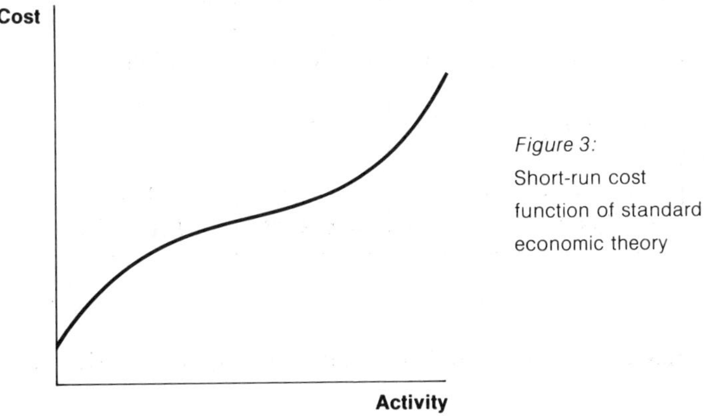

Figure 3:
Short-run cost function of standard economic theory

The shape is justified as follows: in the short-run, with a given stock of facilities, costs will increase rapidly as output increases from a low level, but the cost increases are likely to be at a decreasing rate as the stock of facilities begins to be used more efficiently. When output reaches the level for which the existing facilities is designed, any further output will result in the law of diminishing returns coming into play.

Cost and management accounting routine systems are traditionally based on the linear cost assumption. Marginal costing recognises short-term cost behaviour patterns, dividing costs into variable and fixed elements. This has proved to be a useful simplification for cost-volume-profit analysis purposes (see Chapter 4). The analysis may be useful for deciding on the optimum mix of products and the selling prices to be charged (see Section 2, Chapter 8 and Section 3, Chapter 15). The linear cost model is also extensively utilised in budgeting and in analysing actual performance in relation to budget, especially where standard costing systems are employed (see Section 4).

It is essential always, however, to recognise and understand the assumptions upon which it is based and to use such analysis only in those situations where the underlying assumptions may reasonably apply. For example, it would be wrong to expand output of a particular product, based upon identified variable costs, if as a result substantial increases in fixed costs would be required. It is equally wrong to justify the continuation of a particular product, based on identified variable costs, if its discontinuation would result in considerable saving of attributable fixed costs.

3.2 **(i)** Expected cost per unit for the initial order of 100 units is:

	£ Per Unit
Direct Materials	62.30
Direct Labour	
Dept A: 2.5 hours at £4.00	10.00
Dept B: 9.5 hours at £4.50	42.75
Variable Overhead	
Dept A: 1.5 hours at £2.00 per M/C Hr	3.00
Dept B: 9.5 hours at £1.10 per D.L. Hr	10.45
Fixed Overhead	
Dept A: 1.5 hours at £14.60 per M/C Hr	21.90
Dept B: 9.5 hours at £2.40 per D.L. Hr	22.80
	£173.20

Successive orders will have the same unit cost as above, apart from the learning effect on department B cost. It must be assumed that if direct labour hours reduce, overhead will reduce also.

Department B costs on cumulative output are expected to be:

	100 *Units*	180 *Units*	250 *Units*	310 *Units*
Initial cost per unit	£76.00	£76.00	£76.00	£76.00
× Learning effect	× 1.000	× 0.830	× 0.749	× 0.700
× Cumulative units	× 100	× 180	× 250	× 310
= Total cost	= £7,600	= £11,354	= £14,231	= £16,492

The department B unit cost, and the total unit cost, of successive orders are:

	80 *Units*	70 *Units*	60 *Units*
Dept B costs	(£11,354 – £7,600) ÷ 80 = £46.93	(£14,231 – £11,354) ÷ 70 = £41.10	(£16,492 – £14,231) ÷ 60 = £37.68
+ Other costs	97.20	97.20	97.20
= Total costs (per unit)	144.13	138.30	134.88

(ii) The average cost per unit for the whole contract is:

(76.00 × 0.7) + 97.20 = £150.40.

Careful consideration should be given, before establishing a price to tender for the contract, as to whether the estimated learning effect is realistic and to whether it is likely to have the same effect on overhead costs as on direct labour.

3.3 (a)

Analysis of Fixed and Variable Costs

	Quarters I–III		*Quarter IV*	
	Fixed cost	*Variable cost per unit*	*Fixed cost*	*Variable cost per unit*
	(£'000)	£	(£'000)	£
Material *A*	—	5	—	6 (*Note* 1)
B	—	4	—	4
Production labour	80	10 (*Note* 3)	90 (*Note* 2)	9 (*Notes* 3 & 4)
Factory overheads	50	3	60 (*Note* 5)	3
Depreciation	14	—	14	—
Administration	30	—	30	—
Selling and distribution	20	1	24 (*Note* 6)	1

Note 1 £5 + 20% = £6
2 £80,000 + $12\frac{1}{2}$% = £90,000
3 This is the standard variable labour cost. For production levels in excess of 19,000 units per quarter this cost will rise by 50%
4 (£10 + $12\frac{1}{2}$%) × 0.8 = £9
5 £50,000 + 20% = £60,000
6 £20,000 + 20% = £24,000

(b)

Production Costs—Quarter IV Flexible Budget

Production output—units (000's)	15	18	19 (*Note* 1)	21
Costs	(£'000)	(£'000)	(£'000)	(£'000)
Material *A*	90	108	114	126
B	60	72	76	84
Production labour	225	252	261	288 (*Note* 2)
Factory overheads	105	114	117	123
Depreciation	14	14	14	14
TOTAL PRODUCTION COST	494	560	582	635

Note 1 A budget step point is required at a production level of 19,000 units as variable labour costs per unit change at this level of production.
2 £90,000 + (21,000 × £9) + (2,000 × £4.50) = £288,000

(c) (i)

Profit Statement—Quarter IV

	Activity level					
	Low		*Expected*		*High*	
Sales and Production level—units	15,000		18,000		21,000	
	(£'000)	(£'000)	(£'000)	(£'000)	(£'000)	(£'000)
Sales at £40 per unit		600		720		840
Cost of goods sold						
Opening stocks at £30 × 4,000	120		120		120	
Production costs	494		560		635	
	614		680		755	
Closing stocks at £30	120	494	120	560	120	635
		106		160		205
Administration expenses	30		30		30	
Selling and distribution expenses	39	69	42	72	45	75
PROFIT		37		88		130

Cash receipts—Quarter IV

Cash received from quarter III's sales

	£
Month 7 30% of £200,000	60,000
8 100% of £200,000	200,000
9 100% of £200,000	200,000
	£460,000

Cash received for quarter IV's sales

Month 10 70% of sales

Low sales 70% of £200,000	£140,000
Expected sales 70% of £240,000	£168,000
High sales 70% of £280,000	£196,000

Cash Flow Statement—Quarter IV

	Activity level		
	Low	*Expected*	*High*
Cash Inflows	(£'000)	(£'000)	(£'000)
From previous quarter's sales	460	460	460
From current quarter's sales	140	168	196
	600	628	656
Cash Outflows			
Production costs	480	546	621
Administration expenses	30	30	30
Selling and distribution expenses	39	42	45
	549	618	696
NET INFLOW	51	10	(40)

(c) (ii) As would be expected, profit shows a positive relationship to sales and production levels whereas the cash flow of quarter IV would deteriorate as activity increases. The reason cash flow reduces with increases in activity is that those increases in activity require considerable outflows on production and delivery costs etc but the corresponding inflows from increased sales are, because of the credit terms, largely deferred until the next quarter. This illustrates the point that profit and cash flows are not synonymous and changes in them may not necessarily be the same, or even move in the same direction, in the short-term.
(Flexible budgets and cash budgets are considered further in Section 4).

Solutions to Chapter 4 questions

ANSWERS TO SELF-ASSESSMENT QUESTIONS

4.1 **(a)**

	A Ltd	*B Ltd*
	£'000	*£'000*
Sales	6,000	6,000
Variable costs	3,600	2,400
Contribution	2,400	3,600
Fixed costs	1,800	3,000
Net profit	600	600
Break-even point	$\frac{1,800}{0.4}$	$\frac{3,000}{0.6}$
	= 4,500	= 5,000
Margin of safety	$\frac{1,500}{6,000} \times 100\%$	$\frac{1,000}{6,000} \times 100\%$
	= 25%	= 16.6%

(b)

Sales £'000 (for £250,000 profit)	$\frac{2,050}{0.4}$	$\frac{3,250}{0.6}$
	= 5,125	= 5,417

(c)

New contribution sales ratio	$\frac{50}{110}$	$\frac{70}{110}$
	= 45.45%	= 63.64%
Sales required (£'000)	$\frac{2,400}{0.4545}$	$\frac{3,600}{0.6364}$
	= 5,280	= 5,657

(d) If sales are higher than expected, B Ltd will earn greater profits than A Ltd due to its higher contribution sales ratio. Each additional £ of sales will generate £0.6 additional contribution, as opposed to £0.4 generated by A Ltd. B Ltd will be less profitable than A Ltd if sales are lower than expected as it will lose contribution at a faster rate.

(e) Let x = level of sales at which profits of A Ltd and B Ltd are equal

$$0.45x - 2,000,000 = 0.6x - 3,000,000$$

$$\therefore 0.15x = 1,000,000$$

$$x = £6,666,667$$

Check:

	A Ltd	*B Ltd*
	£'000	*£'000*
Sales	6,667	6,667
Variable costs	3,667	2,667
Contribution	3,000	4,000
Fixed costs	2,000	3,000
Net profit	1,000	1,000

4.2 **(a)**

	£'000
Sales	5,200
Less: Variable costs:	
Raw materials	1,810
Production labour	640
Other production expenses	200
Distribution expenses	300
Administration expenses	50
	3,000
Contribution	2,200
Less: Fixed costs:	
Production labour	160
Other production expenses	800
Distribution expenses	100
Administration expenses	450
	1,510
Net profit	690

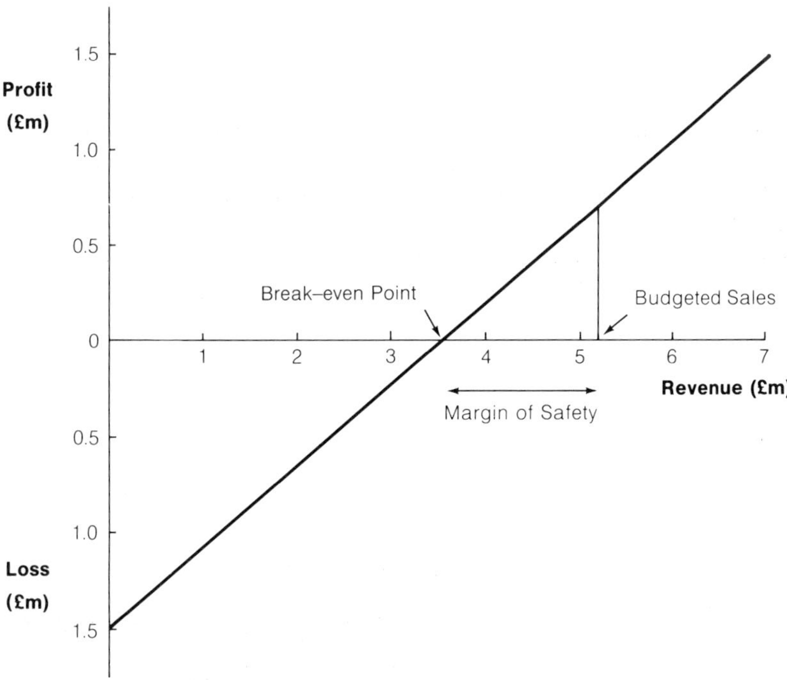

(b) Explanation of graphs:

(i) If an increase in fixed costs is less than compensated by a reduction in variable costs this suggests that the break-even point will be at a higher level of sales and that profit will reduce at budgeted activity. However, the higher the level of activity the greater will be the absolute reduction in variable costs, and the greater the increased contribution, which at some point will be greater than the increase in fixed costs.

On the graph, the new profit line, starting from a lower point due to the increased fixed costs, will rise more steeply due to the increased contribution/sales ratio. Although still below the original profit line at the break-even point and at budgeted sales, the new profit line eventually goes above the original line. The margin of safety is reduced.

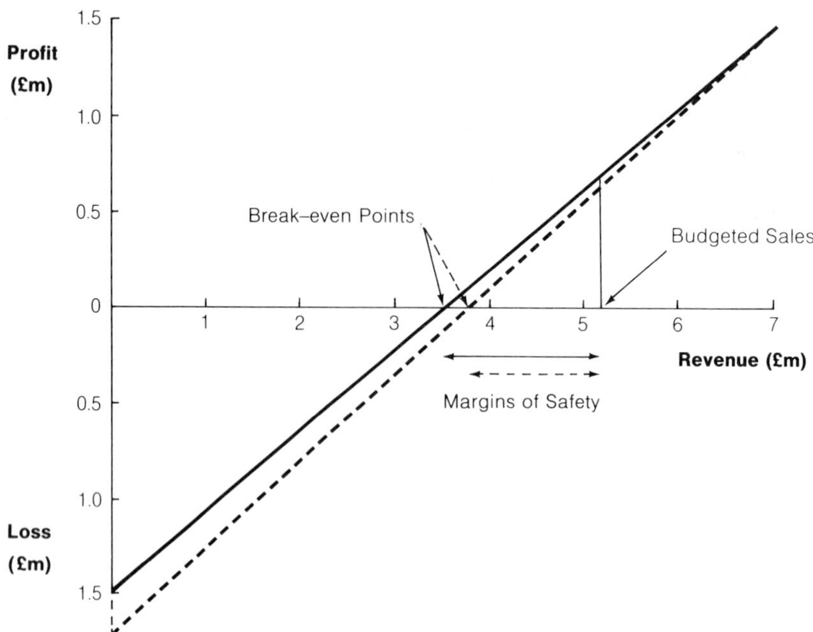

(ii) An increase in selling price will increase the contribution/sales ratio and thus the new profit line will rise more steeply. At the same time the profit will start from a higher point due to the reduced fixed costs. The effect of each of these changes is to reduce the break-even point (ie it occurs at a lower level of sales).

Whether net profit is increased will depend upon the effect of the increased selling price on sales volume. The graph shows increased profit and margin of safety from reduced sales revenue.

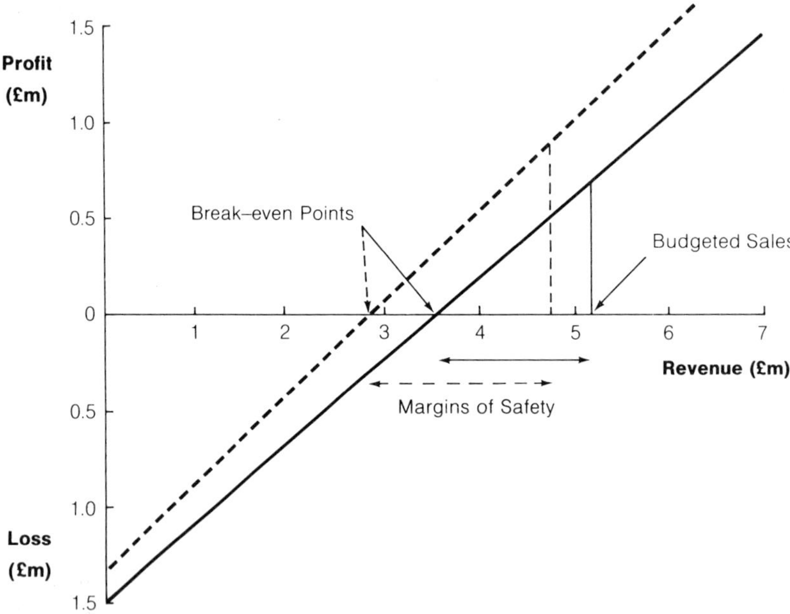

(iii) An increase in variable cost will reduce the contribution/sales ratio and make the profit line less steep. This will move the break-even point to a higher level of sales and will reduce profit and the margin of safety. However, the increased variable cost is combined with an increase in sales volume which, if large enough, could result in increased profits and/or margin of safety.

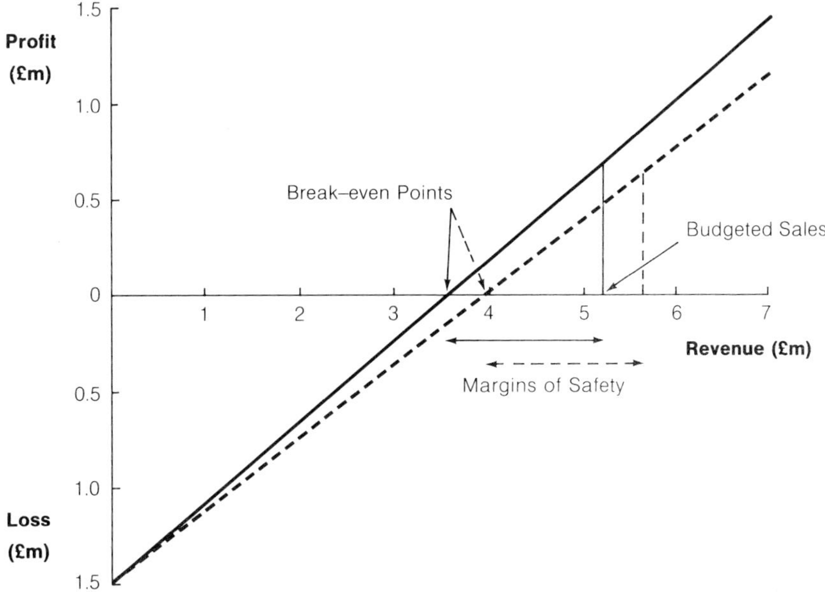

4.3 Contribution (£'000) = 9,600 − 3,840
= 5,760

Net profit before interest (£'000) = 5,760 − 4,320
= 1,440

Operating leverage $= \frac{5{,}760}{1{,}440}$
= 4

Financial leverage $= \frac{1{,}440}{1{,}040}$
= 1.385

Combined leverage $= \frac{5{,}760}{1{,}040}$
= 5.54 (ie 4 × 1.385)

The above calculations indicate that a given percentage change in contribution will result in a change in net profit before interest of 4 times that percentage, and in net profit after interest of 5.54 times that percentage. For example, a 10% increase in contribution will increase net profit before interest by 40%.

The company thus has considerable leverage at current activity level. Of particular significance is the operating leverage, resulting from the fixed/variable cost relationship and the existing level of net profit.

4.4 Sections 4.5 and 4.6 of Chapter 4 provide the answer to this question (see pages 55–58).

ANSWERS TO EXERCISES

4.1 **(a)** The statement is valid as unless the assumptions inherent in a model accurately reflect reality there is little hope that the model itself will be a precise reflection of the real world position. However it must be remembered that the break–even chart is only intended to be a very rough and approximate model and so its assumptions too may be only approximate. Although many of the assumptions may be objected to on the grounds that they do not strictly hold true it is frequently possible to approximate the actual position with sufficient accuracy for the intended purpose within the constraints of a break–even format. Hence the break–even chart is a useful, if general, tool—in fact it has been stated that 'The break–even chart may be compared to the use of a meat axe, not a scalpel' (C T Horngren 'Cost Accounting: a managerial emphasis').

Providing the approximate nature of the chart is borne in mind it can be interpreted to provide useful information. It is when an attempt is made to use the chart as a precise measuring device that it may mislead.

Among the important underlying assumptions of break–even analysis are:

(i) All costs may be classified into fixed and variable elements. This implies that volume is the only cause of cost fluctuation. If it were admitted that factors other than volume were determinants of total costs then the total cost curve could not be accurately represented in a two dimensional form on a breakeven chart.

(ii) Fixed costs remain constant over the relevant range of volumes and variable costs per unit are stable over that range. This assumption allows the relationship between total costs and volume to be stated as a simple linear relationship of the form:

TC = (VC × Volume) + FC where TC = Total costs
VC = Variable costs per unit of volume
FC = Fixed costs

Should this assumption be relaxed then 'fixed' costs may alter and become 'stepped'—in fact this is easily incorporated into the chart—or the variable cost line may become a curve. Implicit in this assumption is the further assumption that both efficiency and productivity are constant over the entire relevant range—if efficiency and/or productivity change then variable costs per unit are liable to change.

(iii) Selling prices per unit are known and stable over the entire relevant range. As with assumptions **(i)** and **(ii)** above for costs this assumption results in total revenues being a linear function of volume. Without this assumption a curvi-linear total revenue function could result.

(iv) Either only one product is being considered or the mix of products is known and constant. If one product is being considered then sales revenues and costs may be expressed as a function of the volume of that product. If several products are being considered then the volume of activity (and hence the total cost) is incapable of a simple description unless the mix of products is known.

(v) A common activity base can be used to describe both sales and production volume. As both sales revenues and total costs are considered simple linear functions of volume it is necessary to express volume for both sales and costs in the same form. For a single product chart that volume may be units or sales revenues; for a multi-product chart the volume will usually be sales revenues.

(vi) There is to be no change in the stock levels. If a change in stock levels is envisaged then the costs incurred will relate to a production volume different from sales.

(b) The discussion in part **(a)** indicates that there are many naive assumptions inherent in break–even analysis. There are many cases where the assumptions are violated—indeed it would be difficult to find a commercial firm for which the assumptions held. However normally over the range of output or volume under consideration the expected connection between volume, cost and revenues may be closely approximated by fitting the facts within the framework of break–even analysis.

Examples of circumstances in which the underlying assumptions are violated include:

(i) *Variable costs per unit remaining stable over the entire relevant range.* This assumption is violated in cases where quantity discounts can be obtained and larger quantities can be obtained at a lower per unit cost than smaller quantities—in fact the quantity discounts may cause the cost curve to be discontinuous, eg for orders of less than 2,000 units the cost is £3 per unit and orders of 2,000 units and over the unit price for the whole order is £2.80 would result in a cost of £5,700 for 1,900 units but a cost of only £5,600 for 2,000 units. Similarly if there is likely to be a change in productivity, due perhaps to the learning curve, then variable costs will alter. These violations result in the simple linear relationship not holding. However over a restricted range, or several restricted ranges, a linear relationship, or a series of linear relationships, may be a close approximation to reality.

(ii) *Selling price is stable.* The volume of sales may well be a function of selling price and consideration may be given to altering the selling price in order to take advantage of the elasticity of demand. The firm may be offering quantity discounts to encourage high sales. In all these cases total sales revenue is not a linear function of volume but again a series of linear relationships may be sufficient to approximate the true relationship for the purpose of providing useful information.

(iii) *Sales mix is known.* Most firms have a range of products and the precise mix of sales will not usually be exactly known. A number of factors including fashion, weather and advertising may alter the actual mix of sales from that expected. To include this on a break–even chart will require a range of total cost curves, corresponding to the cost functions of each sales mix, to be utilised. This will then give a break–even range rather than a point.

(Multi-product situations are considered in Section 2, Chapter 8).

4.2 **(a)**

	Production				
	15,000	20,000	25,000	30,000	35,000
	£	£	£	£	£
Fixed costs	3,000	3,000	3,000	3,000	3,000
Machining costs	1,200	1,600	2,000	2,200	2,400
Binding etc costs	300	400	500	600	700
Total costs	4,500	5,000	5,500	5,800	6,100
Average costs (per 5,000)	1,500	1,250	1,100	967	871
Marginal costs		500	500	300	300

(b) At the break–even point total revenue = total costs
Total revenue = £0.20 × output
For levels of output up to 25,000
$0.20y = 3,000 + 0.08y + 0.02y$
$0.10y = 3,000$
$y = 30,000$ copies.

Breakeven Chart for Silver Fingers A

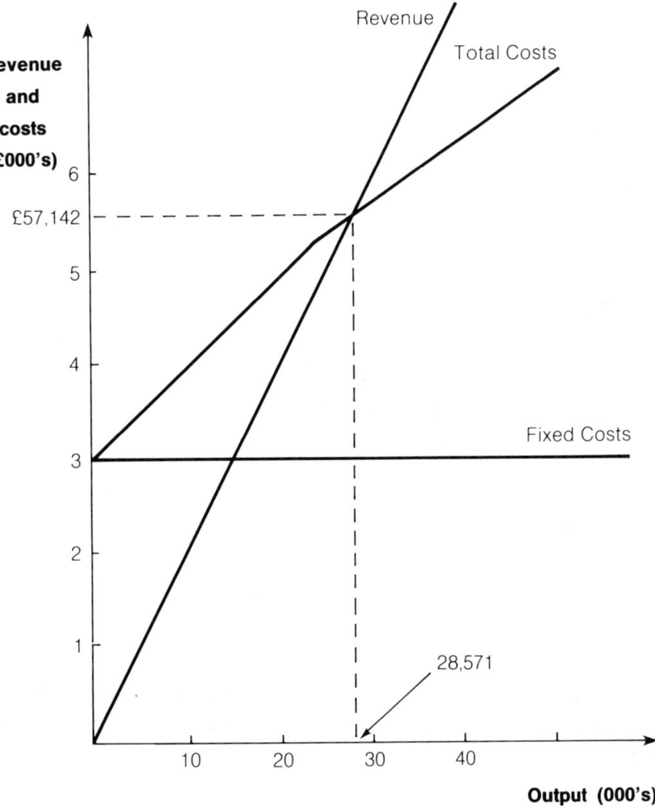

Thus the break–even point is 30,000 copies which is beyond the point where this formula applies.
For levels of output beyond 25,000
$0.20y = 3{,}000 + (25{,}000 \text{ @ £4 per } 100) + 0.04y + 0.02y$
$0.14y = 3{,}000 + 1{,}000$
$14y = 400{,}000$
$y = 28{,}571$ copies.

(c) A number of factors should be considered before the firm decides whether or not to sell a publication to different groups of traders at different prices, especially when these retailers cater for more or less the same consumers.

Once an item has been produced the highest price obtainable would be acceptable without reference to the historical costs of production, which have already been incurred. Thus, in the figures used in the example, the highest price obtainable of £600 would have been acceptable. If the only offer had been £100 this still should have been taken, unless repulping income would have been greater.

In the example the traditional purchasers of the publication are newsagents. Before selling to market traders any loss of newsagents' goodwill needs to be considered. The reaction of the traditional outlets, especially if they still held stocks of the publication, to seeing this sold at cut prices on markets must be gauged. It may be that if the newsagents were offered the publication at a reduced price they would buy the unsold copies themselves.

In this respect the more a market trader has to pay for the publication the less scope he has for cutting its price.

If the 10,000 copies have not yet been bound and finished the costs of doing this must be taken into account. With these costs at £100 per 5,000 copies an offer of more than £200 would be the minimum acceptable.

4.3. **(a)** 3 separate graphs have been prepared:

(i) The cost volume profit chart shows sales and total costs. At 100,000 units, if capacity is expanded, the sales line falls, reflecting the reduction in selling price required in order to increase demand. The cost line rises, reflecting the increase in fixed cost more than offsetting the increased efficiency following expansion of capacity. It is assumed that variable costs will be 50p per unit on all units.

The break–even point, previously 50,000 units, becomes 150,000 units.

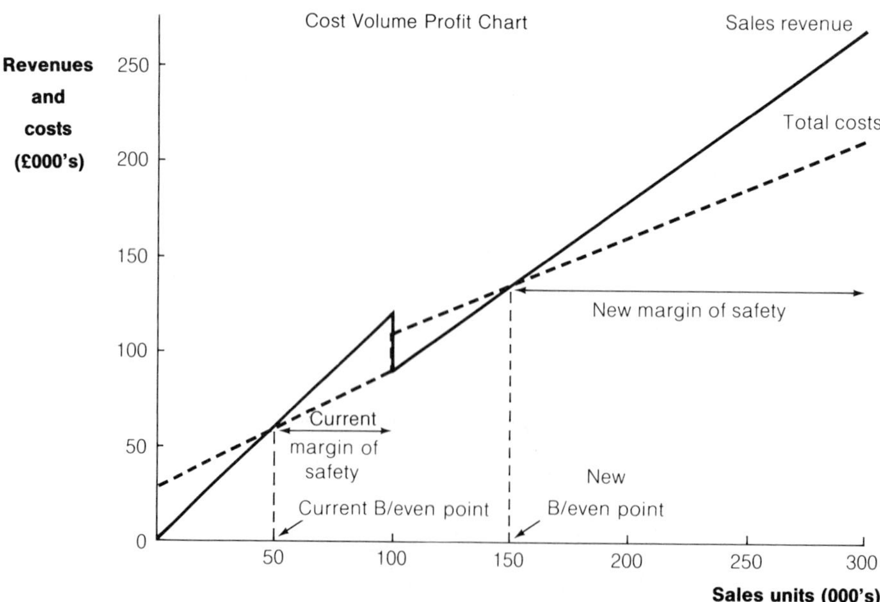

(ii) The same situation is plotted on a contribution volume chart. At 100,000 units, contribution falls (reduced selling price more than offsetting increased efficiency) and fixed costs increase.

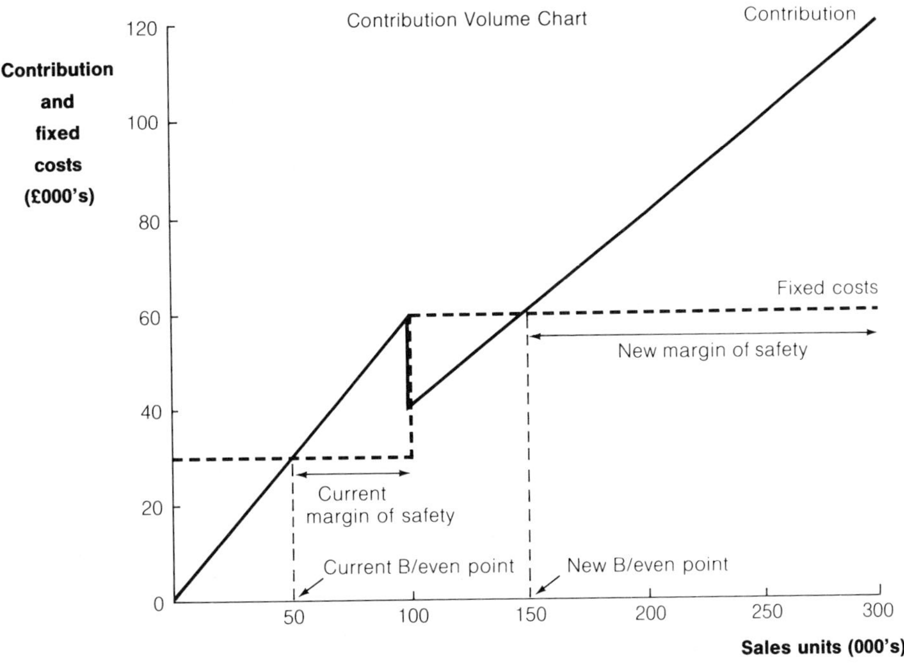

(iii) The same situation is plotted on a profit volume chart. At 100,000 units, profit of £30,000 becomes a loss of £20,000 (ie a reduction of £50,000) if the expansion in capacity and reduction in selling price occurs. Each unit generates 30p less in revenue but costs 10p less in variable cost to produce. Contribution is thus reduced by £20,000 (20p × 100,000). Profit is reduced by £50,000 due, in addition, to an increase in fixed costs of £30,000.

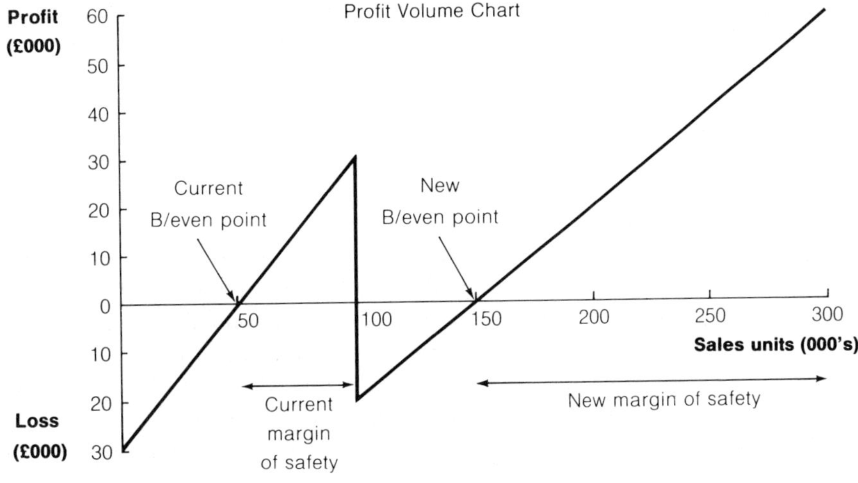

Workings:

	100,000 units (Before re-equipment)		100,000 units (After re-equipment)		300,000 units After re-equipment)	
	£ per unit	£'000	£ per unit	£'000	£ per unit	£'000
Sales revenue	1.20	120	0.90	90	0.90	270
Variable costs	0.60	60	0.50	50	0.50	150
Contribution	0.60	60	0.40	40	0.40	120
Fixed costs		30		60		60
Net profit		30		(20)		60

(b) **(i)** Calculation of break–even point (confirming figures read from the charts in **(a)**):

$$\text{Existing situation} = \frac{30{,}000}{0.6} = 50{,}000 \text{ units}$$

$$\text{Proposed scheme} = \frac{60{,}000}{0.4} = 150{,}000 \text{ units}$$

(ii) Profit (see workings in (a) above)
(iii) Margin of safety:

Existing situation = 50,000 units
or 50% of sales
Proposed scheme = 150,000 units
or 50% of sales

(iv) Profit required = £30,000 (if the question means profit in absolute terms)

$$\text{Sales units required} = \frac{£60{,}000 + £30{,}000}{0.4}$$

$$= 225{,}000 \text{ units}$$

In order to break–even a considerably higher level of sales must be achieved, due to the increase in fixed costs and reduced unit contribution. The break–even point is 3 times the previous level and requires a 50% increase in units sold over the current level. However, the reduction in selling price of 25%, and sale of the product under an additional brand name, are forecast to increase sales by 200%. If this is achievable a doubling of profits will result. An increase in sales of 125% is required in order to maintain profits at the current level. However, the requirement to finance additional fixed and working capital should be considered.

(c) The principal criticisms made by the economist of the accountant's break–even approach are:

(i) The linear total cost line implies that there are constant unit variable costs. The economist would argue that unit variable costs are likely to be higher for very low production, and that they will probably decrease as benefits of scale occur until they eventually start to increase again through inefficiencies coming from managerial diseconomies of very large scale. Total costs are curvi-linear.

(ii) In order to increase sales prices will usually have to be progressively reduced, which again produces a curved line for total revenue.

(iii) Fixed costs are unlikely to remain unchanged over a wide range of production levels.

(iv) Together the straight lines on the accountant's graph imply that infinite profit is available simply by expanding sales and production.

(v) The requirement to earn a satisfactory return on capital is ignored.

It is important to recognise that the economist's model has a fundamental difference of purpose to that of the accountant's model. Whilst the accountant's model enables general cost volume profit analysis to be carried out in practice, the economist's model is a single purpose prescriptive model. It provides a summary explanation of profit maximising behaviour, showing how cost and revenue behaviour determine the optimum price/output decision.

The accountant's model can be used for practical purposes because:

(i) The accountant should be aware of the simplification that the approach uses, and the difficulties and costs associated with obtaining more accurate information usually deter the accountant from adopting the refinements to his approach that the economist would like to see used.

(ii) The accountant will usually have accurate cost and revenue figures for current levels of operation. Most of the accountant's decisions will relate to fairly small movements from the current level of operation and within this narrow range the relationships shown by the break–even graph are likely to be fairly accurately depicted.

It must not be forgotten, however, that an adequate return on capital needs to be earned.

Solutions to Chapter 5 questions

ANSWERS TO SELF-ASSESSMENT QUESTIONS

5.1 Section 5.1 provides the answer to this question (see pages 63 and 64).

5.2 A costing system would provide the necessary basis for the effective planning and control of the transport company's activities. In the process, decisions will be taken as necessary.

Data should be recorded and analysed in such a way that regular reports can be provided of:

(i) the cost and utilisation of drivers.
(ii) the running costs (fuel, oil, tyres) for each vehicle.
(iii) maintenance costs (both breakdown and preventive) for each vehicle, analysed into material, labour, and other items.
(iv) standing charges ie insurance, depreciation, tax.
(v) costs for each depot: staff, power, establishment costs, maintenance.
(vi) central administration costs.
(vii) for each vehicle: kilometres travelled; load capacity utilised; journey times; cost per tonne/kilometre; kilometres per litre; hours out of action due to breakdown, routine maintenance, poor scheduling, or lack of work.

The information described above should be prepared on a monthly/four weekly, or even weekly, basis. The information would be improved by the comparison of actual data with budgets. Management's attention could be drawn to significant variances from budget for appropriate action to be taken.

The collection of cost information as described above would enable total costs per tonne/kilometre to be established for control purposes, as a basis for establishing prices, and so as to determine the profitability/acceptability of different jobs/customers.

Further questions that may be answered better/more easily if the foregoing information is available are:

(i) which vehicles are the most economical in terms of running costs or maintenance costs?
(ii) would sub-contracting of particular loads or of maintenance be worthwhile?
(iii) when should vehicles be repaired or sold?
(iv) what vehicles should be purchased?
(v) how efficient/viable are the different depots?

5.3 (a) *Absorption Costing Statement*

	Container Lorries		Parcel Vans		Total	
	£	% of Sales	£	% of Sales	£	% of Sales
Sales	96,780	100	22,720	100	119,500	100
Less: Cost of sales:						
Fuel & oil	16,450		2,590		19,040	
Drivers' wages	20,850		11,880		32,730	
Repairs & maintenance	3,120		920		4,040	
Road tax	310		310		620	
Vehicle insurance	2,010		1,230		3,240	
Depreciation of vehicles	6,300		2,580		8,880	
	49,040	51	19,510	86	68,550	57
Gross Profit	47,740	49	3,210	14	50,950	43
Less: Office salaries & expenses	26,175		9,245		35,420	
Buildings & equipment insurance & depreciation	895		895		1,790	
	27,070	28	10,140	45	37,210	31
Net Profit/(Loss) before interest and tax	£20,670	21%	£(6,930)	(31%)	£13,740	12%

(b) *Marginal Costing Statement*

	Container Lorries		Parcel Vans		Total	
	£	% of Sales	£	% of Sales	£	% of Sales
Sales	96,780	100	22,720	100	119,500	100
Less: Variable cost of sales:						
Fuel & oil	16,450		2,590		19,040	
Drivers' wages	20,850		11,880		32,730	
Repairs & maintenance	3,120		920		4,040	
Depreciation of vehicles	3,300		1,080		4,380	
Office salaries & expenses	4,839		1,136		5,975	
	48,559	50	17,606	77	66,165	55
Contribution	£48,221	50%	£5,114	23%	£53,335	45%
Less: Fixed costs:						
Road tax					620	
Vehicle insurance					3,240	
Depreciation of vehicles					4,500	
Office salaries & expenses					29,445	
Building & equipment insurance & depreciation					1,790	
					39,595	33
Net Profit before interest and tax					£13,740	12%

(c) Whilst both services provide a contribution to fixed costs in the short-run, in the long-run (on the assumption that costs have been shared reasonably fairly) it appears that the parcel van service is not sufficiently profitable.

Both statements may provide useful information. The marginal cost statement provides useful information especially for short-term decision-making. However, it is important that the longer-term implications are not ignored.

Much depends upon cost behaviour patterns and the ability to identify them, and also the sharing of costs where necessary.

ANSWERS TO EXERCISES

5.1 In general terms, information would be required on both a regular, and also an ad hoc, basis to plan and control and, as part of this ongoing process, make decisions concerning:

1 The operation of different stores.
2 The purchase and sale of different ranges of merchandise.
3 The storage, packaging and transportation of merchandise.
4 The level of head office costs.

Planning is required in order to direct activity, determine resource requirements, and establish targets and means of achieving them. Decisions have to be taken as part of determining the best plan, and on an ongoing basis in order to try to achieve the plan, or to adjust the plan to changed circumstances. This latter arises from the control and evaluation activity where information is provided of actual results in relation to plan. Significant variances can be investigated and appropriate corrective action taken.

Different levels of management at head office, at the regional depots, and at the individual stores, would require cost and/or revenue information and with differing degrees of detail.

Considering the control and evaluation activity first, the type of information which the cost and management accountant may provide includes the following:

(a) analysis by period (eg monthly) of the profitability of each of the department stores. This may be extended to provide an analysis of the gross profit (revenue less direct cost of goods) and the contribution (gross profit less certain allocatable costs eg department labour) of individual sections within each store and in relation to store space occupied.

(b) wages and overhead expenditure, analysed by expense type and by behaviour, incurred at each store, also analysed if meaningful between the various sub-sections of the store.

(c) the capital employed at each store. Particular attention would probably be given to an analysis of stock held at each store using appropriate measures of stock holding efficiency, such as stock turnover ratios.

(d) the gross profit margin of each category of product sold. In addition, an attempt may be made to apportion certain operating costs, both store (eg certain elements of store labour) and non-store (eg warehousing and distribution costs) to products, in order to determine the contribution generated by different products. The contribution may be expressed in absolute money terms, or in relative terms, which may be per £ of sales, per unit of sales, and/or per unit of space occupied.

(e) an analysis of stock holding at the regional depots including stock turnover ratios.

(f) information on the operation of the transport fleet at each of the regional depots. Costs may be collected by individual vehicle with such comparative statistics as maintenance costs per vehicle, and cost of fuel, oil and tyres per tonne/kilometre (or similar).

(g) an analysis of overhead expenditure by department could be provided for each of the functions at head office and at the regional depots.

The above information would provide the basis for establishing plans, which are likely to comprise a formal budgeting system. In the process, and on a continuing basis, the information would assist in making decisions about, and setting targets for, different aspects of the company's business, eg:

(a) determining the optimum allocation of store space to different ranges of products.

(b) setting selling prices.

(c) setting target stock levels at depots and at stores.
(d) determining which products should be sold.
(e) selecting most economical forms of transport and most cost effective routes from the depots to the stores.
(f) determining the required number and location of regional depots.
(g) deciding upon the required level of overhead support in both store and non-store activities.

(Accounting in retail organisations is considered in more detail in Chapter 9).

5.2 **(a)** The benefits which may arise from introducing a job costing system into the company's Plant Maintenance and Repair Department are described below.

(i) Actual costs of repair/maintenance work would be known and this would allow the accountant to charge the appropriate costs to the departments and equipment responsible. This could be of benefit in the following ways:

(a) It could provide additional information to management on the operating costs of equipment; this could be useful for example, if plant replacement is being considered.

(b) As costs could be charged to the department responsible, and not to general expenses, it would encourage department managers to consider the cost implications of any maintenance or repair requests eg it may encourage managers to think in terms of preventive maintenance rather than relying upon periodic expensive repair. Also it may encourage a more careful attitude to the equipment being used.

(c) If the company uses some form of full absorption costing for its products it will be able to construct more accurate overhead absorption rates as the Maintenance and Repair Department costs will be more accurately charged to production departments rather than being 'lost' in general expenses.

(ii) When experience has been obtained in calculating actual costs it may be possible to forecast the (relevant) costs for some of the maintenance and repair work. Once this is possible it will provide useful management decision-making information eg

(a) When deciding whether particular maintenance or repair work should be carried out by an outside contractor, or by the company's maintenance department.

(b) When deciding whether it is worthwhile to repair a particular machine.

(iii) The ability to forecast costs for maintenance and repair work may also be used to assist in the management control process both in the production departments and in the Maintenance and Repair Department. Actual cost of work may be compared with budget, significant variances investigated and if necessary corrective action taken.

(b) The information and procedures required in order to obtain the total cost of individual repair or maintenance jobs are outlined below.

(i) It will be necessary to identify each individual job, with, for example, some form of job or code number. Also it will be necessary to have a job cost card, for each job, where the appropriate costs may be entered.

(ii) The direct material costs may be made up of special material for a particular repair job and materials withdrawn from the maintenance store.

The charge to the jobs for special material will probably be made from the invoices. It will be necessary, therefore, to code the invoices when they have been received from the supplier and are being checked by the Maintenance and Repair Department. A similar system would be required for direct expenses.

The cost of standard materials withdrawn from maintenance store will need to be traced to individual jobs. The degree of sophistication built into this material recording system will depend upon the extent to which standard materials are used. Ideally the quantities of standard materials used on each job would be obtained by using a system based on Material Requisition and Return Notes, which, with appropriate authority, will be presented to the individual responsible for the stores. These notes could then be passed to the cost office for analysis and posting on to the job cards. Also it will be necessary to obtain the actual price of the material issued. This will involve maintaining records of prices paid for materials put into store and adopting some pricing system for charging out material issues eg FIFO, LIFO etc; if only a few standard materials are infrequently used then some form of periodic simple average pricing system may well be adopted.

(iii) Tracing the direct labour cost of maintenance work will involve the maintenance men recording the time spent on each job, their labour grade and consequent hourly rate of pay. These records will be passed to the cost office for analysis and posting to the job cards. Various forms of documentation are used for recording time spent on jobs, but whichever is adopted it will be desirable to attempt to reconcile total attendance time with total recorded direct and indirect time as this will provide some indication of the accuracy of the records being maintained.

(iv) It is inevitable that there will be some indirect costs in the Maintenance and Repair Department, eg overtime premium, indirect time, wages of storekeeper, maintenance of Maintenance Department machines, salary of foreman etc. The only possible means of charging these to jobs will be by using some form of absorption rate, probably using the direct time spent on jobs as the absorption base. As with production absorption rates the Maintenance and Repair Department rate probably will be based upon the budgeted indirect costs, and the budgeted direct hours, for the following year.

(v) In addition to the indirect costs in the Maintenance and Repair Department there will be other service and general factory costs which will be apportioned to this department, eg share of canteen costs, share of building maintenance costs, share of factory rates etc. These costs will be charged to the Maintenance and Repair Department jobs by being included in the absorption rate calculation outlined in (b)(iv) above.

Solutions to Chapter 6 questions

ANSWERS TO SELF-ASSESSMENT QUESTIONS

6.1 (a) Overhead Distribution Sheet

(£'000)	Production Dept			Service Dept		General Factory	*Total*
	A	B	C	X	Y		
Allocation							
Indirect materials	12	24	16	8	12	12	84
Indirect labour	60	40	80	20	40	88	328
Other expenses	—	—	—	—	—	220	220
Apportionment							
General factory	112	64	96	16	32	(320)	—
Service Dept X	11	8.8	17.6	(44)	6.6		—
Service Dept Y	13.59	40.77	36.24		(90.6)		—
	208.59	177.57	245.84	—	—	—	632
Absorption	÷ 20,000 = £10.43 per DLH	÷ 40,000 = £4.44 per DLH	÷ 30,000 = £8.19 per DLH				

(b) Overhead Control Account

	£		£
Indirect materials	85,000	Work-in-progress:	
Indirect labour	332,000	Dept A: 21,200 × 10.43	221,116
		Dept B: 38,600 × 4.44	171,384
Other expenses	217,000	Dept C: 28,100 × 8.19	230,139
			622,639
		Under-absorbed	11,361
	£634,000		£634,000

(c) Overhead absorbed is less than budget due to the fact that hours worked overall were below budget. Additional hours in department A, absorbed at £10.43 per DLH, were more than offset by below budget hours in departments B and C, absorbed at £4.44 and £8.19 per DLH respectively:

Department	**Hours variance versus budget**	**Rate per hour (£)**	**Over/(Under) Absorption (£)**
A	1,200	10.43	12,516
B	(1,400)	4.44	(6,216)
C	(1,900)	8.19	(15,561)
			(9,261)

As hours worked are below budget it may be expected that expenditure on overhead would also be below budget, to the extent that overheads are variable with activity. However, overhead expenditure is £634,000 against a budget of £632,000, an adverse expenditure variance of £2,000. The total under absorption can be explained as:

	£
Under-absorption on below budget hours	9,261
Above budget expenditure	2,000
Rounding	100
	11,361

6.2 **(a)** When considering the way in which service department costs should be controlled, the management accountant must consider a range of aims, eg:

(i) There should be control of the use of the service by user departments.
(ii) There should be control of the efficiency with which the service is provided.
(iii) There should be control of the way in which service costs are included in product costs which will be used for product pricing and stock valuation.
(iv) The motivational implications for the providers and users of a service must be considered when choosing the basis on which to charge for a service.

Use of the service: This is likely to be influenced by the method by which the user is charged for the service. The likely impact of each of a number of possible charge bases is discussed in part **(b)** of the solution.

Efficiency of provision: This could also be influenced by the charge basis used. If the department providing the service can charge out total actual cost to users, there is little incentive for improved efficiency. A system of standard costing and flexible budgetary control can help by monitoring actual performance against an agreed standard.

Inclusion in product costs: Service department costs are charged to user departments and from there to products which pass through and extract benefit from a department. The basis on which the service department cost has been charged to the user department will influence the charge ultimately made to each product unit.

Motivational implications: Data is used by individuals who will each have their own view as to its usefulness and who will be motivated positively or negatively by the way in which it is communicated and presented. Hence in the control of service department costs the accountant must consider the likely attitudes to each charge-out base and the financial reporting of each service.

(b) *Total actual cost*: All costs are passed on to the user departments. There is no incentive for the service department manager to control the cost of the service. The user departments are being charged for any inefficiencies in the provision of the service and any increased costs per unit of service arising from lack of demand for the service. Product costs may be inflated because of the increased service charge, leading to loss of business through prices being higher than they should be.

Standard absorption cost: This approach attempts to overcome the problems associated with charging total actual cost. It will reflect the planned level of efficiency and activity of the service department. The user department knows the costs of the service and where relevant can choose to use more or less of it. Product costs and prices will include a constant element for service costs. The efficiency of the service provision is monitored in the service department where all variances are reported.

Variable cost: This may be implemented on a standard or actual basis. Many argue that the principle of fixed overhead being absorbed by cost units is a highly arbitrary exercise which is not readily understood by management and which is more likely to retard rather than assist in the planning, control and decision-making cycle. The use of variable cost when charging for a service fits in with the operation of a marginal cost system by a company.

Opportunity cost: The company may decide that each service department should operate as a profit centre rather than cost centre. In this situation the service department charge for the service at a rate at which it could be sold externally. In this way the charge may be compared with that of external providers of a similar service (if such exist). The user department may then be allowed to choose whether or not to use the internal service. It may also be claimed that product costs will reflect a more realistic service cost element which could be understated when another cost based approach is used.

No charge: The company may wish to stimulate demand for a service where potential user departments have some discretion over its use eg to stimulate demand for *ad hoc* computer analysis of data. The approach could, however, lead to indiscriminate use of a service so that vital usage is delayed by less important requests.

6.3 **(i)**

	Production Dept			Service Dept		
(£'000)	A	B	C	X	Y	*Total*
Allocation + General factory apportionment (see 6.1)	184	128	192	44	84	632
Service Dept Y	12.6	29.4	25.2	16.8	(84)	—
Service Dept X	17.88	14.31	28.61	(60.8)	—	—
	214.48	171.71	245.81	—	—	632

(ii)

	Production Dept			Service Dept		
(£'000)	A	B	C	X	Y	*Total*
Allocation + General factory apportionment (see 6.1)	184	128	192	44	84	632
Service Dept Y	12.6	29.4	25.2	16.8	(84)	—
Service Dept X	15.2	12.16	24.32	(60.8)	9.12	—
Service Dept Y	1.37	3.19	2.74	1.82	(9.12)	—
Service Dept X	0.46	0.36	0.73	(1.82)	0.27	—
Service Dept Y	0.05	0.12	0.10	—	(0.27)	—
	213.68	173.23	245.09	—	—	632

(iii) Let x = Total overhead of service department X.
Let y = Total overhead of service department Y.
The total overhead of the service departments can be expressed as:

$$x = 44{,}000 + 0.2y$$
$$y = 84{,}000 + 0.15x$$

Rearranging the above equations:

$$x - 0.2y = 44{,}000$$
$$-0.15x + y = 84{,}000$$

Multiplying the first equation above by 5, and leaving the second equation unchanged:

$$5x - y = 220{,}000$$
$$-0.15x + y = 84{,}000$$

Adding the two equations together:

$$4.85x = 304{,}000$$
$$x = £62{,}680$$

Using the second equation, y can be calculated:

$$y = 84{,}000 + (0.15 \times 62{,}680)$$
$$= £93{,}402$$

The apportionment of service dept overhead can be carried out as follows:

	Production Department			
(£'000)	A	B	C	*Total*
Allocation + General factory apportionment (see 6.1)	184	128	192	504
Service Dept X	15.67 (25%)	12.54 (20%)	25.07 (40%)	53.28
Service Dept Y	14.01 (15%)	32.69 (35%)	28.02 (30%)	74.72
	213.68	173.23	245.09	632

6.4 **(a)** Overhead recovery is an attempt to associate with output those costs which although not capable of being associated with individual units of output are nevertheless caused in total by production volume or capacity. Because of the lack of direct causality between some overhead costs and output, a fairly imprecise recovery process must inevitably be used. It is usual to attempt to allocate cost with use and so costs incurred by a cost centre are usually recovered according to some measure of use of a resource provided by that cost centre. Hence a single recovery rate will seldom be considered sufficiently accurate and a separate recovery rate for each cost centre, or group of cost centres, is more usual. Similarly there will usually be separate rates for variable and for fixed production overheads.

The factors to be considered include:

(i) *Cost.*

(ii) *Ease of application.*

(iii) *Determinants, or causes, of cost.* Costs with a similar cause, eg machine costs, should be grouped together. Therefore, if there are many cost causes and cost centres then several recovery rates, one for each cost centre or group of similar cost centres, will be favoured.

(iv) *Production process.* A single production process will facilitate a single recovery rate. Multiple products with different production patterns will require the use of several rates if costs allocated are to appear to be fair and reasonable.

(v) *Accuracy.* Following from (iii) and (iv), a single recovery rate may be sufficiently accurate for some firms but other circumstances may call for the use of multiple rates.

The final choice of the degree to which recovery rates are segregated will be a trade off between costs, ease of use, accuracy and usefulness.

(b) The aim is to use as a base some measure which seems to be associated with the cause of the cost, even where the cost is fixed. The measure must be an element of work done which can be easily recorded and identified with different final products.

Among the methods are:

(i) direct labour hours—useful for labour related overheads.

(ii) direct labour cost—may be useful where skill is rewarded with higher wage rates and where direct labour cost (rather than hours) has a major influence on overhead cost incurred (unlikely with fixed overheads).

(iii) machine hours—useful for machine based costs. Frequently applied for each major grouping of similar machines.

(iv) output—where a variety of overhead costs are incurred influenced by various factors, units of output may be used, especially if a department has few products, with common characteristics.

(v) quantity/value of direct materials—where materials represent a high proportion of total cost and associated overheads are high, such overheads may be absorbed on a direct materials basis.

In any department, overhead costs can be divided into two or more separate parts if desired and each part absorbed into product cost on a different basis.

6.5 **(a)** Both methods include a proportion of fixed production overhead in the stock valuation. With the manager's average actual production cost approach, the amount of fixed overhead attributable to a unit of output would decrease as the level of output rises. Graphically the position would be as follows:

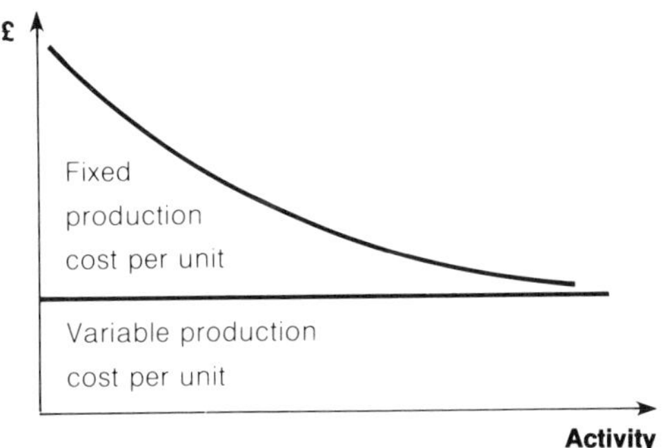

For the accountant's 'normal' production cost method the graph would be:

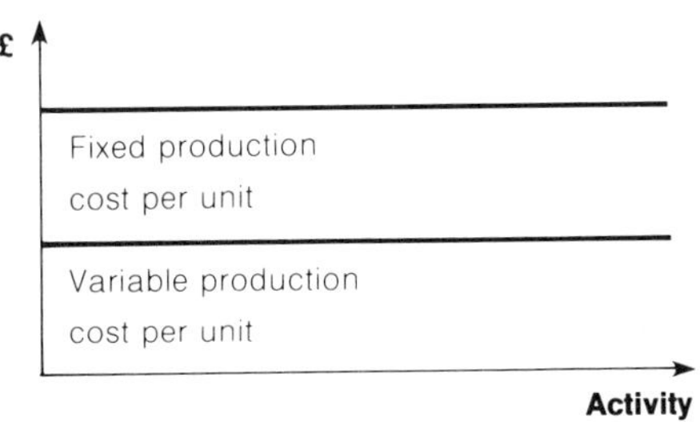

It might be considered that the average actual cost method is inappropriate for levels of output that are well below the 'normal' level whereas the normal production cost method is inappropriate for levels of output that are well above normal, but this would depend upon the precise nature of expectations about future sales levels and the purpose of the information.

(b) With sales fixed at £1,250,000 any increase in production will result in an increase in the physical closing finished goods stock. Since the inventory is being valued using a version of full cost, the value of each unit held in stock will include part of the fixed production cost. Although this fixed cost element will fall as output increases, the net effect is a falling figure for the cost of goods sold and, hence, an increasing profit figure. The following table illustrates the point:

Activity Index—Sales	50	50	50	50
Activity Index—Production	60	80	100	120
Opening Stock	10	10	10	10
Closing Stock	20	40	60	80
Cost of Production				
—*Fixed (£'000)	500	500	500	500
—Variable (£'000)	300	400	500	600
Opening Stock (£'000)	100	100	100	100
	900	1,000	1,100	1,200
Less: Closing Stock (£'000)	267	450	600	733
Cost of Goods Sold (£'000)	633	550	500	467

**Calculation of Fixed Production Costs*

	Current Year (estimated actual)	*Forthcoming Year* (manager's calculations)	*Difference*
Production Activity Index	100	80	20
Production Costs	£1,000,000	£900,000	£100,000
Variable	500,000	400,000	100,000
Fixed	500,000	500,000	—

(c) Calculation of Activity Index for Forthcoming Year (Accountant's Proposal)

Opening Inventory (Index)	10.0
Closing Inventory (Index)	7.5
Reduction in Inventory	2.5
Sales	75.0
Required Production (Activity Index)	72.5

Budgeted Profit and Loss Account
(Accountant's Proposal)

	£	£
Sales		1,687,500
Opening Stock	100,000	
Production Costs	862,500	
	962,500	
Less:		
Closing Stock	75,000	
		887,500
		800,000
Administrative Costs		300,000
Estimated Profit		£500,000

ANSWERS TO EXERCISES

6.1 **(a)** **(i)** *Statement of production order*

(in units)

Orders		*Units*
Ordered but not despatched		1,000
Orders just received		10,000
		11,000
Stock		
Already on hand	5,000	
Work in progress	2,000	
		7,000
Production order		
For customers		4,000
To bring stock to maximum		15,000
Production order to be placed		19,000

(ii) *Statement for material issue*

(in kilos)

Material	*Kilos required per dottie*	*Dotties to be produced*	*Total material requirements (kilos)*
Doh	2	19,000	38,000
Ray	3	19,000	57,000
Mee	1	19,000	19,000
Fah	5	19,000	95,000

(iii) *Statement of material purchase order*

(in kilos)

Material	*Doh*	*Ray*	*Mee*	*Fah*
For production	38,000	57,000	19,000	95,000
Less on hand	3,000	3,000	5,000	20,000
Adjustment for reservation	2,000	nil	nil	1,000
	1,000	3,000	5,000	19,000
	37,000	54,000	14,000	76,000
Plus to make up to maximum	7,000	12,000	7,000	20,000
Purchase order to be placed	44,000	66,000	21,000	96,000

(b) In deciding upon the maximum and minimum levels of stock required for materials to be used in the production of products there are a number of factors which must be considered including:

the demand for the final product; and

the 'lead time' between placing an order for the material and its delivery.

Although there are other considerations these factors will be discussed first. Generally the higher the demand for the final product the greater will be the necessity for higher maximum and minimum stocks of materials used to make it, although the relationship is unlikely to be linear between demand and stocks, as 'economies' will arise in the scale of stocks required to support increasing demand. Then the longer the lead time (and the higher the variability and reliability of this) the higher will be the maximum and minimum stock holdings necessary.

However there are also other factors to be taken into consideration. These will include how well the material keeps in storage. If materials deteriorate quickly, stock levels must be based upon ensuring that the material is used before deterioration sets in. The possibility of technical obsolescence of the material, or its obsolescence through changing patterns in demand, must also be brought into the analysis. If there are seasonal factors in supply, especially if these affect price, they must be looked at. Stock holding costs, which will include costs of storage, handling, insurance, etc must be considered as must the amount of storage space and capital available, and the opportunity costs of these. These factors will all have to be weighed together with the costs associated with stock-outs of material. Such costs include the consequences in immediate terms on production plans and costs (including any ripple effect on the utilisation of resources) and any ultimate effect through lost sales.

In the example, the maximum and minimum stocks of Doh and Mee may be the same because of the workings of a number of the above factors. As both these items go to make the same product, the demand considerations will be the same. However, Mee may be subject to delivery or price fluctuations, have a longer lead-time, only be available on a seasonal basis, or in relatively large quantities. Doh on the other hand may have storage considerations which necessitate lower levels of stock being held.

Definite conclusions are not possible without knowledge of the materials as far as their price, supply, and storage conditions are concerned.

6.2 **(a)** There are two important aspects in the accounting for service department costs. First, control needs to be exercised over each service department's costs. This includes both control of the efficiency with which the service is provided, and control of the use of the service by user departments. Second, the costs have to be passed on if product costs are to be established.

The arguments, which support the view that the costs of service departments in an organisation should be charged to the departments which use the services, are that if the organisation is employing a full absorption cost accounting system, *all* service department costs need to be passed on into the cost of the product and in so doing each service is priced, enabling control over service department and user costs.

The validity of the argument that user departments should be charged depends upon:

(i) Whether an absorption or a marginal costing system is employed. A marginal costing system concentrates attention on short-term variable costs and may result in only variable costs being charged to users. It is, however, possible to make a separate apportionment of fixed costs.

(ii) Understanding of the word 'charged'. If costs have to be included in product costs, it is generally most convenient to do this for production costs by absorption out of production departments, based upon some measure of production activity, for example direct labour hours. Service department costs have to be transferred to production departments. However, 'charged' suggests responsibility for costs. It may instead be an arbitrary apportionment to enable product cost establishment rather than a means of exercising control over both provider and user of the service.

(iii) The nature of the cost. For non-production overheads inclusion in product cost may be very arbitrary and may not be helped by, nor require, apportionment of service department costs to other departments. The issue is likely to be solely whether such apportionment of costs improves control.

Factors affecting the issue of whether the costs of service departments should be charged to users are:

(i) Whether input/output relationships are sufficiently clear. If relationships are unclear the cost may not be passed on as apportionment would not increase product cost reliability nor enable improved cost centre control.

(ii) The extent of the choice as to whether, and as to how much, a centre uses another centre's services. If choice is not available, the buying centre cannot be held responsible for price and thus is not in a position to control its own costs.

(iii) Where the responsibility centre is in the production/administration process. For example, the cost of the factory personnel department may be shared out over other production departments because product cost reliability is improved; the cost of the general personnel department may not be shared out over other administration departments, because this could not be expected to influence product cost reliability.

(iv) It may be wished to stimulate demand for a service where potential user departments have some discretion over its use, for example, to stimulate demand for ad hoc computer analysis of data from the computer centre. This could be achieved by not charging for a service.

(v) Whether indiscriminate use of a service is encouraged if no charge is made.

(vi) Whether there may be adverse consequences in terms of employee motivation as a result of apportionment. For example, assume that a manager is made responsible for a cost budget which includes a share of computer centre costs, whose apportionment is based on numbers of employees. Adverse motivational consequences may result if an increase in computer charges occurs because the costs of the computer centre increase, or because employee numbers in other departments decline. The manager may be less motivated to achieve budget, may be forced to reduce expenditure elsewhere with unfavourable consequences in order to achieve budget, or may seek to obtain the computer service elsewhere at additional cost to the company as a whole.

Key factors affecting employee motivation will be whether the extent of responsibility for different costs can be, and is, clearly established, and whether charges reflect economic reality.

(vii) Whether the cost of providing sophisticated analysis may outweigh the benefits.

(b) **(i)** It is not clear whether maintenance is of a routine preventive nature, or ad hoc in response to problems, or indeed a combination of the two. The treatment in the departmental performance report is unlikely to be effective because:

(1) Time spent, the basis for apportionment, will have no necessary connection with maintenance materials required, especially if maintenance is ad hoc.
(2) Actual costs permit any inefficiency in maintenance to be passed on, which is beyond the control of the supervisor of department A.

One possible approach, which would overcome (1) above, would be to adopt a job costing system in the maintenance department. An alternative approach, especially if maintenance is routine preventive, would be to establish a standard monthly charge to be agreed in advance by the supervisor of department A. This would overcome (2) above. Another alternative would be to charge a standard monthly rate for the fixed costs of the maintenance department, a standard hourly rate for variable costs (other than materials), plus actual maintenance materials used, seeking as far as possible and reasonable to overcome both (1) and (2) above.

(ii) The treatment of power is unlikely to be effective because:

(1) The use of power is unlikely to have any necessary connection with direct wages.
(2) The charge for a department should not be influenced by activity in another department.

The installation of meters may be considered a possibility in order to increase the accuracy of the power costs charged to each department. If this is not a viable proposition, some other measure of power usage may be found as an alternative to the direct wages basis.

(iii) As in the two previous examples (i) and (ii), the production supervisor has little control over the expenditure charged in this way. Indeed he cannot be held responsible at all for a large proportion of the expenditure. The extra handling costs were due to an error on the part of the design department, and therefore the extra charges attributable to the job should have been incorporated in the costs of the design department. Alternatively, the amount should have been classified as an extraordinary cost and written off to profit and loss account.

6.3 **(a)**

Overhead Calculations
(No recognition of reciprocal services)

	General Factory Overhead	*Service Cost Centres*		*Production Cost Centres*	
		1	**2**	**A**	**B**
	£	£	£	£	£
Primary Allocation	210,000	93,800	38,600	182,800	124,800
Apportionment of General Factory Overhead	(210,000)	10,500	21,000	31,500	147,000
	—	104,300	59,600	214,300	271,800
Charges by Service Cost Centre 1		(104,300)	—	91,262	13,038
		—	59,600	305,562	284,838
Charges by Service Cost Centre 2			(59,600)	8,221	51,379
			—	£313,783	£336,217
Budgeted Direct Labour Hours				÷ 120,000	÷ 20,000
Absorption Rates per DLH				= £2.61	= £16.81

(b)

	Production Cost Centres	
	A	**B**
Revised Overhead Absorption Rates	£2.61	£16.81
Current Overhead Absorption Rates	£3.10	£11.00
Increase/(Decrease) as % of Current Rates	(15.8)	52.8

The differences are large and would seem to arise for the following reasons:

1 No distinction has been made between fixed and variable overheads.
2 Overhead is being absorbed on the basis of annual activity (budgeted direct labour hours) rather than normal activity, or rather than a measure of resource availability as opposed to resource utilisation.
3 There is a marked difference in the activity pattern ie there is an increase of 20% in the direct labour hours of production cost centre A and a fall of 50% in the direct labour hours of production centre B.

Taken together the above three reasons result in considerable fluctuation in the overhead absorption rate which would not occur if:

1 Variable overheads alone were absorbed.
or
2 Normal activity, or a measure of resource availability, was used as the denominator.
or
3 Activity, as measured by direct labour hours, was stable.

(c) The quickest and most accurate method of handling reciprocal services, in the two service cost centre situation, is by simultaneous equations.

Let x = Total overhead of service cost centre 1.

Let y = Total overhead of service cost centre 2.

The total overhead of the service departments can be expressed as:

$$x = 104{,}300 + \tfrac{1}{30}y$$
$$y = 59{,}600 + \tfrac{1}{5}x$$

Rearranging the above equations:

$$x - \tfrac{1}{30}y = 104{,}300$$
$$-\tfrac{1}{5}x + y = 59{,}600$$

Multiplying the second equation above by 5, and leaving the first equation unchanged:

$$x - \tfrac{1}{30}y = 104{,}300$$
$$-x + 5y = 298{,}000$$

Adding the two equations together:

$$4\tfrac{29}{30}y = 402{,}300$$
$$y = £81{,}000$$

Using the first equation:

$$x = 104{,}300 + (\tfrac{1}{30} \times 81{,}000)$$
$$= £107{,}000$$

Thus:	*General Factory Overhead*	*Service Cost Centres*		*Production Cost Centres*	
		1	2	A	B
	£	£	£	£	£
Primary Allocation	210,000	93,800	38,600	182,800	124,800
Apportionment of General Factory Overhead	(210,000)	10,500	21,000	31,500	147,000
	—	104,300	59,600	214,300	271,800
Charges by Service Cost Centre 1		(107,000)	21,400	74,900	10,700
Charges by Service Cost Centre 2		2,700	(81,000)	10,800	67,500
		—	—	£300,000	£350,000
Budgeted Direct Labour Hours				÷ 120,000	÷ 20,000
Absorption Rates per DLH				= £2.50	= £17.50

(d) An ideal system of overhead apportionment would be one which clearly indicated the overhead incurred by taking a particular decision. This is a daunting requirement and, invariably, a less ambitious objective would be adopted ie the task of identifying the overhead incurred in taking a routine operating decision such as the decision to adopt a given contract or the decision to operate at a particular level of activity. If the system is charged with this task, then the distinction between fixed and variable overhead is important and when making overhead allocations to cost centres (and cost units) it is necessary to segregate the fixed and variable components. In addition the allocation of variable overhead should normally be on an appropriate activity basis to measure the cost of the services used, whereas fixed overhead should normally be allocated as a standing charge for the services made available rather than the services used.

The floor area occupied by individual cost centres might be proposed as a reasonable basis for the apportionment of fixed general factory overhead when the objective is to apportion on the basis of services made available to them. It is, however, doubtful whether floor space is a good surrogate for available services and its use may only be defensible in that it may be difficult to suggest anything better, assuming that it is agreed that an apportionment should be made. Neither of the methods, discussed for the Isis Engineering Company, distinguishes between fixed and variable expenses of the cost centres. Service Cost Centre 1 has a low level of fixed cost and yet the apportionment of this cost centre's expenses to other cost centres is achieved on the basis of the number of personnel in a cost centre and this is quite likely to be inappropriate for measuring the services absorbed by that cost centre. Prima facie it would seem better to use direct labour hours and a statistical study could be undertaken to determine whether this is appropriate. Service Cost Centre 2 has expenses which are predominantly fixed but these are charged to other departments on the basis of services used, which seems more suitable for allocating variable costs. Service Cost Centre 2 is the plant maintenance section and a peculiarity of such departments is that the work that they undertake in a particular month (and the associated cost of this work) may well be properly attributable to operating activity of past months. It may even be attributable to future operating activity since maintenance work (particularly preventive maintenance) may be carried out in slack production periods. Fixed plant maintenance expenditure may be apportioned on the basis of services made available to other departments (with the problems already mentioned) but the task of allocating variable maintenance costs may require to be tackled by calculating the average variable maintenance cost per machine hour (for example).

Overhead allocation methods which recognise the existence of reciprocal service flows are theoretically superior to methods which ignore their existence but they will provide little benefit if no distinction is made between fixed and variable overheads. Even where this distinction is observed it might be found that the additional complexity of the theoretically superior method may not yield benefits which are large enough to justify its use.

The use of a direct labour hour rate in production cost centre B may be appropriate but, since the cost centre is highly mechanised, the use of machine hour rate(s) should be investigated. Statistical analysis should be useful here.

Solutions to Chapter 8 questions

ANSWERS TO SELF-ASSESSMENT QUESTIONS

8.1 **(a)** The situation described in the question arises from the method of inventory valuation used by Mahler Products together with the fluctuations in the level of finished goods stock that have occurred in the periods under review. The firm is using a full cost (or absorption costing) basis for stock valuation purposes. This method attaches part of the organisation's fixed costs to each item held in stock. In the case of Department A this fixed cost allocation is £12, in the case of Department B it is £16. In the profit and loss account the matching concept requires the use of a stock adjustment process to adjust the cost of production figure to a cost of goods sold figure.

When inventory levels are fluctuating this process of bringing forward fixed costs from past periods and carrying forward fixed costs to future periods can have a considerable effect on the profit calculations. The following table shows the consequences of the full cost method in the current case:

The effect of the inclusion of fixed factory overheads in stock valuations

	1 July–31 December		1 January–30 June	
	1984	1984	1985	1985
	Dept A	Dept B	Dept A	Dept B
	£'000	£'000	£'000	£'000
Fixed overheads brought forward in opening stock of finished goods	36	112	72	96
Fixed overheads carried forward in closing stock of finished goods	72	96	12	160
Profit increased by	36			64
Profit reduced by		16	60	
Net profit as per absorption costing profit and loss account	94	50	53	83
Profit prior to stock adjustment	58	66	113	19

These 'unadjusted profit' figures are in line with the changes in the sales mix between the two periods.

(b) *Mahler Products*
Departmental profit and loss accounts—(marginal cost basis) year to 30 June 1985

	1 July–31 December		*1 January–30 June*	
	1984	1984	1985	1985
	Dept *A*	*Dept* *B*	*Dept* *A*	*Dept* *B*
	£'000	£'000	£'000	£'000
Sales revenue	300	750	375	675
Variable manufacturing costs				
Direct material	52	114	30	132
Direct labour	26	76	15	88
Variable overheads	26	76	15	88
Marginal factory cost of production	104	266	60	308
Add				
Opening stock of finished goods	24	98	48	84
	128	364	108	392
Less				
Closing stock of finished goods	48	84	8	140
Marginal factory cost of goods sold	80	280	100	252
Total contribution	£220	£470	£275	£423
Less				
Fixed overheads				
Fixed factory overheads	132	304	132	304
Fixed administrative and selling overheads	30	100	30	100
Net profit	58	66	113	19

These profit figures are those under the absorption costing basis *before* making the adjustment for fixed factory overhead in the inventory valuations.

8.2 Profit Performance—Year Just Ended

	Product X			Product Y			Product Z			*Total*	
Sales units	45,000			52,500			16,875			114,375	
	£/unit	£	% of sales	£/unit	£	% of sales	£/unit	£	% of sales	£	% of sales
Sales revenue	10.00	450,000	100.0	6.00	315,000	100.0	8.00	135,000	100.0	900,000	100.0
Contribution	3.50	157,500	35.0	3.60	189,000	60.0	3.60	60,750	45.0	407,250	45.3
Fixed costs										330,000	36.7
Net profit										77,250	8.6

Profit Performance—Year Ahead

	Product X			Product Y			Product Z			*Total*	
Sales units	46,922			68,251			11,731			126,904	
	£/unit	£	% of sales	£/unit	£	% of sales	£/unit	£	% of sales	£	% of sales
Sales revenue	10.00	469,225	100.0	5.50	375,380	100.0	8.00	93,845	100.0	938,450	100.0
Contribution	3.50	164,229	35.0	3.10	211,578	56.4	3.60	42,230	45.0	418,037	44.5
Fixed costs										330,000	35.1
Net profit										88,037	9.4

In the year ahead a change in the mix of sales is expected, partly due to the reduction in the selling price of product Y. Apart from an increase in the sales of product Y, (both units and revenue), a small increase in sales of product X is expected, whilst sales of product Z are expected to fall by over 30%. Product X is expected to maintain its 50% share of total sales revenue.

The overall contribution percentage of sales in the year just ended was 45.3%. This is expected to reduce to 44.5% in the year ahead. The effect of the reduced contribution margin on product Y, resulting from the reduction in selling price, more than offsets the increased sales of product Y, the highest contribution percentage of sales product.

In absolute terms, however, total contribution is expected to increase by 2.6%, and net profit by 14%.

The profit volume chart shows the contribution made by each product and the average contribution. In the year ahead the break-even point is at a higher level of sales, due to the reduced average contribution percentage of sales. However, the margin of safety on expected sales for the year ahead is greater, in both absolute and relative terms, compared with the year just ended. Calculations are as follows:

	Year Just Ended	Year Ahead
Break-even point	$\dfrac{330,000}{\dfrac{407,250}{900,000}}$ = £729,281	$\dfrac{330,000}{\dfrac{418,037}{938,450}}$ = £740,816
Margin of safety	£900,000 − £729,281 = £170,719 = 19.0%	£938,450 − £740,816 = £197,634 = 21.1%

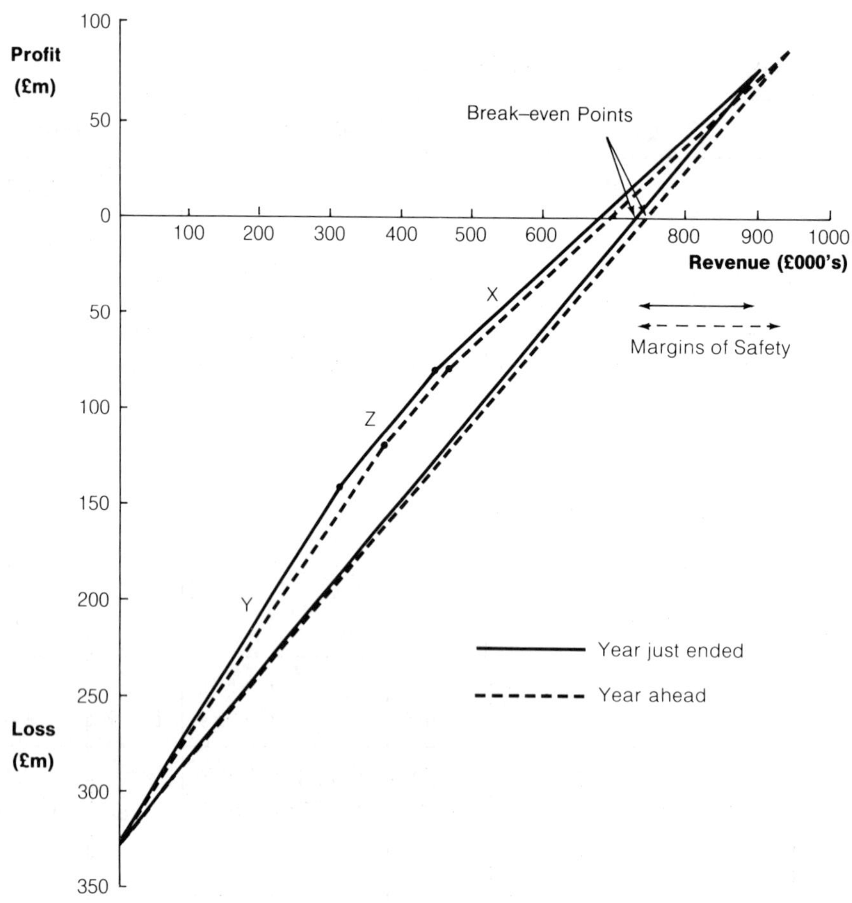

ANSWERS TO EXERCISES

8.2 (a)

Synchrodot Ltd

Budgeted Income Statement for January, February and March 1981

	Product 1	Product 2
Budgeted Sales Quantity	30,000 units	57,000 units
Budgeted Production Quantity	30,000 units	52,500 units
Budgeted Sales Revenue	£450,000	£1,026,000
Budgeted Production Costs		
Direct Material	£60,000	£157,500
Direct Labour	30,000	105,000
Factory Overhead	210,000	532,500
	£300,000	£795,000
Add:		
Budgeted Finished Goods		
Stock at 1 January 1981	(8,000 units) 80,000	(7,500 units) 105,000
	£380,000	£900,000
Less:		
Budgeted Finished Goods		
Stock at 31 March 1981	(8,000 units) 80,000	(3,000 units) 42,000
Budgeted Manufacturing Cost of		
Budgeted Sales	£300,000	£858,000
Budgeted Manufacturing Profit	£150,000	£168,000
Budgeted Administrative and		
Selling Costs (fixed)	30,000	48,000
Budgeted Profit	£120,000	£120,000

(b)

Synchrodot Ltd

Budgeted Income Statements for the two quarters to 30 June 1981

	January/February/March		*April/May/June*	
	Product 1	Product 2	Product 1	Product 2
Budgeted Sales Quantity	30,000 units	57,000 units	30,000 units	57,000 units
Budgeted Production Quantity	30,000 units	52,500 units	24,000 units	60,000 units
Budgeted Sales Revenue	£450,000	£1,026,000	£450,000	£1,026,000
Budgeted Production Costs				
Direct Material	£60,000	£157,500	£48,000	£180,000
Direct Labour	30,000	105,000	24,000	120,000
Factory Overhead	210,000	532,500	204,000	540,000
	£300,000	£795,000	£276,000	£840,000
Add:				
Budgeted Opening Finished				
Goods Stock	32,000	45,000	32,000	18,000
	£332,000	£840,000	£308,000	£858,000
Less:				
Budgeted Closing Finished				
Goods Stock	32,000	18,000	8,000	36,000
Budgeted Manufacturing Cost of Budgeted Sales	£300,000	£822,000	£300,000	£822,000
Budgeted Manufacturing Profit	£150,000	£204,000	£150,000	£204,000
Budgeted Administrative and				
Selling Costs (fixed)	30,000	48,000	30,000	48,000
Budgeted Profit	£120,000	£156,000	£120,000	£156,000

The statements in (a) and (b) above could alternatively be prepared by identifying directly the cost of sales at standard, without reference to opening and closing stocks, which also highlights any under/over absorption of factory overhead using absorption costing.

The absorption costing statement in (a) would be as follows:

	Product 1		Product 2	
		£'000		£'000
Sales revenue	(30,000 units × £15/unit)	450	(57,000 units × £18/unit)	1,026
Production cost of sales (at standard)	(30,000 units × £10/unit)	300	(57,000 units × £14/unit)	798
Gross profit (at standard)	(30,000 units × £5/unit)	150	(57,000 units × £4/unit)	228
Under absorbed factory o'hd*				
production < sales		—	(4,500 units × £8/unit)	36
sales < capacity		—	(3,000 units × £8/unit)	24
Adjusted gross profit		150		168
Administration and selling costs		30		48
Net profit		120		120

The marginal costing statement in (b) would be as follows (it is the same for each quarter as sales are unchanged):

	Product 1		Product 2	
		£'000		£'000
Sales revenue	(30,000 units × £15/unit)	450	(57,000 units × £18/unit)	1,026
Variable cost of sales*	(30,000 units × £4/unit)	120	(57,000 units × £6/unit)	342
Contribution	(30,000 units × £11/unit)	330	(57,000 units × £12/unit)	684
Fixed costs:				
Factory overhead		180		480
Administration and selling costs		30		48
		210		528
Net profit		120		156

*The fixed factory overhead rate per unit is based on practical capacity as follows:

Product 1: £180,000 ÷ 30,000 units = £6/unit
Product 2: £480,000 ÷ 60,000 units = £8/unit

The variable production cost of sales per unit is therefore:

	Product 1	Product 2
	£/unit	£/unit
Total cost of sales (at standard)	10	14
less: standard fixed overhead absorption rate	6	8
	4	6

(c) The difference between the full cost and the marginal cost bases for valuing finished goods stock is that the former attributes an 'appropriate' part of the fixed costs to unsold units of stock whereas the latter identifies all fixed costs as period costs and thus writes them off (against revenue) in the period in which they were incurred. This means that the use of standard marginal cost, as the stock valuation basis, results in profit figures which vary with sales whereas the use of standard full cost treats profit as a function of both sales and production activity. Since Synchrodot's sales are constant for both periods, the marginal cost stock valuation will give constant profit figures but full cost will give varying figures because production varies.

The difference between the profit figures under the two conventions can be considered further, as follows:

(i) When production = sales (as in the first quarter for product 1) profit for the full costing approach is identical with that for the marginal costing method.

(ii) When production > sales (as in the second budget period for product 2) profit for the full costing approach is higher than that calculated under marginal costing. Since physical stock levels are rising full costing relieves the profit and loss account of some fixed overheads by including a higher percentage of such overheads in the closing stock valuation than it does in the open stock valuation.

(iii) With sales > production (as in the first quarter for product 2 and the second quarter for product 1) marginal costing gives a higher profit than full costing. Full costing now charges the profit and loss account with more fixed overhead than does marginal costing, this is because physical stock levels are falling so that the overhead in the closing stock valuation (under full costing) is less than that in the opening valuation.

The Production Director's query as to variations in the average profit per unit sold, shows that he does not appreciate the impact of fixed overheads on profit calculations. The distinction between unit contribution and unit profit should be explained to him.

8.3 *Product Sales*

Product	*Proportion of total sales*	*Sales*	*Sales price per unit*	*No. of units*
	%	(£'000*s*)	£	(000*s*)
A	20	1,000	10	100
B	20	1,000	20	50
C	60	3,000	25	120
		5,000		

Calculation of Fixed Costs

Product	*Quantity produced*	*Direct labour*		*Fixed overhead*		*General depreciation*	
	(000s)	*Per unit* £	*Total* (£'000s)	*Per unit* £	*Total* (£'000s)	*Per unit* £	*Total* (£'000s)
A	100	1.0	100	1.0	100	—	—
B	50	2.0	100	2.0	100	1.0	50
C	120	2.5	300	8.0	960	3.0	360
Total allocated			500		1,160		410
Add: Under-recovery			—		70		20
Total			500		1,230		430

Contribution

	A £	*B* £	*C* £
Per unit			
Sales price	10	20	25
Cash costs			
direct materials	1.5	2.0	6.0
variable overhead	3.0	4.0	4.0
Total cash costs	4.5	6.0	10.0
Cash contribution	5.5	14.0	15.0
Variable depreciation	1.5	4.0	—
Profit contribution	4.0	10.0	15.0
Per £ of sales			
Profit	0.40	0.50	0.60
Cash flow	0.55	0.70	0.60

(a)

Original Plan

Product	*Quantity*	*Profit* *Contribution per unit*	*Profit* *Total contribution*	*Cash Flow* *Contribution per unit*	*Cash Flow* *Total contribution*
	(000s)	£	(£'000s)	£	(£'000s)
A	100	4.0	400	5.5	550
B	50	10.0	500	14.0	700
C	120	15.0	1,800	15.0	1,800
Total contribution			2,700		3,050
Less fixed costs					
direct labour		500		500	
fixed overhead		1,230		1,230	
general depreciation		430		—	
salaries		140		140	
accommodation		40		40	
depreciation of offices		70		—	
			2,410		1,910
Total profit/cash flow			290		1,140

(b) *Contribution per £ of Sales*

		Profit		*Cash Flow*	
(1) *Product*	(2) *Proportion*	(3) *Contribution per £*	(4) (2) × (3)	(5) *Contribution per £*	(6) (2) × (5)
		£	£	£	£
Original plan					
A	0.20	0.4	0.08	0.55	0.11
B	0.20	0.5	0.10	0.7	0.14
C	0.60	0.6	0.36	0.6	0.36
			0.54		0.61
Revised plan					
A	0.20	0.4	0.08	0.55	0.11
B	0.50	0.5	0.25	0.7	0.35
C	0.30	0.6	0.18	0.6	0.18
			0.51		0.64

(i) Sales required = Contribution required ÷ contribution per £ of sales
To equal original profit (in £'000s):
Contribution required = £2,410 + £290 = £2,700
Sales required = £2,700 ÷ 0.51 = £5,294
To equal original cash flow (in £'000s):
Contribution required = £1,910 + £1,140 = £3,050
Sales required = £3,050 ÷ 0.64 = £4,766

(ii) As the fixed costs are unaltered as a result of adopting the alternative plans then the plan with the highest contribution per £ of sales should be chosen.
To maximise profit the original plan (with a profit contribution of £0.54 per £ of sales) is superior to the alternative plan (which has a profit contribution of only £0.51 per £ of sales).
To maximise cash flow the revised plan is superior. The cash flow contributions per £ of sales are: original plan £0.61, revised plan £0.64.

(c) There are many reasons why the analysis may be deficient in practical terms. These include:

(1) Some costs may not be neatly classified into fixed or variable, eg labour costs.
(2) Revenues and total variable costs may be a linear function of activity only over a specified range rather than over the whole potential range of activity. Similarly some 'fixed' costs may be stepped.
(3) Efficiency of production is assumed constant throughout the whole range of activity. This may not be so.
(4) It is unlikely that sales and production will exactly equal each other. Work in progress is ignored.
(5) The classification of expenses between cash and non-cash expenses is frequently difficult.
(6) The analysis assumed certainty concerning the costs and revenues.
(7) Taxation is ignored.
(8) The sales mix is assumed to be absolutely certain.
(9) Volume of activity is assumed to be the only relevant factor affecting cost.

These deficiencies do reduce the usefulness of the results as they cause the final results to be, at best, a first approximation. However, the technique used—break-even, or cost-volume-profit, analysis—is very useful in ascertaining the broad, not detailed, effects of plans. It is useful to ascertain approximately when the firm will break even. Similarly it is useful to ascertain when positive cash flows will be produced, but this will not reduce the need for a detailed cash budget.

(Cash budgets are covered in Section 4).

8.4

Product profitability statement

(£'000) *Product*	*V*	*W*	*X*	*Y*	*Z*	*Total*
Sales	4,400	4,900	6,500	5,100	9,100	30,000
less *Variable Costs*						
Materials	200	600	1,200	1,000	1,500	4,500
Labour	500	800	1,500	1,400	1,800	6,000
Production O'hd	250	350	400	500	720	2,220
Transport	100	300	600	500	500	2,000
Packaging	200	100	200	100	300	900
Sales commission	220	245	325	255	455	1,500
	1,470	2,395	4,225	3,755	5,275	17,120
Contribution	2,930	2,505	2,275	1,345	3,825	12,880
less *Attributable Fixed Costs*						
a) *Discretionary*						
Advertising	500	300	200	300	300	1,600
	2,430	2,205	2,075	1,045	3,525	11,280
b) *Capacity*						
Production O'hd (excl specific plant)	50	50	50	100	40	290
Hire of plant	—	—	—	200	—	200
	50	50	50	300	40	490
	2,380	2,155	2,025	745	3,485	10,790
Depreciation	50	150	300	—	10	510
Attributable Profit	2,330	2,005	1,725	745	3,475	10,280
less *Non-Attributable Fixed Costs*						
Stores	20	60	120	100	150	450
Production O'hd	250	400	750	700	900	3,000
Transport	20	60	120	100	150	450
Administration	660	735	975	765	1,365	4,500
	950	1,255	1,965	1,665	2,565	8,400
Net Profit/(Loss)	1,380	750	(240)	(920)	910	1,880

(a) In the above table the profitability of the five products is shown in absolute terms. On a fully absorbed costing basis, including a share of all costs incurred, products X and Y are unprofitable. However, this includes a share of several costs which, from the information provided, it must be assumed would be unaffected by discontinuation of the product.

In order to advise the managing director the attributable profit should be highlighted. This is the amount of profit generated by products after deducting costs that are directly incurred as a result of their production and sale. Profits of £1,725,000 and £745,000 would be lost if products X and Y were not produced and sold.

This is the long-run situation. It should also be pointed out that production facilities already exist and that, as a result, attributable depreciation is a sunk cost. If the specific plant and equipment has no saleable value the profit lost would be even greater for product X, at £2,025,000. Product Y would be unaffected as it hires plant and equipment on an annual commitment.

It should also be questioned, however, whether non-attributable costs would remain unaffected by the discontinuation of products. All costs are likely, over time, to be to some extent affected by the level of activity. The long-run loss on products X and Y should remain of concern and should be examined further.

(b) (i)

Product	*V* (£'000s)	*W* (£'000s)	*X* (£'000s)	*Y* (£'000s)	*Z* (£'000s)
Existing contribution	2,930	2,505	2,275	1,345	3,825
40% of contribution	1,172	1,002	910	538	1,530
Additional advertising	1,500	900	600	900	900
Additional profit	(328)	102	310	(362)	630

It would be worthwhile pursuing additional advertising for products W, X and Z.

(ii) If funds available were restricted to £1,200,000 then the products with the highest profit per £ of advertising expenditure should be advertised. The additional profits per £ of additional advertising expenditure of those products for which additional advertising would be worthwhile are:

	£
W	0.113
X	0.517
Z	0.700

Hence products Z and X should be advertised. Expenditure should be:

Z	£900,000
X	£300,000

The resulting increase in profits would be:

	£
Z	630,000
X	155,000
	785,000

(Limiting factor situations are considered further in Chapter 14).

(c) Contribution per £ of sales of products V, W and X is £0.6659, £0.5112, and £0.35 respectively. Substitution of V for X would generate contribution of £0.29966 (0.45 × 0.6659) against £0.35 lost, per £ of product X sales lost. Substitution of W for X would generate contribution of £0.25561 (0.50 × 0.5112) against £0.35 lost, per £ of product X sales lost. Neither option would, on the face of it, be worthwhile.

However, if sales of product X could be reduced to zero, and attributable fixed costs could then be saved, the required appraisal is different. Only product V need be considered as potential contribution, as a result of substitution, is higher than product W.

	Product V substituting for Product X £'000
Lost contribution [£6,500,000 × (0.35 – 0.29966)]	(327)
Attributable fixed costs of product X saved (Excl. depreciation of specific plant)	250
	(77)
Depreciation of specific plant	300
	223

Net of all attributable fixed costs, additional profit of £223,000 would be generated by substitution of product V for product X, if product X sales are reduced to zero and discontinued. If, however, the specific plant and equipment used for product X has no value in alternative use then profit would be reduced by £77,000 by such a change.

Solutions to Chapter 9 questions

ANSWERS TO EXERCISES

9.1 **(a)** Cost centres should be set up so as to identify and control the costs of different activities in the warehouse, in line with the responsibility of different managers/supervisors. Cost centres identified in the wholesale warehouse will also depend upon the size of the warehouse, and of the organisation, as the smaller the operation the more flexible will be the organisation of work.

The main functions to be carried out will be:

(i) Buying and ordering
(ii) Goods receiving and unloading
(iii) Stock records and control
(iv) Picking goods against customers' orders
(v) Packing
(vi) Loading
(vii) Sales order processing and invoicing
(viii) General administration

Each of the above functions is likely to be a separate cost centre with cost incurrence made the responsibility of a manager/supervisor.

(b) Performance indicators for the control of costs should provide measures of efficiency in the use of resources. In the wholesale warehouse these will be concerned mainly with the control of premises costs (ie rent and rates; light, heat and power; part of repairs and maintenance) and with control over the use of warehouse staff.

Premises costs will be predominantly fixed, but calculation of cost per square metre occupied can be used to indicate cost trends over time and also for interdivisional or intercompany comparison.

Labour performance control necessitates the keeping of time records and the use of these in calculating such indications as:

(i) Loading/unloading—average labour cost per vehicle unloaded.
(ii) Replenishment—average labour cost per line replenished.
(iii) Picking—labour cost per £ of goods picked.
(iv) Fork-lift truck operation—percentage utilised.

The above indications may lead to consideration of changes in the methods of storing and handling goods, and of the utilisation/size of the labour force.

Repair and maintenance costs (associated both with premises and equipment) should be carefully monitored against different assets and will be an important factor in replacement decisions, where a primary objective should be to minimise the life cycle cost of assets.

Packaging supplies must also be carefully monitored in order to ensure efficient use and minimise/avoid wastage. Cost expressed as a percentage of sales should provide a guide as the cost would be expected to be variable with activity.

Administration costs may also be expressed as a percentage of sales, and year-on-year changes calculated. Each administration operation should be examined separately in order to establish resource requirements.

A further cost, which may not be shown on departmental cost reports, and which may therefore remain hidden, is the interest cost associated with the holding of stocks, and with credit sales. It is important that stock and debtor levels are closely controlled. Stock turnover and debtor/sales ratios should provide assistance in controlling the level of working capital and thus interest cost.

9.2 **(a)** Service costing is the establishment of the cost of providing a service, rather than the cost of producing a product. The service may be provided by departments within a business to other departments (eg personnel, canteen, maintenance) or it may be a separate business on its own providing a service to outside customers (eg transport business, hotel).

A particular difficulty is to define a realistic cost unit (see definition below) that represents a suitable measure of the service provided. Another feature of many service operations is the relatively high level of fixed costs.

(b) In order to establish the cost of anything, costs have to be related to activities, not just in total but in relation to units of each activity. The unit of activity is called the cost unit. The particular cost unit to be used in any given situation will depend upon the nature of the activity being costed. It may be either a production or service activity and thus the cost unit may be a unit of either product or service.

In the transport business, it would be necessary to establish the cost of the service provided, as a basis for charging customers and as a basis for controlling costs. Ultimately, each job undertaken would become a separate cost unit. It would be impossible to identify directly the cost associated with each job undertaken and, therefore, further cost units would be used in order to establish the cost of each job.

Some costs will tend to vary with activity whilst others will be relatively fixed, especially in the short-term, over a given period of time. There would seem to be two possible measures of activity, distance travelled (eg measured in kilometres) and time taken (eg measured in hours). As fixed costs are time based also, time taken could be used as the basis for measuring costs. Cost per hour would become the cost unit. However, many of the variable costs are more directly related to distance rather than time. Thus cost per kilometre would seem more appropriate for these costs. Weight may also be a factor. If this is so, cost per tonne/kilometre may be established. It may in fact be inconvenient, without any guarantee of greater precision, to use both cost in relation to distance and also in relation to time, and thus one only may be used, as indicated by part (b) of the question.

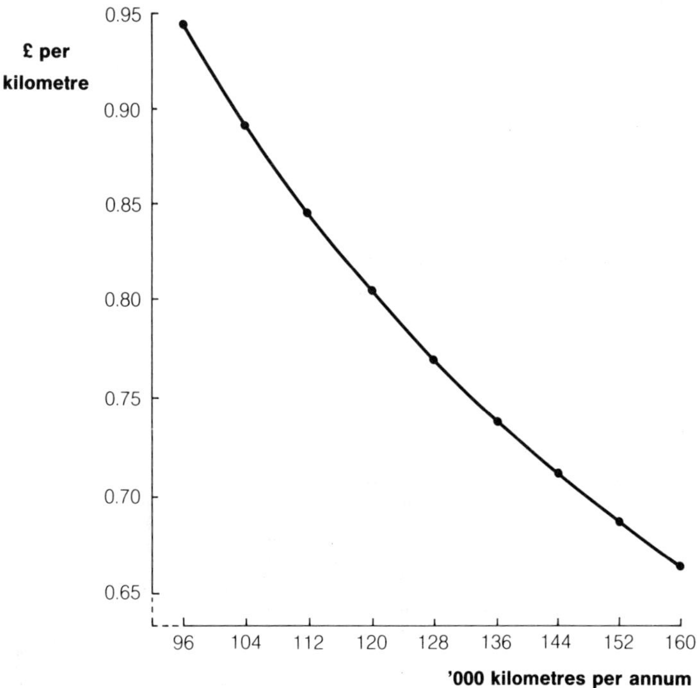

Workings	*Fixed Costs*
	£ per annum
Depreciation, 4 × £4,000	16,000
Basic maintenance, 4 × 2 × £110	880
Vehicle licence, 4 × £140	560
Vehicle insurance, 4 × £450	1,800
Tyres, 4 × 6 × £90	2,160
Drivers, 4 × £8,000	32,000
	53,400

	Variable Costs £ per '000 kilometres
Spares	100
Fuel, 1,000 ÷ 4 × 0.4	100
	200

Cost per kilometre (£)

Capacity usage	*Fixed Cost*	*Variable Cost*	*General Admin.*	*Total*
60% = 96,000 k	0.556	0.2	0.189	0.945
65% = 104,000 k	0.513	0.2	0.178	0.891
70% = 112,000 k	0.477	0.2	0.169	0.846
75% = 120,000 k	0.445	0.2	0.161	0.806
80% = 128,000 k	0.417	0.2	0.154	0.771
85% = 136,000 k	0.393	0.2	0.148	0.741
90% = 144,000 k	0.371	0.2	0.143	0.714
95% = 152,000 k	0.351	0.2	0.138	0.689
100% = 160,000 k	0.334	0.2	0.133	0.667

(c) Fixed costs incurred:

		£
Operating		53,400
General administration		19,700
		73,100
Fixed costs absorbed:		
$\frac{3}{4}$ × 128,000 × 0.571	=	54,816
+ $\frac{1}{4}$ × 96,000 × 0.571	=	13,704
		68,520
∴ Under-absorption	=	4,580

(d) Variable cost = 64 × £0.2 = £12.80
Total cost = 64 × £0.771 = £49.34

9.3 (a)

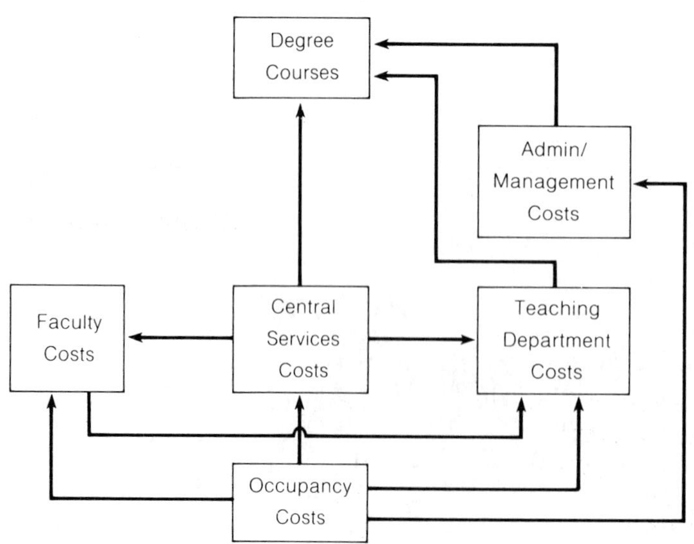

(b) *Average cost per graduate for the polytechnic*

Direct costs:	£'000
Teaching departments	5,525
Faculties	700
Administration/management	1,775
Central services	1,000
Occupancy costs	1,500
	10,500

Average cost per graduate =
£10,500,000/2,500 = £4,200

Cost apportionment

	Degree courses								
	Business Studies	Mechanical Engineering	Catering Studies	Other degrees	Teaching depts	Admin/ mgmt	Faculties	Central services	Occupancy
	£'000	£'000	£'000	£'000	£'000	£'000	£'000	£'000	£'000
Direct costs					5,525	1,775	700	1,000	1,500
Occupancy costs (Note 1)					800	280	300	120	(1,500)
Central services costs (Note 2)	22.4	33.6	22.4	313.6	560		168	(1,120)	
Faculty costs					1,168		(1,168)		
Admin/mgmt costs	51.4	102.7	82.2	1,818.7		(2,055)			
Teaching dept costs	241.6	201.3	563.7	7,046.4	(8,053)				
	315.4	337.6	668.3	9,178.7					
Number of graduates	80	50	120	2,250					
Average cost per graduate	£3,942	£6,752	£5,569	£4,079					

Note 1 *Occupancy cost apportionment*

	Square ft	*£'000*
Teaching departments	20,000	800
Faculties	7,500	300
Administration/management	7,000	280
Central services	3,000	120
	37,500	1,500

Note 2 *Central services apportionment*

	External services cost	*Apportioned savings**	*Central services cost apportionment*
	£'000	£'000	£'000
Faculties	240	72	168
Teaching departments	800	240	560
Degree courses:			
Business studies	32	9.6	22.4
Mech engineering	48	14.4	33.6
Catering studies	32	9.6	22.4
All others	448	134.4	313.6
	1,600	480	1,120

*Savings of £480,000 (£1,600,000 – 1,120,000) is apportioned in proportion to the external services cost ratio.

(c) The variation in cost per graduate from one degree to another may arise for a number of reasons including:

1 The number of years of study required may vary from one degree to another.
2 The teaching methods may differ such that one degree is more labour intensive than another with more small group tutorial work.
3 The extent of specialist laboratory or other equipment will probably be greater in engineering or catering than in business studies.
4 The drop out rate in intermediate years in a degree will affect the ultimate cost per graduate. (In the same way as abnormal losses increase costs in a processing situation.)
5 The percentage of management/admin. cost varies from one degree to another. This may reflect a large area of occupancy for laboratories and cooking areas applicable to mechanical engineering and catering studies but not to business studies.
6 The estimated external costs of service provision suggest that mechanical engineering is more demanding of central services.
7 The figures show the total costs for the year to 30 June 1987 for all years of each degree course. This is divided by the number of graduates from the current final year to give the average cost per graduate. The cohort size may be increasing or decreasing from year to year to a greater extent in one degree as compared with another, thus affecting the teaching and other inputs required.

Average cost per graduate may vary from degree to degree for reasons as itemised above. It is not necessarily correct to directly compare the average cost per graduate for one degree with that of another.

The cost trend for a specific degree through time will give useful additional information, however. It is relevant to monitor whether or not the average cost per graduate in a particular discipline is rising from one year to the next. In order that this trend analysis may be more usefully interpreted, it will be useful to have the figures analysed for each year of each degree. In addition, consideration may be given as to which costs should be included in the analysis. Some effort may be made to analyse costs according to whether or not they are avoidable if a particular degree was discontinued. This would give some indication of the marginal cost per graduate.

The relevance of the cost information might be enhanced if it is used in conjunction with other quantitative and qualitative measures such as cohort pass rates and student satisfaction as indicated from responses to questionnaires.

9.6 (a)

	Retail branches					
£'000	C	G	L	N	Y	Total
Sales	45	60	90	180	120	495
Cost of sales	30	40	60	120	80	330
Gross profit	15	20	30	60	40	165
Staff costs	8	11	14	23	17	73
Occupancy	2	5	6	12	7	32
Head office costs	3	3	3	3	3	15
Advertising	1	1	2	4	2	10
Distribution	1	1	1	1	1	5
	15	21	26	43	30	135
Net profit before discount	—	(1)	4	17	10	30
Discount received	3	4	6	12	8	33
Net profit after discount	3	3	10	29	18	63

(b) When the figures in the above table are calculated, it becomes clear that branch performance referred to in the question has been assessed before discount. After discount, all branches are making a profit. Discount is assumed to apply because cost of sales in the year was £330,000.

In order to assist the decision-maker, two important classifications of cost can be built into the analysis. Costs can be classified:

(i) According to behaviour as either fixed or variable in relation to activity. Apart from the cost of goods and staff costs, all other costs are either stated, or assumed, to be fixed in relation to activity. Staff costs are likely to lie somewhere between the two extremes of fixed and variable. In the very short-term they will be relatively fixed. However, over time, they are likely to respond broadly, if not in direct proportion, with the level of activity. This is demonstrated by a comparison of staff costs and sales in the different branches.

The contribution (sales less cost of sales and staff costs) shows the extent to which profit will be affected by a change in the level of sales in a particular branch. It should be recognised, however, that in the longer-term changes in some fixed costs may result if significant changes in sales occur.

(ii) According to their relationship to a cost object as either direct (attributable) or indirect (non-attributable). The cost object in this analysis is a particular branch. In addition to the variable costs, occupancy costs (including branch rent, rates, heat, insurance etc) are attributable to branches.

The attributable profit (sales less attributable costs) shows the effect on profit of changing the number of branches. It should be recognised, however, that other fixed costs, although not attributable, may in the longer-term be affected by a change in the number of branches.

A comparative branch statement showing contribution and attributable profit follows:

	Retail branches					
£'000	C	G	L	N	Y	Total
Sales	45	60	90	180	120	495
Cost of sales (net)	27	36	54	108	72	297
Staff costs	8	11	14	23	17	73
Contribution	10	13	22	49	31	125
Occupancy	2	5	6	12	7	32
Attributable profit	8	8	16	37	24	93
Contribution % of sales	22.2	21.7	24.4	27.2	25.8	25.3
Attributable profit % of sales	17.8	13.3	17.8	20.6	20.0	18.8

It is difficult to judge performance when comparative size of branches is not given. The occupancy costs would seem to suggest that sales and profit performance is broadly in line with size. The figures demonstrate that all branches are making a contribution, net of attributable costs, with an acceptable percentage of sales. Action should be taken to see if performance at branch G particularly can be improved, as it is not making as effective use of staff and space as the other branches.

Solutions to Chapter 12 questions

ANSWERS TO SELF-ASSESSMENT QUESTIONS

12.1 (Parts **(a)** and **(b)** will be answered together).

The question is concerned with how best to use the stock of material W, as replacement of the material is not possible. However, the optimal use of material Y also arises as further supplies cannot be obtained. It is clear that sale of material Y will not be considered. The material is highly sought after and its present use in the combined cassette deck/tuner/amplifier generates a contribution per unit of material Y of $\left(\frac{260 - 140}{4}\right)$ £30 which is well in excess of its realisable value.

It is important to be clear about the full implications of the three alternatives outlined in part (a) of the question, which include the possible uses of both materials W and Y, (having eliminated the possibility of selling material Y, or buying more). The alternatives are:

(i) 'Sold', which results in:
Sale of material W; production of the combined cassette deck/ tuner/amplifier (using material Y); buying-in of 1,200 units of sub-assembly 149 B.

(ii) 'Converted—alternative I', which results in:
Production of specialist electronic equipment (using both material W and Y); buying-in of 1,200 units of sub-assembly 149 B.

(iii) 'Adapted—alternative II', which results in:
Production of substitute 149 B (using material W); production of the combined cassette deck/tuner/amplifier (using material Y); buying-in of 900 units of sub-assembly 149 B.

The various uses of materials W and Y generate the following incremental profits:

(i) Sale of material W would generate revenue (and profit) of £14,000.

(ii) Using material Y in the production of the combined cassette deck/tuner/amplifier generates a profit of $\left(\frac{1{,}000 \text{ units}}{4} \times £120 \text{ per unit}\right) = £30{,}000$.

(iii) Buying-in 1,200 units of sub-assembly 149 B costs £720,000 (at £60 each). If only 900 units are bought-in, cost would be £630,000 (at £700 each).

(iv) Production of the specialist electronic equipment (using both materials W and Y) would cost £54,000 as follows:

Material X—400 units at £90	£36,000
Labour—10,000 hours at £4	40,000
Variable o'hd—10,000 hours at £2	20,000
Selling and delivery expenses	18,000
Magazine advertising	12,000
	126,000
Revenue—900 units at £200	180,000
	£54,000

(v) Production of the substitute 149 B (using material W) would cost £73,000 as follows:

Material Z—1,000 units at £25	£25,000
Labour—8,000 hours at £4	32,000
Variable o'hd—8,000 hours at £2	16,000
	£73,000

The value placed upon material X in the above calculations is the replacement cost as it is widely used and is available, on the assumption that an immediate order can be satisfied. The book value of existing stock is a past cost and is irrelevant.

The value placed upon material Z is the incremental cost of production which is:

	£/unit
Direct labour—3 hours at £4	12.00
Raw materials	7.00
Variable o'hd—3 hours at £2	6.00
	25.00

No incremental cost has been placed upon either material W or Y in the above calculations. The book value is irrelevant as it is a past cost. The replacement cost is not relevant, as replacement cannot be considered. The cost of materials W and Y will be an opportunity cost through alternative use. The opportunity cost is identified when alternatives are compared.

Several different bases may be used for the analysis. If an uncommitted base is assumed, as far as the use of both materials W and Y is concerned, this would recognise that:

Materials W and Y are already in stock

1,200 units of 149 B would be bought-in.

If the three alternatives are compared with this base the analysis becomes:

	Alternative (i)	Alternative (ii)	Alternative (iii)
Sell W	14,000	—	—
Produce cassette deck etc	30,000	—	30,000
Buy in less 149 B	—	—	90,000
Produce substitute 149 B	—	—	(73,000)
Produce electronic equip	—	54,000	—
	44,000	54,000	47,000

Alternative (ii) is preferred as it generates £7,000 differential profit compared with alternative (iii), and £10,000 more than alternative (i). The value placed upon materials W and Y (ie the opportunity cost) is according to the next best use (ie alternative (iii)). Thus:

Incremental profit from production of electronic equip	£54,000
Less:	
Opportunity cost of mat. W	17,000
Opportunity cost of mat. Y	30,000
	47,000
Differential profit	£7,000

The value placed upon material W is £17,000 as use in the substitute 149 B is the next best use (£90,000 saving – £73,000 incremental cost). The value placed upon material Y is £30,000 (£30 per unit) as use in the combined cassette deck/tuner/amplifier is the next best use.

Other bases may be used which alter the values in the initial analysis. The differential analysis and opportunity costs remain unchanged.

For example, alternative (i) may be assumed in the base. The analysis becomes:

	Alternative (i)	Alternative (ii)	Alternative (iii)
Sell/(not sell) W	—	(14,000)	(14,000)
Produce/(not produce) cassette deck etc	—	(30,000)	—
Buy in	—	—	90,000
Produce substitute 149 B	—	—	(73,000)
Produce electronic equip	—	54,000	—
	—	10,000	3,000

Opportunity costs of materials W and Y appear in the analysis because use of the materials is assumed in the base. These are not necessarily the opportunity costs. Comparing the alternatives, the same differential analysis results as before.

12.2 **(a)** *Marginal cost* is the cost of obtaining an additional unit of output. When decisions are being made as to the activity level to adopt, it is clearly important to know marginal cost and its behaviour as output changes, ie will marginal cost increase, decrease or remain constant if the level of activity is adjusted? This is necessary information for budgetary planning and cost control purposes. A knowledge of marginal cost can also be useful for pricing decisions since it may sometimes be rational to set a price below full cost but (except for promotional purposes) it would not be rational to produce goods for sale at a price below marginal cost. It is commonly assumed in management accounting that marginal cost is constant over the relevant range.

Average variable cost is frequently used by accountants as a surrogate for marginal cost. If marginal cost is constant irrespective of the level of output then marginal cost equals average variable cost. Since accountants assume that constant marginal cost is a common phenomenon, 'marginal cost' is frequently used as a synonym for 'variable cost'. If the marginal cost curve is U shaped then the two will not be equal but average variable cost may be a reasonable approximation to marginal cost and it may be easier to obtain a value for average variable cost. The uses will be as given in the marginal cost section above.

Imputed cost is a notional cost included in cost calculations when it is considered that the costing records are incomplete for a particular purpose. In the calculation of residual income the interest charge is an imputed cost. Similarly in calculating the economic order quantity it is often thought appropriate to include an interest charge on the investment in stock holding. The imputed cost is a form of opportunity cost. It is usually subjective but not less important because of this. Sometimes the term imputed cost is used for that part of a joint cost which is allocated to a particular cost object.

Differential cost is the difference between the outlay involved for one course of action as compared with another. It can also be appropriate to use the term to describe the differences in income between two courses of action. Differential cost is of relevance to decision-making. If alternative levels of output are being considered then the differential cost could be the sum of the marginal costs of the excess units. The calculation could be of use for decision-making purposes where the general rule is that the differential cost should be compared with differential revenue.

(b) *Opportunity cost* is relevant for decision-making because it is specifically the cost of a decision or a potential decision. A decision to use resources in a particular way is often anticipated to have two consequences (1) it opens up the prospect of anticipated (and identified) future benefits and (2) it closes down the opportunity of obtaining alternative future benefits by using the resources in the best alternative way. The opportunity cost of the benefits anticipated in (1) is the benefit foregone (displaced) under (2).

One problem of seeking to use the opportunity cost approach is the fact that often the resources that are being considered for alternative uses are not common. Instead it will more frequently be the case that one bundle of resources is being considered for one use and another overlapping (but not identical) set of resources is being considered for another use. This means that the method requires adjustment by an evaluation of the opportunity cost of the non-common resources.

Opportunity cost is a forward looking concept in that it is the estimate of a future sacrifice. It will change as the estimator's perception of the future changes. Moreover, once a decision has irrevocably been made, its opportunity cost is irrelevant.

The foregoing features of opportunity cost serve to emphasise the difficulty of including it within the framework of a costing system. Costing systems traditionally record the outcome of particular events happening; they do not record what would happen if some other event took place instead. Whilst useful and necessary for decision-making, their inclusion in a costing system as a record of past events would be very subjective and time consuming. In every situation it could not be known what the next best alternative was and what the value would have been. Thus opportunity cost would be used very selectively in costing systems eg the use of an imputed interest charge.

12.3 The following answer provides a comprehensive coverage of the full implications of the situation provided in the question and also considers different ways of carrying out the analysis. It is thus much more extensive than a typical examination answer expected. Both parts of the question are answered together.

A number of different analyses are possible depending upon the alternatives identified and the base adopted. The identification and analysis of relevant costs will depend upon the approach used.

There would seem to be three main possibilities as far as the choice of base is concerned:

(a) adopt a base which assumes that one of the contracts would be carried out;

(b) adopt a base which assumes nothing about accepting either contract, but includes the effect of accepting neither;

(c) adopt a totally uncommitted base as far as the future is concerned.

Analysis (a):

Adopt a base which assumes that one of the contracts would be carried out (eg Great Yarmouth), on the assumption that either one or the other of the contracts *must* be accepted or that both are known to be worthwhile, ie there is no question of accepting neither. There is thus one other alternative, ie carry out the Lowestoft contract.

The identification of avoidable costs and benefits would be as follows:

1 All types of cost and benefit are relevant apart from:
Project manager's salary (past cost)
Project manager's expenses (committed future costs if one or other contract is accepted)
Head Office expenses (committed future cost).

2 Of the relevant types of book depreciation, cost of materials bought and contracted for, and notional interest are past costs and therefore irrelevant (despite the fact that a different amount for depreciation is charged against each contract—this is purely a book-keeping allocation).

Depreciation (ie cost of using plant) is nevertheless relevant to the decision because of the opportunity to sub-contract plant if not required for the contracts, ie there is an opportunity cost of taking on the contracts. It has been assumed that £4,000 would be received from sub-contracting the plant if neither contract were accepted, and that no loss of value arises from its general use (ie depreciation is a function of time).

The materials bought and contracted for have a relevant value through their alternative use. Where there is more than one other alternative use (eg Lowestoft materials) the next best alternative needs to be determined. The value of the materials in store and contracted for which could be used on the Lowestoft job, is the cost saving of £27,000 (ie £30,000 × 90%) that is expected to be achievable next year if the Lowestoft contract was not undertaken, because it has a higher value than could be obtained from the sale of these materials. This value becomes a cost of the Lowestoft contract, ie additional materials would have to be purchased if the Lowestoft contract was accepted.

The materials in store which would be used if the Great Yarmouth contract was accepted, have a saleable value of £12,000 (ie £15,000 × 80%).

Interest is relevant if the cash flows of alternatives differ over time (this has been ignored).

In addition, part of the potential penalty payment is not a future cost from an economic perspective (ie at least £4,000 will be incurred whatever happens). Thus the future cost is the extra £4,000 penalty payment that would be incurred if the Lowestoft contract was accepted.

All other costs of relevant types are future costs.

3 Incremental costs/benefits compared with the base are the differences in the incremental costs/benefits between the two contracts, ie it is the relative cost/benefit levels not the absolute levels of alternatives which are identified in the analysis. Thus opportunity costs and benefits arise in the initial analysis, as follows:

	Lowestoft (£'000)	
Contract price	5	[90 – 85]
Penalty payment	(4)	[(4) – 0]
Materials:		
in store—sale of Great Yarmouth	12	[12 – 0]
—materials for other contract	(10.8)	[(10.8) – 0]
contracted for—materials for other contract	(16.2)	[(16.2) – 0]
to be purchased	3	[(17) – (20)]
Labour—local recruitment	7	[(28) – (35)]
Sub-contract plant	(1)	[0 – 1]
Profit/(Loss)	(5)	

Thus Great Yarmouth should be chosen because it yields £5,000 more profit than Lowestoft.

Analysis (b):
Adopt a base which assumes nothing about choosing Great Yarmouth or Lowestoft but includes the effect of accepting neither, ie:

Sell materials (Great Yarmouth)	£12,000
Use materials on other contract (Lowestoft)	—
Incur extra penalty costs	£ 8,000 extra
Sub-contract plant	£ 4,000

Such an approach would be appropriate where:

(i) the possibility of accepting neither contract is to be considered and it is important therefore to consider whether either contract would be profitable; or
(ii) despite the fact that one or other contract will be accepted it is nevertheless felt desirable to know what profit differences will occur because of this course of action, rather than accepting neither.

The identification of avoidable costs and benefits would be as follows:

1 In addition to the relevant costs in the analysis above, project manager's expenses also become relevant because they would not be incurred if neither contract was accepted.
2 Past costs as before of relevant types of expense.
3 Incremental costs/benefits compared with the base are the incremental costs/benefits that would arise if one or other contract is accepted compared with those that would arise if neither is accepted.

Again, opportunity costs/benefits arise in the initial analysis, eg penalty payment. If Great Yarmouth is chosen, the incremental penalty payment is zero, but there is an opportunity benefit of £8,000 (the increment that would have been incurred if neither contract were accepted) ie there is a net opportunity benefit of £8,000.

	Great Yarmouth		**Lowestoft**	
	£'000		£'000	
Contract price	85	[85 – 0]	90	[90 – 0]
Penalty payment	8	[0 – (8)]	4	[(4) – (8)]
Materials:				
in store—sale of Great Yarmouth	(12)	[0 – 12]		
—materials for other contract			(10.8)	[(10.8) – 0]
contracted for—materials for other contract			(16.2)	[(16.2) – 0]
to be purchased	(20)	[(20) – 0]	(17)	[(17) – 0]
Labour:				
Project manager—travel, etc	(2)	[(2) – 0]	(2)	[(2) – 0]
Local recruitment	(35)	[(35) – 0]	(28)	[(28) – 0]
Sub-contract plant	(3)	[1 – 4]	(4)	[0 – 4]
Profit/(Loss)	21		16	

Thus both contracts are acceptable when compared with the possibility of accepting neither (Great Yarmouth yielding an additional benefit of £21,000 and Lowestoft £16,000). Again Great Yarmouth yields £5,000 more than Lowestoft (£21,000 – £16,000).

Analysis (c):
Adopt a totally uncommitted base as far as the future allocation of relevant resources is concerned.

However, it is important to recognise the situation as it exists. The present situation as far as relevant resources are concerned is as follows:

Materials are in store;
Materials have been contracted for;
Project managers have five year contracts (4 years remaining);
Plant has been acquired;
A penalty payment of at least £4,000 will be incurred.

Whilst the adoption of an uncommitted base will in no way affect the conclusions reached in Analysis (b) above (because all possible alternatives were considered), one should nevertheless consider whether the adoption of an uncommitted base improves the analysis.
The identification of avoidable costs and revenues would be as follows:-

1 Relevant costs and revenues as in (b).
2 Past costs of relevant types as in (b).
3 Avoidable costs/benefits compared with the base are the incremental costs and benefits of each alternative.

	Great Yarmouth	**Lowestoft**	**Neither**
	£'000	£'000	£'000
Contract price	85	90	
Penalty payment	—	(4)	(8)
Materials:			
in store—sale of Great Yarmouth	—	12	12
—materials for other contract	—	(10.8)	—
contracted for—materials for			
other contract	—	(16.2)	—
to be purchased	(20)	(17)	—
Labour:			
Project manager—travel, etc	(2)	(2)	—
Local recruitment	(35)	(28)	—
Sub-contract plant	1	—	4
Profit/(Loss)	29	24	8

Thus the same decision would be reached. However the information is analysed and presented in a different way. All alternatives are looked at in complete isolation from any other opportunity, ie there are no opportunity costs at all in the analysis at this stage. Opportunity costs only arise at the stage of identifying differential costs and benefits (eg if the Great Yarmouth contract is chosen, then the opportunities of realising profit from the Lowestoft contract or from accepting neither have to be foregone). The additional benefit that would arise in the future by choosing each alternative is clear.

Also the information provided in Analyses (a) and (b) can be seen by a comparison of alternatives as follows:

Great Yarmouth v neither	£21,000 (£29,000 – £8,000)
Lowestoft v neither	£16,000 (£24,000 – £8,000)
Great Yarmouth v Lowestoft	£5,000 (£29,000 – £24,000)

Decision Data v Control Data
As has been seen in the above analysis, whenever costs are identified for decision-making the objective should be to identify true economic costs rather than accounting costs.

In the above situation the information provided by the accounting system is not relevant and a special exercise is necessary.

However, even if a special exercise is necessary whether or not it is undertaken may depend not only (a) upon the data provided by the routine information system before the decision, but also (b) upon the data that the system will provide after the decision has been taken.

Let us consider how the information system would record the outcome of the decision. It would be based on the allocation and apportionment of actual costs recorded as follows:

	Great Yarmouth	**Lowestoft**
	£'000	£'000
Contract price	85	90
Variable costs		
Penalty payment	(4)	(8)
Materials	(30)	(47)
Local labour	(35)	(28)
Project manager's expenses	(2)	(2)
	(71)	(85)
Contribution	14	5
Fixed Costs		
Project manager's salary	(5)	(5)
Plant depreciation	(3)	(4)
General administration	(4)	(4)
Interest on plant	(1)	(1)
	(13)	(14)
Net Profit	1	(9)

Clearly only one or other result would be reported depending upon which contract was chosen. Either way management responsible for the contract would not be pleased to find that the basis on which the decision is taken is not reflected in their measured performance. Alternatively, it is possible that the decision on which contract to accept (if either) will be influenced by how the outcome of the decision will be reported.

Longer-term consequences

As has been demonstrated the object of the differential costing process should be to identify the change in costs and benefits that would result from the adoption of particular alternatives and to identify the differences between alternatives. However a further important question that needs to be asked is whether the potential indirect longer-term consequences of such decisions should be considered for two reasons:

(a) even if the decision is a 'one-off', several 'one-offs' together may affect other costs in the long-run.

(b) if the situation is likely to be repeated whilst not necessarily affecting this particular decision, the viability of taking on such business on a long-term basis is an important consideration.

Thus:

(a) If the situation is regarded as a 'one-off', the possible consequences of several such decisions together could be that depreciation, project manager's salary, and general administration are affected. The profit of the Great Yarmouth and Lowestoft contracts could thus be reduced by up to £12,000 and £13,000 respectively, still better than choosing neither but considerably less so.

(b) If these contracts are typical of the contracts entered into by the Anglia Company, then a rather different exercise would be required to identify the likely long-term profitability of such contracts. An attempt should be made to identify the costs (at current price levels) that would be incurred on an ongoing basis, ie:

	Great Yarmouth		**Lowestoft**	
	£'000		£'000	
Contract price	85		90	
Variable costs				
Materials	(35)	(10 × 150% + 20)	(47)	(12 + 18 + 17)
Local labour	(35)		(28)	
Project manager's expenses	(2)		(2)	
	(72)		(77)	
Contribution	13		13	
Fixed costs				
Project manager's salary	(5)		(5)	
Plant depreciation	(3)		(4)	
General administration	(4)		(4)	
	(12)		(13)	
Net profit	1		—	

The above shows that the two contracts have similar contributions and profit. Whilst they both make a short-term contribution, over the longer-term the various fixed costs are likely to become more variable.

Solutions to Chapter 13 questions

ANSWERS TO SELF-ASSESSMENT QUESTIONS

13.1 The contractor has to make a choice between quoting for the contract, which would utilise spare capacity, and selling off/hiring out certain existing resources. The incremental cost of taking on the contract, and the revenue that could be generated from existing resources, will be considered separately.

One area of uncertainty, from the information provided, concerns the estimation of direct labour (incl. labour related variable overhead). The question suggests that the spare capacity is predominantly the existing staff. Apart from the temporary worker, direct labour can therefore be assumed to be a committed future cost. Some labour related overheads may be expected to follow directly from the employment of staff. However, the question states that 80% of the overheads are variable 'at the current level of operations'. It must be assumed, therefore, that such overheads would be incremental to the contract.

The question with the direct labour should be, 'is there likely to be any alternative work?' It is assumed in the solution below that direct labour has no opportunity cost.

Trainees' wages, normal time of supervisory staff, and administrative expenses are also committed future costs which will be incurred whether or not the contract is carried out.

The purchase cost of materials X and Y, the straight line depreciation and the estimating and design cost, are sunk costs.

	Sell off/ Hire out Existing Resources	Incremental Cost of Contract	Differential Cost of Contract
	£	£	£
Direct material:			
Material X	20,000	—	(20,000)
Material Y		(13,000)	(13,000)
Material Other		(12,000)	(12,000)
Direct labour:			
Skilled staff[1]		(6,740)	(6,740)
Trainees		(1,000)	(1,000)
Curing press[2]	2,000	—	(2,000)
Subcontract work		(20,000)	(20,000)
Supervisory staff o'time		(1,000)	(1,000)
	£22,000	£(53,740)	£(75,740)

Notes:

1 Skilled staff cost comprises:

2,720 hours at £2 per hour (£5 × 50% × 80%)	£5,440
+ 13 weeks at £100 per week	£1,300
	£6,740

2 One month depreciation has been assumed to be 4 weeks hire.

Incremental costs of £53,740 would be incurred in carrying out the contract. At the same time the opportunity to earn £22,000 from existing resources would be lost. A price of at least £75,750 would thus be required to justify taking on the contract. There would seem to be scope for tendering below £100,000.

However, it should be of concern that an estimate of the long-term cost of carrying out the contract would not justify such a price.

13.2 (i) It cannot be assumed that R is a loss maker without undertaking some analysis of the figures since the allocation of the joint costs of the distillation plant makes such judgements suspect.

Cost Benefit Analysis of Proposal to Discontinue Processing R Beyond the Split-Off Point

Benefits	
Saving of Mixing Plant's Variable Costs 0.9 (3,000)	£2,700
Saving of other Separable Costs	500
Additional Contribution from External Sale of Mixing Plant's Time 10(500 – 270)	2,300
	£5,500
Costs	
Lost Revenue 500 (10 – 1.5)	£4,250
Benefit	£1,250

(ii) Cost Benefit Analysis of Proposal to Alter the Product Mix in the Distillation Plant

Benefits	
Additional Revenue 300(20 – 12.5)	£2,250
(Assuming that there is a market for the increased volume of Q at the current price)	
Saving in Separable Costs 600 – 300	300
	£2,550
Costs	
Additional Distillation Plant Costs 300 gals @ £1	£300
Additional Variable Cost in Mixing Plant 270 (6 – 3)	810
Lost Contribution from External Sale of Mixing Plant's Time (6 – 3)(500 – 270)	690
	£1,800
Benefit	£750

Revised Profit and Loss Account

Joint Products	*Product P*	*Product Q*	*Product R*
Sales (volume)	700 gals	800 gals	500 gals
Price per gal	£12.50	£20	£1.50
Sales Revenue	£8,750	£16,000	£750
Cost of Changing Product Mix		£300	
Mixing Plant Variable Process Costs	£1,890	£4,320	
Other Separable Costs	£1,400	£800	
Surplus	£5,460	£10,580	£750

Joint Products Surplus Before Charging Joint Distillation Costs		£16,790
Distillation Plant Variable Costs		£7,500
Joint Products Total Contribution		£9,290
Revenue from Outside Sale of Mixing Plant Time 22hrs @ £500	£11,000	
Variable Cost	£5,940	
Contribution from Outside Sale of Mixing Plant Time		£5,060
		£14,350
Fixed Costs		
Distillation Plant	£2,500	
Mixing Plant	£1,350	
		£3,850
Profit		£10,500

Reconciliation

Profit in Original Profit and Loss Account	£5,500
Profit from External Sale of Mixing Plant Time at Original Level 15 hrs @ £200	£3,000
Benefit from Cessation of Processing R in Mixing Plant	£1,250
Benefit from Change in Product Mix	£750
Revised Profit	£10,500

13.3 **(a)** The optimum batch (or order) size is given by the formula

$$B = \sqrt{\frac{2DS}{H}}$$

where
B = optimum batch or order size
D = annual demand
S = 'set up' or ordering costs
H = annual holding costs per unit.

In the context of Pink's circumstances the application of this formula is complicated by the fact that several of Pink's costs are not decision variables and will be incurred irrespective of batch size decisions; these costs must be excluded from the calculations.

Costs to which Pink is committed will not be altered by the decision under consideration and are therefore not relevant for the current application. These costs are:

(i) Skilled labour costs—because skilled labour is being paid idle time and its total costs will not alter as a result of the current decision.

(ii) Fixed overheads—because these are to be incurred whatever batch size is produced.

(iii) Standard cost of manufactured material Dee—because the standard cost includes both skilled labour and fixed overhead costs (see below).

The relevant costs are those which will be altered as a result of the decision. These costs are:

(i) Costs of raw materials purchased from external suppliers.

(ii) Unskilled labour.

(iii) Variable overheads.

(iv) Machine parts.

(v) Incremental cost of manufactured material Dee, ie costs (i)-(iii) above only, and not the full standard cost.

This means that the following are the relevant decision variables:

(i) Demand (D) 4,000 units per annum.

(ii) Set up costs (S) Machine parts £70.

(iii) Annual holding costs. This is comprised of two elements:

- **(a)** cost of storage; and
- **(b)** cost of money tied up in stocks.
- **(a)** Cost of storage per unit of Exe 0.40 × £20 = £8
- **(b)** Costs of financing stocks. Fixed (non incremental) costs associated with stocks should not be included in this analysis. Therefore the incremental costs of stock, on which incremental interest is payable, are

	£	£
Product Dee—relevant costs		
raw materials	8	
labour—unskilled	4	
variable overheads	3	15
Other raw materials		13
Labour—unskilled		7
Variable overheads		5
Incremental cost of production		£40

The cost of money is 15% × £40 = £6 per unit per year

Total annual holding costs (H) per unit are

	£
Storage	8
Cost of money	6
	14

Applying these figures gives an optimum batch size

$$B = \sqrt{\frac{2 \times 4{,}000 \times £70}{£14}} = 200 \text{ units}$$

Cost of current policy

	£
Set up costs 4 × £70	280
Holding costs (average stocks × holding costs)	
$\frac{1{,}000}{2}$ × £14	7,000
Total cost	£7,280

Cost of optimum policy	£
Set up costs $\frac{4,000}{200} \times £70$	1,400
Holding costs (average stocks × holding costs)	
$\frac{200}{2} \times £14$	1,400
	£2,800
Annual savings	£4,480

(b) The economic order quantity is

$$B = \sqrt{\frac{2 \times 10,000 \times £100}{£8}} = 500 \text{ units}$$

This is the order quantity which minimises the total of the holding and the ordering costs associated with Wye. However, the EOQ model does not give explicit consideration to the variation in purchase price per unit and so excludes a potentially important decision variable.

Therefore Pink should order in batches of 500 units unless the benefits of the discounts outweigh the disadvantages of the higher storage or holding costs which result from ordering in higher quantities.

A comparison of total costs shows:

(i) *Purchase price £20.00. Ordering quantity 500*	£
Cost of materials 10,000 × £20	200,000
Cost of ordering $\frac{10,000}{500} \times £100$	2,000
Holding costs $\frac{500}{2} \times £8$	2,000
	£204,000

(ii) *Purchase price £19.80. Order quantity 1,000*	£
Cost of materials 10,000 × £19.80	198,000
Cost of ordering $\frac{10,000}{1,000} \times £100$	1,000
Holding costs $\frac{1,000}{2} \times £8$	4,000
	£203,000

(iii) *Purchase price £19.60. Order quantity 2,000*	£
Cost of materials 10,000 × £19.60	196,000
Cost of ordering $\frac{10,000}{2,000} \times £100$	500
Holding costs $\frac{2,000}{2} \times £8$	8,000
	£204,500

Therefore Pink should order Wyes in batches of 1,000 at a unit price of £19.80.

(c) The economic order quantity model used in part (a) is a simple mathematical model which is useful in determining optimum batch, or order, size and will produce correct results in cases where its assumptions apply and the data requirements of the model are met. However in many cases the real world complications may be difficult to model or data may be difficult to obtain and so application of this simple formulae may only be useful as a guide.

Limitations or difficulties which could be referred to include:

(i) Obtaining correct data—correct incremental figures for holding costs and set up, or ordering, costs may be extremely difficult to obtain.

(ii) Certainty—the model is, strictly, only applicable in cases of certainty. In cases of uncertainty concerning demand or cost structures a more sophisticated approach may be required.

(iii) Speed of production or delivery—the model is useful where orders are fulfilled in full at a given time. Any delay between placing an order and its fulfilment in a single complete delivery, 'lead time', does not affect the size of order. However fulfilment of a single order, or output of a single production run, may be spread over several weeks resulting in a slower build up of stocks and increasing optimum batch, or order, size.

(iv) Quantity discounts—the model indicates the order size which minimises the total of holding costs and set up, or order, costs and ignores any quantity discounts. As was seen in part (b) these discounts may be an important determinant of optimum order size.

(v) Constant rate of demand—the annual demand is assumed constant throughout the year. If there are seasonal variations in demand then this should be reflected in seasonal variations in optimum order quantities.

13.4 (a)

	Wholesale	*Retail*
	£'000	*£'000*
Sales	500	700
Cost of Goods Sold	420	420
Gross Profit	80	280
Selling	21	105
Administration	5.7	32.3
Advertising	31	31
Distribution	15	85
Storage	—	24
Net Profit	7.3	2.7
Net Profit per Customer	£292	£6.75

The company is thus barely profitable, with, on the face of it, little justification for the proposal to employ additional sales representatives so as to supply retailers directly and replace wholesalers.

The above calculations of the costs attributable to the separate wholesale and retail operations are based upon the relationships stated in the question. It should be noted that an equal split of advertising has been made based on the fact that the same cost value of goods are supplied to each operation.

(b) Only average figures are available as a guide to the worthwhileness of re-allocating resources, or of employing additional resources.

A calculation is made below of the contribution currently generated from the wholesale customers, and the contribution that may be made by dealing direct with the 500 retail outlets currently served by the wholesalers. Three different scenarios are considered.

	Sales via wholesalers	Sales direct to retail outlets		
		Scenario 1	Scenario 2	Scenario 3
Wholesale outlets	25	—	—	—
Retail outlets	500	500	500	480
No. of sales reps calls	450	5,625	5,625	5,400
No. of sales reps	1	7	7	6
No. of invoice lines	255,000	255,000	318,750	306,000
	£'000	*£'000*	*£'000*	*£'000*
Sales	500	700	875	840
Variable production cost	294	294	367.5	352.8
Selling	21	147	147	126
Administration	5.7	32.3	40.375	38.76
Distribution	15	85	106.25	102
Storage	—	24	30	28.8
Net contribution	164.3	117.7	183.875	191.64

Assumptions:

A. All scenarios

(i) distribution costs of supplying the retail outlets are all variable and in proportion to sales.

(ii) advertising costs are a discretionary fixed cost and are unaffected by the decision being made.

(iii) other costs are variable in relation to the factors stated in the question.

(iv) invoice lines and sales representatives calls will maintain the same relationship with sales/outlets as at present.

(v) spare production capacity exists sufficient for a 12.5% increase in sales.

B. Scenario 1

(i) the amount of goods sold will remain the same as at present through wholesalers but at prices equivalent to those currently obtained from retail outlets.

(ii) an increase in calls, and thus sales representatives, of 25% will be required to service the 500 retail outlets compared with the existing 400 outlets. As this results in a requirement for 6.25 reps it is assumed that 7 additional reps would be employed. Further sales, (not assumed), may result.

C. Scenario 2

(i) goods sold will be 25% higher than the current level achieved from retail outlets, due to the 500 extra outlets compared with the existing 400 outlets currently directly served. This also represents a 25% increase in sales over that currently achieved from the 500 outlets via wholesalers. Selling prices as per scenario 1.

(ii) calls and sales representatives as per scenario 1.

D. Scenario 3

(i) additional sales representatives will be limited to 6, 20% higher than the existing retail outlet level. Sales outlets and sales have been adjusted accordingly. Further sales may be generated (not assumed) from outlets not visited.

On the basis of the figures it would seem worthwhile to sell direct to all retail outlets, as long as by doing so current average sales per outlet/call can be achieved. However, an important question is what additional distribution costs will be incurred due to the location of the retail outlets currently served by wholesalers. Average costs only have been included in the calculations. A further important question is whether sufficient spare production capacity exists to accommodate the assumed increase in sales. Very broad assumptions only have been made about the mix of sales, cost behaviour, and other relationships. A more thorough study is required.

13.5 (a)

Calculation of Long-Term Monthly Savings from Acceptance of Contractor's Offer

	(£'000s)	(£'000s)
Relevant cost of internal processing (*Note* 1)		
Material *A*	20	
B	60	
C	20	
Plant rental	25	
Variable overhead	2	127
Contractor's cost—20,000 × £4.50		90
Long-term monthly benefit of utilising the contractor		37

Note 1 In the circumstances of this question neither fixed overheads nor the operator's labour costs are avoidable as a result of the decision to be made.

Hence, as they will not be altered by the decision currently being considered they are not decision variables and so may be ignored. If it is wished to bring the figures into the analysis then they must be shown as costs for both alternatives thereby leaving the monthly benefit of £37,000 unaltered.

The contractor's cost of £90,000 per month is more than offset by the saving (opportunity benefit) of £127,000 per month from ceasing internal processing.

However, the total monthly savings of £127,000 would not be achievable for four months, due to expense commitments already made. Lawson is committed to paying for new materials and the plant hire charge during the contract expiry period—hence the following costs may be considered sunk costs for the period of contract expiry and as relevant costs thereafter. The relevant periods are:

	Cost (£'000s)	*Months for which cost is 'sunk'*	*Month from which cost is relevant*
Material *A*	20	1, 2	3
B	60	1	2
C	20	1, 2, 3, 4	5
Hire of plant	25	1, 2, 3	4

There is thus no cost saving for these resources during the contract expiry period from accepting the contractor's offer. The only benefit would be the opportunity to sell off unwanted materials. It would be worthwhile taking delivery of, and selling off, materials B and C for £20,000 (one month only), and £9,000 (for four months) respectively. Lawson should choose not to take delivery of material A if the contractor's offer was accepted as its disposal costs are greater than its salvage value.

A comparison of net relevant costs of contracting over months 1–5, with the relevant costs of internal processing, (including opportunity costs of not selling materials B and C), is as follows:

Comparison of Relevant Costs—Months 1–5

	(£'000*s*)				
	Month				
	1	*2*	*3*	*4*	*5*
Cost of contracting	90	90	90	90	90
Relevant costs of internal processing					
Material *A*	—	—	20	20	20
B	20	60	60	60	60
C	9	9	9	9	20
Hire of plant	—	—	—	25	25
Variable overhead	2	2	2	2	2
Relevant costs of internal processing	31	71	91	116	127
Benefit of contracting	(59)	(19)	1	26	37

(The sale of materials B and C could alternatively have been included as a revenue, reducing the cost of contracting, with nil cost of internal processing).

Therefore Lawson should accept the contractor's offer with effect from month 3. This will entail cancellation of contracts as follows:

Material A—Notice of cancellation given immediately. Material accepted and used for two months.

Material B—Notice of cancellation given at the end of month 1. Material accepted and used for two months.

Material C—Notice of cancellation given immediately. Material accepted and used for two months. Material accepted and sold for months 3 and 4.

Plant —Notice of cancellation given immediately. Not used in month 3.

(b) **(i)** If the plant were owned then only its opportunity value would be relevant to any decision. The monthly depreciation would not be relevant. As the plant has no alternative use its opportunity value is zero. Hence the long-term monthly benefit of contracting is reduced to £12,000, but the optimum decision is unaltered.

(ii) In this case the labour cost becomes an avoidable cost and so should be shown as a relevant cost of internal processing. This would increase the advantage of the external contract by £720 per month (if all labour related overheads are variable costs). Again this would leave the decision unaltered.

However, the possible alternative use of labour should be questioned in any case. If, in part (a), it was reasonable to assume that the labour would be usefully employed elsewhere in the event of ceasing internal processing, it would be a relevant cost anyway.

(iii) If Lawson were required to accept delivery of material A then the additional costs to Lawson of such acceptance of delivery would be £4,000 per month as the total sales revenue (£16,000) would be less than the necessary costs of sale and delivery (£20,000). Therefore this £4,000 should be brought into the analysis for months 1–4 along with the fact that the purchase cost of material A (£20,000) is now committed in months 3 and 4 and is not, therefore, a relevant cost of internal processing. The benefit of contracting would then become:

Month	1	2	3	4	5
Benefit of contracting (£'000*s*)	(63)	(23)	(23)	2	37

Hence Lawson should now accept the contractor's offer with effect from month 4 and continue its own processing for months 1–3. If a penalty payment for non delivery of £0.05 per unit (£2,000 in total, per month) were incurred then the benefit of contracting would become:

Month	1	2	3	4	5
Benefit of contracting (£'000*s*)	(61)	(21)	(21)	4	37

This would leave the revised decision unaltered.

If the penalty payment were £0.15 per unit then Lawson would be advised to accept delivery and sell material A as this latter option is, effectively, equivalent to a penalty of only £0.10 per unit.

13.6 **(a)** The alternative courses of action open to Hilton Ltd are:

(i) To close department K immediately.

(ii) To operate department K for a further year with production and sales of 10,000 units.

(iii) To operate department K for a further year with production and sales of 20,000 units.

The cash flows in each of the situations (i) to (iii) above will be compared with an uncommitted base which recognises the situation as it currently exists. The base for the analysis will simply recognise that:

A quantity of both materials A and B are in stock.

Materials in the other department, currently costing £1.8 per kilo, are being bought and used for all requirements.

The machine is available for use/sale.

The cash flows relating to each of the alternatives, compared with this base, are:

		Alternative		
		(i) *Immediate Closure*	(ii) 10,000 *Units*	(iii) 20,000 *Units*
	Note	(£'000*s*)	(£'000*s*)	(£'000*s*)
Cash Inflow/Savings				
Sales of production		—	90	160
Sale of machine	1	43	35	30
Material B—savings	2, 3	18	9	—
—sales	2	5	—	—
Total inflow/savings		66	134	190
Cash Outflows				
Material A—disposal arrangements	4	2	2	2
—disposal costs		15	10	5
Material B—purchase		—	—	10
Labour—training		—	20	20
—costs		—	30	60
Variable overhead		—	13	26
Foreman	5	2	6	6
Advertising		—	—	15
Total outflows		19	81	144
Net inflow		47	53	46

Note 1 Sales value now £43,000
Sales value in one year = £40,000 − (£0.50 × production level).

Note 2 Immediate closure releases 15,000 kilos of material B which can be used thus:
(i) 10,000 kilos used as substitute in another department—value £18,000;
(ii) 5,000 kilos sold—value 5,000 × £1.

Note 3 An activity level of 10,000 leaves 5,000 kilos of B available to be used as the substitute material.

Note 4 Although this cost has been included for the purposes of analysis, it is common to all options open to Hilton and it may be ignored for the purposes of comparing between those options. A consistent exclusion of this cost would not alter the relative desirability of each option.

Note 5 Immediate closure requires £2,000 paid to the foreman.
Closure after one year requires only salary to be paid to the foreman.

Hilton Ltd would be advised to operate department K at the level of 10,000 units for the forthcoming year and then to close the department and dispose of its remaining assets.

(b) **(i)** If the factory space could be rented for £8,000 then this must be treated as a cash inflow relating to immediate closure. The net inflow relating to immediate closure then becomes £55,000—shown thus:

	(£'000*s*)
Inflows from (a) above	66
Plus rent	8
	74
Outflows	19
	£55

This then becomes the best action and Hilton would be advised to close the department immediately, to dispose of all assets and raw materials and to rent out the factory space for one year.

(ii) A 90% learning curve means that each time production doubles the *average* time taken to produce each unit falls to 90% of the previous average figure.

Average per unit for 5,000 units = 1 hour
Average per unit for 10,000 units = 1 × 0.9 hours = 0.9 hours
Average per unit for 20,000 units = 0.9 × 0.9 hours = 0.81 hours

Production labour costs are:

Production ×	Average time per unit ×	Cost per hour =	Total cost
10,000 units ×	0.9 hours ×	£3	= £27,000
20,000 units ×	0.81 hours ×	£3	= £48,600

Using these figures gives net inflow for each action as follows:

(i) Immediate closure £47,000
(ii) 10,000 units £56,000
(iii) 20,000 units £57,400

Hence Hilton would now be advised to operate department K at 20,000 units for the forthcoming year.

Solutions to Chapter 14 questions

ANSWERS TO SELF-ASSESSMENT QUESTIONS

14.1

	Product 1	Product 2	Product 3	Total
Sales Maxima in money	£57,500	£96,000	£125,000	
Selling Price	£23	£32	£25	
Sales Maxima in physical units	2,500	3,000	5,000	
Machine Time required for one unit of output				
Type A	1	2	3	
Type B	1.5	3	1	
Machine Time required for Sales Maxima				
Type A	2,500	6,000	15,000	23,500
Type B	3,750	9,000	5,000	17,750

Since the usage of B machine time (for production to meet maximum sales) is less than the available machine time of 21,000 hours, whereas the requirement for A machine time is higher than the time available (23,500 hours required, 9,800 hours available), it follows that type A machine time is the limiting factor. The optimal production programme is now determined by ranking the products by means of the unit contribution per hour of type A machine time.

	Product 1	Product 2	Product 3	Total
Unit Contribution	£5	£7	£8	
Type A Machine Time required for one unit of output	1	2	3	
Contribution per hour of Type A machine time	£5	£3.5	£2.67	
Ranking of Products	1	2	3	
Optimal Production Plan				
Units	2,500	3,000	433.33	
Type A Machine Time required	2,500	6,000	1,300	9,800
Contribution	£12,500	£21,000	£3,466.67	£36,966.67
Fixed Overheads				21,000.00
Profit				£15,966.67

14.2 (a) It is first necessary, as a limiting factor situation clearly exists, to establish the additional cost of buying-in, (compared with variable production cost in normal time), per unit of scarce resource (ie metal pressing hours).

	Component			
	A	B	C	D
Variable production cost per unit	£28.50	£27.50	£28.50	£72.00
Buying-in cost per unit	£30.00	£29.50	£26.00	£84.00
Additional cost of buying-in per unit	£1.50	£2.00	(£2.50)	£12.00
Machine hours per unit	1	2	1	6
Additional cost of buying-in per machine hour	£1.50	£1.00	(£2.50)	£2.00
Priority for manufacture	2	3	—	1

Product C would not be manufactured thus reducing the requirement for machine capacity. The remaining three products require machine time as follows:

Component A:	2,000 units × 1 hr =	2,000 hrs
B:	3,500 units × 2 hr =	7,000 hrs
D:	2,800 units × 6 hr =	16,800 hrs
		25,800 hrs

Shortage of capacity still exists. If additional requirements are satisfied by outside purchase of components, the 20,000 hours of press time should be utilised as follows in order to minimise costs:

Component D	16,800
Component A	2,000
	18,800
Component B	1,200
	20,000

5,800 hours of component B would have to be bought-in (2,900 units).

If, on the other hand, second shift operations are being considered in order to overcome the capacity limitation, production should be organised in normal time in such a way as to minimise excess labour costs on the second shift. Labour costs per machine hour should be the deciding factor, with the product with the lowest labour cost per machine hour being produced on the second shift. First, it should be recognised that component C would still be bought-in.

Component B has easily the lowest labour cost per hour of machine time. The utilisation of the 20,000 hours of press time would thus be the same whether a part second shift operation is provided or all additional requirements are bought-in.

(b) If 2,900 units of component B are bought-in, the additional cost would be:

2,900 units × £2.00 per unit = £5,800
(or 5,800 machine hours × £1.00 per hour)

If the 2,900 units are produced on a part second shift, the additional cost would be:

2,900 units × £1.00* per unit	= £2,900
+ 6 × £250	= £1,500
	£4,400

*£4.00 per unit direct labour × 25%.

The balance of components should be provided as follows:

Product C: Buy-in 1,500 units
B: Produce 2,900 units on part second shift.

14.3 At point C, spare capacity exists in Process Z. The use of capacity in Process Z is:

		Operating Hours in Process Z
Product A	$\frac{36,000}{100} \times 5$	1,800
Product B	$\frac{3,000}{100} \times 10$	300
		2,100

Spare capacity in Process Z is thus 300 hours at point C. If full capacity was maintained in Process Y, whilst at the same time substituting production of Product B for Product A, the production schedule would move along the line CF towards F and would gradually eliminate the spare capacity in Process Z. The effect on the spare capacity in Process Z, for every operating hour in Process Y that is transferred from production of A to production of B, would be as follows:

		Spare Capacity in Process Z
Product A	$\frac{-100}{6} = -16.\dot{6}$ units $\times \frac{5}{100} =$	$+0.8\dot{3}$
Product B	$\frac{+100}{8} = +12.5$ units $\times \frac{10}{100} =$	-1.25
		$-0.41\dot{6}$

Thus every hour substituted in Process Y would reduce spare capacity in Process Z by $0.41\dot{6}$ hours. As spare capacity in Process Z at point C is 300 hours, substitution of 720 hours ($300 \div 0.41\dot{6}$) in Process Y would eliminate the spare capacity in Process Z, and thus take the production schedule to point F.

The change in production schedule from C to F would be:

Product A	$-16.\dot{6}$ units × 720 hours = $-$12,000 units
Product B	$+12.5$ units × 720 hours = + 9,000 units

and thus the revised production schedule becomes:

Product A	36,000 − 12,000 = 24,000 units
Product B	3,000 + 9,000 = 12,000 units

Additional contribution generated from the change of 720 hours in Process Y would be £3,000, as each hour allocated to Product B in Process Y generates £37.5 contribution, as opposed to £$33.\dot{3}$ if allocated to Product A. Thus total contribution moves from £81,000 to £84,000.

14.4 (b) The optimal plan given in the question is identified from the optimal tableau by the appearance of the number '1' in a particular column, which if then carried along the row to the far right hand column provides the solution for that variable. For example, in the first row the number '1' appears in the 'S2' column. The far right hand column gives a value of 1,150. The unsatisfied demand for product 2 (S2) is 1,150 units. This is because optimal output of product 2 is 1,850 units compared with the sales maximum established in Self-assessment question 14.1, of 3,000 units.

The shadow prices appear on the bottom row of the tableau. They represent the increase in total contribution that would result from the availability of one more unit of the particular resource (or reduction if equivalent resource is lost).

If unsatisfied demand for product 1 (S1) occurred, (ie if demand for product 1 could be increased), contribution would increase by £1.50 for each additional unit of product 1 produced and sold. The increase of a unit of product 1 could be accommodated by reducing output of product 2 by 0.5 units (with a resulting increase in the unsatisfied demand for that product of 0.5 units). The additional unit of product 1 would yield a contribution of £5 per unit. Contribution from product 2 is £7 per unit and thus £3.50 contribution would be lost. The net gain would be £1.50.

The above changes in units of product are obtained from the column in the optimal tableau that contains the opportunity cost value (in this case £1.50). The S1 column represents unsatisfied demand for product 1. The number '1' represents the increase of 1 unit of product 1 (the solution variable on this row of the tableau) ie it is the extra unit of product 1 that could be sold if there is unsatisfied demand. The number '−0.5' represents half a unit of product 2 (the solution variable on this row of the tableau) that would have to be given up in order to provide the necessary production capacity for one more unit of product 1.

The shadow price of £2.429 for type A machine time indicates that, if an additional hour of time could be obtained, this would increase total contribution by £2.429. This is achieved by making 0.429 of a unit more of product 3 and 0.143 of a unit less of product 2, with the corresponding effect on the unsatisfied demand for those products. The net effect on contribution results from:

Product 3	0.429	units × £8/unit =	£3.43
Product 2	(0.143)	units × £7/unit =	(£1.00)
			2.43

The shadow price of £0.714 for type B machine time indicates that, if an additional hour of time could be obtained, this would increase total contribution by £0.714. This is achieved by making 0.429 of a unit more of product 2 and 0.286 of a unit less of product 3, with the corresponding effect on the unsatisfied demand for those products. The net effect on contribution results from:

Product 2	0.429	units × £7/unit =	£3.00
Product 3	(0.286)	units × £8/unit =	(£2.29)
			0.71

The accountant might make use of the machine time shadow prices if there is the possibility of acquiring extra machine time. The prices can then be interpreted as the upper limit to the premium which Corpach Ltd should be willing to pay to acquire an extra machine hour. Similarly the shadow price of Product 1 is the upper limit to advertising or promotional expense designed to increase the demand for that product by one unit—if such promotional activity is to be profitable. It must be emphasised that the shadow prices only operate within a limited range of machine time (or demand) values.

The figure in the bottom right hand corner of the tableau (35,050) is the total contribution that the programme should yield. It can be checked as follows:

	£
2,500 units of Product 1 produces 2,500 × 5 =	12,500
1,850 units of Product 2 produces 1,850 × 7 =	12,950
1,200 units of Product 3 produces 1,200 × 8 =	9,600
	£35,050

The profit will be £35,050 less the fixed overheads (£18,000) ie £17,050. It should be noted that although the anticipated total contribution has fallen by £1,917, the anticipated profit has increased by £1,083, ie the fixed overheads saved by the fire (£3,000) exceed the lost contribution (£1,917) by £1,083.

(c) LP was not required to obtain a solution for the facts set out in part (a) as there was only one constraint which affected more than one decision variable. This condition ceased to apply to the facts as set out in part (b) so that it was no longer possible to rank products by means of the contribution per unit of limiting factor.

ANSWERS TO EXERCISES

14.1 (a)

	Component 12	Component 14	Product VW	Product XY
	£ per unit	£ per unit	£ per unit	£ per unit
Variable cost	42	32	30	64
Purchase price	60	30	—	—
Selling price	—	—	33	85
Saving from manufacture	18	—	—	—
Additional cost of manufacture	—	(2)	—	—
Contribution	—	—	3	21

Thus: Produce component 12—a saving of £18 per component
Buy in component 14—cheaper to buy in by £2 per component
Produce and sell VW—a contribution of £3 per unit
Produce and sell XY—a contribution of £21 per unit.

The above evaluation is based upon the following assumptions:

(i) Prime costs and variable overheads vary directly with the units produced/sold.

(ii) No additional costs will be incurred as a result of purchasing component 14 eg inspection costs, rejects as a result of poor quality or delivery failures, etc.

(iii) Production of any of the components/products will not alter the fixed costs of the company, in the coming year. Are there any fixed costs specific to any/all the components/products which could be saved if a particular component/product were not produced?

(iv) Limited resources will not restrict the required production of the components/ products identified above and also the production of these items will not restrict the manufacture and sale of other profitable products. If this is not the case then a calculation of the relative profitability/contribution for ALL products sold by the company must be made.

(v) Budgeted variable cost figures as well as budgeted selling prices are accurate.

(b) The additional information given in this section has the following implications:
Note Component 14 is not considered because it is cheaper to buy in than produce.

Special machine requirements	Component 12	Product VW	Product XY
Required production	7,000	5,000	4,000
Machine time required—hours	8	6	12
Machine hours required	56,000	30,000	48,000
		Total = 134,000 hours	

Hours available	80,000
Hours required	134,000
Hours of shortfall	(54,000)

Because of the shortfall in required machine hours a *ranking* process must be pursued.

The ranking may be done on the basis of contribution/saving per machine hour viz:

	Component 12	Product VW	Product XY
	£ per unit	£ per unit	£ per unit
Contribution/saving	18	3	21
÷ MAC machine hours needed	8	6	12
= Contribution/saving per MAC machine hour	£2.25	£0.50	£1.75
Ranking	(1)	(3)	(2)

Thus produce all component 12 = 7,000 × 8 hours = 56,000 hours and produce and sell the balance of time available for product XY being

	80,000
less	56,000
	24,000

hours left divided by 12 hours per unit for product XY means that 2,000 of the saleable 4,000 units of XY can be produced.

Summary

Produce component 12	7,000 units
Produce product XY	2,000 units

Comments: This solution is a short-term decision ie given the constraint of the MAC machine hours of 80,000 per year.

14.2 The criteria* provided in the question would be relevant in the following circumstances: (*see workings at end of answer for calculations)

I *Contribution per unit*

If the whole of the requirements for one component are to be bought-in the ranking order for which component to buy-in is A, B, C. The selection of which component will depend upon availability of production capacity in relation to expected sales demand.

The increase in production capacity if the whole of the requirements for one component are bought-in is:

$$\text{Buy-in A} = \frac{\text{10 hours released}}{\text{36 hours used on B\&C}}$$
$$= 27.8\%$$

$$\text{Buy-in B} = \frac{\text{16 hours released}}{\text{30 hours used on A\&C}}$$
$$= 53.3\%$$

$$\text{Buy-in C} = \frac{\text{20 hours released}}{\text{26 hours used on A\&B}}$$
$$= 76.9\%$$

Thus buying-in of component A offers the highest unit contribution but sales increase would be limited to 27.8%. Component B is next best but sales increase is limited to 53.3%. Buying-in of component C, although least attractive per unit, would enable sales to increase by 76.9%.

The increase in contribution that could result is:

$$\text{Buy-in A} = 1.278 \times £98 = £125.2$$

$$\text{Increase} = \frac{17.2}{108} = 15.9\%$$

$$\text{Buy-in B} = 1.533 \times £94 = £144.1$$

$$\text{Increase} = \frac{36.1}{108} = 33.4\%$$

$$\text{Buy-in C} = 1.769 \times £86 = £152.1$$

$$\text{Increase} = \frac{44.1}{108} = 40.8\%$$

There would be no point buying-in B rather than A until the sales increase is 33.2% $\left[\left(\frac{125.2 - 94}{94}\right) \times 100\%\right]$. There would be no point buying-in C rather than B until the sales increase is 67.6% $\left[\left(\frac{144.1 - 86}{86}\right) \times 100\%\right]$

II *Contribution per production hour*

If the whole of the requirements of one component are to be bought-in, and sales potential exceeds production capacity whichever component is bought-in, buying-in component C provides the highest contribution per hour of production because, despite its higher on-cost, it provides the opportunity for considerably increased production and sales. If it is expected that the sales demand increase will be more than 76.9%, selection of which component to buy-in should be on the basis of contribution per production hour.

111 *Extra cost per production hour saved*

If buying-in of part requirements of components is acceptable/possible the question becomes simply how best to fully utilise the hours available, whatever sales increase is anticipated. Buying-in part requirements of components would give greater flexibility, permitting adjustment of buying-in requirements according to how sales demand turns out.

(a) (1) If the anticipated sales increase is 50% criteria 1 is relevant. Component A would be selected for buying-in first but, as previously established, capacity is only increased by 27.8%. The next best alternative is to buy-in component B which would provide sufficient capacity to satisfy the sales demand. Relative contribution is:

£94 per unit × 1.5 = £141

Alternatively this can be expressed as:

(i) using the information from criteria 11, 45 hours of production × £3.13 per hour = £141

(ii) using the information from criteria 111,

£108 per unit × 1.5	= £162
less 24 hours × £0.875 on-cost =	(£21)
	£141

(2) If the anticipated sales increase is 80% criteria 11 is relevant. Component C would be selected for buying-in. Relative contribution is:

46 hours of production × £3.31 per hour = £152.2

Capacity increase is restricted to 76.9%. Alternatively relative contribution can be expressed as:

(i) using the information from criteria 1,

£86 per unit × 1.769 = £152.2

(ii) using the information from criteria 111,

£108 per unit × 1.769	= £191.1
less 35.4 hours × £1.1 on-cost =	(£38.9)
	£152.2

(b) criteria 111 is relevant whatever the anticipated sales increase. Component B should be bought-in first, then A, and finally C.

(1) If the sales increase anticipated is 50%, then:

Produce C	30 hours	(20 × 1.5)
Produce A	15 hours	(10 × 1.5)
	45	
Produce B	1 hour	(out of 24 hours required)
	46	

Relative contribution is:

£108 per unit × 1.5	= £162
less 23 hours × £0.875 on-cost	= (20.1)
	£141.9

(2) If the sales increase anticipated is 80%, then:

Produce C	36 hours (20 × 1.8)
Produce A	10 hours (out of 18 hours required)
	46 hours

In addition the equivalent of 28.8 hours of component B (16 × 1.8) will be bought-in. Relative contribution is:

£108 per unit × 1.8	=	£194.4
less 8 hours of A × £1.00 on-cost	=	(8.0)
28.8 hours of B × £0.875 on-cost	=	(25.2)
		£161.2

* *Workings*:
Contribution per unit if all components are manufactured:

Selling price	£250
Variable cost	142
Contribution	£108

Additional cost of buying-in (per unit):

Component A	£10	(36 – 26)
Component B	£14	(46 – 32)
Component C	£22	(54 – 32)

		Component bought-in	
Criteria	*A*	*B*	*C*
Contribution per unit	£98 (108 – 10)	£94 (108 – 14)	£86 (108 – 22)
Contribution per production hour	£2.72 ($\frac{98}{36}$)	£3.13 ($\frac{94}{30}$)	£3.31 ($\frac{86}{26}$)
Extra cost per production hour saved	£1.00 ($\frac{10}{10}$)	£0.875 ($\frac{14}{16}$)	£1.10 ($\frac{22}{20}$)

14.3 (a)

Calculation of Variable Costs per Operating Hour

	Department 4	*Department 5*
Budgeted Fixed Overhead	£36,000	£50,400
Normal Hours per annum	1,800	1,800
	£	£
Fixed Overhead per hour	20	28
Overhead Absorption Rate	40	40
Variable Overhead per hour	20	12
Power Cost per hour	40	60
Lost Contribution from outside work	10	—
Total Variable Cost per Operating Hour	£70	£72

Unit Variable Cost of New Product

	£
Direct Material	10
Variable Operating Cost:	
Department 4 0.75(70)	52.5
Department 5 0.33(72)	24
	£86.5

	£	£	£
Selling Prices under Consideration	100	110	120
Variable Cost	86.5	86.5	86.5
Contribution	£13.5	£23.5	£33.5
Demand per annum	1,067*	1,000	500
Total Contribution per annum	£14,404	£23,500	£16,750

*Restricted to production possible from available free time in department 4 assuming that 100% utilisation of capacity is possible and that the use of departmental time for mainline products is more profitable than for the new product.

Available free time = 16 × 50 = 800 hours

At 45 minutes per unit in department 4, production units possible of the new product are 800 × $\frac{60}{45}$ = 1,067 units.

The preferred option is to produce and sell 1,000 units per annum of the new product utilising 750 of the available hours, which represents 15 hours per week in department 4. Requirement for department 5 time is 333 hours (1,000 ÷ $\frac{1}{3}$) which is $6\frac{2}{3}$ hours per week. The best selling price is £110 per unit. Department 4 has one hour per week available for sale at £70 per hour; it is not profitable for department 5 to sell its available time, $9\frac{1}{3}$ hours per week, at the selling price of £70 per hour.

The weekly gain, compared with the alternative of selling the spare time at £70 per hour is:

20 units × £23.5 per unit = £470 (ie £23,500 ÷ 50)

Total weekly gain from utilising the spare capacity on the new product, before considering the opportunity cost of not being able to sell 15 hours per week of processing time in department 4, and assuming that spare time in department 5 is left idle, is:

20 units ×	£110	selling price
	− 45	dept 4 (0.75 × 60)
	− 24	dept 5
	£31	
= £620		

Total gain	£620	
less lost opportunity to sell 15 hours/week	150	(15 × (70–60))
Net gain	£470	

A further £10 contribution would be generated each week by the sale of the spare hour that remains in department 4.

(b) The variable cost of one unit of the new product in the new circumstances is as follows:

Revised Unit Variable Cost of New Product

	£
Direct Material	10
Department 4	
0.75 (60 + 76)	102
Department 5	
0.33 (72 + 27)	33
	£145

Unless the price of the new product can be increased to £145, it does not seem profitable to continue to produce it.

(c) The shadow price of a scarce resource is normally a measure of both the benefit that can be obtained if an additional unit of the scarce resource can be obtained and of the loss that will be suffered if the availability of the resource is reduced by one unit. The opportunity cost of using a resource in a specified way is the benefit that would have been derived from deciding to use it in the most profitable alternative manner. The shadow price is therefore a form of opportunity cost in that it shows the contribution that a unit of the scarce resource makes when it is employed in the best possible way. Any alternative use of the resource can be judged by comparing its contribution with the shadow price (or opportunity cost). The shadow price (and the opportunity cost) do not necessarily apply over the whole of the relevant range of activity and it would therefore be prudent to establish the range for which they do apply.

Solutions to Chapter 15 questions

ANSWERS TO SELF-ASSESSMENT QUESTIONS

15.1 *Working for previous profit made*

	£/unit	£/unit
Selling price		15.00
Variable costs		
Direct materials	5.00	
Direct labour	6.00	
Other direct costs	0.60	
Variable overhead	0.40	
		12.00
Contribution		£3.00

Thus total profit made last year would have been:

Profit = (units sold × unit contribution)—Fixed overhead
= (10,000 × £3)—£20,000
= £10,000

(a) *Selling price if profit is to be maintained at £10,000 with a level of sales and production of 10,000 units during the coming year*

New contribution required
£10,000 = (10,000 × unit contribution)—(£20,000 × 1.05)
£10,000 = 10,000 C—£21,000
£31,000 = 10,000 C
where C = unit contribution

New unit contribution required = £3.10
New Variable Costs

	£	£
Direct materials	5.0 × 1.2	6.00
Direct labour	6.0 × 1.1667	7.00
Other direct costs	0.6 × 1.67	1.00
Variable costs	0.4 × 1.25	0.50
New variable cost per unit		£14.50

Therefore the new selling price required to maintain both profit at £10,000 and sales at the 10,000 units level will be the total variable costs (£14.50) plus the contribution (£3.10) which is £17.60. This is an increase of £2.60 on the previous price of £15.00, an increase of 17.33%. This is below the increase of 17.5% threshold above which price elasticity of demand becomes relevant to the decision.

(b) *The number of units that would have to be sold to enable the previous year's selling price and profit to be maintained.*

With the new variable costs at £14.50 (see above) and the price to remain at £15, a unit contribution of only £0.50 will be made. Using this, the required level of sales can be ascertained:

$$£10,000 = (S \times £0.5) - £21,000$$
$$£31,000 = £0.5S$$
where S = Number of units to be sold.

Therefore 62,000 units would have to be sold if the selling price was to be left at £15 and profits were to be maintained at £10,000 in the coming year.

(c) The situation showing the effect of price changes on sales volume described in this example is what the economist would refer to as the price elasticity of demand. This can be defined as the responsiveness of quantity demanded of a good or service to any change in its price. The general analysis of price elasticity of demand is to ascertain the percentage change taking place in the amount of a good or service demanded, in relation to the percentage change in its price.This can be shown by the formula:

$$\text{Price elasticity of demand} = \frac{\text{Percentage change in quantity demanded}}{\text{Percentage change in price.}}$$

Where the results of applying this equation equal unity this means that any changes in price and demand have offset each other, and so have no effect on the total revenue received from the product. However, when the price elasticity of demand is less than unity, demand is described as being price inelastic. Quantity demanded increases less than proportionately as price falls, causing total revenue received from the product to decrease. When the price elasticity of demand is greater than unity this is referred to as price elastic demand. Quantity demanded increases more than in proportion to decreases in price, and the total revenue received from the product increases. In the example given (as it is not within a significant range for the price rise calculated), the effect of price increases of less than 17.5% have not reached the threshold at which price elasticity of demand becomes relevant. For example, at the price of £17.62, the increase is still slightly below the crucial 17.5%. However, if the price charged was £17.77 the increase in price would have been about 18.5%. The effect would then have been to cause quantity demanded to decrease by 2%, ie from 10,000 units to 9,800. Measuring the effect of the price elasticity within the range of these two alternatives, the revenues in this situation from a price change of to either £17.62 or £17.77 (from £15) would be:

Sales 10,000 @ £17.62 = £176,200
Sales 9,800 @ £17.77 = £174,146

which shows a decrease in total potential revenue in the latter case (price inelastic).

15.2 10,000 units can still be sold at a selling price of £17.625 per unit (£15 per unit + 17.5%). Beyond that price, every 1% increase on £15 per unit (ie an increase of £0.15 per unit) leads to a 2% reduction in demand from the 10,000 unit level (ie a reduction of 200 units). The price/demand relationship is thus:

$$\frac{0.15}{200} = 0.00075 \text{ per unit.}$$

Zero demand will occur where price is increased by 50 times 1% (ie 50 times 2% reduction in demand). The total price increase percentage above £15 will be 67.5% (ie 50% + 17.5%). Selling price at zero demand will occur at a selling price of £25.125 per unit (£15 × 1.675).

Expressing price (P) as a function of output (Q):

$$P = 25.125 - 0.00075Q$$

$$\text{Total revenue} = 25.125Q - 0.00075Q^2$$

$$\text{Marginal revenue} = 25.125 - 0.00150Q$$

$$\text{Marginal cost} = 14.5$$

Profit maximising output is where marginal revenue = marginal cost. Thus:

$$0.00150Q = 10.625$$
$$Q = 7{,}083 \text{ units}$$

Where 7,083 units are sold, selling price = 25.125 – (0.00075 × 7,083)
= £19.813 per unit.

15.3 Cost data is essential data in the determination of pricing policy. It is one of the variables in the economist's profit maximising model, helping to determine the optimum selling price/output relationship. Cost data required is the response of cost to changes in quantity of product produced and sold (or quantity of service provided). This requires a knowledge of cost structures which depend upon the behavioural characteristics of different costs.

If an organisation finds it very difficult, or even impossible, to make an estimate of demand/price relationships it will frequently, and necessarily, resort to cost information as a primary basis for establishing selling price. Costs are more internal to an organisation and are, as a result, easier to forecast than demand, which is particularly dependent on a large number of factors external to, and thus outside the control of, the organisation.

Various pricing formulae based on cost are utilised. These are essentially based on either absorption costing or upon marginal (direct) costing approaches to establishing cost. A percentage mark-up is applied to cost in order to establish the selling price.

The utilisation of absorption costing in pricing policy determination may be either within cost plus formulae, or simply as a guide to whether the optimum price determined by marginal analysis appears satisfactory in the long-run. It is useful in this latter respect as long as the imperfections of absorption costing are recognised.

If absorption costs are used in pricing formulae it is even more important that the following serious limitations should be recognised:

1 Selling price cannot be solely cost related. The likely acceptability of cost plus prices in the market place must always be considered.
2 Unit cost is influenced by volume, which is itself influenced by selling price. There is thus a circular problem which is always present when full cost plus pricing formulae are used. There can be no guarantee that such methods will produce the desired profit.
3 Unit costs are dependent, and in industries with a high indirect/direct cost ratio especially so, on the arbitrary apportionment and absorption of overhead. There can be no guarantee therefore that each product is providing the desired mark-up.

There are thus limitations to the use of absorption cost data in pricing policy especially if used in formulae pricing. However, if marginal costing information is used instead in formulae pricing there are also problems.

In the absence of demand information, marginal cost establishes a minimum price that should be charged in the short-run. To establish normal selling prices required to generate adequate profits a contribution mark-up has to be established. Considerable flexibility is available regarding mark-up on individual products, much more so than with full cost pricing. The limitations of marginal cost plus pricing, however, are that:

1 It provides no indication of whether a particular product/service is paying its way in the long-run.
2 There may be a very large mark-up percentage, because of a high ratio of fixed to variable costs, with little guidance as to how flexibility should be applied.
3 The cost behaviour assumptions may be an oversimplification of reality.

If, however, demand/price relationships can be reasonably determined, marginal cost information has an important role to play in determining pricing policy and has clear advantages over absorption cost information, because of its recognition and identification of the behavioural characteristics of costs.

In the long-run, however, selling prices need to be sufficient to recover all costs and provide an adequate profit. Absorption costing information has a role to play in providing a general guide to the adequacy of selling prices in this respect.

ANSWERS TO EXERCISES

15.1 (a) Fixed Overhead allocated to one unit of Exco $\frac{60,000}{15,000} = £4$

Fixed Overhead allocated to one unit of Wyeco $\frac{300,000}{30,000} = £10$

Variable cost of one unit of Exco 12 – 4 = £8
Variable cost of one unit of Wyeco 24 – 10 = £14
Contribution per unit of Exco 16 – 8 = £8
Contribution per unit of Wyeco 32 – 14 = £18
Contribution per hour of finishing time—Exco 8(1) = £8
Contribution per hour of finishing time—Wyeco 18(2) = £36

∴ Make maximum of Wyeco, ie 40,000 units requiring	20,000 hours
Make balance of Exco, ie 10,000 units requiring	10,000
	30,000*

* Time available in Finishing Department
15,000 hours for manufacturing Exco (15,000 units)
15,000 hours for manufacturing Wyeco (30,000 units)
30,000

(b) $Px = 21 - 0.25x$ (see graph)
$Py = 38 - 0.15y$ (see graph)

where Px is the selling price of a unit of Exco
Py is the selling price of a unit of Wyeco
x is the demand for Exco (in '000s)
y is the demand for Wyeco (in '000s)

$Rx = 21x - 0.25x^2$
$Ry = 38y - 0.15y^2$

where Rx is the total revenue from the sales of Exco
Ry is the total revenue from the sales of Wyeco

$Mx = 21 - 0.5x$
$My = 38 - 0.3y$

where Mx is the marginal revenue of Exco, ie $Mx = \frac{d\,Rx}{dx}$

My is the marginal revenue of Wyeco, ie $My = \frac{d\,Ry}{dy}$

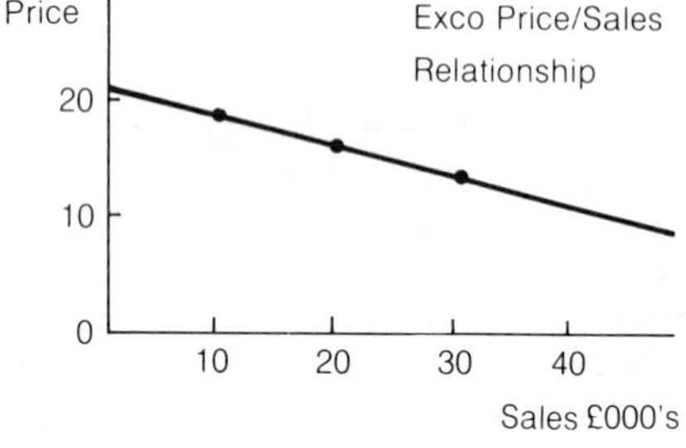

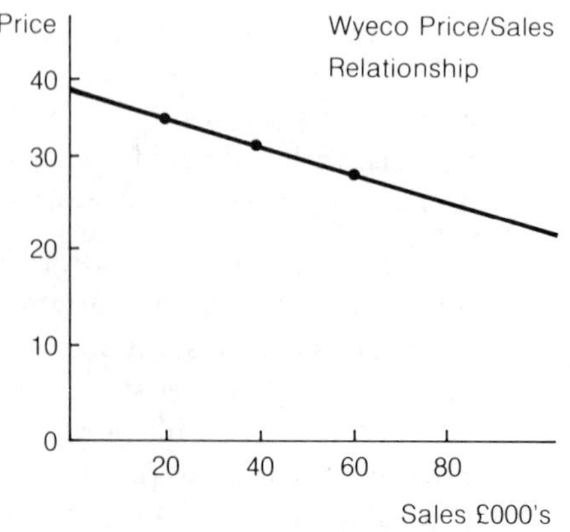

Optimal Level of Output Calculations:
For Exco the optimal level of output is where marginal cost equals marginal revenue ie the value of x for which $8 = 21 - 0.5x$

∴ Optimal Output for Exco is 26,000 units

For Wyeco the optimal level of output is where marginal cost equals marginal revenue, ie the value of y for which $14 = 38 - 0.3y$

∴ Optimal Output for Wyeco is 80,000 units

Optimal Selling Price Calculations:

Optimal Selling Price for Exco

$Px = 21 - 0.25x$

but optimal value for x is 26

∴ Optimal Selling Price is $21 - 0.25(26) =$ £14.50

Optimal Selling Price for Wyeco

$Py = 38 - 0.15y$

but optimal value for y is 80

∴ Optimal Selling Price is $38 - 0.15(80) =$ £26.00

Since this is below the lowest selling price considered by the Sales Director's investigation it should not be accepted without further analysis.

(c) Pricing policy is an area in which theorists have, for long, been aware that their theories seem to be ignored by the business world and in which they have expended much effort in trying to provide a rational justification for the cost plus approach that seems to be used so widely in practice.

The traditional form of economic analysis emphasises that prices are determined by the interaction of the forces of supply and demand. The theorist regards the firm as a profit maximiser and, where it is also a price-maker, it is argued that it should set its selling price by reference to the price that obtains at the profit maximising level of output. The elasticity of demand is of great importance and yet it seems to be totally ignored in the cost plus approach.

The claimed rationality of the theoretical approach does, however, assume that profit maximisation is the overriding goal of the firm and that the firm has the necessary information on its demand and cost functions. These assumptions may apply only rarely in the real world and it may even be rational (in the light of information costs) to seek a satisfactory profit rather than a maximum profit. The following have been claimed as advantages of the cost plus method:

(1) Cost-plus provides a decision rule that can be delegated to junior staff.
(2) The method may be more socially acceptable as producing equitable, defensible prices.
(3) The method may be required in tendering (or pricing) for some public sector projects.
(4) Investment planning may be simplified.

Even in the terms of the traditional goal of profit maximisation, cost plus can be explained as a rational procedure as follows:

(1) Cost plus can give a starting point in the process of price fixing. With this approach the price indicated by the cost plus rule can be adjusted in the light of estimated demand and marginal cost considerations.
(2) Assume that the firm has constructed a master budget and that this has been prepared with full regard to the cost and demand considerations that feature in the theoretical analysis. From this budget, overhead absorption rates can be calculated and mark-up percentages derived. If the firm now uses these overhead absorption rates and profit mark-up percentages it is using them to further a pricing policy which has already been validated by an analysis of the market demand for the firm's services. This argument is particularly relevant to discontinuous production (or jobbing work) where it is not realistic to argue that an analysis of demand should be undertaken whenever there is an inquiry from a prospective customer.

15.2 (a)

Calculation of estimated unit variable cost 1986/87

	Regular grade material	Cheaper grade material
	£	£
Direct material	36.00	31.25
Direct labour	10.50	10.50
Variable overhead	10.50	10.50
	57.00	52.25
Cost of wastage 52.25 (5/95)		2.75
	57.00	55.00

Analysis for regular grade material

Selling price	£80	£84	£88	£90	£92	£96	£100
Demand ('000)	25	23	21	20	19	17	15
Sales revenue (£'000)	2,000	1,932	1,848	1,800	1,748	1,632	1,500
Variable cost (£'000)	1,425	1,311	1,197	1,140	1,083	969	855
Total contribution (profit before charging existing fixed overhead) (£'000)	575	621	651	660	665	663	645

Analysis for cheaper grade material

Selling price	£80	£84	£88	£90	£92	£96	£100
Demand ('000)	25	23	21	20	19	17	15
Sales revenue (£'000)	2,000	1,932	1,848	1,800	1,748	1,632	1,500
Variable cost (£'000)	1,375	1,265	1,155	1,100	1,045	935	825
Total contribution (£'000)	625	667	693	700	703	697	675
Additional overhead (£'000)	30	30	30	30	30	30	30
Profit (before charging existing fixed overhead*) (£'000)	595	637	663	670	673	667	645

*Including the charge of £10,000 arising from a reallocation of existing overhead.

For all levels of demand considered in the analysis, the profit earned for the cheaper grade material is at least as high as it is for the regular grade. For all levels of demand, except 15,000 units, the profit is higher for the cheaper grade. If it can be assumed that the demand estimates and the estimated reject rate for the cheaper grade material are correct, then it can be seen that:

(i) the best price is £92,
(ii) this should lead to the optimal demand level of 19,000 units,
(iii) the cheaper grade material should be utilised, and
(iv) the foregoing should yield a profit of £673,000 − 1.25 (200,000) = £423,000 before charging the £10,000 which is a reallocation of existing overhead (or £413,000 after making such a charge).

It should, however, be noted that the solution is sensitive to minor errors in the estimates. If the demand figure for the £92 price is overstated by 0.5% this would affect the choice of the optimal policy. Also if the reject rate for the cheaper grade material were to be 6% instead of 5%, it would be better to continue with the regular grade of material. Although the optimum solution will change for relatively small alterations to the demand (or cost) estimates, the effect of using a suboptimal price, in the range (say) £90–£94, will have relatively little effect on the profit. For example, with a selling price of £90 the profit can be expected to fall by less than 0.5%. Nevertheless it can be said that the 'cost plus 50%' rule is clearly inappropriate and that the price should be determined by the type of analysis used above.

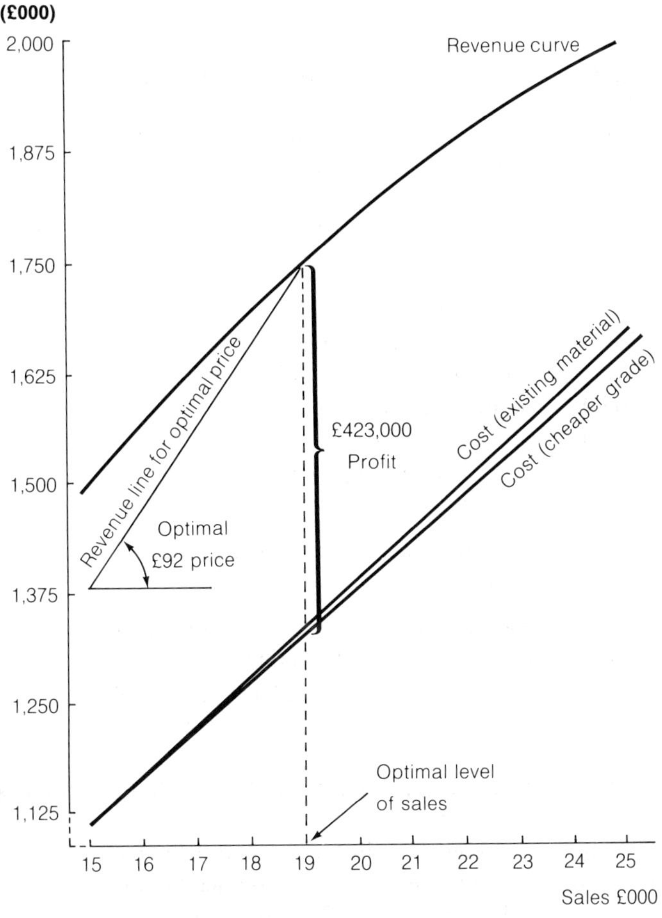

NQ cost-volume-profit chart for 1986/87
N.B. Costs and profit are shown before charging the £10,000 reallocation of existing overhead.

15.3 (a) Consider the range of options available on the outward journey with regard to the split between freight and passenger carriages. The question states that freight must be between 20% and 60% of the carriage capacity on outward journeys.

On the inward journeys, freight will use 20% of the carriage capacity. The number of carriages which will be occupied with passengers will be linked to the price elasticity of demand. The question states that the passenger fares on inward journeys will be the same as that used for the outward journeys. The range of carriage fill options and the average passenger fare per journey (adult/juvenile) which will apply for each is as follows:

Option	*Outward*		*Inward*		*Passenger*
	Freight Carriages	*Passenger Carriages*	*Freight Carriages*	*Passenger Carriages*	*Average Fare per journey* £
A	2	8	2	8	8.250*
B	3	7	2	7	8.625†
C	4	6	2	6	9.000
D	5	5	2	5	9.375
E	6	4	2	4	9.750

* Average passenger fare = $\frac{2}{3} \times £9 + \frac{1}{3} \times £4.50 = £7.50$ where demand is 10 carriages (600 passengers). Where demand is 8 carriages, therefore, the price applicable (based on the price elasticity of demand information) is £7.50 × 1.10 = £8.25.
†Average passenger fare is now £7.50 × 1.15 = £8.625.
Calculation of contribution per double journey

Option	*Revenue per journey* Outward Freight	Outward Passenger	*Inward* Freight	Inward Passenger	*Total Revenue*	*Less: wage cost*	*Contribution per double journey*
	£	£	£	£	£	£	£
A	2,520	3,960	2,400	3,960	12,840	1,200	11,640
B	3,600	3,622.5	2,400	3,622.5	13,245	1,500	11,745
C	4,560	3,240	2,400	3,240	13,440	1,800	11,640
D	5,400	2,812.5	2,400	2,812.5	13,425	2,100	11,325
E	6,120	2,340	2,400	2,340	13,200	2,400	10,800

Illustration of working calculations (eg Option B)

Outward: Freight revenue (600 × £2.20 + 600 × £2.00 + 600 × £1.80) = £3,600

Passenger revenue 7 × 60 × £8.625 = £3,622.50

Inward: Freight revenue 1,200 × £2 = £2,400

Passenger revenue 7 × 60 × £8.625 = £3,622.50

Wages for loading and unloading freight carriages:

(3 + 2) × £300 = £1,500

To maximise profit we should choose option B ie 3 freight carriages and 7 passenger carriages on the outward journey.

Contribution for the year = £11,745 × 2 × 200 =		£4,698,000
Less: Fuel cost 4 × 200 × £500	£400,000	
Misc. other costs	£3,500,000	£3,900,000
Net profit		£798,000

(b) A number of factors could affect the accuracy of the profit maximising strategy calculated in part (a):

Will the mix of passengers be in a mix of adult/juvenile of 2/1? A move towards a greater number of juvenile passengers would reduce the profit.

How accurate is the price/demand relationship for passengers?

Will an even flow of demand be available for every journey? It may be that there will be peaks and troughs depending upon the time of year.

How accurate is the forecast of incremental freight revenue in the face of competition?

Will the craft workshop goods utilise the 20% of freight capacity on every journey?

(c) Answers should focus on the relevant cost and revenue information.

The inward passenger revenues is the only factor to change in each of the options A to E in section (a) of the answer:

We have:

Option	*Inward revenue per journey as per existing prices*	*at £5 per journey*	*Carriage seating costs*	*Net increase on (reduction) in contribution*	*Original contrib.*	*Amended contrib.*
	£	£	£	£	£	£
A	3,960	2,400	nil	(1,560)	11,640	10,080
B	3,622.5	2,400	25	(1,247.50)	11,745	10,497.50
C	3,240	2,400	50	(890)	11,640	10,750
D	2,812.5	2,400	75	(487.50)	11,325	10,837.50
E	2,340	2,400	100	(40)	10,800	10,760

The maximum profit will now be achieved at option D where the mix on the outward journeys is 5 freight and 5 passenger carriages.

The amended profit per annum will be:

Contribution 2 × £10,837.50 × 200	= £4,335,000
less: Cost as before	£3,900,000
Net profit	£435,000

Hence the two tiered price system should not be implemented on financial grounds.

Solutions to Chapter 16 questions

ANSWERS TO SELF-ASSESSMENT QUESTIONS

16.1 (a) (i) The IRR percentage return is at that rate of interest where the cumulative discount factor over eight years is

$$\frac{114{,}000}{27{,}000} = 4.2222$$

$$= \text{approx } 17\%$$

(ii) The cumulative discount factor at 12% (over eight years) is 4.9676. The level of annual saving required in order to provide a 12% return is

$$\frac{114{,}000}{4.9676} = £22{,}949$$

(iii) The cumulative discount factor at 10% (over eight years) is 5.3349. The NPV at 10% is

$$(27{,}000 \times 5.3349) - 114{,}000 = £30{,}042$$

(b) The IRR of the project is approximately 19%. (Cumulative discount factor over six years is 120,000 ÷ 35,000 = 3.4286).

The management accountant should:

(i) Explain that the investment appraisal method used by the chief engineer (ie the ARR % on average net investment) overstates the true economic return. The return is below 20%, rather than being 25%.

Also, the project does not pay for itself in just over three years. The payback method does not provide for any return on the capital invested.

(ii) Ensure that all relevant cash flows have been considered, and valued on a future opportunity cost basis. For example, have installation and commissioning costs of the machine been considered? Will the project affect working capital requirements? How have the cost savings been calculated? The impact of taxation should also be considered.

(iii) Explain that it is inappropriate to use the bank overdraft rate as a guide to the worthwhileness of the return on capital investment projects. A hurdle rate should be established taking into account the required return of the different providers of long-term funds, and the capital mix. The requirement to recover the capital and costs, associated with projects that do not directly contribute to earnings, should also be considered.

(c) (i) Project C can be rejected immediately because the payback period exceeds the project life.

(ii) The payback reciprocal can be used to provide a reasonable approximation (overstated) of the IRR if the life of the project is sufficiently long (say ten years or above) and the return is sufficiently high (say 15% or above). As the return will not be known, a useful guide as to whether reasonable approximation can be made is that project life should be at least twice the payback period.

On this basis no reasonable approximation can be made of the IRR on project A. (If present value tables were being used the cumulative discount factor over five years is 3.3 ie it is the payback. IRR is between 15% and 16% compared with a payback reciprocal of 30%).

The approximate IRR of project B is 25% $\left(\text{ie } \frac{1}{4.0} \text{ years}\right)$. (The IRR is in fact 24%).

Project C will yield no return.

(iii) With a project life nearly four times its payback, project B will have the highest rate of return.

(d) The incremental annual profit required, in order to provide a DCF return of 20%, is

$\frac{£200{,}000}{2.9906}$ (cumulative discount factor at 20% over five years)

= £66,876

\+ 48,000 'fixed' costs

= £114,876 required annual contribution

÷ 0.4 contribution/sales ratio

= £287,190 required annual sales

(The required incremental annual profit of £66,876 can be compared with the £60,606 forecast for the project ie £200,000 ÷ 3.3 years payback.)

16.2 (a) All projects having a positive NPV, when discounted at 10%, should be accepted. The NPV of the four projects is:

Project A:
(115,000 × 2.4869) – 250,000 = £35,994
Project B:
(10,000 × 0.9091) + (140,000 × 0.8264) – 100,000 = £24,787
Project C:
(80,000 × 0.9091) + (60,000 × 0.8264) – 100,000 = £22,312
Project D:
(250,000 × 0.7513) – 200,000 = (£12,175)

Projects A, B and C should be accepted.

(b) The IRR of project B is 23%, and of project C 27%.

Workings (following trial and error calculations):

Project B (at 23% discount rate):

(10,000 × 0.8130) + (140,000 × 0.6610) – 100,000
= £670 (compared with £50,000 at 0%)

Project C (at 27% discount rate):

(80,000 × 0.7874) + (60,000 × 0.6200) – 100,000
= £192 (compared with £40,000 at 0%)

Despite the higher IRR % of project C, project B should be chosen because the NPV is greater when the projects are discounted at the company's cost of capital. This would be confirmed by a calculation of the differential IRR between projects B and C. Comparing B with C, project B has a reduced cash flow of £70,000 in year 1, and an increased cash flow of £80,000 in year 2. The differential IRR is 14% (discount factor of 0.8750 after 1 year ie 70,000 ÷ 80,000) and the present value at 10% is:

((70,000) × 0.9091) + (80,000 × 0.8264) = £2,475 (ie £24,787 – £22,312))

ANSWERS TO EXERCISES

16.1 (a) (i) *Payback period*:

$$\textit{Option 1} = \frac{£278{,}000}{£100{,}000} = 2.78 \text{ years}$$

$$\textit{Option 2} = \frac{£805{,}000}{£250{,}000} = 3.22 \text{ years}$$

(ii) *Accounting rate of return*:

Option 1:

$$\text{Annual depreciation} = \frac{£278{,}000 - £28{,}000}{5}$$

$$= £50{,}000$$

Annual profit = £50,000
(£100,000 cash flow – £50,000 depreciation)

$$\text{Average investment} = \frac{278{,}000 + £28{,}000}{2}$$

$$= £153{,}000$$

$$\text{Accounting rate of return} = \frac{50{,}000}{153{,}000} \times 100\%$$

$$= 33\%$$

Option 2:

$$\text{Annual depreciation} = \frac{£805{,}000 - £150{,}000}{5}$$

$$= £131{,}000$$

Annual profit = £119,000
(£250,000 cash flow – £131,000 depreciation)

$$\text{Average investment} = \frac{£805{,}000 + £150{,}000}{2}$$

$$= £477{,}500$$

$$\text{Accounting rate of return} = \frac{119{,}000}{477{,}500} \times 100\%$$

$$= 25\%$$

(iii) *Net present value* (*at* 15% *cost of capital*):

Option 1:

		£
Year 0		(278,000)
Years 1–5	100,000 × 3.353	335,300
Year 5	28,000 × 0.497	13,900
		71,200

Option 2:

		£
Year 0		(805,000)
Years 1–5	250,000 × 3.353	838,300
Year 5	150,000 × 0.497	74,500
		107,800

(iv) *Internal rate of return*:
Option 1:

$$\text{Approx cumulative discount factor (5 years)} = \frac{268,000}{100,000} = 2.68 = 25\%$$

NPV at 25% =

		£
Year 0		(278,000)
Years 1–5	100,000 × 2.689	268,900
Year 5	28,000 × 0.328	9,200
		100

∴ IRR = 25%

Option 2:

$$\text{Approx cumulative discount factor (5 years)} = \frac{740,000}{250,000} = 2.96 = 20\%$$

NPV at 20% =

		£
Year 0		(805,000)
Years 1–5	250,000 × 2.991	747,700
Year 5	150,000 × 0.402	60,300
		3,000

$$\text{IRR} = 15\% + \left(5 \times \frac{107,800}{104,800}\right)$$

$$= 20.1\%$$

∴ IRR = 20%

(b) Both projects are indicated as being worthwhile when the discounted cash flow returns are compared with the cost of capital.

The payback period, accounting rate of return, and internal rate of return calculations all point to option 1 being preferred. The net present value calculation, on the other hand, favours option 2.

The basic reason for the different ranking provided is that the NPV method is an absolute money measure which takes account of the scale of the investment as well as the quality. The other three appraisal methods provide measures which express return relative to the investment. Investments of comparable relative quality will have the same return regardless of scale. For example, an annual profit of £20 on an investment of £100 will have the same relative return as an annual profit of £200,000 on an investment of £1,000,000. If one is concerned especially with quality then the relative measures would provide the required ranking. However, if the objective is to maximise wealth, investment worth should be measured by the surplus net present value generated, over and above the cost of capital.

If all investment decisions are simple choice situations between 'invest' or 'not invest', the different ranking of projects provided by the different appraisal methods should have no effect on the projects selected, as long as the cut-off point is determined consistently. However, where operational alternatives exist (for example, where a choice has to be made between two different machines for a particular task) ranking becomes critical to the decision. If wealth maximisation is the objective the NPV method provides the correct ranking. The relative measures can still be used, however, but only by converting the appraisal to a simple accept/reject situation. This is done by calculating the differential between alternatives.

In the situation in the question the differential between option 1 and option 2 provides an internal rate of return of 18%, as follows:

NPV at 18% =

		£
Year 0		(527,000)
Years 1–5	150,000 × 3.127	469,100
Year 5	122,000 × 0.437	53,300
		(4,600)

The additional investment of £527,000 in option 2 is worthwhile as the IRR of 18% exceeds the cost of capital.

Finally, it should be recognised that both the payback method and the accounting rate of return method have deficiencies. They do not provide an adequate measure of investment worth. The percentage return resulting from accounting rate of return calculations is not comparable with the cost of capital.

16.2 Although the internal rate of return method of discounted cash flow investment appraisal does give attention to the amount of the capital investment in determining the percentage return, the fact that the attractiveness of an investment is expressed in relative terms means that, in comparing one project with another, the scale of investments will have no influence on ranking. However, while one project may have a higher rate of profit per unit of capital invested than another, if it has fewer units of capital invested, it may make a smaller contribution to the wealth of a business. The net present value method of discounted cash flow investment appraisal provides an absolute, rather than a relative, measure of project worth reflecting both the profit per unit, and the number of units, of capital invested.

Considering the two projects in the question, it can be seen that the scale of project B in year 0 is ten times that of project A. It can also be seen that the profit per unit of project B in each year is less than ten times that of A. It can be concluded that different ranking of the two projects will be provided by the IRR and NPV methods respectively.

Using IRR, project A would be ranked above project B as it produces a return of 20% compared with 15%, ie the profit per unit of capital invested is greater. Using NPV, project B would be ranked higher, with a surplus of £1,441 at a cost of capital of 10%, compared with £308 for project A. This reflects the much greater scale of project B.

If the objective is to maximise the firm's wealth, then the ranking of project NPV provides the correct measure. The IRR method can still be used to make the correct choice, but requires the calculation of the differential IRR. The return on the differential investment of £9,000 is 14%, and thus project B is shown to be preferable.

If properly used, therefore, there should be no conflict between the IRR and NPV methods regarding project selection. It may also be argued that percentage measures are more easily understandable and that the return per unit of investment should be highlighted, particularly as investment outcomes are uncertain. Relative project risk should be a factor in giving priority to different investment proposals. The IRR percentage, when compared with the cost of capital, provides an indication of the margin of safety. A further argument in favour of IRR is that the required return cannot be easily established. The sufficiency of the IRR return can be judged post-calculation. With NPV, the cost of capital has to be established in order to calculate the investment return and thus provide project ranking.

It should also be recognised that if the objective is to maximise the rate of profitability per unit of capital invested, which becomes the relevant criterion in capital rationing situations, a relative measure is required for project ranking and selection. The IRR provides such a measure. The NPV would have to be expressed per unit of capital invested for the method to be appropriate.

Workings:

DCF calculations:

Project A

Year	Undiscounted cash flow £	DCF at 10%		DCF at 20%	
		Discount factor	Cash flow £	Discount factor	Cash flow £
0	(1,000)	1.000	(1,000)	1.000	(1,000)
1	240	0.909	218.2	0.833	199.9
2	288	0.826	237.9	0.694	199.9
3	346	0.751	259.8	0.579	200.3
4	414	0.683	282.8	0.482	199.5
5	498	0.621	309.3	0.402	200.2
	786		308.0		(0.2)

Project B

Year	Undiscounted cash flow £	DCF at 10%		DCF at 15%	
		Discount factor	Cash flow £	Discount factor	Cash flow £
0	(10,000)	1.000	(10,000)	1.000	(10,000)
1	2,300	0.909	2,090.7	0.870	2,001.0
2	2,640	0.826	2,180.6	0.756	1,995.8
3	3,040	0.751	2,283.0	0.657	1,997.3
4	3,500	0.683	2,390.5	0.572	2,002.0
5	4,020	0.621	2,496.4	0.497	1,997.9
	5,500		1,441.2		(6.0)

Differential (*Project B v Project A*)

Year	Undiscounted cash flow £	DCF at 10%		DCF at 15%	
		Discount factor	Cash flow £	Discount factor	Cash flow £
0	(9,000)	1.000	(9,000)	1.000	(9,000)
1	2,060	0.909	1,872.5	0.870	1,792.2
2	2,352	0.826	1,942.7	0.756	1,778.1
3	2,694	0.751	2,023.2	0.657	1,770.0
4	3,086	0.683	2,107.7	0.572	1,765.2
5	3,522	0.621	2,187.1	0.497	1,750.4
	4,714		1,133.2		(144.1)

16.3 **(a)** The graph below gives present value profiles for projects 1 and 2. The workings are shown on pages 578 and 579.

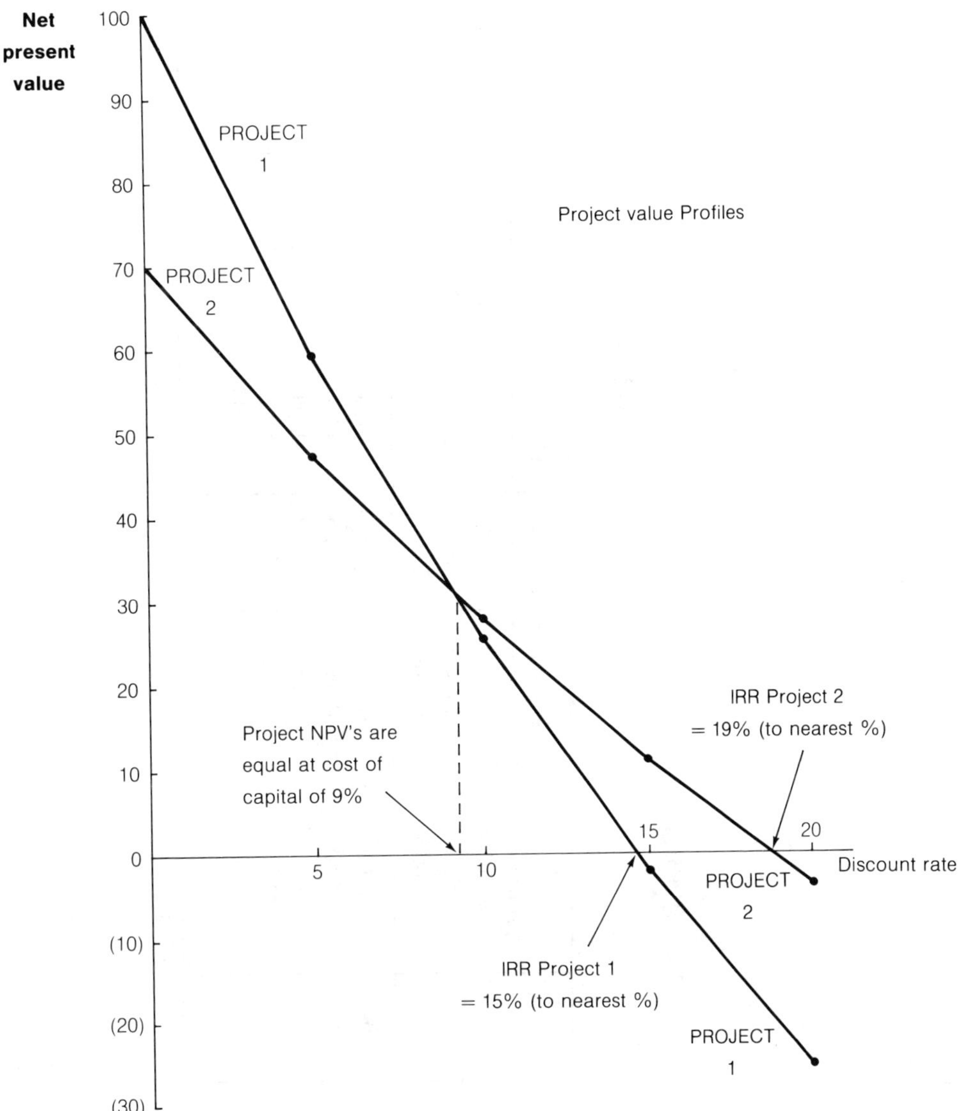

16.3 *Workings*:

Project 1:

Year	Undiscounted cash flow £'000	Discounted at 5%		Discounted at 10%		Discounted at 15%		Discounted at 20%	
		Discount factor	Cash flow £'000	Discount factor	Cash flow £'000	Discount factor	Cash flow £'000	Discount factor	Cash flow £'000
0	(200)	1.000	(200)	1.000	(200)	1.000	(200)	1.000	(200)
1	10	0.952	9.5	0.909	9.1	0.870	8.7	0.833	8.3
2	30	0.907	27.2	0.826	24.8	0.756	22.7	0.694	20.8
3	210	0.864	181.4	0.751	157.7	0.657	138.0	0.579	121.6
4	50	0.823	41.2	0.683	34.2	0.572	28.6	0.482	24.1
	100		59.3		25.8		(2.0)		(25.2)

16.3 *Workings*:

Project 2:

Year	Undiscounted cash flow £'000	Discounted at 5% Discount factor	Cash flow £'000	Discounted at 10% Discount factor	Cash flow £'000	Discounted at 15% Discount factor	Cash flow £'000	Discounted at 20% Discount factor	Cash flow £'000
0	(200)	1.000	(200)	1.000	(200)	1.000	(200)	1.000	(200)
1	120	0.952	114.2	0.909	109.1	0.870	104.4	0.833	100.0
2	90	0.907	81.6	0.826	74.3	0.756	68.0	0.694	62.5
3	50	0.864	43.2	0.751	37.6	0.657	32.9	0.579	29.0
4	10	0.823	8.2	0.683	6.8	0.572	5.7	0.482	4.8
	70		47.2		27.8		11.0		(3.7)

(b) IRR project 1 = 15% (to nearest %)
IRR project 2 = 19% (to nearest %)

(c) If the cost of capital is < 9% (rounded), project 1 would be preferred.
If the cost of capital is >9% (rounded), project 2 would be preferred.
The later cash inflows from project 1 are more heavily discounted the higher the rate of interest in comparison with the earlier cash inflows on project 2.

Solutions to Chapter 17 questions

ANSWERS TO SELF-ASSESSMENT QUESTIONS

17.1 Three alternatives have to be considered:
Alternative 1: keep existing machine.
Alternative 2: purchase new machine and maintain annual output at 5,000 units.
Alternative 3: purchase new machine and increase annual output to 7,000 units with reduction in selling price to £79 per unit.

Annual cash flows from the three alternatives are expected to be as follows:

	Alternative 1		Alternative 2		Alternative 3	
	£ per unit	£'000	£ per unit	£'000	£ per unit	£'000
Sales revenue	88	440	88	440	79	553
Variable costs	(38)	(190)	(33)	(165)	(33)	(231)
(excl labour)	50	250	55	275	46	322
Labour	(30)	(150)	(20)	(100)	(20)	(140)
Contribution	20	100	35	175	26	182

The discount rate (in real terms) applied to the uninflated cash flows (excl labour) will be:

$$\left(\frac{1.16}{1.06} - 1\right) \times 100\% = 9.43\%$$

The discount rate (in real terms) applied to the uninflated labour cash flows will be:

$$\left(\frac{1.16}{1.00} - 1\right) \times 100\% = 5.45\%$$

Approximate cumulative discount factors over five years are:

9.43% = 3.847
5.45% = 4.277

Discounted cash flow calculations are as follows:

	Alternative 1			Alternative 2			Alternative 3		
	Cash flow £'000	Discount factor	Present value £'000	Cash flow £'000	Discount factor	Present value £'000	Cash flow £'000	Discount factor	Present value £'000
Yr 0				(260)	1.000	(260)	(260)	1.000	(260)
Yrs 1–5	250	3.847	961.8	275	3.847	1,057.9	322	3.847	1,238.7
	(150)	4.277	(641.6)	(100)	4.277	(427.7)	(140)	4.277	(598.8)
Yr 6				50	0.583	29.2	50	0.583	29.2
			320.2			399.4			409.1

Purchase of the replacement machine is worthwhile. Selling price should be reduced to £79 if sales of 7,000 units per annum can be achieved as a result.

The analysis could have assumed continuation of the existing situation (ie alternative 1) in the base. The analysis would have identified additional NPV of £79.2 K from alternative 2 (£399.4 K – £320.2 K) and £88.9 K from alternative 3 (£409.1 K – £320.2 K).

ANSWERS TO EXERCISES

17.1 (a) (i) *Base*:

Current situation, including:

Utilisation of facilities contributing £2,000 per annum and with a disposal value of £1,000 in five years' time.

Existing sales demand for other products.

Existing level of fixed costs.

(ii) Alternative:

Invest in new facilities and launch the new product.

(iii) Analysis (of annual net cash inflow).

	£
Contribution from new product	50,000 (in year 1, increasing by £4,000 per annum)
Increase in fixed costs	(5,000)
Loss of some existing products	(2,000)
Reduced demand for other existing products (Lost contribution less fixed costs saved)	(8,000)
Utilisation of facilities released	3,000
	38,000 (in year 1 increasing by £4,000 per annum)

The book value of existing manufacturing facilities is irrelevant as it is a sunk cost. The current disposal value of these facilities need not be included as an alternative, as disposal at this time would clearly not be considered. The disposal value in 5 years time is common to both alternatives (ie stay as at present or launch the new product).

Fixed overhead under-absorption is irrelevant. It is concerned with the internal transfer of costs and has no effect on costs incurred.

Depreciation of £28,000 is not a cash flow. Depreciation is included in the appraisal by identifying investment and disposal cash flows relevant to the project.

(iv) *Investment appraisal*:

Year	*Undiscounted Cash Flow (£'000)*	*Discount Factor (15%)*	*Net Present Value (£'000)*
0	(140)	1.000	(140)
1	38	0.870	33.1
2	42	0.756	31.8
3	46	0.657	30.2
4	50	0.572	28.6
5	54	0.497	26.8
	90		10.5

The investment is worthwhile as there is a positive NPV of £10,500 when cash flows are discounted at the cost of capital.

Alternatively, the IRR of the project could be calculated. Consideration of the total undiscounted cash flow, and the NPV at 15%, indicates that the IRR is likely to be approximately 18%.

Discounting at 18%:

(140) × 1.000 =	(140)
38 × 0.847 =	32.2
42 × 0.718 =	30.2
46 × 0.609 =	28.0
50 × 0.516 =	25.8
54 × 0.437 =	23.6
	(0.2)

The IRR is 18%.

(b) (i) If sales are £100,000 per annum, contribution becomes £50,000 and net cash inflow £38,000.

NPV = 140,000 – (38,000 × 3.352)
= (£12,600)
IRR = Cumulative discount factor of
140,000 ÷ 38,000 = 3.68 (5 years)
= 11%

(ii) If sales are £120,000 in year 1, increasing at the rate of £14,000 per annum, net cash flows become:

(140) × 1.000 =	(140)
48 × 0.870 =	41.8
55 × 0.756 =	41.6
62 × 0.657 =	40.7
69 × 0.572 =	39.5
76 × 0.497 =	37.8
	61.4

NPV is £61,400
IRR becomes 31% (calculations not shown).

17.2 (a) (i) Alternatives:

1 Sell existing equipment
2 Continue as at present
3 Replace existing equipment.

(ii) Base:

Existing book value £15,000 is a sunk cost (whatever happens this has to be charged against future profits).
Working capital zero (ie only required if a decision to continue production is taken).

(iii) Analysis:

	(£)	**Alternative 1** (sell existing equipment)	**Alternative 2** (continue as at present)	**Alternative 3** (replace existing equipment)
Yr 0	Sale of existing equipment	5,000	—	5,000
	Purchase of new equipment		—	(25,000)
	Working capital	—	(4,000)	(10,000)
		5,000	(4,000)	(30,000)
	Annual cash inflows:			
Yrs 1		—	5,000	25,000
2		—	5,000	20,000
3		—	5,000	15,000
4		—	5,000	10,000
5		—	5,000 }	5,000 }
	+ release of working capital	—	4,000 }	10,000 }
	NPV at 14%	5,000	15,300	31,200

Thus alternative 3 is to be preferred.

Alternatively, the analysis could have been carried out assuming a different base as follows:

Base:

As before, plus could sell existing equipment for £5,000.

Analysis:

	(£)	**Alternative 1** (continue as at present v sell existing equipment)	**Alternative 2** (replace existing equipment v sell existing equipment)
Yr 0	Revenue foregone from not selling existing equipment	(5,000)	—
	Purchase of new equipment	—	(25,000)
	Working capital	(4,000)	(10,000)
		(9,000)	(35,000)
	Annual cash inflows:		
Yrs 1		5,000	25,000
2		5,000	20,000
3		5,000	15,000
4		5,000	10,000
5		5,000	5,000
	+ release of working capital	4,000 }	10,000 }
	NPV at 14%	10,300 (ie 15,300–5,000 from previous analysis)	26,200 (ie 31,200–5,000 from previous analysis)

If discontinuation of flibbets is not to be considered, eg if continuation is obviously worthwhile, then a further analysis variant would be as follows:

Base:

Continue with existing equipment.

Analysis:

	(£)	**Alternative** (replace existing equipment v continue as at present)
Yr 0	Sale of existing equipment	5,000
	Purchase of new equipment	(25,000)
	Additional working capital	(6,000)
		(26,000)
	Annual additional cash inflows:	
Yrs 1		20,000
2		15,000
3		10,000
4		5,000
5		—
	+ release of additional working capital	6,000
	NPV at 14%	15,900 (ie 26,200–10,300 from previous analysis)

Using NPV, any of the above approaches would have produced the correct result. Replacement is chosen because it produces additional NPV compared with the other alternatives. The differential NPV can be easily seen whichever way the analysis is carried out. If the DCF internal rate of return method had been employed the final analysis (ie replacement v continuation) would have had to have eventually been carried out in order to calculate the differential IRR.

(b) Smith's 'juggling' is wrong because:

I The Accounting Rate of Return method is an imprecise measure of long-run economic return. Results are not comparable with cost of capital. Discounted cash flow techniques should be used to appraise total project viability.

II In addition, Smith's appraisal of the relevant costs of alternatives contains the following errors:

(i) The appraisal of the viability of replacing the equipment includes the book value of existing equipment £15,000. This is irrelevant as it is a sunk cost. It is a cost which will have to be charged against future profits whichever alternative is chosen. However, having said this, if the existing equipment is sold this (ie: £15,000 book value—£5,000 proceeds) will have to be charged immediately, rather than £15,000 spread over 5 years. Although in no way affecting the economic viability of the alternatives it could have a slight influence if considered a significant sum, because of the effect on short-term profit.

Thus the average profits increase from £4,000 to £6,000 per annum, increasing the viability of replacement.

(ii) In the appraisal of the viability of continuing with the existing equipment the working capital required of £4,000 has been ignored. Thus the return is overstated. It now becomes 44% (ie: 4,000 ÷ 9,000 × 100%).

(iii) Smith's analysis of replacement is inconsistent with the basis for analysing continuation with the existing equipment. Having calculated the return from continuing with existing equipment compared with an uncommitted base he then attempts to compare replacement with continuation. This is acceptable (and indeed is essential if ARR or IRR methods are used) as long as it is recognised that a return in excess of 14% on the differential investment would justify replacement, regardless of the percentage return from continuation.

(iv) In carrying out the differential analysis whilst the differential inflows have been correctly calculated (other than errors resulting from the use of ARR) the differential investment has not. If the equipment is replaced, then the existing equipment can be sold. Thus:

Differential investment	26,000 (31,000 – 5,000)
Differential average annual profit	6,000 (see II(i) above)
ARR = 23%	

As has already been stated ARR does not provide an adequate measure of project viability, but at least in this case would have provided the correct result (ie the extra investment involved in replacement is justified) if the rest of the analysis had been carried out correctly. The true differential % return (ie: using IRR) is in fact approximately 40%, due to the high early cash inflows from replacement.

17.4 Unit contribution/profit:

	£/Unit
Selling price	7.50
Material A 1 kilo at £1.00/kilo	1.00
Material B $\frac{1}{2}$ kilo at £2.20/kilo	1.10
	2.10
Skilled labour $\frac{1}{4}$ hour at £6.00/hour	1.50
Unskilled labour $\frac{1}{4}$ hour at £4.00/hour	1.00
	2.50
Variable overhead	0.50
Total variable cost	5.10
Contribution	2.40
Fixed overhead	2.20
Profit	0.20

Annual contribution =	100,000 × 2.40 = £240,000
[Incl. labour costs	100,000 × (2.50) = (£250,000)
& other	100,000 × 4.90 = £490,000]

In year 1 material B would not be bought, as stock currently exists sufficient for one year's requirements for the new product. Year 1 saving is £110,000 (50,000 kilos at £2.20/kilo). Against this, the opportunity to sell the materials immediately for £80,000 (50,000 kilos at £1.60/kilo) would have to be foregone.

Labour cash flows must be separated from other cash flows in the appraisal, as differential inflation rates apply. If cash flows are appraised at current prices, the cost of capital in real terms must be calculated.

The real terms discount rate for labour cash flows is:

$$[(1.20 \div 1.15) - 1] \times 100\% = 4.35\%$$

Discount factors can be interpolated using 4% and 5% factors.

The real terms discount rate for other cash flows is:

$$[(1.20 \div 1.10) - 1] \times 100\% = 9.09\%$$

Discount factors can be interpolated using 9% and 10% factors.

Investment appraisal:

Year 0: investment	(600,000)
Lost opportunity to dispose of stock of material B	(80,000)
Years 1–10: labour cash outflows (250,000) × 7.98 (cumulative discount factor for 10 yrs at 4.35%)	(1,995,000)
Year 1: other cash flows (excl labour & material B) 600,000 × 0.92 (year 1 discount factor at 9.09%)	550,000
Years 2–10: other cash flows (excl labour) 490,000 × 5.48 (years 2–10 cum. discount factor at 9.09%)	2,685,000
	560,000

On the basis of the above appraisal, the project is worthwhile. Consideration should, however, be given to:

(i) *The likely long-term situation*
Based on the apportionment of a share of all costs incurred, profit generated by the project will only be £20,000 per annum (100,000 units at £0.20 per unit). Further, other assets utilised by the project have an investment cost of £450,000 (based on £0.45 per unit charged and an assumed 10 year life). Whilst they are not deemed to be incremental as a result of this project, such costs have to be recovered in the long-run and are incurred as a result of total investment projects.

(ii) *How post-investment performance will be reported*
Although the incremental analysis supports investment in the project, the full absorption costing system employed will result in product profit being reported at £0.20 per unit. This might not inspire product managers to search for new product opportunities.

Note: The appraisal could alternatively have been carried out in money terms as follows:

Year	Labour cash flows			Other cash flows			Net cash flows		
	Current terms £'000	Inflation factor	Money terms £'000	Current terms £'000	Inflation factor	Money terms £'000	Money terms £'000	Discount factor 20%	Present value £'000
0	—	—	—	(680)	—	(680)	(680)	1.000	(680)
1	(250)	1.15	(287.5)	600	1.10	660	372.5	0.833	310.3
2	(250)	1.15^2	(330.6)	490	1.10^2	592.9	262.3	0.694	182.0
3	(250)	1.15^3	(380.2)	490	1.10^3	652.2	272.0	0.579	157.5
4	(250)	1.15^4	(437.3)	490	1.10^4	717.4	280.1	0.482	135.0
5	(250)	1.15^5	(502.9)	490	1.10^5	789.1	286.2	0.402	115.1
6	(250)	1.15^6	(578.3)	490	1.10^6	868.1	289.8	0.335	97.1
7	(250)	1.15^7	(665.0)	490	1.10^7	954.9	289.9	0.279	80.9
8	(250)	1.15^8	(764.7)	490	1.10^8	1,050.4	285.7	0.233	66.6
9	(250)	1.15^9	(879.5)	490	1.10^9	1,155.4	275.9	0.194	53.5
10	(250)	1.15^{10}	(1,011.4)	490	1.10^{10}	1,270.9	259.5	0.162	42.0
							2,072.9		560.0

Solutions to Chapter 18 questions

ANSWERS TO SELF-ASSESSMENT QUESTIONS

18.2

Decision	Demand	*Opportunity loss* £'000	*Probability*	*Expected Value* £'000
Hire A	10,000	*nil*	0.5	—
	14,000	35,000	0.3	10.500
	16,000	95,000	0.2	19,000
				29,500
Hire B	10,000	25,000	0.5	12,500
	14,000	12,000	0.3	3,600
	16,000	62,000	0.2	12,400
				28,500
Hire C	10,000	65,000	0.5	32,500
	14,000	nil	0.3	
	16,000	nil	0.2	
				32,500

Machine B should be hired because this minimises the opportunity losses.

The company should pay a maximum of £28,500 to secure perfect information.

18.3 Refer to the diagram on page 588. The values shown are mid-points where the problem attaches probabilities to a range. It is assumed that full capacity can be sold.

Discussion and exploration of the problem

The decision tree, including joint probabilities, is a useful means by which the problem can be stated. In preparing the tree, the basic figures and relationships are put into a form which is understandable. The next stage is to find an efficient way in which calculations can be made in order to form a conclusion.

There are numerous ways in which the decision tree for the Wye building can be resolved. Two of the alternatives will be illustrated in order to provide an insight into the issue of applying an efficient manner of carrying out calculations.

The major problem as regards calculating outcomes is to select an appropriate technique. Since the decision is a long-term one, a discounted cash flow approach is suitable. The question states a cost of capital and a product duration, allowing a net present value approach to be adopted.

Initial cost	Fixed cost	Capacity	Contribution @£1.50/unit £'000	Fixed Cost £'000	Joint Probability	Reference (see table later)
£1,050,000 (0.2)	£600,000 (0.3)	625,000 (0.5)	937.5	600	0.03	1
		825,000 (0.5)	1,237.5	600	0.03	2
	£800,000 (0.7)	625,000 (0.2)	937.5	800	0.028	3
		825,000 (0.8)	1,237.5	800	0.112	4
£1,200,000 (0.25)	£600,000 (0.3)	625,000 (0.5)	937.5	600	0.0375	5
		£825,000 (0.5)	1,237.5	600	0.0375	6
	£800,000 (0.7)	625,000 (0.2)	937.5	800	0.035	7
		£825,000 (0.8)	1,237.5	800	0.14	8
£1,350,000 (0.35)	£600,000 (0.3)	625,000 (0.5)	937.5	600	0.0525	9
		825,000 (0.5)	1,237.5	600	0.0525	10
	£800,000 (0.7)	625,000 (0.2)	937.5	800	0.049	11
		825,000 (0.8)	1,237.5	800	0.196	12
£1,450,000 (0.2)	£600,000 (0.3)	625,000 (0.5)	937.5	600	0.03	13
		825,000 (0.5)	1,237.5	600	0.03	14
	£800,000 (0.7)	625,000 (0.2)	937.5	800	0.028	15
		825,000 (0.8)	1,237.5	800	0.112	16

Calculations: *Alternative* 1

The decision tree can be resolved and presented by means of a table:

£'000 Reference	Probability	Cash outflow	Cash inflow per annum	Annuity Value of £1 over 10 years @ 20%	Discounted Future Earnings	Net Present Value
	A	B	C	D	E	F
1	0.03	1,050	337.5	4.192	1,414.8	+364.8
2	0.03	1,050	637.5	4.192	2,672.4	+1,622.4
3	0.028	1,050	137.5	4.192	576.4	−473.6
4	0.112	1,050	437.5	4.192	1,834.0	+784.0
5	0.0375	1,200	337.5	4.192	1,414.8	+214.8
6	0.0375	1,200	637.5	4.192	2,672.4	+1,472.4
7	0.035	1,200	137.5	4.192	576.4	−623.6
8	0.14	1,200	437.5	4.192	1,834.0	+634.0
9	0.0525	1,350	337.5	4.192	1,414.8	+64.8
10	0.0525	1,350	637.5	4.192	2,672.4	+1,322.4
11	0.049	1,350	137.5	4.192	576.4	−773.6
12	0.196	1,350	437.5	4.192	1,834.0	+484.0
13	0.03	1,450	337.5	4.192	1,414.8	−35.2
14	0.03	1,450	637.5	4.192	2,672.4	+1,222.4
15	0.028	1,450	137.5	4.192	576.4	−873.6
16	0.112	1,450	437.5	4.192	1,834.0	+384.0
Expected Value						+448.3

Column E is calculated by multiplying column C by column D.
Column F is column E less column B.
Expected value is the sum of column A multiplied by column F.

It is assumed that fixed costs are specific to the project and not general apportionments of organisation-wide costs.

Cash inflow per annum is therefore approximately equal to contribution, less fixed cost, where fixed cost excludes depreciation.

Alternative 2

Alternative 1 involves a large number of calculations, a number of which are duplicated. Alternative 2 applies a knowledge of the underlying mathematical relationships to derive the same figures as alternative 1 with far fewer calculations.

Expected value of:

	Cost £'000	*Probability*	*Expected Value*
Wye: Initial cost	1,050	0.2	210,000
	1,200	0.25	300,000
	1,350	0.35	472,500
	1,450	0.2	290,000
			£1,272,500
Capacity at a fixed cost:	'000 units		
between £500,000 and £700,000	625	0.5	312,500
	825	0.5	412,500
			725,000 units
between £700,000 and £900,000	625	0.2	125,000
	825	0.8	660,000
			785,000 units

Overall capacity and Fixed Costs

Capacity	*Fixed Costs*	*Probability*	*Expected Value* *Capacity*	*F. Costs*
725,000	£600,000	0.3	217,500	£180,000
785,000	£800,000	0.7	549,500	£560,000
			767,000	£740,000

Cash inflows: 767,000 × £1.50 – £740,000 = £410,500

Discounted Cash Flow Statement

Year	*Cash flow* £	*Discounting rate*	*PV* £'000
0	– 1,272,500	1.000	– 1,272.5
1–10	+ 410,500	4.192	+ 1,720.8
Net Present Value			+ 448.3

Although efficient procedures such as that illustrated above are helpful in preparing answers under tight examination time pressures, there are major dangers and students are advised to use 'safe' procedures where time allows. In a practical situation, the decision tree could be resolved using a spreadsheet or other computer package. Particular care must be exercised in dealing with Internal Rate of Return calculations when short-cuts such as alternative 2 are adopted.

An efficient answer to the question can now be presented.

Answer:

Assumptions:

1 Production remains the limiting factor; full capacity can be sold.

2 Fixed costs are specific to the project and not apportionments of general overhead.

3 Cash inflow can be adequately equated to contribution less fixed cost, which does not include an element of depreciation.

Workings:

Capacity:	*Wye* '000 units	*Prob*	*EV*	*Zed* '000 units	*Prob*	*EV*
Fixed cost £500,000 – £700,000	625	0.5	312.5	1,300	0.6	780.0
	825	0.5	412.5	1,500	0.4	600.0
			725.0			1,380.0
Fixed cost £700,000 – £900,000	625	0.2	125.0	1,300	0.5	650.0
	825	0.8	660.0	1,500	0.5	750.0
			785.0			1,400.0
	725	0.3	217.5	1,380	0.4	552.0
	785	0.7	549.5	1,400	0.6	840.0
			767.0			1,392.0
	£'000		*£'000*	*£'000*		*£'000*
Contribution: Capacity × £1.50			1,150.5			2,088.0
Fixed cost	600	0.3	180.0	600	0.4	240.0
	800	0.7	560.0	800	0.6	480.0
			740.0			720.0

	Wye £'000	*Prob*	*EV*	*Zed* £'000	*Prob*	*EV*
Cash outflow	1,050	0.2	210.0	2,250	0.3	675.0
	1,200	0.25	300.0	2,600	0.3	780.0
	1,350	0.35	472.5	2,900	0.3	870.0
	1,450	0.2	290.0	3,250	0.1	325.0
			1,272.5			2,650.0

Answer:
Discounted Cash Flow Calculations

Year	*Cash flow*	*Disc Rate*	*PV*	*Cash flow*	*Disc Rate*	*PV*
0	−1,272.5	1.000	−1,273	−2,650.0	1.000	−2,650
1	+ 410.5	4.192	+1,721	+1,368.0	4.192	+5,735
Net Present Value			+ 448			+3,085

Comment: Building Zed is clearly the most advantageous option, given a financial quantification of the figures provided. However, the critical factor appears to be the ability of Riddle Company to sell the full capacity of the Zed building in the long-term. This matter should be more fully investigated before a final decision is taken. If necessary, further financial calculations should be produced.

18.4

	Year	*Cash flow* £'000	*Wye* *Disc rate*	*PV* £'000	*Cash flow* £'000	*Zed* *Disc rate*	*PV* £'000
Sensitivity analysis							
– 10% change in cost of capital			@22%			@22%	
	0	−1,272.5	1.000	−1,273	−2,650.0	1.000	−2,650
	1–10	+ 410.5	3.923	+1,610	+1,368.0	3.923	+5,367
				+ 337			+2,717
– 10% change in selling price			@20%			@20%	
	0	−1,272.5	1.000	−1,273	−2,650.0	1.000	−2,650
	1–10	− 88.1	4.192	− 369	+ 463.2	4.192	+1,942
				−1,642			− 708

Workings:

			£
Wye:	Cash flow, years 1–10, before selling price change:		410,500
	Throughput (capacity):	767,000 units	
	Value (@10% of ave. selling price £6.50)		498,550
			£88,050
Zed:	Cash flow, years 1–10, before selling price change:		1,368,000
	Throughput (capacity):	1,392,000 units	
	Value (@10% of ave. selling price £6.50)		904,800
			£463,200

(a) A 10% change in selling price creates a greater change in the outcome of the calculations than does a 10% change in cost of capital. Selling price is more critical than cost of capital, therefore.

(b) The choice of building is unaffected by the analysis; Zed would still be chosen.

(c) Sensitivity analysis confirms the soundness of the original decisions and shows management that Zed would be the correct choice even if their original estimates of selling price, or assessment of cost of capital were to prove incorrect.

By testing all of the variables (including the assumption that full capacity can be sold), two outcomes are possible:

(a) Zed will always be confirmed as the best choice

OR

(b) Under some circumstances (for specific variables) Wye may appear to be the best project. Further work may be necessary to improve knowledge of such circumstances.

Although Zed would be preferred to Wye for selling price and cost of capital variations, the decision to adopt *neither* project would result from a drop of 10% in selling price. Selling price is therefore a critical factor which management must investigate, perhaps through market research.

Sensitivity analysis does not directly reduce uncertainty but it should lead to management action to increase information and knowledge which may lead to more certain decision-making.

ANSWERS TO EXERCISES

18.1 Expected value of demand

	£5.75			£6.25		
	'000 units	*Prob*	*EV*	*'000 units*	*Prob*	*EV*
Pessimistic estimate	35	0.25	8.75	10	0.25	2.5
Most likely estimate	40	0.60	24.0	20	0.60	12.0
Optimistic estimate	50	0.15	7.5	40	0.15	6.0
			40.25			20.5

Expected value of variable cost

	£	*Prob*	*EV*
Optimistic estimate	4.75	0.10	0.475
Most likely estimate	4.90	0.75	3.675
Pessimistic estimate	5.20	0.15	0.78
			4.93

Expected value of contributions

	£5.75	£6.25
Selling price less variable cost of £4.93	£0.82	£1.32
Demand, units	40,250	20,500
Expected value of contribution	£33,005	£27,060

Expected value of fixed cost

£'000	*Prob*	*EV*
25	0.2	5.0
27	0.6	16.2
30	0.2	6.0
		27.2

(a) *Answer*: A selling price of £5.75 should be charged, resulting in an expected profit of £5,805 (£33,005 – £27,200).

However, the alternative of choosing £6.25, whilst more risky, does provide a higher profit potential and should be adopted where a risk-taking policy is appropriate:

	£5.75	£6.25
	£	£
Worst case:		
(35,000 units @ £5.75 – £5.20) – £30,000	–10,750	
(10,000 units @ £6.25 – £5.20) – £30,000		–19,500
Best case:		
(50,000 units @ £5.75 – £4.75) – £25,000	25,000	
(40,000 units @ £6.25 – £4.75) – £25,000		35,000

£6.25 may produce a profit of £35,000 but may equally lead to a loss of £19,500.

(b) An advantage to be gained from the use of probabilities is the ability to ask managers to respond to uncertainty in a more natural manner; by considering future events as ranges of possible outcomes rather than as a single, deterministic outcome. It may therefore be more appropriate for management accountants to request data from managers in the form of 'There is a 20% chance that fixed costs will fall between £24,000 and £26,000' rather than in the form 'the fixed costs will be £25,000 with a probability of 0.2'. The advice provided by management accountants can be no better than the quality of data used in carrying out financial analysis and the ability of the accountant to communicate clearly with managers is likely to be critical to the information process stage of decision taking.

Where a range, rather than a point estimate, is provided, the mid point will be used in the management accountant's calculations.

Note that a decision tree diagram would show 27 calculations of profit. Although, in practice, computerised approaches such as spreadsheets would allow a reasonably efficient means by which a number of permutations can be evaluated, a decision tree approach to this examination problem would increase time pressures. However, the decision tree does provide information from which a stronger answer to (a) can be produced, particularly the range of possible outcomes (the worst case is low demand, high variable cost, high fixed cost; the best case is high demand, low variable cost, low fixed cost) and, using computers, other measures of dispersion. An assessment of the risk of £5.75 and £6.25 can be coupled with the expected value information. It is this reasoning which prompted calculations of best and worst cases for inclusion in the answer to (a).

18.2 An answer should incorporate the following points in the manner prescribed by the question ((**a**) requires a description; (**b**) requires an explanation and a discussion; (**c**) requires a statement ('specify') and an explanation).

(a) It is not possible to state a single point estimate; example: a sales price under certainty may be £5, say, whilst a sales price under uncertainty may take on one of a possible range of values from £4 to £6, say.

It is not possible to predict the outcome of a particular decision; examples: if a person decides to carry an umbrella in case of rain, the umbrella may not be used because the rain does not fall; if a company decides to expand into a new building in anticipation of increased demand, the increased demand may not match anticipations.

Some managers are prepared to take a risk in carrying through a particular decision; others are risk averse. Some decisions are uncertain and subject to risk (may lead to high profits but are also capable of resulting in losses) whilst other decisions are uncertain but low in risk.

(b) **1** Simulation (provide a brief explanation).
Discussion:—a single simulation accounts explicitly for the element of chance which is an inherent part of uncertainty, but does not really assist management
—by conducting a series of simulations, a picture of the range and financial implications of uncertainty can be established.

2 Expected value and decision trees (provide a brief explanation and an illustrative example of a decision tree).
Discussion:—applies subjective probabilities where the decision relates to an original or unique situation
—expected value provides a decision rule based on a single figure derived as the weighted average of possible outcomes, the weighting being probability values
—all data values are used in the analysis
—does not take into account the attitude of the decision-maker towards risk, where expected value is used. Since worst case and best case situations are evaluated within the tree, however, additional analysis can be carried out to evaluate risk.

3 Sensitivity analysis (provide a brief explanation).
Discussion:—management can direct their efforts to those factors or variables which are critical to the decision. Such management action may reduce uncertainty.

(c) Decisions which are taken on the basis of financial analysis should further the objectives of the organisation. The preparer of data for decision-making should ensure that account is taken of uncertainty by considering all possible future outcomes in relation to the decision attribute (eg profit), the scale by which it is measured (eg profit as a percentage of capital employed) and the goal (the particular value or range of values on the scale which the firm seeks to attain), bearing in mind the attitude to risk of the decision taker.
Explanation: The preparer of data for decision-making is seeking to account for economic outcomes in a way which will lead management to take actions to promote organisational objectives. This calls for measurement which must be related to objectives. Ranges of values and attitudes to risk are fundamental aspects of decision taking under uncertainty.

Solutions to Chapter 19 questions

ANSWERS TO SELF-ASSESSMENT QUESTIONS

19.1 This question allows the student to exercise imagination but also demands some discipline in addressing problems of labour control. This answer lists some of the issues which could be raised.
Design requirements:

1 Mundane, repetitive tasks can be carried out by computer, releasing people to do those things which people do better than computers.
Computers can be used to produce information on attendance hours, cost analysis, payroll.
People can be released to meet and discuss labour control issues: ways in which quality, productivity and tasks can be improved to the benefit of all. Ideas similar to the Japanese Quality Circles could be implemented.
2 Information should be geared to 'directing future actions', and to pointing out 'requirements for corrective action' or 'opportunities for improvement'.
3 Information should lead to action. Computers may suggest suitable action which could be taken, perhaps through expert systems, but the action must be carried out by people.

Example to illustrate points 2 and 3:
Department N may be shown to be performing poorly, as measured by a productivity index calculated by the computer (good units of production, or standard hours of good production divided by direct labour hours). Direct labour hours may be collected by person, on portable recording equipment, and analysed in several ways, including analysis by product. Computer analysis reveals that one product is taking significantly longer to process. An expert system suggests that the cause of the problem is most likely to be sub-standard materials. Contacting the supplier and talking through the problem results in departmental productivity returning to normal.

Technical considerations:
1 Data capture eg portable recording equipment, methods of linking recording equipment to the computer, coding and code capturing mechanisms (eg bar codes, visual recognition systems).
2 Processing implications including data integrity (eg computer fraud contingency planning and avoidance).
3 Output requirements eg regularity, and detail contained in reports, mode of reporting (eg on screen, on-line or by printout).

Organisation considerations:
1 Effects of changing to systems with a greater element of technological involvement.
2 Motivation of people to take appropriate corrective action.
3 Implementing the system in a way which is suitable for people within the organisation.

19.2 *Budgeting*: Check by comparison and test the accuracy of; budgets check results by comparing actual results but it is not easy to generalise ways in which budgets are used to test accuracy. Two specific examples illustrate:

1 Some organisations seem to expect budgets to be accurate. Comparing budget with actual results may lead to accounting departments being shown to have failed to produce an accurate budget.

2 Some organisations use budgets to improve the accuracy of monthly financial reporting. A large variance may point to the incorrect omission of an accrual, for instance.

These examples are not to be assumed to be generally applicable or to state how budgets should be used; they merely describe observations made by the author which reveal different ways in which budgets are used for control purposes.
—take to task, call to account, rebuke, reprove; some budgeting systems, especially when linked to responsibility accounting, lead to these aspects of control.
—exercise restraint over, exercise power of authority over, to dominate or command; a later chapter describes the use of some budgets as 'strait-jackets'.

Standard costing: The way in which some standard costing systems operate can lead to comments similar to those given above for budgeting.

Responsibility accounting: —take to task, call to account, rebuke, reprove; responsibility accounting can be used to call people to account and some managers operate responsibility accounting by taking others to task, rebuking and reproving where appropriate.

Auditing: —check or verify and hence to regulate; the process of regulation is by means of a statement of qualification. Auditors check or verify to ensure that a 'true and fair view' is presented by published accounts and hence regulate the quality of reporting to shareholders and other users of financial statements.

—check by comparison and test the accuracy of: analytical review may be given as an example of the auditor exercising control in this manner.

19.3 *Differences*:

1 The machine repair company is faced with a greater degree of uncertainty in its environment because:
   (a) it may be difficult to predict when a machine will break down and therefore require repair
   (b) the type of motor to be repaired can be one out of a possible one thousand different types
   (c) the existence of competitors means that a customer may decide to have a specific repair carried out elsewhere
2 The machine repair company operates probabilistically, therefore, where the milk bottling plant appears to be able to operate deterministically.

Evaluation of purchases cost variance: The milk bottling plant will probably need to analyse the variance to a lesser degree of detail since there should be a smaller number of raw materials (possibly only milk) and fewer processes to which raw materials are issued. Variance evaluation may therefore be more complex for the machine repairer.

The milk bottling plant is likely to operate systems consistent with continuous operation costing whilst the machine repairer is likely to operate specific order costing. Purchase costing reporting systems may therefore be different and this may affect the way in which variances are evaluated.

It is likely that both accountants could be expected to reach similar conclusions about whether the variance in total is significant for the company. At a detailed level, the differences outlined above may lead the accountants to evaluate their variances in manners which differ.

19.4 1 Under negative feedback, action should be taken to comply with the wastage target of 3%. Presumably, the improved performance which created a 2% wastage level will be reversed in order that a 3% result can be reported in the future.

2 Under positive feedback, action would seek to increase the improvements in performance so that future results of better than 2% are achieved. The limit to the application of positive feedback is that no improvement is possible once a zero percent wastage figure has been achieved.

19.5 This question essentially concerns the degree to which a budget should be changed once it no longer represents a fair reflection of suppliers' prices, competitors' actions, customer demand, market prices and other factors of this kind. There is a trade-off between the cost of revising the budget and the cost of inappropriate information provided by the budgeting system. One view may be that, with computers and spreadsheets or financial modelling languages, the cost of revising a budget for known, uncontrollable changes should be low and budgetary control should operate as a double loop system. Another view is that the existence of more than one budget causes confusion and that the system should operate as a closed system so that people know where they stand in relation to a single target. For this latter view, some organisations monitor trends in variances and take corrective action where the trend is inexplicable. The variances can be extrapolated forward to calculate future outputs which can be compared with plan in accordance with the principle of feedforward.

ANSWERS TO EXERCISES

19.1

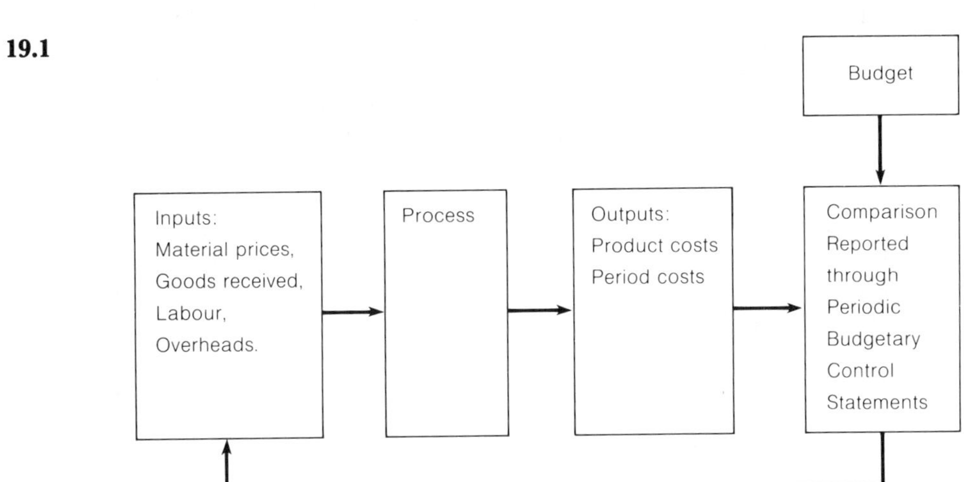

Note: There are numerous ways in which this diagram has been presented by authorities in recent years. The important aspect of a suitable answer is the clear presentation of a system, with inputs and outputs, feedback and the budget operating as an objective.
Circumstances required for the system to operate effectively:

1 Objectives must be clear
2 Inputs must be accurately measured
3 Outputs must be clear and unambiguous
4 There must be a clearly understood model of the way in which the system operates and reflects the organisation
5 Feedback should be frequent and timely.

The chapter provides additional notes on each of these points.

19.2 Control 'consists, in part, of inducing people in an organisation to do certain things and to refrain from doing other things'. An individual's willingness to comply through self control rather than from controls imposed by others can be conducive to the process of getting certain things done whilst other things are not done. An example may be co-operation over productivity. If management believe that a reasonable standard of performance is, say, production of 35 standard hours per employee per week and employee A applies self control and achieves the target, this may be beneficial to both the organisation and to employee A. If employee B lacks self control, as evidenced by poor punctuality and lack of concentration, for instance, and consistently achieves 33 standard hours per week, problems are posed for both the employee and the organisation. Self control can therefore be a positive force in the achievement of organisational objectives.

19.3 *Planning*: It is difficult to see how such an organisation could be persuaded to adopt systematic forecasting or to develop strategies unless the key individuals co-operate. The management accountant would presumably need to hold some influence rather than to rely on rules in the development of formal planning systems. If the central power source does not wish to plan, it is difficult to see how plans can be drawn up and, therefore, it is difficult to see how cybernetic systems based on feedback can be established.

Control: Internal control relies on procedures and the formal definition of duties and responsibilities. It may be difficult to operate internal control in organisations where there are few rules and bureaucracy. Internal controls are both procedural and logical whilst the balance of influence is more critical to the process of taking decisions within the power culture.

Cybernetic systems are possibly equally procedural or logical and additionally may have no objective or plan to form a foundation for feedback, as noted earlier.

The management accountant will have the problem of understanding and responding to organisational politics and thereby having a positive influence on the organisation. There would be no guarantee that budgets, standards or other financial systems would achieve the outcomes expected by the management accountant, however technically or logically sound the systems. For example, a particular reported variance may be used by a manager to change the balance of power and influence, rather than to take corrective action to benefit the organisation.

Solutions to Chapter 20 questions

ANSWERS TO SELF-ASSESSMENT QUESTIONS

20.1 The following points illustrate the questions which could be asked and the types of strategy which could be produced:
Position audit:

1 In which subjects do I have some knowledge from previous studies?
2 How can I find time to study; how much free time is available now, how much time can be made available by not doing certain activities?
3 How much money do I have to spend on courses, books, revision sessions or answers to past examination questions?

Objectives
To pass examinations in order to become a qualified accountant.
To learn as much as possible so as to become expert in accountancy, with sufficient practical experience.

Environmental analysis:
How many students normally pass the examinations?
What are the qualifications, practical experiences and time commitment of other students taking the examinations?

Strengths and weaknesses:
What are my personal strengths and weaknesses?
In which subjects am I strong/weak?

Opportunities and threats:
Are there any special courses or text material available to help pass the examination?
Are there any personal commitments which will make it difficult to devote sufficient time and energy to studies over the period up to the examination?
Can anyone provide personal advice, perhaps based on experience in qualifying as an accountant?

Feedforward:
Based on past and present experience, does it appear that methods of learning which have proved successful/adequate/unsuccessful will prove to be sufficient to meet objectives in the future?

Statement of strategy:
To attend all classes timetabled as part of a programme of study.
To devote, say, fifteen hours per week to reading and attempting self-assessment questions and exercises.
To study for a period of at least thirty weeks, say, before presenting myself for examination.

Note: This answer is an illustration and is not intended to suggest that all points have been covered or that certain questions or strategies are essential to success. The point is that each individual can produce their own strategy and be successful in meeting their objectives.

20.2 There is room for debate on some of these issues. The answer which follows provides a justification for each classification and accepts that other views and other justifications may be equally valid.

1 *Operational control.* The system is concerned with day–to–day control of employees. Measurement is exact; concerned with accurate recording of attendance time. The routine is repetitive; the same procedures are followed week after week. The element of judgement in determining the number of hours attended by a particular employee is minor.

2 *Strategy.* The strategy is to operate a flexible pricing policy with the objective of securing competitive advantage. The judgement of managers is paramount in arriving at a selling price necessary to maximise market share. For instance, one organisation with which the author is familiar increased selling prices to improve its competitive position. Another organisation tries to maintain minimum selling prices. It is difficult to lay down rules or to know exactly the outcomes of a selling price change. A long-term policy of pricing, which gains the acceptance and trust of customers, may be more effective than changing prices short-term, perhaps in direct response to competitors. Another organisation familiar to the author changes prices once a year, despite interim cost increases, as a long-term policy.

3 *Operational control.* The element of judgement is minimal. Calculations are relatively exact. The system is guided by pre-established procedures or decision rules.

4 *Operational control, for the reasons listed under 3 above.*

5 *Operational control, for the reasons listed under 3 above.*

This is the most controversial item in the list. It could be argued that the estimation of cash flows is judgemental and that the project will be of long-term duration, thus making this an example of strategic decision taking. The controversy perhaps suggests that some techniques or procedures are capable of being used for strategic or operational control purposes, dependent on how management implement the system in practice. The author is certainly aware of examples of investment decisions which could not be described under the heading of strategy.

6 *Strategy.* The process is highly judgemental, inexact and long-term.

20.3 As in the case of self-assessment question 20.2, alternative responses may be appropriate. The important aspect of this question is that students should think about relating specific systems to the terms 'strategy', 'management control' and 'operational control' to gain an insight into the usefulness of the framework in considering practical systems.

Strategy	Management Control	Operational Control
1 Budgeting system		
	2 Budgetary control	
	3 Standard costing	
		4 Standard costing
		5 Manufacturing system

1 Budgeting system—may be considered to be of tactical importance and therefore unclassifiable.

6 Budgeting system—there is insufficient detail to know how the system is being operated and this is therefore unclassifiable. Alternatively, the generalised system could be considered an example of management control.

20.4 The examples which follow illustrate the general point, but are not exhaustive.

1 Monthly budgetary control report.

2 A newsletter circulated monthly by the Board of Directors, describing company or personal achievements.

3 A Discounted Cash Flow calculation for a one-off investment decision.

4 A video showing the company's latest television advertisement and explaining how this contributes to marketing strategy.

5 A discussion between the financial director and the management accountant concerning the cash flow implications of buying a new machine.

6 The narrative material included as part of Published Financial Statements prepared in accordance with legislation eg non-quantitative requirements of the Chairman's Report.

ANSWERS TO EXERCISES

20.1 *Feedback control*: Actual results for a particular period are compared with budget. Where differences arise, action is taken to change the inputs which create the results. Improvements in wastage or prices paid for raw materials may result from actions taken. Where action cannot be taken because uncontrollable factors are found to cause divergences from budget, the budget itself may be revised. Budgets commonly operate through a process of negative feedback but there are situations where positive feedback may be beneficial, especially in relation to favourable variances.

Feedforward control: Feedforward is concerned with taking control action where anticipated future outputs deviate from objectives. For example, where variance trends are projected into the future and are found to be unsatisfactory in the light of meeting organisational objectives, corrective action would be initiated. Where feedback is concerned with differences between outputs and objectives related to past periods, feedforward is concerned with differences between outputs and objectives related to future periods.

Noise: Noise is an unwanted component in information processing. A mistake in making out a goods received note or in keying in data at a computer terminal can create 'noisy data'; data with unwanted figures or mistakes. If sufficient noise is present, the message conveyed can be entirely obliterated and no meaningful communications take place. Noise in management information systems is often random and may be unavoidable. Actual results may contain noise where, for example, a one-off circumstance arises; perhaps an employee creates an excessive amount of wastage on a particular day because of personal problems which are quickly overcome. In this case, it is not useful to take corrective action once the deviation from budget is reported. The management accountant needs to develop systems which can tolerate noise. Systems which contain a low ratio of noisy data help in this regard.

Distortion: Distortion changes the form of a message being conveyed by a piece of information. If a manager knows that a cost target of, say, £500,000 is achievable but states that a budget must be set at a minimum of £600,000, distortion has occurred. Variances which result from the budgetary control systems would not be a fair reflection of reality, in this case. The management accountant needs sufficient knowledge to reduce distortion. Knowledge of previous cost trends or budgets may lead to the setting of a budget of £500,000 for the example given, successfully reversing the effects of distortion which were to increase the budgeted allowance by £100,000.

Short-term plan: A budget prepared for a single year is an example of a short-term plan. This can be used as a tactical device or to monitor results as a process of budgetary control. The short-term plan is a means by which management control can be exercised. The short-term plan can be expressed in relative detail and act as both a planning device, in expressing ways in which objectives can be met through short-term actions, and a control device, when incorporated into feedback or feedforward systems.

Long-term plan. The long-term plan, perhaps over a period of five or ten years, is a strategic device which should help the organisation to meet its objectives in the long-term. It may form the basis for short-term planning, or alternatively may incorporate information filtered from the short-term plan. The five year budget would provide a quantification in financial terms of the implications of long-term planning, including a summarised profit and loss account, balance sheet and cash flow statement.

20.2 *Planning*: The budget can provide a financial quantification of the plans of the organisation for both forecasting and strategic purposes. As a forecast, the budget may be used to predict profit, cash and financial position for the foreseeable future. As a strategic tool, the budget can be a means by which the objectives and long-term plans can be communicated throughout the organisation in order to act as a form of motivation. The budget can provide routine, formal and quantified information for planning purposes, in both the long- and short-term.

Control: Cybernetic control works by correcting inputs based on deviations between system's output and the objectives of the system. The budget can reflect a quantification of short-term plans through which objectives can be met. A comparison of actual results and budget can thus enable the company to take corrective action where necessary to ensure that objectives are achieved. Budgetary control systems provide formal, quantified and routine information of deviations between budgets, initially produced as plans, and actual results. Typical corrective actions include negotiating reductions in raw material prices, modifying processes to improve wastage levels and motivating people to improve productivity.

Evaluation: The budget can provide the criterion by which performance and results are evaluated. An adverse variance may, in some circumstances, indicate poor performance. A favourable variance may indicate good performance.

A second aspect is the evaluation of the variances which are reported by the budgetary control system. In a variety of ways (normally associated with the investigation of variances decision), the management accountant may reach the conclusion that certain variances are significant, or material, whilst others are insignificant or immaterial. The result of evaluating variances is that some variances, those considered significant, are the subject of further management activity, with an intention to take corrective action.

Solutions to Chapter 21 questions

ANSWERS TO SELF-ASSESSMENT QUESTIONS

21.1 **1** *Lack of goal congruence* describes the situation where the goals of individuals within an organisation do not coincide with organisational objectives.

2 Argyris found a situation where budgets had the effect of a strait-jacket, applying pressure to improve efficiency and effectiveness. This effect could insult the personal dignity of people, rather than acting as a motivational tool, as intended by accountants.

3 Argyris found that budgets could be a source of *conflict* between accountants and managers. Accountants might see that success comes from finding managers' inefficiencies and examples of ineffectiveness.

4 Merton found that management could behave in a simplistic, rigid and defensive manner where internal control and evaluation targets reward conformity. Managers may act to ensure that targets are met without necessarily improving the underlying performance of their departments. Instead of striving to improve managerial performance, senior managers may respond to emerging problems by introducing further controls. This can lead to an even greater degree of stultified decision-making.

5 *Suboptimisation* describes decisions taken to the benefit of individual divisions but to the detriment of the organisation as a whole.

6 *Dysfunction decision-making* leads to outcomes which defeat the objectives which the decision intends to achieve.

7 *Bias or budget slack* represents distorted information intended to create an allowance between achievable outcomes and budget predictions.

21.2 Contingent factors are the variables which determine the type of management and information systems which are suitable for a particular organisation. The table suggests that rate of change, predictability (ie the ability to predict future outcomes), the behaviour of competitors and the nature of the product range are the major determinants of organisational design, control system assumptions and accounting information system (AIS) characteristics.

A centralised organisation retains power at Head Office and minimises discretion and autonomy at divisional level. Decentralised organisations allow divisions to plan, control and take decisions independently of the centre, or Head Office.

Goal congruence is concerned with the goals or objectives of individuals in relation to the organisation.

Behaviour congruence is concerned with the extent to which the behaviour of individuals is beneficial to the organisation.

Role cultures define responsibilities and tasks in a clear, precise and unambiguous manner. Responsibility accounting is an inherent part of role cultures.

Existential cultures are concerned that individuals meet their own needs.

Functional efficiency relates outputs to inputs for each of the functions, including marketing, production and administration. Divisional effectiveness assumes that control systems should encourage divisions to meet objectives.

Participation promotes the involvement of individual people in contributing to the management process.

Financial performance measures include the ability to comply with cost targets, profit results and return on capital results. Non financial measures include quality performance, wastage levels and labour turnover rates.

Qualitative measures include assessments of labour relations and market standing, including customer relations.

Contingency theory is concerned with the circumstances which influence management and organisational design. The theory argues that there is no single rule of organisation or management which is best for all organisations. It could be argued that the two columns provided in Self-assessment question 21.2 represent extreme types of situation. In designing management accounting systems, issues such as participation, rewards and evaluation criterion need to be resolved. The management accountant may need to assess where a company lies between the two extremes and implement systems with the contingent factors in mind. There is no prescription on management and organisational design acceptable to all authorities and the management accountant therefore needs to apply judgement in designing and implementing systems.

ANSWERS TO EXERCISES

21.3 Contingency theory is concerned with the factors or variables which influence management style and organisational design. Management accountants design and implement systems in ways which can either have beneficial effects or harmful effects of the kind described by Argyris. If there are no universally valid rules of organisation and management, the management accountant cannot expect to be able to design a single system which would be capable of being beneficial for all organisations. There is no single answer to how accountants should produce accounts which have a beneficial effect on the people around them.

Emmanuel and Otley have suggested that organisations experiencing low rate of change, low competitive hostility, which have a homogeneous product range and are able to predict the future with certainty can implement management accounting systems which evaluate performance through short-term budgets. Rewards can be linked to financial performance measures and the participation of management in systems such as budgeting is not necessary. However, many organisations experience a high rate of change, cannot easily predict the future and offer a variety of products within highly competitive markets. It is argued that such organisations need to operate management accounting systems which evaluate performance based on long-term trends, including non-financial and qualitative measures. Rewards should not be linked to financial performance. Divisional managers should be allowed to participate in planning.

Although contingency theory does show that different organisations benefit from different managerial and organisational systems, there is no clear statement acceptable to all authorities. A de-centralised organisation *may* benefit from a profit centre or investment centre approach. A centralised organisation *may* beneficially use cost centres. However, no single statement prescribes the implications of the contingent factors so that the management accountant can avoid the use of judgement in designing systems.

21.5 (a) (i) Budgetary slack is an example of distortion of information. By definition, distortion can be combated by creating adjustments with equal and opposite effect. If a manager, who is known to build in slack of 10%, submits a cost budget of £100,000, the management accountant can create an unbiased budget by budgeting for costs of £90,000.

Budgetary slack can reduce the effects of personal stress and uncertainty and thus be beneficial (Onsi). However, it can also be dysfunctional, as illustrated by pseudo-participation. Returning to the example given above, if the manager knows that the management accountant will reduce a budget by 10%, slack of 20% may be incorporated into the next budgeting cycle. This may give rise to bargaining between the management accountant and the manager. A result might be that the amount of bias becomes unknown, with the consequence that it is impossible to produce an unbiased plan for the organisation. Control is lost because of the lack of a reliable yardstick or gauge against which to measure and monitor results.

(ii) Budget standard setting can be implemented in a variety of ways. This answer will consider two issues: participation and aspiration levels.

Schiff and Lewin found that participation allowed managers to build slack into their budgets. Examples of two dysfunctional consequences are:

—cost standards may be stated at levels which do not take into account planned improvements. The motivation to implement the improvements may thus be lessened, resulting in a loss of control where control is concerned with ensuring that individuals are directed to taking actions of benefit to the organisation.
—increased personnel levels may be planned but recruitment deferred to ensure that short-term targets, as expressed by the annual budget, are met. This can be dysfunctional because the long-term rationale for employing additional staff should ensure that benefits exceed costs. An example is the recruitment of an engineer to carry out preventive maintenance. A saving in salary through deferring recruitment may increase costs of breakdowns and machinery replacement in the long-term.

Hofstede suggested a framework linking budget standard setting with aspiration levels. Aspiration levels are the performance standards which individuals hope to achieve. Loose standards create unambitious aspirations and result in relatively poor performance. As long as tighter budgets lead to more ambitious aspirations, performance improves. Where budgets become so tight as to be discouraging, aspiration levels and performance deteriorate. Stedry found that best performance came from experimental groups who set their aspiration levels after seeing high budget targets.

Managers who expect that improved performance can be achieved by merely setting tighter budget standards are only correct up to a point. Dysfunctional consequences result from excessively tight standards; performance deteriorates. Managers must understand the role of aspiration levels if budgets are to be used to control through motivation.

(iii) Where annual budgets take the place of objectives in feedback systems, it is necessary to ensure that such short-term objectives are consistent with and are likely to achieve organisational objectives in the long-term. Where this is not the case, dysfunctional consequences may arise, as illustrated by the example of deferring recruitment of an engineer to carry out preventive maintenance. It may also be advantageous to encourage individuals to have short- and long-term goals which are congruent with corporate goals.

(b) The physical costs of the technical aspect of the systems:
—manpower to collect, process and issue information; computers; occupancy and materials costs such as stationery.
—cost of designing, implementing and evaluating the system.
Comment: The technical aspects of the system need to be correct, in relation to established practices and criteria such as standard statements of accounting practice (eg where standards are used to value stock, the requirements of SSAP 9 need to be met). These technical aspects partially govern the physical costs of the system. However, the Tavistock Institute pointed out that systems need to optimise both technical and social aspects. Some of the physical costs of the system can thus be expected to arise from the need to design standards in a way which is beneficial to people in the organisation.

—Behavioural costs:

—dysfunctional consequences arising from stress and other factors outlined earlier in the answer.

—Behavioural benefits:

—increased motivation.
—involvement and personal satisfaction associated with participation.

Comment: Standard costing can either create a beneficial or a negative effect upon behaviours within an organisation. Used as a control mechanism, the behavioural consequences of control systems can be related to standards, as to budgets. If a standard is set too loose, less than optimal performance can be expected to result.

—Physical benefits:

—improvements in wastage levels and other quality factors
—increased productivity
—general performance improvement, affecting profits or other organisational objectives directly.

Comment: Standards are intended to promote control. Control is concerned with directing the actions of people. Standards themselves do not create improvements, but when used effectively can be one way in which management encourages people to meet organisational objectives. Standards are implemented *by* people (eg accountants) *for* people (eg managers).

Solutions to Chapter 22 questions

ANSWERS TO SELF-ASSESSMENT QUESTIONS

22.1 1

	Fixed budget £'000	£/unit	*Flexed budget* £'000	*Actual* £'000	*Variance* £'000
	(2,500,000 units)		(based on 2,170,000 units)		
Sales	3,500	1.40	3,038.0	3,255.0	217.0 fav.
Purchases	1,750	0.70	1,519.0	1,714.3	195.3 adv.
Labour	100	—	100.0	108.0	8.0 adv.
Overheads	650	—	650.0	654.0	4.0 adv.
Cost of Sales	2,500	—	2,269.0	2,476.3	207.3 adv.
Gross Profit	1,000	—	769.0	778.7	9.7 fav.
Expenses	650	—	650.0	659.0	9.0 adv.
Net Profit	350	—	119.0	119.7	0.7 fav.

2 Budgeted cost per unit £0.70
Actual cost per unit £0.79 (£1,714,300/2,170,000 units)

Value Variance	Quantity Variance	Total
Method 1		
2,170,000 @ £0.09	£0.70 for 330,000 units	
£195,300 adverse	£231,000 favourable	£35,700 favourable
Method 2		
2,500,000 @ £0.09	£0.79 for 330,000 units	
£225,000 adverse	£260,700 favourable	£35,700 favourable
Method 3		
2,170,000 @ £0.09	£0.79 for 330,000 units	
£195,300 adverse	£260,700 favourable	
	Joint value-quantity variance	
	330,000 units @ £0.09	
	£29,700 adverse	£35,700 favourable

3 The flexed budget statement shows that the selling price charged was greater than budget. Whilst this appears to be favourable, it should be noted that the higher selling price may have reduced demand. The purchases variance is adverse, showing that £195,300 of overspending occurred.

Variance analysis of the comparison between fixed budget and actual expenditure reveals an adverse value variance and a favourable quantity variance. The meaning of the quantity variance is that a saving occurred by selling fewer units. The meaning of the value variance is that overspending occurred. Method 1 reports the same magnitude of variance as reported on the flexed budget statement; £195,300. This must have been caused by paying more for purchases than planned, where 2,170,000 units were purchased for sale.

22.2 Since the management is concerned with the performance of Northern division and evaluation is by means of divisional comparison, variance analysis between Northern-Southern and Northern-Central divisions appears to be sensible.

Northern-Southern

Result Northern division	Southern's prices	Southern's mix	Reference Southern division
L 50,000 @ £4	50,000 @ £4	(30) 30,000 @ £4	30,000 @ £4
M 25,000 @ £5	25,000 @ £5	(30) 30,000 @ £5	30,000 @ £5
N 25,000 @ £6	25,000 @ £6	(40) 40,000 @ £6	40,000 @ £6
£475,000	£475,000	£510,000	£510,000
Wtd. ave. £4.75	£4.75	£5.10	£5.10
(£475,000/100,000)		(£510,000/100,000)	

Northern-Central

Result Northern division	Central's prices	Central's mix	Reference Central division
L 50,000 @ £4	50,000 @ £4.50	(60) 50,000 @ £4.50	60,000 @ £4.50
M 25,000 @ £5	25,000 @ £5.50	(30) 25,000 @ £5.50	30,000 @ £5.50
N 25,000 @ £6	25,000 @ £6.50	(30) 25,000 @ £6.50	30,000 @ £6.50
£475,000	£525,000	£525,000	£630,000
Wtd. ave. £4.75	£5.25	£5.25	£5.25
(£475,000/100,000)	(£525,000/100,000)	(£525,000/100,000)	(£630,000/120,000)

Management information:
Northern division performs equally as well as Southern division, selling a total of 100,000 units at the same selling prices, except with regard to mix. L and M each have a lower than average selling price. North sells 50% and 25% of these products respectively. South sells these products in the proportions 30% and 30%. North sells a bigger proportion of L, which creates an adverse performance but a smaller proportion of M, which is favourable. N has a higher than average selling price. North sells N at a proportion of 25%, 5% below South's 30% mix, thus creating an adverse effect. The overall situation is summarised below.

	Proportions *Northern Division*	*Southern Division*	*Variance* %	*Variance* Units, based on 100,000 total sales	*Variance* £/unit compared with £5.10 weighted ave.	*Variance* £
L	50%	30%	+20%	+20,000	−£1.10	22,000 adv.
M	25%	30%	− 5%	− 5,000	−£0.10	500 fav.
N	25%	40%	−15%	−15,000	+£0.90	13,500 adv.
						35,000 adv.

Northern division sells each of its products at a selling price £0.50/unit lower than Central division. This average £0.50/unit cost Northern division £50,000 during June, when 100,000 units were sold. Additionally, Northern sold 20,000 units less than Central division. If Northern division had increased its sales by those 20,000 units, at the expected weighted average selling price of £5.25, an extra £105,000 of revenue could have been earned.

Northern division could thus improve its performance if it can:
(a) increase its selling prices AND/OR
(b) sell a greater proportion of L and a lower proportion of N AND/OR
(c) sell a greater number of units.

ANSWERS TO EXERCISES

22.1 Flexed budget, assuming that variable costs respond to sales value

	Actual	Flexed budget	Variance
	£	£	£
Sales	6,800,000	6,800,000	—
Cost of goods sold	4,100,000	3,833,333	266,667 adv.
Gross Profit	2,700,000	2,966,667	266,667 adv.
General expenses	2,000,000	1,900,000	100,000 adv.
Net Profit	700,000	1,066,667	366,667 adv.

Flexed budget: workings and assumptions

Fixed budget:	Variable cost of sales 3,500,000 – 1,000,000	£2,500,000
	Sales value	£6,000,000
	%-age of variable cost to sales value	$41\frac{2}{3}$%
	Actual sales	£6,800,000
	Flexed cost of sales ($41\frac{2}{3}$% of £6,800,000, plus £1,000,000 fixed cost)	£3,833,333

It is assumed that general expenses are fixed.

Flexed budget, assuming that variable costs respond to sales units

	Actual	Flexed budget	Variance
	£	£	£
Sales	6,800,000	6,250,000	550,000 fav.
Cost of goods sold	4,100,000	3,604,167	495,833 adv.
Gross Profit	2,700,000	2,645,833	54,167 fav.
General expenses	2,000,000	1,900,000	100,000 adv.
Net Profit	700,000	745,833	45,833 adv.

Workings:

Actual number of units sold (£6,800,000 ÷ £5.44)	1,250,000
Budgeted variable cost per unit: variable cost	£2,500,000
units (£6,000,000 ÷ £5)	1,200,000
£/unit	£2.083
Flexed budget: 1,250,000 units @ £2.083 + £1,000,000	£3,604,167
Sales value: Flexed budget 1,250,000 units @ £5	£6,250,000

It may also be useful to flex the previous year's figures. The following statements compare results with both flexed budget and previous year's cost and revenue structures.

Assuming that variable costs respond to sales value:

	Actual	Flexed Budget	Flex Previous Year
	£'000	£'000	£'000
Sales	6,800	6,800	6,800
Cost of sales	4,100	3,833	3,473
Gross Profit	2,700	2,967	3,327
General expenses	2,000	1,900	1,900
Net Profit	700	1,067	1,427

[Cost of sales: £2,000,000 × 6,800,000/5,500,000 + £1,000,000 = £3,472,727]

Assuming that variable costs respond to sales units:

	Actual	Flexed Budget	Flex Previous Year
	£'000	£'000	£'000
Sales	6,800	6,250	6,250[1]
Cost of sales	4,100	3,604	3,273[2]
Gross Profit	2,700	2,646	2,977
General expenses	2,000	1,900	1,900
Net Profit	700	746	1,077

[1] [1,250,000 units @ £5]
[2] [1,250,000 units @ £1.818 + £1m]

The company should investigate its cost control systems carefully because it appears to be underperforming in cost terms.

22.2

	This Year	*Last Year*	*Variance*
	£	£	£
Sales	6,800,000	5,500,000	
Contribution, assuming fixed cost = £1,000,000	3,700,000	3,500,000	
Contribution target	3,500,000	3,360,000	
	200,000	140,000	
Bonus @ 10%	20,000		
Bonus @ 8%		11,200	8,800

The variance of £8,800 arose from two causes: the increase in contribution for which a bonus was payable and an increase in the bonus percentage:

Result (this year)	200,000	×	10%	20,000
	200,000	×	8%	16,000
Reference (last year)	140,000	×	8%	11,200

The increase in bonus percentage cost the company £4,000 (£20,000 – £16,000) but contribution increased £140,000 (£3,500,000 less £3,360,000), possibly partially due to the efforts of the sales executives, although the implications of figures produced in Exercise 22.1 need to be carefully evaluated. The increased contribution itself cost the company £4,800 (£16,000 – £11,200). These two elements of the increased cost of commission should be evaluated in terms of:

(a) the motivational implications for the sales executives of increasing the commission rate from 8% to 10%.

(b) the extent to which the benefits of £140,000 contribution are related to the costs of £4,800 commission difference. Initial evidence, particularly the increase in sales units from 1,100,000 units last year to 1,250,000 units this year, may suggest that the cost of the commission scheme is justified in terms of benefits to the organisation.

22.3 The major difficulty of this question is defining the problem. Just exactly what information would be helpful to management? The starting point is therefore to define the situation:

OPQ is buying in items which have a DM value. The DM value is initially unknown, but can be calculated in terms of a result and a reference based on budget. Combining this value with the quantity of DM to the £ gives a cost to OPQ of £18, compared with a budget of £20. The average quantity of DM to the £ is known for the result and a budget of 3DM to the £ has been set. There appear to be two variances, therefore:

1 the DM value may differ as between the result and budget

2 the DM to the £ quantity, or exchange, rate may differ as between the result and budget.
Number of units purchased: £540,000/£18 = 30,000 units
Actual DM value: £18 × 3.1 = 55.8 DM
Budgeted DM value: £20 × 3 = 60 DM

Result 30,000 units @ 55.8 DM/unit @ 3.1 DM/£ = £540,000
↓
30,000 units @ 60 DM/unit @ 3.1 DM/£ = £580,645
↓
Reference 30,000 units @ 60 DM/unit @ 3 DM/£ = £600,000

Check, 30,000 units should cost £20 each, which is £600,000.

Value variance: The price of the item fell by 7%, saving £40,645 in the quarter. [£580,645 – £540,000]

Quantity variance: The exchange rate increased, saving £19,355 in the quarter.

If the problem is defined in alternative ways to that given above, different variances would result. This answer illustrates how the general variance approach can be applied to unconventional situations to provide information which may be beneficial to the management process. Other answers, based on carefully defined statements of the problem, may be equally helpful.

ANSWERS TO SELF-TEST QUESTIONS

22.1 2 Variance concerns difference or deviation.

22.2 3

Price paid	£10/unit
Reference	£11/unit
	£1/unit favourable

This is based on result quantity of 30,000 units, giving £30,000 favourable.

22.3 2

Units purchased	30,000 units
Reference	36,000 units (30,000 × 6/5)
	6,000 units favourable

This is based on reference value of £11/unit, giving £66,000 favourable.

22.4 2

'Flexed on the basis of units' must refer to output units. Output units are 30,000 raw material units/5 units of raw material per output unit = 6,000
Budgeted cost allowance per output unit would be based on standard: 6 units @ £11/unit = £66/output unit.

The flexed budget = 6,000 × £66	£396,000
Purchases were 30,000 units @ £10	£300,000
Variance	£ 96,000 favourable

More will be said in later chapters on budgets (fixed and flexible) and standards.

Solutions to Chapter 23 questions

ANSWERS TO SELF-ASSESSMENT QUESTIONS

23.1 Production or sales could be the limiting factor. Production cannot exceed 160,000 units. Production, based on sales as the limiting factor, would be:

Using the relationship: opening stock of finished goods plus production less sales equals closing stock of finished goods:

Sales	100,000 units
less: Opening stock of finished goods	10,000 units
add: Closing stock of finished goods	9,000 units
equals: Production	99,000 units

$$\begin{aligned}[\text{O.S} + \text{P} - \text{S} &= \text{C.S} \\ \therefore \quad \text{P} &= \text{C.S} - \text{O.S} + \text{S} \\ &= \text{S} - \text{O.S} + \text{C.S}]\end{aligned}$$

This shows that sales are the limiting factor. Sales of 100,000 units and Production of 99,000 units would be budgeted.

Materials used in finished production:	
99,000 units @ 10kg/unit	990,000 kg
Materials to be issued:	
Materials used in finished production	990,000 kg
less: materials in opening stock of w.i.p. (4,000 × 10kg × 60%)	24,000 kg
add: materials in closing stock of w.i.p. (24,000 less 10%)	21,600 kg
equals: Materials to be issued to production	987,600 kg
Materials to be purchased:	
Materials to be issued to production	987,600 kg
less: Opening stock of raw materials	50,000 kg
add: Closing stock of raw materials	45,000 kg
equals: Purchases	982,600 kg

Note: There are alternative presentations which would be acceptable and which reflect the relationships between stocks, inputs and outputs equally effectively, for instance:

Input = Output − Opening stock + Closing stock is used consistently above, this is the same as:

Input = Output + Closing stock − Opening stock

OR:

Input = Output + (Closing stock − Opening stock)
= Output + Increase in stocks.

23.2 The inefficient way of preparing a profit and loss account is to prepare the financial accountant's manufacturing, trading and profit and loss account. This will be shown first because many students and some authorities are familiar with the methodology and, therefore, the layout crops up at surprisingly regular intervals. The second presentation adopts the cost accountant's approach, based on a knowledge of the flow of costs through a cost accounting system.

Factors Limited
Manufacturing, trading and profit and loss account
for the budget period ending. . .19x0

	£	£
Raw materials consumed:		
Opening stock (50,000 @ £2)	100,000	
add: Purchases (982,600 @ £2)	1,965,200	
	2,065,200	
less: Closing stock (45,000 @ £2)	90,000	1,975,200
Production overhead		1,000,000
		2,975,200
add: Opening stock of work in progress	72,240	
less: Closing stock of work in progress	65,016	7,224
Manufacturing Cost of Production		2,982,424
Sales (100,000 units @ £50 per unit)		5,000,000
Cost of goods sold:		
Opening stock of finished goods	301,000	
Manufacturing Cost of Production	2,982,424	
	3,283,424	
less: Closing stock of finished goods	270,900	3,012,524
Gross Profit		1,987,476
General expenses		1,500,000
Net Profit		487,476

[Gross Profit is 40% of sales, or turnover and, therefore, cost of sales must be 60% of turnover. Net Profit + Expenses = Gross Profit]

Answer:
Workings: Valuation of work in progress and finished goods stocks.

Product costing:	£/unit
Raw materials (10kg @ £2/kg)	20.00
Production overhead (£1,000,000/99,000)	10.10
	30.10

It is assumed that the planned output from production of 99,000 would approximate to a SSAP 9 definition of normal activity.

Work in Progress:	
Opening stock (4,000 units @ £30.10, 60% complete)	£72,240
Closing stock (£72,240 less 10%)	£65,016
Finished goods:	
Opening stock (10,000 units @ £30.10)	£301,000
Closing stock (£301,000 less 10%)	£270,900

Factors Limited
Budgeted profit and loss for the period ending. . .19x0

	£
Sales (100,000 @ £50.00)	5,000,000
Cost of sales (100,000 @ £30.10)	3,010,000
	1,990,000
less: Under/(Over) recovery of production overhead	2,524
Gross Profit	1,987,476
General expenses	1,500,000
Net Profit	487,476

Workings:

Product costing:	£
Raw materials (10 kg @ £2/kg)	20.00
Production overhead (£1,000,000/99,000)	10.10
Manufacturing cost	30.10

Under/(Over) recovery of production overhead	£
Production work carried out 98,760 units	
Overhead recovered, or absorbed @ £10.10	997,476
Overhead budgeted	1,000,000
	2,524

Production work carried out:	
Production	99,000 units
less: opening stock of w.i.p. (4,000 units, 60% complete)	2,400 units
add: closing stock of w.i.p. (2,400 units less 10%)	2,160 units
	98,760 units

Factors Limited
Budgeted Balance Sheet as at. . .19x0

	£	£	£
Fixed assets			5,000,000
Current assets			
Stocks (90,000 + 65,016 + 270,900)		425,916	
Debtors (5,000,000 × 30/360)		416,667	
		842,583	
Current liabilities			
Creditors (1,965,200 × 30/360 + 1,500,000 × 30/360 + 50% × 1,000,000 × 30/360)	330,433		
Bank overdraft	100,000	430,433	412,150
Capital Employed			5,412,150

There are alternative forms of presentation which would be considered to be acceptable.

23.3 *Workings.*

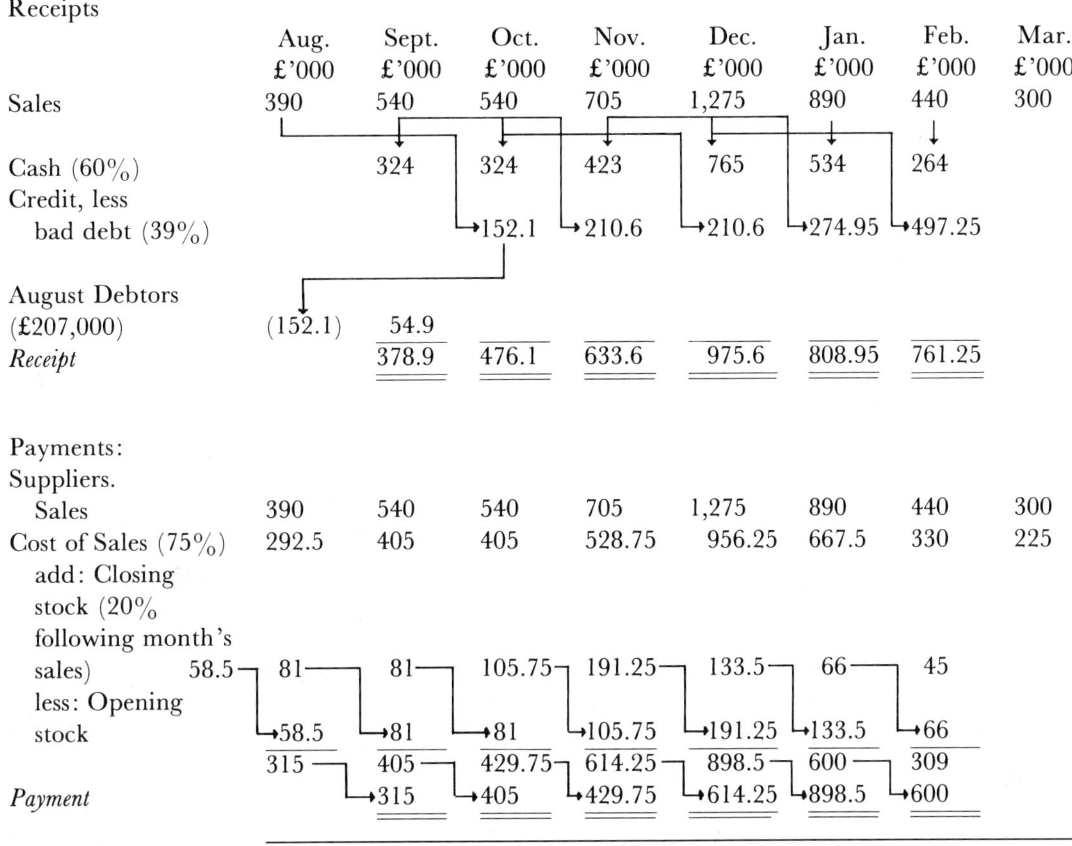

Receipts	Aug. £'000	Sept. £'000	Oct. £'000	Nov. £'000	Dec. £'000	Jan. £'000	Feb. £'000	Mar. £'000
Sales	390	540	540	705	1,275	890	440	300
Cash (60%)		324	324	423	765	534	264	
Credit, less bad debt (39%)			152.1	210.6	210.6	274.95	497.25	
August Debtors (£207,000)	(152.1)	54.9						
Receipt		378.9	476.1	633.6	975.6	808.95	761.25	

Payments: Suppliers.	Aug.	Sept.	Oct.	Nov.	Dec.	Jan.	Feb.	Mar.
Sales	390	540	540	705	1,275	890	440	300
Cost of Sales (75%)	292.5	405	405	528.75	956.25	667.5	330	225
add: Closing stock (20% following month's sales) 58.5	81	81	105.75	191.25	133.5	66	45	
less: Opening stock	58.5	81	81	105.75	191.25	133.5	66	
	315	405	429.75	614.25	898.5	600	309	
Payment		315	405	429.75	614.25	898.5	600	

Budgeted statements:
Debtors: 39% of previous two months' sales.
Creditors are equal to the cost of sales for the period.
Bank interest for profit and loss and Cash for balance sheet taken from Cash flow statement.
Shareholders' capital includes profit.

Silveryseas PLC
Profit and loss budget

	Sept.	Oct.	Nov.	Dec.	Jan.	Feb.	Total
	£	£	£	£	£	£	£
Sales	540,000	540,000	705,000	1,275,000	890,000	440,000	4,390,000
Cost of Sales (75% of sales)	405,000	405,000	528,750	956,250	667,500	330,000	3,292,500
Gross Profit (25% of sales)	135,000	135,000	176,250	318,750	222,500	110,000	1,097,500
Operating costs	100,000	100,000	100,000	130,000	100,000	100,000	630,000
Bad debts (1% of sales)	5,400	5,400	7,050	12,750	8,900	4,400	43,900
Interest: Bank		300					300
Loan	2,400	2,400	2,400	2,400	2,400	—	12,000
Net Profit	27,200	26,900	66,800	173,600	111,200	5,600	411,300

Budgeted Balance Sheet

							Aug.
	£	£	£	£	£	£	£
Fixed assets, less depreciation	1,490,000	1,480,000	1,470,000	1,460,000	1,450,000	1,440,000	1,500,000
Stocks	81,000	105,750	191,250	133,500	66,000	45,000	81,000
Debtors	362,700	421,200	485,550	772,200	844,350	518,700	207,000
Cash	3,900	(15,300)	98,550	339,900	28,350	99,600	30,000
	447,600	511,650	775,350	1,245,600	938,700	663,300	318,000
Creditors	405,000	429,750	614,250	898,500	600,000	309,000	315,000
Interest accrual	2,400	4,800	7,200	9,600			
	40,200	77,100	153,900	337,500	338,700	354,300	3,000
Long-term loan	(120,000)	(120,000)	(120,000)	(120,000)			(120,000)
Capital Employed	1,410,200	1,437,100	1,503,900	1,677,500	1,788,700	1,794,300	1,383,000
Shareholders' cap.	1,410,200	1,437,100	1,503,900	1,677,500	1,788,700	1,794,300	1,383,000

Budgeted Cash Flow Statement

	£	£	£	£	£	£
Receipts	378,900	476,100	633,600	975,600	808,950	761,250
Payments						
Suppliers	315,000	405,000	429,750	614,250	898,500	600,000
Operating costs	90,000	90,000	90,000	120,000	90,000	90,000
Loan					132,000	
	405,000	495,000	519,750	734,250	1,120,500	690,000
Net Cash flow	(26,100)	(18,900)	113,850	241,350	(311,550)	71,250
b/fwd	30,000	3,900	(15,300)	98,550	339,900	28,350
	3,900	(15,000)	98,550	339,900	28,350	99,600
Interest charge	—	300				
c/fwd	3,900	(15,300)	98,550	339,900	28,350	99,600

Budgeted Funds Flow Statement

	£	£	£	£	£	£
Operating profit	27,200	26,900	66,800	173,600	111,200	5,600
Depreciation	10,000	10,000	10,000	10,000	10,000	10,000
	37,200	36,900	76,800	183,600	121,200	15,600
Loan					(120,000)	
	37,200	36,900	76,800	183,600	1,200	15,600
Stocks	—	24,750	85,500	(57,750)	(67,500)	(21,000)
Debtors	155,700	58,500	64,350	286,650	72,150	(325,650)
Creditors	(90,000)	(24,750)	(184,500)	(284,250)	298,500	291,000
Accrual	(2,400)	(2,400)	(2,400)	(2,400)	9,600	
Cash	(26,100)	(19,200)	113,850	241,350	(311,550)	71,250
	37,200	36,900	76,800	183,600	1,200	15,600

23.4 1 The intention of ZBB is to allow no spending unless it can be justified. Where company objectives have been stated, ZBB can be expected to authorise expenditure only in so far as it is in accordance with meeting those objectives. ZBB does not actually state objectives; that is a strategic task. ZBB should provide projects representing alternative means by which organisational objectives can be met. Clear objectives should be stated for each item of expenditure subjected to ZBB.

2 ZBB can be implemented through decision units. It should therefore contribute to the process of defining programs essential to meet organisational objectives.

3 Cost of decision units should be specified.

4 Alternatives are subjected to cost benefit analysis. ZBB can most easily be applied to discretionary cost items rather than the entire budget. The General Motors Budget and Finance procedures are somewhat less specific than ZBB although the analysis given above suggests significant similarities. The ideas which underpin ZBB (definition of decision units, linking decision unit objectives with organisational objectives, analysing alternatives through a cost benefit approach) seem to have much in common with the general approach outlined in the General Motors system.

ANSWERS TO EXERCISES

23.4 1 A budget can be viewed as a model of the financial aspects of the organisation. This model can be computerised through software such as spreadsheets. These models are descriptive and would replicate the processes followed by management accountants, but at computer speeds and levels of accuracy.

2 Budgeting can be an iterative process. Once a computerised model has produced a master budget, management may request revisions and call for bargaining procedures to ensure congruence with objectives. The computer can process the necessary revisions with greater efficiency than could be achieved using manual approaches.

3 Models used by accountants may represent the organisation as a deterministic system or as a stochastic or probabilistic system. Computers are necessary to carry out computations of, say, decision trees because of the volume of calculations necessary to model stochastic systems. Computers therefore provide management accountants with the ability to choose; the accountant can apply judgement in determining whether deterministic or stochastic models are most appropriate. It is probable that manual methods preclude the use of stochastic models for all but the most simple of organisations.

4 Statistical approaches and more sophisticated techniques require the use of computers in practical situations because of the volume of calculations. To use the example of forecasting, statistical approaches including moving averages and exponential smoothing, which may be time consuming, become feasible with the use of computers. Regression and econometric software can be purchased by organisations wishing to adopt these approaches.

5 Optimising models can be processed. Linear programming techniques could be applied where many variables and constraints are possible. Software can be purchased for this purpose.

Note: The examiner would need to mark points raised on merit. There are more than five areas which could be described, for instance sensitivity analysis and simulation were discussed in an earlier chapter and count as areas in their own right. A question such as this one permits the student to draw on knowledge from management accounting in its entirety.

23.5 This problem is typical of a number encountered at this level of study. The situation is original; candidates cannot be expected to have encountered anything similar before. The situation is initially discouraging; there is much to read and assimilate before an answer is attempted. The situation is also somewhat more straightforward than it first appears. The student needs to:

1 find a suitable means of 'gaining entry' to the situation. Similar questions often have a relatively simple 'entry point'. In this case, it is most useful to unravel the question through an understanding of materials, even though this is not specifically called for by the question;

2 apply general principles from throughout accounting studies. For example, the cash flow forecast requested for question (b) applies financial accounting knowledge.

Answer:

(a) Workings:

Materials, £1,000,000 × 1.04 × 1.05 × 1.1 = £1,201,200. Therefore, year 7 is derived directly from year 6 through the application of usage, price and volume indices ie relevant indices.

(i) Year 7 labour cost

	Year 6	Efficiency	Rate	Volume	Year 7
Variable cost*	100,000	× 1.03	× 1.00	× 1.10	113,300
Fixed cost	50,000		× 1.00		50,000
	£150,000				£163,300

* £150,000 less £50,000

It is assumed that the fixed cost element will be affected by labour rate changes.

(ii) Year 7 production overhead

	Year 6	Utilisation	Exp.	Volume	Year 7
Variable cost*	160,000	× 1.03	× 1.05	× 1.10	190,344
Fixed cost	120,000	× 1.03	× 1.05		129,780
Depreciation	30,000				30,000
	310,000				350,124

* £310,000 less £150,000

It is assumed that the fixed cost element will be affected by expenditure level changes. It is also assumed that the fixed cost element will be affected by utilisation changes.

Note: The price level assumption is reasonable. The effect on fixed cost of utilisation levels is less clear and may need to be clarified on a trial and error basis.

(iii) x = £800,000

y = net profit	£196,551
add: financial charges	£124,859
depreciation	£30,000
	£351,410

Financial charges = ((2x − y) × 0.2)/2)

= ((2 × £800,000 − £351,410) × 0.2)/2)

= £124,859

(b) Forecast Profit and Loss Account for Year 8

	Year 6		Performance	Price	Volume		Year 8 £
Sales	2,000,000			× 1.03	× 1.20		2,472,000
Direct material	1,000,000		× 0.95	× 1.20	× 1.20		1,368,000
Direct labour	150,000	100,000	× 0.99	× 1.10	× 1.20		185,680
		50,000		× 1.10			
P. Overhead	310,000	160,000	× 0.99	× 1.12	× 1.20		375,946
		120,000	× 0.99	× 1.12		+ 30,000	
Ad/Selling	100,000		× 1.05	× 1.12			117,600
Distribution	140,000		× 0.95	× 1.12	× 1.20		178,752
Financial							87,088
							2,313,066
Net Profit							158,934

Financial charges: x = £573,449

y = £2,472,000 − £1,368,000 − £185,680 − (£375,946 + £30,000)

− £117,600 − £178,752 = £276,022

Charges = ((2 × 573,449 − 276,022) × 0.2)/2)

= £87,088

Bank overdraft for end of Year 8

Profit for year 8	£158,934
add: non cash items	
Depreciation	£30,000
Funds from operations	£188,934
Bank overdraft b/fwd	£573,449
c/fwd	£384,515

The question does not allow a fuller analysis of funds flow (see answer to (c)).

Forecast Profit and Loss Account for Year 9

	Year 6		Performance	Price	Volume		Year 9 £
Sales	2,000,000			× 1.01	× 1.30		2,626,000
Direct material	1,000,000		× 0.85	× 1.25	× 1.30		1,381,250
Direct labour	150,000	100,000	× 0.97	× 1.15	× 1.30		202,515
		50,000		× 1.15			
P. Overhead	310,000	160,000	× 0.97	× 1.18	× 1.30		405,429
		120,000	× 0.97	× 1.18		+ 30,000	
Ad/Selling	100,000		× 1.00	× 1.18			118,000
Distribution	140,000		× 0.95	× 1.18	× 1.30		204,022
Financial							42,425
							2,353,641
Net Profit							272,359

Financial charges: x = £384,515

y = £2,626,000 – £1,381,250 – £202,515 – (£405,429 + £30,000)

– £118,000 – £204,022 = £344,784

Charges = ((2 × 384,515) – 344,784) × 0.2)/2

= £42,425

Bank overdraft for end of Year 9

Profit for year 9	£272,359
add: non cash items	
Depreciation	£30,000
	£302,359
Bank overdraft b/fwd	£384,515
c/fwd	£82,156

(c) Funds from sources other than operations, for example the issue of shares.
The application of funds, for example the purchase of fixed assets.
Increase/decrease in working capital, for example movement in stock levels.

(d) A stated objective is 'to eliminate the overdraft by the end of year 9'. The projections can be used to test whether this objective can be achieved on the basis of present performance, adjusted for planned changes in this case. Since the overdraft has not been cleared by the end of year 9, the company would presumably seek to implement further changes to its inputs in order to achieve its objective.

Solutions to Chapter 24 questions

ANSWERS TO SELF-ASSESSMENT QUESTIONS

24.1 These situations are intended to provide a focus but, in practice, a diversity of approaches is possible and the answers which follow may only describe one of a number of acceptable responses.

(a) *Materials*: quantities—by means of existing engine specification
wastage—through consultation with factory management aimed at bargaining for a tight but achievable standard
prices—through consultation with buyers, aimed at bargaining for a tight but achievable standard

Labour: labour intensive departments:
time taken—in consultation with work study personnel
productivity/downtime—in consultation with departmental managers/supervisors aimed at bargaining for a tight but achievable standard
wage rates—existing personnel records adjusted for planned wage rate increases agreed with the personnel director
capital intensive departments: treat as overhead

Overheads: determine appropriate departmental absorption rates based on budgets:
—committed costs such as rates would be determined from existing records, adjusted for price changes if necessary
—engineered costs such as the variable element of electricity could be calculated or estimated from analysis of existing records, accounting for cost behaviour
—discretionary costs such as the management accounting department would be subjected to Zero Based Budgeting to ensure that benefits exceed costs and that expenditure is consistent with organisational objectives.

Departmental rates would be machine based in capital intensive departments and labour based in labour intensive departments.

(b) There are two major types of cost: labour, or lecturer costs and occupancy, or the costs of rooms and teaching facilities, and administrative overheads in support of either type of cost. Both types of cost are common to all courses and so the problem of 'joint products' arises. The situation is one of decision-making, since the implication of assessing course viability is that some courses will be found not to be viable and would thus cease to operate.

Given these circumstances, it is not easy to see how a standard costing system is relevant. There are few unambiguous input-output relationships. Perhaps a budgeting technique such as Zero Based Budgeting should be applied, although the common cost problem remains unless it is the viability of the entire accounting department which is questioned, or autonomous packages or courses within the department. Unless sensible incremental standard costs can be established, it is suggested that there is no appropriate method of producing standards for this situation.

[*Note*: In practice, standards such as staff-student ratios are applied to whole departments in order to take decisions on matters such as manning levels. There is some discretion in the United Kingdom higher education sector as to how individual institutions apply standards at a departmental level].

(c) *Materials*: quantities—by means of existing specifications or 'menus'
wastage—from existing records, or through a policy of motivating the workforce to achieve zero wastage
prices—by informal consultation with suppliers

Overheads: (including all employee costs):
determine appropriate process line absorption rates (possibly based on time spent on each line, or a composite time/temperature rate in the case of ovens) based on budget. Budget could be previous year plus a percentage.

[*Note*: A more detailed statement for each of these situations necessitates a more thorough knowledge of the organisation; its objective, policies, processes and human behavioural situation, for instance].

24.2 The report should include the following points:

1 Standard costs are most suitable where there is a clear, measurable output and relationship with input. This appears to be the case for materials. More information would need to be gathered before deciding on the application of standards to labour. Overheads may be suitably controlled through budgeting, including Zero Based Budgeting where appropriate.

2 A wastage less than 6% may be necessary to motivate the production director and thus to improve control. The aim in bargaining a suitable level of wastage would be to change the production director's aspirations from the present 6%. If aspiration levels cannot be changed, 6% would seem to be reasonable since wastage on the trial amounted to 7%, but judgement would need to be applied before finalising wastage levels.

3 A zero defect principle would lead to a standard equal to 2,302kg/8,063, sufficient decimal places being carried. This standard would fully measure quality costs through variance reports and can motivate quality improvements where the impacts of adverse variance reporting are effectively managed. Dysfunctional consequences may arise through inadequate recognition of the effects of aspiration levels; experience and research suggests that an excessively tight standard can lead to a deterioration in performance in general.

4 Once quantity standards have been established, price standards need to be agreed.

5 The cost of seconds would be accounted for in arriving at a perfects cost, except where a zero defects principle applies. The loss in value of items categorised as seconds would be recovered over the perfect items remaining. A standard perfects level, possibly of 90%, would be established. [Where reported production falls below 90%, an adverse variance would later be reported.] Again, in setting a target perfects level, the aim would be to improve control by motivating people to produce results which are congruent with organisational objectives.

6 A zero defects approach would be consistent with an ideal standard. Ideally, no seconds should be produced and thus the cost of perfects would not include the fall in value.

ANSWERS TO EXERCISES

24.1 (a) Where standard costs adequately reflect an SSAP 9 definition of cost and where write-downs to net realisable value have been appropriately made.

In particular:

'Management must exercise judgement to ensure that the methods chosen provide the fairest practical approximation to cost. Furthermore . . . standard costs . . . need to be reviewed frequently to ensure that they bear a reasonable relationship to actual costs obtaining during the period.'

Appendix 1, Paragraph 12.

'Cost is defined . . . as being that expenditure which has been incurred in the normal course of business in bringing the product or service to its present location and condition. This expenditure should include . . . costs of conversion . . . as are appropriate to that location and condition.'

Paragraph 17.

Standards which have been used as the basis for motivation or which have been produced under the marginal costing principle as a basis for decision-making are instances of situations not meeting the above requirements. [Further, appendix 1, paragraph 15, on the treatment of by-products, implies that a system designed to report full quality costs according to the zero defects principle would not meet auditing requirements since products would include a proportion of losses associated with by-products. This implication is not fully clear and would exercise the judgement of the auditor; by-products are not sub-standard goods but the accounting treatment described by SSAP 9 may be applied to sub-standard goods where companies follow consistent management accounting practice.]

(b) Review: Component A, £0.73 appears to be an acceptable standard for financial reporting purposes. The variance is less than 2% of standard cost of sales and the revised standard is close to the standard used in valuing stock.

Component B, £2.16 requires further investigation. The average standard cost for the year to date is £2.05 (£100,245/48,900 units) but the existence of a significant variance of 40% of standard cost of sales suggests a rapidly increasing cost or control problems. Two months' stock is held (8,150/48,900 × 12 months) and it is recommended that the variance against £2.16 be investigated over that period. Where component A is valued approximately half way through its stock period (approximately six months' stock is held and the standard relates to three months ago), component B's value was established outside the period to which the stock relates.

Component C: £1.85 requires further attention. The stock is current (just over two months' stock) and costs appear to be falling significantly, as reflected by a favourable variance and a 16% lower revised standard.

(c) Time taken, including productivity and non-productive time, and rates of pay need to be considered.

24.2 (a)

	£/box
Automatic sowing department	
Seed pellets 40 × 1p × 1.02	0.408
Compost mix 3 × 20p × 1.025	0.615
Boxes 1 × 10p × 1.01	0.101
Operating costs £30,000/125,000 boxes	0.240
	1.364
Germination room	
Input from sowing dept. £1.364 × 1.25*	1.705
Operating costs £50,000/100,000*[1]	0.500
	2.205

* 20% losses over 80% good production = 20/80 = 25%

*[1] 125,000 input, less 20% losses

Growing houses	
Input from germination room £2.205 × 1.111*	2.45
Operating costs £27,000/90,000*[1]	0.30
	2.75

* 10% losses over 90% good production = 10/90 = 11.1%

*[1] 100,000 input, less 10%

(b) In T account form:

Automatic sowing

	£		£
Pellets	52,000	Germination	
Compost	77,700	(125,000 @ £1.364)	170,500
Boxes	14,190		
Operating costs	29,800	Profit and loss	3,190
	173,690		173,690

Germination

	£		£
Automatic sowing	170,500	Growing houses	
Operating costs	50,000	(100,000 @ £2.205)	220,500
	220,500		220,500

Growing houses

	£		£
Germination	220,500	Dispatch	
Operating costs	30,000	(86,000 @ £2.75)	236,500
		Profit and loss	14,000
	250,500		250,500

Diagrammatically:

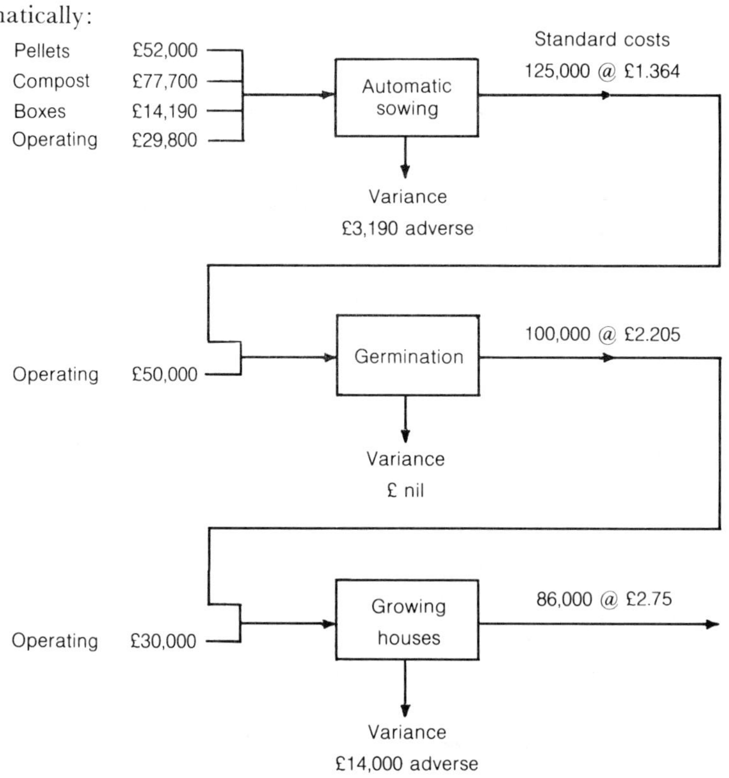

(c) Germination room is performing to standard. Automatic sowing department and growing houses are both showing inefficient operation by comparison with standard. The adverse variance for the sowing department appears to be immaterial, being less than 2% of the standard cost of production. The adverse variance for growing houses, at over 5%, appears to be significant and should be investigated further.

The total departmental variances which have been reported can be subdivided. For example, the £14,000 adverse variance for growing houses can be analysed as follows:

		Variance £
Standard operating costs for input of 100,000 boxes	£27,000	
Actual operating costs	£30,000	3,000 adverse
Standard output for input of 100,000 boxes	90,000 boxes	
Actual output	86,000 boxes	
Abnormal wastage @ standard cost	4,000 boxes @ £2.75	11,000 adverse
		£14,000 adverse

Solutions to Chapter 25 questions

EXAMPLE 25.1—WORKINGS

Product cost workings
Cost behaviour analysis

		Budget	
Output: machine hours	30,000	40,000	50,000
Standard hours (allow 7½% down-time)	27,750	37,000	46,250
Production overheads £	286,750	296,000	305,250

Variable cost per hour (high-low method):

$$\frac{£305,250 - £286,750}{46,250 - 27,750} = \frac{£19,000}{19,000 \text{ hours}} = £1 \text{ per hour}$$

Fixed overhead absorption rate

$$\frac{£296,000 - (37,000 \times £1)}{37,000} = \frac{£259,000}{37,000 \text{ hours}} = £7 \text{ per hour}$$

Quality cost allowance

		£
Beta:	Seconds selling price	2.00
	Cost of production from product cost	7.85
	Loss on sale of seconds	5.85
	Cost of seconds are recovered on perfects produced:	
	£5.85 × 1/6 ÷ 5/6 =	1.17/perfect unit

Raw materials workings

Standard cost of purchases:	£
A 60,000 @ £2	120,000
B 40,000 @ £6	240,000
	360,000

Standard usage of materials:

	Work done	A		B	
	units	kg/unit	kg	kg/unit	kg
Alpha	50,000	0.3	15,000	0.3	15,000
Beta	54,000	0.8	43,200	0.5	27,000
			58,200		42,000

ANSWERS TO SELF-ASSESSMENT QUESTIONS

25.1 Weighted average values: Actual mix

£332,000/92,000 kg = £3.6087
Standard mix
£368,400/100,200 kg = £3.67665

1 *Mix variance*:

Difference between weighted average values for actual and standard mixes	£0.06795 fav.
Issues	92,000 kg
Variance	£6,251 fav.

Yield variance:

Difference between issues and standard usage (92,000 – 100,200)	8,200 kg fav.
Variance (@ £3.67665)	£30,149 fav.
Usage variance (£6,251 + £30,149)	£36,400 fav.

Although the usage variance, the addition of mix and yield variances, agrees with the previous calculation, the individual variances differ because of rounding and the use of approximate mix proportions. In practical systems a degree of difference arises from the number of decimal places carried, as illustrated by this example. Examinations traditionally avoid this by using 'convenient numbers' but there is a trend leading to the use of 'difficult numbers' (which do not provide round answers).

Alternative presentations of the mix variance:

2

Actual issues	*Issues at standard mix*	*Variance*		
kg	kg	kg	£/kg	£
55,000	53,360	1,640 adv.	2	3,280 adv.
37,000	38,640	1,640 fav.	6	9,840 fav.
				6,560 fav.

3 [ACCA syllabus (Horngren and Foster)]

Standard price	*Wtd. average price*	*Variance*	*Variance*	*Variance*
£	£	£	kg	£
2	3.67665	1.67665 fav.	1,640 adv.	2,750 fav.
6	3.67665	2.32335 adv.	1,640 fav.	3,810 fav.
				6,560 fav.

4

Actual price	*Wtd. average price*	*Variance*	*Issues*	*Variance*
£	£	£/kg		£
2	3.67665	1.67665 fav.	55,000	92,216 fav.
6	3.67665	2.32335 adv.	37,000	85,964 adv.
				6,252 fav.

Comment: Since the mathematics can be related to the corner of a three dimensional shape, there are numerous ways of combining the variables to produce non-conventional answers. Each of the presentations above provides a 'correct' variance. Other permutations may equally provide a 'correct' variance; the author has not attempted a rigorous exploration of all permutations, 'correct' or 'incorrect'. Students may therefore have used other procedures to derive the figures £6,252 or £6,560. It would be difficult to fault such procedures if they are accompanied by sensible explanations which could be understood by management.

Explanations:

1 Changes in mix from standard saved approximately £0.07 per kilogramme, resulting in a favourable mix variance of around £6,500 (to the nearest £500), 21% of net profit for the period.

8,200 kg less than expected were used in the production process, saving £30,000 (to the nearest £500).

2 More of material A was used in the process than the standard mix allows, with a consequent saving in material B. Since B is more expensive than A, a favourable variance of around £6,500 arose.

3 Proportionately more of A, which costs below average, was used in the mix, saving £2,750. Proportionately less of B, which costs above average, was used, saving £3,810.

4 Material A is bought in at cost which is below average, saving £92,216 at the issues stage: Material B has a cost greater than average, creating an adverse variance of £85,964.

25.2

Issues		*Issues at standard prices*	*Issues at standard mix*	*Standard usage*
55,000	£116,000	55,000 @ £2	53,360 @ £2	58,200 @ £2
37,000	£230,000	37,000 @ £6	38,640 @ £6	42,000 @ £6
	£346,000	£332,000	£338,560	£368,400

Price variance	(346,000 – 332,000)	£14,000 fav.
Mix variance	(332,000 – 338,560)	£6,560 fav.
Yield variance	(338,560 – 368,400)	£29,840 fav.

From the technical point of view, stocks are valued at standard values, with the consequence that the £14,000 price variance is attributable to purchase quantities. The variance is identical in magnitude to that calculated at the purchase stage, but is strictly explainable as follows:

	Ave. issue value £/kg	*Standard value £/kg*	*Variance £/kg*	*Quantity kg*	*Variance £*
A	$2.10\dot{9}\dot{0}$	2	$0.1\dot{0}\dot{9}$ adv.	55,000	6,000 adv.
B	$6.\dot{2}1\dot{6}$	6	$0.\dot{2}1\dot{6}$ adv.	37,000	8,000 adv.
					14,000 adv.

More conventionally, stock would be valued on an historic cost basis, resulting in a timing difference in the reporting of the price variance.

Comment: The overall materials variance is favourable even though the price variance is adverse. If the same quality of supply has been secured as anticipated in the standard, the effectiveness or efficiency of the purchasing manager should be investigated and steps taken to ensure the continued success of production, as measured by mix and yield variances. If the variances are inter-related, a better quality of supplier, with less economy in terms of purchase prices, has given rise to overall effectiveness and efficiency.

25.3 Both of the variances are favourable, showing that management of labour is leading to improved profits, by comparison with standard. The efficiency variance exceeds 5% of standard cost and can therefore be considered material. An investigation of this variance may reveal an opportunity to apply positive feedback to improve productivity further. Alternatively, the variance may be an illustration of noisy data; for example, a series of uncontrollable, random factors may have caused the favourable conditions.

A calculation of mix variance suggests that grade I and grade II labour can be interchangeable; that by substituting less expensive grade I labour for grade II labour a favourable situation can be created. If the true grades of labour represent different skills and knowledge, such a practice may be dysfunctional; a favourable wages mix variance may be more than offset by adverse usage or productivity variances, for example. Quality or productivity problems may result from ill conceived economies. Before calculating and presenting a variance, the management accountant needs to consider the purpose of the variance report and the consequent actions which may be taken. Additionally, a judgement needs to be made on whether the variance conveys useful information.

The efficiency variance would be subdivided as follows:

Actual hours, standard rate	*Actual hours, standard mix*	*Standard*
(53%) 26,000 @ £2	(49%) 23,833 @ £2	(49%) 25,000 @ £2
(47%) 23,000 @ £2.50	(51%) 25,167 @ £2.50	(51%) 26,400 @ £2.50
49,000	49,000	51,400
£109,500	£110,584	£116,000

The standard mix is I : II 25,000 : 26,400.
[23,833 = (25,000/51,400) × 49,000 : 25,167 = (26,400/51,400) × 49,000]

This shows that a higher proportion of the less expensive grade resulted in a favourable mix variance of £1,084. A saving of 2,400 standard hours, resulting from improved productivity, saved the company £5,416 (2,400 @ £2.2568 average pay). Contingency theory suggests that the extent to which management would benefit from this analysis depends on a variety of factors including those related to management style and organisational form. These factors would be borne in mind by the management accountant in forming judgements about systems design and implementation.

25.4 Workings: Standard hours:

	Alpha	*Beta*
Work done, from direct labour analysis	50,000 units	52,800 units
Standard hours per unit	0.5 (30 mins)	0.25 (15 mins)
Standard hours: total 38,200	25,000	13,200

Statement:

The expenditure variance is £19,500 favourable. This can arise because of two factors:

1 The price paid per unit of variable overhead can vary. In this case, the charge made by suppliers of power may have changed; electricity prices may be different than anticipated, for instance.

2 The usage of variable overheads may have varied from standard. More or less usage of electricity per hour may have been experienced. In this particular situation, the standard envisaged production salaries vary partially in accordance with hours. The categorisation of production salaries as a fixed cost for the period suggests that usage of salaried personnel is no longer a variable overhead commitment. This may suggest that production arrangements have changed since the standards were established.

Where the labour rate variance can be directly traced back to differences between standard rates of pay and rates paid according to personnel and wages records, no such audit trial can as simply exist for variable overheads. The standard rate of £1 combines power costs (hours × power cost per hour, sufficient to produce one standard hour of machine time) and a variable portion of the semi-variable or semi-fixed cost of production salaries (hours × rate per hour, sufficient to produce one standard hour of machine time). The variable overhead expenditure variance therefore reflects a combination of different types of cost.

The efficiency variance derives from the fact that 38,200 standard hours of production were achieved in 39,000 machine hours worked. If part of the 800 hours difference is explained by idle time in excess of the standard allowance, the number of hours excess can be isolated and valued at £1, leaving a variance attributable to the efficiency at which the machines have been operated. It is curious that labour efficiency was favourable for the same period; an investigation to ascertain whether some manual operations have now been mechanised could be helpful.

Both the categorisation of production salaries and the possible interdependence of labour and machine efficiencies suggests that standards need to be reviewed and possibly revised.

25.5 To: Quill PLC Managers
From: Management Accountant
Date:

Fixed overhead variances

1 *Expenditure variance*

Due to a change from standard cost behaviour for production salaried personnel, the £15,500 adverse variance needs to be compared with the £19,500 favourable variance for expenditure on variable overheads. Overall, the position is slightly favourable.

2 *Capacity variance*

Machines worked for 2,000 hours longer than planned for the period. Standards, and hence product profitability, have been assessed on the basis of working 40,000 hours, 37,000 standard hours, allowing for down-time. Profitability increases by using the available capacity more fully. Each extra standard hour of working (approximately 1 hour and five minutes of machine hours) is worth an extra £7 profit, equivalent to the profit from 30 units of Alpha.

Such extra capacity as can be worked should create saleable units in an efficient manner in order to be effective.

Efficiency variance

As reported separately for variable overheads, 38,200 standard hours of production took 39,000 machine hours to achieve. At £7 per hour, this inefficiency cost £5,600.

General recommendation

Although overheads in general were close to standard (actual cost in total £294,000; standard £305,600; variance £11,600 favourable or less than 4% of standard), there are features of the analysis which suggest an investigation, possibly leading to a review of the standards.

25.1.5 Sales variances

Actual gross profit:
Reconciliation of standard and actual gross profit

			£
Standard gross profit (52,800 + 18,240 − 30,000)			41,040
	Variances		
	Favourable	*Adverse*	
	£	£	
Raw materials price		14,000	
mix	6,560		
yield	29,840		
Labour rate	500		
efficiency	6,500		
V. O'hd. rate	19,500		
efficiency		800	
F. O'hd expenditure		15,500	
capacity	14,000		
efficiency		5,600	
Difference		11,700	
	76,900	47,600	29,300 fav.
Actual gross profit, per financial accounts			70,340

25.6

The price variance of £25,000 is attributable to selling prices as follows:

	Selling prices for the period	*Standard*	*Variance*	
	£/unit	£/unit	£/unit	£
Alpha	8.50	8.00	0.50 fav.	24,000 fav.
Beta Perfects	9.50	10.00	0.50 adv.	19,000 adv.
Beta Seconds	1.00	2.00	1.00 adv.	30,000 adv.
				25,000 adv.

Each variance in terms of £/unit has been multiplied by quantities sold to give the total variance.

This analysis shows that a reduction in the price of Beta sales was significant. This was possibly an attempt to sell the seconds in response to the Financial Director's concern about stock levels. Alpha and Beta Perfects each sold at £0.50 variance to the standard price, causing £24,000 favourable and £19,000 adverse variances respectively.

The value of this information can be related to the potential for management action in the selling price area. If the company is a price-taker, management may only be able to take action based on decisions about product range; product price would not be controllable at management level. In this case, double loop feedback would appear most applicable. After investigation, revising the standard may be the only action possible. The variance may convey more information where the company is a price-maker for its perfect quality goods; feedback would probably lead to a revision in the price charged for Beta Perfects.

The mix variance can be explained in the following manner:

	Standard Weighted ave. Profit	*Gross Profit*	*Variance*	*Sales*	*Budgeted Sales*	*Variance*	*Mix Variance*
						£	£
Alpha	0.706122	0.60	0.106122 adv.	48,000	59,184	11,184 adv.	1,187 fav.
Beta Perfects	0.706122	0.98	0.273878 fav.	38,000	47,347	9,347 adv.	2,560 adv.
Seconds	0.706122	nil	0.706122 adv.	30,000	9,469	20,531 fav.	14,497 adv.
							15,870 adv.

The mix variance therefore substantially comprises the effect of de-stocking seconds. This analysis may be useful to management where:

1 The three products are interchangeable.

2 The effects of controllable factors resulting from management action were to create an adverse situation as regards the mix of products.

This does not appear to be valid at face value:

1 Marketing policy would presumably seek to ensure that Perfects and Seconds are not interchangeable or else sales of seconds would reduce the market for perfects with dysfunctional consequences.

2 Management appear to have lowered seconds price to reduce stocks of seconds. This action appears to have been successful and it is thus unfair to report an adverse mix variance.

The mix variance, as calculated, does not therefore appear to convey valuable information. An alternative form of presentation may be to report seconds as a separate variance as follows:

Seconds Variance:	Actual gross profit	(£30,000)
	Budgeted gross profit	nil
	Variance	£30,000 adv.

Perfects Variance:

Actual sales, actual standard profit	Actual sales, budgeted standard profit	Actual sales, budgeted mix	Budget
£52,800	48,000 @ £0.60	47,778 @ £0.60	50,000 @ £0.60
£18,240	38,000 @ £0.98	38,222 @ £0.98	40,000 @ £0.98
£71,040	£66,040	£66,124	£69,200

Price Variance	£5,000 fav.	(71,040 – 66,040)
Mix Variance	£84 adv.	(66,040 – 66,124)
Volume Variance	£3,076 adv.	(66,124 – 69,200)

This case situation should illustrate the application of judgement in preparing information for management. Mindless adherence to procedures and formulae can lead to the preparation of information of doubtful value. A test of valuable information for control purposes is the ability to interpret that information in a manner which logically leads to future actions which benefit the organisation.

The seconds variance illustrates the desirability of revising standards to meet organisational objectives and changing circumstances. A notional value resulting in a reported profit against a price of £1 would be consistent with promoting the profit motive, if the assumption is correct that a price reduction was necessary to reduce stocks.

Marginal Costing Workings
Quality cost allowance:

	£
Selling price of seconds	2.00
Production cost	6.10
Loss on sale of seconds	4.10
1/6 seconds, cost recovered on 5/6;	
Increase in cost of Perfects	
(£4.10 × 1/6 ÷ 5/6)	£0.82

Marginal Costing Workings

Stock revaluation:	Total	Alpha	Beta Perfects	Beta Seconds
Opening finished goods stock:				
Absorption costing valuation		6,000 @ £7.40	5,000 @ £9.02	25,000 @ £2
	£139,500	44,400	45,100	50,000
Marginal costing valuation		6,000 @ £3.90	5,000 @ £6.92	25,000 @ £2
	£108,000	23,400	34,600	50,000
Decrease in stock valuation	£ 31,500			
Closing finished goods stock:				
Absorption costing valuation		8,000 @ £7.40	7,000 @ £9.02	5,000 @ £2
	£132,340	59,200	63,140	10,000
Marginal costing valuation		8,000 @ £3.90	7,000 @ £6.92	5,000 @ £2
	£ 89,640	31,200	48,440	10,000
Decrease in stock valuation	£ 42,700			

Work in Progress
Material values in stock are unaffected.

	Alpha		Beta	
Conversion:				
Equivalent units of opening stock	5,000 @ 50%	2,500	8,000 @ 40%	3,200
Equivalent units of closing stock	10,000 @ 25%	2,500	10,000 @ 60%	6,000
		nil		2,800

Increase in Beta stock		2,800 equivalent units
Absorption costing stock value	£7.85	
Marginal costing stock value	£6.10	£1.75 per unit
Reduction in profits by re-valuing to a marginal costing basis		£4,900

An alternative approach to this calculation would be to value opening and closing stocks on both an absorption and marginal costing basis, as illustrated for finished goods but taking into account degrees of completion and separating material and conversion costs.

Marginal costing operating statement

Quality cost variance

Output value of production:		£
Alpha	50,000 units @ £3.90	195,000
Beta	50,000 units @ £6.10	305,000
		500,000
Input value to finished goods:		
Alpha	50,000 units @ £3.90	195,000
Beta perfects	40,000 units @ £6.92	276,800
Beta seconds	10,000 units @ £2.00	20,000
		491,800
Quality Cost Variance		8,200 adv.

Fixed production overhead:	£
Expenditure for the period	274,500
Budget	259,000
Variance	15,500 adv.

Sales variances

Actual sales, actual standard contribution	*Actual sales, budgeted standard contribution*	*Actual sales, budgeted mix*	*Budget*
£220,800	48,000 @ £4.10	59,184 @ £4.10	50,000 @ £4.10
£98,040	38,000 @ £3.08	47,347 @ £3.08	40,000 @ £3.08
(£30,000)	30,000 @ nil	9,469 @ nil	8,000 @ nil
£288,840	£313,840	£388,480 (nearest £10)	£328,200

Price Variance	(313,840 – 288,840)	£25,000 adv.
Mix Variance	(388,480 – 313,840)	£74,640 adv.
Volume Variance	(328,200 – 388,480)	£60,280 fav.

Calculation of actual standard contribution

	Alpha	*Beta Perfects*	*Beta Seconds*
Sales units	48,000	38,000	30,000
Standard variable cost	£3.90	£6.92	£2.00
Standard cost of sales	£187,200	£262,960	£60,000

	£	£	£
Sales	408,000	361,000	30,000
Standard cost of sales	187,200	262,960	60,000
Standard contribution	220,800	98,040	(30,000)

25.7 (a) Significant variances falling in the range £10,000 – £30,000 are:

Favourable	*Adverse*
Materials yield	Materials price
Overhead rate—variable	Overhead expenditure—fixed
Overhead capacity	Quality cost
Sales volume	Sales price
	Sales mix

Sales appears to be a cause for concern since all variances are significant. Corrective action on quality and the prices paid for materials and fixed overhead should be taken, since these appear to be sources of inefficiency or ineffectiveness. Performance as regards materials yield, variable overhead spending and machine utilisation is good and should be reinforced.

The above interpretation assumes that variances are independent of each other and fairly reflect the operational conditions pertaining to the period. An alternative interpretation which does not rely on these assumptions was made earlier:

1 Production arrangements may have changed:
2 Action may have been taken to reduce the stock of seconds.

Investigation of these matters and a general review of standards would appear to be a sensible course of action. The operating statement may be presenting distorted information and require an alternative approach once more information is available.

(b) Sales variances, at £74,640 adverse for mix and £60,280 favourable for volume are more than twice the size of any other single variance and an investigation should be undertaken with urgency.

(c) Marginal costing rewards (or punishes) sales whilst absorption costing rewards a combination of production and sales. Variable cost variances and variances for sales and fixed overhead which are not affected by volume changes are unaffected.

ANSWERS TO EXERCISES

25.1 *Workings*:

	Budget
Production units: Sales	10,000 units
less: Opening stock of finished goods	(1,000) units
add: Closing stock of finished goods	1,000 units
	10,000 units

There were no work-in-progress stocks budgeted.
Product costing (Quantities based on 10,000 units are provided in the budget)

	£/unit	£/unit
Materials: A 0.5 kg @ £0.30	0.15	
B 0.5 kg @ £0.70	0.35	0.50
Direct labour: Skilled 0.45 hrs @ £3	1.35	
Unskilled 0.26 hrs @ £2.50	0.65	2.00
Fixed overhead £1 per unit		1.00
Variable overhead £0.50 per unit		0.50
		4.00
Standard Profit		1.00
Sales Price		5.00

Note: the question states that £4 is the standard cost. ∴ the above statement is a standard product cost.

There is no information on overhead cost behaviour.

Sales variances

	Actual sales, actual standard profit	*Actual sales, budgeted standard profit*	*Budget*
Sales 11,000 units	£54,000	11,000 @ £1	10,000 @ £1
Cost of sales 11,000 @ £4	£44,000		
	£10,000	£11,000	£10,000
	Price £1,000 adv.		Vol. £1,000 fav.

	Actual
Production units: Sales	11,000 units
less: Opening stock of finished goods	1,000 units
add: Closing stock of finished goods	2,000 units
	12,000 units

Materials variances

Standard usage: A 12,000 units @ 0.5 kg per unit 6,000 kg
B 12,000 units @ 0.5 kg per unit 6,000 kg

Standard mix: A:B 50:50

Stocks of raw materials are not provided ∴ all variances are to be based on issues quantities.

Issues	*Issues at Standard prices*	*Issues at Standard mix*	*Standard usage*
8,000 @ £0.20	8,000 @ £0.30	6,500 @ £0.30	6,000 @ £0.30
5,000 @ £0.80	5,000 @ £0.70	6,500 @ £0.70	6,000 @ £0.70
£5,600	£5,900	£6,500	£6,000

Direct labour variances

Standard hours: Skilled	12,000 units @ 0.45 hours	5,400
Unskilled	12,000 units @ 0.26 hours	3,120
		8,520

Standard mix: Skilled : unskilled 5,400:3,120

Hours worked	*Hours at Standard rate*	*Hours at Standard mix*	*Standard Hours*
6,000 @ £2.95	6,000 @ £3	5,800 @ £3	5,400 @ £3
3,150 @ £2.60	3,150 @ £2.50	3,350 @ £2.50	3,120 @ £2.50
£25,890	£25,875	£25,775	£24,000

Variable overhead variances

Given that there is no information of cost behaviour, two forms of analysis are possible:

1 Based on the assumption that variable overheads vary in relation to labour hours, giving rise to a spending and an efficiency variance.

2 Based on the assumption that variable overheads vary in accordance with activity other than labour hours, in which case a cost variance alone would be appropriate.

The budget appears to show that variable overheads relate to units and so 2 appears to be more appropriate.

Actual expenditure	£7,500
Standard 12,000 units @ £0.50	£6,000
Cost variance	£1,500 adv.

Fixed overheads

The volume variance is the addition of capacity and efficiency variances or the difference between budgeted and standard cost. The following analysis is therefore adequate:

Actual expenditure	£9,010	Spending
Budgeted expenditure (10,000 @ £1)	£10,000	£990 fav.
Standard expenditure (12,000 @ £1)	£12,000	Volume
		£2,000 fav.

Answer: Operating Statement—May 1986

	Favourable	Adverse	£
Budgeted Profit			10,000
Variances:			
Sales price		1,000	
volume	1,000		
Materials price	300		
mix	600		
yield		500	
Labour rate		15	
mix		100	
productivity		1,775	
Variable overhead		1,500	
Fixed overhead			
spending	990		
volume	2,000		
	4,890	4,890	nil
Actual profit			10,000

Usage variance: (mix plus yield)	£100 fav.
Efficiency variance: (mix plus productivity)	£1,875 adv.

Comments:

Sales variances

Viewed as independent, controllable variances, the analysis suggests that sales volume was effectively managed whilst action should be taken to motivate the sales force to secure higher selling prices. If the company took action during the month to increase volume by reducing selling price, this analysis is not entirely helpful. In overall terms, short-term results coincided with budget so that the action created a neutral effect. In the long term, an increased market share would benefit the company but if competitors respond by lowering their prices, the result of this action would be dysfunctional. If the price variance was forced on the company, then action by the sales force appears to have been effective in meeting environmental threats and challenges.

Materials variances

Viewed as independent, controllable variances, yield was inefficient, possibly due to abnormal wastage, whilst the effects of substituting A for B in the mix and paying £0.10 per kilo less for B than expected created favourable results, despite an increase in price for B. Purchasing and product development management were effective but production was ineffective in making positive contributions to profitability.

An investigation may show that the yield variance resulted from the purchasing and product development policies. In this case, the variance analysis presented is not particularly helpful and only provides partial information; information from interpretations needs to take account of the interdependence of variances to create investigations to provide more complete control information.

The mix variance is helpful if the materials are interchangeable. It would be helpful to know the effects of exchanging A for B or vice versa on total quality costs from materials wastage through to returns of sub-standard goods by customers.

Labour variances

In total, labour variances amounted to over 7% of labour cost. In particular, 9,150 hours were required to produce 8,520 hours of work, a productivity level of approximately 93%. Labour control should be investigated with the objective of initiating corrective action.

If investigation shows that low productivity was caused by problems in materials handling, the purchasing and product development policies referred to earlier should be reconsidered because the total variance for materials and labour is £1,490 adverse, leading to a loss of profits of the same amount in comparison with expected profits.

Overheads

Variable overhead was overspent by £1,500 and should be investigated.

Expenditure on fixed overheads was £990 less than budget. A detailed analysis by fixed overhead item, as presented in a statement of budget against actual expenditure by item, or by function, is necessary before this variance can be evaluated.

The volume variance was favourable, reflecting the excess production of 2,000 units by comparison with budget. Of this 2,000 units, 1,000 units were placed in stock; the implications for stock control should be investigated unless the decision to produce 12,000 units was a policy revised since the preparation of the budget. Perhaps the company has recently formed a policy of expansion to meet its long-term objectives.

Solutions to Chapter 26 questions

ANSWERS TO SELF-ASSESSMENT QUESTIONS

26.1 Price variance.

The price paid was £5/kg in each month, a variance of £2/kg against the standard. Usage was constant at 100,000 kg.

Price variance: 100,000 (5–3) = £200,000 adverse/month.

Usage variance

Materials usage: kg	100,000	100,000	100,000	100,000
Standard, output				
@ 2 kg/unit	100,000	90,000	104,000	110,000
Variance kg	nil	(10,000)	4,000	10,000
Variance £	nil	(30,000)	12,000	30,000

The cost trend is constant.

The price variance trend is constant, possibly implying that materials prices are under control.

The usage variance is varying by ± 10%, possibly implying the need for management control. Investigation is advisable.

26.2 The action levels would be set at $\frac{£12{,}500 \pm (2.33 \times £550)}{12}$

$= £935$ and £1,150 (nearest £5)

Standard would be set at £12,500/12 = £1,040 (nearest £5).

The following diagram is a control chart for Chartrend PLC.

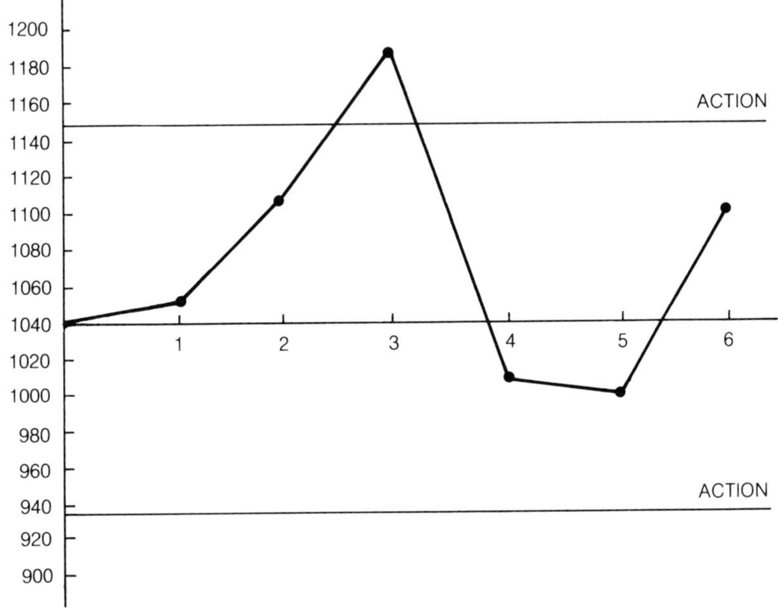

ANSWERS TO EXERCISES

26.2 Information is provided about the decision to investigate variance. If the expected value of investigation is positive, variances should be investigated on a routine basis in the future.

29% of cases:	Investigation costs of £890 incurred No benefits.
9% of cases:	Investigation and Correction costs of £3,910 incurred No benefits.
31% of cases:	£3,910 incurred Benefits: 6 × £8,990 = £53,940 Net Benefit £50,030
18% of cases:	£890 incurred Benefits: 5 years × 12 months × £9,320, discounted.
13% of cases:	£890 incurred No benefits.

The expected value is clearly positive and variances should therefore be investigated on a routine basis.

Solutions to Chapter 27 questions

ANSWERS TO SELF-ASSESSMENT QUESTIONS

27.1 Budget

		£
Contribution	(20,000 units @ £20/unit)	400,000
Fixed cost	(£3,750,000/12)	312,500
		£87,500

Variances

Revision	Original standard cost £30/unit	
	Revised standard cost £35/unit	
	Variance: 19,000 units @ £5/unit adv.	95,000 adv.
Materials	Price 93,100 kg (£6.50 – £6)	46,550 adv.
	Usage £6 (93,100 kg – 19,000 units @ 5kg)	11,400 fav.
Variable overhead	£91,200 – 19,000 units @ £5	3,800 fav.
Fixed overhead	£270,000 – £312,500	42,500 fav.
Sales price*	19,000 units (£51 – £50)	19,000 fav.
Sales volume	£20 (19,000 units – 20,000 units)	20,000 adv.

*Alternatively:

	Actual	Budget
	£	£
Selling price	51	50
Standard cost of sales	30	30
Standard Gross Profit	21	20
Variance	19,000 units	(£21 – £20)

The sales variances are not affected by the revision in this example.

27.2 Planning variance

[Result] Ex Post Standard	Ex Post Standard, Reference Prices		Ex Post Standard Reference Mix		[Reference] Standard
	(15%)	270,000 @ £3	(20%)	360,000 @ £3	100,000 units
	(40%)	720,000 @ £6	(20%)	360,000 @ £6	@ 20 kg/unit
	(30%)	540,000 @ £2	(40%)	720,000 @ £2	@ £3.60/kg
	(15%)	270,000 @ £5	(20%)	360,000 @ £5	
		1,800,000	(100%)	1,800,000	
£7,596,000	£7,560,000		£6,480,000		£7,200,000

Standard weighted average price:

4 kg @ £3	12
4 kg @ £6	24
8 kg @ £2	16
4 kg @ £5	20
20 kg	£72

£72/20 kg = £3.60

Ex Post standard total usage: 100,000 units @ 20 kg less 10%.

Variances:

Price	£36,000 adv.
Mix	£1,080,000 adv.
Yield	£720,000 fav.

Operating variance

Result	Result, Ex Post Standard Prices	Result, Ex Post Standard Mix	[Reference] Ex Post Standard
	(15) 285,000 @ £2.90		270,000 @ £2.90
	(40) 760,000 @ £5.90		720,000 @ £5.90
	(30) 570,000 @ £2.30		540,000 @ £2.30
	(15) 285,000 @ £4.90		270,000 @ £4.90
	1,900,000	1,900,000	1,800,000
£8,132,000	£8,018,000	£8,018,000	£7,596,000

Result total usage: 100,000 units @ 20 kg less 5%
Ex Post Standard Weighted average price £7,596,000/1,800,000 kg
Variances:

Price	£114,000 adv.
Mix	nil
Yield	£422,000 adv.

27.3 Labour and overheads do not appear to vary in accordance with changes in activity and are therefore treated as fixed costs.

The marginal principle is assumed to apply because no absorption information has been provided.

Comparison of budget with forecast 1:
Number of units of output £2,500,000/£2 = 1,250,000
Contribution per unit (£2,500,000 – £1,250,000)/1,250,000 = £1

	Budget	Flexed Budget	Forecast 1	Variance
	£'000	£'000	£'000	£'000
Unit	1,250	1,275	1,275	
Sales	2,500	2,550	2,550	nil
		Materials cost		
Materials	1,250	1,275 →	1,147.5	127.5 fav.
	Sales volume			
Contribution	1,250 →	1,275	1,402.5	127.5 fav.
Labour	250	250	250	nil
Overheads	500	500	500	nil
Net Profit	500	525	652.5	127.5 fav.

Sales Volume Variance: 25,000 units @ £1 Contribution = £25,000
A flexed budget approach is possible because materials vary with units.
The analysis presumes a linear relationship.

Analysis:

	£'000
Budgeted Profit	500.0
Materials cost variance	127.5 fav.
Sales volume variance	25.0 fav.
Forecast 1 Profit	652.5

Extending this method of analysis to Forecast 2 and the Result:

	Forecast 1		Forecast 2		Result
	Static	Flexed	Static	Flexed	
	£'000	£'000	£'000	£'000	£'000
Sales	2,550	2,525	2,525	2,607	2,607
Materials	1,114.7	1,136.2 ↔	1,212	1,251.4 ↔	1,227
Contribution	1,402.5 ↔	1,388.8	1,313 ↔	1,355.6	1,380
Labour	250	250	250	250 ↔	255
Overheads	500	500	500	500 ↔	505
Net Profit	652.5	638.8	563	605.6	620

↔ Variances

Variance analysis summary

	£'000	£'000
Budgeted Profit		500.0
Materials cost variance	127.5 fav.	
Sales volume variance	25.0 fav.	152.5 fav.
Forecast 1 Profit		652.5
Materials cost variance	75.8 adv.	
Sales volume variance	13.7 adv.	89.5 adv.
Forecast 2 Profit		563.0
Materials cost variance	24.4 fav.	
Sales volume variance	42.6 fav.	
Labour cost	5.0 adv.	
Overheads cost	5.0 adv.	57.0 fav.
Result		620.0

Comments:

Analysis of differences between Budget and Forecast 1 and Forecast 1 and Forecast 2 comprise planning variances; changes brought about because information gathered over a period of time reveals knowledge unavailable at the time of preparing the budget or forecast. Significant changes are clearly affecting materials cost at Update but other factors; sales price and volume, labour cost and overhead cost are less subject to uncertainty and are therefore more predictable, at least in the opinion of the planners.

Differences between the latest forecast and the result for a particular period contain an element of planning variance because information may come to light between the time at which forecasts are produced and the end of the period in question. However, these variances are most likely to reflect operational causes; the extent to which actions are leading to control. All variances are less than 2% of their respective reference data and can therefore be considered under control. Both materials and sales management appear to be effective and it is possible that positive feedback action could lead to improved profit results for the future.

Solutions to Chapter 28 questions

ANSWERS TO EXERCISES

28.1 (a) The Intermediate division is constrained by the number of units it can produce. Maximum profit derives from optimising contribution per limiting factor in single constraint situations. The analysis should therefore consider contribution per unit.

	A	B	C
Contribution per unit (Transfer price less variable cost)	13	8	20

Therefore producing most of C maximises profits and leads to production of 10,000 units of A and B (minimum levels) and 30,000 units of C.

Total company profit	A	B	C
	£	£	£
Selling price	56	60	60
Variable cost of both divisions	17	22	26
Total company contribution/unit	£39	£38	£34
Production—units	10,000	10,000	30,000
Contribution £	390,000	380,000	1,020,000
		£1,790,000	
less: Fixed costs (50 + 100 + 75 + 100 + 100 + 200)		£625,000	
Total Company Profit		£1,165,000	

(b) The final division is working without practical constraint. It should seek to maximise contribution. Since it is dependent on Intermediate division's production, the 10,000 unit processing constraint applies.

Contribution for Final division:	X	Y	Z
Selling price	56	60	60
Variable cost (transfer & processing)	30	30	46
	26	30	14

Therefore, 10,000 units of X and Z and 30,000 units of Y would maximise contribution.

Total company profit	X	Y	Z
Quantities—units	10,000	30,000	10,000
Company contribution per unit	£39	£38	£34
Contribution £	390,000	1,140,000	340,000
		£1,870,000	
less: Fixed costs		£625,000	
Total Company Profit		£1,245,000	

(c) The company would wish to minimise production of B and C, with contributions of £38 and £34 respectively, in order to concentrate on the most profitable product A, with a contribution of £39.

Maximum company profit is as follows:

	A	B	C
Quantities—units	30,000	10,000	10,000
Contribution per unit	£39	£38	£34
Contribution £	1,170,000	380,000	340,000
		£1,890,000	
less: Fixed costs		£625,000	
Total Profit		£1,265,000	

(d) Any improvement on the profit of £1,265,000 relies on Final division being able to buy in A, B or C from external sources, for instance:

Intermediate division's optimum contribution comes from A 10,000, B 10,000, C 30,000 giving contribution to the division of (10,000 @ £13 + 10,000 @ £8 + 30,000 @ £20)	£810,000
Final division's optimum contribution: (10,000 @ £26 + 30,000 @ £30 + 10,000 @ £14)	£1,300,000
	£2,110,000

This is £220,000 greater than the £1,890,000 contribution which is optimum for the company as a whole but requires that Final division purchase 20,000 units externally, which does not seem feasible because of the fact that:

'The Final division has sufficient capacity to produce up to 20,000 units more than it is now producing, but, because of the lack of products A, B and C, is limiting production'.

Nothing appears to be lost by the policy of internal transfers, therefore, in financial terms.

In management terms, it is financially sensible to produce in the ratio of A:B:C 30,000:10,000:10,000. Given the present transfer price, such a mix is not attractive to either the Intermediate division or the Final division, assuming that profit based performance measurement applies. A loss of divisional autonomy would result from the company prescribing a product mix. Any other than a centrally imposed mix would give suboptimisation, as divisions seek to optimise their own contribution to the detriment of the company as a whole.

(e) A market based transfer price is being operated. This is ideally effective where a perfect market exists. The implication that Final division cannot secure sufficient quantities to meet its own production capacity and market availability casts doubt on the existence of a perfect market, with a resultant problem of divisional autonomy as noted earlier.

The transfer price system does not promote goal congruence since neither division is motivated to process a mix which meets company objectives of maximising overall profit.

Given that the divisions are vertically integrated, the Final division is dependent on Intermediate division unless external sources of supply are available. A transfer price needs to be fair to Final division in this situation.

28.2 (a)

	£	£
Contribution required		
Residual income		300,000
add: attributable fixed cost	60,000	
interest (£1,600,000 @15%)	240,000	300,000
		£600,000
Contribution required from internal transfers		
Contribution from external sales (80,000 × (£20 – £14))		£480,000
Internal transfers (£600,000 – £480,000)		£120,000

Transfer Price:	
Contribution per unit (£120,000/40,000 units)	£3
Variable cost per unit	£14
Transfer price	£17

(b) For decision-making purposes, group variable cost is the relevant cost. A value of £14 per unit should therefore be built into decision-making analysis. From XY's point of view, the variable cost is equal to the transfer price of £17. Suboptimisation would result from XY division taking a decision which appears to be advantageous at a variable cost of £17 but disadvantageous at a variable cost of £14.

(c) **(i)**

	£
Required contribution	600,000
less: Contribution from external sales ((120,000 capacity − 50,000) × (£20 − £14))	420,000
	£180,000
Transfer price (£180,000/50,000 units + £14)	£17.60

XY should purchase 50,000 units from Company L to maximise its own profits because L would be charging the lowest price and this would minimise XY's costs.

(ii) The opportunity cost to CB of supplying XY with 50,000 units is the contribution foregone on the sale of 10,000 units to external customers.

Average opportunity cost per unit:		
10,000 units @ (£20 − £14)		£60,000
Spread over 50,000 units		£1.20/unit
Transfer price	(£1.20 + £14)	£15.20

XY should purchase 50,000 units from CB to minimise costs.

(iii) The opportunity cost for the first 40,000 components is nil
The opportunity cost for the next 10,000 components is £6/unit

Transfer prices:	First 40,000 units (£0 + £14)	£14
	Subsequent units (£6 + £14)	£20

XY should purchase 40,000 units from CB and 10,000 units from Company M to minimise costs.

(d) Differential group costs

(i)	50,000 units @ £15.50 [Variable cost of purchases]	£775,000
(ii)	50,000 units @ £14 + 10,000 units @ (£20 − £14) [Variable cost of purchases] + [opportunity cost]	£760,000
(iii)	40,000 units @ £14 + 10,000 units @ £18 [Variable cost of components] + [Variable cost of purchases]	£740,000

Option (iii) leads to group profit maximisation.

Reduction in profit from option (i): (£740,000 − £775,000)	£35,000
Reduction in profit from option (ii): (£740,000 − £760,000)	£20,000

The Chartered Association of Certified Accountants

June 1989

Level 2 – Professional Examination

Paper 2.4

Cost and Management Accounting II

Time allowed – 3 hours
Number of questions on paper – 7
The paper is in 2 sections
FIVE questions ONLY to be answered as follows:
Section A – THREE questions ONLY to be answered
Section B – TWO questions ONLY to be answered
Present value and annuity tables to be found on pages 2 and 3

Present Value Table

Present value of 1 i.e. $(1 + r)^{-n}$

where r = discount rate
n = number of years until payment

Discount rates (r)

Years (n)	1%	2%	3%	4%	5%	6%	7%	8%	9%	10%	
1	0·990	0·980	0·971	0·962	0·952	0·943	0·935	0·926	0·917	0·909	1
2	0·980	0·961	0·943	0·925	0·907	0·890	0·873	0·857	0·842	0·826	2
3	0·971	0·942	0·915	0·889	0·864	0·840	0·816	0·794	0·772	0·751	3
4	0·961	0·924	0·888	0·855	0·823	0·792	0·763	0·735	0·708	0·683	4
5	0·951	0·906	0·863	0·822	0·784	0·747	0·713	0·681	0·650	0·621	5
6	0·942	0·888	0·837	0·790	0·746	0·705	0·666	0·630	0·596	0·564	6
7	0·933	0·871	0·813	0·760	0·711	0·665	0·623	0·583	0·547	0·513	7
8	0·923	0·853	0·789	0·731	0·677	0·627	0·582	0·540	0·502	0·467	8
9	0·914	0·837	0·766	0·703	0·645	0·592	0·544	0·500	0·460	0·424	9
10	0·905	0·820	0·744	0·676	0·614	0·558	0·508	0·463	0·422	0·386	10
11	0·896	0·804	0·722	0·650	0·585	0·527	0·475	0·429	0·388	0·350	11
12	0·887	0·788	0·701	0·625	0·557	0·497	0·444	0·397	0·356	0·319	12
13	0·879	0·773	0·681	0·601	0·530	0·469	0·415	0·368	0·326	0·290	13
14	0·870	0·758	0·661	0·577	0·505	0·442	0·388	0·340	0·299	0·263	14
15	0·861	0·743	0·642	0·555	0·481	0·417	0·362	0·315	0·275	0·239	15

	11%	12%	13%	14%	15%	16%	17%	18%	19%	20%	
1	0·901	0·893	0·885	0·877	0·870	0·862	0·855	0·847	0·840	0·833	1
2	0·812	0·797	0·783	0·769	0·756	0·743	0·731	0·718	0·706	0·694	2
3	0·731	0·712	0·693	0·675	0·658	0·641	0·624	0·609	0·593	0·579	3
4	0·659	0·636	0·613	0·592	0·572	0·552	0·534	0·516	0·499	0·482	4
5	0·593	0·567	0·543	0·519	0·497	0·476	0·456	0·437	0·419	0·402	5
6	0·535	0·507	0·480	0·456	0·432	0·410	0·390	0·370	0·352	0·335	6
7	0·482	0·452	0·425	0·400	0·376	0·354	0·333	0·314	0·296	0·279	7
8	0·434	0·404	0·376	0·351	0·327	0·305	0·285	0·266	0·249	0·233	8
9	0·391	0·361	0·333	0·308	0·284	0·263	0·243	0·225	0·209	0·194	9
10	0·352	0·322	0·295	0·270	0·247	0·227	0·208	0·191	0·176	0·162	10
11	0·317	0·287	0·261	0·237	0·215	0·195	0·178	0·162	0·148	0·135	11
12	0·286	0·257	0·231	0·208	0·187	0·168	0·152	0·137	0·124	0·112	12
13	0·258	0·229	0·204	0·182	0·163	0·145	0·130	0·116	0·104	0·093	13
14	0·232	0·205	0·181	0·160	0·141	0·125	0·111	0·099	0·088	0·078	14
15	0·209	0·183	0·160	0·140	0·123	0·108	0·095	0·084	0·074	0·065	15

Annuity Table

Present value of an annuity of 1 i.e. $\frac{1-(1+r)^{-n}}{r}$

where r = interest rate
n = years

Interest rates (r)

Years (n)	1%	2%	3%	4%	5%	6%	7%	8%	9%	10%	
1	0·990	0·980	0·971	0·962	0·952	0·943	0·935	0·926	0·917	0·909	1
2	1·970	1·942	1·913	1·886	1·859	1·833	1·808	1·783	1·759	1·736	2
3	2·941	2·884	2·829	2·775	2·723	2·673	2·624	2·577	2·531	2·487	3
4	3·902	3·808	3·717	3·630	3·546	3·465	3·387	3·312	3·240	3.170	4
5	4·853	4·713	4·580	4·452	4·329	4·212	4·100	3·993	3·890	3·791	5
6	5·795	5·601	5·417	5·242	5·076	4·917	4·767	4·623	4·486	4·355	6
7	6·728	6·472	6·230	6·002	5·786	5·582	5·389	5·206	5·033	4·868	7
8	7·652	7·325	7·020	6·733	6·463	6·210	5·971	5·747	5·535	5·335	8
9	8·566	8·162	7·786	7·435	7·108	6·802	6·515	6·247	5·995	5·759	9
10	9·471	8·983	8·530	8·111	7·722	7·360	7·024	6·710	6·418	6·145	10
11	10·37	9·787	9·253	8·760	8·306	7·887	7·499	7·139	6·805	6·495	11
12	11·26	10·58	9·954	9·385	8·863	8·384	7·943	7·536	7·161	6·814	12
13	12·13	11·35	10·63	9·986	9·394	8·853	8·358	7·904	7·487	7·103	13
14	13·00	12·11	11·30	10·56	9·899	9·295	8·745	8·244	7·786	7·367	14
15	13·87	12·85	11.94	11.12	10.38	9.712	9.108	8·559	8·061	7·606	15

	11%	12%	13%	14%	15%	16%	17%	18%	19%	20%	
1	0·901	0·893	0·885	0·877	0·870	0·862	0·855	0·847	0·840	0·833	1
2	1·713	1·690	1·668	1·647	1·626	1·605	1·585	1·566	1·547	1·528	2
3	2·444	2·402	2·361	2·322	2·283	2·246	2·210	2·174	2·140	2·106	3
4	3·102	3·037	2·974	2·914	2·855	2·798	2·743	2·690	2·639	2·589	4
5	3·696	3·605	3·517	3·433	3·352	3·274	3·199	3·127	3·058	2·991	5
6	4·231	4·111	3·998	3·889	3·784	3·685	3·589	3·498	3·410	3·326	6
7	4·712	4·564	4·423	4·288	4·160	4·039	3·922	3·812	3·706	3·605	7
8	5·146	4·968	4·799	4·639	4·487	4·344	4·207	4·078	3·954	3·837	8
9	5·537	5·328	5·132	4·946	4·772	4·607	4·451	4·303	4·163	4·031	9
10	5·889	5·650	5·426	5·216	5·019	4·833	4·659	4·494	4·339	4·192	10

	11%	12%	13%	14%	15%	16%	17%	18%	19%	20%	
11	6·207	5·938	5·687	5·453	5·234	5·029	4·836	4·656	4·586	4·327	11
12	6·492	6·194	5·918	5·660	5·421	5·197	4·988	4·793	4·611	4·439	12
13	6·750	6·424	6·122	5·842	5·583	5·342	5·118	4·910	4·715	4·533	13
14	6·982	6·628	6·302	6·002	5·724	5·468	5·229	5·008	4·802	4·611	14
15	7·191	6·811	6·462	6·142	5·847	5·575	5·324	5·092	4·876	4·675	15

Section A—THREE questions ONLY to be answered

1 A health clinic is considering the implementation of a project which would extend its ability to provide specialist medical services for a period of five years. The project could be implemented by accepting one of two contracts A or B.

Contract A: The capital costs are payable to the contractor as follows: £500,000 at the commencement of the project and £300,000 at the end of each of years 1 to 3.

Contract B: The overall capital outlay is estimated as being £200,000 at the commencement of the project and £400,000 at the end of each of years 1 to 3. The contractor would share the capital costs on a 50/50 basis in return for a fee of £425,000 payable by the health clinic at the end of year 4, together with the contractor receiving 25% of the additional cash inflows resulting from the provision of the extra specialist services during each of years 1 to 4 inclusive. The contractor's 50% share would apply to each outlay.

The £700,000 of unutilised capital which the health clinic would have at its disposal by accepting contract B could be invested, in the pattern in which it becomes available, in a short-term fitness monitoring scheme which it is estimated would generate cash inflows of £250,000 during each of years 1 and 2 and £150,000 during each of years 3 and 4. The contractor would not receive any share of these cash flows.

The cash inflows accruing to the health club for the additional specialist medical services are estimated at £300,000 in year 1, £400,000 in year 2 and £600,000 in each of years 3 to 5. (All such figures are before any deduction of the contractor's share in contract B.)

Assume that all cash flows arise at year-end points.
Ignore taxation.

Required:

(a) Prepare summaries which enable you to advise management whether to accept contract A or contract B in each of the following situations:

(i) Ignoring the discounting of cash flows; and

(ii) Where the cost of capital is determined as 14% and the discount factors given in Appendix 1 are available. (8 marks)

(b) Advise the health clinic management of the percentage of additional cash inflows from the specialist services payable to contractor B at which they will be indifferent as to the choice between contract A or contract B:

(i) Ignoring the discounting of cash flows; and

(ii) Where the cost of capital of 14% is incorporated into the solution. (6 marks)

(c) (i) Comment on how the structure of contracts A and B might influence the health clinic management in their choice of contract; and

(ii) Comment on quantitative techniques which could be used as part of the alternative choice process. (8 marks)

(22 marks)

2 Sniwe plc intend to launch a commemorative product for the 1992 Olympic games on to the UK market commencing 1 August 1990. The product will have variable costs of £16 per unit.

Production capacity available for the product is sufficient for 2,000 units per annum. Sniwe plc has made a policy decision to produce to the maximum available capacity during the year to 31 July 1991.

Demand for the product during the year to 31 July 1991 is expected to be price dependent, as follows:

Selling price per unit	*Annual sales*
£	Units
20	2,000
30	1,600
40	1,200
50	1,100
60	1,000
70	700
80	400

It is anticipated that in the year to 31 July 1992 the availability of similar competitor products will lead to a market price of £40 per unit for the product during that year.

During the year to 31 July 1992, Sniwe plc intend to produce only at the activity level required to enable them to satisfy demand, with stocks being run down to zero if possible. This policy is intended as a precaution against a sudden collapse of the market for the product by 31 July 1992.

Required:

(Ignoring tax and the time value of money.)

(a) Determine the launch price at 1 August 1990 which will maximise the net benefit to Sniwe plc during the two-year period to 31 July 1992 where the demand potential for the year to 31 July 1992 is estimated as (i) 3,600 units and (ii) 1,000 units. (12 marks)

(b) Identify which of the launch strategies detailed in (a)(i) and (a)(ii) above will result in unsold stock remaining at 31 July 1992.

Advise management of the minimum price at which such unsold stock should be able to be sold in order to alter the initial launch price strategy which will maximise the net benefit to Sniwe plc over the life of the product. (6 marks)

(c) Comment on any other factors which might influence the initial launch price strategy where the demand in the year to 31 July 1992 is estimated at 1,000 units. (4 marks)

(22 marks)

3 Thurbro Ltd make and sell a single product A. The following information is available for use in the budgeting process for the year to 31 December 1990.

(i) *Sales:* selling price per product unit £20

	1990				1991
	Quarter 1	*Quarter 2*	*Quarter 3*	*Quarter 4*	*Quarter 1*
Product units	6,000	4,000	3,600	5,600	4,800

(ii) *Stock levels*

At 31 December 1989: Finished product A 1,500 units
Raw material X 3,500 kilos

Closing stocks of finished product A at the end of each quarter are budgeted as a percentage of the sales units of the following quarter as follows:

At the end of quarters 1 and 2: 25%; At the end of quarters 3 and 4: 35%.

Closing stock of raw material X is budgeted to fall by 300 kilos at the end of each quarter in order to reduce holdings by 1,200 kilos during 1990.

(iii) *Product A unit data*

Material X 4 kilos at £1.60 per kilo
Direct labour 0·6 hours at £3.50 per hour

(iv) *Other quarterly expenditure*

	Quarter 1	*Quarter 2*	*Quarter 3*	*Quarter 4*
	£	£	£	£
Fixed overhead	45,000	48,000	47,000	50,000
Capital expenditure		50,000		

(v) *Forecast balances at 31 December 1989*
Debtors: £40,000 Bad debts provision: £2,000
Bank balance: £22,000 Creditors: materials £9,600
Fixed assets: £500,000 (at cost)

(vi) *Cash flow timing information*
1. Sales revenue: 60% receivable during the quarter of sale, 38% during the next quarter, the balance of 2% being expected bad debts.
2. Material X purchases: 70% payable during the quarter of purchase, the balance of 30% during the next quarter.
3. Direct wages, fixed overhead and capital expenditure: 100% payable during the quarter in which they are earned or incurred.

(vii) Fixed assets are depreciated on a straight-line basis of 5% per annum, based on the total cost of fixed assets held at any point during a year and assuming nil residual value.

(viii) All forecast balances at 31 December 1989 will be received or paid as relevant during the first quarter of 1990.

(ix) Stocks of product A are valued on a marginal cost basis for internal budgeting purposes.

Required:

(a) Prepare a cash budget for Thurbro Ltd for each quarter of the year to 31 December 1990. All relevant working calculations must be shown. (12 marks)

(b) Prepare a budgeted profit-and-loss account for the year to 31 December 1990. (4 marks)

(c) List and quantify the factors which have caused any difference between the budgeted net profit/loss for the year to 31 December 1990 and the movement in the bank balance during 1990. (6 marks)

(22 marks)

4 Genery plc make and sell three types of electronic game for which the following budget/standard and actual information is available for a 4-week period:

	Budget/Standard			
Model	*Sales*	*Unit data*		*Actual Sales*
		Selling price	*Variable cost*	
	(Units)	£	£	Units
A	15,000	50	40	18,000
B	25,000	40	25	21,000
C	10,000	35	22	9,000

Required:

(a) Prepare a summary of sales variances for quantity, mix and volume for each model and in total where individual product standard contribution per unit is used as the variance valuation base. (7 marks)

(b) Prepare an alternative summary giving the same range of variances as in (a) above, but using the budgeted weighted average contribution per unit as the variance valuation base. (5 marks)

(c) Prepare a report to management which specifically comments on each of the following points:

(i) similarities and differences between the variances calculated in (a) as compared with those calculated in (b) above,

(ii) the arguments which may be put in favour of the individual product quantity and mix variances as calculated in (b) above,

(iii) the relevance of the individual product quantity and mix variances to management, and

(iv) the use of product units as the base against which quantity and mix effects are measured. (10 marks)

(22 marks)

Section B – TWO questions ONLY to be answered

5 **(a) Comment on factors likely to affect the accuracy of the analysis of costs into fixed and variable components.** (8 marks)

(b) Explain how the analysis of costs into fixed and variable components is of use in planning, control and decision-making techniques used by the management accountant. (9 marks)

(17 marks)

6 The management accounting information system must be geared to the provision of relevant analysis for a new product.

(a) Identify and comment on information which may be gathered at THREE stages in the introduction of a new product prior to the full production and marketing of the product. (6 marks)

(b) Explain how a feedforward control system will be relevant when considering the full production implementation of the new product, giving specific illustrative examples. (6 marks)

(c) Explain how management control process information will have to be extended in order to accommodate the new product. (5 marks)

(17 marks)

7 **(a) Explain the meaning of each of the undernoted measures which may be used for divisional performance measurement and investment decision-making. Discuss the advantages and problems associated with the use of each.**

(i) Return on capital employed.
(ii) Residual income.
(iii) Discounted future earnings. (9 marks)

(b) Comment on the reasons why the measures listed in (a) above may give conflicting investment decision responses when applied to the same set of data. Use the following figures to illustrate the conflicting responses which may arise:

Additional investment of £60,000 for a 6-year life with nil residual value.
Average net profit per year: £9,000 (after depreciation).
Cost of capital: 14%.
Existing capital employed: £300,000 with ROCE of 20%. (8 marks)

(Solutions should ignore taxation implications.) **(17 marks)**

End of Question Paper

Authors' model answers to this examination paper are on page 651.

Authors' model answers to June 1989 ACCA Cost and Management Accounting 2 paper

The answers which follow seek to develop an understanding of the issues raised by the ACCA June 1989 paper, in the light of material presented throughout the book. There is a tradition that examinations of this standard can be passed by candidates applying different ideas and different approaches. It is therefore important that candidates:

(a) appreciate situations where different assumptions can be taken and clearly state any assumptions made;
(b) relate answers closely to the question.

It is commonly the case that more than one answer can score highly and that no single answer can be considered to be an 'ideal' answer. In producing these answers, the authors have consulted the answers published by the ACCA but have not slavishly followed the ideas presented.

1 **(a)** The answer to this question depends upon the interpretation of the instruction regarding the investment of funds in the short-term fitness monitoring scheme. Investment is stated to be made 'in the pattern in which it becomes available'.

The availability of funds is clearly a limiting factor in the health clinic's investment activity as the short-term fitness monitoring scheme appears not to be a possible investment project if Contract A is accepted.

A reasonable interpretation of 'in the pattern in which it becomes available' would therefore seem to be the difference between the cash outflows required for Contracts A and B. As a result the cash outflows for both Contract A and also Contract B (including the fitness monitoring scheme) would be identical.

An alternative interpretation is that the availability of capital results from the timing of the contractor's contribution. If this is the case, earlier outflows are required for Contract A than for Contract B. A question then arises as to what use would be made of the capital if not required for Contract A before it is required for Contract B. The same question arises, but more significantly, if investment in Contract B is considered without the additional investment in the fitness monitoring scheme, where not just differences in timing, but also an extra £700,000 of capital, becomes relevant.

Yet another factor in funds availability is the cash inflows that are expected to arise from both the specialist medical services and the fitness monitoring scheme. If these are also taken into account the investment in the fitness monitoring scheme would be assumed to take place earlier. Another point worth noting is that, due to the timing of outflows and inflows, it is only in year 0, to a maximum of £500,000, that net outflows are required.

Two different analyses of the situation are carried out below. The first assumes investment timing for the fitness monitoring scheme based on the difference between Contracts A and B. The second is based on fund availability created by the contractor's contribution to capital cost.

In each analysis three alternatives are identified (apart from doing nothing which is the base point for the analysis):

1 Invest in project to provide specialist medical services, accepting Contract A.
2 Invest in project to provide specialist medical services, accepting Contract B.
3 As 2 above, but with investment, in addition, in the fitness monitoring scheme.

Analysis 1

1 Contract A

Year	Cash outflows £'000	Cash inflows £'000	Net cash flows £'000	Discount factor 14%	Net present value £'000
0	(500)	—	(500)	1.000	(500)
1	(300)	300	—	0.877	—
2	(300)	400	100	0.769	76.9
3	(300)	600	300	0.675	202.5
4	—	600	600	0.592	355.2
5	—	600	600	0.519	311.4
	(1,400)	2,500	1,100		446.0

2 Contract B

Year	Cash outflows £'000	Cash inflows £'000	Net cash flows £'000	Discount factor 14%	Net present value £'000
0	(100)	—	(100)	1.000	(100)
1	(200)	225	25	0.877	21.9
2	(200)	300	100	0.769	76.9
3	(200)	450	250	0.675	168.8
4	(425)	450	25	0.592	14.8
5	—	600	600	0.519	311.4
	(1,125)	2,025	900		493.8

3 Contract B and fitness monitoring scheme

Year	Cash outflows		Cash inflows		Net cash flows	Discount factor	Net present value
	Contract B £'000	Fitness monitoring £'000	Contract B £'000	Fitness monitoring £'000	£'000	14%	£'000
0	(100)	(400)	—	—	(500)	1.000	(500)
1	(200)	(100)	225	250	175	0.877	153.5
2	(200)	(100)	300	250	250	0.769	192.2
3	(200)	(100)	450	150	300	0.675	202.5
4	(425)	—	450	150	175	0.592	103.6
5	—	—	600	—	600	0.519	311.4
	(1,125)	(700)	2,025	800	1,000		463.2

Ignoring the discounting of cash flows, Contract A should be accepted as net cash flows over five years of £1,100,000 are anticipated, as opposed to £900,000 and £1,000,000 respectively from the alternative Contract B schemes.

If the cash flows are discounted at 14%, the situation is reversed with the Contract B schemes becoming more profitable than Contract A. The fitness monitoring scheme, however, is not justified in addition to Contract B. This is also demonstrated by the calculation of the net present value of the fitness monitoring scheme on its own, as follows:

Year	Cash outflows £'000	Cash inflows £'000	Net cash flows £'000	Discount factor 14%	Net present value £'000
0	(400)	—	(400)	1.000	(400)
1	(100)	250	150	0.877	131.6
2	(100)	250	150	0.769	115.4
3	(100)	150	50	0.675	33.7
4	—	150	150	0.592	88.8
	(700)	800	100		(30.5)

Analysis 2

1 **Contract A (as before).**

2 **Contract B (as before).**

3 **Contract B and fitness monitoring scheme (revised analysis below).**

Year	Cash outflows		Cash inflows		Net cash flows	Discount factor	Net present value
	Contract B £'000	Fitness monitoring £'000	Contract B £'000	Fitness monitoring £'000	£'000	14%	£'000
0	(100)	(100)	—	—	(200)	1.000	(200)
1	(200)	(200)	225	250	75	0.877	65.8
2	(200)	(200)	300	250	150	0.769	115.3
3	(200)	(200)	450	150	200	0.675	135.0
4	(425)	—	450	150	175	0.592	103.6
5	—	—	600	—	600	0.519	311.4
	(1,125)	(700)	2,025	800	1,000		531.1

The situation, undiscounted, is unchanged as total cash flows are the same. Contract A remains the preferred option. When the cash flows are discounted at 14%, however, Contract B, with the fitness monitoring scheme in addition, now has the highest NPV at £531,100. The different interpretation of the question delays the timing of the cash outflows which reduces their net present value.

(b) The calculations that follow are based upon Analysis 1 in part (a) above (the same principles would apply to calculations based on Analysis 2).

If the cash flows are not discounted, the cash flows given to the contractor would have to be reduced by £200,000 over the four years to make the two contracts equally attractive ie it would provide net cash flows of £1,100,000 for Contract B. The £200,000 as a percentage of total cash inflows of £1,900,000 is 10.53%, and thus the percentage payable to the contractor would have to be 14.47% (ie 25%–10.53%).

If the cash flows are discounted the calculation is more difficult. A higher percentage can be offered as Contract B is preferred to Contract A. The higher percentage must be sufficient to reduce the NPV of Contract B from £493,800 to £446,000, a reduction of £47,800. Each year's cash flow must be taken separately because of the different weighting of each year's discount factor.

If x is the increase in the percentage that could be given to the contractor:

$$\left(\frac{300x}{100} \times 0.877\right) + \left(\frac{400x}{100} \times 0.769\right) + \left(\frac{600x}{100} \times 1.267\right) = 47.8$$

$$2.631x + 3.076x + 7.602x = 47.8$$
$$13.309x = 47.8$$
$$x = 3.59\%$$

the total percentage that could be offered is 28.59%.

(c) **(i)** On the assumption that the decision would be influenced by the discounted, rather than the undiscounted, cash flows, Contract B would be preferred on the basis of the figures. In Analysis 1, Contract B would be selected without the fitness monitoring scheme. If the health clinic wishes to reduce risk, this decision would be reinforced by the fact that outlays, and thus capital at risk, are reduced by the contractor's stake in the project.

In Analysis 2, the discounted figures indicate the selection of Contract B with additional investment in the fitness monitoring scheme. This decision may be reinforced by the fact that risk is spread as it may be assumed that the two investments are at least to some extent independent of each other. Against this it may be argued that such investment has more variables and is thus more susceptible to errors in estimation.

In both Contract B schemes the fact that the contractor has a stake in the project may be seen as an advantage by ensuring that the contract is completed to a high standard. If the health clinic management are prepared to take risks, the fact that the contractor will take a share of profits if the investment is particularly successful may be seen as a disadvantage of investment in Contract B.

(ii) Only single value forecasts for each of the variables, and for the total project cash flows, have been provided, although part (b) of the question provided an example of sensitivity analysis. Further sensitivity analysis could be carried out, in order to provide an indication of the effect on project return, and thus on the viability of the proposed investment, of changes in assumptions regarding future cash flows from each of the variables.

The uncertainty surrounding each of the variables could be quantified by estimating a range of possible cash flows for each variable and attaching a probability of occurrence to each. Best and worst outcomes could be calculated, along with the expected value and the likelihood of achieving the minimum acceptable return. This would provide a greater quantitative basis for exercising choice. However, the analysis and conclusions depend upon the quality of the estimates. It is essential that judgement as well as computation plays a part in the decision.

2 **(a)** Contribution generated from sales in 1990/91 could be:

Sales units	*Contribution per unit*	*Contribution £*
2,000	4	8,000
1,600	14	22,400
1,200	24	28,800
1,100	34	37,400
1,000	44	44,000
700	54	37,800
400	64	25,600

The maximum sales that would be considered in year 1 is 1,000 units, as higher sales result in reduced contribution.

Minimum production over the two years is 2,000 units (all in year 1) and the maximum production is 4,000 units.

(i) If demand in 1991/92 is expected to be 3,600 units at a selling price of £40 per unit, potential contribution is £86,400 (3,600 × £24). Sales in 1990/91 would be restricted to 400 units with a selling price of £80 per unit and total contribution of £25,600. Total contribution over the two years would be £112,000.

Sales in 1991/92 could be reduced if further sales in 1990/91 are justified.

Additional sales and contribution in 1990/91			
Selling price	**Extra units**	**Extra contribution** (see table of figures above)	**Reduced contribution in 1991/92** (units × £24/unit)
70	300	£12,200	(£7,200)
60	300	£ 6,200	(£7,200)

net benefit will be maximised where sales and contribution is:

1 **1990/91**—700 units at a selling price of £70 per unit and total contribution of £37,800.

2 **1991/92**—3,300 units at a selling price of £40 per unit and total contribution of £79,200.

Total contribution over the two years would be £117,000 (ie an increase of £5,000 over the previous calculation).

(ii) If demand in 1991/92 is expected to be 1,000 units, there would be no production in 1991/92 as it has already been established that production in 1990/91 will be 2,000 units and the maximum sales that could be justified in that first year is 1,000 units.

Thus 1,000 units would be sold in each year at the following sales and contribution:

1 **1990/91**—1,000 units at a selling price of £60 per unit and total contribution of £44,000.

2 **1991/92**—1,000 units at a selling price of £40 per unit and total contribution of £24,000.

Total contribution over the two years would be £68,000. The fact that there would be no production in 1991/92 should produce cost savings in addition.

(b) Both solutions in (a) above result in no unsold stock. Stock could be created by selling at higher prices in 1990/91.

In (a)(i) 400 units could be sold at £80 per unit instead of 700 units at £70 per unit. The minimum price for the 300 units would be:

$$\begin{aligned} 700 \times 70 &= 49{,}000 \\ \textit{less}\ 400 \times 80 &= 32{,}000 \\ &\ \underline{17{,}000} \div 300 = £56.67 \text{ per unit} \end{aligned}$$

This would clearly be an unrealistic scenario when the market price in 1991/92 is expected to be £40 per unit.

In (a)(ii) 700 units could be sold at £70 per unit, or 400 units at £80 per unit, instead of 1,000 units at £60 per unit.

At £70 per unit the minimum price for the 300 units of stock made available would be:

$$1{,}000 \times 60 = 60{,}000$$
$$\textit{less}\ 700 \times 70 = 49{,}000$$
$$11{,}000 \div 300 = £36.67 \text{ per unit}$$

This also seems unlikely to be realisable when compared with the market price in 1991/92 of £40 per unit.

At £80 per unit the minimum price for the 600 units of stock made available, in comparison with the recommendations in (a)(ii), would be:

$$1{,}000 \times 60 = 60{,}000$$
$$\textit{less}\ 400 \times 80 = 32{,}000$$
$$28{,}000 \div 600 = £46.67 \text{ per unit}$$

Again this is an unrealistic scenario. In any case if £46.67 per unit could be achieved, Sniwe plc would be better off with a launch price of £70 per unit as any price in excess of £36.67 per unit would be better than the recommendation in (a)(ii).

The selling price required, for any surplus stock, to make launching at £80 per unit more attractive than £70 per unit is in fact £56.67 per unit, as previously calculated.

(c) Where the demand in 1991/92 is estimated at 1,000 units no production is required in that year. It should be considered how the available production capacity could be utilised. However, this is unlikely to affect the pricing of the commemorative product unless additional production capacity was also found to be required in 1990/91.

It may be felt advisable to launch at £70 per unit or £80 per unit in order to provide a stock reserve in case demand in 1991/92 exceeds expectations. This would only be a consideration if the production capacity was not to be utilised for the commemorative product in 1991/92.

3 **Workings**

Note Items in brackets refer to the notes provided in the question.

Quantity budgets:

	Quarter 1	*Quarter 2*	*Quarter 3*	*Quarter 4*
	units	*units*	*units*	*units*
Sales [note (i)]	6,000	4,000	3,600	5,600
add: Closing stock of finished goods [note (ii)]	1,000	900	1,960	1,680
	7,000	4,900	5,560	7,280
less: Opening stock of finished goods [note (ii)]	1,500	→ 1,000	→ 900	→ 1,960
Production	5,500	3,900	4,660	5,320
Material × usage (Production × 4 kg) [note (iii)]	*kg* 22,000	*kg* 15,600	*kg* 18,640	*kg* 21,280

	Quarter 1	*Quarter 2*	*Quarter 3*	*Quarter 4*
	units	*units*	*units*	*units*
add: Closing stock of raw material [note (ii)]	3,200	2,900	2,600	2,300
	25,200	18,500	21,240	23,580
less: Opening stock of raw material [note (ii)]	3,500	3,200	2,900	2,600
Purchases	21,700	15,300	18,340	20,980
Purchases value budget	£	£	£	£
(Purchases quantity × £1.60) [note (iii)]	34,720	24,480	29,344	33,568
Sales value budget (Sales quantity × £20) [note (i)]	120,000	80,000	72,000	112,000

Cash flow timing:

	Quarter 1	*Quarter 2*	*Quarter 3*	*Quarter 4*
	£	£	£	£
Sales value (previous working)	120,000	80,000	72,000	112,000
Receipts [note (vi)]				
60% of current sales	72,000	48,000	43,200	67,200
38% of previous sales		45,600	30,400	27,360
Debtors, *less* bad debt provision [note (v)]	38,000			
	110,000	93,600	73,600	94,560
Payments				
Purchases (previous working)	34,720	24,480	29,344	33,568
Payments, nearest £ [note (vi)]				
70% of current purchases	24,304	17,136	20,541	23,498
30% of previous purchases		10,416	7,344	8,803
Creditors [note (v)]	9,600			
	33,904	27,552	27,885	32,301
Direct wages (Production as previous working × 0.6 × £3.50) [note (iii)]	11,550	8,190	9,786	11,172
Fixed overhead [note (iv)]	45,000	48,000	47,000	50,000
Capital expenditure [note (iv)]		50,000		

Note It is assumed that fixed overhead expenditure excludes depreciation.

Cost of sales [notes (iii) and (ix)]

	£/unit
Materials 4kg @ £1.60	6.40
Direct labour 0.6 hrs @ £3.50	2.10
	8.50

Depreciation [note (vii)]

	£
Cost of assets held (500,000 + 50,000)	550,000
Depreciation (5% of cost of assets)	27,500

Bad debts [note (vi)]

	£
Increase in provision:	
Provision at 31.12.1989, 2% of £112,000	2,240
Provision at 31.12.1988 [note (v)]	2,000
	240

	£
Bad debts written off:	
Provision at 31.12.1988 (bad debts from Quarter 4, 1989)	2,000
Bad debts arising from sales for Quarters 1–3, 1989 (£272,000 from previous workings: £120,000 + £80,000 + £72,000), 2% of sales	5,440
	7,680

End of year debtors (*less* provision for bad debts)

38% of Quarter 4 Sales £112,000 (previous workings) £42,560

End of year creditors
30% of Quarter 4 Purchases £33,568 (previous workings) £10,070 (nearest £)

Answer

(a) *Thurbro Ltd: Cash Budget for the year ending 31 December 1990*

	Quarter 1 £	*Quarter 2* £	*Quarter 3* £	*Quarter 4* £
Receipts				
Sales	110,000	93,600	73,600	94,560
Payments				
Purchases	33,904	27,552	27,885	32,301
Direct wages	11,550	8,190	9,786	11,172
Fixed overhead	45,000	48,000	47,000	50,000
Capital expenditure		50,000		
	90,454	133,742	84,671	93,473
Net Cash Flow	19,546	(40,142)	(11,071)	1,087
Balance brought forward [Quarter 1: note (v)]	22,000	41,546	1,404	(9,667)
Balance carried forward	41,546	1,404	(9,667)	(8,580)

(b) *Thurbro Ltd: Profit and Loss Budget for the year ending 31 December 1990*

	£	£
Sales (19,200 units @ £20)		384,000
Cost of sales (19,200 units @ £8.50)		163,200
Contribution		220,800
Fixed cost		
Overhead	190,000	
Depreciation	27,500	
Bad debts	7,680	225,180
Net Profit/(Loss)		(4,380)

(c)

	£	£
Net loss for the year		(4,380)
Depreciation	27,500	
Capital expenditure	(50,000)	
Stock of A (1,680–1,500) @ £8.50	(1,530)	
Stock of X (2,300–3,500) @ £1.60	1,920	
Debtors (42,560–38,000)	(4,560)	
Creditors (10,070–9,600)	470	(26,200)
Movement in the bank balance		(30,580)

4 Workings

	Actual contribution, sales at standard selling price			*Contribution for standard mix*			*Standard contribution*		
	Units	*£/unit(1)*	*£'000*	*Units(2)*	*£/unit*	*£'000*	*Units*	*£/unit*	*£'000*
A	18,000	10	180.0	14,400	10	144.0	15,000	10	150.0
B	21,000	15	315.0	24,000	15	360.0	25,000	15	375.0
C	9,000	13	117.0	9,600	13	124.8	10,000	13	130.0
	48,000		612.0	48,000		628.8	50,000		655.0

(1) Calculation of contribution £/unit

	Budget/standard unit data		
	Selling price	*Variable cost*	*Contribution*
A	50	40	10
B	40	25	15
C	35	22	13

(2) Total units 48,000

Proportions of individual products are based on budget:

	Budget	*Proportions*	*Actual sales at standard proportions*
A	15,000	30%	14,400
B	25,000	50%	24,000
C	10,000	20%	9,600
			48,000

Budgeted weighted average contribution per unit = £655,000/50,000
= £13.10

Check data: Mix Variance = £628,800 – £612,000 = £16,800 adv.
Quantity Variance = £655,000 – £628,800 = £26,200 adv.

Answer

(a) It is assumed that mix + quantity = volume. This assumption is necessary since the terminology has not been standardised.

Volume variance

	Actual quantity of sales	*Budgeted quantity of sales*	*Variance*		
	Units	*Units*	*Units*	*£/unit*	*£*
A	18,000	15,000	3,000 fav.	10	30,000 fav.
B	21,000	25,000	4,000 adv.	15	60,000 adv.
C	9,000	10,000	1,000 adv.	13	13,000 adv.
					43,000 adv.

Mix variance

	Actual quantities at actual mix	*Actual quantities at budgeted mix*	*Variance*		
	Units	*Units*	*Units*	*£/unit*	*£*
A	18,000	14,400	3,600 fav.	10	36,000 fav.
B	21,000	24,000	3,000 adv.	15	45,000 adv.
C	9,000	9,600	600 adv.	13	7,800 adv.
					16,800 adv.

Quantity variance

	Actual quantities at budgeted mix	*Budgeted quantities*	*Variance*		
	Units	*Units*	*Units*	*£/unit*	*£*
A	14,400	15,000	600 adv.	10	6,000 adv.
B	24,000	25,000	1,000 adv.	15	15,000 adv.
C	9,600	10,000	400 adv.	13	5,200 adv.
					26,200 adv.

(b) Mix variance (all percentage figures are based on actual sales of 48,000 units):

	Actual sales	*Actual sales budgeted mix*	*Variance*	*Contribution*	*Budgeted wtd. ave. contribution*	*Variance*
	Units	*Units*	*Units*	*£*	*£*	*£*
A	18,000 (37%)	14,400 (30%)	3,600 fav. (+7%)	10	13.10	3.10 adv.
B	21,000 (44%)	24,000 (50%)	3,000 adv. (−6%)	15	13.10	1.90 fav.
C	9,000 (19%)	9,600 (20%)	600 adv. (−1%)	13	13.10	0.10 adv.

Variances

A	3,600 fav. @ £3.10 adv.	£11,160 adv.
B	3,000 adv. @ £1.90 fav.	£ 5,700 adv.
C	600 adv. @ £0.10 adv.	£ 60 fav.
		£16,800 adv.

Quantity variance

Actual sales in total	48,000 units
Budgeted sales in total	50,000 units
Variance Units	2,000 units adv.
Budgeted weighted ave.	£13.10/unit
Value	£26,200 adv.

The quantity variance by product

	Actual sales	*Budgeted sales*	*Variance*		
	Units	*Units*	*Units*	*£/unit*	*£*
A	18,000	15,000	3,000 fav.	13.10	39,300 fav.
B	21,000	25,000	4,000 adv.	13.10	52,400 adv.
C	9,000	10,000	1,000 adv.	13.10	13,100 adv.
					26,200 adv.

Note The examiner presents a different variation of the mix variance for the published suggested answer; different presentations are clearly acceptable. This book follows Horngren and Foster, as recommended in the ACCA syllabus.

Date: June 1989

To: Senior Management

From: Management Accountant

Sales Variances for the period——

Introduction

Variance calculations are presented in Appendix A. Method A provides a presentation based on individual product standard contributions whilst Method B is based on budgeted weighted average contribution. The report aims to indicate ways in which performance can be improved through effective management action in the future.

1 Interpretation of the variances

1.1 Both methods of variance presentation show that results fall short of budgeted targets. Achievement of budgeted mix (the proportions of A, B and C sold) would have improved profits by £16,800. Achievement of budgeted quantity sales of 50,000 units would have improved profits by £26,200.

1.2 For mix variance, Method A shows that a higher proportion of Product A was sold than was budgeted. Products B and C were sold in lesser proportions. Since A provides the lowest contribution, the overall contribution is lower than expected. Method B provides a fuller picture, the implications of which are as follows:

(a) Profits decline in the short term where a greater proportion of below average contribution products are sold (Product A) or, conversely, where a lower proportion of above average contribution products are sold (Product B).
(b) Profits improve in the short term by selling a lower proportion of below average contribution products (Product C) or a higher proportion of above average contribution products.

1.3 For quantity variance, Method B shows clearly that each extra unit of sales generated by the salesforce is worth an extra £13.10 profit. Sales for the period were down by 2,000 units at a cost of £26,200. Method A's presentation is less clear; for instance, selling 600 more units of Product A would not have improved the quantity variance by £6,000, as implied by the figures presented, because there would be implications for the mix calculation.

1.4 Overall, the volume variance shows a loss of profits of £43,000 in comparison with budget. This position can be improved by selling more units in total or by selling a greater proportion of Product B.

2 Recommendations for future variance presentation

It is recommended that Method B be adopted in future reporting of mix and quantity variances for the following reasons:

(a) Method A can provide misleading information. For instance, improved sales of Product A create an adverse mix variance whilst presentation implies a favourable variance.
(b) Method B clearly presents the variance analysis implications of improving total sales units performance. Extra units of sale improve the variance by £13.10 per unit.

Since Method B does not have a unique mechanism for reporting the volume variance, other than in a complex fashion or by summarising mix and quantity variances, it is recommended that the Method A format be adopted for reporting volume variances.

3 Limitations to the variances as presented

Variance analysis should lead to management action to improve performance. However, the information provided by variance analysis should be interpreted with care for the following reasons:

(a) Favourable and adverse variances should be viewed in relation to the long-term strategies of the company. The short-term implications of past results should not detract from the necessity to take actions which will benefit the company in the long-term future.
(b) Significant variances should be investigated before action is taken. The volume variance, which is approximately $6\frac{1}{2}\%$ of total contribution, should be investigated.

4 Alternative ways of presenting variances to management

At certain management levels, it may be better to focus on the units sold or proportions of units sold rather than contribution in order to provide useful information. The salesforce may find it better to learn that they were 2,000 units down on a target of 50,000 units or that they should aim for 50% of their sales in the form of Product B, where they only achieved a mix of 44%, 6% down on target. Alternatively, the salesforce may find it useful to know the sales value of the sales variances.

These alternatives provide ways of gaining the increased involvement of people within the organisation by providing information in a form which is relevant to the user. However, assuming that Genery plc has a profit objective, reporting variances on a contribution basis is the only means by which the profit performance of sales can be reliably monitored.

Conclusions

(1) Sales variances should be investigated.
(2) A combination of both Method A and Method B variance reporting should be adopted for the future.

Signed: ____________________

5 **(a)** Two major factors are likely to affect the accuracy of the analysis of costs into fixed and variable components:

1 The actual behaviour patterns of different costs.
2 The methods used to separate costs into estimated fixed and variable components.

Costs have varying patterns of behaviour in response to changes in activity, and the fixed/variable dichotomy can only generally be an approximation of reality. Major influences on actual cost behaviour and thus upon the accuracy of any analysis into fixed and variable components include:

1 **Efficiency and input prices** A change in the level of activity may result in a change in efficiency, or input factor prices may change, and thus certain costs, eg direct materials and direct labour, may not be proportionately variable as is sometimes assumed.
2 **The time period concerned** The analysis of costs into fixed or variable is dependent upon assumptions about the time period concerned. The analysis may well not remain applicable over differing time periods.
3 **Management discretion** The level of some costs incurred will be determined by management discretion. Management may change a cost's behaviour according to how they exercise that discretion.
4 **Changes in capacity/activity** The size of the change in activity will influence requirements for resources. Large changes may necessitate additional resources, or enable reduction of resource requirements, previously assumed to be fixed.
5 **Changes in methods of operation** A change in an organisation's methods of operation may necessitate a re-analysis of fixed and variable costs eg factory automation.

The second major factor affecting the accuracy of fixed/variable cost analysis is the method used to carry out the analysis.

A number of methods are available which differ in their sophistication and, as a result, degree of accuracy. Methods vary from, at one extreme, the exercise of judgement/use of experience in splitting costs into fixed and variable elements, or the use of the high-low method, to, at the other extreme, the use of regression analysis. Regression analysis, which provides a statistical approach to the problem, avoids the inaccuracies inherent in the other methods but still assumes that the cost function is of the form $ax + b$, where 'a' represents the variable cost per unit which is at a constant rate, 'x' is the level of activity, and 'b' is the level of fixed cost.

(b) The analysis of costs into fixed and variable components enables flexible budgeting to be carried out. This enables an organisation to project the outcome of different scenarios of the future where costs are 'flexed' with activity according to the cost behaviour assumptions made.

This also enables more effective control of costs to be exercised, because actual costs can be compared with those expected to be incurred at the particular level of activity.

An analysis of costs into fixed and variable elements is vital for decision making. In any decision-making situation only those costs that will vary depending upon which alternative is accepted are relevant. It should be stressed, however, that the variability of costs depends upon each separate situation under analysis. Nevertheless, general assumptions regarding cost behaviour, which are reflected in marginal costing analysis, may be found useful for product pricing/mix analysis.

6 **(a)** The three stages, together with specific information requirements, could be:

1 Research—specific product costs (applied research).
2 Market research—selling price decision.
3 Development—cost per unit.

1 Research

Specific products can be allocated a research project number so that the costs of specific products can be controlled. Costs accumulated under each project number, in accordance with specific order costing methods, can be compared with budgeted project costs to ensure value for money. Since research is a discretionary cost item, Zero Based Budgeting might be applied at the commencement of each project and as part of a periodic review process. Information would seek to ensure that future benefits, in terms of such factors as competitive advantage or product profitability, exceed costs. Given the nature of research, a high degree of judgement may be anticipated at the stage of evaluating information produced by the management accounting system.

2 Market research

Selling price is often a major determinant of demand and product success. The management accountant can provide information for the selling price decision, which can be tested as part of a market research programme. The management accountant may develop a standard product cost based on information provided either at the research or development stage and suggest a selling price based on a cost-plus basis. Prospective customers could then be asked whether they would be prepared to buy the product at that selling price. Alternatively, given that a high degree of uncertainty may be present, prospective customers may be asked qualitative questions about their willingness to buy the product were it to be sold within certain ranges of prices. For instance, a question might be posed: 'Would you be highly likely/likely/unlikely to buy this product/type of product if it were to be sold at £2.00–£2.50/ £2.50–£3.00/£3.00–£3.50?'. The management accountant could then analyse market research results to provide information on a market based selling price. Such selling price information, when coupled with cost information, can help management to decide on product launch details, packaging, delivery performance and advertising, for instance.

3 Development

At the development stage, the management accountant can provide information on cost per unit so that, for instance, targets can be set for quality performance. Trial runs may be costed and form the basis for standard costs. Such standard costs may be later built into budgets. Information of this nature can be used to motivate development personnel to specify cost-effective products and can later be used to motivate production personnel to optimise quality performance. Standards should be carefully managed so that they avoid the dysfunctional consequences of implementing control systems, at the behavioural level. The impacts of factors such as the learning curve should also be assessed. More generally, SSAP 13 details the information requirements necessary to meet financial accounting needs.

(b) Feedforward systems project present outcomes (and/or variances) in order to measure and evaluate future deviations from planned performance and objectives. Action may then be taken to ensure that future outcomes comply more closely with desired outcomes.

The basis for feedforward is a comparison of projected performance with objectives. Where new products are to be introduced, planned data relating to the products must be incorporated into the projections. An example might be taken from a global production situation. Research and development, in some international computer companies, undertaken in one part of the world, may lead to a new product being manufactured and sold by division X, say, in the United Kingdom. Division X would need to add projections, on such factors as product revenue, product profitability, production capacity, floor area and resources in general, to existing inputs and outputs in order to assess the costs and benefits of the new product in the light of meeting strategic goals. Feedforward mechanisms would seek to ensure that the results of new product decisions further the objectives of the organisation.

(c) Where the new product is comparable with existing products, the management control process should have been designed to have the flexibility to incorporate new products with ease. For instance, the new product will require a product code for sales analysis and profit reporting purposes. The code structure should have been originally designed to accommodate additional items. Where the new product is unique, special arrangements may be necessary, dependent on the characteristics of the product.

The typical systems which would be affected to a greater or lesser extent are:

1 incorporating a standard product costing into the standard costing system;
2 incorporating raw material usage data into stock control systems;
3 incorporating labour and/or machine timings into payroll and/or production capacity reporting systems; and
4 re-assessing information on cost behaviour.

7 **(a)(i)** Return on capital employed is a relative measure based on **net profit** and **capital employed**.

It can be used in investment centres to motivate managers to plan, control and make effective decisions related to costs, revenues and investments. It promotes goal congruence where organisations specify objectives in terms on return on capital employed. It can avoid some situations where investment disincentives arise from the performance measure under profit centre or cost centre structures.

There are potential problems which the management accountant should seek to minimise through systems design and through the way in which the system is operated at a behavioural level. Return on capital employed can lead to suboptimisation, where a divisional decision is sound from the point of view of the division but unsound from the point of view of the organisation as a whole. Accounting assumptions may distort reported measures, where, for instance, the choice of book value of fixed assets may show an improving performance because capital employed reduces as depreciation is charged over time. The management accountant will need to apply judgement in determining appropriate valuation bases for both net profit and capital employed. Particular valuation issues include the treatment of leased assets and the use of replacement or current cost. Strictly speaking, manager's performance should be based on controllable costs, revenues and investments and the management accountant may need to apply judgement in the controllable/non-controllable categorisation. Finally, no account is taken of the time value of money or the pattern of cash inflows and outflows over time.

(ii) Residual income is an absolute measure calculated by deducting a notional interest charge from net profit.

Its advantages include the avoidance of suboptimisation. Notional interest charges can be based on cost of capital for the organisation as a whole. In this way, managers are motivated to accept investments which show an advantageous return.

It may suffer some of the disadvantages or problems associated with valuation bases or controllability, as discussed earlier. It does not account explicitly for the time value of money but analysis shows a relationship between residual income and discounted cash flow techniques.

(iii) Discounted future earnings is an absolute measure of the cash flows associated with a particular investment, discounted to take account of the time value of money.

It is considered to be the most valid and reliable economic measure and overcomes deficiencies of non-cash flow based measures, which:

1 provide a measure of 'return' which is not comparable with cost of capital;
2 cannot account for disparities in the length of lives of alternative projects;
3 provide distorted information on the relationship between projects.

It is not usually associated with divisional performance measurement. Even for investment decisions, it may be perceived to be a 'sophisticated technique' and therefore pose potential problems of acceptance and perceived understanding. There may be problems in determining a suitable cost of capital to apply as a discounting rate. Certain cash flow patterns produce curious discounted future earnings profiles (NPV profiles), as typified by the problem of multiple internal rates of return.

(b)

Return on capital employed

Existing capital employed	20%
Additional investment (£9,000/£60,000)	15%

The additional investment is rejected because it falls short of the existing measure.

Residual income

	£
Average net profit per year	9,000
less: Notional interest (14% × £60,000)	8,400
Residual income	600

The additional investment is accepted because it shows a positive residual income.

Discounted future earnings

		£/annum
Cash flow:	Profit after depreciation	9,000
	Depreciation charge (60,000/6)	10,000
		19,000

Discounted future earnings: £19,000 × 3.889 = £73,891
£3.889 is the present value of an annuity of £1 a year for six years at 14% per annum

The additional investment is accepted because the discounted future earnings (£73,891) exceed the initial investment (£60,000).

Comment Residual income and discounted future earnings methods provide the same advice because the cash flow pattern is constant and both apply cost of capital. Return on capital employed produces different advice, based on a hurdle rate of 20% return on capital employed rather than a cost of capital hurdle rate of 14%. Return on capital employed and residual income are both accruals based, or income and expenditure measures where discounted future earnings is cash based, or a receipts and payments measure.

Index

Page numbers in *italics* refer to figures, those in **bold** refer to tables.

Absolute truth, 8
Absorption cost based transfer prices, 465
Absorption costing, 67, *68*, *71*, 72, 94
compared with marginal costing, 119–42
contribution analysis, 127–9, 130
decision information presentation, 130–4
fixed and variable cost treatment, 130
income determination, 120–4
issues between, 120–30
management information presentation, 124–9
objectives, 119
overhead apportionment and absorption, 120
stock valuation, 120
standard costing variance analysis—
direct labour, 427–8
fixed overheads, 429–30
profit or operating statement, 432–3
quality cost variance, 432
raw materials, 424–7
sales variances, 430–2
variable overheads, 428–9
See also Absorption of overheads
Absorption of overheads, 90–1, 95, 96
predetermined or actual rates, 91–2
resource base, 92
Acard report, 15–16, 290
Acceptability criterion, 174–5
Accounting information system design, 359–60
Accounting rate of return, 264–5, 270–1
closeness of substitutes, 273–4
ease of use and understanding, 273
see also Return on capital employed
Accounts classification method, 34
Administration budgets, 385
Advanced Manufacturing Technology (AMT), 16, 290, 292, 293
Aged debtors list, 341
Algebraic method of apportionment, 89, 90
Apportionment *see* Overheads
Arc elasticity, 244
Argyris budgetary control, 348–9
Aspiration levels, 357–9
Hofstede, 358–9
Stedry on, 357–8
Attributability of costs, 26
Audits—
management audits, 391–2
Avoidable costs and benefits, 185–6, 189

Balance sheet, 3, 5
Batch costing, 106
Bayes decision rule, 312
Becker and Green on participation, 354
Bias, 343–4, 350, 351, 356
see also Slack
Binary digit (BIT), 345
Break-even analysis *see* Cost-volume-profit analysis
Budgetary control, 348–9
behavioural distortions, 350
participation *see* Participation
see also Budgets and budgeting
Budgets and budgeting, 379–404
administration budgets, 385
Budgets and budgeting—*contd*
budget committee, 385
cash budgeting, 379, 386–8
continuous budgeting, 455–6
financial models, 394–5
flexible budgeting, 379
forecasting, 392
functional budgets, 385
incremental budgeting, 385
management audits, 391–2
management by objectives, 391
marketing budgets, 385
objectives—
conflicting nature of, 381
management by, 391
statement of, 379–81
preparation—
bottom-up approach, 381
feedback in, 382, *383*
iterative nature of, 381, *382*
master budget, 382–6
pseudo participation, 381
subsidiary budgets, 382–3, *384*, 385–6
top-down approach, 381
priority based budgeting (PBB), 390
procedures, 386–95
production budgets, 385
Program Planning and Budgeting Systems (PPBS), 390
quantity budgets, 383–4
rolling forecasts, 455–6
standard costing and, 388
uncertainty and, 451–62
decision trees, 452, *453*
ex-ante revision of budgets, 455–6
ex-post revision of budgets, 457–9
joint probabilities, 452
sensitivity analysis, 453–5
simulation, 452
three tier budgeting, 451–2
zero based budgeting, 379, 389–91
see also Budgetary control
Business accounting, 3–7
Business types, *3*, 4–5
By-products, 409–11

Capacity fixed costs, 24
Capital investment decision-making, 263–85
accounting rate of return, 264–5, 270–1
analysis methods, 263–9
appraisal techniques, 269–70
closeness of substitutes, 273–5
compared, 270–2
computation in decision-making, 275
difficulties or misapplication in appraisal, 275
ease of use and understanding, 272
in practice, 272
objectives other than long-term profit, 276
decision data and control data conflict, 298–9
decision types *see* expansion: modernisation: replacement
difficulties and limitations of analysis, 298–300
discounted cash flow, 265–8, 271
internal rate of return, **266**, 267
net present value method, **268**, 269

Capital investment decision-making—*contd*
expansion, 287–90
CVP sensitivity analysis, 289
working capital, 289–90
inflation and, 295–8
information relevant to, 287–303
internal rate of return, **266**, 267
calculation of, 276–81
ranking of projects, 281–4
long-term consequences, 299–300
modernisation, 290–2
benefits from new technology, 291
delivery, 292
flexibility, 292
investment and alternatives, 292–3
operating cost savings, 291
quality, 292
reductions in stockholding, 291–2
net present value method, **268**, 269
ranking of projects, 281–4
payback method, 269, 271
ranking of projects, 281–4
replacement, 293–5
reliability and, 294
timing of, 294
whether to replace, 294
Cash budgeting, 379, 386–8
depreciation, 387
funds flow statement, 387
timing adjustments, 387
Cash flow—
compounding, 265
discounted cash flow *see* Discounted cash flow
Centralisation, 12
Closed system approach, 17
Combined leverage, 54–5
Committed fixed costs, 24
Common cost problem. 146
Communication—
organisational environment and, 17
theory *see* Information
Compounding cash flow, 265
Computer Aided Design (CAD), 16, 291, 292
Computer Aided Manufacture (CAM), 16
Computer Integrated Manufacture (CIM), 16
Computer Numerically Controlled (CNC) machines, 16
Conditional truth, 8
Consensus management, 147
Contingency theory, 17, 351
Continuous budgeting, 455–6
Continuous costing, 106
inventories and, 110–11
profit in, 109–10
Contribution *see* Cost-volume-profit analysis
Control—
control chart approach to variances, 444–5
controllability, 9
cybernetic control *see* Cybernetic control
definition, 326–7
internal control, 329–30, 349
management control, 340–2
operational control, 339–40, *341*
standard costing and, 416–17
see also Control data: Planning and control
Control data—
decision data and, 196–7, 298–9
Cost accounting—
application of, 11–12
communication, 9
forward looking, 8
historical development, 21
internal movements of value, 9
method, 8
objective of, 7–8
responsibility and controllability, 9
routine information *see* Information provision, cost accounting
Cost accounting—*contd*
scope of, 10–11
Cost and revenue analysis, 247–9
Cost behaviour, 23–45
direct and indirect product cost charging and, 80
estimation of, 34–40
accounts classification method, 34
goodness of fit, 39–40
high-low method, 35, *36*
least square regression, 36–9
scattergraph, 34, *35*
visual line of best fit, 36
factors affecting—
activity level, 26
attributability of, 26
degree of control over costs, 27
efficiency and input prices, 26–7
nature of activities, 27
nature of expense, 24–6
time period, 26
fixed costs, *24*, *25*
grid, *28*
learning *see* Learning effect
mixed costs, 25, *26*
over time, 30
patterns of, 23–4
variable costs, *23*, *25*
Cost/benefit relationships, 97
Cost centres—
divisional performance measurement, 159–61
higher education, 146
transport costing, 144
Cost classification, 74–5
Cost coding, 74
Cost ledger control accounts, 72
Cost of capital employed, 56, 57
Cost units, 144–5
Cost-volume-profit analysis, 47–60, 127–9
accountant's model, *55*, 56
content, 55–6
purpose, 56–7
utility of, 57–8
assumptions about costs, 50–1
assumptions of, 47
break-even point, 49
charts—
contribution-volume chart, *51*
cost-volume-profit chart, *50*
profit-volume chart, *51*
contribution, 47, 48
contribution analysis, 127–9, 130
contribution volume chart, 127
cost of capital employed, 56, 57
economist's model, *56*
content, 56
purpose, 56–7
expansion decisions, 289
leverage—
combined, 54–5
financial, 53–4
operating, 52–3
margin of safety, 49
profit, 47, 48
profit volume chart, *57*
relationships, 47–51
revenue, 47, 48
substitute for demand forecasts, 253
variable and fixed costs, 47, 48
Costing—
absorption *see* Absorption costing
batch costing, 106
continuous *see* Continuous costing
job costing, 97
see also Specific order costing
marginal *see* Marginal costing
process costing, 97
see also Continuous costing: Standard process costing

Costing—*contd*
services costing *see* Service organisations
specific order *see* Specific order costing
standard costing *see* Standard costing
standard process costing *see* Standard process costing
transport *see* Transportation
Costs—
attributability of, 26
avoidable costs and benefits, 185–6, 189
direct *see* Direct costs
fixed costs *see* Fixed costs
future costs and benefits, 186
historic cost, 105
holding stock costs, 204–5
indirect *see* Indirect costs
input costs *see* Input costs
internal transfers of, 5
mixed costs, 25, *26*
of customer *see* Customer costs
of information, 20
of losses, 111–12
opportunity costs, 187, 191–2
period costs, 5
product costs, 5, 96–7, 412–13
replacement cost, 105
service costs, 412–13
standard cost, 105
terminology, 21
variable costs, *23*
Cumulative discount factor, 280
Customer costs—
general information requirements, 112–13
identification of, 113
profitability implementation, 113
Cybernetic control, 330–4
feedback, 332, 334
organisational control systems, 334
self regulating systems, 331–5
systems, 330–1

Data processing, 18–19
Debt collection, 341
Decentralisation, 12, 349–50
Decision data—
control data and, 196–7, 298–9
Decision information, 130–4
avoidability, 132
decision events, 131
decision objects,. 131
time horizons, 131
Decision theory, 447
Decision trees, 311–12, 313, 452, *453*
variances and, 445–7
Decision-making, 75, 96, 171, 173–84
acceptability criterion, 174–5
capital investments *see* Capital investment decision-making
decision trees, 311–12, 313, 445–7, 452, *453*
differential costing *see* Differential costing
economic model, 174–81
elements of decisions, 173
ends rationality, 175–7, 251
evaluation of private and public projects, 176
expected profit utility model, 174–5
means rationality—
all possible courses of action, 178
best alternative decisions, 179
effects of alternative courses, 178
successful execution, 179
nature of decisions, 179–81
choice, 180
quantification, 180–1
structure, 180, *182*
time period, 181
necessary conditions for optimal, 173–4
pricing decisions *see* Pricing decisions
profitability and, 176–7

Decision-making—*contd*
profit utility maximisation, 174–5, 176
quantitative decisions, 181
risk and uncertainty, 175, 176
setting objectives, 176
short-term decision making *see* Short-term decision-making
social conscience, 177
standard costing, 416
uncertainty *see* Uncertainty
Depreciation, 385, 387
Desk-top terminals, 18–19
Deterministic orientation, 347, 348
Differential calculus—
profit maximisation using, 250–1
Differential costing, 185–99
avoidable costs and benefits, 185–6, 189
choice of base, 192
concepts in analysis, 186, *187*
difficulties and limitations of analysis—
availability of information, 194–5
communication of information, 195–6
conclusions, 198
decision and control data conflict, 196–7
identification and analysis of information, 195
longer-term consequences, 197
presentation of information, 195–6
problem, 197
solution, 197
framework for analysis, 188
alternative analysis, 190–1
alternatives, 188
analysis, 189–90
avoidable costs and benefits, 189
base, 188–9
problem, 188
future costs and benefits, 186
opportunity costs, 187, 191–2
short-term decision making *see* Short-term decision-making
summary of terms, 187–8
Direct costs, 75, 79–82
cost behaviour, 80
fairness, 80
practicality, 80
product/service, 80–2
direct labour, 81–2
direct materials, 81
flow of materials and labour costs, 82, *83*, *84*
traceability, 79–90
Direct labour, 81–2, *84*
absorption costing, 427–8
standard costing variance analysis, 427–8
standards, 408–9
work study and, 408
Direct product profitability—
profits, 149
utility, 149–51
Discounted cash flow, 265–8, 271
average discount factor, 279
closeness of substitutes, 273–5
computation in decision-making, 275
cumulative discount factor, 280
difficulties or misapplication in appraisal, 275
ease of use and understanding, 272–3
internal rate of return, **266**, 267, 281–4
net present value method. **268**, 269, 281–4
objectives other than long-term profit, 276
ranking of projects, 281–4
Discretionary fixed costs, 24
Distortion, 343–4, 350
Distributions—
discreet and continuous distributions, 313–17
see also Uncertainty
Divisional performance measurement, 157–69
cost centres, 159–61
cost per unit of output, 160

Divisional performance measurement—*contd*
divisionalisation, 350
interactions between divisions, 158
interdependence, 158
types of organisational division, 157–8
inter-company comparisons, 161
inter-divisional comparisons, 160–1, 166–7
league tables, 167
investment centres, 162
monetary and non-monetary measures—
indices, 165–6
percentages and ratios, 164–5
physical quantities, 164
profit centres, 161
quantitative and qualitative measures, 166
standard costing variance analysis, 161
sub-optimisation, 162–4
trends in costs, 160

Education *see* Higher education
Effectiveness, 20
Efficiency, 20
Elasticity of demand *see* **Price elasticity of demand** : Profit elasticity
Electronic point of sale equipment, 148, 150, 151
Elimination method of apportionment, 89–90
Ends rationality, 251
decision-making, 175–7
Environment—
manufacturing, 15–16
organisational, 17–18
Ergonomics, 359, *360*
Evaluation, 350
definition, 327–9
standard costing and, 417
Expansion decisions, 287–90
CVP sensitivity analysis, 289
working capital, 289–90
Expectancy theory, 356–7
Expected profit utility model, 174–5
Expected values, 311–12

Feedback, 332, 334
budget preparation and, 382, *383*
negative and positive, 332
standard costing, 414–15
strategic planning, 339
variance analysis, 365
Feedforward, 339, 365
Filtering, 344
Financial accounting, 3
amount of information, 8–9
cost accounting information and, 72, 74
information flow, *4*, 5
information provision by, 9
method, 8
objective of, 8
recording past, 8
specific order costing and, 108–9
standard costing and, 417
works in isolation, 9
Financial (general) ledger control account, 72
Financial leverage, 53–4
Financial models—
budgets in, 394–5
descriptive, 395
optimising, 395
Fixed costs, *24*
absorption and marginal costing, 130
step fixed cost, *25*
Fixed overheads, 429–30
apportionment, 20
production costs, 120
Flexible budgeting, 379
Flexible Manufacturing Systems (FMS), 16
Forecasting, 392
rolling forecasts, 455–6

Functional budgets, 385
Funds—
investment of, 5
sources, 5
Funds flow statement, 3, 387
Future costs and benefits, 186

Game theory, 447

Health Service *see* National Health Service
Heuristics, 443
High-low method, 35, *36*
Higher education—
common cost problem, 146
cost centres, 146
description of accounting practice, 145–6
future recommendations, 146
incremental budgeting, 385
Jarrett committee, 145–6
Historic cost, 105
Hofstede view of participation, 355
Holding stock costs, 204–5
Hopwood classification of management style, 354

Incremental budgeting, 385
Indices, 165–6
Indirect costs, 75
cost behaviour, 80
cost/benefit relationships, 97
fairness, 80
manufacturing, recording of, *86*
overheads *see* Overheads
practicality, 80
traceability, 79–90
Inflation, 165
capital investment decision-making and, 295–8
input prices and, 27
uncertainty associated with, 412
Information, 342–5
accounting information system design, 359–60
communication theory—
bias, 343–4
distortion, 343–4
filtering, 344
information measurement (bits), 345
noise, 344
one and two way communications, 345
costs of, 20
data and information, 343
decision information *see* Decision Information: Management information
management information *see* **Decision information** : Management information
processing, 18–19
strategy, 19
variance analysis *see* Variance analysis
see also Uncertainty
Information provision, cost accounting, 63–77
absorption costing, 67, *68*, *71*, 72
cost classification, 74–5
cost coding, 74
financial accounting and, 72, 74
general requirements, 65
content, 66–7
form, 67–9
marginal costing, 67, *68*, 72, *73*
process requirements, 70–2
useful information, 63–5
comparability, 64
cost effectiveness, 63
economic reality, 63
objectivity, 64
verifiability, 64
relevance, 63
reliability, 64
timeliness, 63
understandability, 63–4

Information technology—
  data and information processing, 18–19
  desk-top terminals, 18–19
  impact on management accounting, 18, 20
  microcomputers, 19
  on-line processing, 19
  software packages, 19
  see also Manufacturing environment
Input costs, 79–103
  cost behaviour and, 26–7
  direct product/service costs, 80–2
    direct labour, 81–2
    direct materials, 81
    flow of materials and labour costs, 82, *83, 84*
  inflation and, 27
  new technology environment, 94–7
    accounting solutions, 96–7
    existing accounting deficiencies, 95–6
  non-monetary measures, 98
Inter-servicing apportionment, 89–90
  algebraic method, 89, 90
  elimination method, 89–90
  repeated distribution method, 89, 90
Internal control, 329–30, 349
Internal rate of return, **266**, 267
  calculation of, 276–81
    average discount factor, 279
    cumulative discount factor, 280
  ranking of projects, 281–4
Inventories—
  continuous costing and, 110–11
  see also Stock
Investment—
  decision-making *see* Capital investment decision-making
Investment centres—
  divisional performance measurement, 162
  ROCE, 162

Jarrett committee, 145–6
Job costing, 97
  see also specific order costing
Joint probabilities, 317–18, 452
Just In Time (JIT) concept, 15, 16, 94–5, 98, 291–2, 383

Labour—
  cost behaviour and, 27
  direct labour, 81–2, *84*
    absorption costing, 427–8
    standard costing variance analysis, 427–8
    standards, 408–9
    work study and, 408
  learning *see* Learning effect
  productivity calculation, 32–3
  see also Direct labour
League tables, 167
Learning effect, 30–4
  applications, 33–4
  labour productivity calculation, 32–3
  learning curve, 30, *31*, 32
Least square regression, 36–9
Leverage—
  combined, 54–5
  financial, 53–4
  operating, 52–3
Likert classification of management style, 352–3
Linear programming—
  simplex, 232–4
Linear programming based transfer prices, 467
Losses, costs of, 111–12

Managed fixed cost, 24
Management accountant—
  information provision by, 9
  information technology and, 20
Management accounting—
  application of, 11–12
  communication, 9
Management accounting—*contd*
  forward looking, 8
  historical development, 21
  information requirements, 65
    content, 66–7
    form, 67–9
  information strategy, 19
  information technology and, 18
  internal movements of value, 9
  method, 8
  objective of, 8
  organisational environment and, 17–18
  responsibility and controllability, 9
  scope of, 10–11
  structural and locational arrangement, 12
  systems *see* Management accounting systems
  theory and practice, 20–1
Management accounting systems, 347–62
  accounting information system design, 359–60
  budgetary control, 348–9
    participation *see* Participation
  ergonomics, 359, *360*
  motivation *see* Motivation
  negative impact of controls—
    Argyris contribution, 348–9
  organisational theory, 347–8
  participation *see* Participation
  variance analysis *see* Variance analysis
  see also Management style
Management audits, 391–2
Management by objectives, 391
Management control, 340–2
Management information—
  decision information, 130–4
    avoidability, 132
    decision events, 131
    decision objects, 131
    time horizons, 131
  presentation in absorption and marginal costing, 124–9
  see also Information: Management accounting
Management style—
  decentralisation, 349–50
  divisionalisation, 350
  Hopwood classification, 354
  Likert classification, 352–3
  McGregor classification, 353–4
  motivation *see* Motivation
  organisational structure and, 350–4
  participation, 349
  see also Organisational structure
Manufacturing environment—
  Advanced Manufacturing Technology (AMT), 16, 290, 292, 293
  Computer Aided Design (CAD), 16, 291, 292
  Computer Aided Manufacture (CAM), 16
  Computer Integrated Manufacture (CIM), 16
  Computer Numerically Controlled (CNC) machines, 16
  computer technology application, 15
  Flexible Manufacturing Systems (FMS), 16
  Just In Time (JIT) concept, 15, 16, 94–5, 98, 291–2, 383
  new philosophy, 15–16
  Total Quality Control (TQC), 15, 16, 94–5
  see also Modernisation: New technology
Margin of safety, 49
Marginal analysis—
  allocation of scarce resources, 230–5
Marginal cost plus pricing, 254–5
Marginal cost pricing, 255
Marginal costing, 67– *68*, 72, *73*, 94
  break-even point, 121–2
  compared with absorption costing, 119–42
    contribution analysis, 127–9, 130
    decision information presentation, 130–4
    fixed and variable cost treatment, 130
    income determination, 120–4
    issues between, 120–30
    management information presentation, 124–9

Marginal costing—*contd*
  compared with absorption costing—*contd*
    objectives, 1**19**
    overhead apportionment and absorption, 120
    stock valuation, 120
  standard costing variance analysis, 433–4
Market value based transfer prices, 466
Market-Based valuations, 105
Marketing budgets, 385
Master budgets, 382–6
Materials—
  direct materials control, 81, *83*
  standards, 407–8
Maximin criterion, 308, *309*
McGregor classification of management style, 353–4
Means rationality, 252–3
  all possible courses of action, 178
  best alternative decisions, 179
  effects of alternative courses, 178
  objectives, 177–8
  successful execution, 179
Microcomputers, 19
Minimax decision rule, 312–13
Mixed costs, 25, *26*
Modernisation, 290–2
  benefits form new technology, 291
  delivery, 292
  flexibility, 292
  investment and alternatives, 292–3
  operating cost savings, 291
  quality, 292
  reductions in stockholding, 291–2
  see also New Technology
Motivation, 27, 355
  aspiration levels, 357–9
    Hofstede, 358–9
    Stedry on, 357–8
  expectancy theory, 356–7
  see also Participation

National Health Service, 146–8
  consensus management, 147
  early 1980s, 147
  incremental budgeting, 385
  late 1980s, 147–8
  patient costing, 147–8
Negative feedback, 332
Net present value method, **268**, 269
  ranking of projects, 281–4
New technology—
  costing in environment of, 94–7
    accounting solutions, 96–7
    existing accounting deficiencies, 95–6
  see also Information technology: Manufacturing environment: Modernisation
Noise, 344
Non-Monetary costs, 98
Non-Production overhead pricing, 85

Objectives—
  management by objectives, 391
  setting of, 176
On-Line processing, 19
Operating leverage, 52–3
Operating statement, 432–3
Operational control, 339–40, *341*
Opportunity costs, 187, 191–2
Organisational environment, 17–18
  as culture, 17–18
  closed system approach, 17
  communication, 17
  contingency theory, 17
  divisional structures, 17
  hierarchical structures, 17
Organisational structure—
  contingency theory, 351
  cultures, 351
Organisational structure—*contd*
  divisionalisation, 350
  management style and, 350–4
  see also Management style
Organisational theory, 347–8
  deterministic orientation, 347, 348
  voluntarist orientation, 347, 348
Output **valuation**—
  batch costing, 106
  continuous costing, 105, 106
    inventories and, 110–11
    profit in, 109–10
  cost units, 106–7
  costing methods, 105, 106
  customer costs and profitability—
    general information requirements, 112–13
    identifying customer costs, 113
    profitability, 113
  normality and associating costs of losses, 111–12
  process costing, 105, 106
  services costing, 106
  specific order costing, 106, 107–8
    financial accounts and, 108–9
  standard process costing, 106
  valuation bases—
    historic cost, 105
    market-based valuations, 105
    replacement cost, 105
    standard cost, 105
  valuation principles, 107
Overheads, 82–5, 95
  absorption method, 90–1, 95, 96, 428–30
    predetermined or actual rates, 91–2
    resource base, 92
  apportionment and absorption, 120
  budgeted, 388
  fixed overheads, 429–30
    apportionment, 20
  fixed production overhead costs, 120
  inter-servicing apportionment, 89–90
  non-production overheads, 95
    pricing, 85
  production overhead pricing—
    process, 83–4
  responsibility centres, 86–7
    apportionment of overhead—
      choice of, 87–8
      method of, 88–9
  standard costing, 409
  standard costing variance analysis, 428–30
  variable overheads, 428–9
Overtime, 80

Participation, 349, 354–6
  Becker and Green on, 354
  Hofstede view, 355
  pseudo participation, 381
  Schiff and Lewin on, 355–6
  slack, 355–6
  see also Motivation
Patient costing, 147–8
Payback method, 269, 271
  closeness of substitutes, 273–4
  ease of use and understanding, 273
Performance—
  divisional *see* Divisional performance measurement
Performance evaluation, 350
  definition of evaluation, 327–9
  standard costing and, 417
Performance measurement, 467–76
  critique of, 467–72
  divisional *see* Divisional performance measurement
Period costs, 5
Planning and control, 75, 323–35
  budgets and budgeting *see* Budgets and Budgeting
  control definition, 326–7
  evaluation definition, 327–9

Planning and control—*contd*
formal accounting control mechanisms, 329–34
cybernetic control, 330–4
feedback, 332, 334
organisational control systems, 334
self regulating systems, 331–5
systems, 330–1
internal control, 329–30
information, 342–5
communication theory—
bias, 343–4, 350, 351, 356
distortion, 343–4
filtering, 344
information measurement (bits), 345
noise, 344
one and two way communications, 345
data and information, 343
for long and short-term, 337–46
management accounting systems *see* Management accounting systems
management control, 340–2
operational control, 339–40, *341*
planning definition, 325–6
standard costing and, 416–17
strategic planning, 337–9, *341*
uncertainty and, 455–9
ex post revision of budgets and standards, 457–9
ex-ante revision of budgets and standards, 455–7
planning and operating variances, 458–9
variance analysis *see* Variance analysis
Point elasticity, 243–4
Position audit, 338
Positive feedback, 332
Price elasticity of demand, 242–4
arc elasticity, 244
point elasticity, 243–4
Price standards, 408
Price variance, 415
Pricing—
decisions *see* Pricing decisions
transfer pricing *see* Transfer pricing
Pricing decisions, 241–61
cost based approaches, 253–5
long-run cost plus, 254
marginal cost, 255
marginal cost plus, 254–5
rate of return, 254
short-run plus, 254–5
economic approach, 241–53
establishing optimal price and output, 247–51
cost and revenue analysis, 247–9
differential calculus, 250–1
imperfect competition, 241, *242*
limitations—
ends rationality, 251
means rationality, 252–3
sensitivity analysis, 253
market structure, 241–2
price elasticity of demand, 242–4
arc elasticity, 244
point elasticity, 243–4
profit elasticity, 244–6
in practice, 255–6
Priority Based Budgeting (PBB), 390
Probabilities—
joint probabilities, 317–18, 452
Process costing, 97
see also Continuous costing: Standard process costing
Product costs, 5, 96–7, 412–13
Production budgets, 385
Production overhead pricing, 83–4
Profit—
actual standard gross profit, 431
budgeting standard gross profit, 431
direct product profitability—
profits, 149
utility, 149–51
Profit—*contd*
in continuous costing, 109–10
profit or operating statement, 432–3
Profit and loss account, 3, 5
Profit centres, 161
Profit Elasticity, 244–6
Profit utility maximisation, 174–5, 176
Program Planning and Budgeting Systems (PPBS), 390
Programmed fixed cost, 24
Pseudo participation, 381

Quality cost variance, 432
Quantity budgets, 383–4
Quantity variances, 370, 375

Rate of return, 254
Rationality—
ends rationality, 175–7, 251
means rationality *see* Means rationality
Raw material stock control account, 72
Raw materials—
absorption costing, 424–7
standard costing variance analysis, 424–7
Reference value, 371
Repeated distribution method of apportionment, 89, 90
Replacement, 293–5
cost, 105
reliability and, 294
timing of, 294
whether to replace, 294
Residual value, 105
Resource allocation *see* short-term decision-making, allocation of scarse resources
Responsibility accounting, 9
Responsibility centres, 86–7
apportionment of overhead—
choice of, 87–8
method, 88–9
efficiency of, 414–15
Result quantity, 371
Retail organisations—
accounting and technology developments, 148
direct product profitability—
profits, 149
utility, 149–51
electronic point of sale equipment, 148, 150, 151
store performance measurement, 151
unique features and difficulties, 148
Return on capital employed, 162, 349
see also Accounting rate of return: Internal rate of return
Revenue—
cost and revenue analysis, 247–9
Risk—
decision-making and, 175
uncertainty and, 305–6
see also Uncertainty
Roce *see* Accounting rate of return: Return on capital employed
Rolling forecasts, 455–6

Sales variances, 430–2
actual standard gross profit, 431
budgeted standard gross profit, 431
Scattergraph, 34, *35*
Schiff and Lewin on participation 355–6
Scorekeeping, 95, 380
Scrap, 409–11
Service costs, 106, 412–13
Service organisations, 143–56
costing, 106, 143–4
Health Service, 146–8
consensus management, 147
early 1980s, 147
late 1980s, 147–8
patient costing, 147–8

Service organisations—*contd*
higher education—
common cost problem, 146
cost centres, 146
description of accounting practice, 145–6
future recommendations, 146
Jarrett committee, 145–6
retail organisations—
accounting and technology developments, 148
direct product profitability—
profits, 149
utility of, 149–51
electronic point of sale equipment, 148, 150, 151
store performance measurement, 151
unique features and difficulties, 148
transport costing—
cost centres, 144
cost units, 144–5
Short-term decision-making—
allocation of scarce resources, 217–40
limiting factor situations—
single constraint, 217–26
additional resource, 224–5
allocation of resource, 219–22
changed assumptions, 223–6
equal contribution lines, *222*
more users, 223
non-divisibility, 223–4
problem, 218
production potential, 219
production processes, *220*
solution, 218–23
two or more constraints—
additional resource, 236
allocation of resources, 227–9
changed assumptions, 235–6
marginal analysis, 230–5
more users, 235–6
non-divisibility, 236
problem, 226–7
production possibilities, *228*, 229–30
production potential, 227
profitability, 227
simplex linear programming, 232–4
solution, 227–35
problem situations, 201–15
holding stock costs, 204–5
how much to produce and sell, 204–7
how to produce, 208–9
how to sell, 207–8
sell or process further decisions, 203
termination of operations, 210–11
transportation problem, 207–8
what to produce and sell, 202–4
where to produce, 208–9
where to sell, 207–8
whether to produce and sell, 210–11
Simplex linear programming, 232–4
Simulation, 309, **310**, 311, 452
Slack, 355–6
Software packages, 19
Sources of funds, 5
Specific order costing, 97, 106, 107–8
cost units, 106–7
financial accounts and, 108–9
Standard costing, 105, 405–20
budget formulation and, 388
cost recording systems, 413–14
direct labour standards, 408–9
efficiency of responsibility centres, 414–15
engineered costs, 407–9
ex ante revision of standards, 456–7
ex post revision of standards, 457–9
feedback, 414–15
fixed and flexible budgets and, 388
investigations, 415–16
materials standards, 407–8
Standard costing—*contd*
meaning of standard cost, 405–6
operation of systems, 413–16
overheads, 409
preparation, 405–13
price standards, 408
product costs, 412–13
purposes—
decision-making, 416
financial accounting, 417
performance evaluation, 417
planning and control, 416–17
quantity standards, 407–8
service costs, 412–13
type of standard—
attainable, 412
basic, 411
current, 411–12
ideal, 412
uncertainty associated with inflation, 412
variance analysis *see* Variance analysis
wastage, scrap and by-products, 409–11
work study for establishment of, 408
Standard process costing, 106
Statements of cash and funds flow, 3, 387
Stock—
holding costs, 204–5
in quantity budgets, 383–4
see also Inventories: stock valuation
Stock valuation, 5, 7–8, 75
absorption and marginal costing treatment, 120
closing, abnormal costs included in, 107
Strategic planning, 337–9, *341*
feedback, 339
feedforward, 339
management variables, 339
Sub-optimisation, 162–4
Subsidiary budgets, 382–3, *384*, 385–6

Technology *see* Information technology: Manufacturing environment: Modernisation: New technology
Termination decisions, 210–11
Terminology, 21
differential costing, 187–8
Total Quality Control (TQC), 15, 16, 94–5
Transfer pricing, 463–7, 472, 473–6
absorption cost based transfer prices, 465
linear programming based transfer prices, 467
market value based transfer prices, 466
methods, 464–7
negotiated prices, 466–7
purpose, 463–4
variable cost based transfer prices, 466
Transportation, 207–8
cost centres, 144
cost units, 144–5
Truth—
conditional and absolute, 8
Uncertainty, 351
associated with inflation, 412
Bayes decision rule, 312
budgets and standards and, 451–62
decision trees, 311–2, 313, 452, *453*
decision-making and, 175, 176, 305–21
discreet and continuous distributions, 313–17
ex post revision of budgets and standards, 457–9
ex-ante revision of budgets and standards—
continuous budgeting, 455–6
rolling forecasts, 455–6
expected values, 311–2
joint probabilities, 317–18, 452
maximin criterion, 308, *309*
minimax opportunity loss, 312–13
planning and control and, 455–9
reduction in, 318–19
resolving the problem, 308–13
risk and, 305–6

Uncertainty—*contd*
sensitivity analysis, 453–5
simulation, 309, **310**, 311, 452
stating the problem, 306–8
three tier budgeting, 451–2
value of perfect information, 313
Valuation—
of output *see* Output valuation
of stock *see* Stock valuation
Value variances, 370, 375
Variable cost based transfer prices, 466
Variable costs, *23*
step–variable cost, *25*
treatment by absorption and marginal costing, 130
Variable overheads, 428–9
Variance analysis, 363–77
absolute measures, 364, 365
definition, 363–4
feedback, 365
feedforward, 365
implications for management information, 364
interpretation of variances, 441–2
investigation of variances, 442–9
control charts, 444–5
costs of, 442–3, 446
decision theory approach, 447
decision tree approach, 445–7
game theory, 447
heuristics, 443
trends, 443–4
one factor analysis—
calculation, 366
examples, 366–7
price variance, 415
standard costing variance analysis, 421–39

Variance analysis—*contd*
standard costing variance analysis—*contd*
absorption costing—
direct labour, 427–8
fixed overheads, 429–30
profit or operating statement, 432–3
quality cost variance, 432
raw materials, 424–7
sales variances, 430–2
variable overheads, 428–9
marginal costing, 433–4
three factor analysis, 372–4
statement of problem, 372
two factor analysis—
calculation, 368–70
conventional, 370
procedure, 370–1
quantity variances, 370, 375
reference value, 371
result quantity, 371
value variance, 370, 375
variance formulae, 371
Voluntarist orientation, 347, 348

Wastage, 409–11
Work study, 408
Work-In-Progress control account, 72
Working capital—
expansion decisions, 289–90

Zero based budgeting, 379, 389–91
decision unit ranking, 390
implementation of, 389–90
primary rationale for, 389